Handbook of Operations Research

FOUNDATIONS AND FUNDAMENTALS

Handbook of Operations Research

FOUNDATIONS AND FUNDAMENTALS

Edited by

Joseph J. Moder, Ph. D.
Department of Management Science
University of Miami

and

Salah E. Elmaghraby, Ph. D.
Graduate Program in Operations Research
North Carolina State University

VNR VAN NOSTRAND REINHOLD COMPANY
NEW YORK CINCINNATI ATLANTA DALLAS SAN FRANCISCO
LONDON TORONTO MELBOURNE

Van Nostrand Reinhold Company Regional Offices:
New York Cincinnati Atlanta Dallas San Francisco

Van Nostrand Reinhold Company International Offices:
London Toronto Melbourne

Library of Congress Catalog Card Number: 77-21580
ISBN: 0-442-24595-5

Manufactured in the United States of America

Published by Van Nostrand Reinhold Company
135 West 50th Street, New York, N.Y. 10020

Published simultaneously in Canada by Van Nostrand Reinhold Ltd.

15 14 13 12 11 10 9 8 7 6 5 4

Library of Congress Cataloging in Publication Data

Main entry under title:

Handbook of operations research.

Includes index.
1. Operations research. I. Moder, Joseph J.
II. Elmaghraby, Salah Eldin, 1927–
T57.6.H35 001.4′24 77-21580
ISBN 0-442-24595-5

CONTRIBUTORS

Norman I. Agin, Ph.D.
Senior Vice-President and Director of Mathematica, Inc., Princeton, N.J.

U. Narayan Bhat
Professor and Department Head, Department of Computer Science and Operations Research, Southern Methodist University, Institute of Technology, Dallas, Texas.

C. West Churchman
Professor of Business Administration and Research Philosopher at the University of California in Berkeley, California.

Eric V. Denardo
Associate Professor in the School of Organization and Management, Yale University, New Haven, Connecticut.

Peter C. Fishburn
Research Professor of Management Science in the College of Business Administration at the Pennsylvania State University in University Park, Pennsylvania.

Donald P. Gaver
Professor and Associate Chairman for Research in the Department of Operations Research and Administrative Sciences at the Naval Postgraduate School in Monterey, California.

Fred Glover
Professor of Management Science, College of Business, University of Colorado, Boulder, Colorado.

Geoffrey Gordon
IBM Corporation, 205 E. 42nd St., New York, New York.

Ellis L. Johnson, Ph.D.
Research Mathematician, Mathematical Science Department, Research Division, IBM Corp., Yorktown Heights, New York.

Ralph L. Keeney, Ph.D.
Consultant with Woodward-Clyde Consultants, Three Embarcadero Center, San Francisco, California.

Leon S. Lasdon
Professor in the Department of General Business, School of Business Administration, University of Texas at Austin, Texas.

Olvi L. Mangasarian
Professor and Chairman, Department of Computer Science, University of Wisconsin, Madison, Wisconsin.

Philip M. Morse, Ph.D.
Professor Emeritus, Massachusetts Institute of Technology, 126 Wildwood Street, Winchester, Massachusetts.

Hugh J. Miser
Professor in the Department of Industrial Engineering and Operations Research, The University of Massachusetts, Amherst, Massachusetts.

Guillermo Owen
Professor of Mathematical Sciences at Rice University in Houston, Texas.

Elmor L. Peterson
Professor of Industrial Engineering, Management Science and Mathematics, the Department of Industrial Engineering and Management Science, Northwestern University, Evanston, Illinois.

Thomas L. Saaty
Professor of Operations Research, The Wharton School of Business, University of Pennsylvania, Philadelphia, Pennsylvania.

Hans Sagan
Professor in the Department of Mathematics, North Carolina State University, Raleigh, North Carolina.

Walter L. Smith
Professor in the Department of Statistics, The University of North Carolina, Chapel Hill, North Carolina.

Hamdy A. Taha
Professor in the Department of Industrial Engineering, The University of Arkansas, Fayetteville, Arkansas.

Robert M. Thrall
Professor and Chairman of the Department of Mathematical Sciences at Rice University in Houston, Texas.

PREFACE

Operations Research, OR, was officially "born" in the United States as an organized activity in 1952 when the Operations Research Society of America was formed, although the activity had been going on for a number of years prior to that date, starting in Great Britain just before the outbreak of World War II. Interestingly enough, only one pamphlet and one book on the subject were available at that time (in 1948 the pamphlet *Operational Research* was published by P.M.S. Blackett, and in 1952 the book *Methods of Operations Research* by Philip M. Morse and George E. Kimball), and no scientific journals were devoted primarily to it. The next few years witnessed a number of publications on OR, which were either proceedings of conferences on OR (in 1954 and 1957) or booklets sponsored by various institutes and associations such as the Midwest Research Institute (1954), the Railway Systems and Procedures Association (1954), the American Management Association (1956), and the National Industrial Conference Board (1957). In the same period, there appeared the book edited by McCloskey and Trefethen, *Operations Research for Management* (1956), and two bibliographies –one by the OR Group of the Case Institute of Technology (1956, with supplement for 1957) and the other by Riley (1953). The next book of note, *Operations Research*, appeared in 1957 and was edited by three prominent researchers (C. West Churchman, Russell L. Ackoff, and E. Leonard Arnoff) and authored by no less than 14 contributors. It represented, in fact, the most up-to-date thinking in the field as viewed by the specialists and the originators of the ideas. The next five years passed with only a trickle of contributions–from 1957 through 1962, the books published on OR can be counted on the fingers of one hand!

Then the flood came: since 1962, the number of books on OR has run into the hundreds. There are introductory books, specialized books in every facet of OR, progress review books and bibliographies, "reading" books, and so forth. Nor has the burst of activity been confined only to books; the technical journals have multiplied, the professional societies have proliferated, and, most important, the literature on the subject has increased at a high rate. The contributions vary from the totally theoretical—some of which appear in highly specialized mathematical journals—to the totally applied, some of which appear in trade journals. Today, there exist at least three abstracting services in OR.

In this maze of the relevant and the speculative, theoretical and applied, introductory and advanced, there seems to be a definite place for a handbook—an authoritative, concise, complete, and up-to-date survey of the field that is equally useful to specialists who need to "look up" an area outside their expertise, as well as to practitioner's who are interested in knowing what is useful in a particular situation without getting too involved in the theoretical derivation of the results.

Perhaps the best way to introduce this *Handbook* is to contrast what it is and what it is not. It is not a textbook because it sacrifices the most distinguishing aspect of the latter: it does not explain in a thorough and understandable fashion the derivations of the results. It is content with the statement of the premises and the statement of the results based on them. On the other hand, this *Handbook* is not a "survey" book, even though it does attempt to cover the waterfront, because a survey must be critical, giving detailed patterns of advancement as well as avenues of future research. Finally, this *Handbook* is not a catalog, although it does provide, as much as possible, a complete listing of the significant results in the field. But it goes beyond the mere listing, and establishes the connection between theory and practice.

This *Handbook* is intended to serve as a reference book that should appeal to the expert, the practitioner, and the novice alike. It is divided into two volumes. This volume carries the subtitle, *Foundations and Fundamentals*, while the companion volume is subtitled, *Models and Applications*. This division serves to segregate the theory and other philosophical and historical considerations from the practice of OR in either its modeling of common processes or in its application to several fields of human endeavor.

This volume on *Foundations and Fundamentals* is a concise and definitive reference book on the fundamental concepts and methodologies of OR. It is divided into three sections, written by 21 leading authorities in their fields, and offers a panoramic and up-to-date view of OR.

The *first section* (4 chapters) serves as a general introduction to the field. It covers the origin and subsequent development of OR, tracing its growth to its current international status. This is perhaps the most comprehensive exposition of this aspect of OR. This section also covers the professional eduction of the practitioners, and the general approach to the conduct of OR studies. These two topics are usually ignored or glossed over lightly in other publications in OR.

The *second section* (8 chapters) and the *third section* (9 chapters) classify and summarize the theory and methodology of OR. They survey the salient contributions in the various methodologies, giving the most significant theoretical results in clear and concise form. The first classification of methodology appears in the selection of the subjects in each section, with Section 2 dealing with deterministic theory and Section 3 with stochastic or probabilistic theory. The two sections combined cover the various facets of mathematical programming (linear, integer, nonlinear, large scale, geometric, and dynamic); stochastic processes and the theory of queues; graphs and networks; optimal control; value theory and decision analysis; game theory and gaming; search theory; and simulation. To the nonexpert in theory, these two sections offer an introduction and a road map to gaining expertise in a particular methodology. To the expert, on the other hand, the two sections offer a convenient summary and, in many instances, the future areas of research in unsolved problems. The list of references at the end of each chapter should be of valuable service to both types of readers.

The second volume, *Models and Applications*, answers the question of where has the theory of OR been applied? The answer is written by 27 competent authors who have been associated with the different fields of application. Apart from documenting these applications, the volume, which is divided into two sections, provides a perspective and a view of future movement in the applications of OR.

The *first section* (12 chapters) documents the applications to various functional processes that are common to most operational systems, and the degree of success obtained in these applications. The coverage ranges from the standard topics—such as forecasting and project selection, planning, and control—to more uncommon topics in OR literature such as accounting, finance, and human resources management.

The *second section* (8 chapters) concentrates on illustrations of OR applications to human enterprises. It presents a concise and illuminating discussion of the tools that were used, the problems encountered, and the utility derived from them in eight broad areas: the military, health services, education, transportation, urban systems, leisure industries, electric utilities, and process industries.

Despite their comprehensive posture, the two volumes still miss a number of topics in both theory and application. For instance, this first volume carries no mention of the theory of "fuzzy systems," although it may prove to be one of the most innovative and stimulating ideas that has come forth within the past 10 years.* In addition, the second volume has no discussion of OR models and application in a variety of fields, such as management information systems, agriculture, and the railroads, among others.

We have an apology and an explanation to make. The apology is to the readers of this *Handbook* who may have wished to consult it on any, or all, of these topics. The explanation is simply the following: working under the usual constraints of time and space, we had to make some choices and these (as well as many other) topics were excluded from the final product. We trust that we have made the correct choices or at least reached a satisficing solution.

*The interested reader may consult, *Fuzzy Sets and Their Applications to Cognitive Decision Processes*, Zadeh *et al.*, eds., Academic Press, 1975, or the comprehensive bibliography on the subject, *A Bibliography of Fuzzy Systems Theory and Closely Related Topics*, B. R. Gaines and L. J. Kohout, University of Essex, Colchester, Essex, U.K.

The time is now ripe for us to define the audience to whom this *Handbook* is addressed. It is primarily addressed to operations researchers, management scientists, systems analysts, industrial engineers, managers, and others who use quantitative methods in resolving systems-type problems in operational systems. The two volumes are intended to serve as reference books to the expert, novice, and practitioner alike, although each would use it in different ways and for different purposes. This first volume is useful to the specialist from two points of view: first, as a handy resumé of the areas of one's expertise and, second, as a place to "look up" an area outside one's expertise and to discover its essential features and the most important and current references on it. It is useful to the practitioner who is interested in finding out what is useful in a particular situation. And it is useful to the novice, since each chapter includes an easy-to-read introductory section on its subject matter, from which the reader can gain quick and easy familiarity with its more advanced studies. The typical novice is defined as one who has studied the following subjects or their equivalent: a standard college undergraduate course in calculus and matrix algebra, a one-year course in probability and statistics, an elementary course in computers and their programming, and a one-year course in the methodology and techniques of OR.

On the other hand, *Models and Applications*, being an authoritative exposition of the applications of OR methodology in a variety of contexts and operational systems, should have wide appeal to all people engaged in OR, either in theory or practice. It is also accessible to all since the emphasis shifts from theory to utility.

We also believe that this *Handbook* will appeal to persons other than those mentioned previously. In particular, this first volume should be appealing to applied mathematicians, statisticians, computer scientists, and engineers whose interests veer toward the analysis and synthesis of complex systems. With the current emphasis on "applicable" mathematics, more and more mathematicians are finding OR a fertile field of application of their mathematical expertise and acumen. On the other hand, the optimization of engineering design is gaining a strong foothold in traditional disciplines such as mechanical and civil engineering. A select few will find this *Handbook* almost indispenable. As for the second volume, various functional-area specialists (professionals in accounting, finance, personnel management, production and inventory, information systems, and project management) and staff specialists in various operational systems (urban systems, health services, transportation, military, electric utilities, process industries, and leisure industries) will have interest in it, wherein the use of OR in their specific areas is described.

Two college-classroom uses for the *Handbook* follow. Both volumes will find use as a supplement or reference book for undergraduate and graduate students taking the typical one-year professional course in OR methodology and techniques; these courses are taught in departments of industrial and systems engineering or operations research, and to a lesser extent in management science (school of business administration), applied mathematics, and computer science. The main reason for this type of adoption of the *Handbook* is that it presents concise, comprehensive coverage of the foundations and methodology of OR; in the case of the second volume, it indicates to students the rich array of applications of OR theory that may not be adequately covered in their textbook. The second volume will also find use as a supplement in courses in quantitative methods or operations management offered in most MBA programs. The primary objective of these courses is to show how OR is (or can be) used in solving "business" problems. This is consonant with the objective of that volume of the *Handbook*.

This *Handbook* is written by 48 authors who are recognized authorities in their respective fields. It is a distillation of their expertise, deep knowledge, and insight into the theory and practice of OR as it stands in the mid-seventies. It is also a reflection of their individual biases and subjective preferences. We believe that this is how it should be: the reader is presented not with a bland and colorless collection of surveys, but with forceful, and oftentimes provocative, panoramic views of the various topics discussed. The reader may not agree with a particular interpretation or classification—in fact, we suspect that readers will not agree with all of the views expressed in this *Handbook*—but if they are stimulated and informed, we would feel that the mission of the *Handbook* has been accomplished.

Individual differences among authors manifest themselves in several ways. For instance, some chapters contain references to general textbooks in which the topics are discussed in more detail, while others provide almost complete bibliographies. Some authors sketched in a heuristic manner the rationale of their conclusions, while others followed a more formal path. Some authors refrained from passing judgment on the "worthiness" of a particular method in a particular application while others went ahead and expressed their views freely. And so on. We, as editors, did not attempt any "homogenization" of styles or views, and we firmly believe that this "hands-off" policy adds strength and color to the *Handbook*.

Without attempting a formal definition of OR—the reader will find more than one definition in Section 1 of the first volume—one can safely state that OR is primarily concerned with the study of operational systems, where these latter are defined as systems that are subject to human decision (as contrasted to, say, stellar systems, which lie outside the sphere of human decisionmaking, albeit they obey logical laws of nature). One may ask, then, if OR is synonymous with systems theory. In our view, the answer is no; there are differences between the two disciplines. Sometimes the difference is a matter of degree, and sometimes it is in basic outlook. As always, the content of either is highly conditioned by its historical development.

Traditionally, systems theory has been closely related to "hardware" systems (the first "systems engineering," as such, was in the field of telephony), while OR is identified with the "software." OR tends to be concerned with problems that can be represented by mathematical models, which, in turn, can be analytically studied and optimized. Systems theory, on the other hand, although formal in nature, is concerned with problems of greater complexity, and is more global and abstract in its approach. Its components may consist of mathematical models, but may also incorporate social and biological factors that have not been successfully quantified. OR tends to be mostly concerned with smaller-scale problems of existing systems, as contrasted with systems theory, which usually connotes a larger, more encompassing perspective of new systems.

A system is any cohesive collection of items that are dynamically related. Every system does something, and what it does can be regarded as its purpose. Systems theory is primary concerned with the discovery of the mechanisms by which such purpose is achieved and by which equilibrium or self-regulation is maintained. OR is one of the most important inputs to such a theory, providing the quantitative models of the mechanisms that are amenable to such treatment. Thus, OR may be legitimately viewed as one among several disciplines that contribute to the general theory of systems.

A handbook of this size is evidently the outcome of the cooperative effort of a large number of people. In closing, it is our pleasure to acknowlege our indebtedness to them. The editorial advisory committee composed of Drs. R. E. Fetter and David B. Hertz helped guide the formulation of the broad outlines of the structure of this *Handbook*, the scope of its coverage, and its general thrust and orientation. Theirs was a key input at the time of conception of the idea of a handbook. To the 48 contributing authors go our thanks, individually and collectively, for their valuable inputs, and for their patience and understanding in the face of sometimes impatient and sometimes seemingly overcritical editors. Our special thanks go to our colleagues who unselfishly gave of their time and effort to review some of the chapters. In particular, we wish to mention Drs. Jacques Vander Eecken and Willy Gochet, both of the Catholic University of Leuven, and Professors Marianne Gardner and Henry L. W. Nuttle, both of North Carolina State University at Raleigh.

Joseph J. Moder
Miami, Florida

Salah E. Elmaghraby
Raleigh, North Carolina

CONTENTS

Handbook of Operations Research

FOUNDATIONS AND FUNDAMENTALS

SECTION I

Foundations and Philosophy of Operations Research

I-1

THE HISTORY, NATURE, AND USE OF OPERATIONS RESEARCH

Hugh J. Miser
University of Massachusetts

1. THE BEGINNINGS

In 1935, as part of Great Britain's effort to prepare an adequate response to the growing menace of German air power, scientists began an urgent series of experiments aimed at locating aircraft by sending out radio waves from ground stations and then detecting the reflections from the aircraft, a scheme that soon came to be called radar. The work began at Orfordness, on Britain's east coast about 60 miles north of the mouth of the Thames, and continued at Bawdsey, about 10 miles further south, where later the research staff was based and newly designed equipment was installed.

The ensuing three years saw the technical capabilities of the detection equipment established and the practical methods of aircraft tracing and reporting worked out. But to achieve efficient interception the British fighter aircraft needed to be controlled and directed to the appropriate places. Separately—in the interests of secrecy—the "Biggin Hill experiment" proposed by Henry Tizard was mounted during the late months of 1936 and the early ones of 1937. Fighter aircraft from the airfield at Biggin Hill, just south of London, were used to simulate enemy aircraft tracked by ground direction-finding on their own voice radio transmissions. Other fighters were interceptors, also tracked by their own voice transmissions and directed over the same radios. B. G. Dickins led the analysis of the results.

Toward the end of 1937, the two systems—the Bawdsey work on detection and tracking of uncooperative attacking aircraft and the Biggin Hill work on the tracking and direction of cooperative defending fighters—began to be brought together. This work involved the closest possible cooperation between the scientists and the officers and men of the Royal Air Force, so that the best tactical operations of both equipment and men, air and ground crews, could be achieved. "Thus there grew up, between the summer of 1936 and that of 1937, the basic technique of operational control without which the Battle of Britain would not have been won and could hardly have been fought." [Clark, 1965] The work had moved from technical experimentation to the evolution of effective tactics, with the scientists and operating people working together indistinguishably.

As the new tactics were tested further in large-scale air exercises, the scientists turned their attention to measuring how effective they were. It was in connection with such work in 1938 that A. P. Rowe, then in charge of the scientific group at Bawdsey, referred to it as "operational research"—terminology he is thought to have originated.

Thus, it is fair to think of Bawdsey as the birthplace of operations research—still referred to in Britain as operational research—and the period 1935-1938 as the time of gestation of its basic concept.

By 1939, E. C. Williams, a leader of the work at Bawdsey, had moved to the headquarters of the RAF Fighter Command to join a new team under Harold Larnder that continued the work of tactical evaluation and improvement. Within the next two years this scientific work in cooperation with serving military officers had established its worth so convincingly that similar arrangements had been made at the RAF Bomber Command (under B. G. Dickins), the RAF Coastal Command (charged with the air war against submarines), and the British Army's Anti-Aircraft (A.A.) Command.

The major night air raids on Great Britain in the autumn of 1940 presented the A.A. Command with major technical and operational problems. To help with them, P. M. S. Blackett, a physicist who was later to win a Nobel Prize for his work on cosmic rays, joined the staff of the command, and had soon assembled an active and effective group that came to be known as "Blackett's circus." In March 1941 Blackett moved to the Coastal Command, where he established a new operational research section that made important contributions to the effectiveness of this command. In December 1941 Blackett was consulted about the possibility of forming an operational research section for the Admiralty, and wrote a brief memorandum on "Scientists at the Operational Level" that was to have considerable influence on both sides of the Atlantic [Blackett, 1962]. In January 1942 Blackett moved to the Admiralty to establish operations research work there.

Later the operational research section for A.A. Command became the nucleus of the British Army Operational Research Group, and sections had been established in every major British military command, both at home and overseas.

When the United States was brought into the war, both its Navy and Army Air Corps became aware of this successful use of scientists at operational commands. In 1942, Captain W. D. Baker, an antisubmarine-warfare officer with the Atlantic Fleet, requested the establishment of an Anti-Submarine Warfare Operations Research Group and drew from Blackett's 1941 memorandum in describing what he wanted it to do and how it should be manned. To lead ASWORG, later renamed the Operations Research Group and attached to the Headquarters of the Commander-in-Chief, U.S. Navy, Philip M. Morse, a physicist, was recruited from Massachusetts Institute of Technology to be project supervisor, and William Shockley, later to win a Nobel Prize for his work on the transistor, was brought from the Bell Telephone Laboratories to be director of research. During the same period, the U.S. Army Air Corps sent W. Barton Leach, a lawyer then on active duty, to England to study what had been done there; when he brought back a favorable report, he was asked to recruit scientists and to establish an "operations analysis section" at the Eighth Air Force, a bombing force that was then getting itself established in the United Kingdom. The first members of this section arrived on site in October 1942. By the end of the war the Navy's Operations Research Group had grown to over 70 scientists and the USAAF, under Leach's leadership, had established over two dozen operations analysis sections, both at home and at combat commands abroad.

The Royal Canadian Air Force also adopted the operational research concept in 1942, and organized three sections.

Quite independently, Ellis A. Johnson, capitalizing on an expertise in magnetism, developed similar concepts and applied them to the problems of mine warfare; his ideas applied to this offensive tactic played a significant role in the Pacific war [Johnson and Katcher, 1973; Page, et al., 1974].

The Axis powers did not make use of operations research during World War II.

The available historical records do not provide an accurate count of the number of scientists involved in operations research in World War II; however, even a conservative estimate suggests that the number in the British, American and Canadian services totaled well over 700. Their activities, far too various to summarize here, included not only the elements of technical support, evaluating tactical results, and tactical innovation mentioned earlier, but also applying such knowledge to tactical planning and strategic choices. Most important for the future, many of these men saw in these wartime scientific developments the germ of a new science of operating systems and applying the knowledge that it was capable of generating to many peacetime activities.

For sketches of the wartime work, see Air Ministry [1963] and Morse and

Kimball [1946], on which the brief account above is largely based, and Blackett [1962], Johnson and Katcher [1973], Page, et al. [1974], Trefethen [1954], and Waddington [1973].

Since World War II workers have identified many precursors of operations research as it came to be recognized during the war—for example, Lanchester's 1916 model of warfare [Morse and Kimball, 1946], Erlang's development of queuing theory and its applications in Copenhagen in the early years of the twentieth century (see Chapter III-2), and Levinson's work on the problems of retailing beginning in the 1920s [Levinson, 1954]. However, these precursors remained isolated until they joined the mainstream of activity and knowledge that flowed from the history that has just been sketched. Therefore, it is fair to identify the beginnings of operations research as a coherent professional field with a continuous history starting with the work of the World War II analysts.

2. THE SCIENCE OF OPERATIONS RESEARCH

It is clear that many of the early pioneers of operations research (OR) conceived of their work as being scientific; indeed, Blackett's early 1941 memorandum emphasized that the work was the "scientific analysis of operations," and stressed that conditions should be appropriate for such work: "The atmosphere required is that of a first-class pure scientific research institution, and the calibre of the personnel should match this."

In a second memorandum ("A Note on Certain Aspects of the Methodology of Operational Research"), originally written in 1941 but revised in May 1943 [Blackett, 1962], he goes on to say:

> One obvious characteristic of operational research, as at present practiced, is that it has, or should have a strictly practical character. Its object is to assist the finding of means to improve the efficiency of war operations in progress or planned for the future. To do this, past operations are studied to determine the facts; theories are elaborated to explain the facts; and finally the facts and theories are used to make predictions about future operations...
>
> Predictions about the future are of course always subject to much uncertainty, but experience has shown that many more useful quantitative predictions can be made than is often thought possible. This arises to a considerable extent from the relative stability over quite long periods of time of many factors involved in operations. This stability appears rather unexpected in view of the large number of chance events and individual personalities and abilities that are involved in even a small operation. But these differences in general average out for a large number of operations, and the aggregate results are often found to remain comparatively constant.

Morse and Kimball [1946] also observed that "large bodies of men and equipment carrying out complex operations behave in an astonishingly regular manner, so that one can predict the outcome of such operations to a degree not foreseen by most natural scientists."

Thus, the early workers saw clearly that the novelty of what they were doing arose from two sources: the phenomena of operating systems that were being subjected to scientific study, and the administrative arrangements that were evolved to enable the findings to be put to practical use promptly.

These early perceptions remain valid today.

2.1 Science and Its Method

The aim of science is to understand and provide explanations for what occurs in nature, that is, real-world phenomena. Our concept of nature includes both naturally occurring and man-made elements; the phenomena are any happenings or effects exhibited by these elements.

Science begins with carefully disciplined observations of selected phenomena. These facts then lead the scientist to construct theories that fit the facts and constitute an intellectual description and explanation of them. These theories can then be manipulated and extended entirely within the domain of the intellect; more importantly, they can be made to yield predictions of what will happen under various new conditions. These consequences of the theories can then be verified by new observations of the relevant phenomena; if the consequences of one's theory check with the observed facts, his belief in its correctness is strengthened, but, if consequences and facts disagree, then he must discard the theory or modify it.

Kemeny [1959] summarizes the process this way:

> As Einstein has repeatedly emphasized, science must start with facts and end with facts, no matter what theoretical structures it builds in between. First of all the scientist is an observer. Next he tries to describe in complete generality what he saw, and what he expects to see in the future. Next he makes predictions on the basis of his theories, which he checks against the facts again.
>
> The most characteristic feature of the method is its cyclic nature. It starts with facts, ends in facts, and the facts ending one cycle are the beginning of the next cycle. A scientist holds his theories tentatively, always prepared to abandon them if the facts do not bear out the predictions. If a series of observations, designed to verify certain predictions, force us to abandon our theory, then we look for a new or improved theory . . . Since we expect that science consists of an endless chain of progress, we may expect the cyclic process to continue indefinitely.

The process just described is *the method of science*, and *science* is the body of knowledge produced by applying this method to the phenomena of nature.

What unites all of science, then, is its method; what distinguishes one science from another is the domain of nature each has undertaken to understand and explain. Thus, for example, an astronomer looks at the motions of planets, stars, and other bodies in the universe; a geologist examines phenomena of the earth's crust; and so on.

One must be careful not to take this description of the structure of science as a behavioral description of the activities of scientists. While some scientific work does follow this outline, most does not: for example, theories are invented before phenomena are found that fit them (quite common in operations research these days), theories based on phenomena may go unverified for a long time, and so on. In sum, scientists may start anywhere in this outline, and move in any direction to achieve bits and pieces of knowledge. However, the final synthesis of confirmed knowledge is achieved in conformity with the structure of the method of science.

2.2 Operations Research as a Science

In the spirit of this philosophy of science, we may say that OR uses the method of science to understand and explain phenomena of *operating systems*, the natural context it has chosen to explore. Such systems frequently involve men and machines operating in a natural environment, where we understand the word machine to have a very general meaning, ranging all the way from the mechanical devices usually intended by the term to complicated social structures operating according to accepted rules.

Thus, the science of OR observes the phenomena of operating systems, devises theories (in recent years called *models* by many operations-research workers) to explain these phenomena, uses these theories to describe what takes place under altered conditions, and checks these predictions against new observations.

In sum, OR is a science because it employs the method of science to create its knowledge, and it is distinguished from other sciences by undertaking to account for the phenomena of operating systems, a context of nature largely neglected by other sciences.

In view of the steps in the method of science, one can expect any science to develop systematic literature in four categories: the results obtained from observing phenomena and specialized methods for making such observations, the construction of theories (or models), the tailoring of such theories to observations and the derivation of predictions from the results, and the verification of these predictions by comparing them with new observations.

Part II of this handbook describes deterministic theories that have been developed by operations research since World War II: linear programming, integer programming, graph theory, flows in networks, geometric programming, nonlinear programming, large-scale programming, and optimal-control theory. Part III covers eight stochastic theories, largely developed since the war: stochastic processes, the theory of queues, value theory, decision analysis, game theory and gaming, search theory, simulation, and dynamic programming.

Part I of the companion volume, *Handbook of Operations Research: Models and Applications*, describes important models that have been devised for thirteen processes common to many arenas of application: forecasting; accounting; finance and managerial economics; marketing and advertising; personnel management; investment economic analysis; management information systems; computer and information systems; project selection, planning, and control; inventory control; scheduling and sequencing; replacement, maintenance, and reliability; facilities location and layout; and production planning. There is also a section on cost-benefit analysis.

Part II of the companion volume describes how these theories—and others—have been tailored to describe the phenomena in nine of the arenas in which OR was well developed in 1974: military problems, government operations, urban systems, health services, education systems, transportation, public utilities, manufacturing industries, and the process industries.

The results of observations and methods of making them, as well as how they are used in formulating and verifying theories, are usually included in the literature supporting the summaries in Parts I and II of the companion volume. Oddly, OR has not as yet developed a sufficiently specialized literature on these subjects to warrant separate discussion in this handbook. However, one can expect such a literature to emerge in the future.

In any case, it is fair to say that OR workers have, throughout the history of their subject, followed Blackett's advice (from his "Methodology" memorandum): ". . . operations research, like every science, must not copy in detail the technical methods of any other science, but must work out techniques of its own, suited to its own special material and problems. These techniques must not remain rigid but must change with the nature of the problems."

During World War II most of the OR work involved adaptations of methods and approaches from other sciences; in particular, most of the mathematical models were fairly direct constructions using the tools of analysis, probability, and statistics, frequently inspired by conceptual analogies from other sciences. A notable exception was the development in the U.S. Navy's Operations Research Group (ORG) of search theory (see Chapter III-6). Thus, the new theories summarized in Parts II, III of this volume and Part I of the companion volume are largely post-war developments. Lanchester's theory of warfare [Morse and Kimball, 1946] had existed since 1916, and, although explored mathematically during the war, was not applied directly to war-time operations; indeed, it did not achieve significant verification until 1954 [Engel, 1954].

Since World War II, however, the explorations of new phenomena of nature and the construction of theories to account for them has proceeded very rapidly, as Parts I and II of the companion volume amply attest.

3. THE PRACTICE OF OPERATIONS RESEARCH

The science of OR was born in response to pressing operational problems. Thus, throughout the history of the subject, OR workers have done more than develop a science; they have also applied the knowledge gained to solving problems. During the second and third decades of its history, the community of OR workers has grown to be large and varied enough to enjoy some specialization—the growth of a community of theoreticians being particularly notable—but this close relation between research and practice remains a special feature of the subject: the term OR, indeed, comprehends both aspects. In sum, operations research includes both scientific research on the phenomena of operating systems and the associated engineering activities aimed at applying the results of the research.

However, this engineering aspect of OR involves more than just applying knowledge developed by the method of science; it also uses the arts of invention (finding arrangements that work in desired ways) and design (putting inventions together to perform desired tasks or solve important problems), not to mention the various arts of communication, interpretation, and implementation.

Military secrecy kept much of the detail of wartime studies from general publication for a long time; however, by now much of what was done then has been described publicly (see the references in the first section of this chapter). Similarly, industrial and institutional constraints continue to keep much of the work of OR practice from publication. However, the literature, although overbalanced in the theoretical direction by these constraints, does contain records of many fine examples of applied operations-research work—far too many for a compact listing in a handbook. On the other hand, what this means is that even a casual search of the literature will lead one to interesting and excellent examples—and, of course, the chapters in Part V refer to examples in their arenas. Readers interested in early examples now considered classics will find these three papers of interest: Edie, [1954]; Thornthwaite [1953]; O'Brien and Crane [1959].

However, on the arts of invention and design related to the practice of OR, the literature is relatively sparse, and not yet well enough developed to call for a summary chapter in this handbook. The practice of these arts has achieved the most in the military environment [Quade and Boucher, 1968], but significant progress is now appearing in connection with civil-sector problems [Quade, 1975].

On issues of professional concern relating to practice, even the early writers showed concern and offered advice; for example, both Blackett [1962] and Morse and Kimball [1946], based on their wartime experiences, discuss how an analyst should go about his work, the conditions that should surround it, and the relations he should maintain with the users of his findings. In this area, four points deserve to be made here:

1. Chapter I-3 discusses issues relating to the conduct of OR studies.
2. A committee of the Operations Research Society of America (ORSA) has set forth some guidelines for the practice of operations research [Caywood, et al., 1971]. This effort met with considerable early criticism, and it is too early to tell whether or not the concepts, although well based on experience during the war and the first two post-war decades, will endure as permanent guides for practitioners in the changing conditions of the future.
3. The relations between OR groups and their client organizations have been fairly extensively studied; while there is no convenient comprehensive summary of this work, the reader will find [Radnor and Neal, 1973; Neal and Radnor, 1973] convenient entry points for a search of this literature.
4. The rather dry categorizations of this chapter look back at the history of OR, and, no doubt, describe much of its future. However, they almost completely ignore the fact that OR, when its scientific and engineering aspects are taken together, works in a setting provided by society—and, indeed, aims at understanding society's behavior in order to induce changes in it. In fact, OR activity becomes merely a part of the behavior of the system we call society. These perceptions lead naturally to important practical and philosophical issues, which are taken up in the next chapter of this handbook. Thus, the present chapter should be regarded as an introduction to the much more comprehensive social perceptions discussed in Chapter I-2.

4. THE GROWTH OF OPERATIONS RESEARCH, 1945-1975

There is not room in a single chapter of this handbook to set forth a comprehensive history of the growth of OR over the last three decades. In a sense, the other chapters provide much of the material for an intellectual history. Therefore, in very brief compass we shall outline here a few more administrative matters that offer a frame for the substance of OR discussed in the later chapters: some trends in evidence over the period, the creation and growth of professional societies, the founding and growth of journals, the increasing flow of books, and the growth of education.

4.1 Trends

Although most of the war-time OR workers returned to their prewar pursuits at the war's end, an important nucleus remained attached to the military services, which desired to continue an association that had demonstrated its fruitfulness. Indeed, the next decade saw much growth, not only on this foundation, but also through the creation of new arrangements. For example, in the United States, the Navy's ORG became an expanded Operations Evaluation Group with Jacinto Steinhardt as director under a contract with the Massachusetts Institute of Technology. The Air Force expanded its operations analysis sections under the leadership of LeRoy A. Brothers, and in 1948 the Army established its Operations Research Office with Ellis A. Johnson as director under a contract with The Johns Hopkins University. In 1949 the Joint Chiefs of Staff established the Weapons Systems Evaluation Group with Philip M. Morse as the first Technical Director; in the meantime, the Air Force had also established Project RAND at the Douglas Aircraft Corporation, and in 1949 it became The RAND Corporation. By the early 1950s these organizations were staffed with more people than had been involved in operations research in all the Allied countries during the war, and were providing a very wide range of OR and interdisciplinary studies for their client organizations. Similar, but not so extensive, developments took place in Canada and the United Kingdom.

Without the immediate pressures of a war, these organizations turned their attention to the many issues of planning, and developed many of the arts useful in such an endeavor, such as computer simulation (see Chapters III-7 and III-8), cost-benefit analysis (see Chapter II-5 of the companion volume), and systems analysis [Quade and Boucher, 1968]; they also made many significant advances to search theory, game theory and gaming, programming, value theory, and other mathematical techniques. With their relatively large staffs, they were also able to widen the boundaries and extend the horizons of their concerns to a remarkable extent, and to undertake large-scale studies of defense policy. Concurrently, defense contractors added substantial OR work to their proposal, design, and planning activities, and a number of firms whose activities were devoted entirely to research were created and did a substantial amount of defense operations and systems research.

The impacts of this work produced fundamental changes in the ways defense planning was done and major defense decisions were made. However, the impacts were produced, not only by studies, but also by many persons from these organizations taking key posts in defense organizations; for example, the Defense Department Comptroller from 1961 to 1965 was Charles J. Hitch, an economist from RAND who had earlier been President of the Operations Research Society of America, and in 1973 another RAND man, James R. Schlesinger, was appointed Secretary of Defense.

While OR was having this important effect on strategic and weapons planning, it is a puzzling anomaly that it appears to have been unable to influence significantly U.S. military policies with respect to the war in Vietnam.

Concurrently, OR was expanding in a major way into industry and onto university campuses. Indeed, by 1955 the center of gravity of the community's interests had quite clearly shifted away from military work. One index of this shift was the rapid growth after 1954 of a group of workers centering their attention on *management science*, a specialty that can be only marginally differentiated from operations research.

As late as 1955, Philip M. Morse [1955] was able to survey the state of operations research and call for more attention to basic theory, operational experiments, and training new workers in the field. Chapter I-4 gives evidence of the vigor of the response to the call for education, and the chapters in Parts II and III demonstrate the fecundity of the theoretical work over the ensuing two decades; however, the specialized work on operational experimentation is still too scattered and shallow to call for a chapter in this handbook, a fact several of whose aspects have been noted earlier.

The most recent decade has seen the continuing expansion of OR into new contexts, notably such civil-government branches as criminal justice, transportation, urban problems, housing, health care, education, and social services. For example, in the urban field, two notable programs were established in the late 1960s: The Urban Institute was founded in 1968 and The New York City–Rand Institute was set up in 1969. Both have evolved highly varied and effective programs with strong elements of OR permeating their activities [The Urban Institute, 1972; The New York City–Rand Institute, 1972]. Research firms with previous experience in defense analysis have aided materially in the spread of OR approaches to civil-government problems, and there are several hundred OR workers in civil-government agencies of the federal government, scattered, however, in small groups or working individually. Thus, in 1975 it is fair to assess the achievements of OR in civil-government areas as falling far short of the need in the United States, and with significant impacts lying largely in the future [Miser and Cushen, 1975].

The picture for countries other than the United States with well-developed OR communities shows similar features, with, of course, country-by-country variations too numerous to mention here.

A view of the state of OR in 1975 shows several trends, some sympathetic to each other, some partially conflicting. On the one hand, there are the tremendous achievements in theory and application over the last three decades to breed a pride and a comfortable professionalism, particularly in academic programs; on the other hand, there is an influential minority that betrays the philosophical restlessness that Churchman describes in the next chapter and that urges a continual expansion of context and outlook for the subject. On the side, there are critics of the field's shortcomings and failures, as well as those who can see the contributions that have been and can be made. That the field retains its healthy youthful vigor is shown by the facts that there exists a vigorous interchange among all these interests, that the field responds constructively to the differing points of view within it, and that it continues to expand its theories, its contexts, and its outlooks.

4.2 Professional Societies

In April 1948 several scientists who had taken part in the successful development of operations research in England during World War II, and who had had occasional informal meetings to discuss their work, agreed among themselves to act as convenors of an Operational Research Club; J. A. Jukes became its first honorary secretary. Its purpose was to provide a continuing structure for these informal meetings, and six were held each year between September and May in rooms of the Royal Society in London; at them the members discussed the use of operations research in many industries and services, including agriculture, cotton, steel, boots and shoes, coal, electricity, livestock breeding, building, and transport.

The club also founded the *Operational Research Quarterly*, the first issue appearing in March 1950, with Max Davies and R. T. Eddison as joint editors.

On November 10, 1953, the members of the club, recognizing the spread of interest in their subject, voted to become the Operational Research Society, with membership open to any person engaged in operations-research work. The first chairman of the Society was O. H. Wansbrough-Jones.

In the meantime, in the United States the National Research Council had established a Committee on Operations Research in 1949; its chairman was Horace C. Levinson, a man who, although originally an astronomer, had independently pioneered OR in retail merchandising in the 1920s. The purpose of the committee was to foster interest in nonmilitary operations research; to this end, the committee published a pamphlet on *Operations Research, with Special Reference to Non-Military Applications* that was widely circulated. In January 1952 ten persons met in Cambridge, Massachusetts, to consider steps toward founding an American professional society. After a second larger meeting in March to develop the plans further, a founding meeting was held May 26–27 at Arden House, Harriman, New York, at which the Operations Research Society of America (ORSA) came into being. Philip M. Morse, who had been a moving spirit in these developments, was elected its first president. The first meeting of this new society took place in November 1952, when the first issue of the *Journal of the Operations Research Society of America* was published, with Thornton Page as editor; the name was changed to *Operations Research* in 1956.

Another group in the United States founded The Institute of Management Sciences (TIMS) in 1953, an international society, but with most of its members in the United States. William W. Cooper was its first president. The first issue of its journal, *Management Science*, appeared in September 1954, with C. West Churchman as editor.

TABLE 1. THE OPERATIONS RESEARCH SOCIETIES OF THE WORLD

(The societies listed are those adhering to the International Federation of Operational Research Societies in 1974.)

Country	Society	Date Founded	Date Joined IFORS
Argentina	Sociedad Argentina de Investigación Operativa	1960	1962
Australia	Australian Operational Research Society[1]	1959	1960
Belgium	Société Belge pour l'Application des Méthodes Scientifiques de Gestion[2]	1958	1960
Brazil	Sociedade Brasiliera de Pesquisa Operational	1969	1969
Canada	Canadian Operational Research Society	1958	1960
Denmark	Dansk Selskap for Operationanalyze	1962	1963
Finland	Soumen Operaatiotukimussentra Oy	1973	1975
France	Association Française pour la Cybernétique Économique et Technique[3]	1956	1959
Germany	Deutsche Gesellschaft für Operations Research	1961	1962
Greece	Hellenic Operational Research Society	1963	1966
India	Operational Research Society of India	1957	1960
Ireland	Operations Research Society of Ireland	1965	1966
Israel	Operations Research Society of Israel	1966	1969
Italy	Associazione Italiana di Ricerca Operativa	1961	1962
Japan	Operations Research Society of Japan	1957	1961
South Korea	Operations Research Society of Korea	1970	1972
Mexico	Asociación Mexicana de Investigación de Operaciones y Administración Cientifica	1964	1966
Netherlands	Sectie Operationele Research	1958	1960
New Zealand	Operational Research Society of New Zealand	1964	1970
Norway	Norsk Operasjonsanalyseforening	1959	1960
Spain	Sociedad Española de Investigación Operativa	1962	1963
South Africa	Operations Research Society of South Africa	1969	1973
Sweden	Svenska Operationsanalysforeningen	1959	1960
Switzerland	Schweizerische Vereinigung für Operations Research	1961	1963
United Kingdom	Operational Research Society[4]	1948	1959
United States	Operations Research Society of America	1952	1959
USSR	Technical Committee on Operations Research[5]	1970	1972

[1]From 1959 to 1972: The Australian Joint Council for Operational Research.
[2]From 1958 to 1962: a part of the Belgian Statistics Society.
[3]From 1956 to 1964: Société Française de Recherche Opérationnelle.
[4]From 1948 to 1953: Operational Research Club.
[5]A part of the Computer Center of the Academy of Sciences.

Notes: Czechoslovakia adheres to the federation through the Economico-Mathematical Commission of the Czechoslovak Academy of Sciences. The Institute of Management Sciences and the Mathematical Programming Society adhere to the federation as "kindred societies." The Airline Group of IFORS, a special-interest group devoted to operations research on the problems of the world's airlines, also adheres to the federation.

For current names and addresses of officials of these societies, see a recent issue of the federation's journal, *International Abstracts in Operations Research.*

In January 1955 Russell L. Ackoff, then a nominee for Vice President of ORSA, suggested to B. H. P. Rivett, the secretary of the Operational Research Society (ORS), that an international conference on operational research be organized. The idea was seized on immediately, and an organizing committee was formed, with Sir Charles Goodeve as chairman for the ORS and Thornton Page as chairman for ORSA and TIMS. The result was the First International Conference on Operational Research, held at Oxford University, September 2-5, 1957, with 250 delegates from 21 countries in attendance [Davies, Eddison, and Page, 1957]. Subsequent international conferences have been held at Aix-en-Provence (1960), Oslo (1963), Cambridge, Massachusetts (1966), Venice (1969), Dublin (1972), and Tokyo and Kyoto (1975); the proceedings of these conferences provide interesting snapshots of world-wide interest in operations research and its growth [Banbury and Maitland, 1961; Kreweras and Morlat, 1964; Hertz and Melese, 1966; Lawrence, 1970; and Ross, 1973].

At the First International Conference at Oxford initial plans were made for the International Federation of Operational Research Societies (IFORS), which came into being on January 1, 1959, with three initial members: Operational Research Society, Operations Research Society of America, and Société Française de Recherche Opérationnelle (founded in 1956). The first IFORS secretary was Sir Charles Goodeve.

Between 1959 and 1975, twenty-four other national societies joined IFORS, a professional group in Czechoslovakia had adhered through an appropriate governmental organization, The Institute of Management Sciences and the Mathematical Programming Society—although international groups—had adhered under a special arrangement, and a special-interest group had become associated (for the list, see Table 1). However, even this list does not indicate adequately the extent of interest in OR; for example, the Operations Research Society of America, although a national society, in 1974 had members in no less than 67 countries. Thus, it seems fair to conclude that interest in operations research is world-wide.

It is not possible to get an accurate count of how many people world-wide are involved professionally with operations research; however, a crude estimate based on the membership figures supplied by the societies adhering to IFORS yields a result between 25,000 and 35,000 for 1975.

4.3 Journals

The first journal in the field of operations research was the *Operational Research Quarterly*, the second was *Operations Research;* two additional American journals appeared in 1954, and German and French journals were founded in 1956. Table 2 lists the world's OR journals in existence in 1974, and Table 3 lists 22 other journals of significant interest to OR workers, all founded since

TABLE 2. THE OPERATIONS RESEARCH JOURNALS OF THE WORLD.

Journal	Published by	Date Founded
Operational Research Quarterly	Operational Research Society (UK)	1950
Operations Research	Operations Research Society of America	1952
Naval Research Logistics Quarterly	U.S. Office of Naval Research	1954
Management Science	The Institute of Management Sciences	1954
Revue Française d'Automatique, Informatique, Recherche Opérationnelle[1]	Association Française pour la Cybernetique Économique et Technique	1956
Zeitschrift für Operations Research[2]	Deutschen Gesellschaft für Operations Research	1956
Journal of the Operations Research Society of Japan	Operations Research Society of Japan	1957
Cahiers du Centre d'Études de Recherche Opérationnelle	Centre d'Études de Recherche Opérationnelle, Brussels	1959
Revue Belge de Statistique d'Informatique et de Recherche Opérationnelle	Société Belge pour l'Application des Méthodes Scientifiques de Gestion and Société Belge de Statistique	1961
Metra	Metra Group, Paris	1962
INFOR[3]	Canadian Operational Research Society and the Canadian Information Processing Society	1963
Opsearch	Operational Research Society of India	1964
Interfaces	The Institute of Management Sciences and the Operations Research Society of America	1971
Ricerca Operativa	Franco Angeli, editore, Milan, Italy	1971
New Zealand Operational Research	Operational Research Society of New Zealand	1973

[1] During its first ten years, this journal was names the *Revue Française de Recherche Opérationnelle*, and was published by the Société Française de Recherche Opérationnelle, an organization that preceded the one listed above.

[2] This journal was started in 1972 as the successor to *Unternehmensforschung*, which was founded in 1956. Another journal, *Ablauf- und Planungsforschung*, began publication in 1960, but ceased publication about 1972.

[3] Before 1971 this journal was the *Journal of the Canadian Operational Research Society.*

Note: This table lists only journals that center most of their attention on operations research.

1955–indeed, most since 1965. These journals, and the space they devote to OR, exhibit a very substantial growth in the journal literature in OR during the fifteen years ending in 1974.

Operations research is fortunate to have had from 1961 onward an abstracting journal that brings together in one place summaries of all of the world's literature: *International Abstracts in Operations Research* (*IAOR*). Originally, this

TABLE 3. SOME JOURNALS OF SIGNIFICANT INTEREST TO OPERATIONS RESEARCH WORKERS.

Journal	Published by	Date Founded
The Engineering Economist	Engineering Economy Division, American Society for Engineering Education	1955
International Journal of Production Research	Taylor and Francis Ltd., London	1961
Trabajos de Estadistica y de Investigacion Operativa[1]	Instituto de Investigacion Operativa y Estadistica, Consejo Superior de Investigaciones Estadisticas, Madrid	1963
Journal of Applied Probability	Applied Probability Trust and the London Mathematical Society	1964
Transportation Science	Transportation Science Section, Operations Research Society of America	1967
Transportation Research	Pergamon Press, New York	1967
Socio-Economic Planning Sciences	Pergamon Press, New York	1967
Technological Forecasting and Social Change	American Elsevier, New York	1969
Industrial Engineering[2]	American Institute of Industrial Engineers	1969
AIIE Transactions[2]	American Institute of Industrial Engineers	1969
Policy Sciences	American Elsevier, New York	1970
Decision Sciences	American Institute for Decision Sciences	1970
The Bell Journal of Economics and Management Science	American Telephone and Telegraph Co.	1970
Discrete Mathematics	North-Holland, Amsterdam	1971
Mathematical Programming	Mathematical Programming Society	1971
Networks	Interscience, New York	1971
IEEE Transactions on Systems, Man, and Cybernetics[3]	IEEE Systems, Man, and Cybernetics Society	1971
Stochastic Processes and their Applications	North-Holland, Amsterdam	1973
OMEGA	Pergamon Press, New York	1973
Computers and Operations Research	Pergamon Press, New York	1974
Policy Analysis	University of California Press, Berkeley, California	1975
Mathematics of Operations Research	The Institute of Management Sciences and the Operations Research Society of America	1976

[1] From 1950 through 1963 this journal was named *Trabajos de Estadistica.*

[2] A predecessor, the *Journal of Industrial Engineering*, was published between 1949 and 1968.

[3] A predecessor, the *IEEE Transactions on Systems Science and Cybernetics*, was published between 1965 and 1970.

Note: This table contains an arbitrary selection of journals published in western languages. For others, see the references for later chapters in this handbook, and issues of *International Abstracts in Operations Research.*

journal was published by the Operations Research Society of America for IFORS with the cooperation of the societies adhering to the federation; since 1970 the federation has taken over the responsibility for it. The founding editor was Herbert P. Galliher; since 1968 Hugh E. Bradley has been editor. *IAOR* is published by the North-Holland Publishing Company, Amsterdam, The Netherlands, for IFORS.

For the period before 1961, three volumes by James H. Batchelor provide summaries of most of the literature: [Batchelor, 1959] covers the literature through 1957, [Batchelor, 1962] covers the literature for 1958 and 1959, and [Batchelor, 1963] covers the literature for 1960. A fourth volume [Batchelor and Athans, 1964] also provides coverage for 1961, the first year covered by *IAOR*.

Thus, the Batchelor volumes and *IAOR* together cover the world's operations-research literature from its beginnings to the present, and *IAOR* keeps the coverage current.

4.4 Books

At the close of World War II, three books were written to give professional accounts of the war-time OR activities: Morse and Kimball, [1946], Johnson and Katcher [1973], and Waddington [1973]. However, only the first emerged promptly; although its original 1946 government publication was classified, this classification was cancelled in 1948, and a trade publisher issued an edition in 1951. On the other hand, the Johnson and Katcher and Waddington volumes were held up over a quarter of a century by government release procedures. Thus, for a number of years, Morse and Kimball's *Methods of Operations Research* was the only one generally available that gave a coherent professional account of a body of OR work.

For several years in the early 1950s, a number of anthologies of articles and speeches were issued; the most notable and useful was McCloskey and Trefethen's *Operations Research for Management* [1954], which, in addition to articles on methods, cases, and general approaches, included a brief history of the field and a conscientiously prepared bibliography.

The first post-war textbook to emerge from an educational program was Churchman, Ackoff, and Arnoff's *Introduction to Operations Research* [1957], which was widely used and did much to fix the central content of the field.

In the meantime, treatises with particular interests were beginning to appear, such as: the symposium volume on *Activity Analysis of Production and Allocation* edited by Koopmans [1951], McKinsey's *Introduction to the Theory of Games* [1952], Whitin's *The Theory of Inventory Management* [1953], William's *The Compleat Strategyst* [1954], Manne's *Scheduling of Petroleum Refinery Operations* [1956], Bowman and Fetter's *Analysis for Production Management*

[1957], Bellman's *Dynamic Programming* [1957], Luce and Raiffa's *Games and Decisions* [1957], Dorfman, Samuelson, and Solow's *Linear Programming and Economic Analysis* [1958], Gass's *Linear Programming: Methods and Applications* [1958], Magee's *Production Planning and Inventory Control* [1958], McKean's *Efficiency in Government through Systems Analysis* [1958], Morse's *Queues, Inventories and Maintenance: The Analysis of Operations Systems with Variable Demand and Supply* [1958], Vazsonyi's *Scientific Programming in Business and Industry* [1958], Brown's *Statistical Forecasting for Inventory Control* [1959], Beckmann's *Lineare Planungsrechnung* [1959], Berge's *Théorie des Graphes et ses Applications* [1959], Karlin's *Mathematical Methods and Theory in Games, Programming and Economics* [1959], and Saaty's *Mathematical Methods of Operations Research* [1959].

By 1960, both treatises and textbooks at various levels were beginning to appear regularly, and by 1965 this flow had become a flood that had not abated ten years later. Thus, there is not space here to trace the growth further; however, the references for later chapters will guide the reader to the most valuable books in each of the fields treated in this handbook.

On the other hand, a 1969 textbook that set a new standard in the field deserves mention: Wagner's *Principles of Operations Research with Applications to Managerial Decisions* [1969]. It won the Operations Research Society of America's Lanchester Prize for 1969, and has been widely used.

4.5 Education

In the early years after World War II it was quite common for experienced OR workers to visualize their field as one that was not yet ready for an extensive program of formal training; rather, relevant training and research experience in an established field were considered adequate, and perhaps even preferred–thus mirroring the experiences of the pioneers.

However, the organization of educational opportunities proceeded apace. By the early 1950s short courses of varying durations were common in several countries, and university curricula had been started in a number of locations. Within a decade these had become both numerous and strong–as the discussion in Chapter I-4 bears witness. For example, a 1973 report of the Operations Research Society of America lists no less than 53 curricula in the United States [ORSA Education Committee, 1973]; other countries have exhibited similar growth. Thus, today a prospective student can find a wide variety of programs from which to make a choice.

Further, the training gained in them has become recognized as an important qualification for entry into professional work in the field, be it teaching, research, or practice.

5. EXTENSIONS OF OPERATIONS RESEARCH

The history of OR has been marked by continual growth and change. Thus, this field shows an era of discovery and fundamental formulation in the decade of the 1940s, an effort to reach out to new contexts in the decade of the 1950s, a great strengthening of theoretical foundations and academic programs in the decade of the 1960s, and a renewed effort to reach out to new and greatly enlarged contexts in the early 1970s, a movement still at full tide as this chapter is being written. In view of this history, and the state of the field as we observe it in 1975, what extensions of OR can we expect to see in the future?

First, we can expect the strong thrust toward developing theories and models to continue, but with a stronger counterpart activity to check these theories against reality and to modify them for realistic application. This trend will cause more attention to be given to methods of gathering information and data from operating environments, and to ways of experimenting with operating systems. These developments will have their impacts on academic programs, which will move away from their present overemphasis on the theory of OR to more varied emphases, including observation of and experimentation with operating systems, as well as the various arts of practice, including invention, design, and implementation.

Second, the art of systems analysis, so well developed in the military context [Quade and Boucher, 1968], will spread to other contexts; this movement has already begun, but is as yet moving only very slowly [Miser and Cushen, 1975]. This movement will also prompt a growth of interest in the extension of systems analysis called policy science [Quade, 1975], and its extension and application, particularly to problems of civil government at the national level; applications at the lower levels will grow too, but at a slower rate.

Third, operations research will respond to the challenge of the general systems theorists [Laszlo, 1972; Ackoff, 1973] to expand the concept of OR and its application, and, indeed, of what the science itself is. Churchman's argument in the next chapter of this handbook sketches the framework for this development; analysts of the future will think more and more in its terms.

Fourth OR—spurred by thinkers such as Churchman, Ackoff, and Laszlo—will rethink their basic philosophy, now badly scattered and incomplete, in order to achieve a comprehensive point of view relevant to what they are doing and to their expanding ambitions of OR. In doing this, they will, as they always have, keep the scientific and engineering aspects of their subject closely intertwined.

Fifth, OR will continue its currently vigorous efforts to reach out to new arenas of exploration and application.

The roots of all these developments exist in healthy form in 1975; how fast their plants grow will depend on their rate of nourishment, at present unpredictable. However, a balanced, healthy growth of operations research demands that they all grow in an appropriate balance.

6. THE FUTURE OF OPERATIONS RESEARCH

If OR extends itself as the previous section suggests it will—each extension listed there being a response to a currently perceived challenge—then its future holds great promise for its growth in power, scope, and practical importance.

However, there are threats to this future than can be perceived in 1975: a tendency to overemphasize theory, a preference in some quarters for a narrow professionalism, a tendency toward isolation to preserve the status already gained, a hesitancy to respond to major challenges, a history of overselling that sometimes repeats, and an occasional avoidance of risk.

If these threats can be overcome, if the neglected areas of the subject are attended to, if the extensions listed in the previous section are made, if operations research continues to rise to major challenges, and if, as it has throughout its history, it maintains an active cooperation with other specialties relevant to the problem it treats, then the future of OR will be one of expanding importance and utility—and the earned recognition and support that will inevitably ensue. I am confident that this future is the one that we can look forward to.

REFERENCES

1. Ackoff, Russell L., "Science in the Systems Age: Beyond IE, OR, and MS," *Operations Res.* **21**: 666–671 (1973).
2. Air Ministry, *The Origins and Development of Operational Research in the Royal Air Force*, Air Publication 3368, Her Majesty's Stationery Office, London, (1963).
3. Banbury, J. and J. Maitland, (eds.), *Proceedings of the Second International Conference on Operational Research*, Wiley, New York, and Dunod, Paris, (1961).
4. Batchelor, James H., *Operations Research: An Annotated Bibliography* **1**, St. Louis University Press, St. Louis, Missouri, (1959). Covers the literature through 1957.
5. —, *Operations Research: An Annotated Bibliography* **2**, St. Louis University Press, St. Louis, Missouri, (1962). Covers the literature of 1958 and 1959.
6. —, *Operations Research: An Annotated Bibliography* **3**, St. Louis University Press, St. Louis, Missouri, (1963). Covers the literature of 1960.
7. —, and Chris N. Athans, *Operations Research: An Annotated Bibliography* **4**, St. Louis Academy Press, St. Louis, Missouri, (1964). Covers the literature of 1961.
8. Beckmann, Martin, *Lineare Planungsrechnung*, Fachverlag für Wirtschaftstheorie und Oekonometrie, Ludwigshafen, Germany, (1959).
9. Bellman, Richard E., *Dynamic Programming*, Princeton University Press, Princeton, New Jersey, (1957).
10. Berge, Claude, *Théorie des Graphes et ses Applications*, Dunod, Paris, (1958).
11. Blackett, P. M. S., *Studies of War: Nuclear and Conventional*, Hill and Wang, New York, (1962). The material cited is in Part II.
12. Bowman, Edward H. and Robert B. Fetter, *Analysis for Production Management*, Richard D. Irwin, Homewood, Illinois, (1957).
13. Brown, Robert G., *Statistical Forecasting for Inventory Control*, McGraw-Hill, New York, (1959).
14. Caywood, Thomas E., Howard M. Berger, Joseph H. Engel, John F. Magee. Hugh J.

Miser, and Robert M. Thrall, "Guidelines for the Practice of Operations Research," *Operations Res.* **19:** 1123–1148 (1971).

15. Churchman, C. West, Russell L. Ackoff, and E. Leonard Arnoff, *Introduction to Operations Research*, Wiley, New York, (1957).
16. Clark, Ronald W., *Tizard*, Chapter 7, MIT Press, Cambridge, Massachusetts, (1965).
17. Davies, Max, R. T. Eddison, and Thornton Page, (eds.), *Proceedings of the First International Conference on Operational Research*, Operations Research Society of America, Baltimore, Maryland, (1959).
18. Dorfman, Robert, Paul A. Samuelson, and Robert M. Solow, *Linear Programming and Econometric Analysis*, McGraw-Hill, New York, (1958).
19. Edie, Leslie C., "Traffic Delays at Toll Booths," *Operations Res.* **2:** 107–138 (1954).
20. Engel, J. H., "A Verification of Lanchester's Law," *Operations Res.* **2:** 163–171 (1954).
21. Gass, Saul I., *Linear Programming: Methods and Applications*, McGraw-Hill, New York, (1958).
22. Hertz, David B. and Jacques Melese, (eds.), *Proceedings of the Fourth International Conference on Operational Research*, Wiley-Interscience, New York, (1966).
23. Johnson, Ellis A. and David A. Katcher, *Mines against Japan*, Naval Ordnance Laboratory, Silver Spring, Maryland, (1973).
24. Karlin, Samuel, *Mathematical Methods and Theory in Games, Programming, and Economics* **I, II,** Addison-Wesley, Reading, Massachusetts, (1959).
25. Kemeny, John G., *A Philosopher Looks at Science*, Van Nostrand Reinhold, New York, (1959).
26. Koopmans, Tjalling C. (ed.), *Activity Analysis of Production and Allocation*, Wiley, New York, (1951).
27. Kreweras, G. and G. Morlat, (eds.), *Proceedings of the Third International Conference on Operational Research*, English Universities Press, London, and Dunod, Paris, (1964).
28. Laszlo, Ervin, *The Systems View of the World*, George Braziller, New York, (1972).
29. Lawrence, John (ed.), *OR 69: Proceedings of the Fifth International Conference on Operational Research*, Tavistock Publications, London, (1970).
30. Levinson, Horace C., "Experiences in Commercial Operations Research," pp. 265–288 in McCloskey and Trefethen (1954).
31. Luce, R. Duncan and Howard Raiffa, *Games and Decisions*, Wiley, New York, (1957).
32. Magee, John F., *Production Planning and Inventory Control*, McGraw-Hill, New York, (1958).
33. Manne, Alan S., *Scheduling of Petroleum Refinery Operations*, Harvard University Press, Cambridge, Massachusetts, (1956).
34. McCloskey, Joseph F. and Florence N. Trefethen, (eds.), *Operations Research for Management*, Johns Hopkins Press, Baltimore, Maryland, (1954). A second volume with the same title, edited by McCloskey and J. M. Coppinger, appeared in (1956).
35. McKean, Roland N., *Efficiency in Government through Systems Analysis*, Wiley, New York, (1958).
36. McKinsey, J. C. C., *Introduction to the Theory of Games*, McGraw-Hill, New York, (1952).
37. Miser, Hugh J. and W. Edward Cushen, "The Demand for Management-Science Services in the Future in Civil Government," in Michael J. White, Michael Radnor, and David A. Tansik (eds.), *Management and Policy Science in American Government: Problems and Prospects*, Lexington Books, D. C. Heath, Lexington, Massachusetts, (1975).
38. Morse, Philip M., "Where is the New Blood?" *Operations Res.* **3:** 383–387 (1955).
39. ——, *Queues, Inventories and Maintenance: The Analysis of Operational Systems with Variable Demand and Supply*, Wiley, New York, (1958).

40. —— and George E. Kimball, *Methods of Operations Research*, National Defense Research Committee, Washington, D.C., (1946). (Also published by Wiley, New York, 1951.)
41. Neal, Rodney D. and Michael Radnor, "The Relation between Formal Procedures for Pursuing OR/MS Activities and OR/MS Group Success," *Operations Res.* **21**: 451–474 (1973).
42. New York City–Rand Institute, "Research in 1970–1971," *Operations Res.* **20**: 474–515 (1972).
43. O'Brien, G. G. and R. R. Crane, "The Scheduling of a Barge Line," *Operations Res.* **7**: 561–570 (1959).
44. ORSA Education Committee, *Education Programs in Operations Research/Management Science*, Operations Research Society of America, Baltimore, Maryland, (1973).
45. Page, Thornton, George S. Pettee, and William A. Wallace, "Ellis A. Johnson, 1906–1973," *Operations Res.* **22**: 1140–1155 (1974).
46. Quade, Edward S., *Analysis for Public Decisions*, American Elsevier, New York, (1975).
47. —— and W. I. Boucher, *Systems Analysis and Policy Planning: Applications in Defense*, American Elsevier, New York, (1968).
48. Radnor, Michael and Rodney D. Neal, "The Progress of Management-Science Activities in Large US Industrial Corporations," *Operations Res.* **21**: 427–450 (1973).
49. Ross, Miceal (ed.), *Operational Research '72: Proceedings of the Sixth IFORS International Conference on Operational Research*, North-Holland, Amsterdam, and American Elsevier, New York, (1973).
50. Saaty, Thomas L., *Mathematical Methods of Operations Research*, McGraw-Hill, New York, (1959).
51. Thornthwaite, C. W., "Operations Research in Agriculture," *Operations Res.* **1**: 33–38 (1953).
52. Trefethen, Florence N., "A History of Operations Research," pp. 3–35 in McCloskey and Trefethen (1954).
53. Urban Institute, The, "Research, 1968–1971," *Operations Res.* **20**: 516–557 (1972).
54. Vazsonyi, Andrew, *Scientific Programming in Business and Industry*, Wiley, New York, (1958).
55. Waddington, C. H., *OR in World War 2–Operational Research against the U-Boat*, Paul Elek Ltd., London, (1973).
56. Wagner, Harvey M., *Principles of Operations Research with Applications to Managerial Decisions*, Prentice-Hall, Englewood Cliffs, New Jersey, (1969). (2nd Ed., 1975.)
57. Whitin, T. M., *The Theory of Inventory Management*, Princeton University Press, Princeton, New Jersey, (1953).
58. Williams, J. D., *The Compleat Strategyst*, McGraw-Hill, New York, (1954).

I-2

PHILOSOPHICAL SPECULATIONS ON SYSTEMS DESIGN

C. West Churchman
University of California, Berkeley

1. INTRODUCTION

This paper is a philosophical discussion of a very old idea, namely, that humans can consider before they act and that potentially their consideration can produce a better act than the one that would have occurred without any prior consideration. In other words, why should you think before you leap?

The philosophical problem is relevant to the many efforts that are being made today to improve our human condition, by planning, operations research, management science, systems science, information systems, technological assessment, educational evaluation, and so on. Since I am not concerned about the specific characteristics of each of these efforts, but rather about their general philosophical justification, I need a generic label, which I'll call "systems design" (SD). I should emphasize that SD denotes *any* plausible effort to prepare for decisions by means of prior inquiry and, therefore, also includes applied social science, applied psychology, applied theory of altered states of consciousness, and so on.

The basic stipulation of the philosophical inquiry of this paper was given by Descartes in his *Discourse on Method:* all issues are open to discussion, and none shall be taken as settled just because "everyone" agrees. The phrase "few can doubt that . . ." is to be taken as a signal, not of acceptance, but of the obligation to listen to the few.

2. SYSTEMS DESIGN

My purpose here will best be served by first defining SD in a manner which will then enable me to discuss its philosophy: SD is implementing improvement in social systems by means of the best available method of inquiry.

This definition has the relevant advantage of highlighting the philosophical issues of SD. Taking the ideas in reverse, the meaning of "best method of inquiry" is derived from the idea of how knowledge is acquired, or what philosophers call *epistemology*. The meaning of a "social system" is derived from the meaning of social reality, or what philosophers call social *ontology*. The meaning of "improvement" is derived from the meaning of the good, or what philosophers call *ethics*. The meaning of "implementing" is derived from the meaning of translating knowledge into action, or what philosophers call *pragmatics*.

3. "SCIENTIFIC METHOD"

It will be appropriate to abbreviate "best method of inquiry" by "scientific method" because of the historical tradition that "science" is mankind's body of knowledge however acquired. Hence "scientific method" is not the special province of any discipline, but rather is the appropriate method of gaining knowledge in any area of human concern.

We begin with a philosophical discussion of scientific method, and proceed to the other ideas, but we'll see that the route is not linear: what we may learn about social reality, improvement, or implementation will make us revisit the meaning of scientific method. Since this nonlinear journey may be an unusual one for you, it may help to describe at the outset how we'll proceed. We'll start with a fairly obvious and old idea about the meaning of scientific method, and then, by considering one meaning of social reality, we'll find that this first definition of scientific method is inadequate; and we'll try to develop another, richer one. This second definition will lead to a revision of the definition of social reality, which will carry us into the domain of improvement where a first definition will be tried, which pushes us back to reconsidering scientific method and social reality again. If you guess that the journey has no end, you're a good guesser: learning philosophy is learning a restless process of thought.

Scientific method is variously defined in the literature of science, often in terms of the way the writer was trained to do his Ph.D. research. But, as I said, here scientific method is taken to refer to any of the ways in which human knowledge can be produced. In the Western world, two such ways have been identified as especially appropriate: *reason*, or the thought process of inferring consequences from already known principles, and *observation*, or the empirical process of using our senses to tell us what is happening. In the seventeenth and eighteenth centuries, philosophers battled over which process dominated; those who said it was reason were called rationalists, those who said it was observation were called empiricists. In this century there are few pure rationalists or empiricists; the common tendency is to regard scientific method as some judicious combination of these processes. But the important point is that each process must follow certain rules which legitimize the results. Thus, reason must follow orderly rules of deduction, must not indulge in blatant contradictions, must start with plausible or even highly defensible assumptions. Observations must be conducted carefully, according to well-established procedures where the observer does not inject his own biases into the results.

We might sum this up by saying that both reason and observation can be deceptive, but that there are clear and explicit ways of minimizing deception and that these ways are available in principle to all humans, excluding perhaps a subclass who are "mentally deficient."

4. SOCIAL REALITY

All the above sounds very fine and should have us nodding in agreement, which like most agreeable statements is already an indication to the philosopher that it says very little and what little is says may well be wrong. I've bored you with it because it has so often been said with no philosophical justification. The truth is that "scientific method" is an extremely elusive concept. To begin to understand its elusiveness, especially in connection with SD, we should examine the second on the list of SD concepts: social reality. Here again the literature abounds in definitions, of which we can select one: "social reality" consists of a group of humans who are taken to be goal seekers. Their goals really exist, and their actions can be evaluated in terms of whether they do or do not attain these goals. Hence the group is taken to have real choices among a set of possible actions. Finally, and this is the crux of the matter, it is possible to consider an action without taking the action; the consideration consists of evaluating the action in order to estimate its likelihood of attaining the group's goals. The evaluation is "valid" to the extent that what it asserts about the outcome of the action would really occur. It should be pointed out that the "evaluation" can be made of actions already taken, e.g., of existing government programs. Thus, so-called "cost-benefit" studies of educational or health programs all assume this version of social reality.

It can readily be seen that these evaluations are "counterfactuals" in the sense that the results are in the form: if the social group were to do so-and-so, then such-and-such an outcome would occur. For example, if this program were to be funded (or eliminated), then such-and-such benefits and/or costs would occur for society.

Now one might try to "test" these counterfactuals by conducting "social experiments" in which we systematically change certain sectors of society in various ways, e.g., by experimental design techniques, and attempt to use traditional hypothesis-testing methods. But it is highly questionable whether such social experimentation is feasible, or, if so, desirable. It often is far more advantageous to determine the validity of a counterfactual without disturbing social reality. Hence, direct observation and reason may not constitute the appropriate scientific method for SD.

But is there really any difficulty here? After all, engineering and indeed all applied sciences (medicine, agricultural science, etc.) are in the business of trying to assert valid counterfactuals. The methodology seems to be fairly straightforward. One strives to develop a theory about a specific sector of nature; the theoretical assertions say that if such-and-such is the state of a system at a given time, then so-and-so will be the state at another time. The theory is tested by observing how closely it maps "reality," by using the judgment of a community of investigators who develop standards for accepting or rejecting theoretical assertions. Once a theory is accepted, one can then make "counterfactual" assertions of the sort that SD requires. Of course, there are many technical problems involved in the process; logicians, for example, have worried about the epistemological status of counterfactuals. Furthermore, no matter how often and thoroughly a theory has been tested, it may yet fail under new circumstances. But on the whole, relying on counterfactual assertions of applied science seems to work out fairly well, as anyone who steps onto a large jet must feel.

The above account is not so obvious a description of scientific method, but is widely accepted as an adequate description by applied scientists. But from the philosophical point of view, the account is unacceptable for SD. It is unacceptable because of what philosophers call the "self-reflective" paradox. You will note in the account that the "community" of applied scientists is said to establish the standards of acceptable theory. But the community is a "group" and furthermore a group that is seeking a goal: to establish reliable counterfactuals. Such a community of applied scientists is therefore one example of SD's "social reality." The SD question addressed to such a group is whether its choice of actions (i.e., its "scientific method") is to be taken as the best available, or at least as adequate as any other choice. Since the method chosen is very dependent on group agreement among trained applied scientists, the method is certainly suspect from an SD point of view; for example, a great deal of planning and operations research consists of going beyond organizational agreement to policies which no one in the organization has even imagined.

What is "paradoxical" about all this? Why, we apparently need to know what SD is in order to define SD, because SD is the application of "scientific method," and the correct "scientific method" is a legitimate subject matter for SD. I should hasten to point out that the self-reflective paradox is a philosophical issue and need not concern all SD practitioners; after all, it is often sound SD to ignore some problems of an organization, even though they exist and are felt to be critical by many people in the organization. Thus, we have arrived at a definition of a philosopher: someone who is concerned about the self-reflective paradox and attempts to understand it and possibly "solve" it.

I should also point out that SD is not the only area of investigation in which the self-reflective paradox appears. Psychology is another example, since there is one viewpoint of the world in which everything has a psychological base, including the sciences, and therefore including psychology itself. Indeed, this characteristic of an area of inquiry, its susceptibility to the self-reflective paradox, should be regarded as the characteristic which makes the area "basic" or "fundamental."

What is the "solution" of the self-reflective paradox? The soundest reply seems to be that the paradox does not belong in the world view of social reality which assumes that there are problems and solutions. In other words, the paradox does not fit well into the original definition of SD's idea of social reality. What was deficient in the first viewpoint of social reality was SD's own reality. According to this viewpoint, SD stood aside, observed and evaluated the possible actions of the social group, much as a laboratory scientist observes the objects on his bench. But this viewpoint doesn't work because SD is a social reality itself and cannot possibly "pull aside" from itself.

5. IMPROVEMENT

We can gain a better sense of how to modify the earlier concept of social reality if we extend our travels into the third domain of inquiry, "improvement," and the question of how to judge that one action is better than another. This is the age-old question of ethics, and the domain has many confusing pathways. Certainly no one should try to enter it who has not read in the history of ethics since he needs all of the wise guidance he can get, and much of the wisdom of ethics comes to us from our past; it's not an area where only recent citations are relevant.

Ethics is a very practical subject; indeed, it can be considered as the investigation of the practical. Thus, SD must consider the practical questions of who its clients should be, what should be done when the client is seeking the wrong goals, how much to charge for its services, how much of the results should be revealed, and so on. All of these are ethical issues which are essentially practical: they are issues about the practice of SD.

In this story I intend to restrict the conversation about ethics to one central theme, namely, the *scope* of concern about improvement. An SD team may be studying the advertising policy of a firm, say, one that sells cigarettes or machine guns. The ethical issue of scope is whether "improvement" means "increased sales per dollar of advertising" and "increased kill capability," or something much broader like "contribution to health or peace."

6. THE PARADOX OF SD DATA

The issue has a technical base which can help us understand its complexity. Consider, for example, a typical OR study of inventory policy. The purpose of such a policy is to minimize the "costs" of maintaining inventory against various kinds of demand. Too large an inventory runs the risk of tied-up capital, high taxes, obsolescence, and so on. Too little inventory runs the risk of shortages and hence serious delays or loss of patronage. The proper policy is therefore a balance between these (and other) opposing costs. In OR practice, measuring the relevant costs is at least as important as modeling the system mathematically. The clue as to how to measure costs can be seen if we consider one such cost, the cost of funds tied up in inventory, sometimes called the cost of capital. The idea is that a dollar spent on an item that sits on a shelf waiting for future demand is a dollar that cannot be used for other opportunities, like investment in bonds, where it would yield an annual interest. Hence, the cost of capital tied up in inventory is an "opportunity cost," and its measurement consists in estimating the maximum return that would occur if the inventory dollar were to be used in the best alternative opportunity.

But how are we to determine the best alternative? The answer lies in the operations of another subsystem of the organization, the financial system which controls the flow of cash. This system can also be studied by SD, and one result of the study might be an estimate of the optimal use of a dollar which has been released from the inventory system; in this case, the financial system would have provided a measure of the cost of capital *in the inventory system.* The italics are supposed to emphasize that the cost of capital is not a general cost operating across a whole firm or industry, as is sometimes erroneously assumed, but rather a cost that is specific to each subsystem. What should happen to a dollar released from inventory need not be what should happen to a dollar gained by reducing the work-force, for example.

But now another paradox arises. In order to study the inventory system, we need to measure costs, and specifically the cost of capital. To measure the cost of capital we need to study the cash-flow system. But to study the cash-flow system we must also measure some costs (transaction costs, risk costs, etc.) which will inevitably require us to study some other subsystems. The point is that SD is restless; it cannot legitimately measure costs in terms of historical outlays because these outlays may have been based on wrong policies. If so, and SD uses historical data, it is measuring incorrectly.

The same remarks apply to demand. It is very tempting to use past records of demand to forecast demand that will be made on the inventory system. But SD should never find itself in such a forecasting business because if the subsystem which has historically generated demand has been operating incorrectly (and very often it has), then the forecast based on history is an incorrect measure of demand, no matter how elegant the forecasting statistics may be.

This very practical yet philosophical point is often missed in many forecasting studies, where the purpose of the investigator seems to be one of predicting future events on the basis of past patterns of events, or—what is apparently the same thing—on the basis of expert opinion. From the point of view of SD, one has to ask what subsystems are influencing future events and whether these subsystems are judged to be properly designed. It is ridiculous, for example, to forecast a specific technological breakthrough, like the feasible hover-craft or cure for cancer, without considering the linkages of these system sectors to other subsystems of the world.

The same remarks apply to all proposals for "information systems" which store data of various kinds. An information system which is to be used for improving social systems must contain a total subsystem-linkage image, or else the designers cannot judge which "data" really constitute information.

One might be tempted at this point to say that SD is not really in the business of improving social systems by identifying real improvements, but rather its business is to provide "if, then" estimates: "if we were to develop a cheap hovercraft, then it would take 10 years and 30 billions of dollars." The idea is that SD might then avoid the paradox of its requiring a knowledge of all relevant subsystem linkages in order to acquire any meaningful data. But this attempt to make SD's task more modest doesn't resolve the paradox at all, since all estimates like "10 years" and "30 billion dollars" must be based on the way in which the subsystems (finance, management, research, etc.) *ought* to behave. An "if, then" statement based on a very ineffective management subsystem would put SD in the business of supporting bad policies, i.e., into the devil's business.

The philosophical paradox of SD arises because we apparently can see no end to the "linkages" between subsystems which are the sources of the data which SD requires. In the inventory example, the cost of capital is a linkage between the inventory system and the cash-flow system. The cost of liquidity is a linkage between the cash-flow system and the investment system. A firm's social responsibility is a linkage between the firm's total financial system and the social system in which the firm exists. And so it goes—apparently either into an infinite regress or into a vicious circle.

It is important to point out the difference between the *technical* problem of an interlinked system and the *paradoxical* aspect of interlinking systems. It is no news that many machines must be designed by considering the interplay of their parts: there is no such thing as a generally optimal generator, but rather for each design we can estimate the specific generator that does the trick. But all such machine designs assume that certain principles of design are appropriately based on past tests. If we think of the whole world as a machine—or a brain—then we can use brain or machine design principles to help us solve the *technical* problem of linking together subsystems. But such a technical solution by no means resolves the paradox because we need to know some important things about the system which decides that the world is a machine or a brain. Is such an inquiring system operating optimally? The paradox consists of pointing out that there can be no place on which one can stand to answer such a question without again raising the same question.

7. IMPLEMENTATION

Paradox, if it is meaningful, always carries us to other considerations, in this case to yet another domain which I called implementation. If we had allowed the first part of our travels to extend this far, we would have said that implementation would consist in transforming a thought-out solution of a problem into action so that the social group would do what the SD team would propose and, most important, it would do so *because* the SD team had thought out the solution and influenced the group's behavior. So put, implementation would then be another aspect of SD's social reality, in which SD sees itself as really causing a group to veer towards the correct solution. More generally, SD's idea of social reality includes the ability of appropriate inquiry to influence action in appropriate ways.

But this happy viewpoint won't do in the light of what has just been said. For one thing, there must always be a cost of implementation, which is the opportunity foregone for the social group and SD to have done something else. Thus an SD team may devise a wonderful new inventory system, and enlist the assistance of managers and workers in installing it. But all of them might have been engaged in inventing a new product, or analyzing prices, or whatever. Hence, "implementation" for SD cannot simply mean causing a group to put an SD thought into action, because this may not be the best activity for the group to follow. We are being frustrated again by SD on SD.

8. BACK TO "SCIENTIFIC METHOD"

To lessen the frustration, let's try another theory of pragmatics which avoids the trap of problem-solution. This theory starts with the premise that all scientific inquiry—and therefore SD—must begin partially blind and that this blindness in no way detracts from the "science" of the inquiry. Thus, SD may study inventory, but admits that it doesn't know whether this is the "best" area for inquiry, admits that it isn't sure about the appropriate costs and demands, but uses its best judgment to make its first estimates. SD then admits that the "solution" may not be a solution at all and need not, for example, be better than the existing policy. But still implementation will be tried, i.e., the possibly erroneous thought process will be put into action if possible, *not* because the resulting social change is an improvement, but because thereby SD may *learn*, be less blind, see more of its surroundings and understand itself better.

Again, this is not a new idea. It is quite reasonable to view the whole history of the experimental sciences in this manner. In the early stages, e.g., when Galileo wrote his *Dialogues*, both theory and fact were very uncertain. Indeed, Galileo tested his very plausible theory of unobstructed rolling bodies with a defective clock. Had the history of experimental science stopped there, perhaps we would never know whether to believe his test or not. But the process did continue and some theory and some facts became quite solid, though never unshakeable, as the story of Einstein shows. Every finding is subject to further investigation; those findings that continuously "work out" and, more important, both support and are supported by other findings become the lessons that have been learned well and the basis for further learning.

It is important to notice that this "learning" account of scientific method shifts the picture of social reality away from the eventful problem-solving imagery to a wholistic-process imagery. Thus, "improvement" is no longer to be conceived as a specific change for the better in one sector of society, but as a property of the whole system. It follows that we must search for ways of identifying whole-system improvement if we are to make any philosophical sense out of SD's enterprise.

9. "IMPROVEMENT" AS PROGRESS

Here again, history comes to our aid. We are searching for a concept which connotes the gradual maturation of the human system, and the nineteenth century in particular offers us "progress." Having introduced the word, I should hasten to add that it does not mean "growth," nor is it linear. It stands for the continual process of change of the human condition and for the assumption that the overall property of this change *can* be from the worse to the better. Progress is not inevitable; its existence requires the existence of a human will, the will for betterment. The concept of progress, in various forms, underlies all efforts to understand how the plight of the human world can be lessened; to assume that it can be lessened is to assume that progress is really possible. What is needed to make it possible is "global SD."

Until recent decades, it seemed possible to consider science as a prototype of such whole-system development, and even to suggest that the precision of certain physical constants—like the velocity of light *in vacuo*—could be used as surrogates for the real progress of all science from, say, 1500 A.D. to the present. The experience and attitudes of more recent times indicate strongly that "advancement" in science and technology does not necessarily imply progress in the total human system because other ideals of peace and freedom must also be considered. Thus, we are no longer very much impressed by the precision and reliability of physical measurements since this so-called improvement in a subsystem of society can be used by other subsystems for purposes of exploitation and destruction. Naturally, a physicist could respond that the fruits of his inquiry must be used well and that "it's up to the political or managerial system to make sure that they are." But SD can make no such facile reply: it's up to SD to show that a proposed subsystem improvement, like greater precision of measurement or more accurate theory of natural phenomena, is a real whole-system improvement.

10. "SOCIAL REALITY" AND "IMPLEMENTATION" REVISITED

Thus our philosophical inquiry into the meaning of improvement leads us back to the meaning of social reality: is mankind an ideal seeker, a living form which can strive for the betterment of its condition?

In the philosophy of SD, the answer must be "yes," else the SD enterprise becomes a sardonic joke, a struggle to help improve sections of society when the struggle as a whole is a grand illusion. But the answer leads us again to "implementation," which now has a dramatically different meaning from the earlier one. Now the central problem of implementation is to design a society in which the possibility of progress, i.e., ideal seeking, is made secure.

At this point our speculations could readily become reactionary, reacting either to Descartes in the seventeenth century or to St. Paul in the first. One often hears these days that global-systems simulations are only "first approximations," crude and wrong in many ways. But both Descartes and Paul realized that if you believe you have a "first approximation," then you also have an idea about the second, the third, and the "limit," else your "first" is not an "approximation" at all: "Now we see through a glass darkly, but then face to face. Now I know in part; then I shall understand fully . . ." To Paul, the "basic" aspects of mankind's progress lie in faith, hope and love. To Descartes, they lie in the proof of the existence of a benign Supreme Being. Most global simulators do not care to resort to such reactions to our past and indeed ignore them completely and without reflection. None of them seem to wish to forecast what society would be like in the year 2020 if mankind's faith, hope and love with respect to God were restored, although this may be the most important forecast of all. The philosophical point is that none of us who concern ourselves with SD has a sound basis for choosing between Paul and an MIT simulator. If we could only have faith and hope in a Supreme Being, as did the seventeenth-century rationalists, then the implementation problem of SD would seem to be solved: God helps those who help themselves. But the spirit of questioning which characterizes scientific method does not permit any such facile response to the problem of guaranteeing our destiny.

Thus it seems safe to say that today we have no satisfactory theory of implementation from the philosophical point of view. And until we can arrive at a more satisfactory idea of mankind and progress, we must admit we do not have a sound basis for evaluating social change or for evaluating social studies aimed at improving sectors of our society. No university faculty can claim an ability to judge the real quality of an SD research by either students or themselves.

Such a "conclusion" might be taken to be negative, especially by the cynics, but I take it to be altogether very exciting and hopeful. If it were to be more widely recognized, then we might turn away from niggardly criticisms of inadequate research techniques to the more central issues of human progress. Among other things, we'd encourage Ph.D. candidates not to be specific and narrow but broad and comprehensive.

11. "SOCIAL REALITY": THE INDIVIDUAL

But such preaching needs to be checked by reflection in this philosophical journey. The need arises from the reflection that the whole account of progress and social reality leaves out a very important aspect of social reality: the individual. We have been speaking of larger and larger worlds extending to the globe and all future and past globes. These larger images may be real, but so are you, in your here-and-now life.

In the first version of social reality, the individual was seen as a goal seeker; he was, in fact, the limiting case of a group, a group consisting of one person, whose goals presumably were unified since he had no one to combat. In economics, the individual becomes an entity who carries about a utility function for the outcomes of his action. But this "utilitarian psychology" is utterly naive and philosophically suspect, just as is the idea that each individual is an "information processing" entity. The naiveté is well documented in depth psychology, which claims that the unconscious mind has "values" that influence a person's life in critical ways and which conflict with his conscious values. The philosophical suspicion arises with the very plausible speculation that the greatest values of all are two ineffables: the lonely and unique individual and the unique relationship between two such individuals, which we call love.

It is really remarkable how difficult, subtle and exciting the philosophical issues become once we try to view them in terms of the individual. Kant's "never-ending awe" extended outward to the starry heavens and inward to the soul. Nor does the immensity of the world or the universe in the least detract from the importance of the inner man; after all, immensity itself is a creation of man's psyche. Most living creatures don't see an immense world; and, after all, it was Kant's inner psyche which was filled with awe.

Of course, you can stop your philosophical inquiry into the psyche anywhere you wish, at the surface in positivistic behaviorism, a little deeper in attitudinal or motivational psychology, deeper still in analytic psychology, and so on. The philosopher wishes to travel as deeply into the inner psyche as he wishes to travel broadly into the whole system, else "social reality" is only partially explored. This is why SD is not a "discipline" from the philosophical point of view.

Our ignorance of the inner world is immense, and our clues for enlightenment must be found in the most obscure writings of the past, including mysticism and myth. But even in the midst of obscurity we can discern one theme which makes us doubt the philosophical exposition of SD given earlier. It is that individuals, as individuals, should not be classified with respect to society's decisions regarding their lives. The individual is a sacred value; as Kant says, each individual is an end-in-itself which ought not to be used merely for the sake of other ends.

I am less interested here in defending this psychological speculation than in pointing out its consequences, if true, for the philosophy of SD. But I should mention that the speculation is and has been widely held by humans of all walks of life; it is a cornerstone of many religions and doctrines of morality. What it implies is that classifications and comparisons of individuals for the sake of rewarding them, punishing them or otherwise changing them in ways that they themselves do not will to happen are all immoral. One consequence, thoroughly devastating with respect to our earlier speculations about SD, is that the so-called principle of trade-offs of values is absolutely inappropriate with respect to the sacred value of the individual. The trade-off principle states that in determining the decision or policy to be made, we should determine how much of one value (e.g., speed on highways) to trade off for another value (e.g., safety). The principle is the basis for a great deal of SD, e.g., in cost-benefit or cost-effectiveness analysis, mathematical programming, and a whole host of similar techniques. The philosophical speculation says that if an individual is used as a means only, so that his sacred value is sacrificed, then the loss of this value cannot be atoned by trading it off by another value. For example, so runs the speculation, it is immoral to compare the value of a soldier's life versus the value of defending the country. Or, if you deliberately murder another human for the sake of your own goals, you cannot "trade off" this sin by donating a million dollars to your favorite charity. One way to remove sin is through forgiveness; but the methods of attaining forgiveness are lacking in much of SD practice today.

Again, I need to remind you that this speculation is a part of the philosophy of SD, which takes on the joy and frustration of questioning the axioms of SD practice. There is no need as yet to go out and shake fingers at SD practitioners who are busy trading off values; there is a need, on the other hand, to question the foundations of such practice if SD is to remain healthy. Also, it should be recognized why many people reject and are even horrified by many SD recommendations; these critics are not stupid, but rather believe in a totally different picture of social reality. Nevertheless, in my mind's eye I can see the unreflective SD man standing on the right of the king on judgment day and being completely puzzled by the divine pronouncement, "as you did it to one of the least of these my brethern, you did it to me." Surely, he will say to himself, the optimal depends on how many and how important.

Now if you were a well-trained SD type, you might be tempted to sneak around the difficulties presented by the values of the inner life by simply agreeing to write them into the constraint equations: maximize net social benefit subject to never treating anyone as a means only. You can do this, of course, but you'll lack philosophical justification if you do. For one thing, in most models we can readily compute the cost of a constraint and, hence, the cost of avoiding immoral policies. But, as I indicated earlier, morality is never based on trade-offs.

But belief in the existence of the inner life, the psyche, introduces a deeper philosophical speculation which will end my story of the endless philosophical journey. It is the speculation that from the point of view of the inner life, progress and the closely associated ideas of development and maturation have no relevance and cannot be sensibly used to describe the process of the inner life. To be sure, there has been a strong temptation on the part of depth psychologists to transfer the viable ideas about progress in the outer, social world to the life-process of the inner world, but the philosophical speculation argues that this all-too-human intellectual step was erroneous. Even the labels psychopathology, psychotherapy, and mental disease may be inappropriate from the point of view of the inner life, although they clearly have sensible meanings in the outer, social life.

Also, so runs the speculation, the inner life is ineffable and the usual means of communication, e.g., comparison, are not appropriate. That the inner life is essentially ineffable does not imply that we can't talk about it, but rather that we must speak in myths, poems, stories, allegories, in short, in a language far different from that so "effable" a language, mathematics. Thus there may be "progress" in the inner life, but its meaning is essentially ineffable.

Does this philosophical speculation help us better understand SD? It does at least one important thing: it indicates that inquiry into the inner life, through meditation, psychoanalysis, group therapy, religious devotion, etc., is also as much "systems design" as is a large global simulator.

But if we accept the speculation, then we must realize that we evaluators live in two worlds, the outer world of practice and the inner world of the self, and that both worlds are real. But they contradict each other, do they not? The reply may be that the two worlds are dialectical, by which is meant that through contrast we can learn a great deal about each of them.

So it looks as though the outer world dominates after all because there is a purpose to the clash between the two worlds, and the purpose is to learn which is an aspect of progress. But not necessarily. For there are two opposite versions of learning (of course). In the outer world, learning in SD means a shared experience and reasoning to help us better understand the consequences of our actions in the future. Hence, outer learning stretches its significance into the future or into different problem settings. It is learning "from a distance" and, hence, is what people sometimes call Apollonian, since Apollo always shot his arrows at a distance. But learning in the inner world means a direct and unique occasion, not for the sake of anything, but for itself. Such learning touches the essence of the present and is Dionysian, since Dionysius "touches."

12. PAUSE IN THE STORY

At this point the philosophical story can stop itself by its own volition. The nice part about philosophical inquiry is that you can always turn it off simply by introducing a common-sense axiom which you have no intention of examining further. For example, the last section of this article can be successfully ignored by simply denying the existence and/or relevance for SD of the inner life of the type postulated by the philosophical speculation. If you believe that the psyche is a brain or is like a large information-processing computer, then there is no "inner" life other than a set of activities that in principle can be examined and explained. You simply stop philosophizing and start doing other things: designing systems to do such-and-such in the outer world. You'll know you've left the philosophical journey once you hear yourself say: "Well, obviously, . . ." or "It's at least clear that . . ." To a neurologist friend of mine, it's obvious that all psychology in principle is based on neurology; to me it's obvious that his conviction arises out of his own unique psyche.

As for the philosopher, he can end with a joke, to show that he's not all that deadly serious: isn't it marvelous that in order to defend its right to be so precise, SD must be so frustratingly vague?

13. REFERENCES: A PERSONAL NOTE OF APPRECIATION

Over the many years I've acted as an editor of several academic journals, I've become more and more annoyed by our ritualistic style of introducing quotations and proliferating footnotes and references. The reader must constantly shift from the author's style and theme to the name of a book or some other author's style and theme. Too often, the quotation is out of context, or repetitive, or embarrassingly obvious (my ego cringes when I read: "as Churchman says, it is important to consider the large system").

Nevertheless, I do appreciate one function of references: the acknowledgement that so many others were talking to me as I wrote this piece. E. A. Singer's *Experience and Reflection* (University of Pennsylvania Press, 1958) is as always a starting point, counterbalanced to some extent by Carl Jung's writings. Both Singer and Jung acknowledge their debt to the historical writers in philosophy and science.

I've enjoyed immensely the contrasts in SD approaches among the practitioners in the outside world. It's been immensely enlightening to compare Russell Ackoff, Stafford Beer, J. Forrester and George Dantzig. Of course my personal bias goes toward Ackoff's very realistic view of the managerial world.

As for the inner world, the contrasts are even greater. Besides Jung, other Jungians (e.g., Maria Von France and James Hillman) have inspired my remarks about the "no-progress" nature of inner life. Eric Jantsch has been on a trip similar to the one of this paper, of extending SD into other lands of human imagination. Above all, Thomas Cowan, in many articles and countlessly more conversations, has so nicely kept me from drawing conclusions.

I-3

THE CONDUCT OF OPERATIONS RESEARCH STUDIES

Norman I. Agin
Mathematica, Inc.

1. INTRODUCTION

The subject of this chapter is the conduct of operations research (OR) studies. Our goal is to make the reader better able to direct and perform studies and accordingly improve his chances of achieving successful results. Our task is straightforward in the sense that it is easy to list the steps required in the conduct of OR studies. In fact, these steps do not differ significantly from those for the scientific method in general. Even in the particular case of OR studies, the procedural steps have been described by others. See, for example, Hillier and Lieberman [1967] and Wagner [1969].

In another sense, however, the task of this chapter is difficult. The real problem is in being able to aid the reader to properly perform the steps usually necessary for a study. In other words, the difficulty is not identifying the steps of analysis but aiding the practitioner in translating these steps into actions appropriate to his study. As a consequence, the emphasis of the chapter is not on describing the specific steps of OR studies, but rather in bringing these already generally recognized tasks to life—through example and illustration. We concentrate on discussing the "how" not the "what."

William T. Morris [1967] in discussing the steps of the modeling process properly identifies one step as that of writing down the obvious. The same recommendation is appropriate to most undertakings including this one. Thus, we might first ask the obvious. Why be concerned about the proper conduct of an OR study? There are several reasons.

First, the proper conduct of a study ensures the analyst does not make what might be referred to by a statistician as an "error of the third kind." That is, solving the wrong problem right. It is also the proper conduct of the study which ensures that the right problem is not solved wrong. In other words, that any models developed are valid representations of the decision problem being studied, that they are computationally feasible, that the study is completed within cost and time limitations, and that implementation is efficiently and effectively accomplished. In short, that the study succeeds. Also, from a personal point of view, it is the success of a study, as measured by the client, which provides the greatest reward and sense of accomplishment to the practitioner. If the analysis is properly conducted, the study will have an increased chance of management acceptability, and the analyst will be satisfied. For these reasons this chapter is important.

There is one further fact which should be stated: It is that the procedures and guidelines provided in this chapter will not be precisely appropriate to any particular study. Each effort will be different and will require intuition, initiative and imagination on the part of the analyst to successfully define and accomplish his project's objectives. We can only help by providing some general principles and guidelines.

The chapter is organized into sections corresponding to the major steps usually undertaken during the conduct of OR studies. These steps include the following:

1. Definition of objectives
2. Development of the project plan
3. Problem formulation
4. Model development
5. Development of a computational approach
6. Development of program specifications, programming and debugging
7. Data collection
8. Validation
9. Implementation

2. DEFINITION OF OBJECTIVES

The first task of any study is to determine what "management" or the "user" expects to achieve from the project. In other words, what is the project supposed to accomplish.

The definition of objectives should be in terms of the decision or decisions to which the study is oriented. The analyst should take special care to ensure that the goal is not defined in too narrow a context. Nor should he needlessly broaden the objectives of the study in such a way that he attempts to solve all the problems of the corporation in one comprehensive and usually unsuccessful undertaking.

The difficulty in drawing out from a manager the true objectives of a study is an often discussed and illustrated topic. The following extreme, but true, example will illustrate the types of problem definition difficulties which are often faced. A manager asked for a study to examine the consolidation of three of his firms' plants into one. The new plant was to be constructed at a location separate from the three existing plants. A preliminary examination of the economies which would result from the consolidation indicated the plants had no operations in common and that the proposed plan could only result in an increase in costs. The executive should have known this so that prior to an investigation in detail it was decided to review with him what he expected to achieve from the study. Doing this involved several days of discussion. From this, it was discovered that the real issue was an inability for this executive and the union leader at one of the plants to work together. Once this was recognized, a Vice President of Industrial Relations was hired to deal with the union and the idea of consolidation dropped. The undertaking of a study with little or no chance for real success was avoided.

To avoid the risk of not adequately understanding or defining the objectives of a study, the operations researcher is usually instructed to devote effort to problem definition. He is not told how, but rather to do it (which isn't particularly helpful). The advice also suggests establishing a dialogue with the proper managers which is always easier said than done. The real issue, however, is a different one. What we need is an answer to the question of how devoting effort and establishing a dialogue lead to a better understanding of management needs. In other words, how does the operations researcher conduct himself so that after a sequence of discussions with managers he has achieved an understanding of their problems and needs. There are five suggestions which can be made.

1. He should both listen to and hear what he is being told. The obviousness of this is exceeded only by the frequency with which it is not done.
2. He should place himself in the manager's position and look at the problem from this perspective. In other words, he should determine such things as what objectives have been set for the manager, what constraints and political realities influence the manager's behavior and what conflicting aims the manager might be trying to satisfy. As well as possible, he should know the manager's personal characteristics, concerns and biases.
3. He should also understand the organization which his activities will influence. He should be thoroughly familiar with the reporting relations, functions of various groups, prior studies of a related nature, and so forth.
4. He should refrain from pushing his own preconceived notions of the prob-

lem or implicitly adjusting the problem to fit his prior conception of the approach he would like to adopt.

5. Most important, he should not let statements and comments of the manager pass unexamined. Too often, the OR analyst sits and, politely and out of deference, passively listens. This will never get to the root of a problem. He must question and examine. Why do you say that? What do you mean by that? When do you want to do that? These are all questions which should be continually posed by the operations researcher.

Gaining an understanding of the objectives of the study before it begins is, unfortunately, not sufficient. It is also necessary to anticipate and be aware of how objectives may change with time or with the level of management that becomes involved with the study. An example will illustrate the point that while a careful definition of objectives is a necessary prelude to a successful study, it is often not sufficient.

A company in the credit card industry wished to develop a simulation model of their billing practices. The objective of the model, as originally determined, was to aid in operating decisions concerning which card holder accounts should be assigned to the various billing centers and which days during a month different groups of accounts should be billed. The study was under the direction of the Vice President of Operations, who was responsible for decisions related to these matters. A simulation model was designed which represented the pattern of client billing during a month from the company's three billing locations. Since different categories of card holders had varying characteristics, the simulation estimated the charging behavior of the clients as a function of the type of account, geographical location and other pertinent factors. The paying behavior of each account type was also different and this was also represented in the model. Finally, the simulation represented the lag between the occurrence of charges by the card holder, the company's payments to service establishments, the billing to card holders, and the receipt of payment from the card holders. The resulting cash flow projections were to be used as a basis for the decisions mentioned above.

A simulation program was constructed and used. Its success led to a presentation describing the model to several high managers within the company, including the Corporate Treasurer. He recognized that the model could also represent the flow of funds in the banking system and would therefore be useful to him in determining whether there would be an excess or shortage of cash funds during the next several weeks. He wished to use the model to aid in decisions relative to short-term financing. Providing this additional capability required extensions to the model, including reprogramming and retesting. Had all the management objectives of the model been identified initially, the cash flow simulator could have been more efficiently constructed. Although these further uses had been recognized earlier by the study team, there had been no budget allocated to their implementation. As one might guess, the Corporate Treasurer showed no interest in the project until a successful, working simulator of the operational aspects of billing and payments could be demonstrated to him.

The study described above is merely an illustration of a common occurrence with which the operations researcher should be familiar. It has been referred to as the Chinese baseball syndrome. Perhaps the most important accomplishment of this chapter will be to make the operations researcher aware of this condition and thereby permit him to respond to its effect. Its importance derives from the fact that, often when an OR study is accused of having solved the wrong problem, the real difficulty turns out to be a case of the Chinese baseball syndrome.

The game of Chinese baseball is easy to describe. In fact, the rules of the game are identical to the U.S. version except in the following respect. From the time the ball leaves the pitcher's hand, until the time it reaches the catcher's glove, the team in the field is permitted to move the bases in any way they wish. Undoubtedly, the reader will recognize he has often been an unwitting player in the game of Chinese baseball.

3. DEVELOPMENT OF THE PROJECT PLAN

The second step of a study is the development of a project plan. The process of performing an OR study is often a creative one. As a result, the question is often raised, how can there be planning? The answer is clear if one considers planning as the creation of milestones; i.e., points in time at which certain accomplishments are to be completed, rather than the specification of the particular way in which the work is to be done. The former is a necessary control; only the latter is creative. The act of establishing milestones, however, is in itself a stimulus to creativity and accomplishment. Many are familiar with the last one or two days before a deadline in which all the work gets done. Thus, adherence to the time deadlines created by a plan forces creativity (necessity is the mother of invention), pushes the OR analyst to conclusions and, in general, contributes to the success of the project. Conversely, delays and missed deadlines lead to indifferent performance on the part of the analyst and disinterest on the part of management.

Failure to meet schedules frequently occasions additional difficulties. Management is often responsive to problems of immediacy. If the conduct of an OR study is unduly long, the problem, or at least, the manager's perception of it, changes. The result is the operations researcher solves a problem other than the one of current concern. To be sure, the manager may have played Chinese baseball. But, the OR analyst may also have contributed to the difficulty. He may not have properly planned where he should be at each point during the problem solving process, disciplined his conduct and adhered to the required schedule.

A warning is in order. While the development of a work plan is useful to discipline the activities of the analyst and enables him to proceed on schedule, it proves less effective in coping with a characteristic of successful studies called the "greed" syndrome. The greed syndrome results from the manager's recognition that the study may be potentially more useful to him than previously thought. The cash flow simulator study discussed earlier is a good example. The greed syndrome often expands the work required of the analyst. It might also prematurely involve him in the implementation and use of the model and into problems of an operational nature. In many ways, the greed syndrome is a special case of the Chinese Baseball syndrome with equally insidious effects. The saddest of these is the premature expansion of a potentially successful study into one which is never completed. More often, the expansion of the project delays schedules and, when a day of reckoning eventually comes, (about the time of annual budgets) management conveniently forgets they requested all the additional work.

Operationally, a project plan is simply a time schedule for the accomplishment of the project steps. These often correspond to the sections into which this chapter is organized. The plan is usually presented in terms of a Gantt chart as shown in Fig. 1.

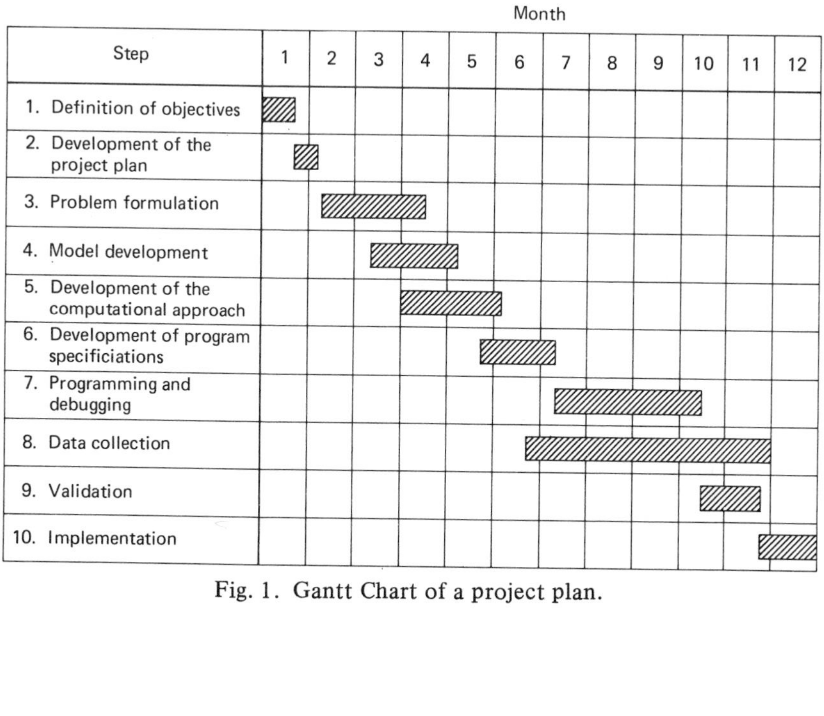

Fig. 1. Gantt Chart of a project plan.

Often the project steps are further divided into tasks. For example, the step concerned with the development of a computational approach may be composed of the following tasks:

1. For each submodel of the problem, develop an appropriate solution method.
2. Describe and document the solution methods. The resulting report will describe the inputs, outputs and computational steps necessary to obtain a solution to each model. The computational steps will be analytically expressed and verbally explained.
3. Test the proposed solution methods on small size, selected sample problems. This step will ensure the feasibility of the methods recommended for solution. It will also serve to ensure the accuracy of the model documentation prior to its translation into a computer program.
4. Revise the solution techniques as indicated by the hand testing.
5. Prepare a summary of the test results and add this to the solution techniques documentation.
6. Prepare and deliver presentations, as appropriate, on the results of this project step.

Development of the project plan in the detail just illustrated is often essential to the determination of valid estimates of the time and resources required to complete a project. Factoring the total study into its constituent steps is the best way to assure valid estimates of the required time, budget and staff are available before the project begins. In other words, the project plan increases the probability that the study can be completed on schedule and within budget.

Often the project plan should focus on the work to be assigned to individual participants. In such a case, it might resemble that illustrated in Fig. 2. The task numbers correspond to those described above for the development of a computational approach.

There are two additional considerations in developing the project plan which should be briefly mentioned. The first of these is the importance of providing for project milestones. As mentioned earlier, these act to discipline the analyst to remain on schedule. Milestones, useful in this respect, include submission of documentation, presentations to management, and the formal initiation of new activities or project steps.

A second consideration is an allocation of resources for the analysis of data collected during the project for purposes which might be unrelated to the project's direct concerns. There are three reasons why this activity is important.

1. The OR analyst, merely because he is collecting data and thinking about an activity, can uncover understandings of more benefit than those associated with the original study. In other words, there is always the chance of a serendipitous discovery. For example, one firm, relying on the monthly management reports provided by their accounting department, believed they were experiencing an

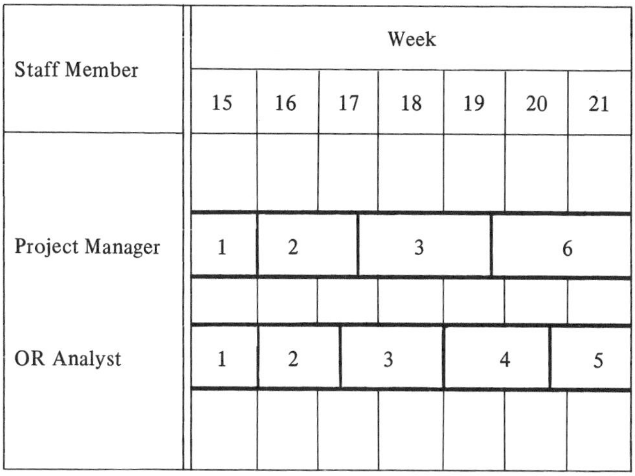
Staff Member
Week
15
16
17
18
19
20
21
Project Manager
1
2
3
6
OR Analyst
1
2
3
4
5

Fig. 2. Staff assignment plan.

enormous increase in cancellations for a particular type of subscriber to their service. To reverse the trend, an expensive marketing campaign, directed at the particular class of subscriber, was about to begin. The cancellation data was being used by an OR group for an unrelated purpose. They discovered, however, that the cancellations were caused entirely by the data processing department. The company was in the process of reclassifying subscribers from the category experiencing the high cancellations into another. Data processing determined the simplest way to do this was to treat the subscribers being reclassified as a cancellation in the one category and a new account in the other. In fact, there were no "real" cancellations and the cost of an expensive and misdirected marketing program was saved.

2. Throughout the problem solving process, it is a responsibility of the operations researcher to report to management and others involved with the project on the progress of the study. Management, however, is results-oriented and during a long project their interest will dissipate, especially if the presentations are concerned only with progress in development rather than what is implemented. Often, a straightforward analysis of data, the preparation of histograms and charts and the presentation of interim results is sufficient to maintain management's interest and support.

3. Finally, such analyses and feedback can help the data collection activity. A good example is provided by a project performed for the U.S. Department of Defense. Its conduct required the collection of large amounts of data in Europe from Army field units. During the one-year study, there were four data collection trips each lasting about one month. The objective of the project was to develop models for determining the economic life of vehicles. These models

would be used by the Department of the Army to aid in fleet procurement decisions. Thus, the result of the project would have no direct bearing or visible benefit to the units which were supplying the data. Success of the project, however, required a high degree of cooperation with these field units. Because of this, some feedback was warranted to make the project meaningful and useful to them and to assure their continued cooperation. Thus, part of the work effort was devoted to the preparation of short analyses and visual presentations using the data collected from each unit. Briefings were presented to unit commanders during each data collection trip. As a result, the field units received direct benefit from the project, they understood their own activities better, and in some cases were able to discover areas in which significant economies or increased effectiveness could be obtained with little effort.

4. PROBLEM FORMULATION

This next step, that of problem formulation, is of fundamental importance to the conduct of an OR study. It marks a significant fork in the road; with one direction leading towards success and satisfaction and the other towards failure and frustration. It involves additional discussions with management, often the first contacts with other staff and line personnel, and the collection of data necessary to gain an understanding of what the problem is, what has occurred in the past, what is likely to occur in the future and what the relationships are between variables of the problem. The conclusion of this task provides the framework for a model of the problem area being studied and establishes the direction of all further work. Its importance warrants a careful discussion.

The first issue of problem formulation is often to decide whether or not the total problem should be broken down into smaller subproblems which can be individually studied either in parallel or sequentially. Doing this is frequently necessary when dealing with large and complicated areas of activity. The process of breaking a large problem into its logical subparts does, of course, lead to suboptimization. Its effect can be minimal, however, if the problem is divided at points of weakest interaction.

To illustrate how one proceeds in this task let us use as an example a production and distribution planning problem and see how it was divided into meaningful, but yet solvable, subparts. The problem was to develop production and shipping plans on a weekly basis over a four-week planning horizon. During the problem formulation stage several questions were identified as important. Some of these were as follows:

1. With only a four-week planning horizon, how could the need for seasonal buildups of inventory be anticipated? Or, asked in another way, what should be the desired level of plant inventory at the end of the four-week planning horizon?

2. What should be the optimal warehouse inventories?
3. How should plant shipments to warehouses be spaced so as to take advantage of the best incentive freight rates?

To deal with all of these issues, yet wind up with a computationally feasible method of solution, meant that the problem had to be subdivided into its principal components. Figure 3 illustrates how this was done. It was decided that five major models would be developed. These were:

1. Forecasting model: This model would generate forecasts of demand for each product on a weekly basis over the four-week planning horizon.
2. Warehouse inventory: Given the demand forecasts, this model would determine optimal inventory levels at the warehouses desired for the end of the planning horizon. From these and based on a knowledge of current inventory levels, minimum production requirements could be determined.
3. Annual planning: This model would use annual sales forecasts, provided by the marketing department, to set aggregate production and inventory levels for each four-week interval during the year. The resulting inventory levels would provide targets for total system inventory for the shorter-horizon production planning model.
4. Production planning: This model would utilize the inventory objectives set by the annual plan and the requirements generated from the warehouse inventory model to set production quantities for each of the next four weeks.

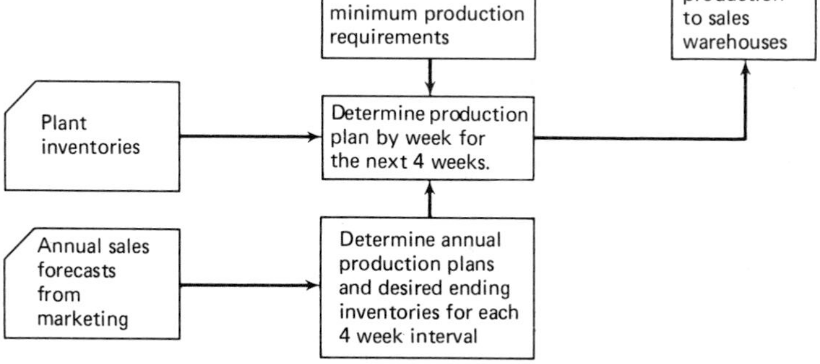

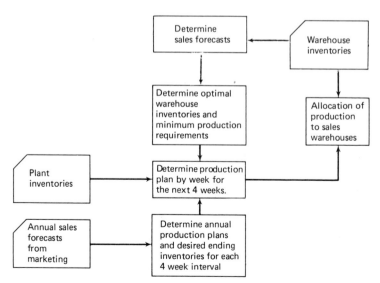

Fig. 3. Formulation of problem subparts.

5. Allocation: Finally, this model would utilize the sales forecasts, warehouse inventories and production plans in order to allocate production to warehouses.

In developing an overall approach to the type of problem illustrated above, the analyst should generally proceed as follows:

1. Start with the central decision problem to which the study is addressed. In the example above this is the four-week planning problem.
2. Ask what inputs and outputs are required of a model for the central problem. This will aid in determining the scope of the submodels which may need to be developed.
3. Determine if there are already existing means of obtaining the required inputs or using the resulting outputs. If so, these can be used. If not, auxiliary models must be defined.
4. For each of the auxiliary models, determine if a full model, a quick and dirty approach, or new manual methods need to be developed.

Following an analysis process of the type outlined above will permit the operations researcher to define manageable problems, better integrate his efforts with current practices and procedures, and increase his chances of successful implementation. At its conclusion he should know what the models he plans to develop are to accomplish and how they are to be used in the context of the management decision problems with which he is dealing.

Some thought should also be devoted, even at this early point, to proper maintenance design. Maintenance is essential for the long term success of an OR study involving the implementation of a new system or new methodologies. If its consideration is left until implementation, chances are maintenance methods will be inadequate and the chances for long term project success substantially decreased. The following checklist will help to ensure successful maintenance design.

1. Will there be means for the continual updating of the model inputs?
2. Will the documentation be adequate to ensure others can improve and update the models?
3. Has provision been made for the operation of the models within the routine activities of the firm? Operations researchers are notoriously poor in assuming responsibility themselves for the routine application of systems they develop. Do executives understand this need?
4. Can the model structure be easily modified to reflect changes in the actions and opportunities being modeled?
5. Has adequate consideration been given to determining ways of using the model to provide information on its weaknesses and errors?

A second issue which must be resolved during the problem formulation phase is to determine the detail in which the models are to be developed. Consideration of the budget available, project schedule, and objectives of the study should be the principal factors which influence this decision. Often in making choices in such matters, the operations researcher mistakenly associates the detail in which he develops a model with its validity. Detail is an incomplete measure of validity. More important, the analyst should ensure he develops what can be referred to as "unbiased" models. Put another way, if the analysis is subject to error, the errors should sometimes be overestimates and sometimes underestimates. On the average, the model should provide "fair" predictions of real world results. The detail with which a model is developed is not necessarily a significant influence on its unbiasedness. We shall later provide several examples of biased models to illustrate this concept.

Once the total problem has been factored into appropriate subparts and an idea of the desired degree of detail obtained, the problem formulation can continue. The next phase of problem formulation involves identifying the scope and dimensions of the models to be developed. For this phase we identify five tasks discussed below. The following example will be used as an illustration in the discussion of these tasks.

The example deals with the design and operation of a vehicle repair and overhaul facility. The type of facility envisioned would be appropriate for any user of a large fleet of vehicles such as a taxi cab company, delivery company, bus company, government motor pool, and so forth. The facility is to handle the unanticipated repair required of vehicles which break down in service. It is also to handle a planned program of maintenance and overhaul. The objective of the study is to aid management in determining the physical size of the repair facility and in setting operating policies with respect to scheduling overhauls. Too much capacity would be expensive to construct and operate, too little would be insufficient to accommodate the demand for service created by the overhaul program and random breakdowns. An inappropriate policy with respect to scheduling the overhauls, on the one hand, would cause vehicles to queue up for repair or overhaul and be out of service for an undue length of time or, on the other hand, would process too few vehicles and therefore not satisfy total fleet overhaul requirements.

4.1 Determination of Problem Dimensions

This first task of the model definition process can be thought of as the determination of the variables of the problem in an analytic statement. For example, specification of problem dimensions might include determination of classifications for products and marketing areas or definition of a planning horizon and the time intervals within the horizon.

In the context of the repair and overhaul facility problem, the determination of problem dimensions corresponds to decisions concerning the types of vehicles to be represented in the model; e.g., cars, $\frac{1}{2}$ ton trucks, $\frac{3}{4}$ ton trucks; the time period of the model, e.g., 4-hour intervals, shifts or days; the types of operations to be performed on the vehicles, e.g., simple repairs, 6000 mile maintenance, major overhauls, and so forth.

Development of the proper dimensions of a model is often taken for granted. This should not be the case. Consider the subtleness of the following example. The problem is one often faced by management and management science staff—that of capacity expansion. It is surprising that most staff groups responsible for such decisions rarely if ever take the initiative in arguing for more capacity prior to repeated requests by production people. This difference in recognition of what should be a common goal of production and staff—that of providing the best level of capacity—should warn the OR analyst and other planning staff that there may be a consistent bias in their approach to such problems. The bias may be in their choice of a planning period for analysis. The following example illustrates the issue. Assume a company has:

Production capacity = 100 units/week
Demand = 400 units/4 weeks

A capacity planning model which considers a four-week time period and plans capital expenditures by trading off added investment costs against possible saving from fewer stockouts and a lesser need for inventory buildups would miss the point of a model which is more detailed in considering the operating environment. The numbers below illustrate why this is the case. If the planning period is a four-week interval:

Production capacity per 4 weeks = 400 units
Demand per 4 weeks = 400
Inventory cost = 0
Lost sales = 0
Additional capacity needed = 0

With the four-week time period the ups and downs of demand are washed out. As a result, it appears there are no holding or penalty costs incurred and capacity is balanced with demand. It follows that new investments would not provide a financial return.

With a weekly time period, however, the following may occur:

	Week 1	2	3	4	Total
Demand	80	130	90	110	400
Production	100	100	100	100	400
Inventory	20	0	10	0	30
Lost sales	0	10	0	0	10

Here we see demand, because of its irregular nature, sometimes exceeds capacity. As a result, inventories must be accumulated to meet peaks and, when they are insufficient, sales are lost. As can be seen, the use of a weekly time period in this case, indicates a financial return to increased plant investment.

This simple example illustrates the notion of bias in models discussed earlier. Using a four-week planning horizon tends to underestimate the attractiveness of new capacity. The model is biased.

4.2 Determination of Controllable Decision Variables

This second step involves determining the variables which are under control of management. They need to be explicitly determined during the problem formulation in order to distinguish between what are the "givens" of the problem and what management is willing to consider as changeable. In other words, what are inputs to the planning problem as opposed to the alternatives or variables of the decision. In the repair and overhaul facility illustration the decision variables might be related to the number of service bays to be constructed and the rules for scheduling planned maintenance and overhaul. Whether or not to build the facility (an alternative might be to not build the facility and use an outside contractor for repair and overhaul work) may not be a decision variable of the problem. Of course, if it is not, this should be the result of an explicit analysis and decision.

Determination of the controllable decision variables may appear to be a simple task. It is not always so and if inadequately considered can often ruin an otherwise successful project. The following example will illustrate this. A company was considering the possibility of closing down one of its major plants; one which contributed a substantial percentage of total company revenues. A careful study was, therefore, deemed appropriate and several consultants hired. One team studied the technology of the production process in order to ensure that the best possible methods of production were being used. Another team developed up-to-date and accurate cost and operating information. An OR team was responsible for developing a methodology for using the information; specifically, to develop a model that would have as input values for the investment in land, machinery, equipment and building, and the fixed and variable costs of operations. The model they planned would also use as inputs estimates of revenue for each product by market area. The model would compute profit or loss, cash flow, return on assets, and other criteria which could be used in deciding whether or not the plant should remain in operation. It would also enable the company's management to consider the effects of various mixes of plant production and ranges on costs and valuations of investment on return on assets which was their key decision criterion. If, for the most likely values for the inputs, return on investment was sufficient to meet the company's standards, the plant would remain operating. If not, it would shut down.

After discussions with operating management and careful consideration it was recognized that essential elements of the decision problem were missing. Specifically, the mix of product produced by the plant and the marketing areas in which the product was being sold were being treated as inputs. This was inappropriate and would clearly bias the results. Because of numerous and complicated product constraints, it was not a simple matter to determine the best mix of production or the extent to which demand in different market areas should be met. After recognizing the need for these additional decision variables, the problem formulation was modified. Product mix and demand satisfied in each market area were treated as decision variables and optimized. This provided a production and distribution plan which would result in a maximum variable profitability for the plant and thus, a fair basis for measuring return on assets. The development of a biased model was averted by the proper choice of decision variables.

4.3 Determination of Uncontrollable Variables

A third task of problem formulation is to determine the uncontrollable variables. These are the aspects of the problem which are not controllable by management but which may change and impact on the operation of the activity being modeled. In the repair facility example, the random breakdown of vehicles is an uncontrollable variable.

Actions taken by competitors in response to decisions adopted by the enterprise being modeled are an often forgotten class of uncontrollable variables in studies that involve aspects of economic competition and industry-wide adaptation to changes. Explicit recognition of such effects is often the most important part of a study. For example, a firm in the flat glass industry wished to model its competitive position. As decision variables, strategies related to capacity expansion and marketing action were identified. The latter variables included alternatives for pricing, product quality, and customer service. The model was to represent the impact of changes in these variables on the company's share of market; it failed, however, to adequately represent the dynamics of competitive behavior. A proper model would have needed to represent the competitors' continual reaction to new strategies of the firm developing the model, as well as the competitors' own initiation of actions designed to optimize their objectives. In general, failure to include such effects can lead to models which are not valid in their representation, and even worse, if adopted, lead to inappropriate and misleading policies.

4.4 Determination of Technology

Determination of technology is the fourth task of problem formulation. The technology is described by the constants and parameters which define limits and relationships between variables. Often complex production technologies have to be modeled. In many instances, fortunately, the technology of a process is rather simple. Ample illustration exists for this in the literature of linear programming which includes mathematical models of such complexity as petroleum refining and blast furnace operation. In the repair facility illustration, the man-hours required for overhaul and repair and failure rates for random breakdowns are examples of the relevant technology.

4.5 Determination of Measures of Effectiveness

The measures of effectiveness are the criteria used to judge the merits of particular solutions to the problem being studied. For the repair facility example, measures might include the number of vehicles awaiting repair, the mean waiting time, the cost of construction, and so forth.

Most OR studies involve several measures of effectiveness. The most important should have come to surface during the definition-of-objectives step. Often the choice of a proper measure is not obvious except in retrospect. Consider the following example provided by Morse and Kimball [1951] in their classic book.

At the beginning of World War II a great number of British merchant vessels were seriously damaged by aircraft attacks. An obvious response was to equip them with antiaircraft guns and this was done for some ships. After nearly a year it was desired to determine whether the guns should be removed from the ships they were on or additional guns installed on the remaining ones. An analysis soon found that in only about 4% of the attacks was an enemy plane shot down. This was indeed a poor showing and seemed to indicate that the guns were not worth the price of installation. On second thought, however, it became apparent that the percentage of enemy planes shot down was not the correct measure of interest. The guns were put on to protect the ship and the proper measure should be whether the ships with guns were less damaged than those without. Figures for this were collected and indicated the guns definitely increased the ships chances of survival.

5. MODEL DEVELOPMENT

The fourth step of an OR study is concerned with model development. The model expresses the interaction between the controllable decision variables, the uncontrollable variables, the technology and the measures of interest. Its proper development is a key requirement for a project's success. If done improperly, the model can be misleading in its inferences or uneconomical in its use. If done properly, the model can contribute substantially to a firm's profit performance or an organization's operating efficiency. Valid model development requires creative insights into the activity being studied. At the same time, it requires that substantial amounts of data be collected and carefully analyzed to ensure a proper understanding of the problem has been achieved.

A first task of model development is a resolution of whether or not the required numbers or relationships are feasible to develop. Often the validity of a study hinges on this question. In the case of most production oriented applications it is relatively simple to estimate the relation between an extra shift of production and the resulting increase in output. It is also reasonable to measure empirically what an extra 50 units in inventory will mean in terms of the probability of a stock out. On the other hand, it is more difficult to accurately ascertain what an additional $5000 in advertising will mean in terms of this year's sales and generally even more difficult to measure the effect on next year's.

Several years ago an agency of the U.S. Government sponsored the development of a simulation model identified by the acronym TEMPER–Technological, Economic, Military, Political Evaluation Routine. TEMPER was an attempt to simulate the coalitions and actions of nations and how these affected the world order. After several months of use, some doubt was cast on the model's validity when its use resulted in Costa Rica attacking the United States. A detailed examination of the model was undertaken with the conclusion that it was not, nor could it be, valid. There was insufficient understanding of the relationships that existed between the controllable decision variables, the uncontrollable variables, and the measures of interest. The model's objectives were too ambitious. Understanding was too limited. And the result merely represented its developers' unadmitted ignorance of relationships which are much too complicated and involved for any of us to even partially understand. Proper understanding of the system being modeled is a prerequisite for project success.

A study requiring too much unknown technology or difficult to construct relationships between variables may be best left unstarted. There is, unfortunately, no valid answer as to how much is too much. The desirability of undertaking a study when little is known about what is being modeled depends to a large extent on how decisions are currently being made. If the process is one involving several staff and managers each of whom contribute their subjective judgments and the decision process is one of discussion and consensus, it may be difficult for the OR study to improve upon results. On the other hand, if the decision process involves but one person with limited input information, a model might nevertheless lead to improved decision-making. Even if there is a lack of understanding of critical parameters and relationships a model can break the problem area into smaller elements each of which can more easily be handled. It can also provide a discipline to the decision-maker requiring him to at least use what information is available in the best possible manner.

As we have said, a model is the explicit statement of the functional relationships which exist between the controllable decision variables, the uncontrollable variables, the technology and the measures of interest. For example, we might have:

c_i = the ith controllable decision variable

u_j = the jth uncontrollable variable

p_k = the kth constant or parameter

w_n = the nth measure of interest

In symbols, then, the model is a function or set of functions f which relates the c_i, u_j and p_k to the w_n, as follows:

$$w_n = f(c_i, u_j, p_k).$$

Although here written as if the w_n are explicit functions of the other variables, this is not necessarily, or even usually, the case.

The relationships which compose a model are generally of several types. These are each discussed in the sections which follow.

5.1 Definitional Relationships

This first type of relationship arises from accounting conventions or physical identities. Examples are:

Assets = Liabilities + Net Worth

Inventory (t) = Inventory (t - 1) + Production (t) - Sales (t)

Definitional relationships are usually easy to develop and, in many cases, require little or no data analysis.

5.2 Empirical Relationships

Empirical relationships also describe the correspondence between two or more variables. They are based on the use of historical data, engineering analysis, experimental evidence, legal prescription or guess work. An example might be the correspondence between a tax provision, T, and taxable corporate income, I. Income under \$25,000 per year is taxed at 22%, while income over \$25,000 per year is taxed at 48%. Thus, the relationship between tax provision and income can be expressed as follows:

$$T = \begin{cases} .22I, \text{ if } I < 25{,}000 \\ 5500 + .48(I - 25000), \text{ if } I \geqslant 25{,}000 \end{cases}$$

A second example is the relationship between raw material costs, R, and sales, S. If, on the basis of past data, raw material costs are consistently about 40% of sales for a particular organizational unit, the formula

$$R = 40S \pm \epsilon$$

would be an example of an empirical relationship. These types of relationships often require statistical analysis to ascertain the numerical parameters involved.

The use and development of empirical relationships involves two special difficulties. First, historical data which are available may not be descriptive of current or future relationships. That is, the correspondence between the variables may reflect modes of operation no longer current. This could be reflected in either a change in the numerical parameters which measure the degree of the relationship or in the structure and nature of the relationship itself. The second difficulty with empirical relationships is that the method of operation to which the data correspond may represent low standards of performance. In such cases, the model will produce plans which do not encourage improved performance nor reflect the results possible from better management control.

5.3 Normative Relationships

The third type of relationships are normative, in the sense that they express how variables should interrelate rather than how they have been related in the past. They may result from management performance standards e.g., top management may insist inventories be less than five days' sales. Often, they are the result of theoretical research in OR techniques. As an illustration, consider the overhaul and repair facility example previously described. Let the vehicles be divided into N classes (class 1 has the highest priority for service and class N the lowest). Let

c = number of service bays

u_i = mean arrival rate for vehicle in class i, $i = 1, \ldots, N$

p = mean service time

w_k = expected waiting time for vehicles in class k, $k = 1, \ldots, N$

Let us further assume that the model developer is satisfied with assuming that all the vehicles have the same exponential distribution of service time (obviously too restricted for the problem described earlier) and that vehicles in each class arrive according to a Poisson arrival rate. Under these assumptions, queuing theory results have determined that w_k, the steady state expected waiting time (including service) for a vehicle in priority class k is

$$w_k = \frac{1}{AB_{k-1}B_k} + \frac{u}{p} \quad \text{for} \quad k = 1, 2, \ldots, N;$$

where

$$A = c! \frac{cp - u}{r^c} \sum_{j=0}^{c-1} \frac{r^j}{j!} + cp,$$

$$B_0 = 1,$$

$$B_k = 1 - \frac{\sum_{i=1}^{k} u_i}{cp} \quad \text{for} \quad k = 1, 2, \ldots, N$$

$$u = \sum_{i=1}^{N} u_i$$

$$r = \frac{u}{p}.$$

The expression for w_k is an example of a normative relationship.

At the conclusion of the model development step, a precise analytic statement of the problem being solved should be available. Understanding of the problem should be sharper and unclear or uncertain relationships identified. The analyst is then ready to develop a computational approach to the problem.

6. DEVELOPMENT OF A COMPUTATIONAL APPROACH

Simultaneously with the model development step, it is necessary to determine how the model is to be solved numerically. This involves several tasks. For example, should a simulation or optimization approach be adopted; should the model recognize the randomness of variables or should a deterministic approach be adopted; should certain nonlinearities be recognized or are linear approximations sufficient; can "state of the art" solution methods be used or must a new method be developed? In short, what assumptions need to be made, and methods developed, in order to make the use of the model computationally practical. This step will also involve the "hand testing" of proposed computational approaches to ensure at least for small test problems, the feasibility and validity of the methods being developed. All this, of course, indicates that problem formulation, model development and design of a solution method overlap as was illustrated in Fig. 1.

An issue which often arises during this step concerns whether an optimization approach to model solution is feasible or whether a heuristic approach is necessary. In either event, for those studies in which it is necessary to develop a computational method, the analyst should start with a best formulation of his problem even if it is clearly unsolvable. From this he can then begin to make simplifving assumptions as needed. The advantages of this approach are several-fold. First, there will exist a realistic problem formulation. The analyst thus is assured of a proper problem understanding. Had he never developed an unsimplified model he may never truly understand the problem with which he is dealing. Second, the analyst is better able to understand the implications of any necessary simplifying assumption in terms of both the realism of his model and the impact of his assumptions on computational feasibility. Finally, if it is necessary to develop a heuristic method for model solution, the analyst is able to start with what would be an optimizing procedure and depart from this. Having such a frame of reference will aid in his chances for developing a computationally efficient, but yet close to optimal, heuristic method.

An example will illustrate the notions introduced above. A truck departure scheduling model needed to be developed. The problem involved specifying the number of trucks to depart from a warehouse during each of 30 4-hour intervals during a week. The departures per period were limited by the loading platforms available and were to be evenly spaced during the week so that labor staffing would be smooth. Additionally, if several trucks were scheduled for the same destination these should be evenly spaced during the week. For example, if 3 trucks were to go to a particular destination they should depart on Monday, Wednesday and Friday. The trucks were provided by common and contract carriers. Thus, besides the requirement for smooth departures in total, each trucker needed to have spaced departures. Otherwise the needed vehicles could not be provided. For example, if a particular trucker was to provide 10 trucks during the week he should be scheduled for 2 departures each day.

The problem could be represented as a gigantic integer programming problem with an objective function representing a numerical measure of departure "smoothness." Although there was no hope of solving the problem as such, its proper formulation provided a valid basis for developing a solution method. It was recognized that for each trucker, and for all trucks in total, separate integer programs could be defined and, because of special structure, solved using a simple algebraic procedure. Finding a feasible solution to the total problem then required only ensuring the total of the individual trucker solutions equalled that desired for the overall problem. A simple heuristic method for achieving this was easily designed. The resulting solution method turned out to be computationally efficient and produced excellent results. Its success was due primarily to the existence of a model representing the real problem and beginning with that in the development of a solution method.

As a final remark on computational methodology, we wish to comment briefly on the choice between obtaining:

a. An optimal solution to a simplified version of the problem;
b. An approximate solution to an exact formulation of the problem.

Experience strongly suggests the desirability of the second choice. In part, this is due to the lack of confidence in a study's results which might evolve from its failure to recognize a significant aspect of a problem. Nothing can turn a manager off faster than a result which is clearly wrong because the model did not take cognizance of a characteristic of a problem he, the manager, believes to be important. In part it is also due to the value of a computer to evaluate the complex interaction of many variables as opposed to dealing with simplified versions of problems. In practice, optimality is at best a fiction, but the many factors which interplay and interact on a decision problem are a fact. Managers need help in considering these. A complete representation of important factors, even if the resulting solution is nonoptimal, will usually be of more value than the optimal solution to a "less rich" problem formulation.

7. DEVELOPMENT OF PROGRAM SPECIFICATIONS, PROGRAMMING AND DEBUGGING

Computer programs are often required as part of an OR study. Because they often take more effort to develop than estimated and are oriented toward the programmer rather than the user, they frequently inhibit the success of the study. The development of programming specifications is to many practitioners an unpleasant task. As a result, it is often improperly performed. This is unfortunate since careful attention to the development of specifications will ensure cost and quality control of the programming work to follow. It also leads to better program documentation and a study more oriented and useful to the user.

We will not discuss the characteristics of good computer program specifications here. They are readily found in any good text on systems analysis and design. What is more important for our purposes is to stress the importance and meaning of one step within this task. That is, the specification of "user oriented" input and output reports and the review of these with the appropriate management and staff. By "user oriented" outputs we mean reports which provide the user with clearly identifiable, well-chosen, and properly arranged outputs, that is, in formats which are already familiar. Not outputs designed for the needs and ease of the programmer, but rather conceived with the requirements and purposes of the manager or staff analyst principally in mind. By "user oriented" inputs we mean a design for the data base which permits the user to provide inputs in readily prepared and easy to update formats. In short, a computer system which puts the burden of data preparation on the computer, not on the user.

What this implies in terms of system design is best illustrated by an example. Presented in Fig. 4 is a sample data bank for a typical production and distribution planning system. The example, which contains only a portion of the infor-

```
CSAMPLE DATA DECK
C
C
C     RUN DESCRIPTION
C     PERIOD         NUMBER         BEGINNING
C                                   MONTH DAY YEAR
      QUARTER        4              JAN     1 1973
C
C
C     PRODUCT FILE
C     CODE           DESCRIPTION
      HARDTOP        TWO-DOOR HARD TOP
      CONV           CONVERTIBLE
C
C
C     PRODUCTION PLANTS FILE
C     CODE           DESCRIPTION
      DETROT         DETROIT, MICHIGAN
      FRFURT         FRANKFURT, GERMANY
C
C
C
C     SALES AREAS FILE
C     CODE           DESCRIPTION
      U.S.           UNITED STATES
      EUROPE         EUROPEAN COMMON MARKET
      JAPAN          JAPAN
C
C
C     PRODUCTION MINIMUMS
C     PLANT          LEVEL/WEEK
      DETROT                500
      FRFURT                 90
C
C
C     ASSEMBLY CAPACITIES
C     PLANT          CATEGORY       CAP/WEEK       PRODUCT        PRODUCT
      DETROT                            1000
      FRFURT                             180
      DETROT         STAT-1             2000       CONV
      FRFURT         SPACE               200       HARDTOP        CONV
      DETROT         SPACE               530       CONV
C
C
C     PRODUCT INVENTORY HOLDING COSTS
C     AREA           PERCENT
      U.S.                20
      EUROPE              20
      JAPAN               25
```

Fig. 4. Sample data bank.

mation needed for such an application, illustrates the ease with which one can prepare and interpret the data bank elements. Virtually anyone knowledgeable in the problem area is able to recognize the data elements and understand their purpose. As a result, the inputs are easy to create, maintain and modify.

The task of programming and debugging is given only passing mention here. Often the OR project will not require computer programming or if it does, already available computer codes can be used: e.g., linear programming routines available from hardware suppliers or through service bureaus. Even when programming is required, it is often performed by others within the company. Nevertheless, the OR analyst may be held responsible for the completion of the programming task on-time and within the budget; an additional reason for the development of good programming specifications and a sensible project plan.

8. DATA COLLECTION

It is during this step that the data needed for validity testing and implementation is collected and analyzed. Previous data collection activities were oriented towards problem definition and model formulation. At the risk of controversy, we suggest that this step is perhaps the only one throughout the conduct of an OR study which is sometimes performed with excessive zeal. There is often an unjustified concern for the accuracy of data used as input to operations research studies. A project for a firm in the can-making industry will illustrate the point. The study was concerned with the development of a production planning model. Needed inputs included can line production rates, average hours per month each line was not operating because of maintenance or repair and the production cost per can per line. An industrial engineer was assigned to the project to develop the required numbers. His enthusiasm for accuracy was exceeded only by the uselessness of his efforts. There were several reasons why highly accurate data were unnecessary. First, the numbers were to be used with estimates of demand which were often in error by more than 50%. Second, the model was not to be used for detailed production planning. Last minute production requests, factors not modeled, and a variety of other reasons limited the model's usefulness to planning purposes. Last, because small differences in the inputs did not effect the model solution. The results simply were not sensitive to the accuracy of the above parameters.

There will, in any project, be inputs to which the model is sensitive and others to which it is not. Much time and effort can often be saved if initial data gathering and processing is limited to obtaining only "ballpark" estimates. The model can then be used to determine to which inputs results are sensitive and additional effort expended to more accurately estimate these.

It is usually during the data gathering phase that the analyst will need to respond to a common management objection to the use of models. The objection, although stated in many ways, essentially amounts to ". . . but we don't have the data. . . ." Usually OR studies are concerned with decisions already being made. The absence of data simply implies these decisions are currently being made in an intellectual vacuum. The difficulty of obtaining the necessary data, therefore, does not preclude the value of the study. Even if the required inputs are merely "guesstimates," the study will probably provide an improvement over existing methods. And, without even "guesstimates," it may help to focus the decision process on the important issues and provide a discipline for the conduct of a logical evaluation of alternatives.

An often valid argument to counter the "no-data" difficulty is to convey to managers an appreciation of the use of mathematical models as a means of resolving the difficulties of estimation by reducing the problem to simpler dimensions. This is best done through the following "convince yourself" exercise. Begin by estimating the area of square inches of the triangle illustrated in Fig. 5. Record your guess.

If you tried to estimate the area directly you have probably discovered the difficulty of the estimation problem. A better approach would be to first

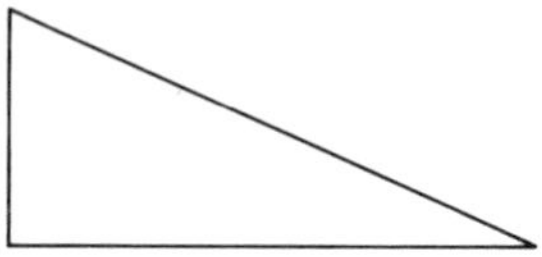

Fig. 5.

develop the relationship between the area of a triangle and its sides (the mathematical model). This is $\frac{1}{2}\,bh$ where b is the base and h is the height. Now estimate the length of the base and the height and compute the area of the triangle using the mathematical model. Record this second estimate. Finally, measure the base and height and compute the true area. You will probably discover your second estimate is more accurate than the first.

The use of OR models aids the decision process in an analogous way. Problems are reduced to the simplest dimensions and variables and the measures of interest expressed in terms of these. More data may need to be acquired but it will be simpler to obtain and its accuracy will be less critical.

9. VALIDATION

The importance of this step cannot be overemphasized. Two aspects are involved. First, determination of how to validate a model and second, conduct of the validation. The former task involves specifying analyses and experiments designed to test the consistency, sensitivity, plausibility, and workability of the model. Each of these is discussed below. Conduct of the validation requires use of the data collected during the prior step for a full test of the model. The results of such a test often necessitate redesign of the model and associated reprogramming.

9.1 Consistency

Are results logical when major parameters are varied especially to extremes? Determining an answer to this question requires an analysis of the model's response to changes in its inputs. The following example illustrates how a consistency test might be made.

An ordering formula is presented below for an inventory problem similar to that which leads to the simple lot size rule. The major difference is that ordering is from a supplier who can only deliver at a finite rate p. Optimization of the appropriate cost model leads to the following ordering rule:

$$Q^* = \sqrt{\frac{2DK}{h}\,\frac{p}{p-D}} \quad \text{for} \quad p > D$$

where

Q^* = the optimal order quantity
D = annual demand
K = fixed cost to order
h = holding cost
p = resupply rate.

Part of the model's consistency test might be to assume an infinite production rate and ensure the above rule reduces to the classic lot size formula. To test this, we would find:

$$\lim_{p \to \infty} \sqrt{\frac{2DK}{h} \frac{p}{p - D}} = \lim_{p \to \infty} \sqrt{\frac{2DK}{h} \frac{1}{1 - \frac{D}{p}}} = \sqrt{\frac{2DK}{h}}$$

which is, as it should be, the usual lot size formula.

9.2 Sensitivity

Are the relative magnitudes of changes in outputs appropriate for small changes in the inputs? This step usually requires a numerical exercise of the model. For example, in the previously described inventory model, values can be assumed for D, K and h and the relation between Q^* and p can be examined. A curve like that shown in Fig. 6 below should result.

9.3 Plausibility

Does the model fit special cases for which actual data are available? An excellent example of this aspect of the validation step is provided by the following example. A mathematical programming model was developed to aid a firm in setting dividend levels to be declared by their 80 foreign subsidiaries in 32 countries. The dividend levels were to be set so as to minimize total taxes paid by the firm subject to constraints reflecting company policies, Department of Commerce "gold flow" limitations, and Internal Revenue Service rules and regula-

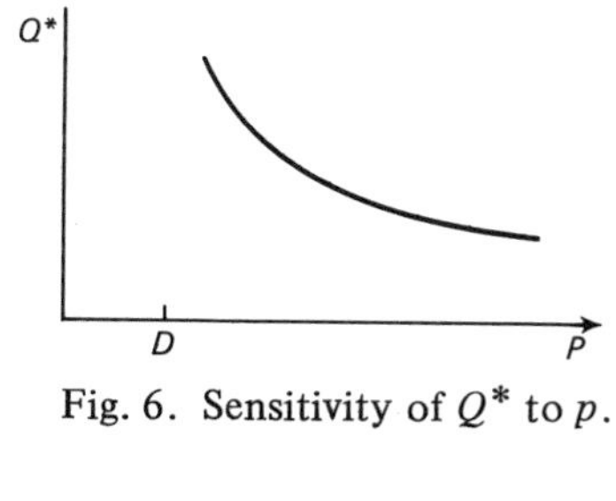

Fig. 6. Sensitivity of Q^* to p.

tions. To validate the model, the data corresponding to a past year were collected including the actual dividends paid. The numbers were input to the model and the value of the objective function determined; it was within .1% of the actual taxes paid. Besides establishing the plausibility of the model, this effort was especially useful in demonstrating the model's validity to the company's tax attorney and management.

9.4 Workability

Is the model easy to solve? If the model is to be used in support of decisions made by line executives, it should be capable of responding within the time frames appropriate for their decisions. Additionally, the effort and resources needed to use the model should be within computer and staff budget limitations. Often this requires the operations researcher to utilize approximations and heuristics even when technically unnecessary.

The following story is believed to be true. One of the U.S. Army agencies had developed a simulation model of tank-versus-tank combat. On the day the 1967 Arab-Israeli War broke out, they were asked by the Joint Chiefs of Staff to use the model to predict the outcome. Their response arrived the next day predicting the war would end in five days. The Joint Chiefs of Staff considered the results unreasonable and suggested the analysts change their numbers, rerun the model and come back with more believable results. They did so, changing their estimate of the number of days the war would last, however, by only one-half a day. By this time, the war was over. Here certainly was a model which was not only valid in its predictions (close enough for government purposes) but also workable in the sense of providing answers within an extremely short interval of time. An inquiry, however, led to the following revelation. The predictions were not provided by the model. Its use would have required weeks, if not months, of prior data collection. Rather, the agency simply asked one of its employees, an ex-German panzer officer who had served with Rommel in the Afrika Corps. The predictions were his.

The second major aspect of validation is the use of test data to evaluate any models developed in a realistic environment. This is especially important for projects involving one-time decisions. Validation of models incorporated into routine operating systems is a more involved process involving parallel operation and formal review. Its discussion is beyond our present scope. The most important aspect of validation for one-time decision projects is intellectual post-processing. This is the set of activities that the analyst should undertake after he utilizes the model but before his evaluation of all alternatives and presentation of results and recommendations to management. The objective of the activity is to gain further insight into the decision problem by questioning the assumptions that underly the model and its use.

The reference by Brown [1970] describes a study in which a corporate staff team at one company evaluated an acquisition opportunity by means of a decision-tree analysis. The computer program they used took four months to develop and another two months to use. In all, 140 computer runs were made before arriving at a recommendation to make the acquisition and to adopt a specific marketing and production strategy. The recommendation was rejected by top management, however, when the company's counsel advised against the acquisition on certain legal grounds. The lawyers discovered that a critical consideration had been omitted from the analysis which rendered it unusable. Had the assumptions been more carefully questioned before the final results were presented to top management, the project might have had a more successful conclusion.

10. IMPLEMENTATION

Too often, the OR analyst believes his responsibility ends with the development and validation of the model. This is not the case. In fact, the real difficulties with a study often only surface during this final project step, that of implementation and maintenance. The effectiveness of the total study will depend heavily on obtaining the cooperation and participation of the various management levels involved in the decision problem being studied or the functions being affected. Much of the resistance which may be encountered can be attributed to nothing more serious than a lack of understanding and a reluctance to change. These can be overcome, but it is the responsibility of the OR analyst to devote the time and patience required. A successful implementation involves the preparation of training materials, the development and presentation of orientation seminars and the use of realistic case study applications. While many managers, by the time a study is completed, may be familiar with any models or systems developed, it is still important to ensure that their understanding is accurate and that suitable materials for training others are available in order to maximize the model's long-term usefulness. It is only when the analyst is willing to cooperate and work in harmony with those whose activities he is studying that the proper partnerships can be formed and the OR study successfully concluded. Implementation is a process of "handholding" without the operations research worker and the manager cannot establish the needed communication and cooperation.

An important but often neglected aspect of a study which involves the implementation of a new system is the short-term problems and disruptions it causes. These are often inevitable regardless of the extent to which the system is previously tested and validated. There are several ways to successfully handle this aspect of the problem of implementation. One way, when possible, is through the conduct of a parallel operation with comparison of test results to the current methods. Care should be taken in this case to ensure beforehand all interested parties understand fully the high likelihood of difficulties. More important, however, is the need for the operations research analyst to have available:

1. A carefully worked out plan for the conduct of the parallel test or tests.
2. A previously tested plan for the comparison of test results to actual data.
3. A means of collecting the test and actual data needed to perform the comparison.
4. The resources necessary to make, on a timely basis, the changes required to correct for problems which may arise.
5. The management approval to conduct subsequent tests as may be necessary.

Those involved and affected by the implementation of a new system must recognize the need for a period of time in order to "iron out the bugs" always found in a new system. Nevertheless, a point is sometimes reached at which management and staff must swallow their pride and admit that the project they have spoken so optimistically about at an earlier time and to which they have devoted so much of their energies, just isn't going to work. It happens, and more times than we care to admit. This chapter may lessen the probability of its occurrence.

REFERENCES

1. Brown, R. V., "Do Managers Find Decision Theory Useful?" *Harvard Business Rev.* (May-June 1970).
2. Hillier, Frederick S. and Gerald J. Lieberman, *Introduction to Operations Research*, Holden-Day, San Francisco, (1967).
3. Morris, William T., "On the Art of Modelling," *Management Sci.*, **13** (12) (August 1967).
4. Morse, Philip N. and George E. Kimball, *Methods of Operations Research*, MIT Press, Cambridge, Massachusetts (1951).
5. Wagner, Harvey M., *Principles of Operations Research*, Prentice-Hall, Englewood Cliffs, N.J., (1969).

I-4

THE EDUCATION OF THE OPERATIONS RESEARCH PROFESSIONAL

Robert M. Thrall
Rice University

1. INTRODUCTION

The history of operations research (OR) is not long in time. Although scattered instances of what now goes under that title can be found much earlier, as a named discipline OR is less than 35 years old and its first appearances as an academic specialization do not go back more than a quarter of a century. There is even still no general agreement as to the best title; some of the alternatives in use are operations research, operations analysis, operational research, management science, and systems analysis.

However, despite its newcomer status OR is now firmly and broadly established academically. Although this development has been worldwide, the present discussion will place primary emphasis on the situation in the United States. Reference 5 summarizes OR programs in 46 universities.

Of necessity the early OR professionals were transfers from other disciplines. Most came from the mathematical, engineering, physical, behavioral and life sciences; however, there was a small but significant representation from other areas. The complexity of the situations faced spawned the formation of interdisciplinary teams whose individual members were specialists able to handle various facets of the problems assigned.

More recently two somewhat opposing trends have become evident. The first is a shift at the operational level from the team of specialists toward individuals each somewhat familiar with most facets of OR problems. The second is the emergence of specialists whose life work is to dig deeper and deeper into some one facet, e.g., inventory theory, simulation or mathematical programming.

The first trend is nurtured by employers who wish operational solutions for their problems, who find "good" solutions obtained quickly more useful than "optimal" solutions obtained only after extensive study. These employers prefer OR professionals who are adept at adapting from existing knowledge and experience to those whose bent and talent are more directed to creative research which expands the base of knowledge. The second trend is nurtured by the whole apparatus of academia which, above all, rewards publication of the results of creative research.

One consequence of these trends is a polarization of OR professionals which influences and complicates OR publication and OR education. This polarization, the breadth and depth of OR and the developing character of OR educational programs indicates the need for multifaceted approach in discussing the education of the OR professional. Such polarization is not unique to OR but spreads across most applied sciences and is a source of educational controversy in almost all professional schools.

In Part 2 of this chapter we deal with the *structure* of OR education and review the major learning channels available to an individual who wishes to become an OR professional. In Part 3 we consider the various *levels* of OR education ranging from the Ph.D. to the casual user. In Part 4 we treat the *subject matter* of OR education. In Part 5 we touch on *recruitment* of OR professionals. By this we mean how to encourage qualified persons, especially students, to opt for careers in OR rather than how to hire an OR professional. I lay no claim that these four facets: structure, level, subject matter, and recruitment are the only possible ones, but they seem to cover what I feel qualified to write about. The references include some papers which are cited and others which are included for supplementary reading.

2. STRUCTURE OF *OR* EDUCATION

The first facet we consider is structure. We may delineate several broad types of OR education: formal, semiformal, informal, and on-the-job. The type designated as "formal" consists of regular university (or college) programs and courses for which credit is earned. "Semiformal" comprises noncredit offerings such as concentrated short courses lasting from two days to six or eight weeks and some extension courses. "Informal" includes meetings of professional societies, symposia, regional seminars, general reading. "On-the-job" refers to education incident to day-to-day OR practice.

2.1 Formal

The subject matter of formal educational programs and courses in OR will be discussed later; our present concern is with organizational structure.

Universities are by nature highly conservative institutions whose power structures are not readily permeated by new groups. It has been said that the only thing harder to achieve in a university than instituting a new program area is terminating an established one even though it has become irrelevant. Accordingly, tactical considerations have led proponents of OR programs to look for soft places in the power structure and to make alliances with existing groups which could be strengthened by infusion of a healthy new topic. A prime example of this is the widespread alliance between OR and industrial engineering. In the 1950s industrial engineering departments did not generally enjoy a high status. However, their existing courses relating to industrial management provided a natural point of entry for OR and there was an extensive invasion which resulted in (a) establishment of OR as a field of concentration at all degree levels, (b) introduction of broadgaged survey courses in OR for nonmajors, and (c) substantial use of OR courses as electives by majors in other engineering departments and elsewhere. As might have been expected, political control of the industrial engineering departments became a struggle between the new OR specialists and the traditionalists. A central bone of contention was how much of the classical program would be required of all industrial engineering students (at each degree level). Questions such as "should statistics courses be upgraded from cook-book level," "how much mathematics should be required," and "what should be the role of computer science courses" were debated at length.

In institutions where the newer groups won control there were a variety of modifications of departmental titles and in some institutions where the traditionalists maintained command interdisciplinary OR programs or even new OR departments were established. The significant fact is that at the present almost all university engineering schools recognize OR as an academic discipline and these engineering-based OR programs tend to operate at a substantially higher mathematical level than corresponding programs in schools of management (business administration).

The title "systems analysis" has been used to designate programs of an OR character closely associated with systems design and found in electrical and aerospace engineering departments. More generally, one can find OR courses scattered rather broadly throughout engineering schools. Frequently in OR, as with statistics, a department may wish to construct a highly specialized course for its own advanced students. Such offerings tend to be expensive in benefit/cost terms except for departments with large student enrollments.

Since OR involves studies which lead ultimately to managerial decisions, it was natural that schools of management should have become heavily involved in OR education. However, the semantics are confusing and we find OR appearing in management schools under a variety of titles including "management science" and "quantitative methods." Sometimes the title is so obscure that an examination of course offerings is required to locate the program. One clue is that in management schools OR and statistics are very frequently organizationally combined.

Although engineering and management schools provide the main bastions for formal OR education there are some other significant academic homes. There is a natural affinity between statistics and OR and each suffers if too far removed from the other. Statistics in the universities has been fragmented into many little pieces. Two of these, in industrial engineering and in management, are now closely allied with OR. In most universities there is a central statistics department which is organizationally separate from the professional schools. In quite a few of these departments there is strong recognition of OR as a specialty area; indeed, in a few cases the departmental title refers to both statistics and OR.

A National Academy of Science Report [See Ref. 7, 1968] included OR as one of the mathematical sciences. There is a rather recent trend toward use of "mathematical sciences" as a departmental (or divisional) title. Where this has occurred OR has usually been included as a subspecialty.

In a few scattered cases computer science and economics have sponsored OR programs, although these tend to be rather narrow in scope. Most of the behavioral sciences offer individual courses or sequences of courses that are important in OR education as is illustrated by course titles such as industrial psychology, law and society, managerial accounting, economic analysis, managerial economics, and urban sociology.

Although the coverage of OR educational programs in Ref. 5 is not comprehensive, the 46 universities listed provide a good sample. They sponsored 58 programs located in the following areas:

Engineering	27
Management	16
OR Departments or Interdisciplinary committees	7
Mathematical Sciences	3
Other	5

A description of formal OR education would be incomplete without some reference to the role of extension and other part-time credit courses designed for persons with full-time regular jobs. These courses are frequently offered in off-campus locations close to (or even within) an industrial or government complex and may be sequenced to fulfill master's degree requirements. Employers may subsidize these programs through such devices as tuition refunds to employees upon successful completion of a course or through guarantees of some funding level.

In summary, formal OR education is now broadly available at all levels from survey courses to doctoral programs; the majority of the programs are located in schools of engineering and management, with a growing number to be found in the mathematical sciences, and with strong supporting courses in the behavioral sciences.

2.2 Semiformal

Since formal OR educational programs are so recent in origin it is not surprising that most of the present OR professionals do not have OR degrees. The person who wished to enter OR (or whose management instructed him to become an instant expert) could have recourse to semiformal programs which arose in universities in the mid 1950s and are now broadly offered by consulting firms. The typical university short courses ran for one or two weeks and ranged in level from very elementary to quite advanced. Government funding was available for a few longer programs which could run as long as eight weeks and were especially directed at potential teachers of OR; such funding has recently been severely pruned, if not cut off altogether.

During the heyday of the short courses the participants came primarily from government and industry, but there was a sprinkling of college and university teachers from institutions which wished to initiate or strengthen existing OR offerings. Some of the advanced courses resembled symposia and were perhaps more important in providing a setting for mutual exchange of information than for their platform deliveries. Indeed, I recall cases where most of the participants were fully qualified to exchange places with the lecturers!

By the end of the 1960s the number of, and attendance at, university based short courses was waning. Simultaneously, offerings of two- or three-day programs by consulting firms were waxing. Typically, each of these would be scheduled at a number of locations, would concentrate on some one topic and would feature practical applications as well as the underlying theory.

This shift in emphasis in semiformal offerings reflects the existence of a large pool of persons with formal OR education who are interested in mastering some new specialty which they perceive as important in their jobs.

In summary, semiformal programs seem likely to continue to play an important role in OR education. Although the number of university short courses has shrunk, there are still some excellent ones, especially at advanced levels and the flexibility of specialized short-short courses sponsored by consulting firms should ensure their continuation at a significant level.

2.3 Informal

Whereas formal education is regarded as preceding and semiformal programs tend to come relatively early in a career, informal education continues as long as an OR professional is active.

A major component of informal education is provided by professional societies through general meetings, special interest groups, regional and local chapters, sponsorship of visiting lecturers and publications. In the United States, the Operations Research Society of America (ORSA) and The Institute of Management Sciences (TIMS) are the major supporting societies. Their general (and regional) meetings provide opportunity for presenting and listening to papers, for informal interchange in the corridors and over a coffee cup, for organizing and participating in special interest sessions, and for becoming generally aware of significant new developments in OR. Local chapters of ORSA and TIMS provide a continuing arena for exchange of information among industrial and university OR professionals, and also mount significant seminars and symposia.

In addition to the two central societies quite a few others have missions which overlap OR; some of these are The Econometric Society, The Psychometric Society, The Society for General Systems Research, The Mathematical Programming Society, The Society for Industrial and Applied Mathematics, The Association for Computing Machinery, The American Statistical Association, and most of the professional engineering societies.

Individual reading of books and journals constitutes a major part of informal education in any field. However, the continuing proliferation of professional journals makes keeping up to date increasingly difficult. Unfortunately, secondary sources in the OR field are limited in coverage; the IFORS International Abstracts concentrates on the major OR journals to the exclusion of locating articles of OR interest that appear elsewhere. Thus a paper describing an application of OR in forest management or in waste water treatment is likely to be missed. This lack of a truly comprehensive indexing of OR papers is a major deficiency and there is little immediate prospect of remedial measures. Important aids to access are expository review papers which survey some topic and provide extensive bibliographies. Also there are many books which collect and reprint major research papers in some area. Handbooks, such as the present one, provide significant aid at the introductory level.

A serendipitous contribution of meeting attendance is the uncovering of literature sources for a topic or application of interest. Consultants are hired for a variety of purposes but one of their major contributions is surely providing references to persons knowledgeable about and references relevant to some topic of immediate concern.

2.4 On-the-Job

Generally, the most effective learning is that which is related to problem solving. A topic that promises to be immediately useful seems to be much easier to master and retain than one whose contribution, however great potentially, is less direct. As a consequence of this, on-the-job learning may provide the most significant education for most OR professionals. Indeed, formal, semiformal and informal education are of little worth to the professional unless he can relate them to his assigned tasks. (This applies equally to the OR teacher who learns really best those topics on which he lectures.)

For the beginner, learning from more experienced colleagues clearly plays a leading educational role; as he begins to work more independently he will learn by solving problems. At this stage his reading will tend to be directed toward very specific objectives and his retention rate is likely to be high.

3. LEVELS OF *OR* EDUCATION

As used here the term "level" refers primarily to the formal component of OR education. It is self-evident that the amount and nature of formal education which is appropriate should depend on the career objective.

An appropriate balance of its professionals between the different levels of formal education is essential for healthy OR growth and development. For example, the OR profession will be damaged if it numbers either too many or too few Ph.D.'s among its members, or if knowledge of OR is limited to full-time OR professionals.

3.1 Doctoral Level

It is quite clear that for a university career of teaching and research in OR the Ph.D. level is essential. The role of the Ph.D. as a union card is adequate justification by itself; however, another sufficient reason is found in the essential nature of the university as the primary institution responsible for extending basic knowledge in every field. With the notable exception of a handful of industrial and government laboratories, creative research on such topics as finding efficient algorithms for large sparse linear programs, or determining optimal policies for multicommodity stochastic inventory problems, or for constructing models for conflict resolution is found primarily in universities, usually aided by federal grants or contracts. The university reward structure encourages publication and so it is not surprising that such a high percentage of OR papers are authored by academics and that these papers are predominantly theoretical in nature. Whether or not the general national furor over too many Ph.D.'s is currently relevant for OR, we must be alert lest an over-emphasis on production of OR doctorates interested only in basic research results in a dangerous imbalance.

This danger is not limited to possible unemployment of the excess doctorates; far worse is the potential impact on publications. When academic jobs are scarce the normal premium on publication is intensified and in academia the more abstract the paper the higher it is valued. If this should result in further increasing the proportion of theoretical to application oriented papers in OR journals there is grave danger of schism between academic and nonacademic OR professionals that would seriously damage both groups.

Before leaving the topic of the role of the Ph.D. in OR we should point out that the possession of a Ph.D. does not automatically render an OR professional useless in solving practical problems. Moreover, there are quite a few nonacademic OR positions where either or both of the union-card and depth-of-knowledge features of the Ph.D. are important. These include some research laboratories and a fairly wide variety of administrative positions. One measure of the viability of the present crop of Ph.D.'s in OR is their current ability to move back and forth between academic and nonacademic posts.

3.2 Master's Level

In the absence of any reliable job census I would hazard the estimate that the need for OR professionals at or just beyond the master's level is at least ten times that for Ph.D.'s. If this estimate is anywhere nearly correct some reforms in our university educational program seem in order.

The nonacademic OR professional typically devotes only a small part of his time to research and that research is primarily adaptive or developmental as opposed to creative. It is not at all clear that the best formal education for such professionals is the predissertation portion of a Ph.D. program. (I will return to this topic in the following section.)

The practicing OR professional probably needs a broader educational base than the theoretician; he should be able to read and to utilize the results found in research papers in almost all OR specialities. In the case of highly technical results he should (1) recognize if he could profit from consulting a specialist and (2) be able to translate a specialist's advice into a usable procedure.

A practitioner who is willing to work on whatever problems arise and is accepted by his colleagues as a dependable co-worker is more likely to be successful in getting an OR based innovation approved and utilized than is one who insists on complete and continuous identification as an OR man. This helps to explain why many corporations are reluctant to hire OR Ph.D.'s.

Requirements for a master's degree vary considerably among institutions; hence, the statement "master's level competence" is ambiguous. The minimal level of one graduate year does not seem generally sufficient as a career base; two years including a thesis may be more than is needed. Somewhere between these extremes one reaches a good operating "journeyman's" level for formal preparation of an OR professional whose chief interest is OR practice. This does not imply that a person with less (or more) formal OR education cannot become an effective practitioner, but until he achieves this recommended level, either through formal education or otherwise, it is difficult to regard him as a real journeyman.

There is, nonetheless, a place in OR for the person who must (at least temporarily) conclude his formal education at the bachelor's level, provided he is willing to continue learning using some of the alternate opportunities.

3.3 Non-OR Majors

Although this chapter relates primarily to the OR professional, some attention should be given to OR education for persons whose use will be mostly casual and indirect. The pervasiveness of OR models makes it attractive and useful for accountants, statisticians, computer scientists, behavior scientists and many engineers to have some knowledge of OR coverage and methodology. The effectiveness of OR is clearly enhanced when the OR professionals deal with colleagues and managers who are not complete novices in the role of model building. Therefore, we are justified in our classification which is rather minimal in formal OR content. Moreover, it is not rare that persons initially planning only for this minimal level become OR converts and transfer to a higher level OR program.

Another topic which should be included in this section is the extent to which OR professionals should have OR as their field of formal concentration. As has been mentioned, the early OR practitioners were all transfers from other disciplines. Does the presence of OR as a recognized academic discipline mean that conversion should no longer be regarded as a significant source of professionals? I believe that few experienced OR professionals would answer this question "yes."

Of necessity, the original converts to OR had no formal OR education, although most of them had graduate degrees in their original disciplines. Thus in discussing converts, the term "level" has two components: (1) the highest level achieved irrespective of discipline, and (2) the level achieved in formal OR. For a non-OR major this second level will not ordinarily be recognized by a degree description. For an MBA it may consist of one or two courses with OR or management science (MS) labels together with many contributory courses in statistics, simulation, accounting and the like. Doctoral candidates in fields such as theoretical physics or core mathematics where jobs are scarce may elect a few OR courses in an attempt to generate a secondary skill. Generally these persons are exceptionally intelligent and, if they combine this native intelligence with a genuine willingness to participate in the nontheoretical parts of OR, they can become first class OR professionals.

4. SUBJECT MATTER

In this section we deal with the formal courses which belong to OR education at the several levels. The chapter titles for this handbook include most of the important subjects in OR, but they do not indicate what basic topics are prerequisites.

4.1 Mathematics Needed for OR Professionals

Table 1 was prepared for convenience in discussing mathematics courses and does not necessarily correspond to actual packaging of mathematics in any institution.

The first two courses listed provide a bare minimum for the casual user of OR. They contain bits and pieces from courses 3, 4, 6, 7 and are not ordinarily intended for students who plan further mathematics electives. (In some instutitions there are sequels to 1, 2 which add the missing portions and result in an end product more or less equivalent to 3, 4, 6, and possibly 7.) Courses 1 and 2 (in either order) make a reasonable one-year sequence for, say, majors in accounting or commerce who wish a basis for an elementary survey course in OR.

TABLE 1. Twenty 3-Hour, 1-Semester Mathematics Courses.

1. Finite Mathematics	11. Modern Algebra
2. Calculus Survey	12. Probability II
3. Calculus I	13. Statistics II
4. Calculus II	14. Combinatorial Analysis
5. Calculus III (several variable)	15. Differential Equations
6. Linear Algebra	16. Difference Equations
7. Probability I	17. Numerical Analysis
8. Statistics I	18. Real Analysis
9. Model Building	19. Complex Analysis
10. Calculus IV (advanced)	20. Topology

An undergraduate who completes courses 3, 4, 6, 7, 8 will be able to handle most standard beginning OR sequences. The model building course 9 is not yet broadly available as a mathematics offering, in part because texts for it have just begun to appear. Its role can be played by an OR course that emphasizes the structure of the modeling process. The eleven courses 3-13 constitute a solid mathematical basis for OR. Selections from courses 14-20 are appropriate for persons who plan careers in methodological research in one (or more) or the OR areas that appear in Sections II and III of this handbook.

4.2 Other Basic Areas

Although mathematics represents the major single preparatory area, a person interested in becoming an OR professional should guard against overemphasizing mathematics to the exclusion of other important topics.

Some computer science is certainly needed. The bare minimum is knowledge of one or more programming languages, and the importance of management information systems indicates the desirability of some formal preparation in information processing systems.

Basic courses in economics, psychology, political science, and sociology are clearly desirable as are also somewhat more technical topics such as human performance, industrial law, and accounting.

4.3 The OR Component

Courses whose titles relate to the chapter titles in Sections II and III of this handbook constitute the quantitative methodological core of OR. The companion volume, *Handbook of Operations Research: Models and Applications*, provides good coverage of applied OR in Section I on Models; the topics treated in Section II on Applications are less likely to be included in formal courses in departments which award OR degrees although they may be found in other parts of a university. They provide excellent and timely areas for student research both at the master's and the Ph.D. levels.

A master's level OR program could be expected to have at least half of its courses in methodological and applied OR with at least two courses in each of these subdivisions. As has been mentioned earlier, the OR practitioner needs breadth more than specialization. A doctoral OR program will ordinarily focus intensively on some one topic either methodological or applied. A methodological major is well advised to include some courses which feature application of his special topic; similarly, an applications major should include some advanced courses in methodologies which are used in his field. However, for the Ph.D., overall breadth need not be an immediate objective since experience shows that a person who has delved deeply into and has achieved some research results in one area can broaden his base as needed through self-study.

Creativity is a rare talent and should not be hampered by artificial requirements of broad coverage. Many OR programs suffer from parochially inspired requirements whose main justification seems to be to shore up dwindling enrollment in some area of waning appeal.

There is a continuing controversy among OR teachers as to the proper balance between subject matter courses and project work which involves practical experience in some industry, government unit, or public institution. If the criterion is *to produce a graduate who is immediately useful to an employer,* there is much to be said for project-centered education. However, this places a burden on the individual to enlarge his/her technical background by self-study or part-time course work. If the criterion is *to produce a graduate who has the background needed to profit by experience,* then subject-matter-centered education seems superior.

Employers who provide extensive on-the-job training for new employees are likely to prefer a candidate with extensive course preparation whereas an employer who is hiring for an immediate task rather than for development of a permanent staff will tend to prefer a candidate with extensive project experience.

This controversy shows no signs of resolution; there seems to be a need for the two types of programs, both at the master's and the Ph.D. levels.

There are still persons who believe that OR specialization provides an inferior product to conversion from a traditional hard discipline. Here again there need be no hard and fast decision. My own opinion is that OR specialization is clearly superior at the master's level, whereas at the doctoral level I believe that both routes are and will continue to be viable.

The titles in Section II of the companion volume, *Handbook of Operations Research: Models and Applications*, indicate a number of career areas for OR practitioners; in most of these, the OR person will be much more effective if he/she has some specialized knowledge of the area. For example, some knowledge of government organization and processes will aid an OR practitioner interested in city planning and similarly effective OR work in health care delivery is clearly enhanced by knowledge of operational procedures in hospitals, clinics, and other health care centers.

Some of this knowledge can be pursued in formal course offerings and much must come from on-the-job experience. The increasing inclusion of OR specialists on the faculties of schools of public health, public administration, conservation, etc., is substantially enhancing the formal course's practical component.

If early in his career an OR student has made a commitment to some particular application he can clearly enhance his likelihood of success by selection of background courses outside the standard OR curriculum. However, such early commitment is not the mode and we seem likely to continue to depend heavily on on-the-job learning. Perhaps offering summer intern positions to potentially interested students could enhance both the quantity and quality of OR practioners in these areas.

5. RECRUITMENT

Any discussion of OR education is without point if there are no candidates for it. Both ORSA and TIMS have been active in encouraging students to consider OR as a profession. They co-sponsor a visiting lecture program, both have student chapters, and both have awards for outstanding student papers. The ORSA Education Committee has prepared a widely distributed booklet, *Careers in Operations Research.* This report is updated from time to time and is available through the ORSA Business Office (428 Preston St., Baltimore, Maryland 21202). See also Ref. 5. The career booklet portrays some capsule biographies of prototype OR professionals, lists some major OR periodicals, and includes a selected bibliography.

Every OR professional has a stake in maintaining a healthy flow of well-qualified and able newcomers. A practitioner can contribute to this by:

1. giving advice and counsel to young persons in his circle of acquaintance,
2. encouraging junior colleagues in his organization to look into the potential of OR,
3. urging his organization to provide summer jobs for OR students,
4. encouraging his organization to participate in work-study OR programs,
5. showing by his own example the advantages of OR as a profession.

His ability to recruit will be enhanced if he keeps aware of recent OR successes and knows something of the history and philosophy of OR.

REFERENCES

1. Bonder, Seth, "Operations Research Education: Some Requirements and Deficiencies," *Operations Res.* **21**: 796–809 (1973).
2. ——, "Operations Research As a Profession," *Management Sci.* **17**: B37-53 (1970).
3. —— (ed.), "Some Papers on Educational Issues in The Management Sciences and Operations Research," *Management Sci.* **17**: B1-36 (1970).
4. Devron, Marc (ed.), NATO Conference: Education and Training on Operational Research I and II, Istanbul Turkey, 31 August–4 September (1970).
5. "Education Programs in Operations Research/Management Science," 54 pp. (1973), a report of the Education Committee of the Operations Research Society of America, 428 East Preston Street, Baltimore, Maryland 21202.
6. Morris, W. T., "On The Art of Modeling," *Management Sci.* **13**: B707-717 (1967).
7. "The Mathematical Sciences: A Report," Publication 1681, National Academy of Sciences, Washington, D. C. (1968) a report of a Committee on Support of Research in the Mathematical Sciences (COSRIMS).

SECTION II

Methodology of OR: Deterministic Models

II-1

LINEAR PROGRAMMING

Hamdy A. Taha
University of Arkansas

1. INTRODUCTION

Linear programming (LP) evolved as the first formal subject of operations research when George B. Dantzig developed his simplex method (SM) in 1947. Prior to this, the need for optimization techniques was recognized by economists and military strategists who were seeking the solution to complex problems evolving from military activities during World War II.

The importance of Dantzig's simplex method became even more recognized when J. von Neumann, father of game theory, developed the concept of duality in 1947. This concept opened many research areas in LP which further enhanced its usefulness and problem-solving capability. The 1950s then witnessed a flood of new algorithms and theoretical developments in the subject. Today, LP stands as one of the best developed optimization techniques from the viewpoints of theory, applications and computations. Indeed, the achievements in LP are directly responsible for progress in the development of algorithms for other mathematical programming problems including integer, stochastic and nonlinear programming.

Undoubtedly, LP owes much of its success as a problem-solving technique to the tremendous advancement in the speed and storage capacity of the digital computer. This is evident by the diverse number of computer codes including the widely used commercial codes of International Business Machines (MPSX),

Control Data (OPHELIE), and Scientific Data Control, London (UMPIRE). In particular, the ability to employ multiple-precision computation has greatly reduced the propagating effect of round-off errors.

The theory of LP has been fully presented in several outstanding books [Dantzig, 1963; Gass, 1975; Hadley, 1962; Koopmans, 1951; Orchard-Hays, 1968; Simmonard, 1966; Spivey and Thrall, 1970]. The objective of this chapter is to provide a unifying presentation of the basic concepts of the subject as well as its scope of applications. The presentation will not include the closely related topics of networks, game theory, and large scale LP's since these are presented independently elsewhere in this book. Due to space limitation (and the immense number of references available for LP), the references at the end of the chapter are confined mainly to the principal works.

2. SCOPE OF LINEAR PROGRAMMING APPLICATIONS

The general LP model may be defined mathematically as

$$\text{maximize (or minimize) } x_0 = \sum_{j=1}^{r} c_j x_j$$

subject to

$$\sum_{j=1}^{r} a_{ij} x_j \,(\leqslant, = \text{or} \geqslant)\, b_i, \quad i = 1, 2, \ldots, m$$

$$x_j \geqslant 0, \quad j = 1, 2, \ldots, r$$

An economic interpretation of the LP model encompassing a wide variety of applications is the following. The modeled system includes several *activities* $j(j = 1, 2, \ldots, r)$ sharing limited *resources* b_i, $i = 1, 2, \ldots, m$. The usage per unit of the jth activity from the ith resource is a_{ij}. In return for this input, the output (cost or profit) per unit of the jth activity is represented by c_j.

The objective of the model is to determine the *level* of each activity, x_j, that optimizes (maximizes or minimizes) the output of all activities without violating the limits stipulated on the resources. It is common to refer to x_0 as the *objective function* and the resource limitations as the *constraints.*

The basic assumptions of the LP model are: (i) proportionality, (ii) additivity, and (iii) nonnegativity. *Proportionality* means that the usage of resources by an activity as well as its contribution to the objective function are directly proportional to the level of the activity. *Additivity*, on the other hand, indicates that the combined usage of resources by all the activities is the sum of individual usages. A similar interpretation is made of the objective function.

The proportionality and additivity assumptions produce completely linear functions. In real life, true linearity is rarely satisfied. However, the linearity assumption results in extremely efficient solution methods, which usually warrant approximating certain nonlinear problems by linear models.

Nonnegativity signifies that no activity can assume a negative level. Although this is a logical assumption in many physical systems, its inclusion in LP models is also a matter of analytic convenience. For there exist situations where the level of activity may be *unrestricted* in sign. A typical situation occurs in *goal programming* models where the constraints of the model cannot be satisfied simultaneously. For example, the different functions of an organization usually operate within conflicting constraints. Suppose these constraints are given as

$$\sum_{j=1}^{n} a_{ij}x_j = b_i, \quad i = 1, 2, \ldots, m$$

The idea of goal programming is to allow some of the constraints to be violated, possibly at a penalty. This may be achieved by adding an *unrestricted* variable (activity) y_i (representing the violated amount) to the left-hand side of the ith constraint. It is interesting to note that when the problem is solved as a LP, the substitution $y_i = y_i^+ - y_i^-, y_i^+$ and $y_i^- \geqslant 0$, must be effected.

Linear programming enjoys a tremendous diversity of applications in military, agriculture, industry, production and inventory control, economics and transportation. A comprehensive bibliography is given in [Gass, 1975, pp. 371-81].

The applications of LP extend to dynamic situations involving a finite number of time periods where the output of one period acts as a (partial) input to the next one. This is particularly the case for production and inventory control problems [Dantzig, 1959; Dzielinski and Gomory, 1965; Johnson, 1957; Manne, 1958]. Other applications acquire this "dynamic" property by including parametric changes in the coefficients of the model. For example, in the oil industry the demand for a certain product may show a time trend even though the basic structure of the model remains unchanged over time. The parametric functions can be handled directly in LP by using sensitivity or parametric analysis [Gass and Saaty, 1955; Saaty, 1959; Saaty and Gass, 1954] (see Section 6 of this chapter).

While LP models are basically deterministic by definition, there are applications in which probabilistic information is included directly in the formulation. An example is the transportation problem in which the demand at destinations is a random variable [Ferguson and Dantzig, 1956]. Other applications include the element of uncertainty in the objective function [Dantzig, 1955; Elmaghraby, 1959; Elmaghraby, 1960; Madansky, 1960]. *Chance-constrained* programming where linear constraints are realized only as probability statements [Charnes and Cooper, 1959] serves as another example of uncertainty. The dominant idea in all these models is to convert (sometimes approximate) the random variation to an equivalent deterministic one. Linear programming has also been used in connection with Markov chains analysis [Wolfe and Dantzig, 1962].

Linear programming applications extend to other scientific disciplines as well. Statistical regression analysis provides a typical example [Wagner, 1962]. The minimax theorem in game theory can be proved directly by LP theory [Dantzig, 1951]. More recently, there have been attempts to extend LP to the complex domain [McCallum, 1972] although no applications of such results have been realized.

Most systems in which LP is applied are actually nonlinear. These systems are usually approximated (by imposing proper assumptions) by linear systems to allow the use of LP formulations. The oil industry is but one situation where linearity is rarely satisfied in the real sense [Garvin, Crandall and Spellman, 1957]. Yet the implementation of the solution (of these approximate models) has produced sufficiently successful results to warrant their continued use.

While certain situations are linearized to allow the use of LP formulations, the nonlinearity in others is sufficiently pronounced that it is inaccurate to impose linearity assumptions on the system. However, although LP is not used at the *formulation* stage of these models, in some cases it can be used to develop a *solution* method. This is accomplished by transforming the nonlinear model to an equivalent LP (or a sequence of LPs) which represents the original model either exactly or approximately. Examples of exact transformations are hyperbolic or fractional programming [Charnes and Cooper, 1962], quadratic programming (QP) [Wolfe, 1959], integer LP [Gomory, 1958; Land and Doig, 1960] and minimax criteria [Dantzig, 1951]. The approximate transformations include separable programming [Charnes and Lemke, 1959; Hartley, 1961; Miller, 1963] and convex programming [Kelley, 1960; Zangwill, 1967]. As an illustration, one exact and one approximate transformation are discussed briefly.

The QP problem may be written as

$$\text{minimize } x_0 = \mathbf{cx} + \mathbf{x}^t\mathbf{Dx}$$

subject to

$$\mathbf{Ax} + \mathbf{IS} = \mathbf{b}$$

$$\mathbf{x}, \mathbf{S} \geqslant \mathbf{0}.$$

where $\mathbf{D}$ is a symmetric $n \times n$ matrix which is assumed to be positive definite and $\mathbf{S}$ is a slack vector of size m. By using the Kuhn-Tucker conditions, it can be shown [Wolfe, 1959] that the necessary and sufficient conditions for $\mathbf{x}$ to be an optimal solution is that there exist the vectors $\boldsymbol{\lambda} \geqslant \mathbf{0}$ and $\mathbf{u} \geqslant \mathbf{0}$ (Lagrangean multipliers) that satisfy the following equations:

$$-2\mathbf{Dx} + \mathbf{A}^t\boldsymbol{\lambda} - \mathbf{Iu} = \mathbf{c}^t$$

$$\mathbf{Ax} + \mathbf{IS} = \mathbf{b}$$

$$u_j x_j = 0, \quad j = 1, 2, \ldots, n$$

$$\lambda_i S_i = 0, \quad i = 1, 2, \ldots, m$$

$$\mathbf{u}, \boldsymbol{\lambda}, \mathbf{S}, \mathbf{x} \geqslant \mathbf{0}$$

The solution of the QP thus reduces to solving the above equations which, with the exception of the conditions $u_j x_j = \lambda_i S_i = 0$, are linear. Linear programming can be used to solve these equations by using "artificial" variables and an objective function which minimizes the sum of these variables. The computational theory of LP is capable of handling the conditions $u_j x_j = \lambda_i S_i = 0$ implicitly (see Section 4 of this chapter).

Separable programming defines problems in which the functions are of the form

$$f(x_1, x_2, \ldots, x_n) = \sum_{j=1}^{n} f_j(x_j)$$

which shows that f can be decomposed additively in terms of the single-variable functions f_j. The main interest is to show how $f_j(x_j)$ can approximate by linear segments.

Suppose the feasible range on x_j is given by $a_j \leqslant x_j \leqslant b_j$, $j = 1, 2, \ldots, n$ and define $a_{k_j j}$, $k_j = 1, 2, \ldots, K_j$ such that

$$a_{1j} \leqslant a_{2j} \leqslant \cdots \leqslant a_{K_j j}$$

where $a_j = a_{1j}$ and $b_j = a_{K_j j}$. Then $f_j(x_j)$ may be approximated linearly by

$$f_j(x_j) \simeq \sum_{k_j=1}^{K_j} \lambda_{k_j} f_j(a_{k_j j})$$

where $\sum_{k_j=1}^{K_j} \lambda_{k_j} = 1$ and $\lambda_{k_j} \geqslant 0$ for all k_j. In this case, x_j is expressed in terms of λ_{k_j} and $a_{k_j j}$ by

$$x_j = \sum_{k_j=1}^{K_j} \lambda_{k_j} a_{k_j j}.$$

The linear approximation is valid only if no more than two *adjacent* λ_{k_j}, for every j, can assume positive values, that is, if λ_t is positive, then only λ_{t-1} or λ_{t+1} can be positive. Again as in QP, this condition can be handled implicitly in the course of LP computations. It is important to observe, however, that while the linear transformations provide an exact solution for QPs, it guarantees an approximate solution only to the separable program, even if the problem has a global optimum.

There is a special class of LP models that are of particular interest because of their special structures as well as their applications. The *transportation* model [Heller and Tompkins, 1956; Kantorvich, 1960; Koopmans, 1947] deals with the transportation of a commodity from m sources to n destinations. The supply available at source i is a_i units and the demand required at destination j is b_j units. The transportation cost per unit from source i to destination j is c_{ij}. Thus, if x_{ij} represents the level of activity (amount transported) from source i to destination j, the model is expressed mathematically as

$$\text{minimize } x_0 = \sum_{i=1}^{m} \sum_{j=1}^{n} c_{ij} x_{ij}$$

subject to

$$\sum_{j=1}^{m} x_{ij} = a_i, \quad i = 1, 2, \ldots, m$$

$$\sum_{i=1}^{n} x_{ij} = b_j, \quad j = 1, 2, \ldots, n$$

$$x_{ij} \geqslant 0, \quad \text{for all } i \text{ and } j$$

The formulation requires that $\sum_{i=1}^{m} a_i = \sum_{j=1}^{n} b_j$, which can always be satisfied by adding a fictitious source or destination to absorb the difference $\left|\sum_{i=1}^{m} a_i - \sum_{j=1}^{n} b_j\right|$.

A direct extension of the transportation model is to allow transshipments so that (part of) a shipment may pass transiently through other sources and destinations before reaching its ultimate destination. The formulation is known as the *transshipment* model [Orden, 1956]. The new information can be accounted for by formulating a transportation model with $m + n$ sources and $m + n$ destinations. A buffer stock $B \geqslant \sum_{i=1}^{m} a_i = \sum_{j=1}^{n} b_j$ is added to the supply at each source and to the demand at each destination, so that the supply at source i is $a_i + B$ for $i = 1, 2, \ldots, m$ and B for $i = m + 1, m + 2, \ldots, m + n$. Similarly, the demand at destination j is B for $j = 1, 2, \ldots, n$ and $b_{j-n} + B$ for $j = n + 1, n + 2, \ldots, n + m$. The unit costs c_{ij} are usually secured from the nature of the problem.

The use of the transportation model extends beyond the above straightforward application. One example is the classical *caterer* problem [Jacobs, 1954] where a caterer is contracted to provide fresh napkins over a period of n days. Fresh napkins are supplied either by buying a new stock or by laundering soiled ones at lower costs. The objective is to satisfy the fresh napkins requirements at the lowest possible cost. The caterer model actually paraphrases a real problem in the Air Force where it is required to estimate the needed number of spare aircraft engines. A second example extends the use of the transportation model to production scheduling [Johnson, 1957]. The model determines the amounts to be produced in each of n periods in order to satisfy given demands without exceeding the production capacities of the periods. A current period may produce for one or more succeeding periods (no backorders allowed). The unit cost of "transporting" a manufactured unit to another period includes the production cost and the inventory holding cost (assuming no shortages).

A special case of the transportation model is the *assignment* problem, which classically seeks the assignment of m operators to n jobs with each operator exhibiting varying degrees of competence on the various jobs. The transportation model specializes to the assignment model by letting $a_i = b_j = 1$ for all i and j. The cost of assigning operator i to machine j represents c_{ij}. An unusual application of the assignment model is the *marriage* problem [Dantzig, 1957], whose solution indicates that monogamy is the best type of marriage(!). The assignment problem is of particular importance because it can be used directly in the development of solution algorithms for the well-known *traveling salesman* problem (TSP) [Dzielinski and Gomory, 1965; Little, et al., 1963].

Another variation of the transportation problem is the *generalized transportation* model which is defined as follows:

$$\text{Minimize } x_0 = \sum_{i=1}^{m} \sum_{j=1}^{n} c_{ij} x_{ij}$$

subject to

$$\sum_{j=1}^{n} p_{ij} x_{ij} \leqslant a_i, \quad i = 1, 2, \ldots, m$$

$$\sum_{i=1}^{m} x_{ij} = b_j, \quad j = 1, 2, \ldots, n$$

$$x_{ij} \geqslant 0.$$

The first application of the generalized model deals with the assignment of different types of aircraft on different routes in order to satisfy the passenger demand at the least possible operating costs [Ferguson, 1955]. Here a_i is the maximum number of passengers on route i and b_j represents the number of available aircrafts of type j. The capacity of one craft of type j on route i is p_{ij} passengers while c_{ij} is the operating cost per aircraft of type j on route i. The objective is to determine x_{ij}, the number of aircraft of type j on route i.

3. PROPERTIES OF LINEAR PROGRAMMING SOLUTIONS

For the purpose of solving LPs, all the constraints are put in equation form by: (1) adding a nonnegative *slack* variable to the left-hand sides of inequalities of the type ($\leqslant$), and (2) subtracting a nonnegative *surplus* variable from the left-hand side of inequalities of the type ($\geqslant$). Also, it is convenient to make all the right-hand side elements b_i nonnegative by multiplying the ith equation by -1 if $b_i < 0$, or realizing that $f_i(x_1, \ldots, x_r) \leqslant b_i$ is equivalent to $-f_i(x_1, \ldots, x_r) \geqslant -b_i$.

After converting all the inequalities into equations, a useful form for expressing LPs in matrix notation is as follows:

$$\text{Maximize (or minimize) } x_0 = \mathbf{cx}$$

subject to

$$\mathbf{Ax} = \mathbf{b}$$

$$\mathbf{x} \geqslant \mathbf{0}$$

where $\mathbf{x} = (x_1, \ldots, x_n)$ is the unknowns or activities vector that, in addition to the original r decision variables of the problem, may now include slack and surplus variables. The right-hand side vector $\mathbf{b} = (b_1, \ldots, b_m)^t$ is assumed nonnegative. The matrix $\mathbf{A}$ now includes the coefficients of any slack and surplus variables.

Another convenient way of defining the above LP is by vector notation. Let $\mathbf{A} = (\mathbf{P}_1, \mathbf{P}_2, \ldots, \mathbf{P}_n)$, then the problem is written as follows:

$$\text{Maximize (or minimize) } x_0 = \sum_{j=1}^{n} c_j x_j$$

subject to

$$\sum_{j=1}^{n} \mathbf{P}_j x_j = \mathbf{b}$$

$$x_j \geqslant 0, \quad j = 1, 2, \ldots, n.$$

It can be assumed, without loss of generality, that $m < n$. If $m > n$, this means at least $n - m$ equations are redundant. Also, if $m = n$ and $\mathbf{A}$ is a full rank matrix, the system $\mathbf{Ax} = \mathbf{b}$ has a unique solution which is a special case. The remaining case, $m < n$, usually signifies that the system $\mathbf{Ax} = \mathbf{b}$ has an infinite number of solutions. If $\mathbf{Ax} = \mathbf{b}$ is inconsistent, then the system has no feasible solution.

The fundamental property governing the development of the solution method for LP is that its entire (bounded) feasible space (usually consisting of an infinite number of points) can be defined in terms of a *finite* number of special feasible points. Theorems 1 and 2 show how these special points can be identified.

THEOREM 1: The optimum solution to a LP, when finite, must be associated with a feasible extreme point of the solution space.

This result is intuitively acceptable since the convex combination (convex hull) of the feasible extreme points yields every feasible solution point satisfying $\mathbf{Ax} = \mathbf{b}$, $\mathbf{x} \geqslant \mathbf{0}$. (Assume for simplicity that the solution space is bounded.) In other words, the feasible extreme points provide sufficient information for identifying the entire solution space of the LP problem.

Theorem 1 shows that a LP can be solved by a simple enumeration of all its feasible extreme points. The question now is: How are the extreme points determined algebraically? Mathematically, an *extreme point* is defined as a feasible point which cannot be expressed as a convex combination of any two other distinct feasible points. From the computational standpoint, this definition is not useful. However, the following theorem shows how extreme points are determined for the linear system $\mathbf{Ax} = \mathbf{b}$ having m equations and n unknowns.

THEOREM 2: The basic solutions of the system $\mathbf{Ax} = \mathbf{b}$ completely identify all its extreme points.

Since a basic solution is identified by a basis, that is, by m *independent* vectors $\mathbf{P}_j$ (out of a total of n), all the extreme points of $\mathbf{Ax} = \sum_{j=1}^{n} \mathbf{P}_j x_j = \mathbf{b}$ are determined by computing $n!/m!(n - m)!$ possible basic solutions of the system. Stated differently, for any extreme point, the variable x_j associated with a vector $\mathbf{P}_j$ *not* in the basis is necessarily at zero level. It is customary to refer to such variables as *nonbasic* variables. On the other hand, if x_j is associated with a basic vector, then it is called a *basic* variable whose value may be positive or zero.

If all the basic variables are strictly positive, the corresponding extreme point (basic solution) is said to be *nondegenerate;* otherwise, if at least one basic variable is zero, the extreme point is *degenerate.* Interestingly, a nondegenerate extreme point is defined by one, and only one, basic solution while a degenerate extreme point is defined by more than one basic solution.

Determination of the extreme points via the basic solutions is the heart of the *simplex method* (SM) for solving LPs. However, rather than enumerate all basic solutions as suggested above, the simplex method starts with a basic *feasible* solution (b.f.s.) to the system $\mathbf{Ax} = \mathbf{b}$ and continues to generate new b.f.s.'s without ever violating the condition $\mathbf{x} \geqslant \mathbf{0}$. In the meantime, every new b.f.s. is selected such that it has the potential to improve the objective value. Consequently, during the course of computations, inferior b.f.s.'s are automatically discarded. The next section formalizes the ideas of the SM.

There is a subtle peculiarity about the fact that (finite) optimal LP solutions, when obtained by the SM, must always be associated with a b.f.s. If the LP has one constraint, then, regardless of the number of activities (variables) in the model, it is already known that at most *one* of these activities can be at positive level in the optimal solution.

If an additional nonredundant constraint is added, then at most *two* activities will be at positive level. In general, the addition of more nonredundant constraints can result in choosing a larger *mix* of activities, even though it may deteriorate the value of the objective function.

The point to be made is that the availability of a large number of activities should seem to induce the utilization of larger mix, a desirable situation in some practical problems. Yet the only way this can be accomplished in LP (assuming the optimum is unique) is by adding more constraints. The trade-off here is that a larger activity mix is achieved at the expense of deteriorating the optimum value of the objective function.

The main reason for the above apparent "paradox" is that the mathematical formulation of the LP concentrates mainly on achieving the optimal value of the objective function, which must occur at an extreme point of the feasible space. Should it be desirable also to expand the activity mix but not at the direct expense of worsening the value of the objective function, an entirely different formulation of the model may be necessary. In this case, the new model may not be linear at all.

Some LP applications deal with physical situations where the variables must be integers. In general, the simplex method does not yield (optimal) integer solutions. An integer solution may be secured by rounding the fractional optimal solution. However, the rounded solution need not be optimal for the ILP. (Exact methods for obtaining optimal integer solutions to LPs are discussed in Chapter II-2.)

A class of LPs for which the SM always yields integer solutions is the transportation model (Section 2). The model satisfies the so-called *totally unimodular* property. A LP is said to satisfy this property if the determinant associated with *every* basis equals ±1. Since

$$\mathbf{B}^{-1} = \text{adj } \mathbf{B}/\det \mathbf{B}$$

$\mathbf{B}^{-1}$, and hence $\mathbf{x_B} = \mathbf{B}^{-1}\mathbf{b}$, is an integer provided $\mathbf{b}$ and the constraint matrix $\mathbf{A}$ are all integers.

The transportation model is proved to possess the totally unimodular property [Hitchcock, 1947]. Unfortunately, it is difficult in general to prove this property for a more general LP.

4. THE SIMPLEX METHOD

An LP problem can generally be put in the form

$$\text{maximize or minimize } x_0 = \mathbf{c_I x_I} + \mathbf{c_{II} x_{II}}$$

subject to

$$\mathbf{A}\mathbf{x}_{\mathrm{I}} + \mathbf{I}\mathbf{x}_{\mathrm{II}} = \mathbf{b} \geqslant \mathbf{0}$$

$$\mathbf{x}_{\mathrm{I}}, \mathbf{x}_{\mathrm{II}} \geqslant 0.$$

This calls for partitioning (and, if necessary, rearranging) the variables into $\mathbf{x}_{\mathrm{I}}$ and $\mathbf{x}_{\mathrm{II}}$ so that the constraint coefficients associated with $\mathbf{x}_{\mathrm{II}}$ form an identity matrix **I**. In a similar manner, the objective coefficients are arranged accordingly so that $\mathbf{c}_{\mathrm{II}}$ gives the objective function coefficients of $\mathbf{x}_{\mathrm{II}}$.

The above form is automatically secured if all the original constraints are of the type ($\leqslant$). In this case, $\mathbf{x}_{\mathrm{II}}$ consists of all slacks and $\mathbf{c}_{\mathrm{II}} = \mathbf{0}$. If some (or all) of the constraints are of the type ($\geqslant$) and/or (=), then the indicated form is obtained by employing *artificial variables.* An artificial variable is added to the left-hand side of a constraint only when it is necessary to complete the identity matrix **I**. However, since these variables are extraneous to the problem, provisions must be made to ensure that they will be at zero level in the optimum solution (provided a b.f.s. exists). One way to accomplish this is to assign a very high penalty to these variables in the objective function. Thus, the elements of $\mathbf{c}_{\mathrm{II}}$ are zeros for slack variables and very high penalties for artificial variables.

The above form provides an automatic starting b.f.s. for the LP, namely, $\mathbf{x}_{\mathrm{II}} = \mathbf{b}$ (it is assumed $\mathbf{b} \geqslant \mathbf{0}$). The idea of the SM is to determine a new b.f.s. from the current one by removing one of the current basic vectors and introducing a nonbasic vector to replace it. The stipulation here is that the new basic (entering) vector must have the potential to improve the objective value while the deleted (leaving) vector must result in a new b.f.s. This leads to the following derivation of the *optimality* and *feasibility* conditions.

Let $\mathbf{x}_B$ and $\mathbf{x}_N$ be the current basic and nonbasic variables and let the columns of $(\mathbf{A}, \mathbf{I})$ be arranged accordingly so that **B** is the basis associated with $\mathbf{x}_B$ and **N** is the matrix associated with $\mathbf{x}_N$. Further let $\mathbf{c}_B$ and $\mathbf{c}_N$ be the elements of $(\mathbf{c}_{\mathrm{I}}, \mathbf{c}_{\mathrm{II}})$ associated with $\mathbf{x}_B$ and $\mathbf{x}_N$. The solution is then represented by

$$\mathbf{x}_B = \mathbf{B}^{-1}\mathbf{b} - \mathbf{B}^{-1}\mathbf{N}\mathbf{x}_N$$

$$x_0 = \mathbf{c}_B\mathbf{B}^{-1}\mathbf{b} - (\mathbf{c}_B\mathbf{B}^{-1}\mathbf{N} - \mathbf{c}_N)\,\mathbf{x}_N.$$

Since at the current iteration $\mathbf{x}_N = \mathbf{0}$, then the current solution is $\mathbf{x}_B = \mathbf{B}^{-1}\mathbf{b} \geqslant \mathbf{0}$ and $x_0 = \mathbf{c}_B\mathbf{B}^{-1}\mathbf{b}$.

Suppose $\mathbf{P}_j$ is the nonbasic vector to be made basic in the next iteration, then the above expressions show that $x_j > 0$ improves the value of x_0 above its current value $\mathbf{c}_B\mathbf{B}^{-1}\mathbf{b}$ if

$$z_j - c_j = \mathbf{c}_B\mathbf{B}^{-1}\mathbf{P}_j - c_j \begin{cases} <\mathbf{0}, & \text{for maximization} \\ >\mathbf{0}, & \text{for minimization} \end{cases}$$

where c_j is the element of x_j in $\mathbf{c}_N$. The *optimality condition* thus for maximization (minimization) problems calls for selecting the entering vector $\mathbf{P}_j$ as the one having the most negative (most positive) $z_j - c_j$ among all nonbasic vectors in **N**. If none exists with negative (positive) $z_j - c_j$, the current basis is optimum.

The *feasibility* condition now determines the leaving vector from among those in **B** such that when x_j becomes basic, the new basic solution remains feasible. From the constraints together with the nonnegativity conditions, the leaving vector $\mathbf{P}_r$ must correspond to

$$\frac{(\mathbf{B}^{-1}\mathbf{b})_r}{(\mathbf{B}^{-1}\mathbf{P}_j)_r} = \min_i \left\{ \frac{(\mathbf{B}^{-1}\mathbf{b})_i}{(\mathbf{B}^{-1}\mathbf{P}_j)_i} \middle| (\mathbf{B}^{-1}\mathbf{P}_j)_i > 0 \right\}$$

where $(\mathbf{B}^{-1}\mathbf{b})_i$ is the ith element of the vector $\mathbf{B}^{-1}\mathbf{b}$, $i = 1, 2, \ldots, m$. If all $(\mathbf{B}^{-1}\mathbf{P}_j)_i \leqslant 0$, then $\mathbf{P}_j$, as selected by the optimality condition, cannot lead to a b.f.s. and the algorithm terminates with the information that the optimum solution is unbounded.

The same optimality and feasibility conditions of the simplex can also be derived by classical methods of optimization, namely, the Lagrangean and Jacobian methods [Taha and Curry, 1971]. Since these methods deal with equality constraints, all constraints are converted to equations by adding the proper slack or surplus variables. The nonnegativity constraints are handled by using the substitution

$$x_j = w_j^2, \quad j = 1, 2, \ldots, n$$

where w_j is unrestricted. A similar substitution is effected for the slack and surplus variables. Thus regardless of the sign of w_j, x_j is always nonnegative. The interesting result is that the use of classical optimization leads exactly to the conditions of optimality and feasibility in the SM.

There are special situations where the change of basis in the simplex tableau (see below) can be made to account for some side conditions, mostly in nonlinear form. Typical examples are the QP and separable programming presented in Section 2. In both cases, the problem used to solve the program is entirely linear except for conditions of the type $xy = 0$, which implies that if $x > 0$ then $y = 0$ and vice versa. This can be accomplished in the SM by allowing this condition to override the optimality condition. Let $\mathbf{P}_x$ and $\mathbf{P}_y$ be the vectors associated with x and y in the linear equations. Suppose $\mathbf{P}_y$ is already in the basis and assume that the optimality condition requires $\mathbf{P}_x$ to enter the solution. If $y > 0$, then $\mathbf{P}_x$ cannot enter the solution unless its associated value of x is zero, or $\mathbf{P}_y$ becomes the leaving vector. Otherwise $\mathbf{P}_x$ is not selected as the entering vector and the next best nonbasic vector, according to the optimality condition, is attempted. This procedure is sometimes referred to as *restricted basis entry* method.

TABLE 1

Basic Vector	$\mathbf{x}_I$	$\mathbf{x}_{II}$	Solution
$\mathbf{x}_0$	$\mathbf{c}_{II}\mathbf{A} - \mathbf{c}_I$	0	$\mathbf{c}_{II}\mathbf{b}$
$\mathbf{x}_{II}$	$\mathbf{A}$	$\mathbf{I}$	$\mathbf{b}$

It can be verified that for any LP, the initial tableau expressed in matrix notation is given as shown in Table 1, while the general tableau resulting from the successive changes in basis (by using the Gauss-Jordan method) is given by Table 2. Notice that the x_0-row yields $z_j - c_j$ and hence the optimality condition is checked by inspecting the x_0-row. Also, the feasibility condition is applied by taking the ratios of the elements of the right-hand side, $\mathbf{B}^{-1}\mathbf{b}$, to the corresponding *positive* elements of $\mathbf{B}^{-1}\mathbf{P}_j$ of the entering vector.

The number of simplex iterations required to solve a LP is primarily controlled by the number of constraints rather than by the number of variables. As a rule of thumb, the number of iterations can be estimated between $1.5m$ and $2m$, where m is the number of constraint equations in the starting tableau.

Although the theory of the SM shows that the optimal solution to a LP is always associated with a b.f.s., two special cases deviate from this result. First, if the objective function is parallel to a binding (nonredundant) constraint at the optimum solution, *alternative optima* exist. These alternative optima yield the same value of the objective function. The situation is recognized in the SM calculations by the fact that all $z_j - c_j$ for all nonbasic x_j satisfy the optimality condition and at least one $z_j - c_j = 0$ for all nonbasic variables. If the vector associated with $z_j - c_j = 0$ can enter the basis, then an alternative basic optimum solution exists. In this case, convex combinations of the alternative basic optima will yield alternative nonbasic optima. On the other hand if the vector associated with $z_j - c_j = 0$ cannot enter the basis, then all alternative optima are necessarily nonbasic.

The second case occurs when the optimality condition shows that a nonbasic vector can improve the solution if introduced into the basis, yet such a vector cannot be made basic. This means that if $z_j - c_j < 0$ (maximization) and $\mathbf{B}^{-1}\mathbf{P}_j \leqslant \mathbf{0}$, introduction of $\mathbf{P}_j$ into the basis cannot yield a b.f.s. Indeed, x_j

TABLE 2

Basic Vector	$\mathbf{x}_I$	$\mathbf{x}_{II}$	Solution
$\mathbf{x}_0$	$\mathbf{c}_B\mathbf{B}^{-1}\mathbf{A} - \mathbf{c}_I$	$\mathbf{c}_B\mathbf{B}^{-1} - \mathbf{c}_{II}$	$\mathbf{c}_B\mathbf{B}^{-1}\mathbf{b}$
$\mathbf{x}_B$	$\mathbf{B}^{-1}\mathbf{A}$	$\mathbf{B}^{-1}$	$\mathbf{B}^{-1}\mathbf{b}$

associated with $\mathbf{P}_j$ can be increased indefinitely without affecting the feasibility of the problem. This means that the new value of the objective function can be increased by an infinite amount, namely, $-(z_j - c_j)x_j$. In this case, the solution is said to be *unbounded.*

Although the basic theory of the SM guarantees convergence to the optimal solution in a finite number of steps, it does not take into account the computational difficulties resulting from machine roundoff errors. The first difficulty is caused when artificial variables are part of the starting basic solution. The use of high penalties in the objective function may create severe machine roundoff errors resulting from the manipulation of a mixture of very large and relatively small numbers. The situation is alleviated by solving the problem in two phases. The Phase I problem is defined as

$$\text{minimize } r_0 = \sum_j x_{R_j}$$

subject to

$$\mathbf{A}\mathbf{x}_{\mathrm{I}} + \mathbf{I}\mathbf{x}_{\mathrm{II}} = \mathbf{b}$$

$$\mathbf{x}_{\mathrm{I}}, \mathbf{x}_{\mathrm{II}} \geqslant \mathbf{0}$$

where x_{R_j} are the artificial variables included in $\mathbf{x}_{\mathrm{II}}$. The new objective function may actually be regarded as a "measure of infeasibility" in the problem. Thus, if $\min r_0 = 0$, the problem has a b.f.s. and the solution associated with $\min r_0$ is used as a starting basis for the original problem. This initiates the Phase II calculations. On the other hand, if $\min r_0 > 0$, this indicates that some of the artificial variables are positive and hence the problem has no feasible solution. This eliminates the need to carry out the Phase II calculations.

The two-phase method accounts for the problem of manipulating very large numbers in the objective function. However, the use of the Gauss-Jordan elimination method to generate the successive simplex tableaus results in the accumulation and propagation of roundoff error to the extent that it distorts the original data of the problem. Consider, for example, the application of the feasibility condition. Suppose $(\mathbf{x}_B)_i = 0$ is the exact value of the ith basic variable and $(\mathbf{B}^{-1}\mathbf{P}_j)_i = 0$ is the corresponding ith constraint coefficient associated with the entering vector $\mathbf{P}_j$. Then the vector associated with $(\mathbf{x}_B)_i$ cannot enter the basis. Suppose now that because of the roundoff error $(\mathbf{x}_B)_i = 10^{-9}$ and $(\mathbf{B}^{-1}\mathbf{P}_j)_i = 10^{-6}$. In this case, $\mathbf{P}_j$ may be eligible to enter the basis.

The *revised simplex* method (RSM) [Dantzig, 1953] is devised to alleviate the roundoff error. The basic steps of the RSM are essentially those of the SM. The main difference is that the Gauss-Jordan eliminations are not used to generate the successive tableaus. Rather, it is evident from Table 2 that the entire tableau can be generated from the *original data* and the current basis inverse $\mathbf{B}^{-1}$. The RSM procedure thus concentrates on minimizing the roundoff error in computing $\mathbf{B}^{-1}$.

In addition to controlling roundoff error, the RSM can also lead to computational savings. In particular, if the constraint matrix **A** contains a large percentage of zero elements, this can be used to reduce the number of multiplication operations. (cf. the regular SM where the elements of the tableau, particularly the zero elements, constantly change from one iteration to the next.) In general, the RSM is known to involve less computations when the density (number of nonzero element to total number of elements) of the matrix **A** decreases and the ratio of the number of constraints to the number of variables decreases [Dantzig, 1963, p. 217].

It appears that the SM (and its variants), after three decades of scrutiny and experimentation, will continue to be the dominant method for solving LPs. A new approach has been suggested recently [Scolnik, 1973; Scolnik, 1973] which forms the optimal basis by introducing the basic vectors one at a time. The method, claimed to be potentially more efficient than the SM, has been quickly proved (by counterexamples) to be invalid for the general LP problem [Gay, 1973; White, 1974].

4.1 Geometric Interpretation of the Simplex Method

The SM can be interpreted geometrically in two different ways [Dantzig, 1951]. The first interpretation illustrates the change of basis which includes the selection of the entering and leaving vectors. The second interpretation illustrates how the successive iterations of the LP are represented by moving from one extreme point to an *adjacent* one in a manner that will improve the value of the objective function. When no further improvements are possible, the optimum is achieved.

Utilizing the matrix notation introduced in Table 2, the current basic solution $\mathbf{x}_B$ and its associated value of the objective function may be written as

$$\begin{pmatrix} \mathbf{B} \\ \mathbf{c}_B \end{pmatrix} \mathbf{x}_B = \begin{pmatrix} \mathbf{b} \\ x_0 \end{pmatrix}$$

This appears equivalently in vector form as

$$\sum_{i=1}^{m} (\mathbf{x}_B)_i \, \mathbf{P}_i^* = \mathbf{b}^*$$

where $(\mathbf{x}_B)_i$ is the ith element of $\mathbf{x}_B$, $\mathbf{P}_i^*$ is the ith vector of $\begin{pmatrix} \mathbf{B} \\ \mathbf{c}_B \end{pmatrix}$ and $\mathbf{b}^* = \begin{pmatrix} \mathbf{b} \\ x_0 \end{pmatrix}$.

The definition shows that $\mathbf{b}^*$ is a *nonnegative* linear combination of $\mathbf{P}_i^*$.

Similarly, for the nonbasic vector $\mathbf{P}_j$

$$\begin{pmatrix} \mathbf{P}_j \\ z_j \end{pmatrix} = \begin{pmatrix} \mathbf{B} \\ \mathbf{c}_B \end{pmatrix} \mathbf{B}^{-1}\mathbf{P}_j = \sum_{i=1}^{m} (\mathbf{B}^{-1}\mathbf{P}_j)_i \, \mathbf{P}_i^*$$

which shows that the vector $(\mathbf{P}_j, z_j)$ is a *linear* combination (not necessarily nonnegative) of $\mathbf{P}_i^*, i = 1, 2, \ldots, m$.

Suppose a LP is defined as

$$\text{maximize } x_0 = c_1x_1 + c_2x_2 + c_3x_3 + c_4x_4$$

subject to

$$x_1\mathbf{P}_1 + x_2\mathbf{P}_2 + x_3\mathbf{P}_3 + x_4\mathbf{P}_4 = \mathbf{b}$$

$$x_j \geqslant 0, \quad j = 1, 2, 3, 4$$

Suppose further that $\mathbf{P}_j = (a_{1j}, a_{2j})^t, j = 1, 2, 3, 4$. The vector representation of the vectors $\mathbf{P}_1$, $\mathbf{P}_2$, $\mathbf{P}_3$ and $\mathbf{P}_4$ is shown on the (a_{1j}, a_{2j}) space in Fig. 1. The basis $\mathbf{B} = (\mathbf{P}_2, \mathbf{P}_4)$ results in a feasible solution because $\mathbf{b}$ can be expressed as a nonnegative linear combination of $\mathbf{P}_2$ and $\mathbf{P}_4$. The vectors $\mathbf{P}_2^* = (\mathbf{P}_2, c_2)$ and $\mathbf{P}_4^* = (\mathbf{P}_4, c_4)$ are also plotted as shown in Fig. 1. Consequently $\mathbf{b}_{(2,4)}^* = (\mathbf{b}, x_0^{(2,4)})$ must, by definition, lie in the cone generated by $\mathbf{P}_2^*$ and $\mathbf{P}_4^*$.

Now, suppose $\mathbf{P}_1$ is the entering vector, then feasibility of the solution is main-

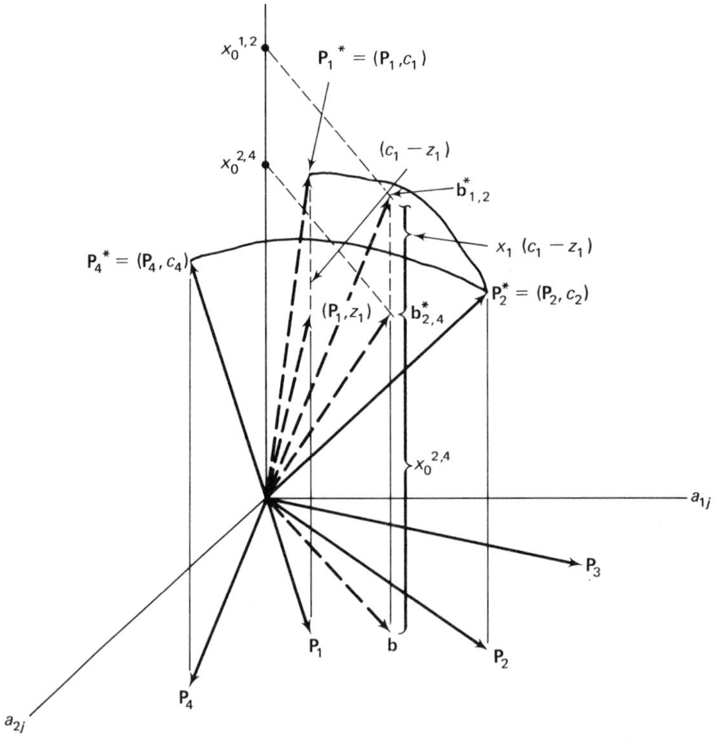

Fig. 1.

tained if $\mathbf{P}_4$ is the leaving vector. (If $\mathbf{P}_2$ leaves instead, then $\mathbf{b}$ can be expressed in terms of $\mathbf{P}_1$ and $\mathbf{P}_4$ only if x_4 is negative, which is infeasible.) $\mathbf{P}_1^* = (\mathbf{P}_1, c_1)$ together with $\mathbf{P}_2^*$ now form the cone in which $\mathbf{b}_{(1,2)}^* = (\mathbf{b}, x_0^{(1,2)})$ lies. This means that the vector $\mathbf{b}_{(1,2)}^* - \mathbf{b}_{(2,4)}^* = (0, 0, x_0^{(1,2)} - x_0^{(2,4)})$ represents the changes in the value of x_0 as a result of introducing $\mathbf{P}_1$ into the basis and dropping $\mathbf{P}_4$. Moreover, the vector $(\mathbf{P}_1, z_1)$ lies in the $(\mathbf{P}_2^*, \mathbf{P}_4^*)$-cone while $\mathbf{P}_1^* = (\mathbf{P}_1, c_1)$ obviously lies in the $(\mathbf{P}_1^*, \mathbf{P}_2^*)$-cone. Thus, $(\mathbf{P}_1, c_1) - (\mathbf{P}_1, z_1) = (0, 0, c_1 - z_1)$.

Now, because $c_1 > z_1$, or $z_1 - c_1 < 0$, (that is, the point $(\mathbf{P}_1, c_1)$ lies above the $(\mathbf{P}_2^*, \mathbf{P}_4^*)$-cone) then, as evident from Fig. 1, the introduction of $\mathbf{P}_1$ into the basis should improve the value of the objective function by $x_1(c_1 - z_1)$, where x_1 is the level of activity 1 in the new solution. If, on the other hand, $z_1 - c_1 \geqslant 0$, then $\mathbf{P}_1$ cannot improve the solution.

An economic interpretation of $z_j - c_j$ thus follows directly from the geometric explanation. If c_j is the profit per unit of the jth activity, z_j should represent its (imputed) cost per unit. Consequently, activity j is promising only if its per unit profit exceeds its per unit cost.

The second geometric interpretation of the SM is illustrated by the following numerical example.

$$\text{Maximize } x_0 = 4x_1 + 3x_2$$

subject to

$$2x_1 + x_2 \leqslant 4$$
$$x_1 + x_2 \leqslant 3$$
$$x_1, x_2 \geqslant 0$$

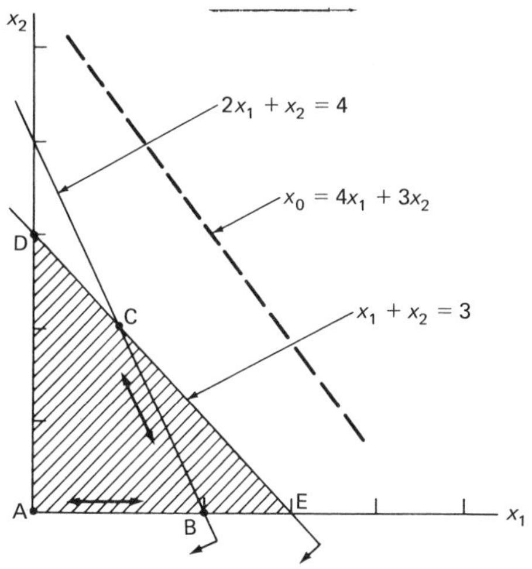

Fig. 2.

Figure 2 represents the feasible space of the problem. Points A, B, C and D represent its feasible extreme points. (Point E represents an infeasible extreme point.)

In this example, the SM starts from A, then moves to B and finally locates the optimal at C. The points A and B (as well as B and C, A and D, and C and D) are called *adjacent* extreme points. The SM always moves from an extreme point to an *adjacent* one provided the new point can improve the value of the objective function. In other words, it is impossible that the SM solution will go directly from A to C. Actually, the SM solution must move along an *edge* of the solution space, which is defined as the line joining two *adjacent* extreme points.

4.2 Degeneracy and Cycling

If, according to the feasibility condition, more than one vector is eligible to leave the basis, the next simplex iteration produces a degenerate solution in which at least one basic variable is zero. This means that subsequent iterations may not produce improvements in the value of the objective function. As a result, it is possible to repeat the same sequence of simplex iterations endlessly without improving the solution, and hence without ever terminating the calculations. This is referred to as *cycling* or *circling.*

Procedures have been devised to ensure that the feasibility condition will select a *unique* leaving vector [Charnes, 1952; Dantzig, 1951; Dantzig et al., 1955; Wolfe, 1957]. The following procedure [Charnes, 1952] appears the most interesting.

Consider the matrix definition of the LP as given in Section 3 of this chapter. Let $\mathbf{P}_j$ be the jth column of $(\mathbf{A}, \mathbf{I})$ and assume $\epsilon(>0)$ is sufficiently small. Define

$$\mathbf{b}_\epsilon = \mathbf{b} + \epsilon \mathbf{P}_1 + \epsilon^2 \mathbf{P}_2 + \cdots + \epsilon^n \mathbf{P}_n$$

From Table 2, if $\mathbf{b}_\epsilon$ represents the right-hand side of the constraint and $\mathbf{B} = (\mathbf{P}_1, \mathbf{P}_2, \ldots, \mathbf{P}_m)$ the current basis, the value of the associated ith basic variable is

$$(\mathbf{X}_{B_\epsilon})_i = (\mathbf{B}^{-1}\mathbf{b})_i + \epsilon^i + \sum_{j=m+1}^{n} \epsilon^j (\mathbf{B}^{-1}\mathbf{P}_j)_i$$

This shows that by selecting $\epsilon(>0)$ sufficiently small and forming $\mathbf{b}_\epsilon$, the leaving variable can be identified uniquely. In practice, it is not necessary really to compute $\mathbf{b}_\epsilon$ since the above idea can be effected by selecting the leaving variable as associated with the *lexicographically* smallest row in the tableau [Dantzig, et al., 1955].

The examples that have been constructed to demonstrate cycling are all mathematical fabrications [Beale, 1955; Hoffman, 1953]. Although the above procedure eliminates cycling, its implementation involves excessive additional computations and its use is usually not warranted in practice.

4.3 Bounded Variables

Many LPs include constraints of the type

$$0 \leqslant \ell_j \leqslant x_j \leqslant u_j < \infty$$

where x_j is the jth variable of the problem and ℓ_j and u_j are given constants. If these constraints are considered explicitly, the size of the problem, particularly the number of constraints, increases drastically. These constraints can be considered implicitly through simple modifications of the structure of the LP or the conditions of the SM. The important result is that from the computational standpoint, only the main constraints $\mathbf{Ax} = \mathbf{b}$ will be used explicitly.

The lower bound constraint, $0 < \ell_j \leqslant x_j$, can be handled directly by using the substitution $x_j = \ell_j + x_j'$, where $x_j' \geqslant 0$. In this case, the upper bound constraint $x_j \leqslant u_j$ becomes $x_j' \leqslant u_j - \ell_j$.

For an upper bound constraint of the type $x_j \leqslant u_j < \infty$, the substitution $x_j = u_j - x_j''$, $x_j'' \geqslant 0$, is not legitimate since the feasibility of x_j is not guaranteed. Procedures for handling the constraints $x_j \leqslant u_j$ *implicitly* in the SM have thus been developed [Dantzig, 1955]. The idea is to modify the feasibility condition so that a variable now becomes infeasible also if it exceeds its upper bound. The interesting result is that a variable may now become nonbasic either at zero level or at its upper bound.

By using the notation for deriving the SM conditions, the upper bound restriction now appears in the picture as follows. Suppose $\mathbf{P}_j$ is the entering vector according to the optimality condition of the SM and let $(\mathbf{x}_B)_i$ be the current ith basic variable. Then

$$(\mathbf{x}_B)_i = (\mathbf{B}^{-1}\mathbf{b})_i - x_j(\mathbf{B}^{-1}\mathbf{P}_j)_i, \quad i = 1, 2, \ldots, m$$

It follows from the conditions $0 \leqslant (\mathbf{x}_B)_i \leqslant u_i$ and $0 \leqslant x_j \leqslant u_j$ that the largest value attained by x_j is given by

$$\theta = \min\ \{\theta_1, \theta_2, u_j\}$$

where

$$\theta_1 = \min_i \left\{ \frac{(\mathbf{B}^{-1}\mathbf{b})_i}{(\mathbf{B}^{-1}\mathbf{P}_j)_i} \,\middle|\, (\mathbf{B}^{-1}\mathbf{P}_j)_i > 0 \right\}$$

$$\theta_2 = \min_i \left\{ \frac{u_i - (\mathbf{B}^{-1}\mathbf{b})_i}{(\mathbf{B}^{-1}\mathbf{P}_j)_i} \,\middle|\, (\mathbf{B}^{-1}\mathbf{P}_j)_i < 0 \right\}$$

If $\theta = \theta_1$, $(\mathbf{x}_B)_i$ becomes nonbasic at zero level and x_j becomes basic. If $\theta = \theta_2$, x_j becomes basic but $(\mathbf{x}_B)_i$ becomes nonbasic at its upper bound. Finally, if $\theta = u_j$, then x_j remains nonbasic but at its upper bound.

It is interesting to note that, for computational purposes, all nonbasic variables are set at zero level by translating the problem to a new origin defined by the substitution $x_k = u_k - x'_k$, $0 \leqslant x'_k \leqslant u_k$, for all x_k which are nonbasic at upper bound.

A more general case of upper bounds is the *generalized upper bounding* [Dantzig and Van Slyke, 1967] where special constraints of the form

$$\sum_{j=1}^{n} x_j = 1$$

appear in the problem. Constraints of this type are used as applications to multi-item scheduling [Lasdon and Terjung, 1971] and in the decomposition algorithm of LP [Dantzig and Wolfe, 1960]. The procedure dealing with generalized upper bounding [Dantzig and Van Slyke, 1967] considers such constraints implicitly, which leads to computational and computer storage savings.

A problem somewhat related to bounded variables is *interval linear programming* [Ben-Israel and Charnes, 1968] which is defined as

$$\text{maximize } \{\mathbf{cx} \mid \mathbf{a} \leqslant \mathbf{Ax} \leqslant \mathbf{b}\}$$

where $\mathbf{a}$ and $\mathbf{b}$ are column vectors. This means that each constraint has a lower and an upper bound. The main assumptions here are that $\mathbf{A}$ has a *full row* rank and $\mathbf{a} \leqslant \mathbf{b}$ so that a bounded feasible solution exists. The full row rank condition guarantees the existence of a *generalized* inverse.

In certain cases, an explicit solution can be obtained for the problem by transforming the variables $\mathbf{x}$ to new variables $\mathbf{z}$ such that $\mathbf{z} = \mathbf{Ax}$, so that $\mathbf{a} \leqslant \mathbf{z} \leqslant \mathbf{b}$ [Zlobec and Ben-Israel, 1970]. In particular, if $\mathbf{A}$ is a nonsingular matrix then ordinary $\mathbf{A}^{-1}$ exists and the problem is transformed to

$$\max \{\mathbf{cA}^{-1}\mathbf{z} \mid \mathbf{a} \leqslant \mathbf{z} \leqslant \mathbf{b}\}$$

whose optimal solution is obviously given $z_i = a_i$ if $(\mathbf{cA}^{-1})_i < 0$, $z_i = b_i$ if $(\mathbf{cA}^{-1})_i > 0$ and $a_i \leqslant z_i \leqslant b_i$ if $(\mathbf{cA}^{-1})_i = 0$. In this case, $\mathbf{x} = \mathbf{A}^{-1}\mathbf{z}$.

Although any LP can be trivially converted to an interval LP, the attainment of a generalized inverse when $\mathbf{A}$ is not a nonsingular matrix may not be a simple task computationally. Thus, with the exception of the case where $\mathbf{A}$ is nonsingular, interval LP is not a promising alternative to the SM. Apparently, however, there are practical applications such as capital budgeting, production planning and control and static Leontief input-output model [Ben-Israel, et al., 1970] in which $\mathbf{A}$ is nonsingular.

5. DUALITY THEORY

An important problem that arises in nonlinear programming (NLP) problems in general and LP in particular is the dual problem. A basic approach to defining duality is through the Lagrangean function and its relationship to the definition of a saddle point.

The Lagrangean function of the NLP

$$\text{maximize } x_0 = f(\mathbf{x})$$

subject to

$$g_i(\mathbf{x}) \leqslant 0, \quad i = 1, 2, \ldots, m$$

where $\mathbf{x} = (x_1, x_2, \ldots, x_n) \in E^n$ is defined as

$$L(\mathbf{x}, \boldsymbol{\lambda}) = f(\mathbf{x}) - \sum_{i=1}^{m} \lambda_i g_i(\mathbf{x})$$

where $\boldsymbol{\lambda} = (\lambda_1, \lambda_2, \ldots, \lambda_m) \geqslant \mathbf{0}$. The point $(\mathbf{x}^*, \boldsymbol{\lambda}^*)$ defines a (global) saddle point of $L(\mathbf{x}, \boldsymbol{\lambda})$ if

$$L(\mathbf{x}, \boldsymbol{\lambda}^*) \leqslant L(\mathbf{x}^*, \boldsymbol{\lambda}^*) \leqslant L(\mathbf{x}^*, \boldsymbol{\lambda}) \quad \text{for all} \quad \mathbf{x} \in E^n \quad \text{and} \quad \boldsymbol{\lambda} \geqslant \mathbf{0}.$$

Let $\overline{L}(\boldsymbol{\lambda}) = \max\limits_{\mathbf{x} \in E^n} L(\mathbf{x}, \boldsymbol{\lambda})$ and $\underline{L}(\mathbf{x}) = \min\limits_{\boldsymbol{\lambda} \geqslant \mathbf{0}} L(\mathbf{x}, \boldsymbol{\lambda})$. Then the problem

$$\max_{\mathbf{x} \in E^n} \underline{L}(\mathbf{x}) = \max_{\mathbf{x} \in E^n} \min_{\boldsymbol{\lambda} \geqslant \mathbf{0}} L(\mathbf{x}, \boldsymbol{\lambda})$$

defines the given NLP since

$$\min_{\boldsymbol{\lambda} \geqslant \mathbf{0}} L(\mathbf{x}, \boldsymbol{\lambda}) = \begin{cases} f(\mathbf{x}), & \text{if } g_i(\mathbf{x}) \leqslant 0, \text{ for all } i \\ -\infty, & \text{if at least one } g_i(\mathbf{x}) > 0. \end{cases}$$

The problem $\max\limits_{\mathbf{x} \in E^n} \underline{L}(\mathbf{x})$ is referred to as the *primal* (given) problem in which case $\min\limits_{\boldsymbol{\lambda} \geqslant \mathbf{0}} \overline{L}(\boldsymbol{\lambda})$ is called the *dual* problem.

The relationships between the primal and dual problems are summarized by the following theorem:

THEOREM 3:

(i) $\underline{L}(\mathbf{x}) \leqslant \overline{L}(\boldsymbol{\lambda})$, $\mathbf{x} \in E^n$ and $\boldsymbol{\lambda} \geqslant \mathbf{0}$.

(ii) If $\underline{L}(\mathbf{x}^*) = \max\limits_{\mathbf{x} \in E^n} \underline{L}(\mathbf{x})$ and $\overline{L}(\boldsymbol{\lambda}^*) = \min\limits_{\boldsymbol{\lambda} \geqslant \mathbf{0}} \overline{L}(\boldsymbol{\lambda})$ and if $\underline{L}(\mathbf{x}^*) = \overline{L}(\boldsymbol{\lambda}^*)$, then $(\mathbf{x}^*, \boldsymbol{\lambda}^*)$ is a saddle point of $L(\mathbf{x}, \boldsymbol{\lambda})$. The converse is true.

Theorem 3 shows that the value of the objective function in the primal sets a lower bound on the value of the objective function in the dual, provided the two problems are bounded. When the two values are equal, the corresponding solutions are optimal for the two problems. More generally, a necessary and sufficient condition for $\mathbf{x}^*$ and $\boldsymbol{\lambda}^*$ to be optima of the primal and dual problem is that $(\mathbf{x}^*, \boldsymbol{\lambda}^*)$ be a saddle point of $L(\mathbf{x}, \boldsymbol{\lambda})$.

Transition from the generalized definition of $L(\mathbf{x}, \boldsymbol{\lambda})$ to the LP case is achieved as follows. Define the primal problem as

$$\text{maximize } x_0 = \mathbf{cx}$$

subject to

$$\mathbf{Ax} \leqslant \mathbf{b}$$
$$\mathbf{x} \geqslant \mathbf{0}$$

The Lagrangean function is

$$L(\mathbf{x}, \boldsymbol{\lambda}) = \mathbf{cx} - \boldsymbol{\lambda}(\mathbf{Ax} - \mathbf{b})$$

The condition $\mathbf{x} \geqslant \mathbf{0}$ is accounted for implicitly as shown below.

The dual problem is thus defined as

$$\min_{\boldsymbol{\lambda} \geqslant \mathbf{0}} \bar{L}(\boldsymbol{\lambda}) = \min_{\boldsymbol{\lambda} \geqslant \mathbf{0}} \boldsymbol{\lambda}\mathbf{b} + \begin{cases} 0, & \text{if } (\mathbf{c} - \boldsymbol{\lambda}\mathbf{A}) \leqslant \mathbf{0} \\ \infty, & \text{if } (\mathbf{c} - \boldsymbol{\lambda}\mathbf{A}) > \mathbf{0} \end{cases}$$

This can be written more explicitly as

$$\text{minimize } \lambda_0 = \boldsymbol{\lambda}\mathbf{b}$$

subject to

$$\boldsymbol{\lambda}\mathbf{A} \geqslant \mathbf{c}$$
$$\boldsymbol{\lambda} \geqslant \mathbf{0}$$

It is interesting that if $\mathbf{x} \in E^n$, that is, $\mathbf{x}$ is an unrestricted vector, the dual problem becomes

$$\min_{\boldsymbol{\lambda} \geqslant \mathbf{0}} \bar{L}(\boldsymbol{\lambda}) = \min_{\boldsymbol{\lambda} \geqslant \mathbf{0}} \boldsymbol{\lambda}\mathbf{b} + \begin{cases} 0, & \text{if } (\mathbf{c} - \boldsymbol{\lambda}\mathbf{A}) = \mathbf{0} \\ \infty, & \text{if } (\mathbf{c} - \boldsymbol{\lambda}\mathbf{A}) \neq \mathbf{0} \end{cases}$$

which show that the dual constraint $\boldsymbol{\lambda}\mathbf{A} \geqslant \mathbf{c}$ when $\mathbf{x} \geqslant \mathbf{0}$ is replaced by $\boldsymbol{\lambda}\mathbf{A} = \mathbf{c}$ when $\mathbf{x}$ is an unrestricted vector. It can be shown similarly that if the primal constraints are of the type $\mathbf{Ax} = \mathbf{b}$, the dual variables $\boldsymbol{\lambda}$ must be unrestricted in sign.

Extending the concept of a saddle point to the LP, it follows that if $(\mathbf{x}^*, \boldsymbol{\lambda}^*)$ is a saddle point, $\mathbf{x}^*$ solves the primal and $\boldsymbol{\lambda}^*$ solves the dual. Moreover, $\mathbf{cx}^* = \boldsymbol{\lambda}^*\mathbf{b}$. The converse is true in the sense that if $\mathbf{x}^*$ and $\boldsymbol{\lambda}^*$ are feasible for the primal and dual problem and $\mathbf{cx}^* = \boldsymbol{\lambda}^*\mathbf{b}$, then $(\mathbf{x}^*, \boldsymbol{\lambda}^*)$ is a saddle point.

Actually, duality and its potential applications in LP were first recognized by John von Neumann when he was first introduced to the SM by George B.

Dantzig [1963, p. 24]. Indeed, every two-person zero-sum game can be represented by a pair of primal and dual LPs. Conversely, every LP can be expressed as a game problem. The concept of saddle points in games relates directly to the concepts that associate the primal and dual solutions [Dantzig, 1951; Tucker, 1950].

If the primal problem possesses no finite solution (that is, unbounded), then from Theorem 3, $\mathbf{cx} \leqslant \boldsymbol{\lambda}\mathbf{b}$ means that

$$(\mathbf{cx} \to \infty) \Longrightarrow (\boldsymbol{\lambda}\mathbf{b} \to \infty).$$

This can be satisfied only if $\mathbf{c} - \boldsymbol{\lambda}\mathbf{A} > \mathbf{0}$, that is, if the dual is infeasible. Conversely, if the primal is infeasible, the dual is either infeasible or bounded. In all these cases, the Lagrangean function possesses no saddle point.

Duality in LP has very important applications. The theory of LP shows that the solution of either problem automatically yields the solution of the other problem. Namely, if $\mathbf{B}$ is the optimal basis in one problem and $\mathbf{c}_B$ is its associated vector in the objective function, the optimal solution to the other problem is $\mathbf{c}_B\mathbf{B}^{-1}$. By using this result, computational savings may be realized by solving the dual rather than the primal. Namely, if the dual problem has a smaller number of constraints than the primal, then it is more efficient to solve the dual.

One of the first exploitations of duality theory is the development of the *dual simplex* method (DSM) [Lemke, 1954]. In the regular SM, the problem starts feasible but nonoptimal and continues to be feasible until optimality is achieved. This is exactly equivalent to considering the dual problem which starts infeasible but (better than) optimal and then maintains optimality while moving the solution toward feasibility. This can be seen since nonoptimality in the (maximization) primal implies

$$z_j - c_j = \mathbf{c}_B\mathbf{B}^{-1}\mathbf{P}_j - c_j = \boldsymbol{\lambda}\mathbf{P}_j - c_j < 0$$

for at least one nonbasic x_j. This shows that the dual is infeasible. At the point where all $z_j - c_j$ satisfies optimality, the dual problem automatically becomes feasible. This observation is the basis for the DSM.

Another interesting application of duality deals with the algorithms for the generalized transportation model of which the transportation model is a special case [Dantzig, 1951]. The definition of the generalized transportation model given in Section 2 is repeated here for convenience.

$$\text{Minimize } x_0 = \sum_{i=1}^{m} \sum_{j=1}^{n} c_{ij} x_{ij}$$

subject to

$$\sum_{j=1}^{n} p_{ij} x_{ij} \leqslant a_i, \quad i = 1, 2, \ldots, m$$

$$\sum_{i=1}^{m} x_{ij} = b_j, \quad j = 1, 2, \ldots, n$$

$$x_{ij} \geqslant 0.$$

The dual of the problem is

$$\text{maximize } \lambda_0 = \sum_{i=1}^{m} a_i u_i + \sum_{j=1}^{n} b_j v_j$$

subject to

$$p_{ij} u_i + v_j \geqslant c_{ij}, \quad \text{for all } i \text{ and } j$$

$$u_i \geqslant 0, \quad \text{for all } i$$

$$v_j \text{ unrestricted, for all } j.$$

From LP theory, for a basic primal variable x_{ij} it must be true that $z_{ij} - c_{ij} = 0$. For the generalized model

$$z_{ij} = p_{ij} u_i + v_j$$

Thus, for all basic x_{ij}, the corresponding dual constraints must be satisfied in equation form, that is,

$$p_{ij} u_i + v_j = c_{ij}, \quad \text{for all basic } x_{ij}$$

Since there are $m + n$ basic variables, there are $m + n$ equations and it is possible to solve uniquely for the corresponding dual variables u_i and v_j. Given the dual values, then

$$z_{ij} - c_{ij} = p_{ij} u_i + v_j - c_{ij}$$

can be evaluated for all nonbasic x_{ij}. If all $z_{ij} - c_{ij} \leqslant 0$, the current basis is optimal; otherwise, the nonbasic vector having the most positive $z_{ij} - c_{ij}$ is selected to become basic.

The importance of the above procedure stems from the fact that the generalized transportation model need not be solved as a regular simplex tableau. In fact, the change of basis can be made by representing the data of the problem in a special tableau format which is much more efficient computationally than the simplex computations. Although the steps of the algorithm are basically those of the SM, the evaluation of $z_{ij} - c_{ij}$ for the purpose of determining the entering vector is a direct contribution of duality theory.

The generalized model can be specialized to the transportation model by putting $p_{ij} = 1$ for all i and j and replacing the first m constraints by strict equations $\left(\text{provided } \sum_{i=1}^{m} a_i = \sum_{j=1}^{n} b_j\right)$. In this case, $z_{ij} - c_{ij} = u_i + v_j - c_{ij}$, where u_i and v_j are unrestricted for all i and j.

Although the transportation method is presented based on duality theory, the exact technique can be presented in an elementary manner by using the so-called *stepping-stone* method [Charnes and Cooper, 1954]. The method, in the apparent sense, seems detached completely from the normal SM computations. However, by employing duality, the two methods are shown to be based on the same steps of the SM.

The transportation method can be extended in a straightforward manner to *capacitated* transportation model that differs only in the presence of the upper bound constraints $0 \leqslant x_{ij} \leqslant d_{ij}$. As in the upper-bounded variables method (Section 4) these constraints are considered implicitly. In this case $u_i + v_j \geqslant c_{ij}$ for all nonbasic variables at zero level and $u_i + v_j \leqslant c_{ij}$ for all nonbasic variables at upper bound. The relationship $u_i + v_j = c_{ij}$ still holds for all basic x_{ij}. Although this method is more efficient than implementing the SM directly, another method called the primal-dual method (P-DM) is known to produce highly efficient results. The basis of this algorithm is developed in the next section.

5.1 Complementary Pivot Theory

The above discussion shows that the optimal solution pair $(\mathbf{x}^*, \boldsymbol{\lambda}^*)$ is a saddle point of the Lagrangean function $L(\mathbf{x}, \boldsymbol{\lambda})$. Another useful representation of the same result is the following theorem.

THEOREM 4: (Complementary slackness [Tucker, 1956]) let $\mathbf{x}$ and $\boldsymbol{\lambda}$ be feasible primal and dual solutions, then a necessary and sufficient condition for $\mathbf{x}$ and $\boldsymbol{\lambda}$ to be optimal for the primal and dual problems is

$$\boldsymbol{\lambda}(\mathbf{b} - \mathbf{A}\mathbf{x}) = 0$$

$$\mathbf{x}(\boldsymbol{\lambda}\mathbf{b} - \mathbf{c}) = 0$$

Since, from the definitions of the primal and dual problems $\boldsymbol{\lambda} \geqslant \mathbf{0}$ and $\mathbf{A}\mathbf{x} \leqslant \mathbf{b}$, the condition $\boldsymbol{\lambda}(\mathbf{b} - \mathbf{A}\mathbf{x})$ is equivalent to $\lambda_i\left(b_i - \sum_{i=1}^{m} a_{ij}x_j\right) = \lambda_i s_i = 0$ for all $i = 1, 2, \ldots, m$, where s_i is the ith slack variable in the primal problem. A similar interpretation applies to the condition $\mathbf{x}(\boldsymbol{\lambda}\mathbf{b} - \mathbf{c}) = 0$.

The complementary slackness theorem implies that at the optimum if $\lambda_i > 0$, then $s_i = 0$, which means that the ith primal resource is exhausted completely. Conversely, if $s_i > 0$, then $\lambda_i = 0$. This result is the basis of an economic interpretation presented in the next section.

Aside from its use in economic interpretations, complementary slackness is the basis for developing the P-DM for LP [Dantzig, et al., 1956]. The motivation behind the development is that if the primal problem does not have an apparent starting b.f.s., then it would be necessary to implement the two-phase procedure

(Section 4). However, the Phase I computations are designed primarily to secure a starting feasible basis without any effort to make it as close as possible to the optimum of the original problem. This is the drawback the P-DM attempts to alleviate.

The primal and dual problems are defined as

Primal	*Dual*
maximize $x_0 = \mathbf{cx}$	minimize $\lambda_0 = \mathbf{b}^t\lambda$
subject to	subject to
$\mathbf{Ax} = \mathbf{b}$	$\mathbf{A}^t\boldsymbol{\lambda} \geqslant \mathbf{c}^t$
$\mathbf{x} \geqslant \mathbf{0}$	unrestricted.

Let $\boldsymbol{\lambda}$ be a feasible solution to the dual and define as associated restricted primal as

$$\text{minimize } x_{R1} + x_{R2} + \cdots + x_{Rm}$$

subject to

$$\mathbf{Ax} + \mathbf{x}_R = \mathbf{b}$$

$$\mathbf{x},\ \mathbf{x}_R \geqslant \mathbf{0}.$$

where the variables $\mathbf{x}_R$ are artificial variables (cf. Phase I of the two-phase method, Section 4). The elements of $\mathbf{x}$ are conditioned, however, so that if $\boldsymbol{\lambda}\mathbf{P}_j > \mathbf{c}_j$, then $x_j = 0$, where $\boldsymbol{\lambda}$ is a b.f.s. of the dual. This means that the only elements of $\mathbf{x}$ that can be positive in the restricted primal are those for which $\boldsymbol{\lambda}\mathbf{P}_j = c_j$.

The dual solution $\boldsymbol{\lambda}$ together with any solution of the restricted primal now satisfies the complementary slackness theorem. The restricted primal is thus solved in the normal manner until its optimal is attained. The optimal solution to the restricted primal is used to obtain a corresponding feasible solution to the dual problem. The new dual solution then defines a new restricted primal in the manner given above and the process of solving it is repeated. At the point where the solution to the restricted primal is feasible with respect to the original problem, (that is, $\mathbf{x}_R = \mathbf{0}$) it is also optimal and the process ends.

The P-DM is actually a generalization of a special P-DM developed for the transportation problem [Ford and Fulkerson, 1956]. The transportation model is very closely related to an earlier development for solving the assignment problem by the Hungarian method [Kuhn, 1955]. But while the P-DM proved highly efficient for the transportation problem, experimentation has shown that its application to general LP's is not as rewarding particularly in comparison with the RSM [Mueller and Cooper, 1955].

5.2 Economic Interpretation of Duality

At the optimal solution, the Lagrangean multipliers, and hence the dual variables, λ_i are expressed in terms of the primal problem as

$$\lambda_i = \frac{\partial x_0}{\partial b_i}, \quad i = 1, 2, \ldots, m$$

This means that the ith dual variable represents the rate of variation of the value of the primal objective function x_0 with the amount of the ith resource. The validity of the result is, by definition, known only in some neighborhood of b_i. However, in LP

$$\boldsymbol{\lambda} = (\lambda_1, \lambda_2, \ldots, \lambda_m) = \mathbf{c}_B \mathbf{B}^{-1},$$

which shows that the interpretation of λ_i is valid so long as the basis $\mathbf{B}$ remains unchanged.

The ith dual variable may be regarded as the marginal price of resource i. Thus, given optimal $\lambda_i > 0$, the value of x_0 can be improved (increased) by increasing the amount of b_i of the ith resource. This result is consistent with the complementary slackness conditions which shows that if $\lambda_i > 0$, then the corresponding ith resource must be satisfied completely. In this respect, it becomes a scarce resource. Conversely, if the ith constraint is abundant, that is, $\sum_{j=1}^{n} a_{ij} x_j < b_i$, then $\lambda_i = 0$, meaning that any increase in the abundant resource cannot affect the value of x_0.

The economic interpretation of the dual variables can be extended meaningfully as follows. Recall from the theory of the SM (Section 4) that if in a maximization problem $z_j - c_j < 0$, an increase in the level of activity j can potentially improve the value of x_0. Now, given

$$z_j = \mathbf{c}_B \mathbf{B}^{-1} \mathbf{P}_j = \sum_{i=1}^{m} a_{ij} \lambda_i$$

and λ_i is the (imputed) price per unit of resource i, then z_j may be interpreted as the price of the resources needed to "produce" one unit of activity j. The condition $z_j - c_j < 0$ thus means that the unit price z_j of the resources needed for one unit of activity j is less than its unit profit c_j. The SM responds to this information by making x_j a basic variable which, if feasibility allows, is equivalent to elevating the value of nonbasic x_j from its current zero level to a positive value. Stated differently, if $z_j - c_j \geqslant 0$, then there is no economic advantage in elevating a nonbasic x_j above its current zero value.

One of the interesting economic interpretations of duality applies to the Leontief input-output model [Dorfman, et al., 1958]. The model deals with an economy which includes a number of interacting industries, with each industry producing a single good by using a single production process. Inputs to each industry include labor as well as goods from other industries and/or external sources. The level of production in each industry must satisfy both the needs of other industries and external demands.

Suppose there are n industries and let x_i be the level of production for industry i. Further, assume that the demand of industry j from industry i is directly proportional to x_j with a_{ij} as the constant of proportionality. If the external demand of the ith good is b_i, the input-output equations of the model are given as

$$x_i \geqslant \sum_{j=1}^{n} a_{ij} x_j + b_i, \quad i = 1, 2, \ldots, n$$

Equivalently, this is put in matrix notation as

$$(\mathbf{I} - \mathbf{A})\mathbf{x} \geqslant \mathbf{b}$$

This shows that

$$\mathbf{x} \geqslant (\mathbf{I} - \mathbf{A})^{-1}\mathbf{b}$$

which would be a feasible solution if $\mathbf{x} \geqslant \mathbf{0}$. In general, meaningful economies automatically result in $\mathbf{x} \geqslant \mathbf{0}$.

To make the problem interesting, suppose c_j is the labor requirement per unit of production in the jth industry. The problem can then be formulated as the following LP.

$$\text{minimize } x_0 = \mathbf{cx}$$

subject to

$$(\mathbf{I} - \mathbf{A})\mathbf{x} \geqslant \mathbf{b}$$
$$\mathbf{x} \geqslant \mathbf{0}.$$

Since $\mathbf{c} \geqslant \mathbf{0}$, and under the assumption that $\mathbf{x} \geqslant \mathbf{0}$ is automatically satisfied, the obvious optimal solution is

$$\mathbf{x} = (\mathbf{I} - \mathbf{A})^{-1}\mathbf{b}$$

(cf. interval LP, Section 4). This gives the level of production in each industry that satisfies the demand for goods at minimum labor requirements.

Consider the dual of the input-output LP.

$$\text{maximize } \lambda_0 = \boldsymbol{\lambda}\mathbf{b}$$

subject to

$$\boldsymbol{\lambda}(\mathbf{I} - \mathbf{A}) \leqslant \mathbf{c}$$
$$\boldsymbol{\lambda} \geqslant \mathbf{0}$$

Again the obvious solution of the dual is

$$\boldsymbol{\lambda} = \mathbf{c}(\mathbf{I} - \mathbf{A})^{-1}$$

The optimal dual values, λ_i, are interpreted as the price per unit demanded of the ith good. This result, incidentally, assumes implicitly that there is a fixed wage rate for all types of labor. This can be seen from the dimensional analysis of the dual solution given above. Namely, $\mathbf{c} = \boldsymbol{\lambda}(\mathbf{I} - \mathbf{A})$ shows that $\boldsymbol{\lambda}$ does not represent monetary values directly since $\mathbf{c}$ represents labor requirements.

The above (simplified) model does not allow the study of the effect of labor demand on the solution. This can be accounted for by treating labor as an industry with external demand, namely, the available labor force.

The given analysis shows that the primal problem can be used to determine the schedule $\mathbf{x}$ satisfying the "bill of goods" $\mathbf{b}$ while the dual problem determines the prices of goods under the assumption that labor is the primary factor in the economy. The model may also be used to study the effect of changing labor wage rate (relative to certain base wage rate) by inflating or deflating the elements of the vector $\mathbf{c}$ to reflect an increase or decrease in wages.

6. SENSITIVITY ANALYSES

Obtaining the optimum solution to a LP cannot be an end by itself. Normally, an OR analyst is interested in the changes in the optimum solution resulting from making changes in the coefficients $\mathbf{c}$, $\mathbf{A}$, and $\mathbf{b}$ of the LP.

Linear programming lends itself neatly to sensitivity or parametric analysis. An examination of Table 2 shows that a current optimal basis of the LP can be changed in two ways:

(i) The basis ceases to be optimal
(ii) The basis ceases to be feasible.

The checks for optimality and feasibility are as follows (see Table 2). A basis $\mathbf{B}$ remains optimal (for a maximization problem) if the condition

$$z_j - c_j = \mathbf{c}_B\mathbf{B}^{-1}\mathbf{P}_j - c_j \geqslant 0$$

is satisfied for all nonbasic $\mathbf{P}_j$. It remains feasible so long as the condition

$$\mathbf{x}_B = \mathbf{B}^{-1}\mathbf{b} \geqslant \mathbf{0}$$

is maintained.

The idea of sensitivity analysis then is to check the optimality and feasibility of the solution as a result of making certain (discrete or parameterized) changes in the coefficients $\mathbf{c}$, $\mathbf{A}$ and $\mathbf{b}$. If the changes occur in the vector $\mathbf{c}$ and/or a *nonbasic* vector $\mathbf{P}_j$, then this can only affect optimality, whereas changes in $\mathbf{b}$ can only affect feasibility. On the other hand, changes in a *basic* vector $\mathbf{P}_k$ can affect both optimality and feasibility since this has a direct effect on the inverse $\mathbf{B}^{-1}$. Indeed, changes in basic $\mathbf{P}_k$ may be such that $\mathbf{B}$ ceases to be a basis.

The cases where either optimality or feasibility are affected can be handled in a straightforward manner by using the SM to recover optimality or the DSM to recover feasibility [Gass and Saaty, 1955; Saaty and Gass, 1954]. The situation is complicated when changes occur in the elements of the basis **B**. Unfortunately, laborious computations are needed [Dantzig, 1963, pp. 271-275] to treat the case where only one element of a basic vector in **B** is changed. In spite of this, there are interesting results which allow meaningful interpretations of such changes.

Suppose that the parameters c_j, a_{ij} and **b** are all functions of a parameter t. Then it can be shown [Saaty, 1959] that the variation of the objective function x_0 with t in the neighborhood of the optimal solution is given by

$$\frac{dx_0}{dt} = -\sum_{i=1}^{m}\sum_{j=1}^{n} \frac{\partial x_0}{\partial b_i}\frac{\partial x_0}{\partial c_j}\frac{da_{ij}}{dt} + \sum_{j=1}^{n}\frac{\partial x_0}{\partial c_j}\frac{dc_j}{dt} + \sum_{i=1}^{m}\frac{\partial x_0}{\partial b_i}\frac{db_i}{dt}$$

If t is taken equal to a_{ij}, then the expression reduces to

$$\begin{aligned}\frac{\partial x_0}{\partial a_{ij}} &= -\left(\frac{\partial x_0}{\partial b_i}\right)\left(\frac{\partial x_0}{\partial c_j}\right)\\ &= -\lambda_i^* x_j^*\end{aligned}$$

where x_j^* and λ_i^* are the optimal primal and dual solutions.

While the expression for $\frac{dx_0}{dt}$ may not be easily interpreted, $\frac{\partial x_0}{\partial a_{ij}}$ shows that the rate of change of the optimal value of x_0 is directly proportional to the product of the associated primal and dual optimal solutions. If λ_i^* and x_j^* are nonnegative, then an incremental increase in a_{ij} would decrease x_0.

Other interesting results concerning incremental changes in a_{ij} can also be derived.

$$\frac{\partial x_0}{\partial a_{ij}} = \frac{\partial x_0}{\partial x_j}\frac{\partial x_j}{\partial a_{ij}} = c_j \frac{\partial x_j}{\partial a_{ij}}$$

Thus, at the optimal x_j^* and λ_j^*, the neighborhood variation of x_j with respect to a_{ij} is

$$\left.\frac{\partial x_i}{\partial a_{ij}}\right|_{x_j^*} = -\frac{\lambda_i^* x_j^*}{c_j}.$$

similarly

$$\left.\frac{\partial \lambda_i}{\partial a_{ij}}\right|_{\lambda_i^*} = -\frac{\lambda_i^* x_j^*}{b_i}$$

Another investigation concerning the variation of optimal x_0 with elements of $\mathbf{A}$ is given in [Mills, 1956].

The study of the parameterization of the coefficients $\mathbf{c}$, $\mathbf{A}$ and $\mathbf{b}$ has been primarily confined to linear variations. For example, for the parameter θ, the objective vector may be parameterized as

$$\mathbf{c}(\theta) = \mathbf{c}^0 + \theta \mathbf{E}$$

where $\mathbf{c}^0$ and $\mathbf{E}$ are constant vectors. However, linear variation is used primarily for analytic convenience since it is possible in this case to obtain closed-form solutions constraining the ranges of values of θ for which solution remains optimal and feasible. If $\mathbf{c}(\theta)$ is represented by *any* nonlinear function, the basic procedures of sensitivity analysis remain unchanged, namely, checking optimality and feasibility. The major problem stems from attempting to solve the nonlinear inequalities representing the optimality and feasibility conditions.

7. DECOMPOSABLE LINEAR PROGRAMS

Consider the LP

$$\text{maximize } x_0 = \mathbf{c}_1\mathbf{x}_1 + \mathbf{c}_2\mathbf{x}_2 + \cdots + \mathbf{c}_n\mathbf{x}_n$$

subject to

$$\begin{aligned}
&\mathbf{A}_1^0\mathbf{x}_1 + \mathbf{A}_2^0\mathbf{x}_2 + \cdots + \mathbf{A}_n^0\mathbf{x}_n \leqslant \mathbf{b}_0\\
&\mathbf{A}_1\mathbf{x}_1\\
&\qquad\quad \mathbf{A}_2\mathbf{x}_2\\
&\qquad\qquad\qquad \ddots\\
&\qquad\qquad\qquad\qquad \mathbf{A}_n\mathbf{x}_n \leqslant \mathbf{b}_n\\
&\qquad\quad \mathbf{x}_1, \mathbf{x}_2, \ldots, \mathbf{x}_n \geqslant \mathbf{0}
\end{aligned}$$

where $\mathbf{x}_1, \mathbf{x}_2, \ldots, \mathbf{x}_n$ are vectors and $\mathbf{A}_1^0, \ldots, \mathbf{A}_n^0, \mathbf{A}_1, \ldots, \mathbf{A}_n$ are matrices. Similarly, $\mathbf{c}_1, \mathbf{c}_2, \ldots, \mathbf{c}_n$, and $\mathbf{b}_0, \mathbf{b}_1, \ldots, \mathbf{b}_n$ are vectors.

This type of problem appears in practical applications where there are groups of activities $\mathbf{x}_1, \ldots, \mathbf{x}_n$ related by common constraints while each group has its own exclusive constraints. The special structure of the problem allows decomposing it into n (almost) independent problems whose constraints are of the type $\mathbf{A}_i\mathbf{x}_i \leqslant \mathbf{b}_i$, $i = 1, 2, \ldots, n$. The advantage here is basically computational, since instead of dealing with the entire problem at one time, decomposition allows considering subproblems that are usually of much smaller sizes.

The general decomposition principle as applied to this problem and its variants can be found in [Dantzig, 1960]. Chapter II-7 on Large Scale Programming also investigates this problem.

8. CONCLUDING REMARKS

The purpose of this chapter has been to give a unified exposition of the principal topics of LP which have been in circulation for the past three decades. It is not presumptuous to conclude that LP has reached the state where no significant new developments can be expected. This, fortunately, is due to the fact that LP theory has reached the level of maturity that makes the technique computationally feasible for relatively large programs.

REFERENCES

1. Beale, E., "Cycling in the Dual Simplex Algorithm," *Nav. Res. Log. Quart.* **2:** 269-276 (1955).
2. Ben-Israel, A. and A. Charnes, "An Explicit Solution of a Special Class of Linear Programming Problems," *Operations Res.* **16:** 1166-1175 (1968).
3. ——, ——, A. Hurter, and P. Robers, "On Explicit Solution of a Special Class of Linear Economic Models," *Operations Res.* **18:** 462-470 (1970).
4. Charnes, A., "Optimality and Degeneracy in Linear Programming," *Econometrica* **20:** 160-170 (1952).
5. —— and W. Cooper, "The Stepping Stone Method of Explaining Linear Programming Calculations in Transportation Problems," *Management Sci.* **1:** 46-69 (1954).
6. ——, ——, "Chance-Constrained Programming," *Management Sci.* **6:** 73-79 (1959).
7. ——, ——, "Programming with Linear Fractional Functionals," *Nav. Res. Log. Quart.* **9:** 181-186 (1962).
8. ——, and C. Lemke, "Minimization of Nonlinear Separable Convex Functionals," *Nav. Res. Log. Quart.* **1:** 301-312 (1959).
9. Dantzig, G., "Application of the Simplex Method to a Transportation Probelm," in Koopmans [35], 359-373.
10. ——, "A Proof of the Equivalence of the Programming Problem and the Game Problem," in Koopmans [35], 330-335.
11. ——, "Maximization of a Linear Function of Variables Subject to Linear Inequalities," Chapter 21 in Koopmans [35].
12. ——, "Computational Algorithm for the Revised Simplex Method," RAND Report RM-1266, The Rand Corporation, Santa Monica, California (1953).
13. ——, "Linear Programming under Uncertainty," *Management Sci.* **1:** 197-206 (1955).
14. ——, "Upper Bounds, Secondary Constraints, and Block Triangularity in Linear Programming," *Econometrica* **23:** 174-183 (1955).
15. ——, "Discrete Value Extremum Problems," *Operations Res.* **5:** 266-277 (1957).
16. ——, "On the Status of Multistage Linear Programs," *Management Sci.* (Oct. 1959).
17. ——, *Linear Programming and Extensions*, Princeton University Press, Princeton, New Jersey (1963).
18. ——, L. Ford, and D. Fulkerson, "A Primal-Dual Algorithm for Linear Programs," 171-181 in H. Kuhn and A. Tucker (eds.), *Linear Inequalities and Related Systems*, Princeton University Press, Princeton, New Jersey (1956).
19. ——, and R. M. Van Slyke, "Generalized Upper Bounding Techniques," *J. Computer and System Sci.* **1:** 213-226 (1967).
20. ——, A. Orden, and P. Wolfe, "Generalized Simplex Method for Minimizing a Linear Form Under Linear Inequality Restraints," *Pac. J. Math.* **5:** 183-195 (1955).

21. ——, and P. Wolfe, "The Decomposition Principle for Linear Programming," *Operations Res.* **8**: 101-111 (1960).
22. Dorfman, R., P. Samuelson, and R. Solow, *Linear Programming and Economic Analysis*, McGraw-Hill, New York (1958).
23. Dzielinski, B. and R. Gomory, "Optimal Programming of Lot Sizes, Inventory, and Labor Allocations," *Management Sci.* **11**: 874-890 (1965).
24. Eastman, W., "Linear Programming with Pattern Constraints," Ph.D. Dissertation, Harvard University (1958).
25. Elmaghraby, S. E., "An Approach to Linear Programming Under Uncertainty," *Operations Res.* **7**: 208-216 (1959).
26. ——, "Allocation Under Uncertainty when Demand Has a Continuous pdf.," *Management Sci.* **6**: 270-294 (1960).
27. Ferguson, A. R. and G. B. Dantzig, "The Problem of Routing Aircraft–A Mathematical Solution," *Aeronau. Eng. Rev.* **14**: 51-55 (1955).
28. ——, and G. B. Dantzig, "The Allocation of Aircraft to Routes–An Example of Linear Programming Under Uncertain Demand," *Management Sci.* **3**: 45-73 (1956).
29. Ford, L. and D. Fulkersen, "Maximal Flow Through a Network," *Canadian J. of Math.* **8**: 399-404 (1956).
30. —— and D. Fulkersen, "A Primal-Dual Algorithm for the Capacitated Hitchcock Problem," *Nav. Res. Log. Quart.* **4**: 47-54 (1957).
31. Frank, M. and P. Wolfe, "An Algorithm for Quadratic Programming," *Nav. Res. Log. Quart.* **3**: 95-110 (1956).
32. Garvin, W., H. Crandall, J. John, and R. Spellman, "Applications of Linear Programming in the Oil Industry," *Management Sci.* **3**: 407-430 (1957).
33. Gass, S., *Linear Programming* (4th ed.), McGraw-Hill, New York (1975).
34. —— and T. Saaty, "The Computational Algorithm for the Parametric Objective Function," *Nav. Res. Log. Quart.* **2**: 39-45 (1955).
35. Gay, D., "On Scolnik's Proposed Polynomial Time Linear Programming Algorithm," TR73-190, Computer Science Department, Cornell University (1973).
36. Gomory, R., "Outline of an Algorithm for Integer Solutions to Linear Programs," *Bull. Am. Math. Soc.* **64**: 275-278 (1958).
37. Hadley, G., *Linear Programming*, Addison-Wesley, Reading, Massachusetts (1962).
38. ——, *Nonlinear and Dynamic Programming*, Addison-Wesley, Reading, Massachusetts (1964).
39. Hartley, H., "Nonlinear Programming by the Simplex Method," *Econometrica* **29**: 223-237 (1961).
40. Heller, I., and C. B. Tompkins, "An Extension of a Theorem of Dantzig," 247-254 in *Linear Inequalities and Related Systems* (H. Kuhn and A. Tucker, eds.), Princeton University Press, Princeton, New Jersey (1956).
41. Hitchcock, F., "The Distribution of a Product from Several Sources to Numerous Locations," *J. Math. Physics* **20**: 224-230 (1941).
42. Hoffman, A., "Cycling in the Simplex Algorithm," National Bureau of Standards, Report No. 2974, December (1953).
43. Jacobs, W. "The Caterer Problem," *Nav. Res. Log. Quart.* **1**: 154-165 (1954).
44. Johnson, S. M., "Sequential Production Planning Over Time at Minimum Cost," *Management Sci.* **3**: 435-437 (1957).
45. Kantorovitch, L., "Mathematical Methods in the Organization and Planning of Production," translated in *Management Sci.* **6**: 366-422 (1960).
46. Kelley, J., Jr., "The Cutting Method for Solving Convex Programs," *J. Indust. Appl. Math.* **8**: 703-712 (1960).

47. Koopmans, T., *Activity Analysis of Production and Allocation*, Wiley, New York (1951).
48. ——, "Optimum Utilization of the Transportation System," *Proceedings of the International Statistical Conferences*, Washington, D.C. (1947).
49. Kuhn, H., "The Hungarian Method for the Assignment Problem," *Nav. Res. Log. Quart.* **2:** 83–97 (1955).
50. Land, A. and A. Doig, "An Automatic Method for Solving Discrete Programming Problems," *Econometrica* **28:** 497–520 (1960).
51. Lasdon, L. S. and R. C. Terjung, "An Efficient Algorithm for Multi-Item Scheduling," *Operations Res.* **19:** 946–969 (1971).
52. Lemke, C., "The Dual Method for Solving the Linear Programming Problem," *Nav. Res. Log. Quart.* **14:** 36–47 (1954).
53. Little, J. D. C., K. G. Murty, D. W. Sweeny, and C. Karel, "An Algorithm for the Traveling Salesman Problem," *Operations Res.* **11:** 979–989 (1963).
54. Madansky, A., "Method of Solution of Linear Programming Under Uncertainty," *Operations Res.* **6:** 197–204 (1960).
55. Manne, A., "Programming of Economic Lot Sizes," *Management Sci.* **14:** 115–135 (1958).
56. McCallum, C., Jr., "Existence Theory for the Complex Linear Complementarity Problem," *J. Math. Anal. and Appl.* **43:** 738–762 (1972).
57. Miller, C., "The Simplex Method for Local Separable Programming," 89–100 in R. Graves and P. Wolfe (eds.), *Recent Advances in Mathematical Programming*, McGraw-Hill, New York (1963).
58. Mills, H., "Marginal Values of Matrix Games and Linear Programs," 183–193 in H. Kuhn and A. Tucker (eds.), *Linear Inequalities and Related Systems*, Princeton University Press, New Jersey (1956).
59. Mueller, R. and L. Cooper, "A Comparison of the Primal Simplex and Primal-Dual Algorithms in Linear Programming," *Communications of the ACM* **18:** 115–121 (1965).
60. Orchard-Hays, W., *Advanced Linear Programming Computing Techniques*, McGraw-Hill, New York (1968).
61. Orden, A., "The Transshipment Problem," *Management Sci.* **2:** 276–285 (1956).
62. Saaty, T., "Coefficient Perturbation of a Constrained Extremum," *Operations Res.* **7:** 294–302 (1959).
63. ——, and S. Gass, "Parametric Objective Function (Part I)," *Operations Res.* **2:** 316–319 (1954).
64. Scolnik, H., Untitled preliminary report presented at the Eighth International Symposium on Mathematical Programming, Stanford University, California (Aug. 1973).
65. ——, "A New Approach to Linear Programming," *SIGMAP Newsletter* (Nov. 1973).
66. Simonnard, M., *Linear Programming* (translated by W. S. Jewell), Prentice-Hall, New Jersey (1966).
67. Spivey, W. A. and R. M. Thrall, *Linear Optimization*, Holt, Rinehart and Winston, New York (1970).
68. Taha, H. and G. Curry, "Classical derivation of the Necessary and Sufficient Conditions for Optimal Linear Programs," *Operations Res.* **19:** 1045–1050 (1971).
69. Tucker, A., "Linear Programming and Theory of Games," *Econometrica* **18:** 189 (1950).
70. ——, "Dual Systems of Homogeneous Linear Relations," 3–18 in H. Kuhn and A. Tucker (eds.), *Linear Inequalities and Related Systems*, Princeton University Press, Princeton, New Jersey (1956).
71. Vienott, A. F. and G. B. Dantzig, "Integral Extreme Points," *SIAM Rev.* **10:** 371–372 (1968).

72. Wolfe, P., "A Technique for Resolving Degeneracy in Linear Programming," RAND Report RM 2995-PR, Santa Monica, California (1957).
73. ——, "The Simplex Method for Quadratic Programming," *Econometrica* **27**: 382–398 (1959).
74. —— and G. Dantzig, "Linear Programming in a Markov Chain," *Operations Res.* **10**: 702–710 (1962).
75. Wagner, H. M., "Linear Programming and Regression Analysis," *J. Amer. Stat. Assoc.* **57**: 572–578 (1962).
76. White, W. W., "A Commentary on the 'New Approach to L.P.'," *SIGMAP Newsletter*, (April 1974).
77. Zangwill, W., "The Convex Simplex Method," *Management Sci.* **14**: 221–238 (1967).
78. Zlobec, S. and A. Ben-Israel, "On Explicit Solution of Interval Programs," *Israel J. Math.* **8**: 12–22 (1970).

II-2

INTEGER PROGRAMMING AND COMBINATORICS

Fred Glover
University of Colorado

1. INTRODUCTION

Integer programming (IP) and combinatorics are closely linked. In the broadest sense their domains are identical, though in practice some problems are popularly viewed to fall more in the province of one than the other. "Combinatorics," as spoken of here, is the field of "combinatorial optimization," whose problems characteristically have the form of seeking a "best" subset of items (decisions, actvities, etc.) satisfying particular criteria from a structured finite set of alternatives. "Best" is evaluated in terms of maximizing or minimizing some functional. The *structure* of the finite set, whatever it may be, is the feature to be exploited in devising a systematic method to solve the problem, rather than simply enumerating and comparing all alternatives (which in problems of real world significance can require astronomical amounts of computation). A remarkable number of practical problems fall into the IP/combinatorics area. Those associated with the "combinatorics" label usually are problems that are conveniently expressed in the specialized terminology of graph or matroid theory. Those associated with the "integer programming" label usually are more conveniently expressed in mathematical programming terminology. Then there is a no-man's-land of problems that fall under either or both labels according to the flavor the author wishes to impart to them.

This chapter focuses primarily (though not exclusively) on those problems and formulations that commonly find expression in IP terminology. (The graph theoretic branch of combinatorics is covered in Chapter II-3.)

Loosely speaking, IP is the domain of mathematical optimization in which some or all of the problem variables are required to assume integer (whole number) values. The nonlinear character of the integer requirement is subtle enough to accommodate an unexpected variety of other nonlinearities, permitting most "nonlinear" IPs to be sorted into a linear component and an integer component. Consequently, IP is frequently regarded as the domain of linear mathematical optimization (specifically, "linear programming") in which some or all of the problem variables are integer-constrained.

1.1 An Illustration

A very simple example of an IP is that of a gardener who needs 107 pounds of fertilizer for his lawn, and has the option of buying it either in 35-pound bags at \$14 each or in 24-pound bags at \$12 each. His goal is to buy (at least) the 107 pounds he needs at the cheapest cost. Letting x_1 be the number of 35-pound bags he buys and letting x_2 be the number of 24-pound bags he buys, he seeks to

$$\text{minimize } 14x_1 + 12x_2$$

subject to

$$35x_1 + 24x_2 \geqslant 107$$

$$x_1, x_2 \geqslant 0 \quad \text{and integer.}$$

The "and integer" stipulation means that the gardener can't buy half or a third of a bag of fertilizer, but must buy a whole bag or none at all. Without this stipulation the problem is an example of an ordinary LP problem.

1.2 Significance of the Integer Restriction

To get a very rudimentary grasp of how the integer restriction can affect the character of the problem, consider what would happen if the restriction were missing. The gardener would then observe that fertilizer in the 35-pound bags costs 40¢ a pound and fertilizer in the 24-pound bags costs 50¢ a pound, and immediately perceive that his best policy would be to buy 3-2/35 of the 35-pound bags. However, in the presence of the integer restriction, his best policy is to buy only 1 of the 35-pound bags and buy 3 of the 24-pound bags. Clearly, his best policy has changed drastically, which is not unusual when requiring the variables to be integer valued. (In fact, an example exists [Glover, 1972] of a "conditional transportation problem" that can be summarized by a 5 X 5 cost matrix and whose LP solution can be rounded in more than a million ways, none of which yields a feasible–let alone optimal–solution.)

1.3 Areas of Application

In the foregoing example, the interpretation and relevance of the integer restriction was clear, as it would also be if one wished to determine an optimal number of airplanes, cargo ships, or human beings. However, a variety of problems that seem on the surface to have little or nothing to do with "integer constrained linear optimization" can nevertheless be given an IP formulation. Indeed, the requirement of discreteness indirectly, if not directly, pervades many significant classes of problems and provides IP with application in an uncommonly wide variety of theoretical and practical disciplines. Production sequencing, job shop scheduling, logistics, plant location, assembly line balancing, mineral exploration, capital budgeting, resource allocation, and facilities planning constitute a few of the important industrial problem areas that frequently fall within the wider domain of IP.

The uses of IP are not confined to industry, however, and also find application in many other combinatorial optimization problems arising in engineering and scientific contexts. Computer design, system reliability, prime implicant selection, signal coding, and energy storage system design all give rise to classes of problems with IP formulations.

Integer programming also has applications to economic analysis. The assumption of continuity underlying traditional economic theory is incompatible with the existence of indivisible plants, set up costs, and developmental expenditures. Conclusions reached by marginal analysis must, therefore, often be amended (or stated with appropriate qualification) to accommodate considerations which are the focus of IP.

1.4 Mathematical Formulation of Linear and Integer Programs

A standard formulation of the LP problem is, in matrix notation,

$$\text{Minimize } \mathbf{cx}$$

subject to

$$\mathbf{Ax} \leqslant \mathbf{b}$$

$$\mathbf{x} \geqslant \mathbf{0}$$

where $\mathbf{c} = (c_j)_{1\times n}$, $\mathbf{x} = (x_j)_{n\times 1}$, $\mathbf{A} = (a_{ij})_{m\times n}$ and $\mathbf{b} = (b_i)_{m\times 1}$. The matrix inequality $\mathbf{Ax} \leqslant \mathbf{b}$ can be used to summarize constraints of the form $\mathbf{Dx} \geqslant \mathbf{d}$ and $\mathbf{Dx} = \mathbf{d}$ by the well-known equivalences

$$\mathbf{Dx} \geqslant \mathbf{d} \iff -\mathbf{Dx} \leqslant -\mathbf{d}$$

and

$$\mathbf{Dx} = \mathbf{d} \iff \begin{array}{c} \mathbf{Dx} \leqslant \mathbf{d} \\ -\mathbf{eDx} \leqslant -\mathbf{ed} \end{array}$$

where **e** denotes the vector all of whose components equal 1, interpreted to be a row or column vector according to context. (Thus $-\mathbf{eDx} \leqslant -\mathbf{ed}$ sums the row inequalities of $\mathbf{Dx} \leqslant \mathbf{d}$ and reverses their sign.) Also, a problem with the objective to maximize **dx** can be accommodated by the foregoing minimization formulation by letting $\mathbf{c} = -\mathbf{d}$.

1.5 Pure and Mixed Integer Programs

A LP problem in which all components of **x** are additionally constrained to be integer is called a *pure* IP problem and one in which only some of the components of **x** are additionally constrained to be integer is called a *mixed* IP problem. Variables that are not integer constrained are called *continuous* variables. (Thus, in the ordinary LP problems all variables are continuous.)

The words "integer programming" often have reference to the pure integer problem but we allow them also to refer to the more general mixed problem depending on the setting.

2. EXAMPLES OF IP PROBLEMS

2.1 The Knapsack (or Loading) Problem

One of the simplest IP problems is the *knapsack* problem, so called because it can be interpreted as a problem of selecting a best set of items to go in a hiker's knapsack, given the value he attaches to these items and an upper limit on the amount of weight he can carry. The resultant model is a linear objective function subject to a single linear constraint, both in integer variables. For example:

$$\text{maximize } 7x_1 + 5x_2 + 9x_3 + 6x_4 + 3x_5$$

subject to

$$54x_1 + 35x_2 + 57x_3 + 46x_4 + 19x_5 \leqslant 100$$

and

$$x_j \geqslant 0 \text{ and integer}, \quad j = 1, \ldots, 5.$$

In practice the variables of a knapsack problem are often constrained to satisfy

$$x_j \leqslant 1$$

in which case it is sometimes called the "0-1" knapsack problem. More generally, the variables may be required to satisfy $x_j \leqslant U_j$, in which case it is called the "bounded variable" knapsack problem.

The knapsack problem is extremely easy to solve as an ordinary LP simply by ranking the variables according to the ratios of the objective function coefficients to the constraint coefficient (the so-called "Greedy Algorithm"). That is, writing the problem as

$$\text{maximize } \sum d_j x_j$$

subject to

$$\sum a_j x_j \leqslant b$$

$$x_j \geqslant 0 \text{ and integer}$$

where $d_j > 0$ and $a_j > 0$ for all j, the variables are ranked by a "primed indexing" so that

$$d_{1'}/a_{1'} \geqslant d_{2'}/a_{2'} \geqslant \cdots$$

where $1', 2', \ldots$ constitute a permutation of the numbers $1, 2, \ldots$. Then the problem is solved by taking $x_{1'}$ as large as possible without violating the constraint $\sum a_j x_j \leqslant b$ (or any bound imposed on $x_{1'}$, as in the 0–1 problem), then taking $x_{2'}$ as large as possible subject to the value already assigned $x_{1'}$, and so on. Thus in the above example we have

$$1' = 5, \quad 2' = 3, \quad 3' = 2, \quad 4' = 4, \quad 5' = 1$$

and the optimal solution for the unbounded and continuous problem is

$$x_5 = 100/19, \quad x_3 = x_2 = x_4 = x_1 = 0$$

while the optimal solution for the 0–1 problem is

$$x_5 = 1, \quad x_3 = 1, \quad x_2 = 24/35, \quad x_4 = x_1 = 0.$$

A frequently encountered generalization of the knapsack problem is the so called "multi-dimensional" knapsack problem whose formulation "minimize $\mathbf{cx}$ subject to $\mathbf{Ax} \leqslant \mathbf{b}$, etc.," is characterized by $\mathbf{c} \leqslant \mathbf{0}$ and $\mathbf{A} \geqslant \mathbf{0}$. An obvious and sometimes useful property of the multidimensional knapsack problem is that any fractional (i.e., "not totally integer") $\mathbf{x}$ vector that satisfies $\mathbf{Ax} \leqslant \mathbf{b}$ can be rounded down to produce an integer $\mathbf{x}$ that satisfies $\mathbf{Ax} \leqslant \mathbf{b}$. Practical applications of the multidimensional knapsack problem arise in capital budgeting, forestry, and cargo loading.

We have given an extended description of the knapsack problem not only for historical interest but also because, in spite of its apparent simplicity, this problem reappears in several guises and contexts in IP. (The problem of the gardener described at the beginning of this article is one form of the knapsack problem.) In fact, a number of solution techniques in IP can be interpreted as a direct extension of a "knapsack method," or involve the creation of "knapsack subproblems" whose solution provides valuable information for the solution of the original problem. More will be said about this subsequently.

2.2 The Fixed Charge Problem

The fixed charge problem is characterized by "one shot" outlays (or set up costs) that are incurred in the process of starting or renewing a business venture. For example, a manager who is faced with deciding which of several machines to buy, automobile plants to build, oil wells to drill, or land areas to develop, must account not only for the continuing costs of operation (once the projects are underway) but also for the initial *fixed cost* required to initiate the projects. This type of problem, especially in the presence of imbedded networks, is one of the most frequently occurring problems in practical applications.

A typical fixed charge problem has the form:

$$\text{Minimize } \mathbf{cx} + \boldsymbol{\alpha}\mathbf{y}$$

subject to

$$\mathbf{Ax} \leqslant \mathbf{b}$$

$$\mathbf{x} \geqslant \mathbf{0}, \quad \mathbf{y} \geqslant \mathbf{0}$$

where the vectors $\mathbf{x}$ and $\mathbf{y}$ have the same dimension and $x_j > 0$ implies $y_j = 1$. (Here, of course, $\mathbf{c}$, $\mathbf{A}$ and $\mathbf{b}$ are not intended to represent the $\mathbf{c}$, $\mathbf{A}$ and $\mathbf{b}$ of the general IP formulation given earlier.) The stipulation that $x_j > 0$ implies $y_j = 1$ conveys the meaning that to make, buy, or process any positive amount of x_j incurs a fixed charge of $\alpha_j (> 0)$. It may be noted that $x_j = 0$ automatically implies $y_j = 0$ at any minimizing solution, since whenever $x_j = 0$ and $y_j = 1$ a better solution can always be obtained by setting $y_j = 0$ (without causing any of the constraints to become unsatisfied). However, the preceding formulation is not acceptable for IP since the constraint "$x_j > 0$ implies $y_j = 1$" is "logical" rather than linear. To put the problem in acceptable form, we assume the existence of a bound U_j so that $x_j \leqslant U_j$ is satisfied for all values of x_j compatible with $\mathbf{Ax} \leqslant \mathbf{b}$, $\mathbf{x} \geqslant \mathbf{0}$. Then the constraint

$$U_j y_j \geqslant x_j$$

always holds for $y_j = 1$, and moreover, if y_j is integer valued, then $x_j > 0$ implies $y_j \geqslant 1$ and hence $y_j = 1$ in a minimizing solution (by the same reasoning that shows $x_j = 0$ implies $y_j = 0$). Thus, the IP formulation of the fixed charge problem may be written

$$\text{minimize } \mathbf{cx} + \boldsymbol{\alpha}\mathbf{y}$$

subject to

$$\mathbf{Ax} \leqslant \mathbf{b}$$

$$\mathbf{x} - \mathbf{Uy} \leqslant \mathbf{0}$$

$$\mathbf{x} \geqslant \mathbf{0}, \quad \mathbf{y} \geqslant \mathbf{0}, \quad \mathbf{y} \text{ integer}$$

where $\mathbf{U} = (U_j)$. It is also possible to add the constraint $\mathbf{y} \leqslant \mathbf{e}$ (i.e., $y_j \leqslant 1$ for all j) to explicitly acknowledge that the y_j are 0-1 variables, but this is unnecessary under the assumption that $\boldsymbol{\alpha} > \mathbf{0}$, as already noted.

2.3 The Harmonious Expedition Problem and the Combinatorial Matching Problem

The harmonious expedition problem involves a group of explorers who wish to embark on an expedition and take along as many of their members as possible. However, certain pairs of members do not get along, and if one of the pair goes on the expedition the other will stay home. The problem may be formulated as a 0-1 integer program by defining

$$x_j = \begin{cases} 1 & \text{if member } j \text{ goes along} \\ 0 & \text{if member } j \text{ stays home} \end{cases}$$

Then the objective is to

$$\text{maximize } \sum x_j$$

subject to the constraints

$$x_h + x_k \leqslant 1$$

for those pairs of members h and k who are not compatible. The formulation is completed by requiring $1 \geqslant x_j \geqslant 0$ and x_j integer for all j.

The harmonious expedition problem is closely related to the *maximum cardinality matching problem* from combinatorial graph theory. Figure 1 shows a "typical" graph consisting of nodes (points) and edges (lines) connecting them. A *matching* in such a graph is defined to be a set of edges that share no common endpoints. Thus, by the numbering of the edges shown in Fig. 1, edges 1 and 4 constitute a matching, while edges 5 and 7 do not (since edges 5 and 7 share a node in common). The maximum cardinality matching problem is to determine a matching containing the largest number of edges. Its formulation is the same as that of the harmonious expedition problem by defining

$$x_j = \begin{cases} 1 & \text{if edge } j \text{ is in the matching} \\ 0 & \text{if edge } j \text{ is not in the matching} \end{cases}$$

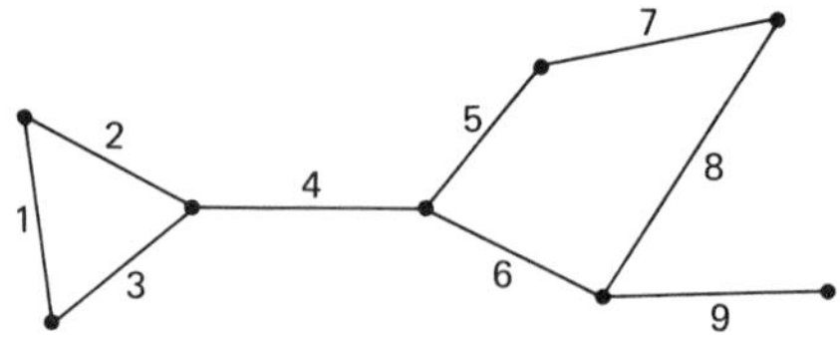

Fig. 1.

introducing the constraints $x_h + x_k \leqslant 1$ for those pairs of edges h, k that share a common endpoint.

A simple generalization of the harmonious expedition problem arises by attaching a "worth" d_j to each member j, and seeking to maximize the "total worth" $\sum d_j x_j$ of the expedition rather than the number of members that go along. The corresponding generalization of the graph theory problem is called the maximum weight matching problem, and arises by assigning a weight to each edge and seeking a matching whose edge weights sum to the greatest value. Other generalizations readily come to mind. For example, in the harmonious expedition problem, one may identify sets rather than pairs of members that constitute an "inharmonious group." If S denotes such a set, and $|S|$ denotes the number of its elements, then one may enforce

$$\sum_{j \in S} x_j \leqslant |S| - 1$$

to assure that at least one member of S stays home.

2.4 The Efficacious Expedition Problem and the Combinatorial Covering Problem

In this problem a group of explorers seeks to *minimize* the number of members who embark on an expedition. However, for each of several critical skills there must be at least one member possessing that skill who goes on the expedition in order for the expedition to be carried out successfully. Defining the variables x_j as for the harmonious expedition problem, and letting S_i denote the set of members possessing the ith skill, the problem is to

$$\text{minimize } \sum x_j$$

subject to the constraints

$$\sum_{j \in S_i} x_j \geqslant 1$$

Again the formulation is completed by stipulating $1 \geqslant x_j \geqslant 0$ and x_j integer.

There is, as might be suspected, a closely related problem from combinatorial graph theory, in this case called the *minimum cardinality covering problem.* A *cover* (or covering) is a set of edges whose endpoints include all nodes of the graph. Thus, in Fig. 1, the edges 1, 2, 3, 4, 5, 8, 9 constitute a cover, but the edges 1, 3, 5 and 9 do not. (No edge covers the node at the intersection of edges 7 and 8.) A minimum cardinality cover is one containing the fewest number of edges, and its formulation is the same as that of the efficacious expedition problem; x_j is defined as for the matching problem and letting S_i denote the set of edges that intersect at a node i (thus yielding one constraint for each node of the graph).

Immediate generalizations of these problems arise by assigning weights to edges and requiring the nodes to be multiply covered.

2.5 A Delivery Problem

A company delivers merchandise to its customers each day by truck (or railroad, air, barge, etc.). There are a variety of feasible delivery routes, each one accommodating a specified subset of customers and capable of being traveled by a single carrier in a day. Each route also has a "cost" associated with it, which may be just the length of the route, or the cost of fuel to travel the route, etc. The goal is to select a set of routes that will make it possible to provide a delivery to each customer and, subject to this, minimize total cost.

Define

$$x_j = \begin{cases} 1 & \text{if route } j \text{ is selected} \\ 0 & \text{if not} \end{cases}$$

and create an **A** matrix whose jth column has (constant) entries

$$a_{ij} = \begin{cases} 1 & \text{if customer is on route } j \\ 0 & \text{if not} \end{cases}$$

Denoting the cost of route j by c_j, the delivery problem may be written

$$\text{minimize } \mathbf{cx}$$

subject to

$$\mathbf{Ax} = \mathbf{e}$$

$$\mathbf{x} \geqslant \mathbf{0} \quad \text{and integer,}$$

where as before **e** is a vector of 1's (a column vector in this case).

The delivery problem may also include a constraint of the form

$$\sum x_j \leqslant k,$$

which restricts the total number of routes selected to be no more than k (because, for example, the company can operate at most k trucks on a given day).

Note that for the specified form of **A**, the constraints "$\mathbf{Ax} = \mathbf{e}$, $\mathbf{x} \geqslant \mathbf{0}$ and integer" automatically imply $x_j = 0$ or 1 for each j (this would also be true if $\mathbf{Ax} = \mathbf{e}$ were replaced by $\mathbf{Ax} \leqslant \mathbf{e}$). We assume of course that there are no columns of **A** that are all 0's (which would correspond to a route without any customers). The matrix equation $\mathbf{Ax} = \mathbf{e}$ stipulates that each customer will receive exactly one delivery each day.

2.6 Multiple Alternative Problems

A variety of "dichotomous" or "multiple alternative" situations can be accommodated by the introduction of appropriately defined 0-1 variables. Problems to which such multiple alternative situations are relevant range from the design of a nuclear reactor complex to the determination of demand reservoir locations for a water resource allocation project.

The common ingredient in these problems is a set of contraining relations

$$\mathbf{A}^{(1)}\mathbf{x} \leqslant \mathbf{b}^{(1)}$$
$$\mathbf{A}^{(2)}\mathbf{x} \leqslant \mathbf{b}^{(2)}$$
$$\vdots$$
$$\mathbf{A}^{(r)}\mathbf{x} \leqslant \mathbf{b}^{(r)}$$

out of which at least q are required to be satisfied while the remaining $r - q$ may be satisfied or not. Corresponding to each $\mathbf{b}^{(k)}$ let $\mathbf{M}^{(k)}$ denote a vector of the same dimension (which may be different for different k) whose components are sufficiently large that $\mathbf{A}^{(k)}\mathbf{x} \leqslant \mathbf{b}^{(k)} + \mathbf{M}^{(k)}$ will be satisfied for all $\mathbf{x}$ vectors relevant to the problem under consideration. Thus, the constraint

$$\mathbf{A}^{(k)}\mathbf{x} \leqslant \mathbf{b}^{(k)} + y_k \mathbf{M}^{(k)}$$

where y_k is a 0-1 variable, corresponding to $\mathbf{A}^{(k)}\mathbf{x} \leqslant \mathbf{b}^{(k)}$ for $y_k = 0$ and to $\mathbf{A}^{(k)}\mathbf{x} \leqslant \mathbf{b}^{(k)} + \mathbf{M}^{(k)}$ for $y_k = 1$. For at least q of the inequalities $\mathbf{A}^{(k)}\mathbf{x} \leqslant \mathbf{b}^{(k)}$ to hold, at least q of the y_k must be 0. This is accommodated by introducing the constraints $\mathbf{A}^{(k)}\mathbf{x} \leqslant \mathbf{b}^{(k)} + y_k \mathbf{M}^{(k)}$ for $k = 1, \ldots, r$ and requiring

$$\sum y_k \leqslant r - q.$$

This latter constraint may also be replaced by

$$\sum y_k = r - q$$

to accomplish the same result.

2.7 Zero-One Polynomial Problems

Nonlinear 0-1 programming problems of the form

$$\text{Minimize } f(\mathbf{x})$$

subject to

$$g_i(\mathbf{x}) \leqslant 0 \qquad i = 1, \ldots, m$$
$$x_j = 0 \text{ or } 1 \text{ for all } j$$

where f and g_i are polynomials, can be replaced by equivalent linear 0-1 programming problems by the rules

(a) Replace all nonzero powers of x_j by x_j itself (since for $x_j = 0$ or 1, $x_j = x_j^2 = x_j^3$ etc.)
(b) Replace each cross product $\Pi_{j \in Q} x_j$ by a 0-1 variable x_Q which is required to satisfy

$$x_Q \geqslant \sum_{j \in Q} x_j + 1 - |Q|$$

and

$$x_Q \leqslant \left(\sum_{j \in Q} x_j \right) \Big/ |Q|$$

where $|Q|$ denotes the number of elements in Q.

The justification of the second rule follows from the fact that the indicated lower bound for x_Q is always redundant until $\sum_{j \in Q} x_j = |Q|$, (which occurs when $x_j = 1$ for all $j \in Q$), in which case it implies $x_Q \geqslant 1$, and the indicated upper bound always requires $x_Q < 1$ (hence $x_Q = 0$) until $\sum_{j \in Q} x_j = |Q|$, in which case it permits $x_Q = 1$. Thus $x_Q = 1$ if $x_j = 1$ for all $j \in Q$ (and $x_Q = 0$ otherwise), which identifies the value of x_Q to be the same as that of $\Pi_{j \in Q} x_j$. Ways have been developed for expressing these polynomials still more effectively [Glover, 1972].

2.8 Equivalence of a Bounded Variable Integer Program to a 0-1 Integer Program

There are several ways to express an integer program in bounded variables as a problem in 0-1 variables.

To illustrate, suppose each integer variable x_j of the original problem can be required to satisfy $0 \leqslant x_j \leqslant U_j$ for some finite upper bound U_j. Then we may replace x_j by the linear expression

$$x_{0j} + 2x_{1j} + 4x_{2j} + \cdots + 2^r x_{rj}$$

where each x_{ij} is a 0-1 variable and r is the unique integer for which $2^r \leqslant U_j < 2^{r+1}$ Two other ways to replace an integer variable by a weighted sum of 0-1 variables arise simply by taking all weights equal to 1 (yielding an ordinary sum of U_j different variables) and by taking the weights to be the positive integers $1, 2, 3, \ldots, U_j$, with the added restriction that the sum of the 0-1 variables associated with these latter weights not exceed 1.

Because of the generality of the 0-1 problem, and because a high percentage of practical problems exhibit "naturally occurring" 0-1 variables, a good deal of attention has been devoted to methods and results for the 0-1 case. In fact, a variety of NLP can be expressed as IP problems (within a desired degree of approximation) by the use of 0-1 variables. Two of the more significant ways of doing this follow.

2.9 Piecewise Linear Approximation of a Separable Nonlinear Function

A nonlinear function $f(\mathbf{x})$ ($\mathbf{x} = (x_j)_{n \times 1}$) is called *separable* if it can be written in the form $f(\mathbf{x}) = f_1(x_1) + f_2(x_2) + \cdots + f_n(x_n)$, where each f_j is a function of the single variable x_j. If the functions f_j are sufficiently well-behaved, it may be possible to fit them with reasonable piecewise linear approximations without too much difficulty. In this context we shall for convenience drop the j subscript and understand $f(x)$ to designate one of the functions $f_j(x_j)$ where now x is a single variable rather than a vector. For example, such a function $f(x)$ and its linear approximation $L(x)$ might be as shown in the following diagram, where $f(x)$ is the curved line and $L(x)$ is the broken straight line.

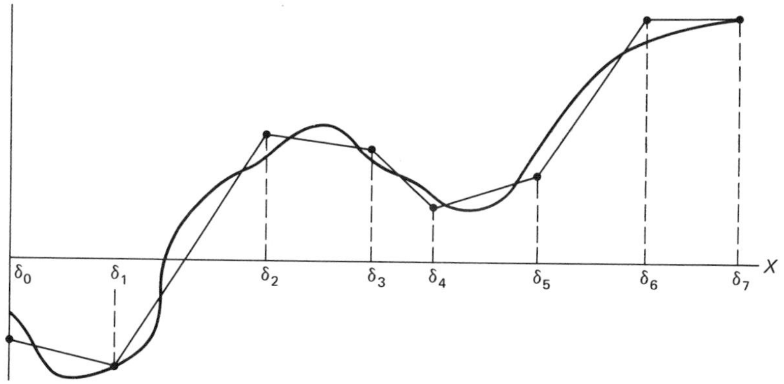

The domain of these functions has been divided into intervals $[\delta_{k-1}, \delta_k]$, $k = 1, \ldots, 7$ over which $L(x)$ is an unbroken straight line. We let α_k denote the slope of $L(x)$ on the interval $[\delta_{k-1}, \delta_k]$ and observe that if $x \in [\delta_{k-1}, \delta_k]$ then $L(x) = L(\delta_{k-1}) + \alpha_k(x - \delta_{k-1})$. This fact makes it possible to represent $L(x)$ by a linear function as follows. Let y_k be a 0-1 variable and let z_k be a continuous variable with the interpretation that $y_k = 1$ corresponds to $x \in [\delta_{k-1}, \delta_k]$ and z_k is nonzero only if $y_k = 1$, in which case it represents the quantity $x - \delta_{k-1}$. Then, $L(x)$ may be expressed as

$$\sum_{k=1}^{r} (L(\delta_{k-1}) y_k + \alpha_k z_k)$$

given the constraints

$$\sum_{k=1}^{r} y_k = 1$$

and

$$(\delta_k - \delta_{k-1}) y_k \geqslant z_k \geqslant 0,$$

$$y_k \geqslant 0 \text{ and integer}; \quad k = 1, \ldots, r$$

This representation can be made valid even if $L(x)$ is not continuous. To do this, one selects the δ_k so that $L(x)$ is continuous on the half-open interval $[\delta_{k-1}, \delta_k)$, and interprets $y_k = 1$ to mean $x \in [\delta_{k-1}, \delta_k)$, whereupon z_k is constrained to satisfy $(\delta_k - \delta_{k-1}) y_k - \epsilon \geqslant z_k \geqslant 0$, for ϵ a small positive number.

It is also quite possible to make the representation valid when $L(x)$ is defined over disjoint intervals. In particular, if $L(x)$ is defined only at the points δ_k, then one can simply represent $L(x)$ by $\sum_{k=1}^{r} L(\delta_k) y_k$, without any reference to the z_k variables.

There is another way to represent $L(x)$ which, however, requires $L(x)$ to be continuous. Under this assumption, $L(x)$ may be written

$$L(0) + \sum_{k=1}^{r} \alpha_k z_k$$

where now the z_k have the interpretation of equaling the length of the interval $[\delta_{k-1}, \delta_k]$ if $x > \delta_k$, equaling $x - \delta_{k-1}$ (as before) if $x \in [\delta_{k-1}, \delta_k]$, and equaling 0 if $x < \delta_{k-1}$. (Thus, $\sum z_k = x$.) This interpretation is assured by imposing the constraints

$$y_{k-1}(\delta_k - \delta_{k-1}) \geqslant z_k \geqslant y_k(\delta_k - \delta_{k-1})$$

$$y_k \geqslant 0 \quad \text{and integer}; \quad k = 1, \ldots, r$$

where by convention $y_0 = 1$. Then "$y_k = 1$" corresponds to "$x \geqslant \delta_k$." The constraints imply that $1 \geqslant y_1 \geqslant y_2 \cdots \geqslant y_r$, and that each z_k assumes exactly the value indicated by the foregoing discussion.

This second way of representing $L(x)$ can be slightly modified to accommodate discontinuous functions and functions defined over disjoint intervals by including the 0-1 variables in the expression for $L(x)$.

If the function $L(x)$ that approximates $f(x)$ is *convex*, and if the problem objective is to minimize $f(x)$, then the quantity $L(0) + \sum \alpha_k z_k$ provides an acceptable linear expression for $L(x)$ without introducing 0-1 variables y_k. The only stipulation required is that

$$\delta_k - \delta_{k-1} \geqslant z_k \geqslant 0 \qquad k = 1, \ldots, r$$

This follows from the fact that

$$\alpha_1 \leqslant \alpha_2 \leqslant \cdots \leqslant \alpha_k$$

and is implied by the convexity of $L(x)$.

3. SOLUTION METHODS FOR INTEGER PROGRAMMING PROBLEMS

The number of solution methods—and special variations for special cases—that have been proposed for IP problems are legion. However, nearly all of them can be described in terms of a single framework. We will describe this framework, and then provide illustrations of a few of the more popular methods that are special instances of it.

Methods for solving IP problems typically proceed by generating a succession of related problems which we will call *descendants* of the original problem. For each descendant, an associated *relaxed problem* is identified that is easier to solve than the problem it came from (which will be called its *source* problem). The solution to the relaxed problem determines the resolution of its source; i.e., whether the source may be discarded or replaced by one or more descendants of its own (hence, which are also descendants of the original problem). Thereupon, one of the descendants is selected which has not yet been discarded or replaced and the process repeats until no more unresolved descendants remain. In a variety of methods (as, for example, cutting methods), the resolution of a problem gives rise to exactly one descendant, though there is typically a choice among several alternatives to provide the identity of this descendant.

We will now characterize the nature of descendants and relaxed problems more precisely.

3.1 Descendants

In the same way that a relaxed problem has a source, a descendant problem has a parent (an immediate predecessor from which the descendant "issues"). A collection of immediate descendants of a given problem is required to have the property that at least one of these descendants has the same optimal solution as its parent. In case the parent problem has multiple optima, the restriction is that some nonempty subset of these optima must constitute the set of optimal solutions for one of its descendants.

Two common examples of descendant problems with these properties will be given. In the so-called cutting approach, an inequality or equation—called a "cut"—is deduced that is satisfied by all solutions to the parent. (To be useful, the cut usually must not be satisfied by the optimum for the relaxed problem which has been solved in lieu of the parent.)· The cut is then appended to the parent to yield a single new problem which has exactly the same set of optimal solutions as the problem from which it descended.

In the branch and bound approach, for the second example, a collection of inequalities (or equations) is deduced, so that each admits some subset of the solutions to the parent problem as feasible, and so that the union of these subsets includes all feasible solutions to the parent. Each of the derived inequalities–or "provisional cuts"–is adjoined to the parent problem separately from the others (since it is not known in advance which one will admit an optimum solution to the parent as feasible), thus creating a collection of descendants having the properties indicated.

In still other approaches (such as certain graph theory methods), nothing is added to the parent problem, but the manner in which the problem is "represented" is modified, based on the solution to the relaxed problem, to produce a single descendant for which the process is repeated.

3.2 Relaxed Problems

The principal characteristic of a relaxed problem is that its constraints are less restrictive–i.e., admit a larger (or no smaller) range of feasible solutions–than the constraints of its source problem. Frequently, a relaxed problem is created simply by discarding some of the constraining conditions of its source. For example, in IP a commonly employed relaxed problem is the ordinary LP problem (which arises by dropping the integrality requirements). A relaxed problem may also have a different objective function than its source, provided the optimum objective function value for the relaxed problem does not exceed that for the source (in the minimization context).

These stipulations immediately give rise to the following "double inequality": optimal objective function value for the relaxed problem $\leqslant$ optimal objective function value for the source problem $\leqslant$ objective function value for the source problem for any feasible solution to the source.

It follows that, whenever solutions can be found that make the first and the last quantities in this double inequality equal, then the middle quantity is compelled to equal the other two quantities, and an optimal solution has been found for the source problem.

Duality theories for LP, NLP and combinatorial programming involve the specification of a problem which is an instance of a relaxed problem as just defined, and thus which causes the double inequality to hold. The dual problem in each of these duality theories is to find a "strongest" relaxed problem from among the problems in its category–i.e., a relaxed problem that makes the first quantity in the double inequality the largest.

Only a strongest relaxed problem can possibly force the double inequality to hold as an equality and thereby serve as a tool for identifying an optimal solution to the source problem. (However, even a strongest relaxed problem—from those in the category specified by a particular duality theory—may not be able to force equality, in which case the resulting condition is known as a "duality gap.")

In view of these remarks, the methods that derive from the framework under consideration may properly be called *duality exploiting* methods. In fact, one of the important features of these methods is that they give a means for solving the source problem even when duality gaps occur. The manner in which they do this relies on the iterative creation of descendants to serve as source problems, and on making use of three useful properties of their associated relaxed problems:

(a) Whenever a relaxed problem lacks a feasible solution, then so does its source;
(b) the optimum objective function value for a relaxed problem provides a lower bound for the optimum objective function value for the source problem; and
(c) if an optimal solution to a relaxed problem yields the same objective function value for the source problem as for the relaxed problem (which it automatically does if the two objective functions are the same), and if this solution is feasible for the source problem, then it is also optimal for the source problem.

Consequently, whenever conditions (a) or (c) hold, the process of solving the relaxed problem "disposes of" the source problem, thereby accomplishing a hard task (solving the source) by undertaking an easier one (solving the relaxed problem). Moreover, if a ceiling has been established for the optimum objective function value of the source problem, so that the optimum must fall below this ceiling if it is to be acceptable (as commonly occurs in branch and bound methods), then the solution of the relaxed problem also disposes of the source problem under condition (b), provided the lower bound identified by this condition equals or exceeds the imposed ceiling.

Utilizing these observations, we now state the general procedural format for "duality exploiting" methods in IP and combinatorial optimization.

3.3 Duality Exploiting Methods: General Framework

1. Begin with a "problem list" that contains the original problem as its only member.
2. Select a problem from the list. (If there are no problems on the list at this point, the method stops and the best solution so far found is optimal for the original problem. If no such "candidate" solutions were found, the original problem has no feasible solution.)

3. Solve a relaxed problem—or a collection of relaxed problems—corresponding to the selected problem.

   - If a relaxed problem lacks a feasible solution (cf. condition (a)), discard the selected problem and return to Step 2.
   - If the optimum objective function value for a relaxed problem equals or exceeds the ceiling given by the objective function value for the best candidate solution for the original problem so far found (cf. condition (b)), discard the selected problem and return to Step 2.
   - If neither of the preceding situations apply, and if an optimal solution to a relaxed problem is optimal for the selected problem (cf. condition (c)), then check this solution to see if it is feasible for the original problem. (The check is unnecessary for standard branch and bound and cutting approaches—as previously characterized—since for these the set of feasible solutions to each selected problem is a subset of the feasible solutions to the original problem.) If feasibility for the original problem is established, then record this solution as the new best candidate solution for the original problem, and return to Step 2.
   - If none of the preceding circumstances apply, treat the selected problem as a parent problem and generate a set of one or more descendants (as by the use of cuts, provisional cuts, an updated problem representation, etc.), so that these descendants have the properties previously stipulated. Add these descendant problems to the list (in place of their parent) and return to Step 2.

Some comments about the foregoing framework are in order. First, standard techniques for obtaining successively stronger relaxed problems can be used in Step 3. These techniques apply to relaxed problems that are created by replacing some subset of the constraints of the source problem with a nonnegative linear combination of these constraints, where this linear combination is either absorbed into the objective function, as in generalized Lagrangean approaches, or used to form one or more "summarizing" constraints, as in the surrogate constraint approaches. (These two types of relaxation approaches will be discussed in more detail later.) All of the techniques for creating successively stronger relaxed problems utilize some variant of the following simple strategy:

(a) solve the current relaxed problem;

(b) if the solution is not feasible for the source problem, identify a subset of the violated constraints and a subset of the "oversatisfied" constraints (so that at least one of these subsets is nonempty) and modify the relaxed problem by increasing the weights of the linear combination associated with the first set and by decreasing the weights associated with the second set. The amount of increase or decrease may vary for each constraint, in a given set, but the net change is made sufficiently great so that the previous solution to the relaxed problem becomes nonoptimal relative to the modified form of the relaxed problem. (The Frank-Wolfe algorithm is a popular technique of this type [Frank and Wolfe, 1956; Hogan, 1971].) In fact, many of the penalty function methods for nonlinear programming utilize essentially the same strategy, except that the "weights" may apply to functions other than linear ones.

Another comment is that, as an adjunct to Step 2 or 3, one can optionally employ heuristic approaches to generate "trial solutions" to the selected problem, whereupon these solutions can be tested to see whether they provide improved candidate solutions for the original problem.

Further, in addition to this option, there are three main places in the duality exploiting framework where choice enters: in selecting the next problem from the list; in choosing a relaxed problem (or collection of relaxed problems) for a given source problem; in deciding which cut or which set of provisional cuts, etc., should be generated to produce the new descendant problems. Each of these choice areas is critical to efficient implementation [see Balas, 1973; Garfinkel and Nemhauser, 1972; Geoffrion, 1973; Ross and Glover, 1974; Salkin, 1970; Sommer, 1972; Tomlin, 1971].

Another thing to be noted is that provisional cuts must tend to be a great deal stronger (more restrictive) than ordinary cuts if, as often happens, the branch and bound option is to be preferred to cutting, since the use of provisional cuts leads to two or more descendants of each given problem, and these descendants must somehow be easier to solve than the single descendant of the cutting approach if the total solution time of branch and bound is not to suffer. But there is one advantage to branch and bound that may be extracted even if some of the provisional cuts are rather weak, provided at least some of them are sufficiently strong. For problems that require excessive amounts of computer time to solve optimally, it may nevertheless be possible that relatively good candidate solutions can be found early in the game using branch and bound, and hence the method may be arbitrarily stopped at a reasonable cut-off point and the best solution found to that time used in lieu of a guaranteed optimum.

3.4 Accommodating Primal and Primal-Dual Methods in the Duality Exploiting Framework

A class of methods not subsumed by the preceding framework is the class of "primal" methods. Nevertheless, these methods are easily characterized, and can be incorporated into the foregoing framework as an alternative means of providing trial solutions to the problem selected in Step 2, or as a means of improving a candidate solution generated in Step 3, or even in some cases, as a means of completely solving a relaxed problem or its source.

A method classified as "primal" proceeds by producing a succession of feasible solutions, each better (or no worse) than its predecessor. The "primal strategy" operates by imposing all constraints of the source problem, plus a number of additional constraints which require admissible solutions to be "nearly the same" as the current feasible solution to the source. (In the primal simplex method, for example, the additional constraints compel all current nonbasic variables except one to equal 0, thus allowing a very limited deviation from the solution associated with the current basis. In the primal max flow method, similarly, all flow changes are restricted to occur on an elementary path which currently has a positive "net capacity," again compelling a modified solution to lie close to the current one.) The resulting more highly constrained problem is typically much easier to solve than its source (just as an appropriately generated relaxed problem is much easier to solve than its source), and will always yield a feasible solution at least as good or better than the one currently at hand.

Primal methods that are guaranteed to obtain an optimal solution are much harder to come by in IP than in LP [Hu, 1969; Young, 1965; Young, 1968; Zionts, 1974], but the "primal strategy" can still be a viable solution technique. In fact, the primal methods for IP are actually "primal-dual" methods, insofar as they may be interpreted as combining problem relaxation with problem restriction.

The duality-exploiting framework becomes a framework for both primal and primal-dual methods simply by incorporating the primal strategy in Step 3. Moreover, the use of cuts (and provisional cuts) in a primal strategy can be carried out in a manner that assures these cuts are valid for the source problem. Specifically, cuts derived in the process of generating a succession of restricted problems by a primal approach may be inferred relative only to constraints shared in common with the source problem. (This is in fact one way of interpreting the known primal IP methods.) Thus in the general primal-dual framework, the generation of cuts or provisional cuts to create descendant problems can be guided by an imbedded primal strategy.

3.5 Some Examples of Specific Methods

For a clearer understanding of how the foregoing framework can be applied, illustrations will be provided of some of the more popular methods that occur as variants of this framework.

3.5.1 A Cutting Plane Method. For the pure IP problem, where all variables are integer-valued, a commonly employed method is that proposed by Gomory [1963]. An equation from the Tucker form of a LP tableau (see Chapter II-1) may be written as

$$x_i = a_{io} + \sum_{j \in N} a_{ij}(-t_j),$$

where x_i is an integer variable and the $t_j, j \in N$, are the current nonbasic variables, assumed to be constrained to nonnegative integer values. A cut equation implied by this equation is

$$S = -f_{io} - \sum_{j \in N} f_{ij}(-t_j)$$

where S is a nonnegative integer variable, and the constants f_{ij} are the "positive fractional parts" of the constants a_{ij}; that is $f_{ij} = a_{ij} - [a_{ij}]$, where the square brackets represent the largest integer not exceeding the quantity inside. Since x_i does not have to be nonnegative, the cut can be taken from any equation obtained as some integer linear combination of tableau equations.

A standard method for using such cuts results from the general framework by selecting the relaxed problem to be the ordinary LP problem at Step 3 (Section 3.3). A cut is then obtained from an equation for which a_{io} is not an integer (hence $f_{io} > 0$), thereby producing a single descendant (having the same set of feasible solutions as its parent). For each successive descendant selected at Step 2, the relaxed LP problem is solved in Step 3 by "postoptimizing" with the DSM.

Recently, a number of advances have been made in cutting theory by reference to subadditive functions [Burdet, 1973; Gomory, 1972; Gomory and Johnson, 1972; Jeroslow, 1974] and specially constructed convex domains [Balas, 1970, 1973; Burdet, 1972; Glover, 1973; Jeroslow, 1973; Young, 1971]. Stronger cuts obtained from these advances may permit cutting methods to be applied with greater efficiency than in the past.

3.5.2 A Branch and Bound Method. A simple procedure that has had some success in certain mixed-integer problem applications is the "Dakin branching scheme" [Dakin, 1965] of branch and bound, which again takes the relaxed problem of Step 3 to be the ordinary LP. This approach generates two descendants from a given problem by reference to an integer variable x_i whose current LP solution value, x_i^*, is noninteger. These descendants arise by respectively (i.e., separately) adjoining the two constraints $x_i \leqslant [x_i^*]$ and $x_i \geqslant [x_i^*] + 1$ to the parent problem.

More elaborate branch and bound schemes employ "penalty calculations" from relaxed problems that may differ from the LP problem. These penalties yield a lower bound on the amount by which compelling $x_i \leqslant [x_i^*]$ or $x_i \geqslant [x_i^*] + 1$ will cause the optimum objective function value for a descendant problem to differ from that of its parent, thereby allowing some descendants to be discarded immediately, and allowing others to be put "on the bottom" of the problem list as unlikely possibilities for yielding an improved candidate solution.

Some of the relaxed problems from which penalties and other typical uses of relaxed problems derive will now be discussed.

3.5.3 Problem Relaxation. Perhaps the most common generic form of problem relaxation is "generalized Lagrangean relaxation," which incorporates a subset of the problem constraints into the objective function.

Using the notation by which the LP and IP problems were earlier defined, the Lagrangean approach associates nonnegative weights u_i with a subset of the problem inequalities (with index set P, say) to create the modified objective function

$$\text{minimize} \sum_{j=1}^{n} c_j x_j + \sum_{i \in P} u_i \left(\sum_{j=1}^{n} a_{ij} x_j - b_i \right)$$

The constraints thus absorbed into the objective function are "dropped" from the constraint set for the relaxed problem. The updated objective function coefficients of the SM for LP problems arise by exactly this technique (here the constraints "taken up" are those corresponding to the nonbasic variables). In fact, most duality theory of mathematical programming is based on this type of relaxation, so it cuts a very wide swath indeed. Variations in the application of this approach are covered in [Everett, 1963; Fisher and Shapiro, 1973; Geoffrion, 1973, 1971; Held and Karp, 1970; Shapiro, 1971].

A second form of problem relaxation that has found considerable application in IP is "surrogate constraint relaxation," which replaces subsets of problem constraints by one or more "surrogate constraints." A surrogate constraint likewise may be expressed in terms of nonnegative weights u_i, $i \in P$, used to define the Lagrangean (though the *values* of these weights that give a strongest relaxation are usually different for the two approaches). The original objective function remains unchanged, but the constraints associated with the index set P are replaced by

$$\sum_{i \in P} u_i \sum_{j=1}^{n} a_{ij} x_j \leqslant \sum_{i \in P} u_i b_i$$

Although of recent vintage [Balas, 1967; Geoffrion, 1969; Glover, 1968], surrogate constraint relaxation in some cases provides stronger penalties than Lagrangean relaxation, and a new mathematical programming duality theory has emerged from this type of relaxation [Glover, 1973; Greenberg, 1973, 1970] that may lead to increased use. The use of knapsack methods to solve more general problems than knapsack problems occurs primarily in this setting.

The remaining form of relaxation commonly employed is a "group theoretic" relaxation that arises by dropping the nonnegativity conditions on the variables that are basic in an optimal LP solution, but retaining all integer restrictions. This relaxation can actually be viewed as an instance of generalized Lagrangean relaxation, and can be supplemented by further use of this type of relaxation, but is of unique interest due to the special group theory structure it provides. Studies of this form of relaxation may be found in [Gomory, 1967, 1972; Gomory and Johnson, 1972; Hu, 1969; Shapiro, 1971].

Finally, a duality that accommodates both generalized Lagrangean and surrogate constraint relaxation–and their composite–in a single framework is now available [Glover, 1973] and combinations of these approaches are beginning to find use in practice [Ross and Glover, 1974].

3.5.4 Practical Considerations. Some aspects of solving IP problems in practice deserve mention, together with a few accompanying cautions.

First of all, some IP problems seem to be inherently difficult to solve, regardless of the method employed. Thus, while simple approaches such as rounding may be clearly futile for such problems, there may also be no other method (currently known) that is capable of producing an optimal or even a feasible integer solution in a reasonable length of time.

Secondly, even for those problems that can be solved relatively efficiently by existing IP methods, it is a useful precaution to be skeptical about the presumed optimality of an "optimal" solution. The real world situations which IP formulations are sometimes called upon to model can be rather complex, and, the question of imperfect data entirely aside, it is easy to overlook certain aspects of these situations that should be reflected in the constraints or the objective function. In such instances an optimal IP solution may be hazardous to implement unless a number of checks and safeguards are used to make sure that the solution exhibits characteristics appropriate to the situation modeled. Indeed, on the positive side, obtaining absurd or inappropriate optimal solutions is a very useful way to identify unreasonable assumptions and inadequate information that may have gone into the model, thereby permitting an improved model to be developed.

4. INTEGER PROGRAMS WITH SPECIAL STRUCTURES

Some IP problems, such as the classical "transportation" and "assignment" problems discussed in many LP textbooks, have the fortunate property that the LP solution, or more precisely, every extreme point solution automatically assigns integer values to the variables. Consequently, the standard LP methods are entirely sufficient to solve these problems and no special IP techniques are required.

There are also other IP problems with very special structures, but that do not have the "integer extreme point" property. Most of those discussed earlier in this chapter are of such a type. For these, the LP solution generally does not provide an integer solution, and other approaches must be sought. Precisely what approach should be used to solve a specially structured problem? This question is a very difficult one, and a great deal less is known about matching IP methods to problem structures than one would prefer. Nevertheless, ignorance is not total on this issue, and guidelines are in the process of being established [Geoffrion, 1973; Geoffrion and Marsten, 1972; Klingman, Glover and Stutz,

1972; Ross and Glover, 1974; Sommer, 1972; Williams, 1973]. These guidelines must be taken cautiously, however, for approaches that initially seem ineffective in certain contexts are sometimes found to be far more effective when slightly modified or when implemented in a slightly different way. But the question of matching methods to problems also has other facets. Some problems have more than one IP formulation, and a problem that appears almost wholly intractable under one formulation may be readily solved under another. Recent disclosures in this area can be found in [Fisher and Shapiro, 1973; Geoffrion and Marsten, 1972; Glover, 1972; Sommer, 1972; Williams, 1973; Williams, 1973].

A still more basic issue for some problems is whether they should be formulated as IPs at all. Virtually every mathematical programming problem whose functions map into the field of real numbers can be approximated to an arbitrary degree of accuracy (if not precisely) by a corresponding IP problem. However, it is a pertinent question whether such "artificial" IPs are worth the bother to formulate, or whether it would be better to tackle these problems in their "natural" form with an appropriately designed solution technique. To make matters murkier, the question of what constitutes a "natural" or an "artificial" form for a problem is itself a rather difficult one. Part of the issue is clearly empirical; a new algorithm may change an "artificial" formulation into a "natural" one by readily solving problems posed in that formulation. Important advances in this area are provided by the special solution methods developed for "lattice point" and "disjunctive" problems [Cabot and Hurter, 1968; Klingman and Glover, 1973; Klingman, Glover and Stutz, 1972].

On the other hand, it is also true that part of the question of whether an IP formulation is natural or not has to do with the issue of sheer size. A variety of NLPs and combinatorial optimization problems tend to "blow-up" when formulated as IPs. A problem that appears to involve a modest number of parameters and restrictions in a nonlinear or combinatorial formulation may easily turn out to have a staggering number of variables and constraints in an IP guise. Another caution at this point: it's not entirely clear that size should be the bugbear it is sometimes taken to be. Frequently accompanying the problem "blow up" is a corresponding reduction in its "density." That is, the problem matrices corresponding to these large IPs are usually exceedingly sparse, containing only a small number of nonzero elements. The development of special computer techniques for handling sparse matrices has been very active in recent years and may conceivably revise some of our opinions about the formidability of certain classes of "large" IPs in the near future. This is particularly true for problems involving imbedded networks, due to substantial recent advances in handling network structures [Charnes, et al., 1973; Glover, et al., 1974].

On the other hand, special problem structures often suggest special approaches for accommodating them. It is a truism that there nearly always exists a special method that is more efficient for such problems than a general method. (Again, applications involving imbedded networks offer a case in point.) Indeed, the general method itself, adapted and tailored to the special structure, is usually an example of a "more efficient special method." It frequently occurs that special methods devised for combinatorial (and even some nonlinear) problems are in fact refinements of more general IP methods.

Finally, a truly significant area that is forever being rediscovered, fleetingly heralded for its importance, and then somehow submerged in the rush to devise more foolproof and rigorously founded approaches, is that of heuristics. In the present context, heuristics refer to intelligent schemes for obtaining "good" solutions. Such schemes typically provide no assurance of obtaining optimal solutions, or even ultimately of obtaining *any* solution. A systematic cataloguing of the features of good heuristic methods in IP and combinatorics is not an easy thing, though a few attempts have been made [Bradley, 1971; Cooper and Drebes, 1967; Glover, 1967; Hillier, 1969].

In the real world, the mathematical guarantee of "convergence to an optimum in a finite number of steps" can amount to a warranty that a solution will be obtained one day before doomsday (optimistically speaking, in the case of some IP problems). Consequently, the usefulness of a particular algorithm can well be said to depend on its "heuristic content." In this view, which gradually seems to be gaining in favor, the active pursuit of heuristic principles may hold promise of unlocking doors that presently remain closed, leading to the efficient implementation of IP in what are presently "hard" problem areas.

REFERENCES

1. Balas, Egon, "Discrete Programming by the Filter Method," *Operations Res.* **19**: 915–957 (1967).
2. ——, "The Intersection Cut–A New Cutting Plane for Integer Programming," *Operations Res.* **19**: 19–39 (1970).
3. ——, "Integer Programming and Convex Analysis: Intersection Cuts from Outer Polars," *Math. Prog.* **2**: 330–382 (1972).
4. ——, "On the Use of Intersection Cuts in Branch and Bound," paper presented at the Eighth International Symposium on Mathematical Programming, Stanford (August 1973).
5. Beale, E. M. L., "Sparseness in Linear Programming," in *Large Sparse Sets of Linear Equations*, pp. 1–15, ed. J. K. Reid, Academic Press, London (1971).
6. Benders, J. F., "Partitioning Procedures for Solving Mixed-Variables Programming Problems," *Numerische Mathematik* **4**: 238–252 (1962).
7. Bowman, V. J., and G. L. Nemhauser, "Deep Cuts in Integer Programming," *Opsearch* **8**: 89–111 (1971).
8. Bradley, G. H., "Heuristic Solution Methods and Transformed Integer Linear Programming Problems," Yale Report No. 43 (March 1971).
9. Bradley, G. H., P. L. Hammer, and L. A. Wolsey, "Coefficient Reduction for Inequalities in 0-1 Variables," *Math. Prog.* **7**: 263–282 (1974).

10. Burdet, C. A., "Polaroids: A New Tool in Non-Convex and in Integer Programming," *Nav. Res. Log. Quart.* **20:** 13–24 (1973).
11. —— and E. L. Johnson, "A Subadditive Approach to the Group Problem of Integer Programming," released by the Mathematical Sciences Department, IBM Watson Research Center, Yorktown Heights, New York (September 1973).
12. Cabot, V. A., "An Enumeration Algorithm for Knapsack Problems," *Operations Res.* **18:** 306–311 (1970).
13. —— and A. P. Hurter, "An Approach to 0–1 Integer Programming," *Operations Res.* **16:** 1206–1211 (1968).
14. Charnes, A., F. Glover, D. Karney, D. Klingman, and J. Stutz, "Past, Present and Future of Development, Computational Efficiency, and Practical Use of Large-Scale Transportation and Transhipment Computer Codes," *Computers and Operations Reseach*, **2:** 71–82 (1975).
15. Cooper, L. and C. Drebes, "Investigations in Integer Linear Programming by Direct Search Methods," Report No. COO-1493-10, Washington University (1967).
16. Dakin, R. J., "A Tree Search Algorithm for Mixed Integer Programming Problems," *Computer J.* **8:** 250–255 (1965).
17. Everett, H., "Generalized Lagrange Multiplier Method for Solving Problems of Optimum Allocation of Resources," *Operations Res.* **11:** 399–417 (1963).
18. Fisher, M. L., and J. F. Shapiro, "Constructive Duality in Integer Programming," *SIAM J. Appl. Math.* **27:** 31-52 (1974).
19. Frank, M., and P. Wolfe, "An Algorithm for Quadratic Programming," *Nav. Res. Log. Quart.* **3:** 95–110 (1956).
20. Garfinkel, R. S. and G. L. Nemhauser, *Integer Programming*, John Wiley & Sons, New York (1972).
21. Geoffrion, A. M., "An Improved Implicit Enumeration Approach for Integer Programming," *Operations Res.* **17:** 437–454 (1969).
22. ——, "Lagrangean Relaxation for Integer Programming," *Math. Programming Study*, **2:** 82-114 (1974).
23. ——, "Duality in Nonlinear Programming," *SIAM Rev.* **13-1:** 1–37 (January 1971).
24. —— and R. E. Marsten, "Integer Programming Algorithms: A Framework and State-of-the-Art Survey," *Management Sci.* **18:** 465–491 (1972).
25. Glover, F., "Surrogate Constraints," *Operations Res.* **16:** 741–749 (1968).
26. Glover, Fred, "Heuristics for Integer Programming Using Surrogate Constraints," *Decision Sciences*, **8:** 156–166 (1977).
27. ——, "Convexity Cuts and Cut Search," December 1969, published in *Operations Res.* **21:** 123–134 (1973).
28. ——, "Improved Linear Representations of Nonlinear Integer," *Management Sci.* **22:** 455–460 (1975).
29. ——, "Surrogate Constraint Duality in Mathematical Programming," *Operations Res.* **23:** 434–451 (1975).
30. ——, D. Karney, D. Klingman, and A. Napier, "A Computation Study on Start Procedures, Basis Change Criteria, and Solution Algorithms for Transportation Problems," *Management Sci.* **20:** 793–813 (1974).
31. Gomory, R. E., "An Algorithm for Integer Solutions for Linear Programs," in *Recent Advances in Mathematical Programming*, pp. 269–302, R. L. Graves and P. Wolfe, eds., McGraw-Hill (1963).
32. ——, "An Algorithm for the Mixed Integer Problem," RM-2597, RAND Corporation (1960).
33. ——, "Faces of an Integer Polyhedron," *Proc. Nat. Acad. of Sci.* **57:** 16–18 (1967).

34. —— and E. L. Johnson, "Some Continuous Functions Related to Corner Polyhedra," *Math. Prog.* **3**: 23–85 (1972).
35. —— and E. L. Johnson, "Some Continuous Functions Related to Corner Polyhedra, II," *Math. Prog.* **3**: 359–389 (1972).
36. Greenberg, Harvey J., "The Generalized Penalty Function Surrogate Model," *Operations Res.* **21**: 162–178 (1973).
37. —— and W. P. Pierskalla, "Surrogate Mathematical Programs," *Operations Res.* **18**: 924–939 (1970).
38. Hammer, P. L. and S. Rudeanu, "Boolean Methods in Operations Research and Related Areas," Springer-Verlag, Berlin-Heidelberg-New York (1968).
39. Hammer, P. L., E. L. Johnson, and U. N. Peled, "Facets of Regular 0–1 Polytopes," *Math. Prog.* **8**: 179–206 (1975).
40. Held, M. and R. M. Karp, "The Traveling Salesman Problem and Minimum Spanning Trees," *Operations Res.* **18**: 1138–1162 (1970).
41. Hillier, F. S., "Efficient Heuristic Procedures for Integer Linear Programming with an Interior," *Operations Res.* **17**: 600–637 (1969).
42. ——, "A Bound-and-Scan Algorithm for Pure Integer Linear Programming with General Variables," *Operations Res.* **17**: 638–679 (1969).
43. Hogan, W. W., "Convergence Results for Some Extensions of the Frank-Wolfe Method," Working Paper No. 169, Western Management Science Institute, University of California, Los Angeles (January 1971).
44. Hu, T. C., *Integer Programming and Network Flows*, Addison-Wesley (1969).
45. Jeroslow, R. G., "The Either-Or Cut from Convex Domains," Carnegie-Mellon University (September 1973).
46. ——, "The Principles of Cutting-Plane Theory: Part I," preliminary report, Carnegie-Mellon University (February 1974).
47. Klingman, D. and F. Glover, "The Generalized Lattice Point Problem," *Operations Res.* **21**: 141–156 (1973).
48. Klingman, D., F. Glover, and J. Stutz, "The Disjunctive Facet Problem: Formulation and Solution Techniques," *Management Sci.* **22**: 582–601 (1974).
49. McDaniel, D. and M. Devine, "Alternative Benders-Based Partitioning Procedures for Mixed Integer Programming," School of Industrial Engineering, University of Oklahoma (May 1973).
50. Lemke, C. E. and K. Spielberg, "Direct Search Zero-One and Mixed Integer Programming," *Operations Res.* **15**: 892–914 (1967).
51. Padberg, Manfred W., "Equivalent Knapsack-type Formulations of Bounded Integer Linear Programs," Management Sciences Research Report No. 227, Carnegie-Mellon University (September 1970).
52. Ross, T. and F. Glover, "Strong Penalty Calculations for a Class of 0–1 Programs," MSRS 74-5, University of Colorado (April 1974).
53. Salkin, H. M., "On the Merit of the Generalized Origin and Restarts in Implicit Enumeration," *Operations Res.* **18**: 549–554 (1970).
54. Shapiro, J. F., "Generalized Lagrange Multipliers in Integer Programming," *Operations Res.* **19**: 68–76 (1971).
55. Sommer, D., "Computational Experience with the Ophelie Mixed Integer Code," Control Data Corp., Minneapolis (May 1972).
56. Sommer, D. and F. Glover, "Pitfalls of Rounding in Discrete Management Decision Problems," *Decision Sciences* **6**: 211–220 (1975).
57. Tomlin, J. A., "An Improved Branch and Bound Method for Integer Programming," *Operations Res.* **19**: 1070–1075 (July-August 1971).
58. ——, "Survey of Computational Methods for Solving Large Scale Systems," Technical

Report 72-25, Department of Operations Research, Stanford University (October 1972).
59. Williams, A. C., "Some Modeling Principles for M.I.P.'s," paper presented at the VIII International Symposium on Mathematical Programming, Stanford University (August 1973) (author at Mobil Oil Corp., Princeton, N.J.).
60. Williams, H. P., "Experiments in the Formulation of Integer Programming Problems," *Math. Programming Study* **2,** 180-197 (1974).
61. Young, R. D., "Hypercylindrically Deduced Cuts in Zero-One Integer Programming," *Operations Res.* **19:** 1393-1405 (1971).
62. ——, "A Primal (All-Integer) Integer Programming Algorithm," *J. of Res., Nat. Bureau of Stand. Section B, Math. and Mathematical Physics* **69B (3):** 213-250 (July-September 1965).
63. ——, "A Simplified Primal (All-Integer) Integer Programming Algorithm," *Operations Res.* **16:** 750-782 (1968).
64. Zionts, Stanley, *Linear and Integer Programming*, Prentice-Hall (1974).

II-3

GRAPH THEORY: SOME METHODS AND APPLICATIONS

Thomas L. Saaty
University of Pennsylvania

1. INTRODUCTION

Even though some people have attempted to treat it as a theory, for the most part graph theory is not an integrated theory. Instead, it is basically a variety of ideas arising from attempts to solve concrete problems. Perhaps some historical perspective will help illustrate this point.

Graph theory had its origins in the eighteenth century in the town of Königsberg, Prussia, where some people wondered whether one can take a tour of the city, crossing each of the seven bridges once and only once. The famous mathematician, Euler, both mathematically formulated and solved this problem. His answer (in the negative to this problem) will be studied later.

In the nineteenth century there arose in England another formidable problem of mathematics which properly belongs in graph theory. It is the four color problem: is it possible to color any map drawn in the plane or on a sphere with four colors so that no two neighboring regions have the same color? Only very recently has this problem been solved. We shall have more to say about it below.

In the twentieth century, graph theory gradually acquired status until it became recognized as a formal discipline with the publication of König's book, *Theorie der endlichen und unendlichen Graphen* in the 1930s [König, 1950].

In simple terms a graph represents relations between sets of objects and graph theory is directed towards studying some of the many possible properties of these objects within the representation. To be more specific, a graph is a collection of points and lines connecting these points. Such connections can have many characteristics and graph theory is essentially the study of these characteristics. Note that a graph here is not the kind of graph one sees in analytic geometry and calculus books where position of points and slopes and lengths of lines play such an important part. There is a freer form here, with the important considerations being which points are connected to which other points. Sometimes the order of connection is also important.

Because of the generality of graph theory, its boundaries and basic concepts have been extended far. At present, graphs are used to model a variety of problems that deal with the discrete arrangements of objects. Here is a list of some [Busacker and Saaty, 1965] : Design and Analysis of Communication Networks; Analysis of Electrical Networks; Analysis of Printed Circuits Boards; Signal Flow Graphs and Feedback Theory; Wiring Panel Problems; Computer Flow Charts; Study of Automation; Analysis and Synthesis of Logical Networks; Scheduling Problems; Most Efficient Production Line; Logistics; Information Retrieval; Information Theory; Investment Strategy; Brand Analysis; Traffic Studies; Distribution of Utilities; Simulation; Data Flow; Economic Problems; Sensitivity of a Structure; Game Theory; Genetics; Biology; Behavioral Science; Puzzles; Genealogy; Architectural Design; Wind Effects on Trajectories; The ISING Problem; Crystallography; Cryptography; Feynman Diagrams; Chemical Identification; Chemical Reaction Mechanisms; Theorem Proving.

Aside from its usefulness in all these areas of applications, graph theory is an interesting subject on its own because it furnishes a host of unsolved problems which are easy for junior mathematicians and laymen to understand, but are exceedingly challenging and difficult to solve, even for the experts.

Essentially, graph theoretic problems come in two forms. One form asks "are there any and if so, how many or at most how many" objects which have a certain property. The other asks "how" to construct a graph or subgraph satisfying a certain property. Sometimes one also characterizes graphs by giving conditions which they must satisfy in order to have a certain property. We will illustrate this later.

Extensive research is going on in all facets of the subject. The *Journal of Combinatorial Theory* published by the Academic Press is dedicated to combinatorial and graph theories. Books that are proceedings of symposia on the subject are being published regularly. I have confined the list of references mostly to books because otherwise it would be impossible to do justice to the literature as a whole. An excellent bibliography has appeared in the book edited by Harary on *Proof Techniques in Graph Theory* [Harary, 1969b].

To give the reader an overview of the field, I have attempted to structure the subject in a chart along the various lines of its development. Some of the concepts delineated in the chart will be defined later. Many are not defined because,

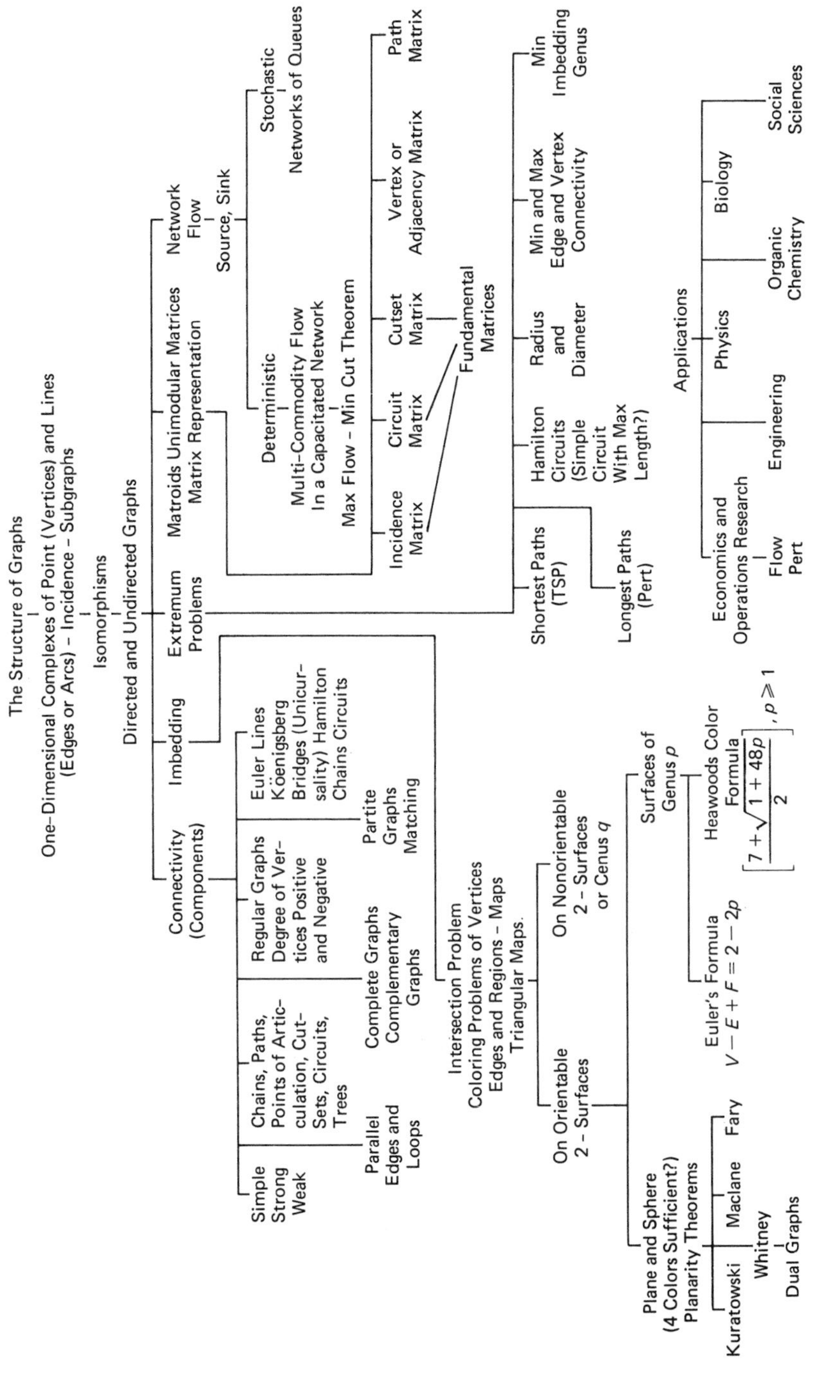
The Structure of Graphs
One-Dimensional Complexes of Point (Vertices) and Lines (Edges or Arcs) - Incidence - Subgraphs
Isomorphisms
Directed and Undirected Graphs
Connectivity (Components)
Imbedding
Extremum Problems
Matroids Unimodular Matrices Matrix Representation
Network Flow
Source, Sink
Deterministic
Multi-Commodity Flow In a Capacitated Network
Max Flow - Min Cut Theorem
Stochastic
Networks of Queues
Simple Strong Weak
Chains, Paths, Points of Artic-culation, Cut-Sets, Circuits, Trees
Regular Graphs Degree of Ver-tices Positive and Negative
Euler Lines Köenigsberg Bridges (Unicur-sality) Hamilton Chains Circuits
Parallel Edges and Loops
Complete Graphs Complementary Graphs
Partite Graphs Matching
Incidence Matrix
Circuit Matrix
Cutset Matrix
Vertex or Adjacency Matrix
Path Matrix
Fundamental Matrices
Intersection Problem
Coloring Problems of Vertices Edges and Regions - Maps Triangular Maps.
On Orientable 2 - Surfaces
On Nonorientable 2 - Surfaces or Cenus q
Plane and Sphere (4 Colors Sufficient?) Planarity Theorems
Kuratowski
Maclane
Fary
Whitney
Dual Graphs
Euler's Formula $V - E + F = 2 - 2p$
Surfaces of Genus p
Heawoods Color Formula $\left[\frac{7 + \sqrt{1 + 48p}}{2}\right], p \geqslant 1$
Shortest Paths (TSP)
Longest Paths (Pert)
Hamilton Circuits (Simple Circuit With Max Length?)
Radius and Diameter
Min and Max Edge and Vertex Connectivity
Min Imbedding Genus
Applications
Economics and Operations Research
Flow Pert
Engineering
Physics
Organic Chemistry
Biology
Social Sciences

due to space limitation, it is pointless to introduce them and not write more about them. It would be difficult to give an interesting (nondry) condensed presentation of the entire subject and hence I have attempted to focus attention on some of the main highlights from each of the major areas of the chart. Nevertheless, references in all areas are given in the chart.

The study of graphs can be divided into five major areas of interest: Connectivity, Imbedding, Extremum Problems, Matrices and Matroids, and Network Flows (see chart). As we shall see these fields are not independent of one another but are interrelated with substantial overlap.

After laying down some basic definitions and concepts we shall go into the first four areas of interest, since Network Flow is presented separately in Chapter II-4 of this handbook. Integer programming, discussed in Chapter II-2, also touches on graph theory. Whenever space and brevity permit we shall (1) define basic and related terminologies, (2) present a concrete example for motivation, (3) construct a model and/or count the number of cases with a given property, (4) briefly indicate an algorithm and illustrate a proof, and (5) give related applications. At the same time, we will indicate some unsolved problems whenever possible.

2. BASIC DEFINITIONS

A *graph* is an ordered pair (V, E) where V is a nonempty set, called the set of *vertices; E* is an unordered binary relation on V, (i.e., if $(u \,\&\, v)$ is in $V \,\&\, V$ then $(u \,\&\, v) = (v \,\&\, u)$). E is called the set of *edges.* An edge in E is said to be *incident* with the vertices it joins. The above is the definition of an *undirected graph* which is completely defined by listing all vertices and stating which pairs have a connecting edge. A *directed graph* is an ordered pair (V, E) with V being the set of vertices, and E being an ordered relation on V (i.e., $V \times V$). Then E is called a set of *arcs.* The first and second vertices of an arc are called the *initial* and *terminal* vertices respectively.

A graph (V', E') is a *subgraph* of the graph (V, E) if V', E' are contained in V, E; respectively. Throughout the chapter we shall limit our discussion to graphs with finite number of edges, called *finite graphs.*

A *loop* is an edge, both of whose end points coincide. The *degree* (or valence) of a vertex is the number of edges incident with that vertex. *The multiplicity* of a pair of vertices is the number of edges joining them.

In an undirected (directed) graph a sequence of n edges (arcs) $e_1, \ldots, e_n$ is called an *edge (arc) progression* of length n if there exists an appropriate sequence of $n + 1$ (not necessarily distinct) vertices $v_0, v_1, \ldots, v_n$ such that e_i is incident with $(v_{i-1} \,\&\, v_i)$, $i = 1, \ldots, n$. The edge (arc) progression is *closed* (*open*) if $v_0 = v_n$ $(v_0 \neq v_n)$. If $e_i \neq e_j$ for all i and j, $i \neq j$, the edge (arc) progression is called a *chain(path) progression.* The set of edges (arcs) is said to form a *chain(path).* The chain(path) is a *circuit(cycle)* if $v_0 = v_n$. If the vertices are also distinct, we have a *simple chain(cycle).* The length of (number of edges in) a longest simple circuit is called the *circumference* of the graph. Frequently one abbreviates a "simple circuit" ("simple cycle") by a "circuit" ("cycle"). In all these cases the definitions are concerned with tracing a set of edges in the graph without repetition of any edge. However, in an edge progression, for example, vertices may be encountered more than once.

A graph is *connected* if every pair of vertices can be joined by a chain. A graph which is not connected may be decomposed into a finite number of connected subgraphs called *components* or *pieces.* The *connectivity* of a graph is the smallest number of vertices which can be removed to disconnect the graph. A *cutset* of a graph is a minimal set of edges whose removal increases the number of components. A graph is *complete* if every vertex is connected by an edge to every other vertex. A graph is *bipartite* if its vertices can be partitioned into two sets so that every edge joins a vertex of one set with a vertex of the other set. (Note that not every vertex of one set need be incident with every vertex of the other). A connected graph is *regular* if all its vertices have the same degree.

In an undirected graph a *tree* is a connected subgraph without circuits. It is a *spanning tree* if it includes all the vertices of the graph. A directed tree has a *root* at a vertex v if there is a path from v to every other vertex. The edges of a graph which belong to a spanning tree are called *branches.* All other edges are called *chords.*

A directed graph is said to be *strongly connected* if for every two vertices u and v there is a path from u to v and a path from v to u. In a connected graph, a vertex is said to be an *articulation point* if the vertex can be removed leaving behind an unconnected graph.

A graph is *planar* if it can be embedded (drawn) in a plane such that no two edges meet except at a vertex.

A *planar map* is a planar graph together with the regions or faces (often called countries) into which its simple circuits divide the plane such that each edge bounds exactly two regions. (Two adjacent edges which bound the same two regions may be replaced by a single edge bounding these regions.) More generally, a map M is a graph G together with a surface S on which G is drawn in such a way that edges intersect only at their end points. The map M is said to be an embedding of the graph G in the surface S.

A *proper n-coloring* of a map is an assignment of one of n colors to each country such that no two countries having a boundary edge in common are colored the same. (Hereafter we shall only be concerned with proper colorings).

A surface is *nonorientable* if one can choose a direction of rotation about a

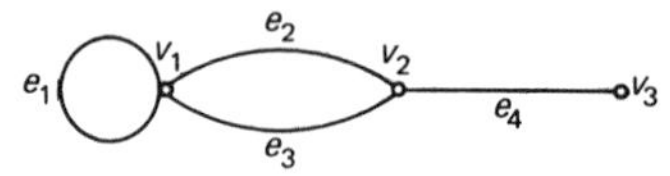

Fig. 1.

point and then move the point around the surface with preservation of the direction of rotation and arrange it so that when the point is returned to the original position the direction of rotation is different from the original one. (The Möbius strip is such an example.) Otherwise the surface is *orientable.*

A *factor* of a graph G is a subgraph which includes all the vertices but is not totally disconnected. An *n-factor* is regular of degree n. A graph G is a sum of factors if it is their edge disjoint union. In that case one has a *factorization* of G.

Two graphs are said to be *isomorphic* iff there is a 1-1 correspondence between their vertices which is also a 1-1 correspondence between their edges, with all the incidences preserved.

Remark: An isomorphism of a graph with itself is called an *automorphism.* An automorphism is a permutation of the vertices which preserves adjacency. An automorphism followed by another automorphism is also an automorphism. Actually this set of automorphisms forms a group known as the *group of the graph.* The problem as to when a given abstract group is isomorphic with the group of some graph has been solved. Its answer is that every group is the group of some graph [Harary, 1969a].

It may be helpful to the reader to relate the relevant definitions to Figs. 1 and 2.

In this graph e_1 is a loop; e_2 and e_3 are parallel edges; v_2 and v_3 are adjacent vertices; e_2 and e_4 are adjacent edges. Denote the number of elements in a set S as $|S|$, so $|V|$ is the number of vertices and $|E|$ is the number of edges.

In Fig. 2, $e_1 e_2 e_3 e_4 e_2$ is an edge progression; $e_1 e_2 e_3 e_4$ is a chain; $e_1 e_2 e_3 e_4 e_8 e_7$ is a circuit; $e_1 e_2 e_3$ is a simple chain; $e_2 e_3 e_4$ is a simple circuit; e_5 is a cutset.

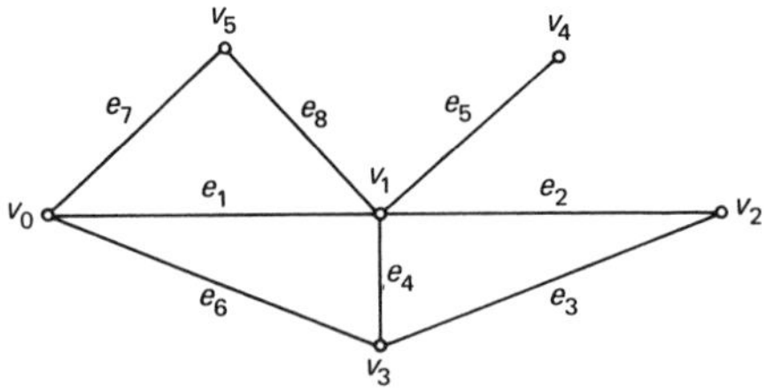

Fig. 2.

3. CONNECTIVITY

3.1 Euler Path

One of the earliest problems in graph theory is known as the "Königsberg bridge problem" and intrigued the inhabitants of this Prussian town until solved by Euler in 1736. Euler wrote:

> In the town of Königsberg in Prussia there is an island A, called "Kneiphof," with the two branches of the river (Pregel) flowing around it (as shown in Fig. 3). There are seven bridges, a, b, c, d, e, f, and g, crossing the two branches. The question is whether a person can plan a walk in such a way that he will cross each of these bridges once but not more than once.

We can associate a vertex with each land region and join two vertices with an edge whenever there is a bridge between corresponding regions. This gives a graph associated with the map (Fig. 4).

A *Euler path* in a graph G is a path containing each edge of G exactly once. Euler showed that such a path is possible if and only if no more than two vertices of G have odd degree and G is connected (an obviously necessary condition). Since there are four vertices of odd degree, the answer to the Königsberg bridge problem is negative. If the graph has exactly two odd vertices, A and B, then a Euler path must have A and B as end vertices. If no vertices are odd, the graph contains a closed Euler path.

To show how to construct a Euler path, let G be any graph with exactly two odd vertices A and B. Starting at vertex A, follow a set of edges as far as possible without repeating any edge. This path cannot dead-end at an even vertex because each time such a vertex is crossed by the path, two of its edges are used. Also the path cannot stop at A because the first edge of the path is adjacent to vertex A leaving an even number of unused edges for subsequent crossings through A. Thus, the path dead-ends only at the other end vertex B. If all edges are included in the path, then it is the desired Euler path. If not, we delete

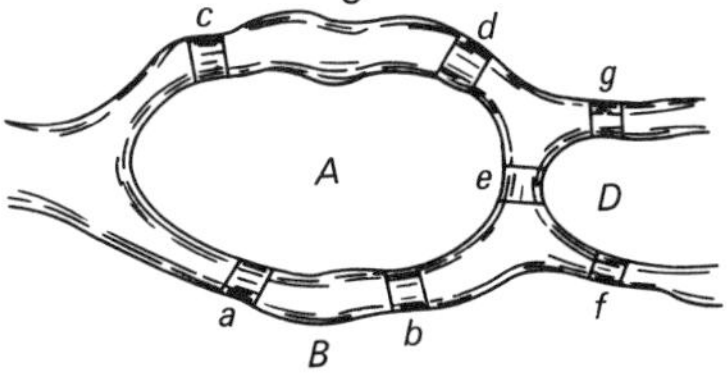

Fig. 3. Map.

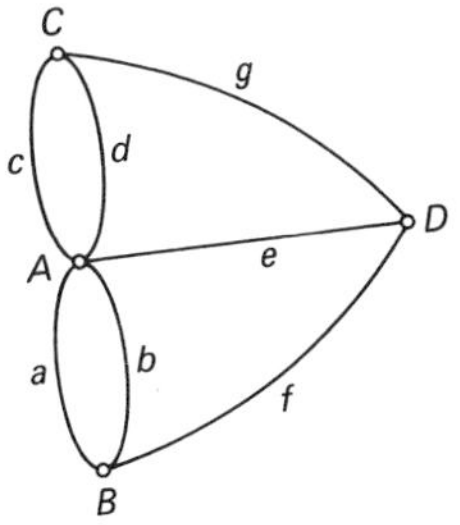

Fig. 4. Graph.

its edges from G and obtain a new graph G', whose vertex degrees are all even since the path meets each vertex through an even number (possibly zero) of edges with the exception of A and B. Since G is connected, there is a vertex C on the path which is contained in an edge of G'. We construct a new path in G' starting at C, which must return to C because all vertex degrees of G' are even. We enlarge the first path to the "spliced" path from A to C, then along the second path from C to C and finally from C to B. We repeat the process until all edges of G are included. It can be shown by a similar argument that a graph with $2n > 0$ odd vertices can be covered by exactly n paths. (See [Busacker and Saaty, 1965])

An interesting problem has to do with arranging city streets as one-way or two-way streets for traffic control purposes. Whenever possible, as many streets as possible are to become one-way streets. What are the conditions to be satisfied by the street plan so that one can go from any point of the city to any other? It turns out that one can do this if all the streets lying on circuits are oriented in the same way and all the streets not on any circuit are left as two-way streets.

3.2 Hamiltonian Path

The Irish mathematician Sir William Rowan Hamilton invented a game in the nineteenth century and sold it for 25 pounds. It consisted of a dodecahedron (See Fig. 5) whose vertices were assigned names of famous cities and the problem was to pass a string from one vertex to another (all marked by nails) passing through each vertex only once and covering all vertices.

A graph G is said to be *Hamiltonian* if there is a simple circuit (called a *Hamiltonian circuit*) which passes through all the vertices of G. The graph of Fig. 5 has such a circuit but the one in Fig. 6 does not, although it has a simple path which passes through all vertices (known as a *Hamiltonian path*). A graph with a Hamiltonian circuit is called a *Hamiltonian Graph*. A complete graph always has a Hamiltonian circuit. The following statement is equivalent to the four-color problem: Every Hamiltonian planar graph is four-colorable.

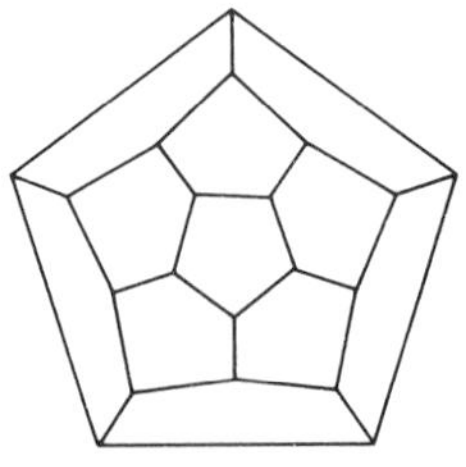

Fig. 5.

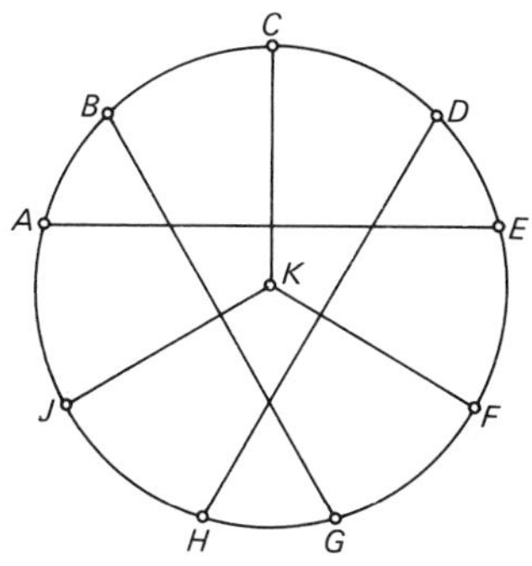

Fig. 6.

The traveling salesman problem (TSP) is a member of a more general class of mathematical programming problems. It can be simply stated as follows:

Find a route for a traveling salesman who has to visit $(n - 1)$ cities in sequence and return to his home city, such that the total mileage of his journey is minimized and each city is visited exactly once. Thus among all Hamiltonian circuits in the complete graph on n vertices we wish to find one the total sum of the lengths of whose arcs is a minimum. An algebraic formulation and attack on this unsolved problem (as far as finding an efficient algorithm is concerned) is given in Hu [1969].

The routing of a school bus that has to collect students from certain sections of a city is also a TSP. The problem of scheduling a number of jobs on a single machine in which the total changeover time (time to prepare the machine for the subsequent job) is to be minimized is equivalent to the TSP. Each city corresponds to a job; the distance between cities corresponds to the changeover time for each pair of jobs, and the total travel distance corresponds to the total changeover time.

3.3 A Hamiltonian Circuit in a Directed Graph

The map below (Fig. 7) represents a one-way street system of a certain university city, the direction in which travel is allowed being indicated by arrows. An undergraduate living at A wishes to cycle round the city, visiting each intersection just once, and returning to A. What route must he take?

3.4 Regular Graphs

A problem concerning regular graphs deals with shortest circuits. Suppose G is a regular graph of degree r, without loops, and suppose the length of a circuit

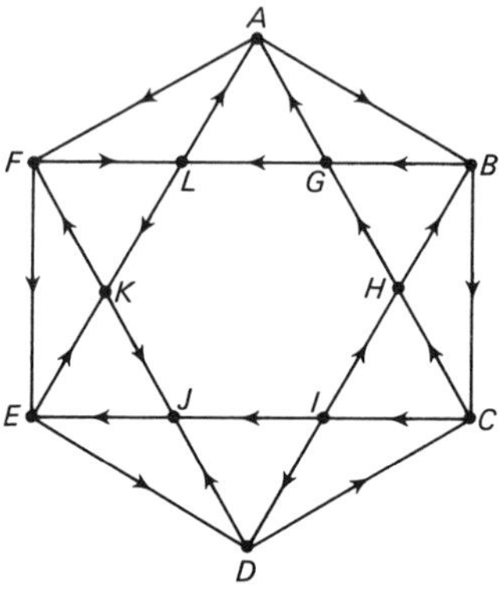

Fig. 7.

is measured by the number of its edges. The shortest circuits in G, if they exist, are called *girdles* and the length of a girdle is called the *girth* of G. We cite below certain results among several which have been found [Sachs, in Fiedler (1964), pp. 91-97].

Denote by $G(n, r, k)$, for $r \geqslant 3$ and $k \geqslant 2$, a graph having order n, being regular of degree r, and having girth k. The following theorem concerns such graphs.

For any three integers $r \geqslant 3$, $k \geqslant 2$, and $d \geqslant 1$ a graph $G = G(n, r, k)$ can always be constructed having these properties:

1. G has a Hamiltonian circuit.
2. The girdles of G are mutually disjoint and the collection of all girdles is a 2-factor Q of G.
3. If the edges of Q are removed from G, the remaining graph decomposes into $r - 2$ 1-factors.
4. The number of girdles contained in G is divisible by d.

3.5 Trees and Spanning Trees

Let $T_{n,k}$ denote the number of graphs with $n + k - 1$ labeled vertices $P_1, P_2, \ldots,$ P_{n+k-1} which consist of k disjoint trees as subgraphs and are such that the points $P_1, P_2, \ldots, P_k$ belong to different subgraphs. Cayley gives the following formula for $T_{n,k}$

$$T_{n,k} = k(n + k - 1)^{n-2}$$

Clearly $T_{n,1} = T_n$, where T_n is the number of trees in a complete graph.

The number $T_{n,k}$ can be interpreted as follows: If there are $n + k - 1$ cities among which k cities are lying on the bank of the same river (or sea), then $T_{n,k}$ is the number of such minimal railway nets connecting some of the cities, that it is possible to go from any city to any other by traveling by railway along the net and eventually traveling by ship from one of the cities lying at the river to another such city. Thus, the railway-nets in question will consist of k subnets, such that every city lying at the bank of the river belongs to another subnet, and if the cities A and B belong to the same subnet, one can go by railway from A to B, but if A and B belong to different subnets, one can travel from A to B by going first by train to the harbor-city belonging to the same subnet as A, then by ship to the harbor-city belonging to the same net as B and finally by train to B.

Incidentally it was also Cayley who conjectured that the number of trees in a complete graph with n labeled vertices is n^{n-2}. A proof of this fact is given in [Busacker and Saaty, 1965].

An algorithm for constructing a spanning tree of minimum length in a connected graph $G(V, E)$ with n vertices is as follows:

(1) Let $i = 1$;
(2) Choose the shortest edge of G as the first edge of the spanning tree T, call it t_i;
(3) Increase i by one;
(4) Among the edges of G, not yet chosen, choose the shortest edge which does not form a circuit with the edges formerly chosen. Call this new edge t_i;
(5) If $i < (n - 1)$ go to Step (3), otherwise stop.

One can prove that the edges $t_1, \ldots, t_{n-1}$ (where the length of $t_i <$ the length of t_{i+1} for $i = 1, 2, \ldots, n - 2$) found above, form the unique minimum spanning tree of G, if the lengths of the edges in G are all distinct.

Figure 8 is an example to which this algorithm has been applied yielding a minimum spanning tree whose edges are indicated on the right. Here are examples of applications of spanning trees. It is desired to connect n cities by railroad lines in such a way that no superfluous connections are built. In how many ways can the system be constructed? Suppose that the cost of construc-

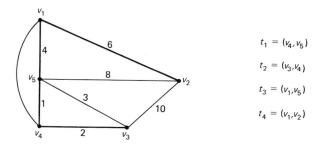

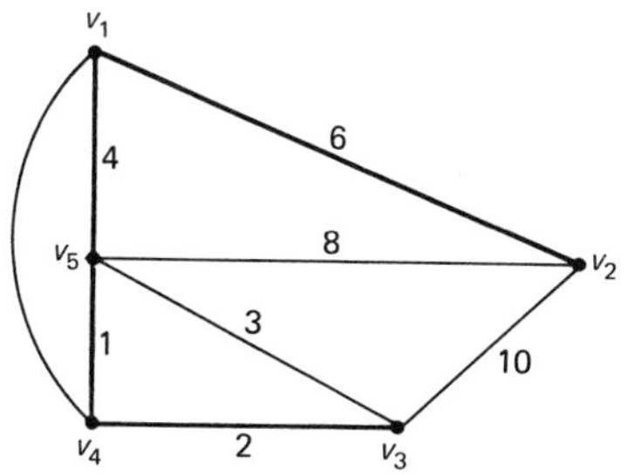

$t_1 = (v_4, v_5)$

$t_2 = (v_3, v_4)$

$t_3 = (v_1, v_5)$

$t_4 = (v_1, v_2)$

Fig. 8.

tion of railroad lines is known and equals $u(a, b)$ for a pair of cities a and b. How can one build a road net connecting all the cities at the smallest possible cost? A similar question arises when building electrical networks. These problems can be restated in terms of spanning trees of a graph.

Trees can be used in the study of dynamic storage allocation for computers. A computer program may consist of several subprograms invoked, or called, from higher level programs. Although with recursive subprograms, a sequence of calls from the highest level program to a given subprogram may contain loops, we will consider only sequences which are simple chains for simplicity's sake. As a consequence, the sequences of invocation has no loops. Since all subprograms must have been called from some other subprogram, the graph of invocations is a tree [Holt, 1961].

Associated with each subprogram are certain demands for the use of core (fast) storage in the computer—for the storage of the subprogram itself, for its data, and for the record keeping information needed to keep track of the storage assigned to it. The latter information is needed by the allocator to know what portions of storage belong to the subprogram so the storage space may be free for other uses when the subprogram (including all of its descendants) is no longer active.

An example (Fig. 9) will illustrate how this is done: The S_i are subprograms and the direction of an arc joining two subprograms is from the calling program to that called.

A particular subprogram, S_4, for example remains in fast storage until the whole program is complete or the space it occupies in storage is needed for other subprograms. Note that if a particular subprogram is active, all subprograms on the path between this subprogram and the root are also considered active. When storage in the core is exhausted, the allocator gets more by moving an inactive subprogram to auxiliary storage (which is large, but slow). Now the storage

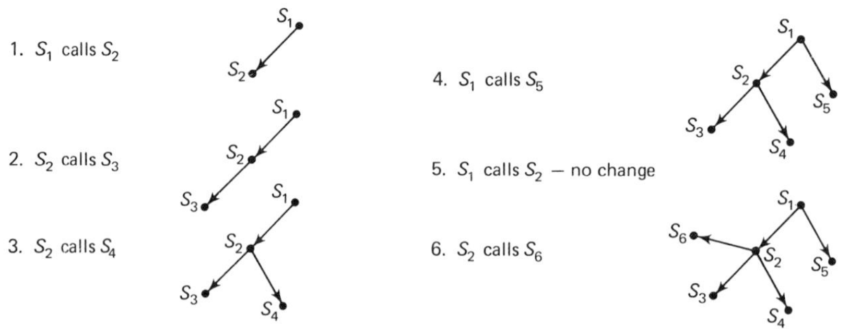

Fig. 9.

which that subprogram occupied is free for other uses. Later, if that subprogram is needed, it will be retrieved from auxiliary storage.

If the allocator were to scan these trees, it would need to keep track of which nodes remained to be scanned. This requires a variable amount of storage (push down list scan). To prevent this, the tree is "threaded" with chords as follows:

Let $L(v_0)$ be the tree distance from the root v_p to v_0 which is any vertex other than v_p. For each such v_0, let v_k, $k = 1, \ldots, n$ be the n vertices adjacent to v_0 for which $L(v_k) > L(v_0)$. For each v_k, $k = 1, \ldots, n$ add an arc from v_{k-1} to v_k (for $k > 2$ this is a chord of the tree). Connect v_p by arcs to $v \neq v_0$ vertices adjacent to it (if any). Each vertex v_k is connected (by a path) to every vertex to which v_0 is connected. The new set of arcs also forms a rooted tree with the same number of vertices (and edges) as the original (Fig. 10).

Example:

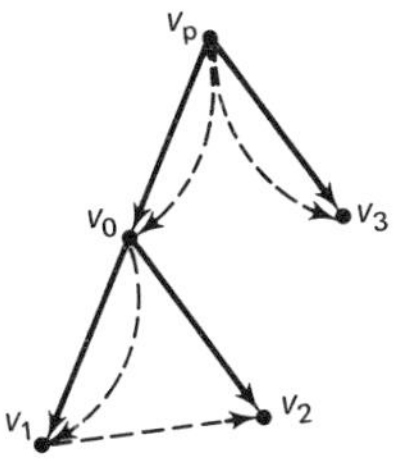

The original tree is represented by solid lines, the new one by dotted lines.

Fig. 10.

3.6 Shortest and Longest Paths

Algorithms for shortest and longest paths (or chains as the case may be) for travel between two points of a connected graph have several applications. The utility of studying shortest path problems evokes immediate intuitive apprecia-tion involving economy of effort. Longer paths occur in critical path planning where it is desired to time-sequence a production process in order to complete its various phases in a synchronous manner. Those that take the longest time must be constantly and carefully supported with men and materiél. Shorter ones can be appropriately deferred. The immediate effect of such algorithms on the real world was to revolutionize transportation routing problems.

The following is the fundamental problem of shortest chains.

If to every edge a_{ij} of the network is associated a distance d_{ij}, we are interested in finding a chain from v_0 to v_t with the sum of $\{d_{ij}\}$ in the chain a minimum. However, some treat the more general problem of finding a shortest chain from v_0 to any vertex v_i. Such algorithms are discussed in Chapter II-4 and will not be pursued here.

3.7 Matching

Assigning people to jobs or pairing people off according to various schemes are important practical problems. Determining whether it is possible to carry out an assignment and the best way to do it is a problem of matching.

The mathematical formulation of this problem is: given a bipartite graph (V_1, V_2, E), what is the largest number of arcs such that no two arcs are adjacent?

Definition. A *matching in a bipartite graph* G is a subset of the edges E, no two of which are adjacent. A matching is *maximal* if it is not a proper subset of any other matching. The *deficiency* of a set of vertices A contained in V_1 denoted by $\delta(A)$ is given by $|A| - |R(A)|$ where $|A|$ is the number of vertices in A and $|R(A)|$ is the number of vertices in V_2 that are adjacent to A. The deficiency of a bipartite graph G, denoted by $\delta(G)$ is the maximal value of the deficiencies of all subsets of V_1.

THEOREM. In a bipartite graph G the maximal number of vertices in V_1 that can be matched into V_2 is equal to $|V| - \delta(G)$.

PROBLEM. *We now attempt an algebraic formulation of the matching problem in a bipartite graph as a transportation problem. Consider a simple network* (V_1, V_2, E) *in which we first regard each vertex of* V_1 *as a source and each vertex of* V_2 *as a sink. Let* c_{ij} *be equal to zero or one depending on whether there is an arc from vertex* i *in* V_1 *to vertex* j *in* V_2 *or not. Let* X_{ij} *denote flow along each arc. Then* X_{ij} *again assumes the two values zero or one. Next we regard the vertices of* V_2 *as sources and those of* V_1 *as sinks. We then maximize the total number of vertex disjoint arcs along which there is flow.*

Thus, the maximal matching problem is converted to the following transportation problem:

$$\text{maximize } Z = \sum_{i,j \in V_1, V_2} X_{ij}$$

subject to

$$\sum_{j \in V_2} c_{ij} X_{ij} \leqslant 1, \quad i \in V_1$$

$$\sum_{i \in V_1} c_{ij} X_{ij} \leqslant 1, \quad j \in V_2$$

4. EXTREMAL GRAPHS

In the following two illustrations we are concerned with the problems of counting how many objects of a special kind there are in a particular type of graph, viz., a complete graph. The first deals with a directed complete graph and the second with an undirected one.

4.1 How Many Cycles in a Directed Complete Graph?

The problem of counting cycles in directed graphs occurs in statistics. The method of paired comparisons is a way of ranking a set of objects by having an observer select from each possible pair the object he prefers. If he prefers object a to object b, and b to c, but c to a, this introduces an inconsistency into the ranking.

The data can be represented as a directed graph by letting a point stand for each object and drawing an arrow from point a to point b if the observer prefers object a to object b. If he prefers a to b, b to c, but c to a, this forms a three-cycle in the graph. Since such cycles represent inconsistencies, they are undesirable. Statisticians therefore want the sharpest possible upper bounds on their number.

Kendall and Babington Smith in 1940 found the maximum number of three-cycles that a directed graph on a given number of points can have, but did not consider the number of longer cycles. Colombo in 1964 extended this result to the maximum number of four-cycles.

The three-cycle and four-cycle problems are similar in that three or four points of a directed graph can have at most one three- or four-cycle, respectively.

It turns out in this case that the maximum number of three-cycles in a complete directed graph is

$$\frac{n^3 - n}{24} \qquad n \text{ odd}$$

$$\frac{n^3 - 4n}{24} \qquad n \text{ even}$$

A similar result exists for the case of four-cycles and little is known about the five-cycle case. The problem remains unsolved in general.

4.2 Planarity and Crossings

There is a classic puzzle known as the "three utilities–three houses" problem which has as its basis a nonplanar graph. The problem is to connect the three utilities with each of the three houses in such a way that the connecting pipelines do not intersect. It is easily shown that this problem is not solvable in the plane. That is, no matter how the edges are drawn in the plane there is at least one intersection at other than a vertex. One way of drawing the graph with one intersection is shown in Fig. 11a. In Fig. 11b an imbedding of the graph on a torus is shown. This imedding on the torus which is a surface of genus 1 eliminates the intersection. For our purpose the *genus* of a surface is essentially the number of holes in the surface or the maximum number of simple closed curves which can be drawn on the surface without disconnecting it if cut along these

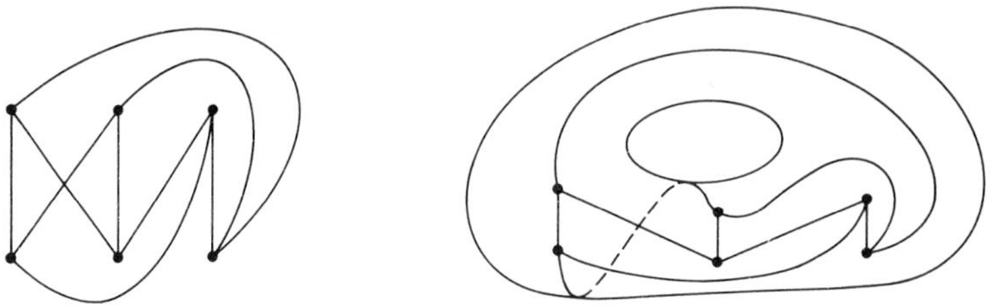

(a) (b)

Fig. 11.

curves. Note that the torus would not be disconnected, i.e., one can still travel on a path from any point to any other, if it is cut along any simple closed curve on the surface and passing through (along) the hole. A cut along a second single closed curve would disconnect it. A sphere would always be disconnected by such a cut, and hence its genus is zero.

There are a number of theorems which prescribe conditions for a graph to be planar. Note first that for planarity Euler's formula is necessary but not sufficient. Here is a known characterization. (See Busacker and Saaty [1965] for others.)

KURATOWSKI'S THEOREM: A graph is nonplanar iff it contains a subgraph which is isomorphic up to vertices of degree two with one of the two Kuratowski graphs K_5 and $K_{3,3}$ (see Fig. 12).

Two graphs are isomorphic up to vertices of degree two if they are isomorphic after possible additions or suppressions of some vertices of degree two.

It is clear then that many graphs that are drawn in the plane are actually nonplanar. Thus, no matter how they are drawn, some of their edges intersect. A question naturally arises as to how to draw a given nonplanar graph in the plane so that the number of intersections of its edges is minimal. It is probably easier

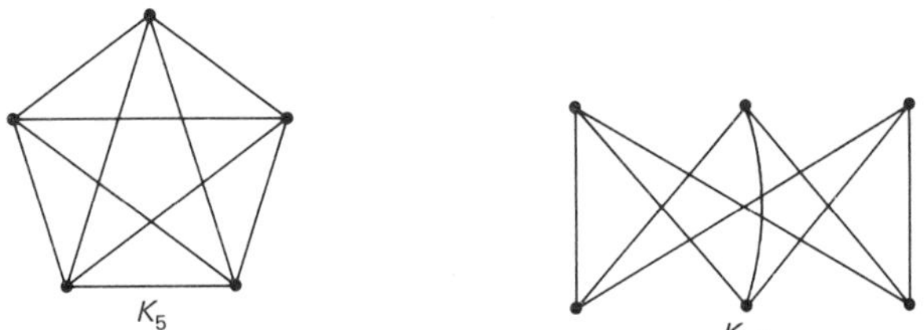

K_5
The complete graph on 5 vertices

(a)

$K_{3,3}$
The utilities graph

(b)

Fig. 12.

to try and answer this question for known classes of graphs such as bipartite and complete graphs.

For bipartite graphs, the problem appears in printed circuits where it is desired to minimize the number of crossovers. For complete graphs the problem has an interesting origin. In a brick factory there are m ovens in which bricks are baked. The bricks are then loaded on a small special-rail car at each oven and pushed to any one of n platforms where a loading truck may be available. Since each oven must be connected by rail to each loading platform, the rail lines have a great number of intersections. As the cars go over the intersections they are often derailed, causing spillage of bricks and a traffic jam within the factory. The problem is to construct the rails from the ovens to the destinations with a minimum number of crossings and thus minimize the hazards of derailment.

This problem may be solved within the framework of graph theory, where the rail lines correspond to edges of a graph connecting vertices (corresponding to the ovens) to other vertices (corresponding to the loading platforms). One condition is imposed, and that is that no three edges may intersect at the same point unless it is a vertex. Two edges, however, may intersect at an intermediate point.

There is a conjecture that the minimum number of intersections I_n of the edges of a complete graph on n vertices drawn in the plane in which two edges intersect in at most one point and two edges with a vertex in common have no intersections, is given by

$$I_n = \frac{n(n-2)^2(n-4)}{64} \qquad \text{for } n \text{ even}$$

$$I_n = \frac{(n-1)^2(n-3)^2}{64} \qquad \text{for } n \text{ odd}$$

In a complete graph every vertex is connected to each other vertex by one edge. We shall use K_n to denote a complete graph on n vertices and call it minimal (maximal) if it has a minimum (maximum) number of intersections. Saaty [1970] gives a realization scheme. Thus we know that I_n cannot exceed the above bounds. The problem is to show that equality holds.

Consider each vertex of the graph K_n and its $n - 1$ connecting edges (its star) to the remaining vertices. The removal of this vertex and its star, eliminates all intersections falling on these edges. The result is a complete graph on $n - 1$ vertices. Any other vertex of the complete graph on n vertices has the same or a different number of intersections on its star. In general, if x_i, $i = 1, \ldots, n$ is the number of intersections on the edges connecting the ith vertex then the total number of intersections of K_n is $\frac{1}{4}\sum_{i=1}^{n} x_i$ since each intersection is counted exactly four times, once for each of the four vertices of the two edges defining the intersection. Thus we have:

If x_i, $i = 1, \ldots, n$ *is the number of intersections falling on the star of the* ith *vertex of a complete graph* K_n, *then the total number of intersections in the graph is given by* $\frac{1}{4} \sum_{i=1}^{n} x_i$.

A necessary condition on the minimum number of intersections I_n *of a complete graph* K_n, *is that it satisfy the relation*

$$I_n \geqslant \frac{n}{n-4} I_{n-1} \quad n \geqslant 5$$

$$I_n = 0 \qquad n \leqslant 4$$

Note that by the theorem of Kuratowski $I_5 = 1$. We have proved the validity of the conjecture up to $n = 10$ (see Figs. 13-18 for realization in the plane which the reader will have no problem in generalizing). The problem remains unproven in general.

The complete m by n bipartite graph consists of m "dark" vertices, n "light" vertices, and the mn edges joining vertices of different types. Zarankiewicz (whose work is also discussed in [Busacker and Saaty, 1965]) has conjectured that the minimum value of the crossing number in this case is

$$\left[\frac{m}{2}\right] \cdot \left[\frac{m-1}{2}\right] \cdot \left[\frac{n}{2}\right] \cdot \left[\frac{n-1}{2}\right]$$

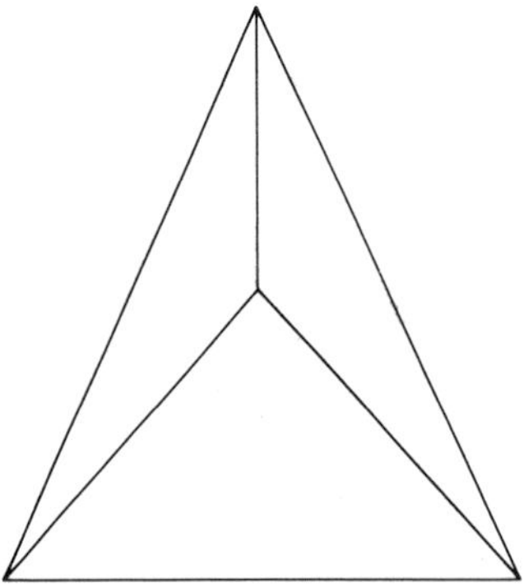

$I_4 = 0$

Fig. 13.

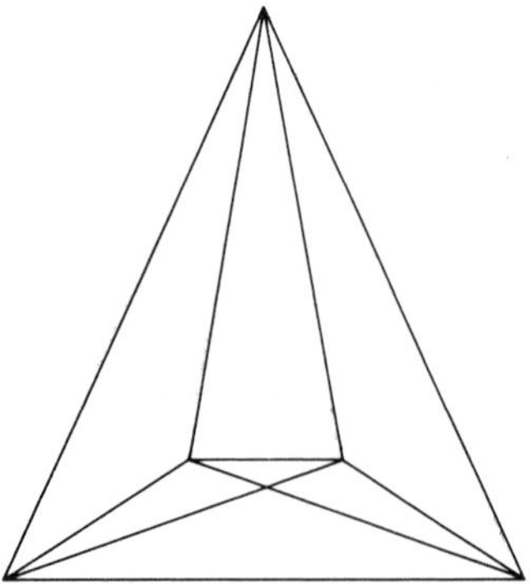

$I_5 = 1$

Fig. 14.

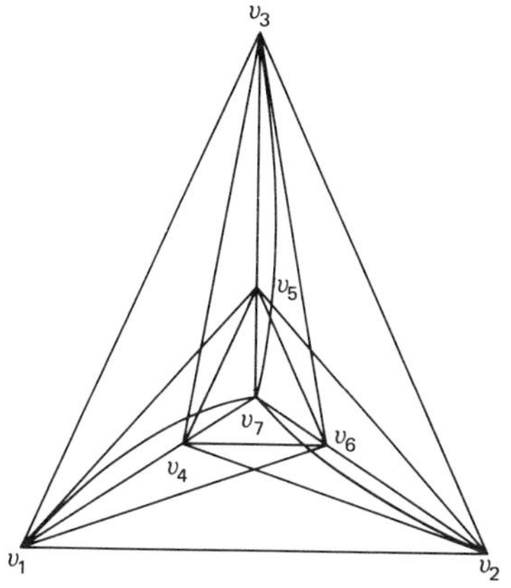

$l_7 = 9$

Fig. 15.

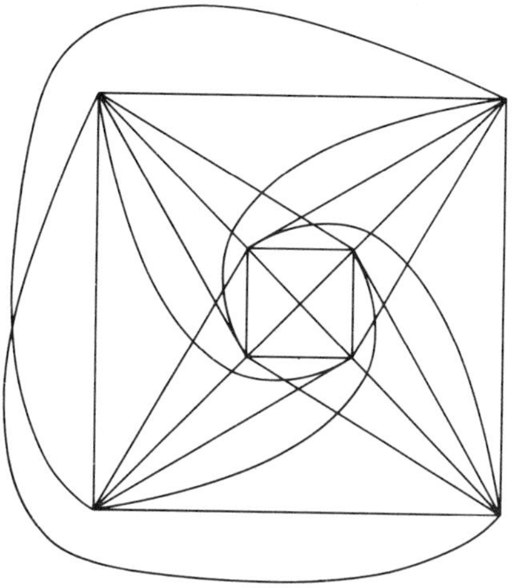

$l_8 = 18$

Fig. 16.

Where $[x]$ denotes the largest integer $\leqslant x$. A realization scheme for this number is also described in the reference. This conjecture also remains unproved. Its solution would take care of the brick factory problem.

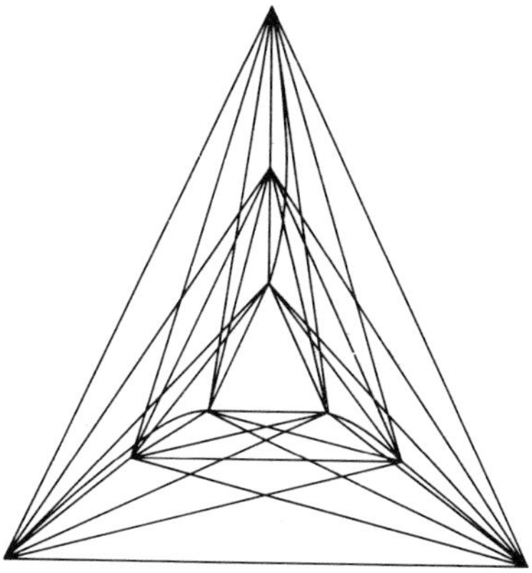

$l_9 = 36$

Fig. 17.

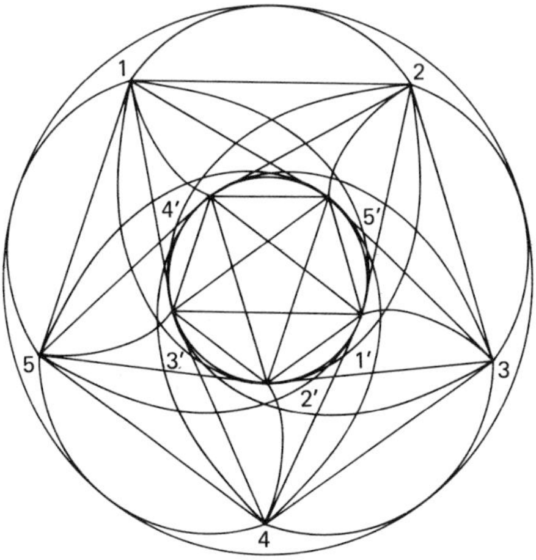

$l_{10} = 60$

Fig. 18.

5. IMBEDDING

In previous illustrations we dealt with concepts of connectivity and with extremum (maximum and minimum) problems arising in graph theory. It is opportune for us to discuss further the idea of imbedding graphs in surfaces as it ties closely with planarity.

5.1 Planar Graphs and Their Duals

Planar graphs were also characterized by H. Whitney as those graphs having a planar dual-map. The following theorem and corollary, due to Edmonds [1965] extend this characterization to more complicated surfaces.

Let M be a map which is an imbedding of a graph G in a surface S. The *dual map* of M is defined to be a map N having the same surface S, with an imbedded graph H satisfying the following conditions.

1. The dual of the dual map N is M.
2. Each vertex of the imbedded graph G_M is interior to a region of N.
3. Each region of M contains exactly one vertex of H_N.
4. Each edge of G_M intersects one edge of H_N precisely once.

As an example of a map and its dual, Fig. 19 shows a graph G (solid edges, vertices v_i) imbedded in the plane; the dual map is also in the plane with the graph H (dash edges, vertices p_j).

A one-to-one mapping of the edges of a graph G onto the edges of a graph H is called a *surface duality* if G can be imbedded in a map M with surface S and H can be imbedded in map N with the same surface in such a way that N is the dual map of M and edges which correspond to each other under the given edge mapping cross each other in the dual maps M and N. We have:

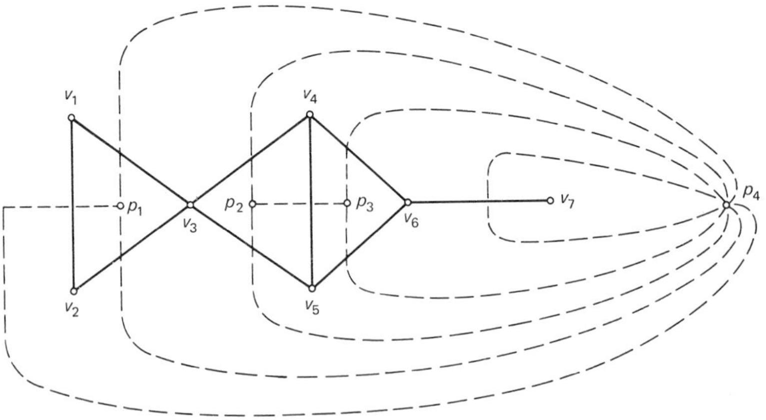

Fig. 19.

THEOREM. A one-to-one map of the edges of a connected graph G onto the edges of a connected graph H is a surface duality iff

1. for each vertex v of G the edges meeting v correspond to the edges of a connected subgraph of H and every vertex in this connected subgraph has even degree;
2. for each vertex w of H the edges meeting v correspond to the edges of a connected subgraph of G and every vertex in this connected subgraph has even degree.

   Suppose now that M is an imbedding of a graph G with surface S. If N is a dual map with graph H, then the number of vertices $|V_G|$ of G equals the number of regions $|R_N|$ of N. Also $|V_H| = |R_M|$, and $|E_G| = |E_H|$. Thus, by Euler's formula which relates the number of vertices, edges and regions

3. $$|V_G| - |E_G| + |R_M| = |V_H| - |E_H| + |R_N| \equiv \chi;$$

   χ is called the *characteristic* of the graph G. For a planar graph $\chi = 2$ (see also Section 5.2).

Corollary: A necessary and sufficient condition for a connected graph G to be imbeddable in a surface of given characteristic χ is that there exist an edge correspondence between G and some graph H such that the conditions of the theorem and Condition (3) are satisfied.

For a graph to be planar it must be imbeddable in an orientable surface of characteristic two. For a connected graph to be planar the conditions of the corollary are essentially those of Whitney, namely there must exist a planar dual.

An Unsolved Problem: Kuratowski characterized planar graphs as those graphs not containing a subgraph isomorphic to within vertices of degree two to either of the Kuratowski graphs. Thus the Kuratowski graphs are definitive for a surface of genus zero.

The generalized problem, as yet unsolved, is to find a family of graphs which are to be excluded from those graphs which can be drawn in an orientable surface of given genus g. What is desired is a theorem to the effect that any graph not having a subgraph isomorphic to some graph in the family can be imbedded in the surface of genus g. The genus $g(G)$ of a graph G is the minimum genus of an orientable surface in which G can be imbedded. Finding the genus of a graph can sometimes be accomplished by an indirect method. The following two theorems show that finding the genus of a graph G can be reduced to obtaining the genuses of subgraphs relative to certain decomposition of G.

Let B be a subgraph of G and suppose B is maximal in the sense that deleting any one vertex of B and the edges incident with it leaves the remainder connected. B is then called a *block* of G. There is a unique collection B of blocks B_i for G such that $G = \bigcup_i B_i$, $B_i \in B$. B is called the *block decomposition* of G [Harary 1969a].

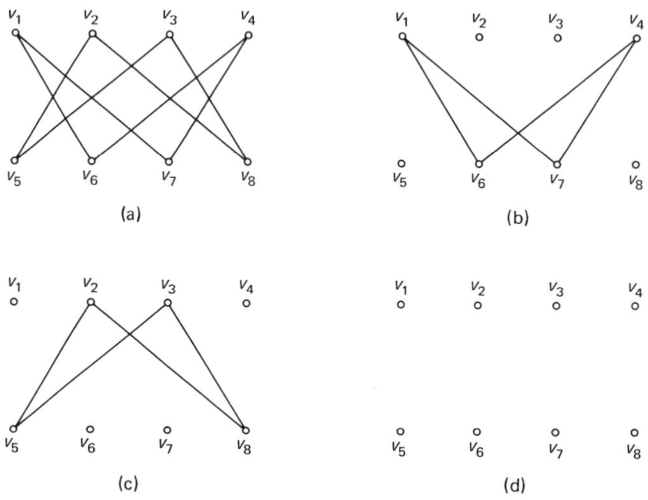

Fig. 20.

Trivial examples of this decomposition are provided by the complete graph, which has a single block since deleting any vertex and its incident edges leaves the rest connected, and the null graph, with each vertex a block. The graph in Fig. 20(a) has the block decomposition shown in Figs. (b), (c), and (d). We have

THEOREM. If G is a connected graph having n blocks $B_1, \ldots, B_n$, then $g(G) = \sum_{j=1}^{n} g(B_j)$.

In this theorem the graph G is assumed to be connected. We now show that this is not an essential requirement. Suppose that G is not connected and consists of m distinct components. Construct a graph $G' \supset G$ by adding one vertex v and m edges, each edge connecting one of the components with v.

It is easily seen that if the vertex v and any edge were added to a block B of G, then B would not be a block of G'. For, removing the other endpoint of the edge disconnects v from the vertices in B. Thus, each of the added edges is a block of G' and a block of genus zero.

Thus we have the following result:

THEOREM. The genus of any graph (connected or not) is the sum of the genuses of its blocks.

The notions of a minimal imbedding and block decomposition for a graph G can be combined to show that finding a minimal imbedding for G is essentially equivalent to finding one for each of the blocks of G.

Denote by $r(G)$ the maximum number of regions in $[S - G_M]$ for all maps M with an orientable surface S. We have:

THEOREM. If G is a connected graph having n blocks $B_1, \ldots, B_n$, then the number of regions $r(G)$ in a minimal imbedding is

$$r(G) = 1 - n + \sum_{i=1}^{n} r(B_i).$$

Above we defined a planar graph to be essentially a graph which can be imbedded in a surface of genus zero. An interesting question is, for a given graph G, what is the minimum number of planar subgraphs whose union is G. This number is called the *planar thickness* of G, and is denoted by $t(G)$.

It is easy to show, using Euler's formula, that for any planar graph H having m edges and n vertices, $m \leqslant 3(n - 2)$. Using this fact we can find a lower bound for $t(G)$ in the following special case:

Let G denote the complete graph on n vertices, then $t(G) \geqslant \left[\frac{n+7}{6}\right]$, where [ ] denotes the greatest integer function [Beineke and Harary, 1965].

We also have: If $n \neq 9$ and $n \neq 4 \pmod 6$, then $t(G) = \frac{n+7}{6}$ where G is the complete graph on n vertices.

Generalizations to genus one thickness $t_1(G)$, that is the minimum number of subgraphs which can be imbedded in a torus and whose union is G, and the genus two thickness $t_2(G)$ have also been studied. It has been shown that, if G denotes the complete graph on n vertices, then $t_1(G) = \frac{n+4}{6}$ and $t_2(G) = \frac{n+3}{2}$.

5.2 The Four Color Problem

After careful analysis of information regarding the origins of the four-color conjecture, Kenneth O. May concludes that:

> It was not the culmination of a series of individual efforts but flashed across the mind of Francis Guthrie while coloring a map of England . . . his brother communicated the conjecture, but not the attempted proof to DeMorgan in October, 1852.

His information also reveals that DeMorgan gave it some thought and communicated it to his students and to other mathematicians, giving credit to Guthrie. In 1878 the first printed reference to the conjecture, by Cayley, appeared in the *Proceedings of the London Mathematical Society*. He wrote asking whether the conjecture had been proved. This launched its colorful career involving a number of equivalent variations, conjectures, and false proofs. Only very recently has a computer-assisted (and quite lengthy) proof been given to this problem by Appel and Haken [1976].

The reader will find a rich source of information regarding the problem in Ore's famous book [Ore, 1967] *The Four Color Problem.*

That four colors are necessary can be seen from the following example:

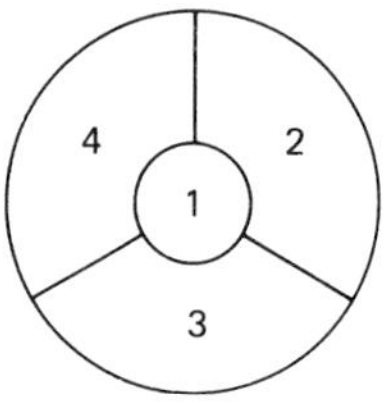

Fig. 21.

It can be proven without difficulty by using the dual graph that five colors suffice to color any planar map. Here we give a short direct proof that six colors suffice. A map is *cubic* if the vertices of its graph are all of degree three. Any map can be reduced to a cubic map by replacing any vertex of degree different from three by a polygon which has as many sides as the degree of the vertex and connecting each of its vertices to one vertex with which the given vertex was adjacent. After six-coloring the resulting cubic map, each such artificial polygon is shrunk back to the original vertex, resulting in a six-coloring of the given map.

Consider Euler's formula $n - m + r = 2$, which holds for any planar map with n vertices, m edges and r regions. Substitute $n = 2m/3$ (for a cubic map). This gives $6(r - 2) = 2m$. Since $6r > 6(r - 2) = 2m$ we prove that six colors are sufficient to color any cubic map. This is clear when $r < 6$. If $r \geqslant 6$, then there must be at least one region bounded by five or less edges. To see this, note that otherwise substituting the fact that $3n \leqslant 2m$ (always true) and $6n \leqslant 2m$ (by assumption) in Euler's formula we have $0 \geqslant 6$, a contradiction. Applying induction, we may assume that all maps are six-colorable for $r - 1$ regions. If we remove a less than six-sided region of the map and extend the edges of its neighbors in such a way that each vertex is of degree three and the entire removed region is covered by its five neighbors as in Fig. 22 below, we can six-color the map and then reinstate the removed region, coloring it with the sixth color not appearing in any of its five neighbors.

Note that the four-color problem only asks for a proof of the sufficiency of four colors. There is also the question of how to color any map. This is a construction problem which one would have to face up to when actually coloring a map. There is no theory available for this problem.

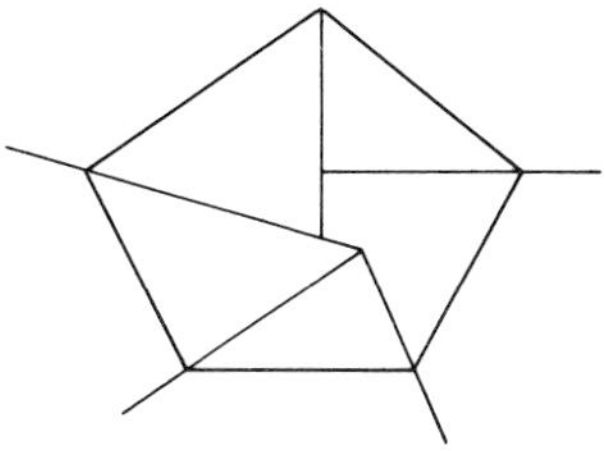

Fig. 22.

The *chromatic number* $\gamma(G)$ of a graph G is the smallest number of colors needed to color the vertices of the graph so that no two vertices connected by an edge have the same color. This is the same as dividing the vertices into subsets such that no two vertices in a subset have a common edge. Note that for the minimality of the number of subsets one would attempt to maximize the size of each subset. Some useful applications relate to an affiliate of the chromatic number known as the *cliquomatic number* $\chi(G)$. A clique in a graph G is a maximal complete subgraph (a complete subgraph not contained in any other complete subgraph of G). The cliquomatic number of a graph is the smallest number of cliques in the graph which includes all the vertices. The chromatic number of a graph G on n vertices is equal to the cliquomatic number of the graph (known as the *complementary* graph of G) obtained from a complete graph on n vertices with all the edges of G deleted. The proof of this assertion is found in B. Roy [1969].

Examples of applications are the following:

A member of a university faculty was given the job of scheduling n examinations to be taken by $N \geqslant n$ students. Any number of exams could be scheduled during the same period of time, but in such a way that no two tests to be taken by the same student are scheduled for the same period. The problem is to determine the minimum number of groupings and do the scheduling so that no conflict occurs.

As a second problem, a firm has demand for an expensive repair machine which each of n truck terminals needs occasionally. Only some of the terminals are directly connected by roads. The times when a terminal needs this equipment are random and difficult to predict. When a terminal needs the equipment, it is crucial that it be delivered within a certain time period. The time period requirement can be satisfied by shipping the equipment from one terminal to another, but in general, because of the route layout, it cannot be satisfied if the shipment requires transit through another terminal. This is due to the considerable delay caused by the extra handling and layover at the intermediate terminal. It is desired to make a minimum number of machines available in such a way that when needed, no repair machine has to go through an intermediate terminal.

A third problem deals with a network of cities visited by an airline. Spare engines are left in parts of the network so that they could be loaded on the first departing plane to the next scheduled stop where the engine is needed. It is essential that no spare engine should travel to an intermediate stop before reaching its destination. What is the minimum number of engines needed and how should they be distributed?

A final problem occurs in a small zoo where is is necessary to keep the number of cages to a minimum, and hence, it is desired to keep all animals which do not pose a threat to each other in the same cage. What is the minimum number of cages?

Welsh and Powell [1967] give an algorithm for obtaining an approximation $y'(G)$ to the chromatic number $\gamma(G)$ of a graph G. This approximation satisfies

$$\gamma(G) \leqslant y'(G) \leqslant \max_i \min \{d_i + 1, i\};$$

where d_i is the degree of the ith vertex after indexing the vertices $v_i, i = 1, \ldots, n$ according to descending degree, i.e., $d_1 \geqslant d_2 \geqslant \cdots \geqslant d_n$. It is pointed out that the difference between the two extremes of the above inequality can be arbitrarily large for certain graphs.

The algorithm begins by forming a set T_1. To form T_1 one begins with the highest degree vertex v_1 and then systematically moving down the degree ranking and adding the vertex next in degree that is not adjacent to v_1 then again choosing the vertex next in rank not adjacent to either and so on each time adding a vertex not adjacent to any of the previous ones. The set T_1 is assigned one color. To form the next subset T_2 one now begins with the highest degree vertex not in T_1 and repeats the process on the remaining vertices not in T_1. Thus T_2 is assigned a second color. The procedure is continued until every vertex belongs to some $T_i, i = 1, \ldots, m$ and each T_i is assigned a different color.

5.3 Stability (Relation to Coloring)

An *internally stable* set of vertices of a graph is a set of vertices no two elements of which are adjacent. The *coefficient of internal stability* $\alpha(G)$ of a graph G is the maximum number of vertices in G that form a stable set. We have $\alpha(G)$ $\gamma(G) \geqslant n$. A set of vertices is *externally stable* if every vertex not in the set is joined by an edge to some vertex in the set. The smallest number of vertices satisfying this property is called the *coefficient of external stability* of G. A *kernel* in G is a subset of vertices that is both internally and externally stable. A graph need not have a kernel or it may have several. If a graph does not have a circuit of odd length, it has a kernel [Berge, 1961].

6. SOME FUNDAMENTAL THEOREMS

The following are a few of the well-known theorems in graph theory which cannot be elaborated on for lack of space, but which the reader should be familiar with [Busacker and Saaty, 1965; Harary, 1969a].

Euler's Theorem (first theorem of graph theory): In any finite graph the sum of the degrees of the vertices is equal to twice the number of edges. (It is interesting to note that the number of vertices of odd degree is even.)

Menger's Theorem: The minimum number of vertices (articulation points) whose removal separates two nonadjacent vertices of a graph (so that each belongs to a different component) is equal to the maximum number of disjoint chains connecting the two vertices.

König's Theorem: A graph is bipartite iff it has no circuits of odd length. (This implies that a map is colorable with two colors iff every vertex is of even degree.)

Heawood's Map Coloring Theorem: For every positive integer p, the chromatic number of a graph embedded in an orientable surface of genus p is at most

$$\frac{7 + \sqrt{1 + 48p}}{2}$$

Brooks' Theorem: If k (>2) is the maximum degree of any vertex in a graph without loops and without complete subgraphs on $k + 1$ vertices, then the graph is k-colorable.

Ramsey's Problem: What is the smallest integer $r(m, n)$ such that every graph with $r(m, n)$ vertices contains the complete graph on m vertices or the complement of the complete graph on n vertices? This is a generalization of the problem that in any party with six people, there are three mutual acquaintances or three nonacquaintances. It is known that [Harary, 1969a]

$$r(m, n) \leqslant \binom{m + n - 2}{m - 1}.$$

There is a formal theory for answering some of the counting problems in graph theory. It would require a few pages to introduce *Polya's enumeration theorem* here. Instead of doing so we refer the reader to Busacker and Saaty [1965] and Harary [1969a].

7. MATRICES

7.1 Matrix Representations

Another topic mentioned in the Chart (Section 1) is that of matrix representation of graphs. There are various kinds of matrices associated with graphs. Because they are given an algebraic structure, we can use algebraic techniques to facilitate the solutions of many graph theory problems.

Here is a list of important matrix representations of graphs. (See Berge [1961] and Seshu and Reed [1961]).

1. The incidence matrix A:
   a. For an undirected graph, the *incidence matrix* has for row labels the vertices and for column labels the edges. An entry in the matrix is 1 whenever a vertex is incident with an edge. Otherwise, the entry is 0. ($a_{ij} = 1$ if v_i is incident with e_j. $a_{ij} = 0$ otherwise.)
   b. For a directed graph, the entry is +1 when the vertex incident with an arc is the initial vertex of the arc (hence the arc is directed away from the vertex). The entry is −1 if the vertex is directed toward the arc. If a vertex is not incident with an arc, the entry is 0.
2. The *circuit matrix C:*
   a. For an undirected graph the circuit matrix has for row labels the simple circuits of the graph and for column labels the edges of the graph. An entry, $a_{ij} = 1$ if circuit C_i includes edge e_j. Otherwise $a_{ij} = 0$.
   b. For a directed graph, $a_{ij} = 1, -1$ or 0 depending on whether circuit C_i is oriented the same, differently, or not at all with respect to arc e_j.
3. The *circuit-basis matrix* is a submatrix of the circuit matrix whose row labels are the simple circuits corresponding to the chords associated with a given spanning tree.
4. The *cutset matrix* K is analogous to the circuit matrix except that the circuit labels for the rows are replaced by cutset labels.
5. The *cutset basis matrix* is associated with a spanning tree of a graph. The row labels are cutsets each of which consists of a tree branch and the chords joining the vertices of subtrees formed by deleting the branch. These cutsets form a basis for the cutsets.
6. The *adjacency* or *vertex matrix* **V** has for row and column labels the vertices of the graph and a_{ij} is the number of edges joining vertex i, to vertex j in the undirected case. In the directed case a_{ij} is the number of edges directed from vertex i to vertex j.
7. The *edge matrix* has for row and column labels the edges of the graph and a_{ij} is the number of vertices incident with the 2 edges i and j.
8. The *path matrix* **D** of a connected graph with ordered vertices has for row labels all the paths from the first to the last vertex and for column labels the edges. In an undirected graph, $a_{ij} = 1$ if path i contains edge j; otherwise $a_{ij} = 0$. In the directed case, $a_{ij} = 1$ if arc e_j is directed the same way as the path and $a_{ij} = -1$ if arc e_j is directed in the opposite sense to the path. Otherwise $a_{ij} = 0$.
9. The *node-to-datum-path matrix* is formed by choosing a vertex as the datum

vertex in a spanning tree of a directed connected graph. From each nondatum vertex, there is a path directed from the nondatum vertex to the datum vertex in the tree. Then the elements d_{ij} of the node-to-datum-path matrix are defined by:

d_{ij} = +1, if the ith branch is in the jth path (vertex j) and is oriented in the same direction as the path.
= −1, if the ith branch is in the jth path (vertex j) and oriented in the direction opposite to that of the jth path.
= 0, if the ith branch is not in the jth path.

Note that the matrix **D** is a square matrix of order (number of branches) by $(n - 1)$.

Matrix representations have imparted substantial contributions to the study of graphs. To go into the details of the theory is beyond the scope of this chapter. We list some of the basic matrix representation theorems:

1. The rank (the maximum number of linearly independent columns) of the incidence matrix, **A**, of a connected graph (directed or undirected) with n vertices is $(n - 1)$.
2. The rank of the circuit matrix, **C**, of a connected graph with m edges and n vertices is $(m - n + 1)$.
3. The rank of the cutset matrix of a connected graph with n vertices is $(n - 1)$.
4. The rank of the path matrix is $m - n + 2 - c$ where c is the number of independent circuits in those separable subgraphs between the terminal vertices whose removal from the graph does not remove either of the terminal vertices.
5. The product $\mathbf{AP}'$ of the incidence matrix **A**, and the transpose, $\mathbf{P}'$ of the path matrix, $\mathbf{P}'$, is a matrix all of whose rows except the first and last have zero elements and whose first and last row elements are all 1.
6. The incidence matrix, **A**, and the transpose, $\mathbf{C}'$ of the circuit matrix, **C**, when arranged using the same order of edges as the incidence matrix, are orthogonal, i.e., $\mathbf{AC}' = \mathbf{0}$.
7. The circuit matrix, **C**, and the cutset matrix, **K**, of any graph satisfy $\mathbf{CK}' = \mathbf{0}$ (orthogonality condition).
8. A square $(n - 1) \times (n - 1)$ submatrix of the incidence matrix of a connected graph is nonsingular if the columns of this submatrix correspond to the branches of a tree.
9. Let **B** be a submatrix of **C**, the circuit matrix of a connected graph. Let **B** have $n - m + 1$ rows and be of rank $n - m + 1$. A square matrix **B** of order $n - m + 1$ is nonsingular, iff the columns of this submatrix correspond to the set of chords for some spanning tree of the graph.

10. Nonsingular $(n - 1) \times (n - 1)$ submatrices of the incidence matrix $\mathbf{A}$ are in 1-1 correspondence with the spanning trees of the graph.
11. Nonsingular $(n - m + 1) \times (n - m + 1)$ submatrices of the circuit matrix $\mathbf{C}$ are in 1-1 correspondence with the complements of the spanning trees of the graph.
12. Nonsingular $(n - 1) \times (n - 1)$ submatrices of the cutset matrix $\mathbf{K}$ are in 1-1 correspondence with the spanning trees of the graph.
13. Let $\mathbf{A}_s$ be an $(n - 1) \times m$ submatrix of $\mathbf{A}$. Partition $\mathbf{A}_s$ in terms of the chords and branches of a spanning tree as $\mathbf{A}_s = [\mathbf{A}_{11} : \mathbf{A}_{12}]$. Then the circuit basis matrix $\mathbf{C}$, is given by $\mathbf{C} = [\mathbf{I} : -\mathbf{A}_{11} \mathbf{A}_{12}]$.
14. If the columns of $\mathbf{A}$, $\mathbf{C}'$ and $\mathbf{K}$ of a directed graph are arranged in similar order of chords and branches for a spanning tree (the same tree for all), so that $\mathbf{A} = [\mathbf{A}_{11} : \mathbf{A}_{12}]$, $\mathbf{C} = [\mathbf{I} : \mathbf{C}_{12}]$ and $\mathbf{K} = [\mathbf{K}_{11} : \mathbf{I}]$, then the following relations hold: $\mathbf{K} = \mathbf{A}_{12}^{-1} \mathbf{A}$ and $\mathbf{K}_{11} = -\mathbf{C}'_{12} = \mathbf{A}_{12}^{-1} \mathbf{A}_{11}$.
15. The matrix $\mathbf{V}^n$ gives the number of arc progressions of length n between any two vertices of a directed graph.
16. Let the $(n - 1) \times m$ incidence matrix $\mathbf{A}$ (with the row corresponding to the datum vertex omitted) of a connected directed graph be partitioned according to chords and branches of a spanning tree as shown: $\mathbf{A} = [\mathbf{A}_{11} : \mathbf{A}_{12}]$. The node-to-datum-path matrix, $\mathbf{D}$, is related to $\mathbf{A}_{12}$ by $\mathbf{A}_{12} \mathbf{D} = \mathbf{I}$.
17. Two graphs are isomorphic if they have the same incidence matrices to within a permutation of rows and columns.
18. The determinant of a nonsingular submatrix of $\mathbf{A}$ is ± 1.
19. For an interchange graph, $G'(V', E')$ of $G(V, E)$ developed by a 1-1 correspondence of the elements of E' with the elements of V and a 1-1 correspondence of the elements of V' with the elements of E preserving the incidence relations of G, the edge matrix of G is the vertex matrix of G' and the vertex matrix of G is the edge matrix of G'.

7.2 An Application of the Adjacency Matrix [Kuhn, 1971]

Consider the two graphs in Fig. 23 below:

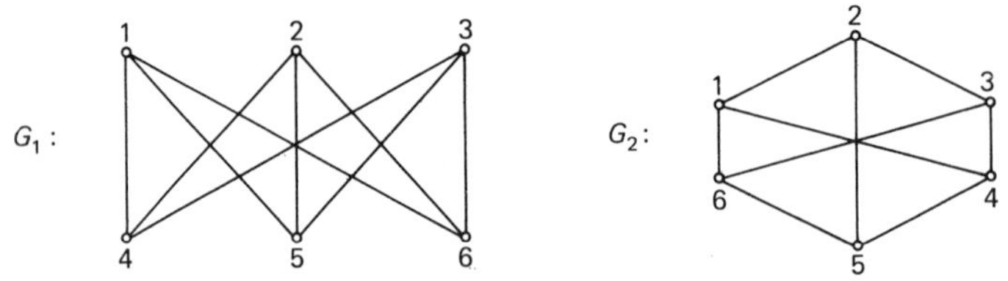

Fig. 23.

They have the vertex adjacency matrices $\mathbf{A}_1$ and $\mathbf{A}_2$ given below:

$$G_1 \to \mathbf{A}_1 = \begin{bmatrix} 0 & 0 & 0 & 1 & 1 & 1 \\ 0 & 0 & 0 & 1 & 1 & 1 \\ 0 & 0 & 0 & 1 & 1 & 1 \\ 1 & 1 & 1 & 0 & 0 & 0 \\ 1 & 1 & 1 & 0 & 0 & 0 \\ 1 & 1 & 1 & 0 & 0 & 0 \end{bmatrix} \qquad G_2 \to \mathbf{A}_2 = \begin{bmatrix} 0 & 1 & 0 & 1 & 0 & 1 \\ 1 & 0 & 1 & 0 & 1 & 0 \\ 0 & 1 & 0 & 1 & 0 & 1 \\ 1 & 0 & 1 & 0 & 1 & 0 \\ 0 & 1 & 0 & 1 & 0 & 1 \\ 1 & 0 & 1 & 0 & 1 & 0 \end{bmatrix}$$

The following mapping shows that G_1 and G_2 are isomorphic:

$$\begin{array}{ccc} G_1 & & G_2 \\ 1 & \to & 1 \\ 2 & \to & 3 \\ 3 & \to & 2 \\ 4 & \to & 5 \\ 5 & \to & 4 \\ 6 & \to & 6 \end{array}$$

This is merely reordering the vertices of G_1 to obtain G_2. In the adjacency matrices we are simultaneously reordering the rows and columns, which can be accomplished by a similarity transformation using a permutation matrix. $\mathbf{A}_2 = \mathbf{P}\mathbf{A}_1\mathbf{P}'$ where

$$\mathbf{P} = \begin{bmatrix} 1 & 0 & 0 & 0 & 0 & 0 \\ 0 & 0 & 1 & 0 & 0 & 0 \\ 0 & 1 & 0 & 0 & 0 & 0 \\ 0 & 0 & 0 & 0 & 1 & 0 \\ 0 & 0 & 0 & 1 & 0 & 0 \\ 0 & 0 & 0 & 0 & 0 & 1 \end{bmatrix} \quad \text{or} \quad p_{i,j} = \delta_{p(i),j}. \quad \text{(Kronecker's Delta)}$$

and $\mathbf{P}'$ is the transpose of $\mathbf{P}$.

Therefore, G_1 and G_2 are isomorphic iff there exists a permutation matrix $\mathbf{P}$ such that $\mathbf{A}_1 = \mathbf{P}\mathbf{A}_2\mathbf{P}'$. But, finding $\mathbf{P}$ may not be easy and it turns out that the following is true:

G_1 and G_2 are isomorphic implies that $\mathbf{A}_1$ and $\mathbf{A}_2$ have the same eigenvalues. However, this condition is not sufficient because the two graphs below have the indicated eigenvalues.

and

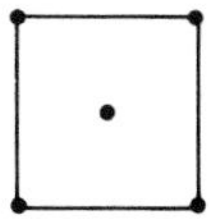

have $\lambda = \pm 2, 0, 0, 0$

It is possible to extend these ideas and tighten the conditions to obtain a complete characterization of isomorphism.

7.3 Matroids

Matroids have come to play a prominent role in the study of graphs. There are many ways of defining matroids (see the book by Wilson [1972] and an article by him in the *American Mathematical Monthly* Wilson, [1973]). One definition of a matroid is that it is a finite set of edges together with a collection of nonempty subsets (called circuits) with the property that no circuit properly contains another and if two distinct circuits contain an edge then there is a circuit in the union of these two circuits which does not contain that edge. Matroids come in a variety such as uniform, graphic, cographic, representable, algebraic, transversal, gammoids, and Fano matroids. Some of these types of matroids have been shown to be related. Very important characterizations of graphic matroids have been given by Tutte in a series of papers. This type of characterization is related to such questions as when a given matrix may be the circuit or cutset matrix of a graph.

8. TWO APPLICATIONS

8.1 A Business Application Using Matrices

Matrices of graphs have been used to study problems of production. Products are constructed from several items where each type of item may be used to produce more than one product. The number of units used from each item to make the product is known. The graph consists of vertices representing the items and other vertices representing the products. As many arcs are drawn from a vertex representing an item to a vertex representing a product as there are units of that item used in the product. A loop is drawn from each item vertex to itself to indicate that the item may be needed by itself regardless of its participating in the manufacture of a product. The result is a bipartite graph with multiple arcs. A vertex adjacency matrix for this directed graph is constructed, whose only nonzero entries are in the last column representing the products and also the main diagonal where they are equal to unity.

A new matrix is constructed whose rows are all the vertices of the graph and whose columns indicate the delivery times. Its entries indicate the number of units needed for each item and for the final product.

If the two matrices are multiplied the result gives the sales matrix for the total period being considered. The graph theoretic representation serves as a method of systematizing the process.

8.2 Modeling with Graphs [Busacker and Saaty, 1965]

An illuminating illustration of the use of graph theory in problem solving is the problem known as *instant insanity.* The six faces of each of four cubes are colored with four colors. Since there are six faces each cube would have more than one face colored with the same color. The coloring of the cubes is different so two cubes are not necessarily colored the same way. The problem is to stack the cubes vertically in such a way that we have a rectangular prism and each of the rectangles on the side has all four colors appearing in it—not necessarily in the same order.

Of course, the problem may not have a solution. For example, if all three faces meeting at a corner of each cube are colored with the same color for all four cubes, then that color appears in the stack at least eight times instead of the required four and the problem has no solution.

First, we draw four points as corners of a square and let each represent a different color. Then we label the cubes 1 to 4. Each cube has three pairs of opposite faces. We take the first cube and draw lines connecting the vertices associated with each pair of opposite faces and label these three lines with number one. We do the same for each of the other three cubes. In all, we have 12 lines. Three labeled 1, three labeled 2, etc.

Next we decompose the problem into two parts. We solve the problem for one pair of opposite rectangles in the stacking and then for the other pair. We note that in each pair each cube is used once and each color appears twice, once in each rectangle. Thus, we draw the four points associated with the colors and choose four lines from the diagram that are labeled 1, 2, 3, 4 (thus each cube is used once) but in such a way that each point is incident with two lines. When this is done, the same procedure is repeated for the remaining pair of opposite rectangles. Adjustment in the choice of lines for the first pair of rectangles may be necessary to solve the problem for the second pair. The solution for the two parts are independent. Given the solution of one partition, the other is obtained by a rotation around an axis passing through the centers of the two opposite faces of the cubes which appear in the first solution. It is also easy to arrange the appearing of colors so that they alternate from one rectangle to the one on the opposite side. In this manner the problem is solved.

9. POSTSCRIPT

Although graph theory has a large number of unsolved problems, it is difficult to single out one or two of these problems as the most important. The four color conjecture perhaps has been the most challenging because it attracted the attention of so many great minds for so long even though its solution may not make a significant difference to the activity in the field.

Among the most important and far reaching attempts have been those of Gian-Carlo Rota of MIT and his associates to create a unifying theory for discrete mathematics which includes the subject of graphs.

Applications of graph theory to model real life problems will continue and expand primarily because quantification in the social and decision sciences calls for discrete models. However, greater use of the subject in concrete applications has been made in the decision sciences than in sociology, anthropology and allied fields where existing approaches to measurement in spite of slow progress are among the most difficult or challenging problems these fields are facing today. Graphs may be called to use in modeling but it is hard to say in what form and to solve what behavioral problems. Without doubt, modern mathematics is undergoing great evolution through progress made in graph theory and combinatorial theory and other fields of discrete mathematics.

REFERENCES

Books

1. Berge, Claude, *Theory of Graphs and its Applications*, John Wiley, New York (1961) (first appeared in French, 1958).
2. Berge, Claude and A. Ghouila-Houri, *Programming, Games and Transportation Networks*, John Wiley and Sons, New York (1965).
3. Bessonov, L. A., *Elements of Graph Theory*, Uchebn, Posobie Vses. Zaochn, Energ. Instituta (Moscow, 1964).
4. Busacker, R. and T. L. Saaty, *Finite Graphs & Networks*, McGraw-Hill, New York (1965).
5. Capobianco, M., J. B. Frechen, M. Krolik (Eds.), *Recent Trends in Graph Theory*, Springer-Verlag, New York (1971).
6. Chartrand, G. and S. F. Kapoor (Eds.), *The Many Facets of Graph Theory*, Springer-Verlag, New York (1969).
7. Domschke, Wolfgang, *Kurzeste Wege in Graphen: Algorithmen, Verfahrensvergleiche*, Verlag Anton Hain Meisenheim Am Glan (1972).
8. Dynkin, E. B. and W. A. Uspenski, *Multicolor Problems*, D. C. Heath and Company, Boston (1952) (Original in German).
9. Elmaghraby, S. E., "Some Network Models in Management Science," Springer-Verlag, New York, Lecture Notes in O. R. and Math. Systems, No. 29 (1970).
10. Erdos, P. and G. Katona (Eds.), *Theory of Graphs: Proceedings of the Colloquium held at Tihany, Hungary in September, 1966*, Academic Press, New York (1968).
11. Fiedler, M., (Ed.), *Theory of Graphs and its Applications*, Proc. Symp. Smolenice, Czech., June 17-20, 1963, Academic Press, New York (1964).
12. Ford, L. R. and D. R. Fulkerson, *Flows in Networks*, Princeton University Press (1962).
13. Frank, H. and I. T. Frisch, *Communication, Transmission and Transportation Networks*, Addison-Wesley, New York (1971).
14. Grossman, I. and W. Magnus, *Groups and Their Graphs*, Random House, New York (1964).
15. Grunbaum, Branko, *Convex Polytopes*, Interscience Publishers, New York (1967).

16. Harary, F. (Ed.), *Graph Theory and Theoretical Physics*, Academic Press, New York (1967).
17. ——, *Graph Theory*, Addison Wesley, Reading, Massachusetts (1969a).
18. —— (Ed.), *Proof Techniques in Graph Theory*, Academic Press, New York (1969b). (Proceedings of the Second Ann Arbor Graph Theory Conference, February, 1968).
19. —— and L. Beineke (Eds.), *A Seminar on Graph Theory*, Holt, Rinehart & Winston, New York (1967).
20. —— and D. Cartwright, *Structural Models: An Introduction to the Theory of Directed Graphs*, John Wiley & Sons, New York (1965).
21. Harary, F. and R. Z. Norman, *Graph Theory as a Mathematical Model in Social Science*, University of Michigan, Ann Arbor, Michigan (1953).
22. Hu, T. C., *Integer Programming and Network Flows*, Addison Wesley, Reading, Massachusetts (1969).
23. Kim, W. H. and Chien, R. T., Topological Analysis and Synthesis of Communication Networks, Columbia University Press, New York (1962).
24. König, D., *Theorie der endlichen und unendlichen Graphen*, Chelsea, New York (1950).
25. Lietzmann, W., *Visual Topology*, American Elsevier, New York (1965).
26. Liu, C. L., *Introduction to Combinatorial Mathematics*, McGraw-Hill (1968).
27. Moon, J. W., *Topics on Tournaments*, Holt, Rinehart & Winston, New York (1968).
28. Ore, O., *Graphs and Their Uses*, Random House, New York (1963).
29. ——, *Theory of Graphs*, Colloquium Publications, Vol. 38, American Mathematical Society, Providence, Rhode Island (1961).
30. ——, *The Four Color Problem*, Academic Press, New York (1967).
31. Read, Ronald C. (Ed.), *Graph Theory and Computing*, Academic Press, New York (1972).
32. Ringel, G., Farbungsprobleme auf Flachen und Graphen, VEB Deutsche Verlag der Wissenschaften, Berlin (1959).
33. Rosenstiehl, P., (Ed.), *Theory of Graphs*, International Symposium, Rome, (July 1966), Gordon and Breach, New York (1967).
34. Roy, Bernard, *Algebre Moderne et Theorie des Graphes, Tome 1:* Notions et resultats fondamentaux, Dunod, Paris (1969).
35. ——, *Algebre Moderne et Theorie des Graphes, Tome 2:* Applications et problemes specifiques., Dunod, Paris (1969).
36. Saaty, T. L., *Optimization in Integers and Related Extremal Problems*, McGraw-Hill, New York (1970).
37. Seshu, S. and M. B. Reed, *Linear Graphs and Electrical Networks*, Addison-Wesley, Reading, Massachusetts (1961).
38. Tutte, W. T., *Recent Progress in Combinatorics*, (Proceedings of the Third Waterloo Conference on Combinatorics, May, 1968), Academic Press, New York (1969).
39. ——, *Connectivity in Graphs*, University of Toronto Press (1966).
40. Wilson, R. J., *Introduction to Graph Theory*, Oliver and Boyd, Edinburgh, and Academic Press, New York (1972).

Articles

41. Appel, K. and W. Haken, "A Proof of the Four Color Theorem," *Discrete Mathematics* **16,** No. 2: pp. 179–180 (October 1976).
42. Beineke, L. and F. Harary, "The Thickness of a Complete Graph," *Canadian J. Math.* **17:** 850–859 (1965).
43. Colombo, U., Dui circuiti nei grafi completi. Boll. Un. Mat. Ital. **19:** 153–170 (1964).

44. Edmonds, J., "On the Surface Duality of Linear Graphs," *J. of Res. Nat. Bureau of Stand.* **96B** (January–June 1965).
45. Holt, A. W., "Program Organization and Record Keeping for Dynamic Storage Allocation," *Comm. ACM* **4:** 422–431 (October 1961); also in *Information Processing*: 539–544 (1962).
46. Kendall, M. and B. Babington Smith, "On the Method of Paired Comparisons," *Biometrika* **33:** 239–251 (1940).
47. Kuhn, William W., *An Algorithm for Graph Isomorphism Using Adjacency Matrices*, Ph.D. Thesis, University of Pennsylvania (1971).
48. Saaty, Thomas L., "Thirteen Colorful Variations on Guthrie's Four Color Conjecture," *The Am. Math. Monthly* **79,** No. 1: 2–43 (January 1972).
49. Welsh, D. J. and M. P. Powell, "An Upper Bound for the Chromatic Number of a Graph and its Application to Time-Tabling Problems," *Computer J.* **10:** 85–86 (1967).
50. Wilson, R. J., "An Introduction to Matroid Theory," *The Am. Math. Monthly* **80,** No. 5: 500–525 (May 1973).

II-4

FLOWS IN NETWORKS

Ellis L. Johnson
IBM, Thomas J. Watson Research Center

1. INTRODUCTION

In this chapter we present some algorithms and theory for the network flow problem (NFP) and indicate extensions and applications. The reference list should provide a starting point for recent work in the area. No historical survey is given; instead the focus here is on an exposition incorporating recent developments. However, credit should be given to Ford and Fulkerson [1962] for the major development of the subject.

We begin with two special cases of the NFP: shortest paths and maximum flows. Both are interesting in themselves but become more important as alternating steps in the primal-dual algorithm or method (P-DM). We emphasize performing both halves of the P-DM in an efficient way.

Relations with LP are given along with the out-of-kilter, SM, and DSM versions of the algorithm.

Applications are mentioned with emphasis on the project planning problem. Finally, extensions to flows with gains, multiterminal, and multicommodity flows are mentioned.

2. SHORTEST PATHS

2.1 Definitions

A simple example of a NFP is to send one unit of flow from any one of a set S_0 of nodes, called the *sources*, to any one of another set S_T of nodes, called the *sinks*, at the least cost. When the costs are nonnegative, there are particularly attractive algorithms for solving this shortest path problem.

We are given a network G with *node* set V and *arc* set E where each arc $e \in E$ is an ordered pair $e = (i,j)$ of distinct nodes. The arc $e = (i,j)$ is *from i to j*. A *flow* is a vector ($\mathbf{x}_e$: $e \in E$) satisfying some set of *flow constraints* defined in terms of the net flow f_i out of node i, where

$$f_i = \sum_{e=(i,j)} x_e - \sum_{e=(k,i)} x_e.$$

If f_i is negative, then $-f_i$ is the net flow into node i. The flow constraints for our shortest path problem are

$$\sum_{i \in S_0} f_i = 1, \qquad f_i \geqslant 0, \;\; i \in S_0,$$

$$f_i = 0, \qquad i \notin S_0 \cup S_T,$$

$$\sum_{i \in S_T} f_i = -1, \qquad f_i \leqslant 0, \;\; i \in S_T.$$

More general NFPs will involve flow constraints of the form $f_i = b_i, i \in V$.

The unit *cost* of arc e is some number c_e. The objective is to minimize total cost of the flow: $\sum c_e x_e$. When all $c_e \geqslant 0$, an answer to the previously stated problem will be a chain from source to sink. A *path* is a sequence $i_0, e_1, i_1, e_2, i_2, \ldots, i_{L-1}, e_L, i_L$ of, alternately, nodes and arcs such that $e_k = (i_{k-1}, i_k)$ or $e_k = (i_k, i_{k-1})$. A *chain* is a simple, directed path, that is, the nodes $i_0, i_1, \ldots, i_L$ are are distinct, and each edge $e_k = (i_{k-1}, i_k)$. To be precise, the problem here is a shortest chain problem.

2.2 Algorithm for the Shortest Chain from Some Source to Some Sink

Assume all $c_e \geqslant 0$. The algorithm here is a simple modification of Dijkstra's algorithm for the shortest path problem [Dijkstra, 1959; Johnson, 1972]. (For a general survey of some shortest path problems and methods, see Dreyfus [1969].)

Step 0: Let the *candidate set* S_c consists of the sources, $S_c = S_0$, and let $d_i = 0$ for $i \in S_0$ and $d_i = \infty$ otherwise.

Step 1: Choose $i^* \in S_c$ giving the minimum of $d_i, i \in S_c$. This d_i is the shortest distance (using length c_e) from a source to i^*, and arc e_i (to be defined for all $i \in S_c$ except for the sources) is the last arc in the path. If i^* is a sink, then terminate. Otherwise, go to the Step 2.

Step 2: *Scan* node i^*; that is, for each arc $e = (i^*, j)$ replace d_j by min $\{d_j, d_i + c_e\}$. If d_j was ∞, put j in S_c. If d_j becomes smaller, let $e_j = e = (i^*, j)$.

Step 3: Remove i^* from S_c and go to Step 1 unless S_c is empty in which case terminate.

This algorithm may terminate without reaching any sink. In that case, there is no directed path from a source to a sink. By ignoring the termination condition in Step 1, we can find a shortest chain from the sources to all other nodes which can be reached. The total amount of work in Step 2 is at most of order $|E|$, the number of arcs, provided the graph is arranged so that for each node we can find the arcs out of that node without, for example, having to look through the edge list.

In Step 1, the total work required by simply going through S_c in order to find the min is at most of order $|V|^2$. This number can be reduced when $|V|^2 < E$ by using a binary sort, or 2-sort [Johnson, 1972]. The total work is then at most $|E|(2 \log |V| - \log |E|)$. However, the work in Step 3 becomes, at most, of order $|V| \log |V|$. Both of these steps require, in practice, much less work.

The flow problem is solved by backtracking from the sink reached, using arcs e_j and making the flow $x_e = 1$, until a source is reached, for which $e_j = 0$.

There is a class of shortest path problems with some negative costs c_e which can still be solved using network flow techniques (see Section 5) but cannot be solved with the algorithm in this section. In order to define that class, define a *directed circuit* to be a chain except that $i_o = i_L$. A *negative directed circuit* is a directed circuit such that the sum of the costs on the edges of the circuit is negative. Then the problem can be solved as a NFP provided there are no negative directed circuits. If there are negative directed circuits the problem is much harder (equivalent to the TSP).

3. MAXIMAL FLOWS

3.1 Augmenting Chains

Another special case of the flow problem is to send the most possible flow from source to sink when each arc e has a capacity α_e^0; that is, the flow x_e must satisfy $0 \leqslant x_e \leqslant \alpha_e^0$. The flow requirements are

$$\sum_{i \in S_0} f_i = Q, \qquad f_i \geqslant 0, \quad i \in S_0,$$

$$f_i = 0, \qquad i \notin S_0 \cup S_T,$$

$$\sum_{i \in S_T} f_i = -Q, \quad f_i \leqslant 0, \ i \in S_T,$$

and the problem is to maximize Q. Here, costs on arcs are not considered.

We now describe an algorithm for finding a max flow. First, a device (to be used in Section 4 for the general NFP) will be described. The flows x_e will be suppressed and reflected implicitly in revised capacities on arcs and oppositely directed copies of arcs. The given capacities α_e^0 of arcs will remain fixed, and α_e will be used to denote revised capacities, which change during the course of the algorithm.

Given any arc $e = (i, j) \in E$, expand E to include *the opposite arc* $e' = (j, i)$ which is in one-to-one correspondence with the *given arc e*. It is important to keep track of corresponding arcs; that is, if e is given and e' is its opposite arc, then e is the *reverse arc* of e' and e' is the *reverse arc* of e. In general, $\alpha_e = \alpha_e^0 - x_e$ and $\alpha_{e'} = x_e$, where x_e is the flow at any given iteration of the algorithm.

An augmenting chain is a chain from a source to a sink such that each arc in the chain has positive capacity. A *flow augmentation* along an augmenting chain consists of decreasing the capacity of each arc in the chain by θ and increasing by θ the capacity of the reverse arc of each arc in the chain. Translated into a flow change, this change increases the flow out of the source by θ and sends θ more flow to the sink. The largest value for θ, without violating any $0 \leqslant x_e \leqslant \alpha_e^0$, is the value of the smallest (revised) capacity along the chain.

Starting with zero flow means every given arc e has $\alpha_e = \alpha_e^0$ and every opposite arc has zero capacity. With that start, $Q = 0$. We can look for an augmenting chain using a scanning procedure similar to that used in finding shortest paths. In fact, we could use the same algorithm as in Section 1 by letting $c_e = 0$ if $\alpha_e = 0$ and $c_e = \infty$ if $\alpha_e = 0$. That algorithm is restated using the terminology of Ford and Fulkerson [1962].

Step 0: Let the sources be *labeled* but *unscanned.* Every other node is *unlabeled.*

Step 1: Choose any labeled, unscanned node i.

Step 2: Scan node i; that is, for each arc $e = (i, j)$ with $\alpha_e > 0$, if j is unlabeled then let it be labeled and unscanned and let $e_j = e = (i, j)$. If any sink becomes labeled then terminate with an augmenting chain. Otherwise go to Step 3 after looking at every arc (i, j).

Step 3: Let i be labeled and scanned. Go to Step 1 unless there are no more labeled, unscanned nodes, in which case terminate.

In the previous terminology, the labeled, unscanned nodes are the candidate set. Step 1 is simple here because all d_i are zero for i labeled. Scanning is slightly more simple because all d_i are zero or infinity.

If the termination is in Step 2, then there is an augmenting chain. Making a flow augmentation along that chain results in a larger flow Q and that chain becomes no longer augmenting because at least one arc in it reaches capacity zero, while its reverse arc reaches full capacity; that is, some $\alpha_e = 0$.

By alternately repeating Steps 1-3 and making flow augmentations, we eventually terminate in Step 3, provided all initial capacities are integer, because every flow augmentation is integer and the capacities remain integer. Assuming there is some max possible value of Q, the algorithm terminates because Q is increased by at least one with every flow augmentation.

It is easily seen that this algorithm will find an augmenting chain if there is one. It is also easily seen that any flow giving the max possible value of Q will not permit existence of an augmenting chain. However, it is not easily seen that any flow with no augmenting chain will give the largest possible value of Q. In order to prove this, we turn to the max flow-min cut theorem, which can be interpreted as an instance of the LP duality theorem.

First, one remark should be made. In the present framework, an augmenting chain may include an opposite arc of a given arc so that the flow augmentation reduces the flow in the given arc. Thus, our augmenting chains are called augmenting paths in terms of the given arcs.

3.2 Max Flow-Min Cut

This material is due to Ford and Fulkerson [1962, Chapter 1]. If we form the set L of labeled nodes at the termination of the algorithm, the given arcs $e = (i, j)$, $i \in L$, $j \notin L$, must have $x_e = \alpha_e^0$ and the given arcs $e = (i, j)$, $i \notin L$, $j \in L$, must have $x_e = 0$. Let $C = \{e\colon\ i \in L, j \notin L\}$ (see Fig. 1). Then $\sum_{e \in C} \alpha_e^0 \geqslant Q$ because there is no way to get more than that much flow across from L to the complement L^c of L. The value $\sum_{e \in C} \alpha_e^0$ associated with the cutset (L, L^c) is thus an upper bound on Q.

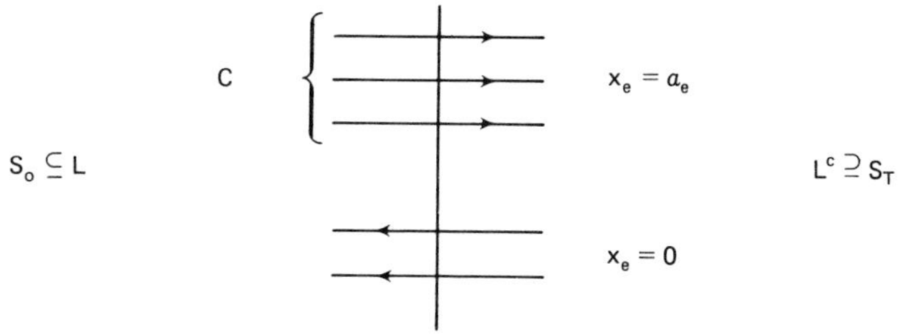

Fig. 1.

We must show our flow achieves $Q = \sum_{e \in C} \alpha_e^0$. Intuitively, it should be clear that flow $\sum_{e \in C} \alpha_e^0$ crosses from L to L^c, so it must go to a sink because no flow goes back from L^c to L. The reader interested in a purely network proof which is complete and precise is referred to Ford and Fulkerson [1962].

3.3 Edmonds-Karp Max Flow Algorithm [1972]

The method given in Section 3.1 will converge, but the number of flow augmentations may be as many as the value Q of the max flow. This section gives a method for finding a max flow which will require no more than $\frac{1}{2}|V||E|$ flow augmentations.

In the max flow algorithm of Section 3.1, every arc has length zero or infinity, and the distances to nodes are all zero or infinite. Suppose instead we arbitrarily say every arc (with positive capacity) has length one instead of zero. This length has no connection with cost, if any, of the arc, and the distances to nodes are only used in Step 1 to decide which nodes to scan next. If fact, the correct node will be chosen if we simply choose the node first labeled. That is, if the shortest path algorithm of Section 2.2 is applied to a network with all arcs having length one, we can keep the candidate set as a list and add new nodes to the bottom of the list while choosing i^* in Step 1 to be the node at the top of the list.

The bound on the number of flow augmentations follows from the fact that in the sequence of shortest path problems solved no node gets closer to a source and whenever an arc reaches zero capacity (so its length becomes infinity) the reverse arc is not in a shortest path until the distance to one of the two incident nodes becomes two larger. In Fig. 2, if arc (i, j) is in a flow augmenting chain and reaches zero capacity, then $d_j = d_i + 1$. Now, d_j does not decrease by putting infinite length on arc (i, j). If arc (j, i) is in a flow augmentation, it must be in the shortest path to node i so $d_i' = d_j' + 1$ at that time. This new d_i' is at least two more than when arc (i, j) was dropped. Thus, an arc and its reverse arc can only reach zero capacity $\frac{1}{2}|V|$ times because no node can be further than $|V|$ from a source, unless it is distance ∞ in which case it remains so. Since every flow augmentation puts some new arc at zero capacity and there are $|E|$ arcs, there can be no more than $\frac{1}{2}|V||E|$ flow augmentations.

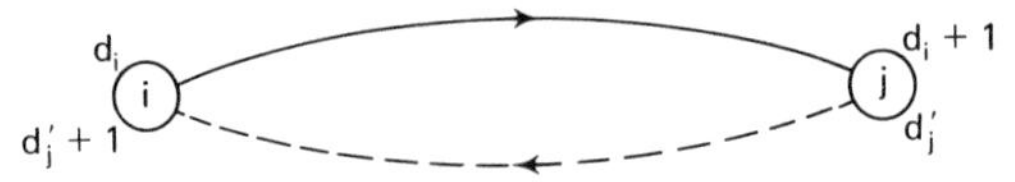

Fig. 2.

4. PRIMAL-DUAL ALGORITHM

4.1 Min Cost Flow

Section 2 dealt with a shortest path problem or, equivalently, a min cost flow problem for a flow of one or, equivalently, a min cost flow problem with infinite capacities on the flow in every arc. In Section 3, capacities on arcs are introduced, but the problem dealt with was only to find a max flow, not a least cost flow. This max flow problem can be solved by successively finding augmenting chains (Section 3.1) which can be done in such a way (Section 3.3) that it can be interpreted as successively finding shortest paths with each arc having length either one or infinity.

To solve the general min cost flow problem, defined below, we will alternately solve a shortest path problem and a max flow problem. The shortest path step will provide us with a dual change, and the max flow step gives a primal change. Bounds of $|V|^2$ and $|V|^3$ can be placed on the order of work required for these steps, so they are of approximately the same difficulty.

By comparison with the earlier P-DM, we combine several dual changes into one step avoiding a sequence of "non-breakthroughs." By comparison with earlier connections drawn between shortest paths and network flows, the shortest path problems solved here all involve nonnegative lengths on arcs.

To begin, the *min-cost flow problem* is to find real numbers x_e, $e \in E$, satisfying:

$$0 \leqslant x_e \leqslant \alpha_e^0, \quad e \in E, \quad \text{(capacity constraints)};$$

$$f_i = b_i, \quad i \in V, \quad \text{(exogenous flow constraints)};$$

and minimizing $\sum c_e x_e$. Here, f_i is defined to be

$$f_i = \sum_{e=(i,j)} x_e - \sum_{e=(k,j)} x_e,$$

where the first sum is the flow out of node i and the second is the flow into node i. If b_i is positive, then the flow constraint $f_i = b_i$ says that there must be a net flow out of node i, so b_i is a supply at node i. If b_i is negative, then $-b_i$ is the demand at node i.

In order for there to be a solution to the problem, $\sum b_i$ over all nodes i must be zero; that is, in the entire network, demand must equal supply. Because of the capacity constraints, there may still be no solution.

We begin with any values x_e^0, $0 \leqslant x_e^0 \leqslant \alpha_e^0$, $e \in E$, and π_i^0, $i \in V$. If not given, these can all be zero. Initially, all of the infeasibilities are transferred to the flow constraints by changing x_e^0 to be:

$$x_e^0 = \alpha_e^0 \quad \text{if} \quad \pi_i^0 - \pi_j^0 > c_e, \quad \text{or}$$

$$x_e^0 = 0 \quad \text{if} \quad \pi_i^0 - \pi_j^0 \leqslant c_e,$$

where $e = (i, j)$. Now, the nodes $i \in V$ are partitioned as follows:

$$i \text{ is an } outer \text{ node if } \quad f_i^0 < b_i,$$

$$i \text{ is an } inner \text{ node if } \quad f_i^0 > b_i,$$

$$i \text{ is a } satisfied \text{ node if } \quad f_i^0 = b_i.$$

As in Section 3.1, for each arc $e = (i, j)$, there is introduced an opposite arc $e' = (j, i)$. Given a flow x_e, the arc e has capacity $\alpha_e^0 - x_e$ and the opposite arc has capacity x_e. Instead of changing the flow values, we change the capacities (simultaneously for the pair of reverse arcs). The cost of a reverse arc e' is $-c_e$.

4.2 Shortest Path Step

For each arc $e = (i, j)$ whether given or opposite, let the length of the arc be $\lambda_e = c_e - (\pi_i - \pi_j)$ unless the arc has zero capacity in which case its length is infinite. Now, apply the shortest path algorithm of Section 2.2 using lengths λ_e and letting the set of sources be the outer nodes and the set of sinks be the inner nodes.

For our purposes, the distances d_i, $i \in V$, are more important than the path itself. The max flow routine below can make use of the path, but here changes in $\pi_i, i \in V$, will be made. The d_i satisfy:

$$d_i + \lambda_e \geqslant d_j, \qquad e = (i, j) \text{ and } \alpha_e > 0.$$

Hence, if $\pi_i' = \pi_i - d_i$, then

$$\lambda_e' = c_e - (\pi_i' - \pi_j') = c_e - (\pi_i - \pi_j) + d_i - d_j$$
$$= d_i + \lambda_e - d_j \geqslant 0$$

Hence, changing π_i to π_i' will result in new nonnegative lengths λ_e' such that there is at least one zero distance path from a source to a sink. That path is the one found by the shortest path algorithm, because for arc e in that path, $d_i + \lambda_e = d_j$ so $\lambda_e' = 0$.

If the shortest path algorithm terminates with no path to a sink, then the problem is infeasible. The reason is that, similar to the max flow problem, the labeled nodes form a cut set and a set L containing the sources such that no arc goes from L to L^c. Even if we ignore the length c_e' and use the max flow routine of Section 3.1, the same set L of nodes will be labeled and the proof of infeasibility here is along the same lines as the proof of max flow in Section 3.

The details of that proof will be omitted, but let us remark that here any initial flow could have been given and any subset of the supplies and demands could be satisfied. Nevertheless, once there is no path from a source, or outer node, to a sink, or inner node, there is no way to further reduce the infeasibilities of the problem.

4.3 Maximum Flow Step

In this step, only arcs with $\lambda_e = 0$ are considered. Among such arcs, there is at least one augmenting chain: the shortest path found in Section 4.2. After the max flow routine terminates, there is no further augmenting chain, so there is no chain from any source to any sink using arcs with $\lambda_e = 0$.

During an augmentation, if some f_i reaches the value b_i, then that node immediately becomes a satisfied node and ceases to be a source or a sink. Since there are only $|V|$ nodes, this occurrence can take place at most $|V|$ times. When it does happen, we must, in principle, begin the max flow routine anew, but in practice, particularly when a sink becomes satisfied, it is possible to continue without starting over.

When the initial capacities α_e^0, flows x_e^0, and node requirements b_i are all integer, every flow augmentation is an integer amount. Since there are bounds of order $|V|^3$ or less for both the dual (shortest path) step and the primal (max flow) step and since these steps alternate with each primal step resulting in an integer decrease in the primal infeasibility, a bound can be placed on the total work which could be required. This bound is $|V|^3$ times the initial primal infeasibilities summed over the nodes.

On the other hand, each dual step results in an improved dual solution. When the initial costs c_e and initial solution π_i^0 are all integer, this improvement is by an integer amount. Thus another bound for the most work required is $|V|^3$ times the difference between the initial dual objective value and the opt objective value.

When neither the primal nor dual is integer, there is no good bound on the most required work [Zadeh, 1973]. The question of whether there exists an algorithm for this problem with a polynomial bound on the most required work is an open question. Zadeh [1973] shows that for the usual algorithms (primal simplex, primal-dual, etc.) there are counter-examples to a polynomial bound.

4.4 Complementary Slackness

The proof that this algorithm produces an opt solution will be indicated by means of the complementary slackness conditions of LP. These conditions say, here, that a flow x_e, $e \in E$, is opt if there is some π_i, $i \in V$, such that x_e satisfies the capacity and exogenous flow constraints and, in addition, one of the following holds for each arc $e = (i, j)$:

$$x_e = 0 \quad \text{and} \quad \pi_i - \pi_j < c_e; \quad \text{or}$$

$$0 \leqslant x_e \leqslant \alpha_e \quad \text{and} \quad \pi_i - \pi_j = c_e; \quad \text{or}$$

$$x_e = \alpha_e \quad \text{and} \quad \pi_i - \pi_j > c_e.$$

Initially, these conditions hold. In the max flow step, only arcs with $\pi_i - \pi_j = c_e$ are used, and $0 \leqslant x_e \leqslant \alpha_e$ is maintained. In the shortest path step, if $x_e = 0$ then only the given arc is present and $\pi_i - \pi_j \leqslant c_e$ is imposed. If $x_e = \alpha_e$, then only the reverse arc (j, i) is present, and $\pi_j - \pi_i \leqslant -c_e$ is maintained. If $0, < x_e < \alpha_e$, then $\pi_i - \pi_j = c_e$ (and $\pi_j - \pi_i = -c_e$), so $\lambda_e = 0$. Thus $d_i = d_j$ because both arcs (i, j) and (j, i) are present with length zero. Hence, $\pi_i - \pi_j$ does not change in the dual step when $0 < x_e < \alpha_e$. The changes which can take place are illustrated in Fig. 3a. In Fig. 3b, the case of piece-wise linear, convex cost on an arc is illustrated. The slope of the cost is, then, a monotone increasing step function. This case can be treated by using four arcs with costs and capacities, respectively: c_1 and α_1; c_2 and $\alpha_2 - \alpha_1$; c_3 and $\alpha_3 - \alpha_2$; and c_4 and $\alpha_4 - \alpha_3$. It can also be treated directly with primal changes in the horizontal direction and dual changes in the vertical direction.

4.5 Out-of-Kilter

The presentation here of the primal-dual algorithm does allow any initial solution x_e^0, π_i^0 but immediately shifts all of the infeasibility to the flow constraints while assuring that every arc satisfies the complementary slackness conditions illustrated in Fig. 3a. There are other possible initialization procedures, and the question is undoubtedly of practical importance. On the other hand, the problem can be attacked directly with a given x_e^0 and π_i^0, as explained below (see pp. 162-9 of Ford and Fulkerson [1962]). We suppose for sake of discussion, that $f_i = b_i$ for all nodes i.

For each arc e, compare the point $(x_e, \pi_i - \pi_j)$ to the heavy line as shown in Fig. 3a. An arc is *out of kilter* if the point is not on the line. If, for example,

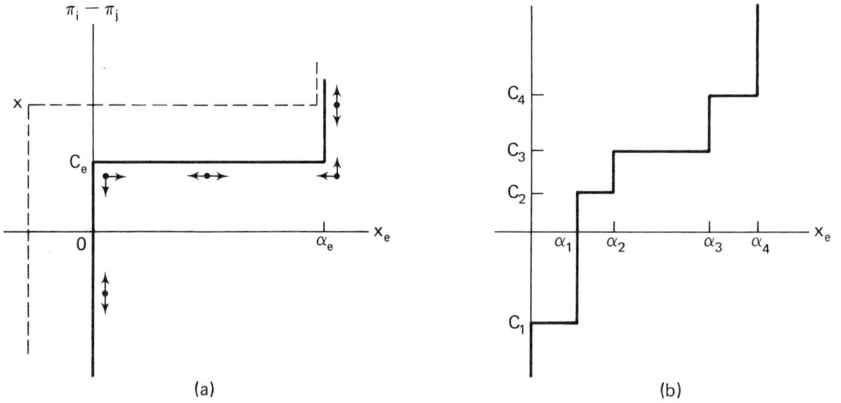

Fig. 3.

the point is to the left of the line, then temporarily replace the cost c_e by $\pi_i - \pi_j$ and the lower bound on flow (previously zero) by x_e. In other words, only allow x_e to increase and $\pi_i - \pi_j$ to decrease. The dotted line in Fig. 3a illustrates the new complementary slackness conditions. In this way, no variable gets more "out-of-kilter"; that is, further from the true complementary slackness line.

Choose any one out-of-kilter arc $e = (i, j)$. If it is to the left of the line, increase x_e until either $x_e = 0$ if $\pi_i - \pi_j \leqslant c_e$ or until $x_e = \alpha_e$ if $\pi_i - \pi_j > c_e$. Now there is excess flow into node j and deficit flow into node i. Make j a source and i a sink and apply the primal-dual algorithm described earlier. It is not necessary to think of increasing x_e at all, but instead just make node j a source and node i a sink. In any case, the problem is treated as before except that only one arc at a time is treated as though it were out-of-kilter.

5. SHORTEST PATHS REVISITED

In Section 2, lengths of arcs are assumed to be nonnegative. Here, that assumption is dropped, but in order for the algorithm to find the true shortest chain, there must be no negative length circuit. However, the algorithm will detect negative length circuits and can be used to find such circuits if they exist.

Two versions of the problem will be treated: a single source-single sink (that is, to find the shortest path from the source to the sink); and the problem of simply finding a negative circuit if there is one.

Treating the problem as a flow problem, we begin by placing a capacity of one on each negative length arc and then setting the flow to one. In terms of our convention of reverse arcs, we replace an arc $e = (i, j)$ with a length $c_e < 0$ by the arc (j, i) with a cost of $-c_e$. Now, however, there is one unit of excess flow out of node i and one into node j. After changing each arc with $c_e < 0$ in this way, some flow values f_i are generated. For this problem, b_i is zero originally, except for the source and sink where b_i is +1 and −1, respectively. Clearly, the sum of the infeasibilities is of order less than $|V|^2$.

Applying the method of Section 4 results in termination in at most $|V|^2$ flow augmentations and each flow augmentation requires solving at most one shortest path problem with nonnegative length as in Section 2.

Let us remark on the dual variables for this problem. If a number λ_i at each node i is subtracted from all arcs out of node i and added to all arcs into node i, then the resulting problem is the same because any simple path goes into a node once and out of it once, if at all, except for the source and sink.

The resulting lengths are $c_e' = c_e - \lambda_i + \lambda_j$. The dual LP problem (see Section 6.4 below) is to find $\lambda_i, i \in V$, such that all $c_e' \geqslant 0$, for given arcs e [Nemhauser, 1972].

A negative length circuit will be easily seen at the conclusion of the algorithm by looking for a circuit including some given arc e having $c_e < 0$ and for which

$c'_e = c_e - (\lambda_i - \lambda_j)$ is also less than zero. This circuit will have negative length using length c'_e on the arcs, because every arc with flow in it has $c'_e = 0$ unless $c_e < 0$ and then $c'_e \leqslant 0$. But the total length around the circuit is the same in c_e as in c'_e.

The algorithm may terminate with a negative length path from source to sink. In that case, the path is opt if there is no flow around a negative length circuit, and then there may or may not be a negative length circuit. Even if the path from source to sink has negative length, we cannot know if it is opt if there is flow around a negative circuit. Whenever there is flow around a negative circuit, the method fails in the sense that the path will not in general be opt. In that case, network flow methods cannot be used, and the problem is much harder.

The problem of simply finding a negative circuit is the same except that $b_i = 0$ for all $i \in V$ so that there is no source or sink. With that formulation, the algorithm will always find one or more negative circuits if there is one.

6. LINEAR PROGRAMMING

6.1 Basic Solutions and Trees

A LP is a problem of the form: minimize $\mathbf{z} = \mathbf{cx}$ subject to $\mathbf{Ax} = \mathbf{b}$ and $\mathbf{0} \leqslant \mathbf{x} \leqslant \boldsymbol{\alpha}$. In this Section, we relate a special class of LP to NFPs and give results about those LPs using descriptions involving networks.

These LPs always have opt solutions with integer x_j whenever the $\boldsymbol{b}$ and $\boldsymbol{\alpha}$ are integer. The matrices $\mathbf{A}$ are totally unimodular [Hoffman and Kruskal, 1956]. This fact leads to the solution of several interesting combinatorial problems [Fulkerson, 1966].

Suppose in a LP the coefficient matrix $\mathbf{A}$ has entries either 0, +1 or −1 and that every column has at most two nonzero entries. In addition, for any column with two nonzero entries, those entries must be a +1 and a −1. Corresponding to such a matrix $\mathbf{A}$, form a network with a node for each row of $\mathbf{A}$. For each column $\mathbf{e}$ of $\mathbf{A}$, let there be an arc from node i if $a_{ik} = +1$ and to node j if $a_{jk} = -1$. Columns with only one nonzero entry will correspond to one-ended arcs or *slacks*. See Fig. 4 for an example. The LP will correspond to a NFP on this network. The matrix $\mathbf{A}$ is called a *node-arc incidence matrix* of the network. The only additional generality introduced here is in allowing slacks. They can be changed to two ended arcs by simply introducing a redundant equation to $\mathbf{Ax} = \mathbf{b}$; that is, add up the rows of $\mathbf{A}$, take the negative, and do the same for $\mathbf{b}$. In Fig. 4, the additional row and the dotted lines illustrate this change. In this form, the problem is exactly the NFP of Section 4.

In a LP, introducing a redundant row is unnatural. In fact, we do the opposite and eliminate redundant rows until $\mathbf{A}$ is of full row rank. In this case, it is easily seen that $\mathbf{A}$ has full row rank if and only if every connected component of the

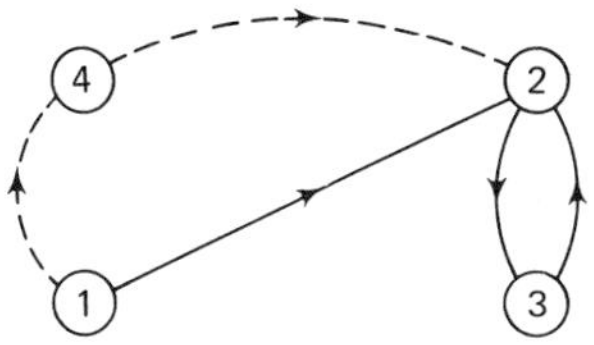

Nodes	Arcs				
1	1			1	
2	−1	1	−1		−1
3		−1	1		

[0 0 0 −1 1]

Fig. 4.

corresponding network has at least one slack. Thus, in a problem with no slacks, we introduce them by deleting rows. In a connected component with no slacks, any row is redundant and can be deleted. If the b_i for nodes i in that component sum to zero, then an equation is indeed redundant. Otherwise, the system is inconsistent and has no solution.

Henceforth, assume **A** to have full row rank. Since connected components of the network can be treated separately, we may as well assume the corresponding network consists of only one component which has at least one slack.

A *basic solution* to a LP is a solution x such that the column of **A** corresponding to x_j with $0 < x_j < \alpha_j$ are linearly independent. In order to identify basic solutions of a NFP, we must know which sets of columns of **A** are linearly independent when **A** is a node-arc incidence matrix. Some definitions are needed.

A *tree* is a connected network with no slacks and containing no circuit. Thus, in a tree there is a unique simple path between every pair of nodes. A *rooted tree* is a tree together with one slack. The slack is the *root* of the tree.

THEOREM 1. A set of columns from a node-arc incidence matrix is linearly independent iff the arcs and slacks corresponding to the columns from one or more trees or rooted trees.

Proof: For a complete proof see Dantzig [1963, pp. 356–357]. Here, only an outline will be given.

Define an *A-circuit* to be either a circuit (a simple path which closes back to its beginning) or a *doubly-rooted path* (a simple path with a slack at each end). The theorem is equivalent to the assertion that A-circuits correspond to minimal, dependent sets of columns of **A**. This equivalence is seen by the fact that a rooted tree contains no A-circuit, and deleting any arc of an A-circuit gives a tree or rooted tree.

It is easy to see that A-circuits do correspond to dependent columns of **A** and are thus forbidden in the network corresponding to any set of independent columns of **A**. Figure 5 gives an example for a circuit and a doubly-rooted path illustrating the linear combinations required to show dependence.

The converse half of the theorem is equivalent to the assertion that if no A-circuits are present, then the columns of **A** are independent. That fact is illustrated

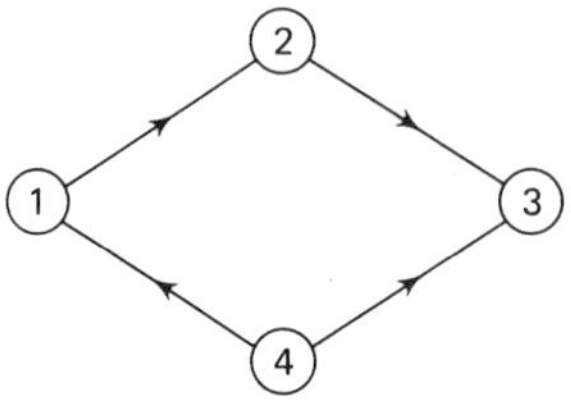

Nodes	Arcs				
	+1	+1	−1	+1	
1	1			−1	= 0
2	−1	1			= 0
3		−1	−1		= 0
4			1	1	= 0

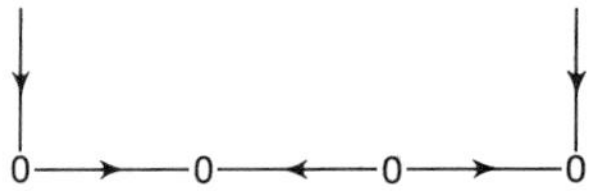

Nodes	Arcs					
	+1	+1	−1	+1	−1	
1	−1	1				= 0
2		−1	−1			= 0
3			1	1		= 0
4				−1	1	= 0

Fig. 5.

for a rooted tree in Fig. 6. In fact, the square submatrix corresponding to a rooted tree is triangular. The proof of this fact involves the simple lemma that a tree of more than one node has at least two ends, one of which is not the root. An *end* of a tree is a node met by exactly one arc of the tree. Thus, the row corresponding to an end of a tree has only one nonzero entry. Deleting that end of a tree and the incident arc results in a smaller rooted tree whose corresponding matrix is formed by deleting a row and column of the original matrix.

6.2 Adjacent Vertices

The preceding section gives necessary and sufficient conditions for a flow to correspond to a basic solution or, in other words, to correspond to a vertex of the polyhedron of solutions. In this section, we give conditions for two such vertices to be adjacent; that is, connected by an edge of the polyhedron. The

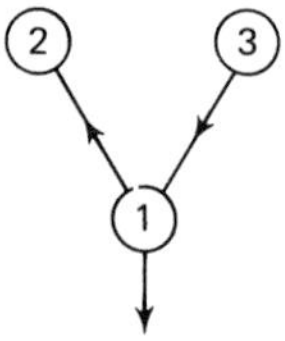

Nodes	Arcs		
1	+1	+1	−1
2		−1	
3			+1

Fig. 6.

question of adjacency is of interest in studying LP methods since the SM moves from one vertex to an adjacent one.

The following theorem summarizes the results.

THEOREM 2. A flow $\mathbf{x}$ corresponds to a vertex of the polyhedron P iff the arcs e_j with $0 < x_j < \alpha_j$ do not include any A-circuits. Two such flows $\mathbf{x}^1$ and $\mathbf{x}^2$ correspond to adjacent vertices iff the set of arcs e with $x_e^1 \neq x_e^2$ contains exactly one A-circuit.

Proof: Recall that an A-circuit is either a circuit or a doubly-rooted path. The first assertion of the theorem is equivalent to Theorem 1.

To outline the proof of the second assertion, let $\mathbf{x}^1$ and $\mathbf{x}^2$ be flows corresponding to vertices and let the set of arcs e with $x_e^1 \neq x_e^2$ contain one A-circuit. Let a be an arc of that A-circuit. Once x_a is fixed between x_a^1 and x_a^2, and every x_e with $x_e^1 = x_e^2$ is set to that common value, a unique flow is defined. That flow $\mathbf{x}$ is on the line segment joining $\mathbf{x}^1$ and $\mathbf{x}^2$, and that flow cannot be written as the midpoint of two other flows unless they also have $x_e = x_e^1 = x_e^2$ for all e such that $x_e^1 = x_e^2$. Therefore, that line segment must be an edge of the polyhedron.

The converse is proven along similar lines.

6.3 Primal Simplex Method (SM)

The primal SM moves from one primal feasible solution to a better one and maintains the conditions:

$$0 < x_k < \alpha_k \quad \text{implies} \quad c_k = \pi_i - \pi_j \quad \text{where} \quad e_k = (i, j),$$

so that once the other two conditions

$$x_k = 0 \quad \text{implies} \quad c_k \geqslant \pi_i - \pi_j, \quad \text{and}$$

$$x_k = \alpha_k \quad \text{implies} \quad c_k \leqslant \pi_i - \pi_j$$

are satisfied, then the solution is optimal.

In discussing the SM, two points should be emphasized. First, the usual tableau discussion of the SM actually involves moving from one basis to another. Hence, there may be several dual changes for each primal change (due to primal degeneracy). Here, the discussion is in terms of moving from vertex to vertex and not from basis to basis.

Secondly, we will address the question of whether a change from one vertex to another is along an edge of the polyhedron; that is, whether the vertices are adjacent or not. In the case of the primal SM, this question is equivalent to the same question considered for the special case of the max-flow routine.

For simplicity, we consider the case where there are no slacks and only mention modifications necessary when they are present.

Clearly, a flow is opt iff there is no circuit around which the flow can be changed in one direction while decreasing the total cost. If we adopt the same convention as earlier of introducing a reverse arc which is present whenever the flow is positive and of deleting the original arc whenever the flow is at capacity, then we can say that a flow is opt iff there is no negative length (directed) circuit [Klein, 1967]. In Section 5, finding such a circuit was considered. There the role of the dual variables was discussed. To summarize, we can assign numbers π_i to the nodes i and change c_e to $c_e' = c_e - (\pi_i - \pi_j)$, for $e = (i,j)$, without changing the length of a circuit. Thus, the dual variables are used to demonstrate optimality by bringing $c_e' \geqslant 0$ for all e. Alternatively, there is a negative circuit, and increasing the flow around it will force some arc to capacity breaking up that negative circuit. Convergence of this algorithm can be proven in the all-integer case (including the cost coefficients c_e) by showing the flow not only gets better, but always improves by an integer amount.

This method is not really the SM because the solution may be nonbasic, and, even if basic, the changes may not be between adjacent vertices.

A modification of this method which is much closer to the SM is as follows. Pick any arc with negative reduced cost c_e' (say the most negative). Now, every other negative reduced cost is temporarily replaced by zero (we can think of increasing its original cost until the reduced cost is zero). Now for the chosen negative c_e', say $e = e_0 = (i_0, j_0)$, make i_0 a sink and j_0 a source and find the shortest path from j_0 to i_0. If the distance becomes as large as $-c_{e_0}'$, then terminate and make the dual changes $\pi_i = \pi_i - d_i$, which changes c_{e_0}' to zero. This case results in a smaller number of arcs with negative reduced costs. Otherwise, we find the shortest path to i_0, make changes in dual variables so that c_{e_0}' remains negative, but now there is a zero distance path from j_0 to i_0 so that a flow change can be made around a negative circuit. Make all of the flow changes possible and repeat the procedure, either with the same e_0 or another one having negative costs. To make the flow changes, we can use the max flow methods of Section 3 using only arcs having zero reduced cost. The question of whether we are really doing the SM or not comes back to what is done in the max flow step.

Clearly, if we start with $c_e' = 0$ for every arc e having $0 < x_e < \alpha_e$, then this method maintains that condition. The only questions concerning the relation to the SM are whether such arcs always form a rooted forest and whether we move to an adjacent rooted forest as described in Section 5.2. These questions only concern what happens in the max flow step and can be answered in general for the max flow problem, as will be done in Section 6.5. The same remarks apply to the P-DM or out of kilter method of Section 4.

6.4 Dual Simplex Method (DSM)

The dual problem of a NFP is of interest in itself as is seen from the example in Section 7 below where the original problem is actually the dual problem of a NFP.

The theorems here on basic solutions are rather different than for the primal problem but the proofs are similar and are omitted. Some additional definitions are required. As before, we consider the problem in equality form $\mathbf{Ax} = \mathbf{b}, \boldsymbol{\alpha} \geqslant \mathbf{x} \geqslant \mathbf{0}$, minimize $z = \mathbf{cx}$, where any slack variables are explicitly written in the $\mathbf{A}$ matrix and represented in the network as one-ended arcs. Assume that $\mathbf{A}$ has full row rank so that each connected component of the network has at least one slack. We have previously defined a rooted forest in Section 6.1. A *maximal rooted forest* is defined to be a rooted forest such that every node is in a tree and every tree has a root.

THEOREM 3. A solution π_i, $i \in V$, to the dual problem is basic in the dual problem iff the arcs with zero reduced cost $c'_e = c_e - \pi_i + \pi_j$ include a max rooted forest. The corresponding primal solution is to set $x_e = \alpha_e$ if $c'_e < 0$, $x_e = 0$ if $c'_e > 0$, and x_e arbitrary when $c'_e = 0$. The existence of a max rooted forest using arcs e with $c'_e = 0$ assures that the flow constraints $\mathbf{Ax} = \mathbf{b}$ can be satisfied, but perhaps with infeasible flow values x_e.

THEOREM 4. Two basic dual solutions $\boldsymbol{\pi}^1$ and $\boldsymbol{\pi}^2$ are adjacent on the dual polyhedron iff the arcs which have zero reduced costs for both $\boldsymbol{\pi}^1$ and $\boldsymbol{\pi}^2$ do not include a max rooted forest but there is at least one other arc such that adding that one arc to the set would result in existence of a max rooted forest.

The DSM maintains a max rooted forest with 0 reduced costs and such that except for the arcs in the forest all the arcs are feasible and satisfy complementary slackness. Begin an iteration by choosing an arc, necessarily in the rooted forest, having flow x_e outside the feasible range $(0, \alpha_e)$. Now send as much flow through that arc as possible only using arcs with 0 reduced costs. For example, if $x_e < 0$, $e = (i, j)$, then make j a source and i a sink and use the max flow routine in Section 3 but only use arcs with zero reduced costs. Any other such arcs with infeasible flow can be prevented from becoming more infeasible.

Once the max flow step has terminated, a dual change can be made. The dual change is to increase or decrease, by the same amount, all π_k on nodes k of the trees left without a root when arc e is deleted. One increases or decreases these π_k depending on arc e. For example, if $x_e < 0$, $e = (i, j)$, and node j is in the unrooted tree as in Fig. 7, then increase π_j and all the other nodes in that tree formed by removing e. What stops the increase in π_j is that some arc which previously had positive reduced costs (otherwise it would have been used in the max flow step) now has zero reduced costs and is directed away from the tree for which the π_k are changing. Since we have a max rooted forest, we can now change the flow around a circuit or doubly-rooted path so as to make $x_e = 0$ while the dual change caused $c'_e = 0$. Now, we still have a max rooted forest with zero reduced cost and every arc not in that forest is feasible, $0 \leqslant x_e \leqslant \alpha_e$, and satisfies complementary slackness.

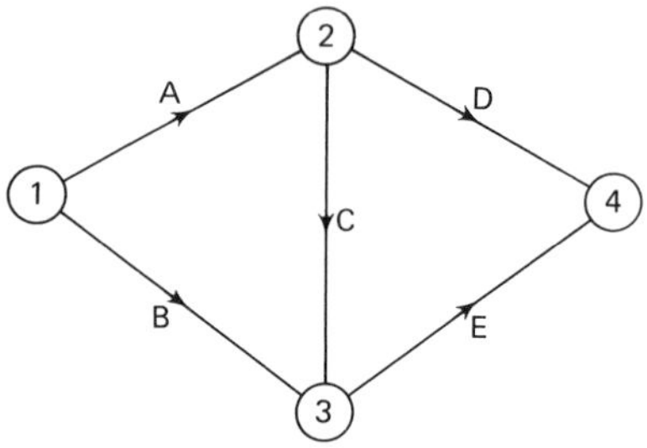

Fig. 7.

The question of whether or not the primal is basic is irrelevant here since we are focusing on the dual problem.

Early work on dual methods was done by Balas and Hammer [1962].

6.5 Basic Solutions

The question of whether a flow remains primal basic is only concerned with the max flow step. Thus, we focus on the problem of keeping a solution basic for a max flow problem in a capacitated network.

In the simple algorithm given in Section 3.1 a solution can be kept basic by giving preference to arcs e having $0 < x_e < \alpha_e^0$. In the convention used in Section 3, we give preference to arcs e for which both e and its reverse arc e' have positive capacity. These arcs must not contain a circuit or form a path from a source or sink to a source or sink in order for the solution to be basic.

Assume each connected component of these arcs is a tree. In Step 2 of Section 3.1 if node j is in such a tree then immediately label every node of that tree and use the arcs of the tree to reach those nodes. In this way, the tree of arcs e_j formed in Step 2 will either contain or be disjoint from any tree of arcs having $0 < x_e < \alpha_e^0$.

Johnson [1966] has pointed out the advantages of a triple-label method for storing trees in this context. Glover, et al., [1974] have used that method very successfully in a primal Simplex code. Srinivasan and Thompson [1973] report a two-fold increase in speed using it. Both Glover, et al. [1974] and Srinivasan and Thompson [1973] report results from extensive testing and show development of very fast codes. Their experience seems to indicate that the primal SM requires least storage and runs fastest. An improved labeling method of Glover et al. [1974] uses only 2 labels. See Barr, et al. [1974] and Kennington, et al. [1974] for other computational comparisons.

To keep a basic solution in the Edmonds-Karp algorithm of Section 3.3 is not so easy. Shortest edge-distance may not be consistent with preference to using arcs e having $0 < x_e < \alpha_e^0$. A further modification is needed, and the following one seems to work. Keep a number d_i on each node i such that d_i is never increased (d_i corresponds roughly to the number of edges in a path from a source to node i). Use the shortest path algorithm but when a new node i leaves the candidate list, replace d_j on the tree of arcs having $0 < x_e < \alpha_e^0$ including node i by max $\{d_j, d_i\}$.

7. APPLICATIONS

Many applications are included in the references [Bennington, 1974; Busacker and Saaty, 1965; Elmaghraby, 1970; Kelley, 1961; Veinott, 1971; Zangwell, 1969]. There are the obvious transportation and communication applications as well as the assignment application. Others are not of this type (see for example [Veinott, 1971]). Here, we go into some detail in giving one example where the initial problem is the dual problem to a NFP. The example is the use of CPMs for project planning (see pp. 151-162 of Ford and Fulkerson [1962] and also [Kelley, 1961]).

The problem is to find start and finish times of interdependent jobs so that a given overall completion time is met and so that certain jobs are finished before other jobs are started. In order to present the ideas, we will present a simple example of this type and show its formulation as a NFP.

Let there be five jobs, A, B, C, D and E such that A must be completed before C or D can start, and B and C must be completed before E starts. In Fig. 8, the arcs correspond to completions and starts of jobs. Let the normal completion times for A, B, C, D, E be 30, 25, 1, 20 and 22, respectively.

Suppose job C cannot be shortened but jobs A, B, D and E can be at costs of 1, 2, 3, 4 dollars per unit time, respectively. Let τ_A, τ_B, τ_D, τ_E, represent the decrease in time for jobs A, B, D, E so that the actual completion times are $30 - \tau_A$, $25 - \tau_B$, $20 - \tau_D$, $22 - \tau_E$. Let the problem be to complete all jobs in a time of 40 while minimizing costs for shortening the jobs. By placing a time t_i

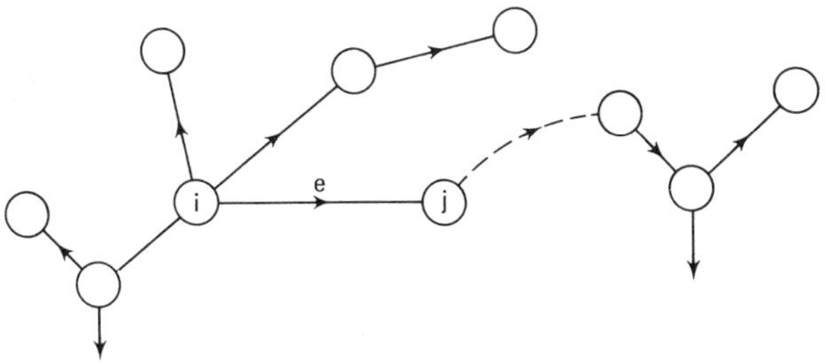

Fig. 8.

at nodes $i = 1, 2, 3, 4$, the problem can be stated as:

$$\text{minimize } \tau_A + 2\tau_B + 3\tau_D + 4\tau_E$$

subject to

$$\tau_A \geqslant 0, \quad \tau_B \geqslant 0, \quad \tau_D \geqslant 0, \quad \tau_E \geqslant 0,$$
$$t_2 \geqslant t_1 + (30 - \tau_A),$$
$$t_3 \geqslant t_1 + (25 - \tau_B),$$
$$t_3 \geqslant t_2 + 1,$$
$$t_4 \geqslant t_2 + (20 - \tau_D),$$
$$t_4 \geqslant t_3 + (22 - \tau_E),$$
$$t_4 - t_1 = 40.$$

This problem is the dual (Section 6.4) to a NFP. The primal problem is to send flows $x_A, \ldots, x_E$ giving a flow of Q from node 1 to node 4 while minimizing $40Q - (30x_A + 25x_B + x_C + 20x_D + 22x_E)$. The constraints are $0 \leqslant x_A \leqslant 1$, $0 \leqslant x_B \leqslant 2, 0 \leqslant x_C, 0 \leqslant x_D \leqslant 3, 0 \leqslant x_E \leqslant 4$,

$$Q = x_A + x_B,$$
$$x_A = x_C + x_D,$$
$$x_B + x_C = x_E,$$
$$x_D + x_E = Q.$$

In this case, the flow can be interpreted as dollars, so that when the flow equals the cost of reducing the time for a job then the job can be shortened. So long as the job is shortened, that flow value must be maintained.

For this problem, the opt flow values are $Q = 3, x_A = 1, x_B = 2, x_C = 1, x_D = 0, x_E = 3$, and the completion times are 17, 18, 1, 23, 22 for A, B, C, D, E respectively. Note that job D has excess time for completion.

The networks associated with this type of activity analysis are required to be without directed circuits. The longest, or critical, path is the longest path from start to finish where the lengths of arcs are the completion times. Because of the absence of circuits, these longest path problems can be solved by methods similar to those of Section 2 for finding shortest paths (see Busacker and Saaty [1965] pp. 128-135 for further details and references).

8. FLOWS WITH GAINS

The NFP with gains [Jewell, 1962] is similar to the flow problem except that the flow entering an arc e is multiplied by a factor k_e while passing through the arc. In terms of the coefficient matrix, the column corresponding to $e = (i, j)$ has +1 in row i and $-k_e$ in row j. The k_e can be positive or negative.

For the flows with gains problem, columns corresponding to circuits are linearly independent iff the product of the gains k_e around the circuit is not equal to 1. Thus, a basis may include such a circuit. However any connected component of basic arcs can include at most one such circuit.

For this problem, a full basis consists of trees each of which includes either one slack or one additional arc forming a circuit. A basis change can involve an arc or slack entering and an arc or slack in the path to the root dropping (as in Fig. 3a), or an arc entering to form a circuit and an arc of that circuit dropping (as in Fig. 3b), or an arc between trees can enter and an arc or slack in either path to the root can drop.

For this problem, there is no better proof of convergence than the usual Simplex proof, and there are counter examples to convergence when the solution is not kept basic [Johnson, 1966].

For a discussion of the structure of the basis, see Chapter 21 of Dantzig [1963].

9. MULTI-TERMINAL AND MULTICOMMODITY FLOWS

The multi-terminal problem concerns the requirement that a network allow a given flow between pairs of nodes, but where no consideration of simultaneous flows sharing the capacities of arcs is given. Usually a symmetric problem is treated: if arc (i, j) has capacity α_{ij} then arc (j, i) is present and has the same capacity. Then, the symmetric function $v(i, j)$, on all pairs i and j of nodes, given by the max flow value between i and j is called a *flow function.* In Gomory and Hu [1961] (see also Ford and Fulkerson [1962, Section IV-2]), it is proven that a nonnegative, symmetric function v on all pairs of nodes is a flow function iff

$$v(i, j) \geqslant \min_k \{v(i, k), v(k, j)\}.$$

Furthermore, every flow function can be realized by a tree which is the min spanning tree of the complete, undirected graph with each edge (i, j) having length $v(i, j)$.

Gomory and Hu [1961] give a way of finding the flow function of a given network by reducing it to such a tree having the same flow function. To do so, they solve only $n - 1$ flow problems.

The multicommodity flow problem requires sending specified, or maximal, flow between pairs of nodes simultaneously; that is, the total flow in an arc must not exceed its capacity. For each node pair i and j with a flow required from i to j, we say that flow is of a different commodity. Jewell [1966] treated this problem by a decomposition involving linking individual flows by certain circuit adjustments. Gregoriadis and White [1972] use a dual method so that they can frequently be working on individual flows.

In the case of two commodities, Hu [1963], Rothchild and Winston [1966], and Sakarovitch [1973] have given results which extend some of the integrality results for flows and allow one to find max flows in a way requiring only twice as much work as for one commodity.

The interesting structure of a multicommodity flow problem results from the structure of the basis of the LP:

$$0 \leqslant x_e^k,$$

$$\mathbf{A}\mathbf{x}^k = \mathbf{b}^k, \quad k = 1, \ldots, K,$$

$$\sum_{k=1}^{K} x_e^k \leqslant \alpha_e,$$

where **A** is a node-arc incidence matrix of a network. A basis **B** will always have the form

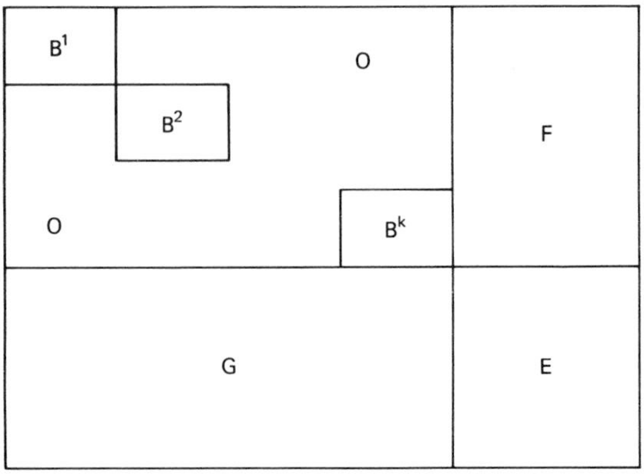

where each $\mathbf{B}^k$ is the node-arc incidence matrix of a spanning, rooted forest of the network, each column of **F** is either all 0's or corresponds to an arc in some block $\mathbf{B}^k$, and each column of **G** has exactly one 1 in it. The $\mathbf{B}^k$ are all triangular, and if they are used to eliminate **G** (or, equivalently **F**) then the resulting matrix has $\mathbf{E} - \mathbf{G}\overline{\mathbf{F}}$ in place of **E**, where

$$\bar{F} = \begin{bmatrix} B^1 & & \\ & \ddots & \\ & & B^k \end{bmatrix}^{-1} F.$$

Where a column of **F** has an arc in block k, that column of $\overline{\mathbf{F}}$ is the incidence column of arcs in $\mathbf{B}^k$ needed to form that arc. The matrix $\mathbf{E} - \mathbf{G}\overline{\mathbf{F}}$ is the incidence matrix of edges verses circuits formed by the arcs in **F** when adjoined to the rooted spanning trees in $\mathbf{B}^k$.

REFERENCES

1. Balas, E. and P. L. Hammer, "On the Transportation Problem I and II," Cahiers du Centre d'Etudes de Recherche Operationalle **4**: 38–116 and 131–160 (1962).
2. Barr, R. S., F. Glover, and D. Klingman, "An Improved Version of the Out-of-Kilter Method and a Comparative Study of Computer Codes," *Math. Prog.* **7**: 60–87 (1974).
3. Bennington, G. E., "Applying Network Analysis," *Indust. Eng.* **6**: 17–25 (1974).
4. Berge, C. and A. Ghouila-Houri, *Programming, Games and Transportation Networks*, Methuen and Co., Ltd., London, (1965).
5. Busacker, R. G. and T. L. Saaty, *Finite Graphs and Networks*, McGraw-Hill, New York (1965).
6. Dantzig, G. B., *Linear Programming and Extensions*, Princeton University Press, Princeton, New Jersey (1963).
7. Dijkstra, E. W., "A Note on Two Problems in Connection with Graphs," *Numerische Mathematik* **1**: 269–271 (1959).
8. Dreyfus, S. E., "An Appraisal of Some Shortest-Path Algorithms," *Operations Res.* **17**: 395–412 (1969).
9. Edmonds, J. and R. M. Karp, "Theoretical Improvements in Algorithmic Efficiency for Network Flow Problems," *J. ACM* **19**: 248-264 (1972).
10. Elmaghraby, S. E., *Some Network Models in Management*, Springer-Verlag, New York (1970).
11. Ford, L. R., Jr. and D. R. Fulkerson, *Flows in Networks*, Princeton University Press, Princeton, New Jersey (1962).
12. Frank, M. and I. T. Frisch, *Communication, Transmission, and Transportation Networks*, Addison-Wesley, Reading, Massachusetts (1971).
13. Fulkerson, D. R., "Flow Networks and Combinatorial Operations Research," *American Mathematical Monthly* **73**: 115–138 (1966).
14. Glover, F., D. Kafney, D. Klingman, and A. Napier, "A Computations Study on Start Procedures, Basis Change Criteria, and Solution Algorithms for Transportation Problems," *Management Sci.* **20**: 793–813 (1974).
15. Glover, F., D. Klingman, and J. Stutz, "An Augmented Threaded Index Method for Network Optimization," *INFOR* **12**: 293–298 (1974).
16. Gomory, R. E. and T. C. Hu, "Multi-terminal Network Flows," *J. Indust. Appl. Math.* **9**: 551–570 (1961).
17. Grigoriadis, M. D. and W. W. White, "A Partitioning Algorithm for the Multi-Commodity Network Flow Problem," *Math. Prog.* **3**: 157–177 (1972).
18. Hoffman, A. J. and J. B. Kruskal, "Integral Boundary Points of Convex Polyhedra," in H. W. Kuhn and A. W. Tucker (eds.), *Linear Inequalities and Related Systems*, Annals of Mathematics Study No. 38, Princeton University Press, Princeton, New Jersey, pp. 233–246 (1956).
19. Hu, T. C., "Multi-Commodity Network Flows," *Operations Res.* **11**: 344–360 (1963).
20. ——, *Integer Programming and Network Flows*, Addison-Wesley, Reading, Massachusetts (1969).

21. Jewell, W. S., "Optimal Flows with Gains," Second International Conference on Operations Research, Aix-en-Provence, France (1960), *Operations Res.* **10:** 476–522 (1962).
22. ——, "A Primal-Dual Multi-Commodity Flow Algorithm," Report ORC 66-24, Operations Research Center, Univ. of Calif., Berkeley, California (1966).
23. Johnson, E. L., "Networks and Basic Solutions," *Operations Res.* **14:** 619–624 (1966).
24. ——, "On Shortest Paths and Sorting," IBM RC 3691, IBM Research, Yorktown Heights, New York (1972).
25. Kelley, J. E., Jr., "Critical Path and Planning and Scheduling, Mathematical Basis," *Operations Res.* **9:** 296–320 (1961).
26. Kennington, J. L., R. W. Langley, and C. M. Shetty, "Efficient Computational Devices for the Capacitated Transportation Problem," *Nav. Res. Log. Quart.* **21:** 637–648 (1974).
27. Klein, M., "A Primal Method for Minimum Cost Flows," *Management Sci.* **14:** 205–220 (1967).
28. Maurrus, J. F., "Optimization of the Flow through Networks with Gains," *Math. Prog.* **3:** 135–144 (1972).
29. Nemhauser, G. L., "A Generalized Permanent Label Setting Algorithm for the Shortest Path between Specified Nodes," *J. Math. Anal. and Appl.* **38:** 328–334 (1972).
30. Rothschild, B. and A. Winston, "On Two-Commodity Flows," *Operations Res.* **14:** 377–387 (1966).
31. Sakarovitch, M., "Two Commodity Network Flows and Linear Programming," *Math. Prog.* **4:** 1–20 (1973).
32. Srinivasan, V., and G. L. Thompson, "Benefit-Cost Analysis of Coding Techniques for the Primal Transportation Algorithm," *J. ACM* **20:** 194–213 (1973).
33. Veinott, A. F., Jr., "Least d-majorized Network Flows with Inventory and Statistical Applications," *Management Sci.* **17:** 547–567 (1971).
34. Zadeh, N., "A Bad Network Problem for the Simplex Method and Other Minimum Cost Flow Algorithms," *Math. Prog.* **5:** 255–266 (1973).
35. Zangwill, W., "A Backlogging Model and a Multi-Echelon Model of a Dynamic Economic Lot Size Production System–A Network Approach," *Management Sci.* **15:** 506–527 (1969).

II-5

GEOMETRIC PROGRAMMING

Elmor L. Peterson
Northwestern University

1. INTRODUCTION

Since its inception by Zener [1961, 1962] and Duffin [1962a, 1962b], geometric programming (GP) has undergone rapid development, especially with the appearance of the first book on the subject by Duffin, Peterson, and Zener [1967]. Although its essence and scope have recently been broadened and amplified by Peterson [1970, 1973, 1976], major advances in theory, computation, and application are still occurring as more workers enter the field. The main purpose of this chapter is to summarize the present state of the subject and to indicate some of the directions in which it is developing. To keep the length of this chapter within reasonable limits, only the most fundamental aspects are presented, and then only within the context of n-dimensional Euclidean space E_n. (Just to list all relevant papers would itself require several additional pages.) Consequently, some important topics have been omitted, but a much more extensive treatment can be found in [Peterson 1976]; and an even more thorough treatment with complete proofs is presently being prepared as part of [Peterson, 1979]. Since both of those treatments completely subsume the present treatment, only prior references (when available) are cited herein.

Research sponsored by the Air Force Office of Scientific Research, Air Force Systems Command, USAF, under Grant No. AFOSR-73-2516A. The United States Government is authorized to reproduce and distribute reprints of this paper for governmental purposes notwithstanding any copyright notation hereon.

Contrary to popular belief GP is not just a very useful technique for studying the very important class of "posynomial" optimization problems. It is really a very general, multifaceted approach that is also very useful for studying other important classes of optimization problems. Some examples are: non-linear network flow problems (both single-commodity and multicommodity), discrete optimal control problems with linear dynamics, optimal location problems of the generalized Fermat type, (l_p constrained) l_p regression problems, ordinary programming problems, (quadraticly constrained) quadratic programming problems, and general algebraic programming problems. The theory of GP includes (1) very strong existence, uniqueness, and characterization theorems, (2) useful parametric and economic analyses, (3) illuminating decomposition principles, and (4) powerful numerical solution techniques.

This chapter can serve either as an up-to-date handbook of the most fundamental aspects of GP or as a modern introduction to the subject (including an enlightening review of the original posynomial case).

With respect to notation, the context alone dictates whether a given vector $\mathbf{v}$ in E_n is to be interpreted as a "column vector," or as a "row vector." In all cases, the symbol $\langle \cdot, \cdot \rangle$ indicates the usual "inner product" function.

2. PROBLEM FORMULATION AND EXAMPLES

Geometric programming provides a mechanism for formulating and studying in "separable" form many important (usually inseparable) optimization problems. The key to this mechanism is the exploitation of the linearities that are present in a given problem. Such linearities frequently appear as linear equations or linear inequalities, but they can also appear in much more subtle guises, such as matrices associated with nonlinearities.

We shall begin with unconstrained problems and then proceed to (the more complicated) constrained problems. In each case we consider important examples that arise in operations research.

2.1 The Unconstrained Case

Classical optimization theory and ordinary mathematical programming are concerned with the minimization (or maximization) of an arbitrary real-valued function g over some given subset $\mathcal{S}$ of its non-empty domain $\mathcal{C} \subseteq E_n$. In GP, the subset $\mathcal{S}$ is required to be the intersect of the function domain $\mathcal{C}$ with an arbitrary cone $\mathcal{X} \subseteq E_n$ (which is, in fact, a vector space for most examples). For purposes of easy reference and mathematical precision, the resulting GP Problem $\mathcal{A}$ is now given the following formal definition in terms of classical terminology and notation.

PROBLEM $\mathcal{A}$. *Using the "feasible solution" set*

$$\mathcal{S} \triangleq \mathcal{X} \cap \mathcal{C},$$

calculate both the "problem infimum"

$$\varphi \triangleq \inf_{\mathbf{x} \in \mathcal{S}} g(\mathbf{x})$$

and the "optimal solution" set

$$\mathcal{S}^* \triangleq \{\mathbf{x} \in \mathcal{S} \,|\, g(\mathbf{x}) = \varphi\}.$$

Each optimization problem can generally be formulated as Problem $\mathcal{A}$ in more than one way by suitably choosing the function g and the cone $\mathcal{X}$. For example, one can always let g be the "objective function" for the given problem simply by choosing $\mathcal{X}$ to be E_n, but that choice is generally not the best possible choice. The reason is that most problems involve a certain amount of linearity (due to the presence of linear equations, linear inequalities, matrices, etc.), which can be conveniently handled through the introduction of an appropriate *nontrivial* subcone $\mathcal{X} \subset E_n$. The presence of such a subcone $\mathcal{X}$ is one of the distinguishing features of GP.

Example 1: Perhaps the most striking example of the utility of GP comes from using it to study the *minimization of signomials*. This was first done by Zener [1961, 1962] and Duffin [1962a, 1962b], and served as the initial development (as well as the main stimulus for subsequent developments) of GP.

A "signomial" (sometimes termed a "generalized polynomial") is any function with the form

$$P(\mathbf{t}) = \sum_{i=1}^{n} c_i t_1^{a_{i1}} t_2^{a_{i2}} \cdots t_m^{a_{im}},$$

where the coefficients c_i and the exponents a_{ij} are arbitrary constants but the independent variables t_j are restricted to be positive. After much experience in the physical sciences, engineering and OR, Zener clearly recognized that many optimization problems of practical importance can be accurately modeled with such functions. In many cases they come directly from the laws of nature and/or economics. In other cases this functional form gives a good fit to empirical data over a wide range of the variables t_j. Actually, the signomials that occur in such cases frequently have positive coefficients, in which event they are termed "posynomials."

The presence of the "exponent matrix" $[a_{ij}]$ (which is of course associated with algebraic nonlinearities) is the key to applying GP to signomial optimization. To effectively place the problem of minimizing $P(\mathbf{t})$ in the format of

Problem $\mathcal{A}$, simply make the change of variables

$$x_i = \sum_{j=1}^{m} a_{ij} \log t_j, \qquad i = 1, 2, \ldots, n;$$

and then use the laws of exponents to help infer that minimizing $P(\mathbf{t})$ is equivalent to solving Problem $\mathcal{A}$ when

$$\mathcal{C} \triangleq E_n, \;\; g(\mathbf{x}) \triangleq \sum_{i=1}^{n} c_i e^{x_i}, \;\; \text{and } \mathcal{X} \triangleq \text{column space of } [a_{ij}].$$

The advantages of studying this Problem $\mathcal{A}$ rather than its signomial predecessor are numerous. For example, unlike the signomial P, the exponential function g is completely separable (in that it is a sum of terms, each of which depends on only a single independent variable x_i). Moreover, if P is actually a posynomial, then g is of course strictly convex (even though P itself clearly need not even be convex). Consequently, if $\mathbf{t}^*$ minimizes a posynomial P, then the corresponding $\mathbf{x}^*$ must be a unique optimal solution to Problem $\mathcal{A}$; in which event the set of all $\mathbf{t}$ that minimize P can be obtained from $\mathbf{x}^*$ simply by solving the displayed system of equations (a task that is relatively easy because the system is clearly linear in terms of $\log t_j$, $j = 1, 2, \ldots, m$). In [Duffin, Peterson and Zener, 1967], [Avriel and Williams, 1970], [Duffin and Peterson, 1972a, 1972b, 1972c, 1973], as well as [Abrams and Bunting, 1974], and some of the references cited therein, these properties and others that are too complicated to describe here have been combined into a very comprehensive existence, uniqueness, and characterization theory for signomial (and especially posynomial) optimization. Moreover, in [Falk, 1973] the complete separability induced into signomial optimization forms the basis for a branch-and-bound algorithm that converges to *globally* optimal solutions to (intrinsically nonconvex) signomial optimization problems.

Example 2: Our second example comes from the *minimization of quadratic functions*

$$Q(\mathbf{z}) = (\tfrac{1}{2})\langle \mathbf{z}, \mathbf{H}\mathbf{z}\rangle + \langle \mathbf{h}, \mathbf{z}\rangle,$$

where $\mathbf{H}$ is an arbitrary constant matrix and $\mathbf{h}$ is an arbitrary constant vector.

A factorization of the coefficient matrix $\mathbf{H}$ (which is of course associated with quadratic nonlinearities) is the key to effectively applying GP to quadratic programming. More specifically, linear algebra is used to compute matrices $\mathbf{D}$ and $\mathfrak{D}$ such that $\mathbf{H} = \mathbf{D}^t\mathbf{D} - \mathfrak{D}^t\mathfrak{D}$, where the superscript t indicates the transpose operation. In terms of $\mathbf{D}$ and $\mathfrak{D}$ the quadratic function

$$Q(\mathbf{z}) = (\tfrac{1}{2})(\langle \mathbf{D}\mathbf{z}, \mathbf{D}\mathbf{z}\rangle - \langle \mathfrak{D}\mathbf{z}, \mathfrak{D}\mathbf{z}\rangle) + \langle \mathbf{h}, \mathbf{z}\rangle.$$

Of course, the expression $-\langle \mathfrak{D}\mathbf{z}, \mathfrak{D}\mathbf{z}\rangle$ is not present when $Q(\mathbf{z})$ is positive semidefinite (i.e., a convex function).

From elementary linear algebra we now infer that minimizing $Q(\mathbf{z})$ is equivalent to solving Problem $\mathcal{A}$ when

$$\mathcal{C} \triangleq E_{2m+1}, \quad g(\mathbf{x}) \triangleq (\tfrac{1}{2})\left(\sum_{i=1}^{m} x_i^2 - \sum_{i=m+1}^{2m} x_i^2\right) + x_{2m+1},$$

$$\text{and } \mathfrak{X} \triangleq \text{column space of} \begin{bmatrix} \mathbf{D} \\ \mathfrak{D} \\ \mathbf{h} \end{bmatrix}.$$

Notice that, unlike the quadratic function Q, the quadratic function g is completely separable, a fact that can be exploited both theoretically and computationally.

It is useful to introduce some additional parameters into the preceding function g so that a much broader class of optimization problems can be studied. In particular, we redefine g so that

$$g(\mathbf{x}) \triangleq \sum_{i=1}^{m} p_i^{-1} |x_i - b_i|^{p_i} - \sum_{i=m+1}^{2m} p_i^{-1} |x_i - b_i|^{p_i} + x_{2m+1} - b_{2m+1},$$

where b_i and p_i are arbitrary constants, and $|\cdot|$ designates the absolute value function. Notice that the function g is still completely separable and can be specialized to the quadratic case by choosing $b_i = 0$ and $p_i = 2$ for each i.

Another interesting specialization is obtained by choosing $p_i = p$ for each i while choosing $\mathfrak{D} = 0$ and $\mathbf{h} = \mathbf{0}$. The resulting problem consists essentially of finding the "best l_p-norm approximation" to the fixed vector $(b_1, \ldots, b_m)$ by vectors in the column space of the matrix $\mathbf{D}$, a fundamental problem in *linear regression analysis.*

A detailed analysis of this rather broad class of optimization problems can be found in [Peterson, Ecker, 1970] and the references cited therein.

Example 3: Our third example comes from the *optimal location* of a new facility relative to existing facilities. We suppose that there are p existing facilities with fixed locations $\mathbf{b}^1, \mathbf{b}^2, \ldots, \mathbf{b}^p$ in E_m, and we assume that for each facility i there is a cost $d_i(\mathbf{z}, \mathbf{b}^i)$ of choosing the new facility location $\mathbf{z}$ relative to $\mathbf{b}^i$. In many instances the functions d_i are just "metrics" that reflect the cost of shipping matériel between the two locations. The problem then is to choose a new location $\mathbf{z}$ that minimizes the total cost $d(\mathbf{z}) = \sum_{i=1}^{p} d_i(\mathbf{z}, \mathbf{b}^i)$.

In this problem statement there is no matrix that serves as the key to effectively applying GP. However, minimizing $d(\mathbf{z})$ is clearly equivalent to solving Problem $\mathcal{A}$ when

$$\mathcal{C} \triangleq E_{pm}, \quad g(\mathbf{x}) \triangleq \sum_{i=1}^{p} d_i(\mathbf{x}^i, \mathbf{b}^i), \quad \text{and } \mathcal{X} \triangleq \text{column space of } \begin{bmatrix} \mathcal{I} \\ \mathcal{I} \\ \cdot \\ \cdot \\ \cdot \\ \mathcal{I} \end{bmatrix},$$

where $\mathbf{x} = (\mathbf{x}^1, \mathbf{x}^2, \ldots, \mathbf{x}^p)$ and there are a total of $p(m \times m)$ identity matrices $\mathcal{I}$.

Notice that, unlike the function d, the function g is at least partially separable in that it is a sum of terms, each of which depends on only a single independent vector variable $\mathbf{x}^i$. This separability occurs in even more complicated location problems and has been exploited both theoretically and computationally in [Peterson and Wendell, 1978] and the references cited therein.

Example 4: The fourth example comes from *discrete optimal control with linear dynamics* (or DP with linear transition equations). We suppose that for each "stage" i there is a cost $g_i(\mathbf{r}^i, \mathbf{d}^i)$ that depends on the ith "state" $\mathbf{r}^i$ and the ith "decision" $\mathbf{d}^i$, where the domain of the cost function g_i is the Cartesian product $R_i \times D_i$ of the ith "state set" R_i and the ith "decision set" D_i. We also suppose that the "initial state" $\mathbf{r}^1$ is determined by the "initial decision" $\mathbf{d}^1$ through the equation $\mathbf{r}^1 = \mathbf{B}_1 \mathbf{d}^1$ and that each subsequent state $\mathbf{r}^i$ is determined by both the ith decision $\mathbf{d}^i$ and the $(i-1)$th state $\mathbf{r}^{i-1}$ through the "transition equation" $\mathbf{r}^i = \mathbf{A}_i \mathbf{r}^{i-1} + \mathbf{B}_i \mathbf{d}^i$, where $\mathbf{A}_i$ and $\mathbf{B}_i$ are constant matrices. Given that there is a total of p stages, the problem is to make sequential decisions $\mathbf{d}^i$ that minimize the total cost $\sum_{i=1}^{p} g_i(\mathbf{r}^i, \mathbf{d}^i)$.

The presence of the matrices $\mathbf{A}_i$ and $\mathbf{B}_i$ is the key to applying GP to discrete optimal control. To effectively place the preceding control problem in the format of Problem $\mathcal{A}$, simply let

$$\mathbf{x} = (\mathbf{r}^1, \mathbf{d}^1, \mathbf{r}^2, \mathbf{d}^2, \ldots, \mathbf{d}^{p-1}, \mathbf{r}^p, \mathbf{d}^p)$$

and then observe that the preceding control problem is equivalent to Problem $\mathcal{A}$ when

$$\mathcal{C} \triangleq \mathop{\times}_{i=1}^{p} (R_i \times D_i), \quad g(\mathbf{x}) \triangleq \sum_{i=1}^{p} g_i(\mathbf{r}^i, \mathbf{d}^i), \quad \text{and}$$

$$\mathcal{X} \triangleq \{\mathbf{x} \mid \mathbf{r}^1 = \mathbf{B}_1 d^1, \text{ and } \mathbf{r}^i = \mathbf{A}_i \mathbf{r}^{i-1} + \mathbf{B}_i \mathbf{d}^i, \; i = 2, \ldots, p\}.$$

The partial separability of g and the "sparsity" of the matrix whose columns span $\mathfrak{X}$ has been exploited both theoretically and computationally in [Dinkel and Peterson 1978] and the references cited therein.

There is another important example that ought to be mentioned—the *analysis of multicommodity transportation networks*. It differs drastically from the examples just given, in that $\mathfrak{X}$ is not generally a vector space but is instead a polyhedral cone generated by certain "feasible path vectors." Such problems are thoroughly studied in [Hall and Peterson, 1976] and some of the references cited therein.

The reader who wishes to avoid the complications inherent in constraints can skip the next section and begin with Section 2.3.

2.2 The Constrained Case

To generalize GP by incorporating explicit constraints into the preceding problem formulation, we introduce two non-intersecting (possibly empty) positive-integer index sets I and J with finite cardinality $o(I)$ and $o(J)$, respectively. In terms of these index sets I and J we also introduce the following notation and hypotheses:

1. For each $k \in \{0\} \cup I \cup J$ there is a function g_k with domain $C_k \subseteq E_{n_k}$, and there is a set $D_j \subseteq E_{n_j}$ for each $j \in J$.
2. For each $k \in \{0\} \cup I \cup J$ there is an independent vector variable $\mathbf{x}^k$ in E_{n_k}, and there is an independent vector variable $\boldsymbol{\kappa}$ with components κ_j for each $j \in J$.
3. $\mathbf{x}^I$ denotes the Cartesian product of the vector variables $\mathbf{x}^i$, $i \in I$, and $\mathbf{x}^J$ denotes the Cartesian product of the vector variables $\mathbf{x}^j$, $j \in J$. Hence, the Cartesian product $(\mathbf{x}^0, \mathbf{x}^I, \mathbf{x}^J) \triangleq \mathbf{x}$ of $\mathbf{x}^0$, $\mathbf{x}^I$, and $\mathbf{x}^J$ is an independent vector variable in E_n, where
$$n \triangleq n_0 + \sum_I n_i + \sum_J n_j.$$
4. there is a cone $X \subseteq E_n$.

For purposes of easy reference and mathematical precision, the resulting GP *Problem* A is now given the following formal definition in terms of classical terminology and notation.

PROBLEM A. *Consider the objective function G whose domain*

$$C \triangleq \{(\mathbf{x}, \boldsymbol{\kappa}) | \mathbf{x}^k \in C_k, \ \ k \in \{0\} \cup I, \ \ \textit{and} \ \ (\mathbf{x}^j, \kappa_j) \in C_j^+, \ \ j \in J\}$$

and whose functional value

$$G(\mathbf{x}, \boldsymbol{\kappa}) \triangleq g_0(\mathbf{x}^0) + \sum_J g_j^+(\mathbf{x}^j, \kappa_j),$$

where

$$C_j^+ \triangleq \{(\mathbf{x}^j, \kappa_j) | \textit{either } \kappa_j = 0 \textit{ and } \sup_{d^j \in D_j} \langle \mathbf{x}^j, \mathbf{d}^j \rangle < +\infty, \textit{ or } \kappa_j > 0 \textit{ and } \mathbf{x}^j \in \kappa_j C_j\}$$

and

$$g_j^+(\mathbf{x}^j, \kappa_j) \triangleq \begin{cases} \sup_{d^j \in D_j} \langle \mathbf{x}^j, \mathbf{d}^j \rangle & \textit{if } \kappa_j = 0 \textit{ and } \sup_{d^j \in D_j} \langle \mathbf{x}^j, \mathbf{d}^j \rangle < +\infty \\ \kappa_j g_j(\mathbf{x}^j/\kappa_j) & \textit{if } \kappa_j > 0 \textit{ and } \mathbf{x}^j \in \kappa_j C_j. \end{cases}$$

Using the feasible solution set

$$S \triangleq \{(\mathbf{x}, \boldsymbol{\kappa}) \in C | \mathbf{x} \in \mathbf{X}, \textit{ and } g_i(\mathbf{x}^i) \leq 0, \ i \in I\},$$

calculate both the problem infimum

$$\varphi \triangleq \inf_{(\mathbf{x}, \boldsymbol{\kappa}) \in S} G(\mathbf{x}, \boldsymbol{\kappa})$$

and the optimal solution set

$$S^* \triangleq \{(\mathbf{x}, \boldsymbol{\kappa}) \in S | G(\mathbf{x}, \boldsymbol{\kappa}) = \varphi\}.$$

Of course, the unconstrained case occurs when $I = J = \phi, g_0 : C_0 \triangleq g : \mathcal{C}$, and $\mathbf{X} \triangleq \mathfrak{X}$.

When $D_j = E_{n_j}$ (which is frequently the situation), a simplification results from noting that $\sup_{\mathbf{d}^j \in D_j} \langle \mathbf{x}^j, \mathbf{d}^j \rangle < +\infty$ iff $\mathbf{x}^j = \mathbf{0}$, in which event $\sup_{\mathbf{d}^j \in D_j} \langle \mathbf{x}^j, \mathbf{d}^j \rangle = 0$. In particular then, the functional domain

$$C_j^+ = \{(\mathbf{x}^j, \kappa_j) | \kappa_j \geq 0 \textit{ and } \mathbf{x}^j \in \kappa_j C_j\};$$

and the functional values

$$g_j^+(\mathbf{x}^j, \kappa_j) = \kappa_j g_j(\mathbf{x}^j/\kappa_j)$$

with the understanding that $0 g_j(\mathbf{0}/0) \triangleq 0$.

In defining the feasible solution set S it is important to make a sharp distinction between the *cone condition* $\mathbf{x} \in X$ and the *constraints* $g_i(\mathbf{x}^i) \leq 0$, $i \in I$, both of which restrict the vector variable $(\mathbf{x}, \boldsymbol{\kappa})$. In many cases the cone X is polyhedral (and hence is finitely generated); and in most examples of practical significance X is actually a vector space (and hence has a finite basis). Consequently, the cone condition $\mathbf{x} \in X$ can frequently be automatically satisfied and therefore explicitly eliminated by a linear transformation of $\mathbf{x}$ that results from the introduction of generating vectors or basis vectors for X (whereas the generally nonlinear constraints $g_i(\mathbf{x}^i) \leq 0$, $i \in I$, usually cannot be explicitly eliminated by even a nonlinear transformation). Nevertheless, even when it is possible to do so, we do not explicitly eliminate the cone condition $\mathbf{x} \in X$, because such a linear transformation would clearly introduce a common vector variable into the arguments of g_0, g_i, and g_j^+. Such a common vector variable only tends to camouflage one of the extremely useful characteristics of GP—its (partial) separability. Such separability is clearly present even when the functions $g_k : C_k$, $k \in \{0\} \cup I \cup J$ are inseparable.

Since each optimization problem can generally be formulated as Problem A in more than one way by suitably choosing the functions $g_k : C_k, k \in \{0\} \cup I \cup J$ and the cone X, a very important aspect of applied GP is the exploitation of this flexibility in such a way that a given inseparable problem is formulated as an equivalent Problem A with as much function separability as possible. As in the unconstrained case, the key to such a formulation is usually the introduction of an appropriate nontrivial cone X to handle the linearities that are present in a given problem. Such linearities frequently appear as linear equations or linear inequalities, but they can also appear in rather subtle guises, such as matrices associated with nonlinearities.

The function separability induced in the objective function for each of the unconstrained examples given in Section 2.1 can also be induced in any constraint function of the same general type. We now use signomial optimization to illustrate the general procedure for doing so.

Example 5: First, make the following choices:

$$I = \{1, 2, \ldots, p\} \quad \text{and} \quad J = \phi;$$

$$C_k \triangleq E_{n_k} \quad \text{and} \quad g_k(\mathbf{x}^k) \triangleq \sum_{[k]} c_q e^{x_q} - d_k,$$

where

$$[k] = \{m_k, m_k + 1, \ldots, n_k\}$$

and

$$1 = m_0 \leqslant n_0, \quad n_0 + 1 = m_1 \leqslant n_1, \ldots, n_{p-1} + 1 = m_p \leqslant n_p = n;$$

$$X \triangleq \text{column space of } [a_{qr}], \quad \text{where} \quad [a_{qr}] \text{ is any } n \times m \text{ matrix.}$$

Now, note that all functions in Problem A are completely separable.

To relate Problem A to *constrained signomial optimization,* explicitly eliminate the vector space condition $\mathbf{x} \in X$ by the (essentially linear) transformation

$$x_q = \sum_{r=1}^{m} a_{qr} \log t_r, \qquad q = 1, 2, \ldots, n.$$

By virtue of the laws of exponents, Problem A is now clearly equivalent to the following (generally inseparable) signomial optimization problem:

$$\text{Minimize} \sum_{[0]} c_q \prod_{1}^{m} t_r^{a_{qr}} \quad \text{subject to} \quad \sum_{[k]} c_q \prod_{1}^{m} t_r^{a_{qr}} \leqslant d_k,$$

$$k = 1, 2, \ldots, p, \quad \text{and} \quad \mathbf{t} > \mathbf{0}.$$

Of course, the preceding procedure is usually reversed in practice; that is, the signomial form of Problem A tends to occur more often than Problem A in real-world applications, but is transformed into problem A so that the complete separability of the resulting exponential functions can be exploited. Actually, signomial optimization problems (as well as more general "algebraic optimization problems") should usually be reduced to much simpler signomial optimization problems prior to their transformation to an appropriate Problem A. To see how to reduce such problems to signomial optimization problems in which each signomial has at most two terms, both of which have the same sign, consult [Duffin, 1970] and [Duffin and Peterson, 1973, 1972b]. If such problems could be further reduced to signomial problems in which each signomial has only a single term, all algebraic optimization problems (and hence essentially all optimization problems involving only continuous functions) could be reduced to (finite-dimensional) linear programming problems. Even though such a reduction will not be accomplished in the future, the reductions given in the preceding references are already starting to be exploited, both theoretically and computationally.

The reader who is interested in the applications of signomial and posynomial optimization should consult the recent book by Zener [1971] as well as the comprehensive list of papers compiled in [Rijckaert, 1973].

The procedure for inducing function separability into constrained versions of each of the other three examples given in Section 2.1 will be left to the imagination of the interested reader, who can also consult the references already cited in Section 2.1.

Three ways in which to view LP from a GP point of view are given in [Peterson, 1973, 1976], but none of the three ways have yet had other than pedagogical influence on LP. A way of viewing "ordinary programming" (the subject of Chapter II-6) from a GP point of view is also given in [Peterson, 1973, 1976], and results in a partially separable formulation that helps to strengthen some of the theorems of ordinary programming.

In all of the examples given here, the index set J is empty. Probably the most important example for which J is not empty is the "chemical equilibrium problem"—a problem that lies outside the scope of OR but is thoroughly discussed in [Peterson, 1976] and the references cited therein. The reason for including J in the present problem formulation is that it is a prerequisite for the duality symmetry described in Section 3.3.3.

2.3 A Summary

Experience seems to indicate that any optimization problem involving matrices, linear equations, affine sets, or cones (and even certain other optimization problems, such as optimal location problems) can probably be transformed into a GP problem that is considerably more separable and hence much more amenable to analysis and solution than the original problem. This is especially true for each of the preceding examples, but the complete exploitation of this fact is way beyond the scope of this chapter.

In the remaining part of this chapter we present only the most basic theory of GP—a theory that is equally applicable to all problem classes and does not, for the most part, actually require separability of the functions $g:\mathcal{C}$ and $g_k:C_k$, $k \in \{0\} \cup I \cup J$. Such function separability does, however, become extremely useful when specific problem classes are to be thoroughly investigated and solved.

3. BASIC THEORY

The basic theory of GP can be conveniently partitioned into several topics. Certain "optimality conditions" describe important properties possessed by all optimal solutions, and in many cases collectively characterize all optimal solutions. Appropriate "Lagrangians" provide important "saddle-point" characterizations of optimality, and can also be used to introduce the even more significant concepts of "duality." The latter topic provides important "existence and uniqueness theorems" for optimal solutions, as well as useful "algorithmic stopping criteria." Duality is also a key ingredient in "parametric programming" and "post-optimality analysis."

Since many important problem classes are unconstrained and since the theory for the unconstrained case is far simpler than that for the constrained case, we initially limit our attention to the unconstrained case. Actually, in doing so, there is no loss of generality, as explained in Section 3.2.

3.1 The Unconstrained Case

Let $\mathcal{Y}$ be the "dual" of the cone $\mathcal{X}$; that is,

$$\mathcal{Y} \triangleq \{\mathbf{y} \in E_n \mid 0 \leqslant \langle \mathbf{x}, \mathbf{y} \rangle \quad \text{for each } \mathbf{x} \in \mathcal{X}\}.$$

Rather elementary considerations show that $\mathcal{Y}$ is generally a closed convex cone. Moreover, $\mathcal{Y}$ is "polyhedral" (i.e., "finitely generated") when $\mathcal{X}$ is polyhedral; and $\mathcal{Y}$ is the "orthogonal complement" $\mathcal{X}^{\perp}$ of $\mathcal{X}$ when $\mathcal{X}$ is actually a vector space. In fact, $\mathcal{Y}$ can be computed via elementary linear algebra for each of the examples given in Section 2.1.

Some of the following subsections can be omitted on first reading. In particular, either Section 3.1.1 (on optimality conditions) or Section 3.1.3 (on Lagrangian saddle points) can be omitted without serious loss of continuity. Moreover, Section 3.1.2 can be omitted by those readers who are already sufficiently familiar with the "conjugate transformation, subgradients and convex analysis."

3.1.1 Optimality Conditions. We begin with the following fundamental definition.

Definition. *A* critical solution *(stationary solution, equilibrium solution, P solution) for Problem* $\mathcal{A}$ *is any vector* $\mathbf{x}^*$ *that satisfies the following P* optimality conditions

$$\mathbf{x}^* \in \mathcal{X} \cap \mathcal{C}, \quad \nabla g(\mathbf{x}^*) \in \mathcal{Y}, \quad \text{and} \quad 0 = \langle \mathbf{x}^*, \nabla g(\mathbf{x}^*) \rangle.$$

If the cone $\mathcal{X}$ is actually a vector space (which is the case for each of the examples given in Section 2.1), then $\mathcal{Y} = \mathcal{X}^{\perp}$ and hence the last P optimality condition $\mathbf{0} = \langle \mathbf{x}^*, \nabla g(\mathbf{x}^*) \rangle$ is obviously redundant and can be deleted from the preceding definition. Furthermore, if $\mathcal{X}$ is actually the whole vector space E_n (which is the situation in the unconstrained case of ordinary programming), then $\mathcal{Y} = E_n^{\perp} = \{\mathbf{0}\}$ and hence the remaining P optimality conditions clearly become the (more familiar) optimality conditions $\mathbf{x}^* \in \mathcal{C}$ and $\nabla g(\mathbf{x}^*) = \mathbf{0}$.

The following theorem gives two convexity conditions that guarantee the necessity and/or sufficiency of the P optimality conditions for optimality.

THEOREM 1. Under the hypothesis that g is differentiable at $\mathbf{x}^*$,

1. given that $\mathcal{X}$ is convex, if $\mathbf{x}^*$ is an optimal solution to Problem $\mathcal{A}$, then $\mathbf{x}^*$ is a critical solution for Problem $\mathcal{A}$ (but not conversely),
2. given that g is convex on $\mathcal{C}$, if $\mathbf{x}^*$ is a critical solution for Problem $\mathcal{A}$, then $\mathbf{x}^*$ is an optimal solution to Problem $\mathcal{A}$.

It is worth noting that g is differentiable for most of the examples given in Section 2.1. Moreover, $\mathcal{X}$ is polyhedral and hence convex for each of those examples, and g is convex on $\mathcal{C}$ for important special cases of each of those examples. Consequently, the P optimality conditions frequently characterize the optimal solution set $\mathcal{S}^*$ for Problem $\mathcal{A}$.

Characterizations of $\mathcal{S}^*$ that do not require differentiability of g, but do require the concepts described in the following section, are given in Section 3.1.3.

3.1.2 The Conjugate Transformation, Subgradients and Convex Analysis. The conjugate transformation evolved from the classical Legendre transformation but was first studied in great detail only rather recently by Fenchel [1949, 1951]. For a very thorough and modern treatment of both transformations see the recent book by Rockafellar [1970]. We now briefly describe only those of their properties that are relevant to GP. All such properties are quite plausible when viewed geometrically in the context of two and three dimensions.

The conjugate transformation maps functions into functions in such a way that the "conjugate transform" $\omega : \Omega$ of a given function $w : W$ has functional values

$$\omega(\zeta) \triangleq \sup_{\mathbf{z} \in W} [\langle \zeta, \mathbf{z} \rangle - w(\mathbf{z})].$$

Of course, the domain Ω of ω is defined to be the set of all those vectors $\boldsymbol{\zeta}$ for which this supremum is finite, and the conjugate transform $\omega:\Omega$ exists only when Ω is not empty.

The conjugate transform of a separable function is clearly the sum of the conjugate transforms of its individual terms—a fact that simplifies the conjugate transform computations for many of the GP examples given in Section 2.1. In particular, such computations frequently reduce to elementary (differential calculus) exercises in the convex case—the only case in which the conjugate transformation proves to be extremely effective.

Geometrical insight into the conjugate transformation can be obtained by considering the "subgradient" set for w at $\mathbf{z}$, namely,

$$\partial w(\mathbf{z}) \triangleq \{\boldsymbol{\zeta}\in E_\eta \,|\, w(\mathbf{z}) + \langle\boldsymbol{\zeta}, \mathbf{z}' - \mathbf{z}\rangle \leqslant w(\mathbf{z}') \quad \text{for each} \quad \mathbf{z}' \in W\}.$$

Subgradients are related to, but considerably different from, the more familiar gradient. The gradient provides a "tangent hyperplane" while a subgradient provides a "supporting hyperplane" (in that the defining inequality obviously states that the hyperplane with equation $w' = w(\mathbf{z}) + \langle\boldsymbol{\zeta}, \mathbf{z}' - \mathbf{z}\rangle$ intersects the "graph" of w at the point $(\mathbf{z}, w(\mathbf{z}))$ and lies entirely "on or below" it). It is, of course, clear that a subgradient may exist and not be unique even when the gradient does not exist. On the other hand, it is also clear that a subgradient may not exist even when the gradient exists. There is, however, an important class of functions whose gradients are also subgradients—the class of convex functions. In fact, the notions of gradient and subgradient coincide for the class of differentiable convex functions defined on open sets, a class that arises in many of the examples given in Section 2.1.

To relate the conjugate transform to subgradients, observe that if $\boldsymbol{\zeta}\in\partial w(\mathbf{z})$ then $\langle\boldsymbol{\zeta}, \mathbf{z}'\rangle - w(\mathbf{z}') \leqslant \langle\boldsymbol{\zeta}, \mathbf{z}\rangle - w(\mathbf{z})$ for each $\mathbf{z}' \in W$, which in turn clearly implies that $\boldsymbol{\zeta} \in \Omega$ and that $\omega(\boldsymbol{\zeta}) = -[w(\mathbf{z}) + \langle\boldsymbol{\zeta}, -\mathbf{z}\rangle]$. Hence, $\omega(\boldsymbol{\zeta})$ is simply the negative of the intercept of the corresponding supporting hyperplane with the w'-axis. Consequently, the conjugate transform ω exists when w has at least one subgradient $\boldsymbol{\zeta}$, a condition that is known to be fulfilled when w is convex. Actually, the conjugate transform ω restricted (in the set-theoretic sense) to the domain $\bigcup_{\mathbf{z}\in W} \partial w(\mathbf{z})$ is termed the "Legendre transform" of w and has been a major tool in the study of classical mechanics, thermodynamics, and differential equations (as described, for example, in [Courant and Hilbert, 1953]). Usually, the domain Ω of the conjugate transform ω consists of both $\bigcup_{\mathbf{z}\in W} \partial w(\mathbf{z})$ and some of its limit points.

When it exists, the conjugate transform $\omega:\Omega$ is known to be both convex and "closed;" that is, its "epigraph" (which consists of all those points in $E_{\eta+1}$ that are "on or above" its graph) is both convex and (topologically) closed. Moreover, the conjugate transform of $\omega:\Omega$ is the "closed convex hull" $\overline{w}:\overline{W}$ of $w:W$; and thus the conjugate transformation maps the family of all closed convex functions onto itself in one-to-one symmetric fashion. Consequently, the conjugate transformation is its own inverse on the family of all such functions; and given two such "conjugate functions" $w:W$ and $\omega:\Omega$, the relations $\zeta \in \partial w(\mathbf{z})$ and $\mathbf{z} \in \partial\omega(\zeta)$ are equivalent and hence "solve" one another.

In GP we must deal with both an arbitrary cone Z and its "dual"

$$\mathcal{Z} \triangleq \{\zeta \in E_\eta \mid 0 \leqslant \langle \mathbf{z}, \zeta \rangle \quad \text{for each} \quad \mathbf{z} \in Z\},$$

which is clearly itself a cone. Now, it is obvious that the conjugate transform of the zero function with domain Z is just the zero function with domain $-\mathcal{Z}$. Consequently, the theory of the conjugate transformation implies that $\mathcal{Z}$ is convex and closed (a fact that can be established by more elementary considerations). Furthermore, if the cone Z is also convex and closed, the symmetry of the conjugate transformation readily implies that the dual of $\mathcal{Z}$ is just Z. If, in particular, Z is a vector space in E_η, this symmetry readily implies the better-known symmetry between orthogonal complementary subspaces Z and $\mathcal{Z}$.

In convex analysis the "relative interior" (ri$W$) of a convex set $W \subseteq E_\eta$ is defined to be the "interior" of W "relative to" the "Euclidean topology" for the "affine hull" of W (i.e., the "smallest affine set [or linear manifold]" containing W). The reason is that the (ri$W$) defined in this way is not empty, even when the interior of W is empty.

This completes our prerequisites for the remaining subsections of this section.

3.1.3 Lagrangian Saddle Points. Let $h:\mathcal{D}$ be the conjugate transform of the function $g:\mathcal{C}$; that is,

$$\mathcal{D} \triangleq \{\mathbf{y} \in E_n \mid \sup_{\mathbf{x}\in\mathcal{C}} [\langle \mathbf{y}, \mathbf{x}\rangle - g(\mathbf{x})] < +\infty\} \quad \text{and} \quad h(\mathbf{y}) \triangleq \sup_{\mathbf{x}\in\mathcal{C}} [\langle \mathbf{y}, \mathbf{x}\rangle - g(\mathbf{x})].$$

If $h:\mathcal{D}$ exists (which is the case, for example, when $g:\mathcal{C}$ is convex), then $h:\mathcal{D}$ is a closed convex function that inherits any separability present in $g:\mathcal{C}$. In fact, $h:\mathcal{D}$ can be computed via the calculus in the convex case for each example given in Section 2.1.

The following definition is of fundamental importance.

Definition. *For a consistent Problem* $\mathcal{A}$ *with a finite infimum* φ, *a* P vector *is any vector* $\mathbf{y}^*$ *with the two properties*

$$\mathbf{y}^* \in \mathcal{D} \quad \textit{and} \quad \varphi = \inf_{\mathbf{x}\in\mathcal{X}} L_g(\mathbf{x};\mathbf{y}^*),$$

where the (*geometric*) Lagrangian $L_g(\mathbf{x};\mathbf{y}) \triangleq \langle \mathbf{x}, \mathbf{y}\rangle - h(\mathbf{y})$.

It should be noted that L_g is generally as easy to compute as $h:\mathcal{D}$.

The following "saddle-point theorem" provides several characterizations of optimality via P vectors.

THEOREM 2. Given that $g:\mathcal{C}$ is convex and closed, let $\mathbf{x}^* \in \mathfrak{X}$ and let $\mathbf{y}^* \in \mathfrak{D}$. Then $\mathbf{x}^*$ is optimal for Problem $\mathfrak{A}$ and $\mathbf{y}^*$ is a P vector for Problem $\mathfrak{A}$ iff the ordered pair $(\mathbf{x}^*; \mathbf{y}^*)$ is a "saddle point" for the Lagrangian L_g, that is,

$$\sup_{\mathbf{y} \in \mathfrak{D}} L_g(\mathbf{x}^*; \mathbf{y}) = L_g(\mathbf{x}^*; \mathbf{y}^*) = \inf_{\mathbf{x} \in \mathfrak{X}} L_g(\mathbf{x}; \mathbf{y}^*);$$

in which case L_g has the saddle-point value $L_g(\mathbf{x}^*; \mathbf{y}^*) = g(\mathbf{x}^*) = \varphi$. Moreover, $\sup_{\mathbf{y} \in \mathfrak{D}} L_g(\mathbf{x}^*; \mathbf{y}) = L_g(\mathbf{x}^*; \mathbf{y}^*)$ iff $\mathbf{x}^*$ and $\mathbf{y}^*$ satisfy both the feasibility condition $\mathbf{x}^* \in \mathcal{C}$ and the subgradient condition $\mathbf{y}^* \in \partial g(\mathbf{x}^*)$; in which case $L_g(\mathbf{x}^*; \mathbf{y}^*) = g(\mathbf{x}^*)$. Furthermore, $L_g(\mathbf{x}^*; \mathbf{y}^*) = \inf_{\mathbf{x} \in \mathfrak{X}} L_g(\mathbf{x}; \mathbf{y}^*)$ iff $\mathbf{x}^*$ and $\mathbf{y}^*$ satisfy both the feasibility condition $\mathbf{y}^* \in \mathcal{Y}$ and the orthogonality condition $0 = \langle \mathbf{x}^*, \mathbf{y}^* \rangle$; in which case $L_g(\mathbf{x}^*; \mathbf{y}^*) = -h(\mathbf{y}^*)$.

Since the second assertion of Theorem 2 gives certain conditions that are equivalent to the first saddle-point equation, and since the third assertion of Theorem 2 gives other conditions that are equivalent to the second saddle-point equation, Theorem 2 actually provides four different characterizations of all ordered pairs $(\mathbf{x}^*; \mathbf{y}^*)$ of optimal solutions $\mathbf{x}^*$ and P vectors $\mathbf{y}^*$.

Of course, each of those four characterizations provides a characterization of all optimal solutions $\mathbf{x}^*$ in terms of a given P vector $\mathbf{y}^*$, as well as a characterization of all P vectors $\mathbf{y}^*$ in terms of a given optimal solution $\mathbf{x}^*$.

The symmetry of the preceding statement suggests that all P vectors may, in fact, constitute all optimal solutions to a closely related optimization problem. Actually, the appropriate optimization problem can be motivated by the following inequalities

$$\inf_{\mathbf{x} \in \mathfrak{X}} L_g(\mathbf{x}; \mathbf{y}^*) \leqslant \sup_{\mathbf{y} \in \mathfrak{D}} \left[\inf_{\mathbf{x} \in \mathfrak{X}} L_g(\mathbf{x}; \mathbf{y}) \right] \leqslant \inf_{\mathbf{x} \in \mathfrak{X}} \left[\sup_{\mathbf{y} \in \mathfrak{D}} L_g(\mathbf{x}, \mathbf{y}) \right]$$
$$\leqslant \sup_{\mathbf{y} \in \mathfrak{D}} L_g(\mathbf{x}^*; \mathbf{y}),$$

which are valid for each $\mathbf{y}^* \in \mathfrak{D}$ and each $\mathbf{x}^* \in \mathfrak{X}$, by virtue of the single fact that $\mathbf{x}$ and $\mathbf{y}$ reside in independent sets $\mathfrak{X}$ and $\mathfrak{D}$ respectively (i.e., the vector $(\mathbf{x}; \mathbf{y})$ resides in a Cartesian product $\mathfrak{X} \times \mathfrak{D}$). In particular, note that each of these inequalities must be an equality when $(\mathbf{x}^*; \mathbf{y}^*)$ is a saddle-point for L_g; in which case $\mathbf{x}^*$ is obviously an optimal solution to the minimization problem $\inf_{\mathbf{x} \in \mathfrak{X}} \left[\sup_{\mathbf{y} \in \mathfrak{D}} L_g(\mathbf{x}; \mathbf{y}) \right]$, and $\mathbf{y}^*$ is obviously an optimal solution to the maximization problem $\sup_{\mathbf{y} \in \mathfrak{D}} \left[\inf_{\mathbf{x} \in \mathfrak{X}} L_g(\mathbf{x}; \mathbf{y}) \right]$. Now, when g is convex and closed, the definition of L_g and the symmetry of the conjugate transformation clearly imply that the preceding minimization problem is essentially Problem $\mathfrak{A}$. Consequently, it is not unnatural to consider the preceding maximization problem simultaneously with Problem $\mathfrak{A}$ and term it the "geometric dual problem" $\mathfrak{B}$.

PROBLEM $\mathcal{B}$. *Using the feasible solution set*

$$\mathcal{T} \triangleq \{\mathbf{y} \in \mathcal{D} \mid \inf_{\mathbf{x} \in \mathcal{X}} L_g(\mathbf{x}; \mathbf{y}) \text{ is finite}\}$$

and the objective function

$$\mathcal{H}(\mathbf{y}) \triangleq \inf_{\mathbf{x} \in \mathcal{X}} L_g(\mathbf{x}; \mathbf{y}),$$

calculate both the problem supremum

$$\Psi \triangleq \sup_{\mathbf{y} \in \mathcal{T}} \mathcal{H}(\mathbf{y})$$

and the optimal solution set

$$\mathcal{T}^* \triangleq \{\mathbf{y} \in \mathcal{T} \mid \mathcal{H}(\mathbf{y}) = \Psi\}.$$

Even though Problem $\mathcal{B}$ is essentially a "max-min problem"—a type of problem that tends to be relatively difficult to analyze—the minimization problems that must be solved to obtain the objective function $\mathcal{H}: \mathcal{T}$ have trivial solutions. In particular, the definition of L_g and the hypothesis that $\mathcal{X}$ is a cone clearly imply that $\inf_{\mathbf{x} \in \mathcal{X}} L_g(\mathbf{x}; \mathbf{y})$ is finite iff $\mathbf{y} \in \mathcal{Y}$, in which case $\inf_{\mathbf{x} \in \mathcal{X}} L_g(\mathbf{x}; \mathbf{y}) = -h(\mathbf{y})$. Consequently, $\mathcal{T} = \mathcal{Y} \cap \mathcal{D}$ and $\mathcal{H}(\mathbf{y}) = -h(\mathbf{y})$, so Problem $\mathcal{B}$ can actually be rephrased in the following more direct way:

Using the feasible solution set $\mathcal{T} = \mathcal{Y} \cap \mathcal{D}$, calculate both the problem *infimum* $\psi \triangleq \inf_{\mathbf{y} \in \mathcal{T}} h(\mathbf{y}) = -\Psi$ and the optimal solution set $\mathcal{T}^* = \{\mathbf{y} \in \mathcal{T} \mid h(\mathbf{y}) = \psi\}$.

When phrased in this way, Problem $\mathcal{B}$ closely resembles Problem $\mathcal{A}$, and is in fact a GP problem. Of course, the geometric dual Problem $\mathcal{B}$ can actually be defined in this way—an approach that is exploited in the following subsection. Nevertheless, the preceding derivation serves as an important link between Lagrangians and duality.

3.1.4 Duality. As in the preceding subsection, let $h: \mathcal{D}$ be the conjugate transform of the function $g: \mathcal{C}$.

Now, consider the following GP Problem $\mathcal{B}$.

PROBLEM $\mathcal{B}$. *Using the feasible solution set*

$$\mathcal{T} \triangleq \mathcal{Y} \cap \mathcal{D},$$

calculate both the problem infimum

$$\psi \triangleq \inf_{\mathbf{y} \in \mathcal{T}} h(\mathbf{y})$$

and the optimal solution set

$$\mathcal{T}^* \triangleq \{\mathbf{y} \in \mathcal{T} \mid h(\mathbf{y}) = \psi\}.$$

It should be noted that Problem $\mathcal{B}$ is generally as easy to compute as $h:\mathcal{D}$ and $\mathcal{Y}$. Moreover, Problem $\mathcal{B}$ is always a convex programming problem, because both $h:\mathcal{D}$ and $\mathcal{Y}$ are always convex and closed (even when $g:\mathcal{C}$ and $\mathcal{X}$ are not convex and closed).

Problems $\mathcal{A}$ and $\mathcal{B}$ are termed *geometric dual problems.* When both $g:\mathcal{C}$ and $\mathcal{X}$ are convex and closed, this duality is clearly symmetric, in that Problem $\mathcal{A}$ can then be constructed from Problem $\mathcal{B}$ in the same way that Problem $\mathcal{B}$ has just been constructed from Problem $\mathcal{A}$. This symmetry induces a symmetry on the theory that relates $\mathcal{A}$ to $\mathcal{B}$, in that each statement about $\mathcal{A}$ and $\mathcal{B}$ automatically produces an equally valid "dual statement" about $\mathcal{B}$ and $\mathcal{A}$. To be concise, each dual statement will be left to the reader's imagination.

Unlike the usual min-max formulations of duality in mathematical programming, both Problem $\mathcal{A}$ and its geometric dual Problem $\mathcal{B}$ are minimization problems. The relative simplicity of this min-min formulation will soon become clear, but the reader who is accustomed to the usual min-max formulation must bear in mind that a given duality theorem will generally have slightly different statements depending on the formulation in use. In particular, a theorem that asserts the equality of the min and max in the usual formulation will assert that the sum of the mins is zero (i.e. $\varphi + \psi = 0$) in the present formulation.

The following definition is almost as important as the definition of the dual Problems $\mathcal{A}$ and $\mathcal{B}$.

Definition. *The* extremality conditions *(for unconstrained GP) are:*

(I) $$\mathbf{x} \in \mathcal{X} \quad \text{and} \quad \mathbf{y} \in \mathcal{Y}$$

(II) $$0 = \langle \mathbf{x}, \mathbf{y} \rangle$$

(III) $$\mathbf{y} \in \partial g(\mathbf{x}).$$

Extremality conditions (I) are simply the "cone conditions" for Problems $\mathcal{A}$ and $\mathcal{B}$ respectively. Extremality condition (II) is termed the "orthogonality condition", and extremality condition (III) is termed the "subgradient condition."

If the cone $\mathcal{X}$ is actually a vector space (which is the case for each of the examples given in Section 2.1), then $\mathcal{Y} = \mathcal{X}^{\perp}$ and hence the orthogonality condition (II) is redundant and can be deleted from the preceding definition (and everywhere that definition is used).

The following "duality theorem" is the basis for many others to come.

THEOREM 3. If $\mathbf{x}$ and $\mathbf{y}$ are feasible solutions to Problems $\mathcal{A}$ and $\mathcal{B}$ respectively (in which case the extremality conditions (I) are satisfied), then $0 \leqslant g(\mathbf{x}) + h(\mathbf{y})$, with equality holding iff the extremality conditions (II) and (III) are satisfied; in which case $\mathbf{x}$ and $\mathbf{y}$ are optimal solutions to Problems $\mathcal{A}$ and $\mathcal{B}$ respectively.

The following important corollary is an immediate consequence of Theorem 3.

Corollary 3A: If the dual Problems $\mathcal{A}$ and $\mathcal{B}$ are both consistent, then

(i) the infimum φ for Problem $\mathcal{A}$ is finite, and $0 \leqslant \varphi + h(\mathbf{y})$ for each $\mathbf{y} \in \mathcal{T}$,
(ii) the infimum ψ for Problem $\mathcal{B}$ is finite, and $0 \leqslant \varphi + \psi$.

The strictness of the inequality in conclusion (ii) plays a crucial role in almost all that follows.

Definition. *Consistent dual Problems* $\mathcal{A}$ *and* $\mathcal{B}$ *for which* $0 < \varphi + \psi$ *have a* duality gap *of* $\varphi + \psi$.

It is well known that duality gaps do not occur in finite LP but they do occasionally occur in infinite LP where this phenomenon was first encountered by Duffin [1956] and Kretchmer [1961]. Although duality gaps occur very frequently in the present (generally nonconvex) formulation of GP, we shall eventually see that they can occur only very rarely in the convex case, in that they can then be excluded by very weak conditions on the geometric dual Problems $\mathcal{A}$ and $\mathcal{B}$. Yet, they do occur in the convex case, and examples (due originally to J. J. Stoer) can be found in Appendix C of [Peterson, 1970].

Geometric programming Problems $\mathcal{A}$ that are convex are usually much more amenable to study than those that are nonconvex, mainly because of the relative lack of duality gaps in the convex case. Duality gaps are undesirable from a theoretical point of view because we shall see that relatively little can be said about the corresponding geometric dual problems. They are also undesirable from a computational point of view because they usually destroy the possibility of using the inequality $0 \leqslant g(\mathbf{x}) + h(\mathbf{y})$ to provide an *algorithmic stopping criterion.*

Such a criterion results from specifying a positive tolerance ϵ so that the numerical algorithms being used to minimize both $g(\mathbf{x})$ and $h(\mathbf{y})$ are terminated when they produce a pair of feasible solutions $\mathbf{x}^\dagger$ and $\mathbf{y}^\dagger$ for which $g(\mathbf{x}^\dagger) + h(\mathbf{y}^\dagger) \leqslant 2\epsilon$. Because conclusion (i) to Corollary 3A, along with the definition of φ shows that $-h(\mathbf{y}^\dagger) \leqslant \varphi \leqslant g(\mathbf{x}^\dagger)$, we conclude from the preceding tolerance inequality that

$$\left| \varphi - \frac{g(\mathbf{x}^\dagger) - h(\mathbf{y}^\dagger)}{2} \right| \leqslant \epsilon.$$

Hence, φ can be approximated by $[g(\mathbf{x}^\dagger) - h(\mathbf{y}^\dagger)]/2$ with an error no greater than $\pm\epsilon$. Moreover, duality (i.e. symmetry) implies that ψ can be approximated by $[h(\mathbf{y}^\dagger) - g(\mathbf{x}^\dagger)]/2$ with an error no greater than $\pm\epsilon$.

Note though that Problems $\mathcal{A}$ and $\mathcal{B}$ have a duality gap iff there is a positive tolerance ϵ so small that $2\epsilon < \varphi + \psi$. Because the definitions for φ and ψ imply that $\varphi + \psi \leqslant g(\mathbf{x}) + h(\mathbf{y})$ for feasible solutions $\mathbf{x}$ and $\mathbf{y}$, we infer that when ϵ satisfies the preceding inequality there are no feasible solutions $\mathbf{x}^\dagger$ and $\mathbf{y}^\dagger$ for which $g(\mathbf{x}^\dagger) + h(\mathbf{y}^\dagger) \leqslant 2\epsilon$; in which event the algorithms being used are never terminated.

The following corollary provides a useful characterization of dual optimal solutions $\mathbf{x}^*$ and $\mathbf{y}^*$ in terms of the extremality conditions.

Corollary 3B: If the extremality conditions have a solution $\mathbf{x}'$ and $\mathbf{y}'$, then

(i) $$\mathbf{x}' \in \mathcal{S}^* \quad \text{and} \quad \mathbf{y}' \in \mathcal{T}^*$$

(ii) $$\mathcal{T}^* = \{\mathbf{y} \in \mathcal{Y} \cap \partial g(\mathbf{x}') \mid 0 = \langle \mathbf{x}', \mathbf{y} \rangle\}$$

(iii) $$0 = \varphi + \psi.$$

On the other hand, if the dual Problems $\mathcal{A}$ and $\mathcal{B}$ are both consistent and if $0 = \varphi + \psi$, then $\mathbf{x} \in \mathcal{S}^*$ and $\mathbf{y} \in \mathcal{T}^*$ iff $\mathbf{x}$ and $\mathbf{y}$ satisfy the extremality conditions.

The first part of Corollary 3B shows that Problems $\mathcal{A}$ and $\mathcal{B}$ can be viewed as "variational principles" for finding solutions to the extremality conditions. Actually, in many contexts (such as the network problems alluded to in Section 2.1), the extremality conditions are, in one form or another, the natural objects of study (rather than either Problem $\mathcal{A}$ or Problem $\mathcal{B}$). Needless to say, Corollary 3B shows that the lack of a duality gap is fundamental in all such contexts.

It is worth noting that if $g:\mathcal{C}$ is convex and closed, then the symmetry of the conjugate transformation implies that the subgradient condition (III) can be replaced by the equivalent subgradient condition

(IIIa) $$\mathbf{x} \in \partial h(\mathbf{y})$$

without changing the validity of Corollary 3B.

In that case Corollary 3B and its (unstated) dual are of direct use when $0 = \varphi + \psi$ and *both* $\mathcal{S}^*$ and $\mathcal{T}^*$ are known to be nonempty; because they then provide a method for calculating all optimal solutions from the knowledge of only a single optimal solution. For example, if $\mathbf{x}^*$ in $\mathcal{S}^*$ is a known optimal solution to Problem $\mathcal{A}$, then

$$\mathcal{T}^* = \{\mathbf{y} \in \mathcal{Y} \cap \partial g(\mathbf{x}^*) \mid 0 = \langle \mathbf{x}^*, \mathbf{y} \rangle\};$$

and for each $\mathbf{y}^* \in \mathcal{T}^*$, the set

$$\mathcal{S}^* = \{\mathbf{x} \in \mathcal{X} \cap \partial h(\mathbf{y}^*) \mid 0 = \langle \mathbf{x}, \mathbf{y}^* \rangle\}.$$

The definition of the Lagrangian L_g (in Section 3.1.3) and the fact that $\mathcal{X}$ is a cone readily imply that the cone condition $\mathbf{y} \in \mathcal{Y}$ and the orthogonality condition $0 = \langle \mathbf{x}, \mathbf{y} \rangle$ can both be replaced by the single equivalent condition $L_g(\mathbf{x}; \mathbf{y}) = \inf_{\mathbf{x}' \in \mathcal{X}} L_g(\mathbf{x}' : \mathbf{y})$. Moreover, if $g:\mathcal{C}$ is convex and closed, conjugate transform theory readily implies that the subgradient condition $\mathbf{y} \in \partial g(\mathbf{x})$ can be replaced by the equivalent condition $\sup_{\mathbf{y}' \in \mathcal{D}} L_g(\mathbf{x};\mathbf{y}') = L_g(\mathbf{x};\mathbf{y})$. Consequently, the saddle-point condition discussed in Section 3.1.3 is equivalent to the extremality conditions when $g:\mathcal{C}$ is convex and closed. Nevertheless, it seems that the extremality conditions given in the definition are the most convenient to work with.

The following theorem provides an important tie between dual Problem $\mathcal{B}$ and the P vectors defined in Section 3.1.3.

THEOREM 4. Given that Problem $\mathcal{A}$ is consistent with a finite infimum φ,

1. if Problem $\mathcal{A}$ has a P vector, then Problem $\mathcal{B}$ is consistent and $0 = \varphi + \psi$,
2. if Problem $\mathcal{B}$ is consistent and $0 = \varphi + \psi$, then $\{\mathbf{y}^* \mid \mathbf{y}^*$ is a P vector for Problem $\mathcal{A}\} = \mathcal{T}^*$.

An important consequence of Theorem 4 is that, when they exist, all P vectors for Problem $\mathcal{A}$ can be obtained simply by computing the dual optimal solution set $\mathcal{T}^*$. However, there are cases in which the vectors in $\mathcal{T}^*$ are not P vectors for Problem $\mathcal{A}$; though such cases can occur only when $0 < \varphi + \psi$, in which event Theorem 4 implies that there can be no P vectors for Problem $\mathcal{A}$.

The absence of a duality gap (i.e., the assumption that $0 = \varphi + \psi$) is crucial to the preceding computational and theoretical techniques, as well as others to come. Although there are numerous conditions that guarantee the absence of a duality gap, the most useful and widely used ones can be viewed as special manifestations of the hypotheses in the following theorem. In addition to guaranteeing the absence of a duality gap, this GP version of "Fenchel's theorem" also serves as a very important existence theorem.

THEOREM 5. Suppose that both $g:\mathcal{C}$ and $\mathcal{X}$ are convex and closed. If the dual Problem $\mathcal{B}$ has a feasible solution $y^\circ \in (\mathrm{ri}\,\mathcal{Y}) \cap (\mathrm{ri}\,\mathcal{D})$, and if Problem $\mathcal{B}$ has a finite infimum ψ, then $0 = \varphi + \psi$ and $\mathcal{S}^* \neq \phi$.

There are several facts about relative interiors that help in the application of Theorem 5. For example, if the cone $\mathcal{Y}$ is actually a vector space, then $(\mathrm{ri}\,\mathcal{Y}) = \mathcal{Y}$ and hence the hypothesis $\mathbf{y}^\circ \in (\mathrm{ri}\,\mathcal{Y}) \cap (\mathrm{ri}\,\mathcal{D})$ is implied by the hypothesis $\mathbf{y}^\circ \in \mathcal{Y} \cap (\mathrm{ri}\,\mathcal{D})$. Also, if the set $\mathcal{D}$ turns out to be a vector space, then $(\mathrm{ri}\,\mathcal{D}) = \mathcal{D}$ and hence the hypothesis $\mathbf{y}^\circ \in (\mathrm{ri}\,\mathcal{Y}) \cap (\mathrm{ri}\,\mathcal{D})$ is implied by the hypothesis $\mathbf{y}^\circ \in (\mathrm{ri}\,\mathcal{Y}) \cap \mathcal{D}$; which in turn is always satisfiable when $\mathcal{D} = E_n$.

Theorem 5 and the preceding facts are the key ingredients needed to show that there are no duality gaps for many of the examples given in Section 2.1, such as:

1. posynomial programming problems (Example 1) that are "canonical" (as defined in [Duffin, Peterson, 1966] or [Duffin, Peterson, Zener, 1967]),
2. convex l_p programming problems (Example 2) that are "canonical" (as defined in [Peterson, Ecker, 1970]),

3. optimal location problems (Example 3) whose costs $d_i(\mathbf{z}, \mathbf{b}^i) = \|\mathbf{z} - \mathbf{b}^i\|_i$ for some "norm" $\|\cdot\|_i$ (as first shown in [Peterson, Wendell, 1978]),
4. discrete optimal control problems (Example 4) that are "canonical" (as defined in [Dinkel, Peterson, 1978]).

It is worth mentioning here that, when both $g:\mathcal{C}$ and $\mathfrak{X}$ are convex and closed, the absence of a duality gap can actually be characterized in terms of the changes induced in the problem infimum φ by small changes in certain problem input parameters–a characterization that is given in the following section.

3.1.5 Parametric Programming and Post-Optimality Analysis. For both practical and theoretical reasons, Problem $\mathcal{A}$ should not be studied entirely in isolation. It should also be embedded in a parameterized family $\mathcal{F}$ of closely related GP problems $\mathcal{A}(\mathbf{u})$ that are generated by simply translating (the domain $\mathcal{C}$ of) g through all possible displacements $-\mathbf{u} \in E_n$, while keeping $\mathfrak{X}$ fixed. (For gaining insight, we recommend making a sketch of a typical case in which n is 2 and $\mathfrak{X}$ is a one-dimensional vector space.) Problem $\mathcal{A}$ then appears in the parameterized family $\mathcal{F}$ as problem $\mathcal{A}(\mathbf{0})$ and is studied in relation to all other GP problems $\mathcal{A}(\mathbf{u})$, with special attention given to those problems $\mathcal{A}(\mathbf{u})$ in $\mathcal{F}$ that are close to $\mathcal{A}(\mathbf{0})$ in the sense that (the "norm" of) $\mathbf{u}$ is small.

The parameterized family $\mathcal{F}$ of all problems $\mathcal{A}(\mathbf{u})$ (for fixed $g:\mathcal{C}$ and $\mathfrak{X}$) is termed a *GP family*. For purposes of easy reference and mathematical precision, Problem $\mathcal{A}(\mathbf{u})$ is now given the following formal definition, which should be compared with the formal definition of Problem $\mathcal{A}$ at the beginning of Section 2.1.

PROBLEM $\mathcal{A}(\mathbf{u})$. *Using the feasible solution set*

$$\mathcal{S}(\mathbf{u}) \triangleq \mathfrak{X} \cap (\mathcal{C} - \mathbf{u}),$$

calculate both the problem infimum

$$\varphi(\mathbf{u}) \triangleq \inf_{\mathbf{x} \in \mathcal{S}(\mathbf{u})} g(\mathbf{x} + \mathbf{u})$$

and the optimal solution set

$$\mathcal{S}^*(\mathbf{u}) \triangleq \{\mathbf{x} \in \mathcal{S}(\mathbf{u}) \mid g(\mathbf{x} + \mathbf{u}) = \varphi(\mathbf{u})\}.$$

Note that (in a rather general set-theoretic sense) the symbols $\mathcal{A}$, $\mathcal{S}$, φ and $\mathcal{S}^*$ now represent functions of $\mathbf{u}$, though they originally represented only the particular functional values $\mathcal{A}(\mathbf{0})$, $\mathcal{S}(\mathbf{0})$, $\varphi(\mathbf{0})$ and $\mathcal{S}^*(\mathbf{0})$ respectively. Needless to say, the reader must keep this notational discrepancy in mind when comparing subsequent developments with previous developments.

For a given $\mathbf{u}$, Problem $\mathcal{A}(\mathbf{u})$ is either consistent or inconsistent, depending on whether the feasible solution set $\mathcal{S}(\mathbf{u})$ is nonempty or empty. It is, of course, obvious that the parameterized family $\mathcal{F}$ contains infinitely many consistent Problems $\mathcal{A}(\mathbf{u})$. The domain of the infimum function φ is taken to be the corresponding nonempty set $\mathcal{U}$ of all those vectors $\mathbf{u}$ for which $\mathcal{A}(\mathbf{u})$ is consistent. Thus, the range of φ may contain the point $-\infty$; but if $\varphi(\mathbf{u}) = -\infty$ then the optimal solution set $\mathcal{S}^*(\mathbf{u})$ is clearly empty.

Due to the pre-eminence of Problem $\mathcal{A}(\mathbf{0})$, we shall find it useful to interpret Problem $\mathcal{A}(\mathbf{u})$ as a perturbed version of $\mathcal{A}(\mathbf{0})$, so we term the set

$$\mathcal{U} \triangleq \{\mathbf{u} \in E_n \mid \mathcal{S}(\mathbf{u}) \text{ is not empty}\}$$

the *feasible perturbation set* for Problem $\mathcal{A}(\mathbf{0})$ (relative to the family $\mathcal{F}$).

The functions φ and $\mathcal{S}^*$ usually show the dependence of optimality on actual external influences and hence are of prime interest in "cost-benefit analysis" and other such subjects. In fact, for the examples given in Section 2.1, it is easy to see that the perturbation vector $\mathbf{u}$:

1. alters in Example 1 the (log of the absolute value of the) signomial coefficients c_i (which are generally determined by such external influences as design requirements, performance requirements, matériel costs, and so forth),
2. alters in the linear regression analysis case of Example 2 the vector $(b_1 \ldots, b_m)$ being optimally approximated.
3. alters in Example 3 the fixed facility locations $\mathbf{b}^i$, provided that each cost $d_i(\mathbf{z}, \mathbf{b}^i) = \|\mathbf{z} - \mathbf{b}^i\|_i$ for some "norm" $\|\cdot\|_i$,
4. translates in Example 4 the "state sets" R_i and the "decision sets" D_i.

The properties of the parameterized family $\mathcal{F}$ brought out in the following theorem are of fundamental theoretical significance and also have rather obvious applications in parametric programming.

THEOREM 6. The feasible perturbation set $\mathcal{U}$ is given by the formula

$$\mathcal{U} = \mathcal{C} - \mathcal{X}.$$

Moreover, if both $\mathcal{C}$ and $\mathcal{X}$ are convex, then so is $\mathcal{U}$, and the point-to-set function $\mathcal{S}$ is "concave" on $\mathcal{U}$ in that

$$\delta_1 \mathcal{S}(\mathbf{u}^1) + \delta_2 \mathcal{S}(\mathbf{u}^2) \subseteq \mathcal{S}(\delta_1 \mathbf{u}^1 + \delta_2 \mathbf{u}^2)$$

for each "convex combination" $\delta_1 \mathbf{u}^1 + \delta_2 \mathbf{u}^2$ of arbitrary points $\mathbf{u}^1, \mathbf{u}^2 \in \mathcal{U}$. Furthermore, if both $g{:}\mathcal{C}$ and $\mathcal{X}$ are convex, then so is Problem $\mathcal{A}(\mathbf{u})$ for each $\mathbf{u} \in \mathcal{U}$, and the infimum function φ is either finite and convex on $\mathcal{U}$ or $\varphi(\mathbf{u}) \equiv -\infty$ for each $\mathbf{u} \in (\text{ri}\,\mathcal{U})$.

In cases for which $\mathcal{X}$ is actually a vector space, the following theorem reduces a study of the parameterized family $\mathcal{F}$ to a study of only those Problems $\mathcal{A}(\mathbf{u})$ in $\mathcal{F}$ for which $\mathbf{u} \in \mathcal{Y} = \mathcal{X}^\perp$. In such cases, it is convenient to adopt the notation $\mathbf{u}_{\mathcal{X}}$

and $\mathbf{u}_{\mathcal{Y}}$ for the "orthogonal projection" of an arbitrary vector $\mathbf{u} \in E_n$ onto the orthogonal complementary subspaces $\mathcal{X}$ and $\mathcal{Y}$ respectively.

THEOREM 7. Suppose that $\mathcal{X}$ and $\mathcal{Y}$ are orthogonal complementary subspaces of E_n. Then, for each vector $\mathbf{u} \in E_n$, either the feasible solution sets $\mathcal{S}(\mathbf{u})$ and $\mathcal{S}(\mathbf{u}_{\mathcal{Y}})$ are both empty, or both are nonempty, with the latter being the case iff $\mathbf{u} \in \mathcal{U}$, in which case $\mathcal{S}(\mathbf{u}) = \mathcal{S}(\mathbf{u}_{\mathcal{Y}}) - \mathbf{u}_{\mathcal{X}}$ and $\varphi(\mathbf{u}) = \varphi(\mathbf{u}_{\mathcal{Y}})$. Furthermore, if $\mathbf{u} \in \mathcal{U}$, then either the optimal solution sets $\mathcal{S}^*(\mathbf{u})$ and $\mathcal{S}^*(\mathbf{u}_{\mathcal{Y}})$ are both empty, or both are nonempty and $\mathcal{S}^*(\mathbf{u}) = \mathcal{S}^*(\mathbf{u}_{\mathcal{Y}}) - \mathbf{u}_{\mathcal{X}}$.

In addition to its rather obvious applications in parametric programming the preceding reduction theorem and its (unstated) dual can be used to relate the present GP formulation of duality to both the original Fenchel formulation of duality [Fenchel, 1951] and the more recent Rockafellar formulations of duality [Rockafellar, 1967a, 1968, 1970]. All such relations can be found in [Peterson, 1970].

The following GP version of a theorem due originally to Rockafellar [1967a, 1968, 1970] provides a direct link between the infimum function φ and the dual Problem $\mathcal{B}$. This link serves as the key to deriving very important properties of φ via conjugate transform theory.

THEOREM 8. The infimum function φ is finite everywhere on its domain $\mathcal{U}$ and possesses a conjugate transform iff the dual Problem $\mathcal{B}$ is consistent, in which case the dual objective function $h:\mathcal{T}$ is the conjugate transform of $\varphi:\mathcal{U}$.

Although this theorem has a relatively simple and direct proof (due originally to Rockafellar), it can also be viewed as an immediate corollary to other theorems that produce micro-economic interpretations of the dual Problem $\mathcal{B}$. In fact, a detailed analysis of the situation (given in [Peterson, 1970]) shows that a rather interesting class of micro-economic problems can be solved explicitly in terms of Problem $\mathcal{B}$.

The following corollary plays a crucial role in most applications of Theorem 8.

Corollary 8A: If the dual Problem $\mathcal{B}$ is consistent, then the conjugate transform of its objective function $h:\mathcal{T}$ is the closed convex hull $\overline{\varphi}:\overline{\mathcal{U}}$ of the infimum function $\varphi:\mathcal{U}$ (which is, of course, identical to $\varphi:\mathcal{U}$ when $\varphi:\mathcal{U}$ happens to be both convex and closed).

The preceding theorem and its corollary provide *a method for constructing, without the use of numerical optimization techniques, the closed convex hull $\overline{\varphi}:\overline{\mathcal{U}}$ of $\varphi:\mathcal{U}$* (which, by virtue of Theorem 6, is essentially the desired infimum function $\varphi:\mathcal{U}$ when both $g:\mathcal{C}$ and $\mathcal{X}$ are convex). In particular, if the dual feasible solution set $\mathcal{T}$ is not empty (which, as indicated by Theorem 6, is the only really interesting nontrivial case), it can of course be covered with a "mesh"

$$\mathcal{M} \triangleq \{\mathbf{y}^1, \mathbf{y}^2, \ldots, \mathbf{y}^s\} \subseteq \mathcal{T} \triangleq \mathcal{Y} \cap \mathcal{D}.$$

From Corollary 8A and conjugate transform theory $\overline{\varphi}$ is clearly bounded from below on $\overline{\mathfrak{U}}$ by the (polyhedral) approximating function $\overline{\varphi}_b$ whose functional values

$$\overline{\varphi}_b(\mathbf{u}) \triangleq \max_{i=1,2,\ldots,s} [\langle \mathbf{y}^i, \mathbf{u}\rangle - h(\mathbf{y}^i)] \quad \text{for each} \quad \mathbf{u} \in \overline{\mathfrak{U}}.$$

Moreover, the conjugate inequality (for $\overline{\varphi}:\overline{\mathfrak{U}}$ and $h:\mathcal{T}$) can be used to show that

$$\overline{\varphi}(\mathbf{u}) = \langle \mathbf{y}^i, \mathbf{u}\rangle - h(\mathbf{y}^i) \quad \text{for each} \quad \mathbf{u} \in \partial h(\mathbf{y}^i) - \{\chi \in \mathcal{X} \mid \langle \chi, \mathbf{y}\rangle = 0\},$$
$$i = 1, 2, \ldots, s;$$

and the convexity of $\overline{\varphi}$ then implies that $\overline{\varphi}$ is bounded from above by "affine interpolations" between such functional values. Furthermore, it is a consequence of conjugate transform theory that these lower and upper approximations can be made with arbitrary accuracy simply by choosing the mesh $\mathfrak{M}$ to be sufficiently "dense" in $\mathcal{T}$. To be practical though, this method requires an explicit construction of the dual objective function $h:\mathcal{T}$, a construction that is rather easy for virtually all of the important (convex) examples given in Section 2.1.

The preceding corollary also helps to motivate the following definition.

Definition. *Problem* $\mathcal{A}(\mathbf{u})$ *is said to be* quasi-consistent *if the closed convex hull* $\overline{\varphi}:\overline{\mathfrak{U}}$ *of the infimum function* $\varphi:\mathfrak{U}$ *exists and if* $\mathbf{u} \in \overline{\mathfrak{U}}$, *in which case* $\overline{\varphi}(\mathbf{u})$ *is termed the* quasi-infimum *for Problem* $\mathcal{A}(\mathbf{u})$.

Since $\mathfrak{U} \subseteq \overline{\mathfrak{U}}$, each consistent Problem $\mathcal{A}(\mathbf{u})$ is quasi-consistent, but not conversely.

The following theorem leads to a complete explanation of duality gaps, and is also at the heart of many postoptimal "sensitivity analyses."

THEOREM 9. Suppose that the dual Problem $\mathcal{B}$ is consistent. Then, its infimum ψ is finite if and only if Problem $\mathcal{A}(\mathbf{0})$ is quasi-consistent, in which case

$$0 = \overline{\varphi}(\mathbf{0}) + \psi \quad \text{and} \quad \partial\overline{\varphi}(\mathbf{0}) = \mathcal{T}^*.$$

The following corollary identifies duality gaps as simply the difference between $\varphi(\mathbf{0})$ and $\overline{\varphi}(\mathbf{0})$.

Corollary 9A: Suppose that the dual Problems $\mathcal{A}(\mathbf{0})$ and $\mathcal{B}$ are both consistent. Then, Problem $\mathcal{A}(\mathbf{0})$ is quasi-consistent and

$$\varphi(\mathbf{0}) - \overline{\varphi}(\mathbf{0}) = \varphi(\mathbf{0}) + \psi.$$

The preceding corollary helps to motivate the following definition.

Definition. *A consistent Problem* $\mathcal{A}(\mathbf{u})$ *for which* $\varphi(\mathbf{u}) = \overline{\varphi}(\mathbf{u})$ *is said to be* normal.

The following corollary formalizes the equivalence of normality and the lack of a duality gap, while showing that either condition guarantees the validity of an equation on which many sensitivity analyses are based.

Corollary 9B: Suppose that the dual Problems $\mathcal{A}(\mathbf{0})$ and $\mathcal{B}$ are both consistent. Then, Problem $\mathcal{A}(\mathbf{0})$ is normal iff Problems $\mathcal{A}(\mathbf{0})$ and $\mathcal{B}$ have no duality gap, in which case

$$\partial\varphi(\mathbf{0}) = \mathcal{T}^*.$$

An additional prerequisite for sensitivity analyses is provided by the following definition.

Definition. *A consistent Problem* $\mathcal{A}(\mathbf{u})$ *with a finite infimum* $\varphi(\mathbf{u})$ *is termed* stable set *(relative to the family* $\mathcal{F}$*) when the (one-sided) "directional derivative"*

$$D_{\mathbf{d}}\varphi(\mathbf{u}) \triangleq \lim_{s \to 0^+} \frac{\varphi(\mathbf{u} + s\mathbf{d}) - \varphi(\mathbf{u})}{s}$$

exists and is finite for each feasible direction $\mathbf{d}$ *(i.e., each direction* $\mathbf{d}$ *such that* $\mathbf{u} + s\mathbf{d} \in \mathcal{U}$ *for sufficiently small* $s > 0$*).*

The following theorem ties stability directly to the existence of certain subgradients, and shows how each guarantees normality.

THEOREM 10. Let both $g:\mathcal{C}$ and $\mathcal{X}$ be convex, and suppose that Problem $\mathcal{A}(\mathbf{0})$ is consistent and has a finite infimum $\varphi(\mathbf{0})$. Then, Problem $\mathcal{A}(\mathbf{0})$ is stably set iff $\partial\varphi(\mathbf{0})$ is not empty, in which case Problem $\mathcal{A}(\mathbf{0})$ is normal.

Given a consistent Problem $\mathcal{A}(\mathbf{0})$ with a known finite infimum $\varphi(\mathbf{0})$, a *sensitivity analysis* consists of estimating other infima $\varphi(\mathbf{u})$ for very small $\mathbf{u}$. First-order estimates can, of course, be based on the directional derivatives $D_{\mathbf{u}}\varphi(\mathbf{0})$ when Problem $\mathcal{A}(\mathbf{0})$ is stably set. In that case, the defining equation for $D_{\mathbf{u}}\varphi(\mathbf{0})$ provides the usual estimation formula

$$\varphi(\mathbf{u}) \approx \varphi(\mathbf{0}) + D_{\mathbf{u}}\varphi(\mathbf{0}),$$

whose use requires a computation of $D_{\mathbf{u}}\varphi(\mathbf{0})$. Toward that end, Fenchel [1951] and, more recently, Rockafellar [1970] have appropriately extended the well-known formula $D_{\mathbf{u}}\varphi(\mathbf{0}) = \langle \mathbf{u}, \nabla\varphi(\mathbf{0})\rangle$ by showing that $D_{\mathbf{u}}\varphi(\mathbf{0}) = \max_{\mathbf{y} \in \partial\varphi(\mathbf{0})} \langle \mathbf{u}, \mathbf{y}\rangle$ when φ is convex on $\mathcal{U}$—which is indeed the case when both $g:\mathcal{C}$ and $\mathcal{X}$ are convex, by virtue of Theorem 6. Moreover, Corollary 9B shows that the preceding formula can be rewritten as

$$D_{\mathbf{u}}\varphi(\mathbf{0}) = \max_{\mathbf{y} \in \mathcal{T}^*} \langle \mathbf{u}, \mathbf{y}\rangle$$

when the dual Problem $\mathcal{B}$ is consistent and there is no duality gap—which is almost always the case, as indicated by Theorem 6, Theorem 8, and (Fenchel's) Theorem 5. Consequently, it is of interest to know $\mathcal{T}^*$ in addition to $\varphi(\mathbf{0})$ and $\mathcal{S}^*(\mathbf{0})$, so that the preceding displayed formulas can be used to estimate $\varphi(\mathbf{u})$ for a very small $\mathbf{u}$. But $\mathcal{T}^*$ can usually be calculated from an arbitrary $\mathbf{x}^* \in \mathcal{S}^*(\mathbf{0})$ by employing the extremality conditions, as explained after Corollary 3B.

To further characterize duality gaps, we also embed the dual Problem $\mathcal{B}$ in a parameterized family $\mathcal{G}$ of closely related GP problems $\mathcal{B}(\mathbf{v})$ that are generated by simply translating (the domain $\mathcal{D}$ of) h through all possible displacements $-\mathbf{v} \in E_n$, while keeping $\mathcal{Y}$ fixed. Problem $\mathcal{B}$ then appears in the parameterized family $\mathcal{G}$ as problem $\mathcal{B}(\mathbf{0})$ and is studied in relation to all other GP problems $\mathcal{B}(\mathbf{v})$, with special attention given to those problems $\mathcal{B}(\mathbf{v})$ in $\mathcal{G}$ that are close to $\mathcal{B}(\mathbf{0})$ in the sense that (the "norm" of) $\mathbf{v}$ is small.

Naturally, the symbols $\mathcal{B}$, $\mathcal{T}$, ψ and $\mathcal{T}^*$ now represent functions of $\mathbf{v}$, though they originally represented only the particular functional values $\mathcal{B}(\mathbf{0})$, $\mathcal{T}(\mathbf{0})$, $\psi(\mathbf{0})$ and $\mathcal{T}^*(\mathbf{0})$ respectively. Needless to say, the reader must keep this notational discrepancy in mind when comparing subsequent developments with previous developments.

Since the main results having to do with the *dual GP family* $\mathcal{G}$ are essentially dual to those already given for the family $\mathcal{F}$, we shall feel free to use them without further discussion.

The following important theorem involves the dual families $\mathcal{F}$ and $\mathcal{G}$ in a reflexive (i.e., self-dual) way.

THEOREM 11. Let both $g:\mathcal{C}$ and $\mathcal{X}$ be convex and closed, and suppose that the dual Problems $\mathcal{A}(\mathbf{0})$ and $\mathcal{B}(\mathbf{0})$ are both consistent. Then, the following three conditions are equivalent:

(i) Problem $\mathcal{A}(\mathbf{0})$ is normal,
(ii) Problem $\mathcal{B}(\mathbf{0})$ is normal,
(iii) Problems $\mathcal{A}(\mathbf{0})$ and $\mathcal{B}(\mathbf{0})$ do not have a duality gap.

Moreover, if any of these three conditions are satisfied, then $\partial\varphi(\mathbf{0}) = \mathcal{T}^*$ and $\partial\psi(\mathbf{0}) = \mathcal{S}^*$.

There are various degrees of consistency, ranging all the way from (the very weak) quasi-consistency through (the intermediate) consistency to "strong consistency."

Definition. *Problem* $\mathcal{B}(\mathbf{v})$ *is said to be* strongly consistent *if* $\mathbf{v} \in (\mathrm{ri}\,\mathcal{V})$. *Since* $(\mathrm{ri}\,\mathcal{V}) \subseteq \mathcal{V}$, *each strongly consistent Problem* $\mathcal{B}(\mathbf{v})$ *is consistent, but not conversely.*

The following theorem indicates the importance of strong consistency.

THEOREM 12. Each strongly consistent dual Problem $\mathcal{B}(\mathbf{0})$ with a finite infimum $\psi(\mathbf{0})$ is stably set (and hence normal).

Since $(\mathrm{ri}\,\mathcal{V})$ is "almost all" of $\mathcal{V}$, Theorem 12 implies that almost all consistent problems $\mathcal{B}(\mathbf{0})$ with a finite infimum $\psi(\mathbf{0})$ are normal, so Theorem 11 shows that duality gaps are rather rare phenomena when both $g:\mathcal{C}$ and $\mathcal{X}$ are convex and closed. Nevertheless, duality gaps can occur when both $g:\mathcal{C}$ and $\mathcal{X}$ are convex and closed, and examples (due originally to J. J. Stoer) can be found in Appendix C of [Peterson, 1970].

3.2 Relations Between the Constrained and Unconstrained Cases

The constrained case can, of course, be specialized to the unconstrained case, simply by letting both index sets I and J be empty while choosing $g_0 : C_0$ to be $g:\mathcal{C}$ and X to be $\mathfrak{X}$. A somewhat surprising fact is that this specialization can be reversed; that is, the unconstrained case can actually be specialized to the constrained case.

To do so, let the functional domain

$$\mathcal{C} \triangleq \{(\mathbf{x}^0, \mathbf{x}^I, \boldsymbol{\alpha}, \mathbf{x}^J, \boldsymbol{\kappa}) \in E_n \mid \mathbf{x}^0 \in C_0; \mathbf{x}^i \in C_i, \alpha_i \in E_1, \text{ and } g_i(\mathbf{x}^i) + \alpha_i \leqslant 0, i \in I; (\mathbf{x}^j, \kappa_j) \in C_j^+, j \in J\};$$

and let the functional value

$$g(\mathbf{x}^0, \mathbf{x}^I, \boldsymbol{\alpha}, \mathbf{x}^J, \boldsymbol{\kappa}) \triangleq g_0(\mathbf{x}^0) + \sum_J g_j^+(\mathbf{x}^j, \kappa_j) \triangleq G(\mathbf{x}, \boldsymbol{\kappa}),$$

while letting the cone

$$\mathfrak{X} \triangleq \{(\mathbf{x}^0, \mathbf{x}^I, \boldsymbol{\alpha}, \mathbf{x}^J, \boldsymbol{\kappa}) \in E_n \mid (\mathbf{x}^0, \mathbf{x}^I, \mathbf{x}^J) \in X; \boldsymbol{\alpha} = \mathbf{0}; \boldsymbol{\kappa} \in E_{o(J)}\}.$$

Then, (the unconstrained) Problem $\mathcal{A}$ is clearly identical to (the constrained) Problem A. The additional independent vector variable $\boldsymbol{\alpha}$ with components α_i, $i \in I$ may seem superfluous, but is included so that the induced family $\mathcal{F}$ is essentially identical to a family F that includes certain important constraint parameters μ_i (as described in Section 3.3.4).

Of course, the preceding choice of $g:\mathcal{C}$ and $\mathfrak{X}$ also induces a choice of the dual Problem $\mathcal{B}$ and dual family $\mathcal{G}$ corresponding to Problem $\mathcal{A}$ (i.e., Problem A). In fact, computations of the resulting conjugate transform $h:\mathfrak{D}$ and dual cone $\mathcal{Y}$ (given in [Peterson 1978]) show that the induced dual Problem $\mathcal{B}$ and dual family $\mathcal{G}$ are essentially identical to the dual Problem B and dual family G respectively described in Sections 3.3.3 and 3.3.4. This identification turns out to be highly significant because it provides an efficient mechanism for extending to the constrained case most of the important theorems already described for the unconstrained case.

3.3 The Constrained Case

Only the key ideas and results from the unconstrained case are generalized here, but hopefully the reader can easily fill in the remaining details by using Section 3.1 as a guide.

Let Y be the "dual" of the cone X; that is

$$Y \triangleq \{\mathbf{y} \in E_n \mid 0 \leqslant \langle \mathbf{x}, \mathbf{y} \rangle \quad \text{for each} \quad \mathbf{x} \in X\}.$$

Of course, the fact that $\mathbf{x} \triangleq (\mathbf{x}^0, \mathbf{x}^I, \mathbf{x}^J)$ means that $\mathbf{y} \triangleq (\mathbf{y}^0, \mathbf{y}^I, \mathbf{y}^J)$, with $\mathbf{y}^I$ and $\mathbf{y}^J$ constructed in the same manner as $\mathbf{x}^I$ and $\mathbf{x}^J$.

3.3.1 Optimality Conditions. We begin with the following fundamental definition.

Definition. *A* critical solution (*stationary solution, equilibrium solution, P solution*) *for Problem A is any vector* $(\mathbf{x}^*, \boldsymbol{\kappa}^*)$ *for which there is a vector* $\boldsymbol{\lambda}^*$ *in* $E_{o(I)}$ *such that* $(\mathbf{x}^*, \boldsymbol{\kappa}^*)$ *and* $\boldsymbol{\lambda}^*$ *jointly satisfy the following* P optimality conditions

$$\mathbf{x}^* \in X,$$

$$g_i(\mathbf{x}^{*i}) \leqslant 0, \quad i \in I,$$

$$\lambda_i^* \geqslant 0, \quad i \in I,$$

$$\lambda_i^* g_i(\mathbf{x}^{*i}) = 0, \quad i \in I,$$

$$\mathbf{y}^* \in Y,$$

$$0 = \langle \mathbf{x}^*, \mathbf{y}^* \rangle,$$

and

$$\langle \mathbf{x}^{*j}, \mathbf{y}^{*j} \rangle = g_j^+(\mathbf{x}^{*j}, \kappa_j^*), \quad j \in J,$$

where

$$\mathbf{y}^{*0} \triangleq \nabla g_0(\mathbf{x}^{*0}), \mathbf{y}^{*i} \triangleq \lambda_i^* \nabla g_i(\mathbf{x}^{*i}), \quad i \in I, \text{ and } \quad \mathbf{y}^{*j} \triangleq \nabla g_j(\mathbf{x}^{*j}/\kappa_j^*), \quad j \in J.$$

For ordinary programming, it is worth mentioning that the P optimality conditions are essentially the (more familiar) "Kuhn-Tucker optimality conditions."

The following important concept from ordinary programming plays a crucial role in the constrained case of GP.

Definition. *For a consistent Problem A with a finite infimum* φ, *a* Kuhn-Tucker vector *is any vector* $\boldsymbol{\lambda}^*$ *in* $E_{o(I)}$ *with the two properties*

$$\lambda_i^* \geqslant 0, \quad i \in I, \text{ and } \varphi = \inf_{\substack{(\mathbf{x}, \boldsymbol{\kappa}) \in C \\ \mathbf{x} \in X}} L_0(\mathbf{x}, \boldsymbol{\kappa}; \boldsymbol{\lambda}^*),$$

where the (ordinary) Lagrangian $L_0(\mathbf{x}, \boldsymbol{\kappa}; \boldsymbol{\lambda}) \triangleq G(\mathbf{x}, \boldsymbol{\kappa}) + \sum_I \lambda_i g_i(\mathbf{x}^i)$.

The following theorem gives two convexity conditions that guarantee the necessity and/or sufficiency of the P optimality conditions for optimality.

THEOREM 13. Under the hypotheses that g_k is differentiable at $\mathbf{x}^{*k}$, $k \in \{0\} \cup I$ and that g_j^+ is differentiable at $(\mathbf{x}^{*j}, \kappa_j^*)$, $j \in J$,

1. given that X is convex, if $(\mathbf{x}^*, \boldsymbol{\kappa}^*)$ is an optimal solution to Problem A, and if $\boldsymbol{\lambda}^*$ is a Kuhn-Tucker vector for Problem A, then $(\mathbf{x}^*, \boldsymbol{\kappa}^*)$ is a critical solution for Problem A relative to $\boldsymbol{\lambda}^*$ (but not conversely),
2. given that g_k is convex on C_k, $k \in \{0\} \cup I \cup J$, if $(\mathbf{x}^*, \boldsymbol{\kappa}^*)$ is a critical solution for Problem A relative to $\boldsymbol{\lambda}^*$, then $(\mathbf{x}^*, \boldsymbol{\kappa}^*)$ is an optimal solution to Problem A, and $\boldsymbol{\lambda}^*$ is a Kuhn-Tucker vector for Problem A.

3.3.2. Lagrangian Saddle Points. Let $h_k : D_k$ be the conjugate transform of the function $g_k : C_k$, $k \in \{0\} \cup I \cup J$, and let these sets D_j determine the sets D_j, $j \in J$ postulated at the beginning of Section 2.2.

The following definition is of fundamental importance.

Definition. *Consider the function H whose domain*

$$D \triangleq \{(\mathbf{y}, \boldsymbol{\lambda}) \mid \mathbf{y}^k \in D_k, \;\; k \in \{0\} \cup J, \;\; \textit{and} \;\; (\mathbf{y}^i, \lambda_i) \in D_i^+, i \in I\}$$

and whose functional value

$$H(\mathbf{y}, \boldsymbol{\lambda}) \triangleq h_0(\mathbf{y}^0) + \sum_I h_i^+(\mathbf{y}^i, \lambda_i),$$

where

$$D_i^+ \triangleq \{(\mathbf{y}^i, \lambda_i) \mid \textit{either } \lambda_i = 0 \;\; \textit{and} \;\; \sup_{\mathbf{c}^i \in C_i} \langle \mathbf{y}^i, \mathbf{c}^i \rangle < +\infty,$$

$$\textit{or} \;\; \lambda_i > 0 \;\; \textit{and} \;\; \mathbf{y}^i \in \lambda_i D_i\}$$

and

$$h_i^+(\mathbf{y}^i, \lambda_i) \triangleq \begin{cases} \sup\limits_{\mathbf{c}^i \in C_i} \langle \mathbf{y}^i, \mathbf{c}^i \rangle & \textit{if} \;\; \lambda_i = 0 \;\; \textit{and} \;\; \sup\limits_{\mathbf{c}^i \in C_i} \langle \mathbf{y}^i, \mathbf{c}^i \rangle < +\infty \\ \lambda_i h_i(\mathbf{y}^i / \lambda_i) & \textit{if} \;\; \lambda_i > 0 \;\; \textit{and } \mathbf{y}^i \in \lambda_i D_i. \end{cases}$$

For a consistent Problem A *with a finite infimum φ, a P* vector *is any vector $(\mathbf{y}^*, \boldsymbol{\lambda}^*)$ with the two properties*

$$(\mathbf{y}^*, \boldsymbol{\lambda}^*) \in D \;\; \textit{and} \;\; \varphi = \inf_{\substack{\mathbf{x} \in X \\ \boldsymbol{\kappa} \geq 0}} L_g(\mathbf{x}, \boldsymbol{\kappa}; \mathbf{y}^*, \boldsymbol{\lambda}^*),$$

where the (geometric) Lagrangean $L_g(\mathbf{x}, \boldsymbol{\kappa}; \mathbf{y}, \boldsymbol{\lambda}) \triangleq \langle \mathbf{x}, \mathbf{y} \rangle - H(\mathbf{y}, \boldsymbol{\lambda}) - \sum_J \kappa_j h_j(\mathbf{y}^j)$.

For a given Problem A note that the geometric Lagrangean L_g is entirely different from the ordinary Lagrangian L_0. Unlike the geometric Lagrangean

L_g, the ordinary Lagrangian L_0 simply reduces to the objective function G when $I=\phi$, but L_0 exists even when the conjugate transforms $h_k:D_k$, $k\in\{0\}\cup I\cup J$ do not exist. However, Corollary 17B in Section 3.3.3 shows that Kuhn-Tucker vectors and P vectors are closely related.

The following saddle-point theorem provides several characterizations of optimality via P vectors.

THEOREM 14. Given that $g_k:C_k$, $k\in\{0\}\cup I\cup J$ is convex and closed, let $(\mathbf{x}^*,\boldsymbol{\kappa}^*)$ be such that $\mathbf{x}^*\in X$ and $\boldsymbol{\kappa}^*\geqslant \mathbf{0}$, and let $(\mathbf{y}^*,\boldsymbol{\lambda}^*)\in D$. Then, $(\mathbf{x}^*,\boldsymbol{\kappa}^*)$ is optimal for Problem A and $(\mathbf{y}^*,\boldsymbol{\lambda}^*)$ is a P vector for Problem A iff the ordered pair $(\mathbf{x}^*,\boldsymbol{\kappa}^*;\mathbf{y}^*,\boldsymbol{\lambda}^*)$ is a "saddle point" for the Lagrangean L_g, that is,

$$\sup_{(\mathbf{y},\boldsymbol{\lambda})\in D} L_g(\mathbf{x}^*,\boldsymbol{\kappa}^*;\mathbf{y},\boldsymbol{\lambda}) = L_g(\mathbf{x}^*,\boldsymbol{\kappa}^*;\mathbf{y}^*,\boldsymbol{\lambda}^*) = \inf_{\substack{\mathbf{x}\in X\\ \boldsymbol{\kappa}\geqslant \mathbf{0}}} L_g(\mathbf{x},\boldsymbol{\kappa};\mathbf{y}^*,\boldsymbol{\lambda}^*);$$

in which case L_g has the saddle-point value $L_g(\mathbf{x}^*,\boldsymbol{\kappa}^*;\mathbf{y}^*,\boldsymbol{\lambda}^*)=G(\mathbf{x}^*,\boldsymbol{\kappa}^*)=\varphi$. Moreover,

$$\sup_{(\mathbf{y},\boldsymbol{\lambda})\in D} L_g(\mathbf{x}^*,\boldsymbol{\kappa}^*;\mathbf{y},\boldsymbol{\lambda}) = L_g(\mathbf{x}^*,\boldsymbol{\kappa}^*;\mathbf{y}^*,\boldsymbol{\lambda}^*)$$

iff $(\mathbf{x}^*,\boldsymbol{\kappa}^*)$ and $(\mathbf{y}^*,\boldsymbol{\lambda}^*)$ satisfy both the feasibility conditions

$$(\mathbf{x}^*,\boldsymbol{\kappa}^*)\in C,$$
$$g_i(\mathbf{x}^{*i})\leqslant 0, \qquad i\in I,$$

and the subgradient and "complementary slackness" conditions

$$\mathbf{y}^{*0}\in\partial g_0(\mathbf{x}^{*0}),$$

either $\lambda_i^*=0$ and $\langle\mathbf{x}^{*i},\mathbf{y}^{*i}\rangle = \sup_{c^i\in C_i}\langle\mathbf{c}^i,\mathbf{y}^{*i}\rangle$,

or $\lambda_i^*>0$ and $\mathbf{y}^{*i}\in\lambda_i^*\partial g_i(\mathbf{x}^{*i})$, $i\in I$,

$$\lambda_i^* g_i(\mathbf{x}^{*i})=0 \qquad i\in I,$$

either $\kappa_j^*=0$ and $\langle\mathbf{x}^{*j},\mathbf{y}^{*j}\rangle = \sup_{\mathbf{d}^j\in D_j}\langle\mathbf{x}^{*j},\mathbf{d}^j\rangle$,

or $\kappa_j^*>0$ and $\mathbf{y}^{*j}\in\partial g_j(\mathbf{x}^{*j}/\kappa_j^*)$, $j\in J$;

in which case $L_g(\mathbf{x}^*,\boldsymbol{\kappa}^*;\mathbf{y}^*,\boldsymbol{\lambda}^*)=G(\mathbf{x}^*,\boldsymbol{\kappa}^*)$.

Furthermore,

$$L_g(\mathbf{x}^*,\boldsymbol{\kappa}^*;\mathbf{y}^*,\boldsymbol{\lambda}^*) = \inf_{\substack{\mathbf{x}\in X\\ \boldsymbol{\kappa}\geqslant \mathbf{0}}} L_g(\mathbf{x},\boldsymbol{\kappa};\mathbf{y}^*,\boldsymbol{\lambda}^*)$$

iff $(\mathbf{x}^*,\boldsymbol{\kappa}^*)$ and $(\mathbf{y}^*,\boldsymbol{\lambda}^*)$ satisfy both the feasibility conditions

$$\mathbf{y}^*\in Y,$$
$$h_j(\mathbf{y}^{*j})\leqslant 0, \qquad j\in J,$$

and the orthogonality and complementary slackness conditions

$$0 = \langle \mathbf{x}^*, \mathbf{y}^* \rangle,$$

$$\kappa_j^* h_j(\mathbf{y}^{*j}) = 0 \qquad j \in J;$$

in which case $L_g(\mathbf{x}^*, \boldsymbol{\kappa}^*; \mathbf{y}^*, \boldsymbol{\lambda}^*) = -H(\mathbf{y}^*, \boldsymbol{\lambda}^*)$.

3.3.3. Duality. Let $h_k : D_k$ be the conjugate transform of the function $g_k : C_k$, $k \in \{0\} \cup I \cup J$, and let these sets D_j determine the sets $D_j, j \in J$ postulated at the beginning of Section 2.2.

Now, consider the following GP Problem B.

PROBLEM B. *Consider the objective function H whose domain*

$$D \triangleq \{(\mathbf{y}, \boldsymbol{\lambda}) \mid \mathbf{y}^k \in D_k, k \in \{0\} \cup J, \text{ and } (\mathbf{y}^i, \lambda_i) \in D_i^+, i \in I\}$$

and whose functional value

$$H(\mathbf{y}, \boldsymbol{\lambda}) \triangleq h_0(\mathbf{y}^0) + \sum_I h_i^+(\mathbf{y}^i, \lambda_i),$$

where

$$D_i^+ \triangleq \{(\mathbf{y}^i, \lambda_i) \mid \text{either } \lambda_i = 0 \text{ and } \sup_{\mathbf{c}^i \in \mathrm{C_i}} \langle \mathbf{y}^i, \mathbf{c}^i \rangle < +\infty,$$

$$\text{or } \lambda_i > 0 \text{ and } \mathbf{y}^i \in \lambda_i \mathrm{D}_i\}$$

and

$$h_i^+(\mathbf{y}^i, \lambda_i) \triangleq \begin{cases} \sup_{\mathbf{c}^i \in C_i} \langle \mathbf{y}^i, \mathbf{c}^i \rangle & \text{if } \lambda_i = 0 \text{ and } \sup_{\mathbf{c}^i \in C_i} \langle \mathbf{y}^i, \mathbf{c}^i \rangle < +\infty \\ \lambda_i h_i(\mathbf{y}^i/\lambda_i) & \text{if } \lambda_i > 0 \text{ and } \mathbf{y}^i \in \lambda_i D_i. \end{cases}$$

Using the feasible solution set

$$T \triangleq \{(\mathbf{y}, \boldsymbol{\lambda}) \in D \mid \mathbf{y} \in Y, \text{ and } h_j(\mathbf{y}^j) \leq 0, \ j \in J\},$$

calculate both the problem infimum

$$\psi \triangleq \inf_{(\mathbf{y}, \boldsymbol{\lambda}) \in T} H(\mathbf{y}, \boldsymbol{\lambda})$$

and the optimal solution set

$$T^* \triangleq \{(\mathbf{y}, \boldsymbol{\lambda}) \in T \mid H(\mathbf{y}, \boldsymbol{\lambda}) = \psi\}.$$

Problems A and B are, of course, termed *geometric dual problems*. When $g_k : C_k$, $k \in \{0\} \cup I \cup J$ and X are convex and closed, this duality is clearly symmetric, in that Problem A can then be constructed from Problem B in the same way that Problem B has just been constructed from Problem A. Actually, this duality is the only completely symmetric duality that is presently known for general (closed) convex programming with explicit constraints.

The following definition is almost as important as the definition of the dual Problems A and B.

Definition. *The* extremality conditions *(for constrained GP) are:*

(I) $$\mathbf{x} \in X \quad \textit{and} \quad \mathbf{y} \in Y$$

(II) $$g_i(\mathbf{x}^i) \leqslant 0, \quad i \in I \quad \textit{and} \quad h_j(\mathbf{y}^j) \leqslant 0, \quad j \in J,$$

(III) $$0 = \langle \mathbf{x}, \mathbf{y} \rangle$$

(IV) $$\mathbf{y}^0 \in \partial g_0(\mathbf{x}^0),$$

(V) $$\textit{either } \lambda_i = 0 \quad \textit{and} \quad \langle \mathbf{x}^i, \mathbf{y}^i \rangle = \sup_{\mathbf{c}^i \in C_i} \langle \mathbf{c}^i, \mathbf{y}^i \rangle$$

$$\textit{or} \quad \lambda_i > 0 \quad \textit{and} \quad \mathbf{y}^i \in \lambda_i \partial g_i(\mathbf{x}^i), \qquad i \in I,$$

(VI) $$\textit{either } \kappa_j = 0 \quad \textit{and} \quad \langle \mathbf{x}^j, \mathbf{y}^j \rangle = \sup_{\mathbf{d}^j \in D_j} \langle \mathbf{x}^j, \mathbf{d}^j \rangle$$

$$\textit{or} \quad \kappa_j > 0 \quad \textit{and} \quad \mathbf{y}^j \in \partial g_j(\mathbf{x}^j/\kappa_j), \qquad j \in J,$$

(VII) $$\lambda_i g_i(x^i) = 0, \quad i \in I, \quad \textit{and} \quad \kappa_j h_j(\mathbf{y}^j) = 0, \quad j \in J.$$

When $C_i = E_{n_i}$ (which is frequently the situation), a simplification results from noting that $\langle \mathbf{x}^i, \mathbf{y}^i \rangle = \sup_{\mathbf{c}^i \in C_i} \langle \mathbf{c}^i, \mathbf{y}^i \rangle$ iff $\mathbf{y}^i = \mathbf{0}$. In particular then, the corresponding extremality condition (V) can be replaced by the equivalent extremality condition

$$\lambda_i \geqslant 0 \quad \text{and} \quad \mathbf{y}^i \in \lambda_i \partial g_i(\mathbf{x}^i), \qquad i \in I.$$

Extremality conditions (I) are simply the "cone conditions" for Problems A and B respectively, and extremality conditions (II) are simply the "constraints" for Problems A and B respectively. Extremality condition (III) is termed the "orthogonality condition," extremality conditions (IV) through (VI) are termed the "subgradient conditions," and extremality conditions (VII) are (of course) termed the "complementary slackness conditions."

The following duality theorem is the basis for many others.

THEOREM 15. If $(\mathbf{x},\boldsymbol{\kappa})$ and $(\mathbf{y},\boldsymbol{\lambda})$ are feasible solutions to Problems A and B respectively (in which case the extremality conditions (I) through (II) are satisfied), then $0 \leqslant G(\mathbf{x},\boldsymbol{\kappa}) + H(\mathbf{y},\boldsymbol{\lambda})$, with equality holding iff the extremality conditions (III) through (VII) are satisfied; in which case $(\mathbf{x},\boldsymbol{\kappa})$ and $(\mathbf{y},\boldsymbol{\lambda})$ are optimal solutions to Problems A and B respectively.

The preceding theorem has two important corollaries that are left to the imagination of the reader because they differ only slightly from the two corollaries to (the analogous) Theorem 3. The first corollary is fundamental to the definition of "duality gap" and is helpful in studying the constrained version of the algorithmic stopping criterion presented in Section 3.1.4. The second corollary provides a useful characterization of dual optimal solutions $(\mathbf{x}^*, \boldsymbol{\kappa}^*)$ and $(\mathbf{y}^*, \boldsymbol{\lambda}^*)$ in terms of the extremality conditions.

It is worth noting that if $g_0 : C_0$ is convex and closed, then the symmetry of the conjugate transformation implies that the subgradient condition (IV) can be replaced by the equivalent subgradient condition

$$\text{(IVa)} \qquad \mathbf{x}^0 \in \partial h_0(\mathbf{y}^0).$$

Likewise, if $g_i : C_i$, $i \in I$ is convex and closed, then the subgradient condition (V) can be replaced by the equivalent subgradient condition

$$\text{(Va)} \quad \textit{either } \lambda_i = 0 \text{ and } \langle \mathbf{x}^i, \mathbf{y}^i \rangle = \sup_{\mathbf{c}^i \in C_i} \langle \mathbf{c}^i, \mathbf{y}^i \rangle,$$

$$\text{or } \lambda_i > 0 \text{ and } \mathbf{x}^i \in \partial h_i(\mathbf{y}^i/\lambda_i), \qquad i \in I;$$

and if $g_j : C_j$, $j \in J$ is convex and closed, then the subgradient condition (VI) can be replaced by the equivalent subgradient condition

$$\text{(VIa)} \quad \textit{either } \kappa_j = 0 \text{ and } \langle \mathbf{x}^j, \mathbf{y}^j \rangle = \sup_{\mathbf{d}^j \in D_j} \langle \mathbf{x}^j, \mathbf{d}^j \rangle,$$

$$\text{or } \kappa_j > 0 \text{ and } \mathbf{x}^j \in \kappa_j \partial h_j(\mathbf{y}^j), \qquad j \in J.$$

These equivalent subgradient conditions (IVa) through (VIa) are, of course, especially helpful when using the extremality conditions to compute all primal optimal solutions $(\mathbf{x}^*, \boldsymbol{\kappa}^*)$ in S^* from the knowledge of only a single dual optimal solution $(\mathbf{y}^*, \boldsymbol{\lambda}^*)$ in T^*.

It should be emphasized that Problem A need not always be solved directly. Under appropriate conditions it can actually be solved indirectly by solving either the extremality conditions (I-VII) or Problem B. In some cases it may be advantageous to solve the extremality conditions (I-VII), especially when they turn out to be (essentially) linear (e.g., linearly constrained quadratic programming). In other cases it may be advantageous to solve Problem B, especially when the index set J is empty (e.g., quadratically constrained quadratic programming and posynomial constrained posynomial programming); in which event Problem B has no constraints (even when Problem A does). Of course, in all such cases the absence of a duality gap is crucial.

The definition of the Lagrangian L_g (in Section 3.3.2) and the fact that X is a cone readily imply that the cone condition $\mathbf{y} \in Y$, the constraints $h_j(\mathbf{y}^j) \leqslant 0$, $j \in J$, the orthogonality condition $0 = \langle \mathbf{x}, \mathbf{y} \rangle$, and the complementary slackness conditions $\kappa_j h_j(\mathbf{y}^j) = 0, j \in J$ can all be replaced by the single equivalent condition $L_g(\mathbf{x}, \boldsymbol{\kappa}; \mathbf{y}, \boldsymbol{\lambda}) = \inf_{\substack{\mathbf{x}' \in X \\ \boldsymbol{\kappa}' \geq 0}} L_g(\mathbf{x}', \boldsymbol{\kappa}'; \mathbf{y}, \boldsymbol{\lambda})$. Moreover, if $g_k : C_k, k \in \{0\} \cup I \cup J$ is convex and closed, conjugate transform theory implies that the constraints $g_i(\mathbf{x}^i) \leq 0, i \in I$, the subgradient conditions (IV) through (VI), and the complementary slackness conditions $\lambda_i g_i(\mathbf{x}^i) = 0, i \in I$ can all be replaced by the two equivalent conditions $\boldsymbol{\kappa} \geq \mathbf{0}$ and $\sup_{(\mathbf{y}', \boldsymbol{\lambda}') \in D} L_g(\mathbf{x}, \boldsymbol{\kappa}; \mathbf{y}', \boldsymbol{\lambda}') = L_g(\mathbf{x}, \boldsymbol{\kappa}; \mathbf{y}, \boldsymbol{\lambda})$. Consequently, the saddle-point condition discussed in Section 3.3.2 is equivalent to the extremality conditions when $g_k : C_k$, $k \in \{0\} \cup I \cup J$ is convex and closed. Nevertheless, it seems that the extremality conditions given in the definition are the most convenient to work with.

The following theorem provides an important tie between dual Problem B and the P vectors defined in Section 3.3.2.

THEOREM 16. Given that Problem A is consistent with a finite infimum φ,

1. if Problem A has a P vector, then Problem B is consistent and $0 = \varphi + \psi$,
2. if Problem B is consistent and $0 = \varphi + \psi$, then $\{(\mathbf{y}^*, \boldsymbol{\lambda}^*) \mid (\mathbf{y}^*, \boldsymbol{\lambda}^*)$ is a P vector for Problem A$\} = T^*$.

The following theorem provides an important tie between dual Problem B and the Kuhn-Tucker vectors defined in Section 3.3.1.

THEOREM 17. Given that Problems A and B are both consistent and that $0 = \varphi + \psi$, if there is a "minimizing sequence" $\{(\mathbf{y}^q, \boldsymbol{\lambda}^q)\}_1^\infty$ for Problem B (i.e. $(\mathbf{y}^q, \boldsymbol{\lambda}^q) \in T$ and $\lim_{q \to +\infty} H(\mathbf{y}^q, \boldsymbol{\lambda}^q) = \psi$) such that $\lim_{q \to +\infty} \boldsymbol{\lambda}^q$ exists and is finite, then $\boldsymbol{\lambda}^* \triangleq \lim_{q \to +\infty} \boldsymbol{\lambda}^q$ is a Kuhn-Tucker vector for Problem A.

The following corollary ties the dual optimal solution set T^* directly to Kuhn-Tucker vectors.

Corollary 17A: Given that Problems A and B are both consistent and that $0 = \varphi + \psi$, each dual optimal solution $(\mathbf{y}^*, \boldsymbol{\lambda}^*) \in T^*$ provides a Kuhn-Tucker vector $\boldsymbol{\lambda}^*$ for Problem A.

The following corollary ties the set of all P vectors $(\mathbf{y}^*, \boldsymbol{\lambda}^*)$ directly to the set of all Kuhn-Tucker vectors $\boldsymbol{\lambda}^*$.

Corollary 17B: Given that Problem A is consistent with a finite infimum φ, each P vector $(\mathbf{y}^*, \boldsymbol{\lambda}^*)$ for Problem A provides a Kuhn-Tucker vector $\boldsymbol{\lambda}^*$ for Problem A.

As the preceding theory indicates, the absence of a duality gap is a highly desired situation. The following GP version of "Fenchel's theorem" provides useful conditions that guarantee both the absence of a duality gap and the existence of primal optimal solutions $(\mathbf{x}^*, \boldsymbol{\kappa}^*) \in S^*$.

THEOREM 18. Suppose that both $g_k : C_k$, $k \in \{0\} \cup I \cup J$ and X are convex and closed. If

(i) problem B has a feasible solution $(\mathbf{y}', \boldsymbol{\lambda}')$ such that

$$h_j(\mathbf{y}'^j) < 0 \quad j \in J,$$

(ii) problem B has a finite infimum ψ,

(iii) there exists a vector $(\mathbf{y}^+, \boldsymbol{\lambda}^+)$ such that

$$\mathbf{y}^+ \in (riY),$$

$$\mathbf{y}^{+k} \in (\mathrm{ri}D_k), \qquad k \in \{0\} \cup J,$$

$$(\mathbf{y}^{+i}, \lambda_i^+) \in (\mathrm{ri}D_i^+), \qquad i \in I,$$

then $0 = \varphi + \psi$ and $S^* \neq \phi$.

Note that the vector $(\mathbf{y}^+, \boldsymbol{\lambda}^+)$ in hypothesis (iii) need not be a feasible solution to Problem B. However, $(\mathbf{y}^+, \boldsymbol{\lambda}^+)$ is obviously such a solution when J is empty (which is the case for all examples described in Section 2.2). Consequently, hypothesis (i) can clearly be replaced by the hypothesis

(i′) J is empty

without disturbing the validity of Theorem 18. Moreover, when the cone Y is in fact a vector space (which is the case for all examples described in Section 2.2), the condition $\mathbf{y}^+ \in (\mathrm{ri}Y)$ is implied by the weaker condition $\mathbf{y}^+ \in Y$.

Theorem 18 can be used to show that there are no duality gaps for the constrained versions of problem classes (1) through (3) listed after Theorem 5. Furthermore, its (unstated) dual can be used to strengthen the "Kuhn-Tucker-Slater theorem" in ordinary programming.

3.3.4. Parametric Programming and Post-Optimality Analysis. As mentioned in Section 3.2, the parameterized family F into which Problem A is to be embedded can be obtained by translating the prescribed domain $\mathcal{C}$ (given at the beginning of Section 3.2) through all possible displacements $-\mathbf{u}$, while keeping the prescribed cone $\mathfrak{X}$ fixed.

Now, the structure of $\mathcal{C}$ obviously induces a partitioning of the components of $\mathbf{u}$ into vectors $\mathbf{u}^0$, $\mathbf{u}^I$, μ, $\mathbf{u}^J$, and $\mathbf{u}_J$ that correspond respectively to the vectors $\mathbf{x}^0$, $\mathbf{x}^I$, $\boldsymbol{\alpha}$, $\mathbf{x}^J$, and $\boldsymbol{\kappa}$. Clearly, each component u_j, of $\mathbf{u}_J$ does not influence the problem infimum, but simply translates through $-u_j$ only the optimal value of κ_j (if such a value exists). Hence, setting u_j equal to zero deletes from the resulting family $\mathfrak{F}$ only problems $\mathfrak{A}(\mathbf{u})$ that are essentially superfluous. Consequently, the family F is actually taken to be the resulting family $\mathfrak{F}$ with all such superfluous problems deleted. Of course, the vectors $\mathbf{u}^0$, $\mathbf{u}^I$, $\mathbf{u}^J$ and $\boldsymbol{\mu}$ still needed to parameterize F constitute a single vector parameter $(\mathbf{u},\boldsymbol{\mu})$ where $(\mathbf{u}^0, \mathbf{u}^I, \mathbf{u}^J) \triangleq \mathbf{u}$.

The parameterized family F of all problems $A(\mathbf{u},\boldsymbol{\mu})$ (for fixed $g_k : C_k, k \in \{0\} \cup I \cup J$ and X) is termed a *GP family*. For purposes of easy reference and mathematical precision, Problem $A(\mathbf{u},\boldsymbol{\mu})$ is now given the following formal definition, which should be compared with the formal definition of Problem A at the beginning of Section 2.2.

PROBLEM $A(\mathbf{u},\boldsymbol{\mu})$. *Consider the objective function $G(\cdot + \mathbf{u}, X)$ whose domain*

$$C(\mathbf{u}) \triangleq \{(\mathbf{x},\boldsymbol{\kappa}) \mid \mathbf{x}^k + \mathbf{u}^k \in C_k,\ k \in \{0\} \cup I,\ \text{and}\ \ (\mathbf{x}^j + \mathbf{u}^j, \kappa_j) \in C_j^+, j \in J\},$$

and whose functional value

$$G(\mathbf{x} + \mathbf{u}, \boldsymbol{\kappa}) \triangleq g_0(\mathbf{x}^0 + \mathbf{u}^0) + \sum_J g_j^+(\mathbf{x}^j + \mathbf{u}^j, \kappa_j),$$

where

$$C_j^+ \triangleq \{(\mathbf{c}^j, \kappa_j) \mid \text{either}\ \kappa_j = 0\ \ \text{and}\ \sup_{\mathbf{d}^j \in D_j} \langle \mathbf{c}^j, \mathbf{d}^j \rangle < +\infty,\ \ \text{or}\ \ \kappa_j > 0\ \ \text{and}\ \ \mathbf{c}^j \in \kappa_j C_j\}$$

and

$$g_j^+(\mathbf{c}^j, \kappa_j) \triangleq \begin{cases} \sup_{\mathbf{d}^j \in D_j} \langle \mathbf{c}^j, \mathbf{d}^j \rangle & \text{if}\ \ \kappa_j = 0\ \ \text{and}\ \ \sup_{\mathbf{d}^j \in D_j} \langle \mathbf{c}^j, \mathbf{d}^j \rangle < +\infty, \\ \kappa_j g_j(\mathbf{c}^j/\kappa_j) & \text{if}\ \ \kappa_j > 0\ \ \text{and}\ \ \mathbf{c}^j \in \kappa_j C_j. \end{cases}$$

Using the feasible solution set

$$S(\mathbf{u},\boldsymbol{\mu}) \triangleq \{(\mathbf{x},\boldsymbol{\kappa}) \in C(\mathbf{u}) \mid \mathbf{x} \in X,\ \text{and}\ \ g_i(\mathbf{x}^i + \mathbf{u}^i) + \mu_i \leqslant 0, \quad i \in I\},$$

calculate both the problem infimum

$$\varphi(\mathbf{u},\boldsymbol{\mu}) \triangleq \inf_{(\mathbf{x},\boldsymbol{\kappa}) \in S(\mathbf{u},\boldsymbol{\mu})} G(\mathbf{x} + \mathbf{u}, \boldsymbol{\kappa})$$

and the optimal solution set

$$S^*(\mathbf{u},\boldsymbol{\mu}) \triangleq \{(\mathbf{x},\boldsymbol{\kappa}) \in S(\mathbf{u},\boldsymbol{\mu}) \mid G(\mathbf{x} + \mathbf{u}, \boldsymbol{\kappa}) = \varphi(\mathbf{u},\boldsymbol{\mu})\}.$$

Of course, Problem A appears in the parameterized family F as Problem $A(\mathbf{0}, \mathbf{0})$; and the symbols A, S, φ and S^* now represent functions of $(\mathbf{u},\boldsymbol{\mu})$, though they originally represented only the particular functional values $A(\mathbf{0}, \mathbf{0})$, $S(\mathbf{0}, \mathbf{0})$, $\varphi(\mathbf{0}, \mathbf{0})$ and $S^*(\mathbf{0}, \mathbf{0})$ respectively–a notational discrepancy that must be kept in mind when comparing subsequent developments with previous developments.

For the signomial Example 5 in Section 2.2, it is worth noting that the perturbation vector $(\mathbf{u},\boldsymbol{\mu})$ alters the (log of the absolute value of the) signomial coefficients c_q and the constraint upper bounds d_k.

To extend the unconstrained theorems given in Section 3.1.5 into corresponding constrained theorems:

1. each hypothesis that the set $\mathcal{C}$ be convex should be replaced by the hypothesis that the sets C_0 and C_j^+, $j \in J$ along with the functions $g_i : C_i$, $i \in I$ be convex,
2. each hypothesis that the function g: $\mathcal{C}$ be convex (closed) should be replaced by the hypothesis that the functions $g_k : C_k$, $k \in \{0\} \cup I$ and the functions $g_j^+ : C_j^+$, $j \in J$ be convex (closed),
3. each hypothesis that the cone $\mathfrak{X}$ be convex (closed) should be replaced by the hypothesis that the cone X be convex (closed),
4. make the obvious notational alterations in both the hypotheses and the conclusions, as well as the definitions.

In carrying out (4): the symbol $\mathcal{G}$ should be replaced by the symbol G, the symbol $\mathbf{v}$ should be replaced by the symbol $(\mathbf{v}, \boldsymbol{\nu})$, where $(\mathbf{v}^0, \mathbf{v}^I, \mathbf{v}^J) \triangleq \mathbf{v}$ translates sets and $\boldsymbol{\nu}$ influences constraint upper bounds.

REFERENCES

1. Abrams, R. A., and M. L. Bunting, "Reducing Reversed Posynomial Programs," *SIAM J. Appl. Math.*, **27**: 629–640 (1974).
2. Avriel, M., and A. C. Williams, "Complementary Geometric Programming," *SIAM J. Appl. Math.* **19**: 125–141 (1970).
3. Courant, R., and D. Hilbert, *Methods of Mathematical Physics*, **I**, Interscience, New York (1953).
4. Dinkel, J. J., and E. L. Peterson, "Discrete Optimal Control (with Linear Dynamics) via Geometric Programming," *J. Math. Anal. and Appl.*, to appear (probably 1978).
5. Duffin, R. J., "Infinite Programs," *Linear Inequalities and Related Systems*, H. W. Kuhn and A. W. Tucker (Eds.), Princeton Univ. Press, Princeton, New Jersey, 157–170 (1956).
6. ——, "Dual Programs and Minimum Cost," *SIAM J. Appl. Math.* **10**: 119 (1962a).
7. ——, "Cost Minimization Problems Treated by Geometric Means," *Operations Res.* **10**: 668 (1962b).
8. ——, "Linearizing Geometric Programs," *SIAM Rev.* **12**: 211–227 (1970).
9. Duffin, R. J., and E. L. Peterson, "Duality Theory for Geometric Programming," *SIAM J. Appl. Math.* **14**: 1307–1349 (1966).
10. ——, "Geometric Programs Treated with Slack Variables," *J. Appl. Anal.*, **2**: 255–267 (1972a).
11. ——, "The Proximity of (Algebraic) Geometric Programming to Linear Programming." *Math. Prog.* **3**: 250–253 (1972b).
12. ——, "Reversed Geometric Programs Treated by Harmonic Means," *Indiana Univ. Math. J.* **22**: 531–550 (1972c).
13. ——, "Geometric Programming with Signomials," *J. Optimization Theory and Applic.* **11**: 3–35 (1973).
14. Duffin, R. J., E. L. Peterson, and C. Zener, *Geometric Programming – Theory and*

Applications, Wiley, New York (1967); Russian translation by D. Babayev, Mir, Moscow (1972).
15. Falk, J. E., "Global Solutions of Signomial Programs," Technical Report #T-274, George Washington Univ. Prog. in Logistics, Washington, D.C. (June 1973).
16. Fenchel, W., "On Conjugate Convex Functions," *Canadian J. Math.* **1**: 73–77 (1949).
17. ——, "Convex Cones, Sets and Functions," Mathematics Department mimeographed lecture notes, Princeton Univ., Princeton, New Jersey (1951).
18. Hall, M. A., and E. L. Peterson, "Traffic Equilibria Analyzed via Geometric Programming," *Proc. Int. Symp. Traffic Equilibrium Methods*, M. Florian (Ed.), 53–105, Springer-Verlag Lecture Notes in Economics and Mathematical Systems, No. 118, New York (1976).
19. Kretschmer, K. S., "Programmes in Paired Spaces," *Canadian J. Math.* **13**: 221(1961).
20. Peterson, E. L., "Symmetric Duality for Generalized Unconstrained Geometric Programming," *SIAM J. Appl. Math.* **19**: 487–526 (1970).
21. ——, "Mathematical Foundations of Geometric Programming," Appendix to "Geometric Programming and Some of Its Extensions," *Optimization and Design*, M. Avriel, M. J. Rijckaert and D. J. Wilde (Eds.), 244–289 Prentice-Hall, Englewood Cliffs, N.J. (1973).
22. ——, "Geometric Programming," *SIAM Review*. **18**: 1–51 (1976).
23. ——, "Constrained Duality via Unconstrained Duality in Generalized Geometric Programming," *J. Opt. Theory and Applic.*, to appear (probably 1978).
24. ——, "The Mathematical Foundations of Convex and Nonconvex Programming," to appear (probably 1979).
25. Peterson, E. L., and J. G. Ecker, "Geometric Programming: Duality in Quadratic Programming and lp–approximation, I," Proc. *Int. Sym. Math. Prog.*, H. W. Kuhn (Ed.), 445–480, Princeton Univ. Press, Princeton, New Jersey (1970).
26. Peterson, E. L., and R. E. Wendell, "Optimal Location via Geometric Programming," to appear (probably 1978).
27. Rijckaert, M. J., "Engineering Applications of Geometric Programming," *Optimization and Design*, M. Avriel, M. J. Rijckaert and D. J. Wilde (Eds.), 196–220 Prentice-Hall, Englewood Cliffs, N.J. (1973).
28. Rockafellar, R. T., "Duality and Stability in Extremum Problems Involving Convex Functions," *Pac. J. Math.* **21**: 167–187 (1967a).
29. ——. "Duality in Nonlinear Programming," *Amer. Math. Soc. Lects. Appl. Math.* **11**, G. B. Dantzig and A. F. Veinott (Eds.), 401–422 Amer. Math. Soc., Providence, Rhode Island (1968).
30. ——. Convex Analysis, Princeton Univ. Press, Princeton, N.J. (1970).
31. Zener, C., "A Mathematical Aid in Optimizing Engineering Designs," *Proc. Nat. Acad. of Sci.* **47**: 537–539 (1961).
32. ——. "A Further Mathematical Aid in Optimizing Engineering Designs," *Proc. Nat. Acad. Of Sci.* 48: 518–522 (1962).
33. ——. Engineering Design by Geometric Programming, Wiley, New York (1971).

II-6

NONLINEAR PROGRAMMING

O. L. Mangasarian
University of Wisconsin

1. INTRODUCTION

The primal nonlinear programming (NLP) problem is to

$$\text{minimize} \quad f(x_1, x_2, \ldots, x_n)$$

subject to

$$\begin{aligned} g_j(x_1, x_2, \ldots, x_n) &\leqq 0, \quad j = 1, \ldots, m \\ h_j(x_1, x_2, \ldots, x_n) &= 0, \quad j = 1, \ldots, k \end{aligned} \tag{1}$$

By using vector notation the above problem can be written more succinctly as

$$\text{minimize} \quad f(\mathbf{x})$$

subject to

$$\begin{aligned} g(\mathbf{x}) &\leqq 0 \\ h(\mathbf{x}) &= 0 \end{aligned} \tag{1'}$$

where f: $R^n \to R$, g: $R^n \to R^m$ and h: $R^n \to R^k$, that is f, g and h are functions which map each point of the n-dimensional real Euclidean space R^n into R, R^m and R^k respectively.

Problems such as (1) arise frequently in the decision [Dantzig and Veinott,

1968] and physical sciences [Fox, 1971, Stark and Nichols, 1972] and their systematic study beginning in the late 1940s [John, 1948] has grown into the discipline of NLP. In this survey we shall be concerned with the theory and computational algorithms of NLP. In Section 2 we shall discuss various optimality conditions. Besides their intrinsic importance optimality conditions play an important role in the computational algorithms also. In Section 3 we shall dwell briefly on one type of duality in NLP. Beginning with Section 4 we shall be discussing various computational algorithms of NLP. In Section 4 we shall discuss one-dimensional minimization problems. In Section 5 we shall discuss unconstrained minimization algorithms, that is the problem: $\underset{\mathbf{x}\in R^n}{\text{minimize}}\, f(\mathbf{x})$. Finally in Section 6 we shall discuss a variety of algorithms for solving Problem (1).

We begin with a few paragraphs on notation and definitions.

We shall be interested in various types of "solutions" of Problem (1). A point $\bar{\mathbf{x}}$ in R^n satisfying $g(\bar{\mathbf{x}}) \leqq 0$ and $h(\bar{\mathbf{x}}) = 0$ is said to be: a *solution* or *global solution* of Problem (1) iff $f(\bar{\mathbf{x}}) \leqq f(\mathbf{x})$ for all $\mathbf{x}$ satisfying $g(\mathbf{x}) \leqq 0$ and $h(\mathbf{x}) = 0$; a *local solution* of Problem (1) iff $f(\bar{\mathbf{x}}) \leqq f(\mathbf{x})$ for all $\mathbf{x}$ satisfying $g(\mathbf{x}) \leqq 0$, $h(\mathbf{x}) = 0$ and $\|\mathbf{x} - \bar{\mathbf{x}}\| \leqq \delta$ for some $\delta > 0$ where $\|\mathbf{x} - \bar{\mathbf{x}}\| = \left(\sum_{j=1}^{n} (x_j - \bar{x}_j)^2\right)^{1/2}$; a *unique local solution* of Problem (1) iff $f(\bar{\mathbf{x}}) < f(\mathbf{x})$ for all $\mathbf{x} \neq \bar{\mathbf{x}}$ satisfying $g(\mathbf{x}) \leqq 0$, $h(\mathbf{x}) = 0$ and $\|\mathbf{x} - \bar{\mathbf{x}}\| \leqq \delta$ for some $\delta > 0$.

We shall also make use of the concepts of *convex* and *concave functions.* More general concepts can be found in [Mangasarian, 1969]. A function f defined on a set X in R^n is said to be convex at $\bar{\mathbf{x}}$ (with respect to X) iff

$$\begin{gathered} \mathbf{x} \in X, \quad 0 < \lambda < 1, \quad (1 - \lambda)\mathbf{x} + \lambda\bar{\mathbf{x}} \in X, \\ \text{imply:} \quad (1 - \lambda) f(\bar{\mathbf{x}}) + \lambda f(\mathbf{x}) \geqq f((1 - \lambda)\bar{\mathbf{x}} + \lambda\mathbf{x}) \end{gathered} \tag{2}$$

If the last inequality of Condition (2) is strict ($>$) for $\mathbf{x} \neq \bar{\mathbf{x}}$ then f is *strictly convex at* $\mathbf{x}$, and if it is reversed ($\leqq$) then f is *concave* at $\bar{\mathbf{x}}$. The function f is *convex on* X if it is convex at *each* $\bar{\mathbf{x}}$ in X.

We shall use vector notation quite frequently. If $\mathbf{x}$ and $\mathbf{y}$ are in R^n, then x_i and y_i, $i = 1, \ldots, n$, denote their respective components, $\mathbf{xy} = \sum_{i=1}^{n} x_i y_i$ is the scalar product of $\mathbf{x}$ and $\mathbf{y}$, and $\mathbf{xy}^T$ is the $n \times n$ matrix whose ijth element is $x_i y_j$. Superscripts will denote specific vectors such as $\mathbf{x}^1$ and $\mathbf{x}^2$ in R^n say. Exponentiation will be distinguished by enclosing the quantity raised to a power by parentheses. If f: $R^n \to R$ is differentiable at $\bar{\mathbf{x}}$ then $\nabla f(\bar{\mathbf{x}}) = \left(\frac{\partial f(\bar{\mathbf{x}})}{\partial x_1}, \ldots, \frac{\partial f(\bar{\mathbf{x}})}{\partial x_n}\right)$ and if f is twice differentiable at $\bar{\mathbf{x}}$ then $\nabla^2 f(\bar{\mathbf{x}})$ is the $n \times n$ Hessian matrix whose *ij* element is $\dfrac{\partial^2 f(\bar{\mathbf{x}})}{\partial x_i \partial x_j}$. We shall say that a function is differentiable (twice differentiable) *around* $\bar{\mathbf{x}}$ if it is differentiable (twice differentiable) in a neighborhood of $\bar{\mathbf{x}}$. The symbol ■ will mark the end of a statement of a theorem or of an algorithm.

2. OPTIMALITY CONDITIONS

Necessary optimality conditions are those conditions which some type of solution of Problem (1) must satisfy. Sufficient optimality conditions are conditions which when satisfied guarantee that the point is some type of solution of Problem (1). We give first some of the best known optimality conditions which involve first derivatives only and hence are called *first order optimality* conditions.

2.2 First Order Kuhn-Tucker Conditions [Kuhn and Tucker, 1951; Mangasarian, 1969]

(Necessity) Let $\bar{\mathbf{x}}$ be a local or global solution of Problem (1) and let f, g and h be differentiable at $\bar{\mathbf{x}}$. Let g and h satisfy a first order constraint qualification at $\bar{\mathbf{x}}$ [Mangasarian, 1969] such as this: h is continuously differentiable at $\bar{\mathbf{x}}$, $\nabla h_i(\bar{\mathbf{x}})$, $i = 1, \ldots, k$, are linearly independent and there exists a $\mathbf{z}$ in R^n satisfying $\nabla g_i(\bar{\mathbf{x}})\mathbf{z} > 0$ for $i = 1, \ldots, m$ such that $g_i(\bar{\mathbf{x}}) = 0$, and $\nabla h_j(\bar{\mathbf{x}})\mathbf{z} = 0$ for $j = 1, \ldots, k$, then $\bar{\mathbf{x}}$ and some $\bar{\mathbf{u}}$ in R^m and $\bar{\mathbf{v}}$ in R^k satisfy the Kuhn-Tucker conditions

$$\begin{aligned} \nabla f(\mathbf{x}) + \sum_{i=1}^{m} \bar{u}_i \nabla g_i(\bar{\mathbf{x}}) + \sum_{i=1}^{k} \bar{v}_i \nabla h_i(\bar{\mathbf{x}}) &= 0 \\ \bar{u}_i g_i(\bar{\mathbf{x}}) &= 0, \quad i = 1, \ldots, m \\ g(\bar{\mathbf{x}}) &\leqq 0 \\ h(\bar{\mathbf{x}}) &= 0 \\ \bar{\mathbf{u}} &\geqq 0. \end{aligned} \tag{3}$$

(Sufficiency) Conversely if f and g are differentiable and convex at $\bar{\mathbf{x}}$, h is linear and the Kuhn-Tucker conditions (3) are satisfied, then $\bar{\mathbf{x}}$ is a global solution of Problem (1). ■

The Kuhn-Tucker conditions (3) are merely a statement that a linear combination of the gradients of the objective function with a positive weight, the gradients of the active inequality constraints ($g_i(\bar{\mathbf{x}}) = 0$) with nonnegative weights, and the gradients of the equality constraints must vanish at $\bar{\mathbf{x}}$. A constraint qualification is imposed to rule out singular solutions at which the Kuhn-Tucker conditions cannot hold. For example the origin in R^2 is the global solution of the problem: minimize x_1 subject to $(x_1)^4 - x_2 \leqq 0$ and $-(x_1)^3 + x_2 \leqq 0$, but neither a constraint qualification nor the Kuhn-Tucker conditions (3) are satisfied there. In the absence of convexity, the conditions (3) cannot rule out stationary points such as the origin for the function $(x)^3$. To rule out such stationary points, conditions involving second order derivatives have been developed [Fiacco and McCormick, 1968].

2.3 Second Order Kuhn-Tucker Conditions

(Necessity) Let $\bar{\mathbf{x}}$ be a local or global solution of Problem 1 and let f, g and h be twice continuously differentiable around $\bar{\mathbf{x}}$. Let g and h satisfy a first order constraint qualification such as that of Section 2.2 and a second order constraint qualification such as: $\nabla g_i(\bar{\mathbf{x}})$, $i \in \{i \mid g_i(\bar{\mathbf{x}}) = 0,\ i = 1, \ldots, m\}$ and $\nabla h_j(\bar{\mathbf{x}})$, $j = 1, \ldots, k$, are linearly independent. Then $\bar{\mathbf{x}}$ and some $\bar{\mathbf{u}}$ in R^m and $\bar{\mathbf{v}}$ in R^k satisfy the Kuhn-Tucker conditions (3), *and* for every $\mathbf{y}$ in R^n such that $\mathbf{y}\nabla g_i(\bar{\mathbf{x}}) = 0$, $i \in \{i \mid g_i(\bar{\mathbf{x}}) = 0, i = 1, \ldots, m\}$, and $\mathbf{y}\nabla h_j(\bar{\mathbf{x}}) = 0$ for $j = 1, \ldots, k$, it follows that

$$\mathbf{y}\nabla_{11}\mathbf{L}(\bar{\mathbf{x}}, \bar{\mathbf{u}}, \bar{\mathbf{v}})\mathbf{y} \geqq 0 \tag{4}$$

where the Lagrangean $\mathbf{L}$ is defined as

$$\mathbf{L}(\mathbf{x}, \mathbf{u}, \mathbf{v}) = f(\mathbf{x}) + \sum_{i=1}^{m} u_i g_i(\mathbf{x}) + \sum_{i=1}^{k} v_i h_i(\mathbf{x}) \tag{5}$$

and $\nabla_{11}\mathbf{L}$ is the $n \times n$ Hessian matrix of second partial derivatives of $\mathbf{L}$ with respect to its first argument $\mathbf{x}$. (Sufficiency) Conversely, let f, g and h be twice differentiable at $\bar{\mathbf{x}}$, let $\bar{\mathbf{x}}$ and some $\bar{\mathbf{u}}$ in R^m and $\bar{\mathbf{v}}$ in R^k satisfy Conditions (3), *and* let for every nonzero $\mathbf{y} \in R^n$ such that

$$\begin{aligned}
&\mathbf{y}\nabla g_i(\bar{\mathbf{x}}) = 0 && \text{for } i = 1, \ldots, m,\ g_i(\bar{\mathbf{x}}) = 0 \text{ and } \bar{u}_i > 0\\
&\mathbf{y}\nabla g_i(\bar{\mathbf{x}}) \leqq 0 && \text{for } i = 1, \ldots, m,\ g_i(\bar{\mathbf{x}}) = 0 \text{ and } \bar{u}_i = 0\\
&\mathbf{y}\nabla h_j(\bar{\mathbf{x}}) = 0 && \text{for } i = 1, \ldots, k,
\end{aligned} \tag{6}$$

it follows that

$$\mathbf{y}\nabla_{11}\mathbf{L}(\bar{\mathbf{x}}, \bar{\mathbf{u}}, \bar{\mathbf{v}})y > 0. \tag{7}$$

Then $\bar{\mathbf{x}}$ is a unique local solution of Problem (1). ■

The second order sufficient optimality condition plays an important role in some of the superlinearly convergent algorithms that we will discuss in Section 6. It should be noted also that second order sufficient optimality conditions can also apply to linear programming problems in which case, since $\nabla_{11}\mathbf{L}(\bar{\mathbf{x}}, \bar{\mathbf{u}}, \bar{\mathbf{v}}) = 0$, the Conditions (6) must imply that $\mathbf{y} = \mathbf{0}$. For such a case $\bar{\mathbf{x}}$ would be the unique solution to the linear program. Condition (4) is trivially satisfied by all solutions of linear programs.

More recently there have been efforts [Rockafellar, 1971, 1973a, 1973b, 1974; Buys, 1972; Mangasarian, 1975] directed towards relating solutions of nonlinear programming problems to solutions of nonlinear equations. The objective of such relation is to employ the vast machinery for solving nonlinear equations [Ortega and Rheinboldt, 1970; Ostrowski, 1966] in attacking nonlinear programming problems. One such relationship is embodied in the following optimality conditions which involve no inequalities whatsoever.

2.4 First Order Augmented Lagrangean Optimality Conditions [Mangasarian, 1975]

(Necessity) Let $\overline{\mathrm{x}}$ be a local or global solution of Problem 1 and let f, g and h be differentiable at $\overline{\mathrm{x}}$. Let g and h satisfy a first order constraint qualification at $\overline{\mathrm{x}}$ such as that of Section 2.2. Then $\overline{\mathrm{x}}$ and some $(\overline{\mathrm{y}}, \overline{\mathrm{z}})$ in $R^m \times R^k$ constitute a stationary point of the augmented Lagrangean function $M(\mathrm{x}, \mathrm{y}, \mathrm{z})$

$$M(\mathrm{x}, \mathrm{y}, \mathrm{z}) = f(\mathrm{x}) + \frac{1}{4r} \sum_{i=1}^{m} \left((rg_i(\mathrm{x}) + y_i)_+^4 - (y_i)^4\right) + \sum_{i=1}^{k} \left(\frac{r}{2} (h_i(\mathrm{x}))^2 + z_i h_i(\mathrm{x})\right) \tag{8}$$

where r is any fixed positive number and the notation $(\beta)_+^4$ denotes 0 if $\beta < 0$ and $(\beta)^4$ if $\beta \geqq 0$. In particular we have that

$$\nabla_1 M(\overline{\mathrm{x}}, \overline{\mathrm{y}}, \overline{\mathrm{z}}) = 0, \quad \nabla_2 M(\overline{\mathrm{x}}, \overline{\mathrm{y}}, \overline{\mathrm{z}}) = 0, \quad \nabla_3 M(\overline{\mathrm{x}}, \overline{\mathrm{y}}, \overline{\mathrm{z}}) = 0 \tag{9}$$

where $\nabla_i M$ denotes the gradient of M with respect to its ith argument, $i = 1, 2, 3$. (Sufficiency) Let f and g be differentiable and convex at $\overline{\mathrm{x}}$, let h be linear and let Conditions (9) hold. Then $\overline{\mathrm{x}}$ is a global solution of Problem (1). ■

Note that the Conditions (9) involve no inequalities of any sort, neither inequalities on any of the variables nor constraint inequalities. Thus, tools of nonlinear equations theory [Ortega and Rheinholdt, 1970] can be employed directly to solve Conditions (9). The relation between the optimal Kuhn-Tucker multipliers $\overline{\mathrm{u}}, \overline{\mathrm{v}}$ of Conditions (3) and the optimal $\overline{\mathrm{y}}, \overline{\mathrm{z}}$ of Conditions (9) are given by

$$\begin{aligned} \overline{u}_i &= (\overline{y}_i)^3, \quad i = 1, \ldots, m \\ \overline{v}_i &= \overline{z}_i, \qquad i = 1, \ldots, k \end{aligned} \tag{10}$$

For more details concerning the augmented Lagrangean see Mangasarian [1975 a and b], Arrow, et al. [1973], and Rockafellar [1971, 1973a, 1973b, 1974].

Another optimality condition that may be useful computationally is that associated with exact penalty functions. An exact penalty function from R^n into R associated with Problem (1) is a function whose local or global minima for *finite* values of a parameter that it contains are associated with local or global minima of Problem (1). In general such functions are continuous but only piecewise differentiable [Zangwill, 1967; Pietrzykowski, 1969; Howe, 1973; Evans, et al., 1973]. However some exact penalty functions are differentiable locally [Fletcher, 1973]. We shall confine ourselves here to a simple piecewise differentiable exact penalty function.

2.5 Exact Penalty Optimality Conditions

(Necessity) Let $\bar{\mathbf{x}}$ be a local or global solution of Problem (1) and let either: (a) f, g and h be continuously differentiable around $\bar{\mathbf{x}}$ and let one of the following constraint qualifications hold (1) the system $\nabla f(\bar{\mathbf{x}})\mathbf{y} \leqq 0$, $\nabla g_i(\bar{\mathbf{x}})\mathbf{y} \leqq 0$, $i \in \{i \mid g_i(\bar{\mathbf{x}}) = 0,\ i = 1, \ldots, m\}$, $\nabla h(\bar{\mathbf{x}})\mathbf{y} = 0$ has no solution $\mathbf{y} \neq 0$ in R^n, (2) $\nabla g_i(\bar{\mathbf{x}})$, $i \in \{i \mid g_i(\bar{\mathbf{x}}) = 0,\ i = 1, \ldots, m\}$, $\nabla h_i(\bar{\mathbf{x}})$, $i = 1, \ldots, k$ are linearly independent, (b) or let f and g be convex on R^n, let h be linear and let the Slater constraint qualification hold, that is there exists an $\tilde{\mathbf{x}}$ such that $g(\tilde{\mathbf{x}}) < 0$ and $h(\tilde{\mathbf{x}}) = 0$. Then there exists a real number $r_0 > 0$ such that for all $r \geqq r_0$: $P(\bar{\mathbf{x}}, r) \leqq P(\mathbf{x}, r)$ for all $\mathbf{x}$ in some open neighborhood of $\bar{\mathbf{x}}$, where

$$P(\mathbf{x}, r) = f(\mathbf{x}) + r\left[\sum_{i=1}^{m} g_i(\mathbf{x})_+ + \sum_{i=1}^{k} |h_i(\mathbf{x})|\right]$$

and $g_i(\mathbf{x})_+$ denotes $g_i(\mathbf{x})$ if $g_i(\mathbf{x}) \geqq 0$ and 0 if $g_i(\mathbf{x}) < 0$. (Sufficiency) If for all $r \geqq r_0 > 0, P(\bar{\mathbf{x}}, r) \leqq P(\mathbf{x}, r)$ for all $\mathbf{x}$ in some set S containing $\bar{\mathbf{x}}$ and some feasible point of Problem (1), then $\bar{\mathbf{x}}$ solves Problem (1) subject to the extra condition that $\mathbf{x} \in S$. (Note that S may be taken as R^n or a sufficiently large neighborhood of $\bar{\mathbf{x}}$.) ■

Note also that in the sufficiency part, no differentiability, convexity or even continuity was assumed on f, g or h.

Finally we give one additional optimality condition which will be useful in connection with gradient projection algorithms.

2.6 First Order Gradient Projection Optimality Conditions [Levitin and Polyak, 1966]

(Necessity) Let $\bar{\mathbf{x}}$ be a solution of Problem (1), let g be continuous and convex on R^n, let h be linear and let f be differentiable at $\bar{\mathbf{x}}$. Then for any $n \times n$ symmetric positive definite matrix $\mathbf{H}$ the gradient projection condition

$$Q(\bar{\mathbf{x}} - \mu \mathbf{H} \nabla f(\bar{\mathbf{x}})) = \bar{\mathbf{x}} \quad \text{for each} \quad \mu \geqq 0$$

holds, where $Q(\mathbf{z})$ is the projection of $\mathbf{z}$ on $X = \{\mathbf{x} \mid g(\mathbf{x}) \leqq 0, h(\mathbf{x}) = 0\}$, that is

$$\mu \|\mathbf{H} \nabla f(\bar{\mathbf{x}})\|_{\mathbf{H}^{-1}} = \underset{\mathbf{y} \in X}{\text{minimum}} \|\bar{\mathbf{x}} - \mu \mathbf{H} \nabla f(\bar{\mathbf{x}}) - y\|_{\mathbf{H}^{-1}} \quad \text{for each} \quad \mu \geqq 0$$

where $\|x\|_{H^{-1}} = (xH^{-1}x)^{1/2}$
(Sufficiency) If under the same assumptions, the gradient projection condition holds for *some* $\mu > 0$ and f is convex at $\bar{x}$, then $\bar{x}$ is a solution of Problem (1). ■

3. DUALITY

Associated with the minimization Problem (1) is a maximization problem which under suitable conditions gives the same extremum as Problem (1). In particular we have the following *dual problem* [Wolfe, 1961] to the *primal problem* (1)

$$\text{maximize } L(x, u, v) = f(x) + \sum_{i=1}^{m} u_i g_i(x) + \sum_{i=1}^{k} v_i h_i(x)$$

subject to

$$\nabla_1 L(x, u, v) = \nabla f(x) + \sum_{i=1}^{m} u_i \nabla g_i(x) + \sum_{i=1}^{k} v_i \nabla h_i(x) = 0 \qquad u \geqq 0 \tag{11}$$

There are also other dual formulations [Rockafellar, 1970; Mangasarian and Ponstein, 1965]. The dual problem can give rise to lower bounds to the minimum value of Problem (1) and also to computational algorithms for solving Problem (1) [Buys, 1972]. For more details concerning duality theory as presented here see [Mangasarian, 1969].

3.1 Weak Duality Theorem

Let f and g be differentiable on R^n and let h be linear. Then

$$\left.\begin{array}{l} g(x^1) \leqq 0, \quad h(x^1) = 0 \\ \nabla_1 L(x^2, u^2, v^2) = 0, \quad u^2 \geqq 0 \\ f \text{ and } g \text{ convex at } x^2 \end{array}\right\} \quad \text{imply } f(x^1) \geqq L(x^2, u^2, v^2).$$ ■

3.2 Duality Theorem

Let f, g and h be differentiable on R^n, let $\bar{x}$ be a local or global solution of the primal Problem (1) and let a first order constraint qualification such as that of Section 2.2 be satisfied at $\bar{x}$. If f, g and h are twice differentiable at $\bar{x}$, then $\bar{x}$ and some $\bar{u}$, $\bar{v}$ in $R^m \times R^k$ satisfy the first order Kuhn-Tucker conditions for the dual Problem (11) and $f(\bar{x}) = L(\bar{x}, \bar{u}, \bar{v})$. If f and g are convex on R^n and h is linear, then $\bar{x}$ and some $\bar{u}, \bar{v}$ in $R^m \times R^k$ constitute a global solution of the dual Problem (11) and $f(\bar{x}) = L(\bar{x}, \bar{u}, \bar{v})$. ■

3.3 Strict Converse Duality Theorem

Let f, g and h be differentiable on R^n and let $(\bar{\mathbf{x}}, \bar{\mathbf{u}}, \bar{\mathbf{v}})$ be a local or global solution of the dual Problem (11). If the $n \times n$ Hessian matrix $\nabla_{11}L(\bar{\mathbf{x}}, \bar{\mathbf{u}}, \bar{\mathbf{v}})$ is nonsingular, then $(\bar{\mathbf{x}}, \bar{\mathbf{u}}, \bar{\mathbf{v}})$ satisfy the first order Kuhn-Tucker Conditions (3) of the primal Problem (1). If in addition f and g are convex at $\bar{\mathbf{x}}$ and h is linear, then $\bar{\mathbf{x}}$ is also a global solution of the primal Problem (1). ■

4. ONE DIMENSIONAL MINIMIZATION ALGORITHMS

Because many algorithms of unconstrained and constrained optimization require the minimization of a function along a line we give in this section algorithms for solving the following problem

$$\left.\begin{array}{ll}\text{minimize} & f(x)\\ \text{subject to} & a \leqq x \leqq b\end{array}\right\} \tag{12}$$

where f is a function defined on the real line segment $[a, b]$. Often in using one dimensional minimization as part of an n-dimensional optimization algorithm, the upper bound b will be missing from Problem (12). However it will be known that the derivative $f'(a) < 0$. For such problems we first search for b such that $f'(b) > 0$ and then solve Problem (12).

4.1 Golden Section and Fibonacci Search Algorithms [Wilde, 1964; Kowalik and Osborne, 1968]

Let $a^0 = a$, $b^0 = b$. Having a^i, b^i, determine a^{i+1}, b^{i+1} as follows:

(i) Define

$$\ell^i = b^i - \tau^i(b^i - a^i), \quad r^i = a^i + \tau^i(b^i - a^i)$$

where for golden section

$$\tau^i = \tau = (\sqrt{5} - 1)/2 \cong 0.618$$

and for Fibonacci search

$$\tau^i = \frac{F_{n-i-1}}{F_{n-i}}, \quad i = 0, 1, \ldots, n-3, \quad \tau^{n-2} = \frac{1+\epsilon}{2} \quad \text{or} \quad \frac{1-\epsilon}{2}$$

where $n (n \geqq 2)$ is a prescribed number of allowable function evaluations, ϵ is any small positive number less than 1, and F_j are the Fibonacci numbers: $F_0 = F_1 = 1$, $F_j = F_{j-1} + F_{j-2}, j \geqq 2$.

(ii) Set

$$a^{i+1} = \ell^i, \quad b^{i+1} = b^i \quad \text{if} \quad f(\ell^i) > f(r^i)$$

$$a^{i+1} = a^i, \quad b^{i+1} = r^i \quad \text{if} \quad f(\ell^i) \leqq f(r^i)$$ ■

4.2 Convergence of Golden Section and Fibonacci Search Algorithms

Assume that f has a minimum solution $\bar{x}$ in the interval $[a, b]$ and that f is unimodal on $[a, b]$, that is for ℓ, r in $[a, b]$ and $\ell < r$, if $f(\ell) > f(r)$ then $\bar{x} \in [\ell, b]$, if $f(\ell) < f(r)$ then $\bar{x} \in [a, r]$ and if $f(\ell) = f(r)$ then $\bar{x} \in [\ell, r]$. After $n(n \geqq 2)$ function evaluations a minimum solution $\bar{x}$ is in $[a_{n-1}, b_{n-1}]$ where

$$b_{n-1} - a_{n-1} = \begin{cases} (0.618)^{n-1}(b - a) & \text{for golden section} \\ \dfrac{1}{F_n}(b - a) \quad \text{or} \quad \dfrac{1+\epsilon}{F_n}(b - a) & \text{for Fibonacci search} \end{cases} \qquad \blacksquare$$

Fibonacci search has the property of giving the smallest final interval length $b_{n-1} - a_{n-1}$ for a fixed number n of allowable function evaluations. However golden section is in general preferred because it is simpler to implement and it does not require a knowledge of n in advance. For other methods see Danilin [1971]. Since $b^i - a^i$ is the maximum error in the ith step, an estimate of the *rate* of convergence is given by the relation between $b^i - a^i$ and $b^{i-1} - a^{i-1}$. We have then $b^i - a^i = 0.618\ (b^{i-1} - a^{i-1})$ for golden section, $b^i - a^i = \dfrac{F_{n-i}}{F_{n-i+1}} \cdot (b^{i-1} - a^{i-1})$ for Fibonacci search where it can be shown that F_{n-i}/F_{n-i+1} approaches 0.618 as i and n approach ∞. Because of the foregoing *linear* relation between $(b^{i-1} - a^{i-1})$ and $(b^i - a^i)$ we say that golden section has a *linear convergence rate* and Fibonacci search has an *asymptotic linear* convergence rate. To improve on these rates, we would like to get a ratio between the errors at the ith and $(i - 1)$th steps which tends to zero rather than to a positive constant. Such rates of convergence a are termed *superlinear* because they are better than any linear convergence rate. One such method is the secant method (also called sometimes *regula falsi*). This is a discrete version of Newton's method for finding a zero of the derivative f' of f in $[a, b]$ if it exists. Newton's method itself consists of linearizing f' around the current point and taking the zero of the linearized function as the next point of the iteration. In particular we have the following secant algorithm.

4.3 Secant Algorithm [Ortega and Rheinboldt, 1970; Shampine and Allen, 1973]

Start with two distinct points x^0, x^1 in $[a, b]$ such that $f'(x^0) \neq f'(x^1)$. Having x^i, x^{i-1} compute x^{i+1} as follows

$$x^{i+1} = x^i - \frac{f'(x^i)}{\dfrac{f'(x^i) - f'(x^{i-1})}{x^i - x^{i-1}}} \qquad \blacksquare$$

4.4 Convergence of the Secant Algorithm

Let $\left|\dfrac{f'''(x)}{2f''(y)}\right| \leqq M$ for some M and all x, y in some interval $[a', b']$ containing $[a, b]$ and let $M|\hat{x} - x^0| < 1$ and $M|\hat{x} - x^1| < 1$ where $\hat{x}$ is a zero of f' in $[a', b']$, that is $f'(\hat{x}) = 0$. Then the sequence $\{x^i\}$ converges to $\hat{x}$. If in addition $f''(x) > 0$ for all x in $[a', b']$, then the unique solution $\bar{x}$, of $\min_{x \in [a,b]} f(x)$, is given by

$$\bar{x} = \hat{x} \text{ if } a \leqq \hat{x} \leqq b, \quad \bar{x} = a \text{ if } \hat{x} < a, \quad \text{and } \bar{x} = b \text{ if } \hat{x} > b. \quad \blacksquare$$

It can be shown that a bound on the error of the secant algorithm is given by

$$|x^i - \hat{x}| < \frac{\delta^{F_i}}{M}$$

where $\delta = \max\ \{M(x^0 - \hat{x}),\ M(x^1 - \hat{x})\} < 1$ and F_i is the ith Fibonacci number defined earlier under Fibonacci search. If we let e^i denote this error bound then

$$e^{i+1} = \delta^{F_{i-1}} e^i.$$

For large i, $\delta^{F_{i-1}}$ tends to $\delta^{0.724(1.618)^{i-1}}$ which approaches zero as i approaches ∞. Hence the convergence rate is superlinear and is of order 1.618 per function evaluation. This is better than the order $\sqrt{2} = 1.414$ per function evaluation of Newton's method for one dimensional problems.

5. UNCONSTRAINED MINIMIZATION ALGORITHMS

We shall be concerned here with the problem

$$\underset{x \in R^n}{\text{minimize}}\ f(\mathbf{x}) \tag{13}$$

where f: $R^n \to R$. Because of space limitations we shall limit ourselves to two of the most effective algorithms for solving Problem (13): the Davidon-Fletcher-Powell variable metric method and the method of conjugate gradients. Both of these methods have two important properties: (1) They have a superlinear rate of convergence and (2) They find the minimum of a strictly convex quadratic function in n steps or less. The variable metric algorithm imitates the Newton method by computing $\mathbf{x}^{i+1} - x^i = -\lambda^i \mathbf{H}^i \nabla f(\mathbf{x}^i)$ where $\mathbf{H}^i$ is an approximation in a certain sense to $\nabla^2 f(\mathbf{x}^i)^{-1}$ and λ^i is a stepsize. The approximation is achieved by forcing $\mathbf{H}^i$ to satisfy the quasi-Newton condition $\mathbf{H}^{i+1}(\nabla f(\mathbf{x}^{i+1}) - \nabla f(\mathbf{x}^i)) = \mathbf{x}^{i+1} - \mathbf{x}^i$ which must hold if f were a strictly convex quadratic function. The conjugate direction methods, on the other hand, picks directions p^i in R^n which satisfy the *conjugacy relation* $p^i \nabla^2 f(\mathbf{x}^i) p^{i-1} = 0$. For a strictly convex quadratic function, the n first such directions are linearly independent and are orthogonal to $\nabla f(\mathbf{x}^n)$, the gradient at the nth point, which must then vanish, so that $\mathbf{x}^n$ is optimal.

5.1 Variable Metric Algorithm (Davidon-Fletcher-Powell) [Fletcher and Powell, 1963]

Start with any $\mathbf{x}^0$ in R^n. Let $\mathbf{H}^0 = \mathbf{I}$, the $n \times n$ identity matrix. Having $\mathbf{x}^i$ and $\mathbf{H}^i$ determine $\mathbf{x}^{i+1}$ and $\mathbf{H}^{i+1}$ as follows:

(1) Let $\mathbf{p}^i = -\mathbf{H}^i \nabla f(\mathbf{x}^i)$. Compute $\mathbf{x}^{i+1} = \mathbf{x}^i + \lambda^i \mathbf{p}^i$ where λ^i is the first nonnegative root of $\nabla f(\mathbf{x}^i + \lambda \mathbf{p}^i)\mathbf{p}^i = 0$, or, $\lambda^i \geqq 0$ and $f(\mathbf{x}^i + \lambda^i \mathbf{p}^i)$ is the first local minimum of $f(\mathbf{x}^i + \lambda \mathbf{p}^i)$ subject to $\lambda \geqq 0$.

(2) If $\mathbf{y}^i = 0$ or $\mathbf{z}^i = 0$ where $\mathbf{z}^i = \mathbf{x}^{i+1} - \mathbf{x}^i$ and $\mathbf{y}^i = \nabla f(\mathbf{x}^{i+1}) - \nabla f(\mathbf{x}^i)$ set $\mathbf{x}^i = \bar{\mathbf{x}}$ and stop. Else compute

$$\mathbf{H}^{i+1} = \mathbf{H}^i + \frac{\mathbf{z}^i \mathbf{z}^{i^T}}{\mathbf{z}^i \mathbf{y}^i} - \frac{(\mathbf{H}^i \mathbf{y}^i)(\mathbf{H}^i \mathbf{y}^i)^T}{\mathbf{y}^i \mathbf{H}^i \mathbf{y}^i}$$ ∎

5.2 Convergence and Rate of Convergence of the Variable Metric Algorithm [Powell, 1971; Broyden, et al., 1973]

If $f(\mathbf{x}) = \frac{1}{2}\mathbf{x}C\mathbf{x} + a\mathbf{x}$ and C is positive definite, then the algorithm in Section 5.1 arrives at the unique minimum solution $\bar{\mathbf{x}}$ in n or less steps. More generally if f is twice continuously differentiable on R^n and $\alpha\|\mathbf{y}\|^2 \leqq \mathbf{y}\nabla^2 f(\mathbf{x})\mathbf{y}$ for some $\alpha > 0$ and all $\mathbf{x}$, $\mathbf{y}$ in R^n, then the sequence $\{\mathbf{x}^i\}$ generated by the algorithm in Section 5.1 terminates at or converges to $\bar{\mathbf{x}}$, the unique solution of Problem (13). If, in addition, $\|\nabla^2 f(\mathbf{y}) - \nabla^2 f(\mathbf{x})\| \leqq R\|\mathbf{y} - \mathbf{x}\|$ for some $R > 0$ and all $\mathbf{x}$, $\mathbf{y}$ in R^n, then $\|\mathbf{x}^{i+1} - \bar{\mathbf{x}}\| \leqq \delta^i \|\mathbf{x}^i - \bar{\mathbf{x}}\|$, where $\lim_{i \to \infty} \delta^i = 0$, that is $\{\mathbf{x}^i\}$ converges superlinearly to $\bar{\mathbf{x}}$. ∎

5.3 Conjugate Directions Algorithm [Fletcher and Reeves, 1964; Polyak, 1969b; Polak and Ribière, 1969]

Start with any $\mathbf{x}^0$ in R^n and set $\mathbf{p}^0 = -\nabla f(\mathbf{x}^0)$. Having $\mathbf{x}^i$, $\mathbf{p}^i$ determine $\mathbf{x}^{i+1}$, $\mathbf{p}^{i+1}$ as follows:

(1) $\mathbf{x}^{i+1} = \mathbf{x}^i + \lambda^i \mathbf{p}^i$, where λ^i is the first nonnegative root of $\nabla f(\mathbf{x}^i + \lambda \mathbf{p}^i)\mathbf{p}^i = 0$, or, $\lambda^i \geqq 0$ and $f(\mathbf{x}^i + \lambda^i \mathbf{p}^i)$ is the first local minimum of $f(\mathbf{x}^i + \lambda \mathbf{p}^i)$ subject to $\lambda \geqq 0$.

(2) If $\nabla f(\mathbf{x}^i) = 0$, set $\bar{\mathbf{x}} = \mathbf{x}^i$ and stop. Otherwise compute

$$\mathbf{p}^{i+1} = -\nabla f(\mathbf{x}^{i+1}) + \alpha^{i+1}\mathbf{p}^i$$

where

$$\alpha^{i+1} = \frac{\|\nabla f(\mathbf{x}^{i+1})\|^2}{\|\nabla f(\mathbf{x}^i)\|^2} \quad \text{(Fletcher-Reeves)}$$

or

$$\alpha^{i+1} = \frac{(\nabla f(\mathbf{x}^{i+1}) - \nabla f(\mathbf{x}^i))\nabla f(\mathbf{x}^{i+1})}{\|\nabla f(\mathbf{x}^i)\|^2} \quad \text{(Polyak-Polak-Ribière)}$$ ■

5.4 Convergence and Rate of Convergence of the Conjugate Gradient Method [Zoutendijk, 1970; McCormick and Ritter, 1974, 1972; Cohen, 1972]

Let $\|\nabla f(\mathbf{y}) - \nabla f(\mathbf{x})\| \leqq M\|\mathbf{y} - \mathbf{x}\|$ for some $M > 0$ and all $\mathbf{y}$ and $\mathbf{x}$ in R^n. If $f(\mathbf{x}) = \frac{1}{2}\mathbf{x}C\mathbf{x} + a\mathbf{x}$ and C is positive definite, then the conjugate direction algorithm arrives in n or less steps at $\bar{\mathbf{x}}$, the unique minimum. More generally: (a) If the set $\{\mathbf{x} \mid f(\mathbf{x}) \leqq f(\mathbf{x}^0)\}$ is bounded, then the Fletcher-Reeves algorithm either terminates at a stationary point $\bar{\mathbf{x}}$, that is $\nabla f(\bar{\mathbf{x}}) = 0$ or at least one accumulation point $\bar{\mathbf{x}}$ of the sequence $\{\mathbf{x}^i\}$ is stationary. (b) If f is twice continuously differentiable on R^n, then the Polyak-Polak-Ribière algorithm Section 5.3 either terminates at a stationary point $\bar{\mathbf{x}}$ or each accumulation point $\bar{\mathbf{x}}$ of the sequence $\{\mathbf{x}^i\}$ is stationary. If in addition the set $\{\mathbf{x} \mid f(\mathbf{x}) \leqq f(\mathbf{x}^0)\}$ is bounded and $\alpha\|\mathbf{y}\|^2 \leqq \mathbf{y}\nabla^2 f(\mathbf{x})\mathbf{y} \leqq M\|\mathbf{y}\|^2$ for some $M \geqq \alpha > 0$ and all $\mathbf{x}$, $\mathbf{y}$ in R^n, then the Polyak-Polak-Ribière conjugate directions algorithm in Section 5.3 is n-step superlinearly convergent; that is

$$\|\mathbf{x}^{n(i+1)} - \bar{\mathbf{x}}\| \leqq \delta^i\|\mathbf{x}^{ni} - \bar{\mathbf{x}}\|, \quad \lim_{i\to\infty} \delta^i = 0$$

provided that $\mathbf{p}^i$ is reset to $-\nabla f(\mathbf{x}^i)$ after each n steps. ■

6. CONSTRAINED MINIMIZATION ALGORITHMS

Constrained optimization problems form the core of nonlinear programming and the typical programming problem is that given by Problem (1). The difficulty of the problem depends on whether the functions f, g, h are linear, quadratic or neither. In particular we can distinguish the following classes of programming problems:

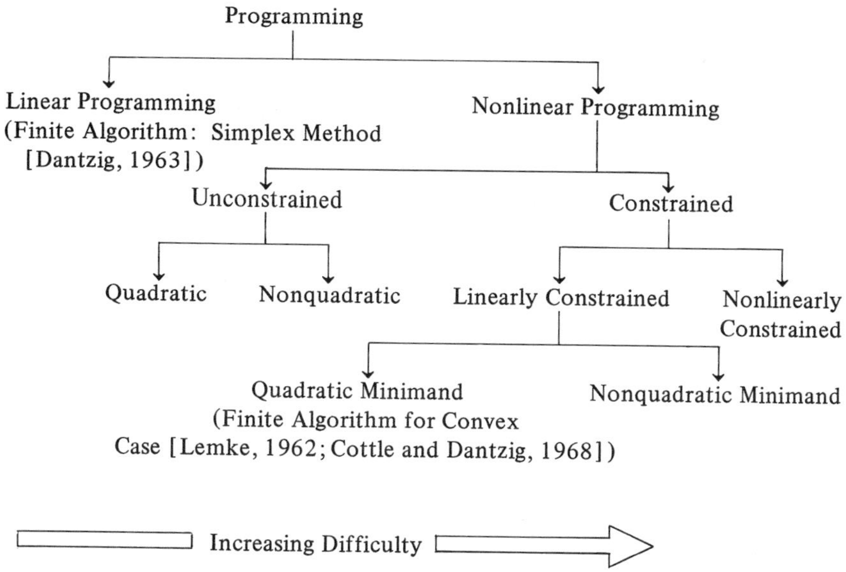

We shall concentrate here on algorithms for solving the rightmost problems given in the above table, that is, problems which are nonlinearly constrained, and, linearly constrained problems with a nonquadratic minimand. We shall give a number of algorithms for solving such problems.

We begin with penalty function algorithms. The basic idea here is to reduce the constrained problems to a sequence of "unconstrained" problems, the solutions of which approach a solution of the original problem. This is done by combining the constraints with the objective function in such a way that minimizing the combined "penalty function" penalizes constraint violation. Penalty function algorithms can be classified as follows:

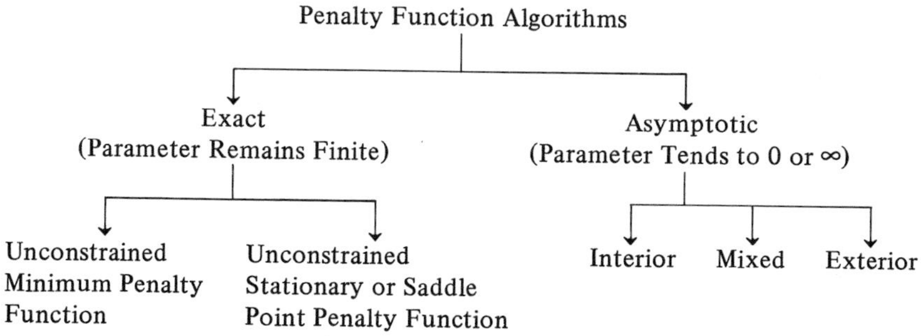

Each of these methods has its advantages and disadvantages which we shall mention after describing each algorithm.

6.1 Asymptotic Interior Penalty Algorithm [Fiacco and McCormick, 1968]

For any decreasing sequence of real positive numbers $\{r^i\}$ converging to zero, find solutions, $\mathbf{x}^i$, of the problems: minimize $P^i(\mathbf{x})$ subject to $g(\mathbf{x}) < 0$ where

$$P^i(\mathbf{x}) = f(\mathbf{x}) - r^i \sum_{j=1}^{m} \frac{1}{g_j(\mathbf{x})}, \quad \text{for all } i$$

or

$$P^i(\mathbf{x}) = f(\mathbf{x}) - r^i \sum_{j=1}^{m} \log(-g_j(\mathbf{x})), \quad \text{for all } i$$

If the set $X^0 = \{\mathbf{x} | g(\mathbf{x}) < 0\}$ is not empty and $\underset{\mathbf{x} \in X^0}{\text{infimum}} f(\mathbf{x}) = \underset{\mathbf{x} \in X}{\text{infimum}} f(\mathbf{x})$, where $X = \{\mathbf{x} | g(\mathbf{x}) \leqq 0\}$, and if f and g are continuous on X, then every accumulation point of the sequence $\{\mathbf{x}^i\}$ is a solution of minimize $f(\mathbf{x})$ subject to $g(\mathbf{x}) \leqq 0$ (which is Problem (1) but without the equality constraints $h(\mathbf{x}) = 0$). ■

The main difficulties with the above algorithm are that equality constraints cannot be handled and the penalty parameter r^i must approach zero which creates conditioning problems [Lootsma, 1969, 1972; Murray, 1971]. To avoid the former difficulty we consider exterior penalty function algorithms which can handle both equalities and inequalities.

6.2 Exterior Penalty Algorithm [Fiacco and McCormick, 1968]

For any increasing sequence of real positive numbers $\{r^i\}$ which tends to $+\infty$, find solutions $\mathbf{x}^i$ of the unconstrained problems: $\underset{x \in R^n}{\text{minimize}}\, P^i(\mathbf{x})$, where

$$P^i(\mathbf{x}) = f(\mathbf{x}) + r^i \left[\sum_{j=1}^{m} (g_j(\mathbf{x})_+)^2 + \sum_{j=1}^{k} (h_j(\mathbf{x}))^2 \right]$$

where $g_j(\mathbf{x})_+$ denotes $g_j(\mathbf{x})$ if $g_j(\mathbf{x}) \geqq 0$, and 0 if $g_j(\mathbf{x}) < 0$. If f, g and h are continuous on R^n and Problem (1) possesses a solution, then every accumulation point $\bar{\mathbf{x}}$ of the sequence $\{\mathbf{x}^i\}$ is a solution of Problem (1).

Again the exterior penalty algorithm suffers from conditioning difficulties as r^i approaches ∞. To overcome these difficulties exact penalty function methods will be discussed shortly. However the parameter r^i need not approach $+\infty$ if we are willing to accept some feasibility tolerance $\epsilon > 0$ for the accumulation point $\bar{\mathbf{x}}$, that is $\sum_{j=1}^{m} (g_j(\bar{\mathbf{x}})_+)^2 + \sum_{j=1}^{k} (h_j(\bar{\mathbf{x}}))^2 \leqq \epsilon$. Then the sequence $\{r^i\}$ need not tend to $+\infty$ but rather $\lim_{i\to\infty} r^i > \dfrac{2|f(\hat{\mathbf{x}}) - f(\mathbf{x}^0)|}{\epsilon}$, where $\hat{\mathbf{x}}$ is an arbitrary feasible point, that is $g(\hat{\mathbf{x}}) \leqq 0$, $h(\hat{\mathbf{x}}) = 0$, and x^0 is a solution of the first iteration $\min_{\mathbf{x}\in R^n} P^0(\mathbf{x})$. Mixed penalty methods [Fiacco and McCormick, 1968] are a combination of exterior and interior penalty method. A typical mixed penalty function for Problem (1) is given by

$$P^i(\mathbf{x}) = f(\mathbf{x}) - r^i \sum_{j\in J_1} \log(-g_j(\mathbf{x})) + \frac{1}{r^i}\left[\sum_{j\in J_2} (g_j(\mathbf{x})_+)^2 + \sum_{j=1}^{k} (h_j(\mathbf{x}))^2\right]$$

where J_1 is any subset of indices of the inequality constraints for which there exist an interior, that is there exists an $\hat{\mathbf{x}}$ such that $g_j(\mathbf{x}) < 0$, for $j \in J_1$. J_2 is the set of indices of the remaining inequality constraints. The subproblems to be solved here are: minimize $P^i(\mathbf{x})$ subject to $g_j(\mathbf{x}) < 0, j \in J_1$ and the sequence $\{r^i\}$ is a decreasing sequence tending to 0. If f, g and h are continuous and $-\infty < \operatorname{infimum}_{\mathbf{x}\in X} f(\mathbf{x}) = \operatorname{infimum}_{\mathbf{x}\in X^1\cap X^2} f(\mathbf{x})$ where $X = \{\mathbf{x} | g(\mathbf{x}) \leqq 0, h(\mathbf{x}) = 0\}$, $X^1 = \{\mathbf{x} | g_j(\mathbf{x}) < 0, j \in J_1\}$ and $X^2 = \{\mathbf{x} | g_j(\mathbf{x}) \leqq 0, j \in J_2, h(\mathbf{x}) = 0\}$, then each accumulation point of the sequence $\{\mathbf{x}^i\}$ solves Problem (1), provided it has a solution.

More recently there have been attempts at inventing penalty functions in which the parameter remains finite. Such penalty functions are called exact. Unfortunately exact penalty functions are in general nondifferentiable [Zangwill, 1967; Pietrzykowski, 1969; Howe, 1973] or only locally differentiable [Fletcher, 1972], or an unconstrained stationary or saddle point must be found rather than an unconstrained minimum [Rockafellar, 1971, 1973a, 1973b, 1974; Arrow, *et al.*, 1973; Mangasarian, 1975].

6.3 Exact Minimum Penalty Algorithm [Zangwill, 1967; Pietrzykowski, 1969; Howe, 1973]

For an increasing sequence of real numbers $\{r^i\}$ find unconstrained local (global) minima $\mathbf{x}^i$ of $P(\mathbf{x}, r^i)$ where $P(\mathbf{x}, r)$ is defined in Section 2.5. Stop when $\mathbf{x}^i$ is feasible, that is $g(\mathbf{x}^i) \leqq 0$ and $h(\mathbf{x}^i) = 0$. $\mathbf{x}^i$ is a local (global) solution of Problem (1). ∎

Note the advantage of this algorithm over asymptotic penalty methods is the finiteness of r^i.

The main disadvantage is that $P(\mathbf{x}, r)$ is in general piecewise differentiable at most. Special methods must be used to minimize it [Polyak, 1969a].

We turn now to the final type of penalty function methods, namely, the exact stationary point penalty algorithm.

6.4 Exact Stationary Point Penalty Algorithm (Augmented Lagrangean)

For some positive number $r > 0$ find a root $(\bar{\mathbf{x}}, \bar{\mathbf{y}}, \bar{\mathbf{z}})$ of the $m + n + k$ equalities (Eq. (9)). The vector $\bar{\mathbf{x}}$ and the vectors $\bar{\mathbf{u}}$ and $\bar{\mathbf{v}}$ given by Eqs. (10) satisfy the first order Kuhn-Tucker conditions (3). If in addition f and g are convex at $\bar{\mathbf{x}}$, and h is linear then $\bar{\mathbf{x}}$ is a global solution of Problem (1). ■

Specific methods for solving the equalities (Eq. (9)) are given in [Mangasarian, 1975a]. For a compendium of methods for solving nonlinear equations see [Ortega and Rheinboldt, 1970].

We next turn to the method of feasible directions. The basic idea here is to find a direction which simultaneously decreases the minimand and at the same time remains feasible. A tolerance ϵ^i to prevent jamming or zig-zagging must be introduced in the algorithm [Zoutendijk, 1960]. Note that in this method g can be nonlinear but h must be linear.

6.5 Feasible Directions Algorithm [Zoutendijk, 1960; Zangwill, 1969]

Start with an $\mathbf{x}^0 \in X = \{\mathbf{x} | g(\mathbf{x}) \leqq 0, h(\mathbf{x}) = 0\}$, where h is linear, and some fixed positive number $\epsilon^0 > 0$. Having $\mathbf{x}^i, \epsilon^i$ determine $\mathbf{x}^{i+1}, \epsilon^{i+1}$ as follows. Solve the linear program

$$\underset{\delta, q}{\text{minimize}} \; \{\delta \,|\, \nabla f(\mathbf{x}^i)\mathbf{q} \leqq \delta, \;\; \nabla g_j(\mathbf{x}^i)\mathbf{q} \leqq \delta, \;\; j \in I_N(\mathbf{x}^i, \epsilon^i)$$

$$\nabla g_j(\mathbf{x}^i)\mathbf{q} \leqq 0, \;\; j \in I_L(\mathbf{x}^i, \epsilon^i), \;\; \nabla h(\mathbf{x}^i)\mathbf{q} = 0\}$$

where

$$I_N(\mathbf{x}^i, \epsilon^i) = \{j \,|\, -\epsilon^i \leqq g_j(\mathbf{x}^i) \leqq 0, \;\text{ and }\; g_j \;\text{ is nonlinear}\}$$

$$I_L(\mathbf{x}^i, \epsilon^i) = \{j \,|\, -\epsilon^i \leqq g_j(\mathbf{x}^i) \leqq 0, \;\text{ and }\; g_j \;\text{ is linear}\}$$

Call a solution of the linear program $\delta^i, \mathbf{q}^i$. If $\delta^i = 0$ stop, else set

$$\epsilon^{i+1} = \begin{cases} \epsilon^i & \text{if } \epsilon^i \leqq -\delta^i \\ \dfrac{\epsilon^i}{2} & \text{if } \epsilon^i > -\delta^i \end{cases}$$

Set $\mathbf{p}^i = \nu^i \mathbf{q}^i$ where $\nu^i = \max \{1, \frac{1}{2}, \frac{1}{4}, \ldots\}$ such that $\mathbf{x}^i + \mu \mathbf{p}^i \in X$ for all $\mu \in [0, 1]$. Determine $\mathbf{x}^{i+1} = \mathbf{x}^i + \lambda^i \mathbf{p}^i$ such that $f(\mathbf{x}^i + \lambda^i \mathbf{p}^i) = \underset{0 \leqq \lambda \leqq 1}{\text{minimum}} \; f(\mathbf{x}^i + \lambda \mathbf{p}^i)$

or $\lambda^i = \max \{1, \frac{1}{2}, \frac{1}{4}, \ldots\}$ such that $f(\mathbf{x}^i) - f(\mathbf{x}^i + \lambda^i \mathbf{p}^i) \geqq -\frac{1}{4}\nabla f(\mathbf{x}^i)\mathbf{p}^i$. If f has continuous first partial derivatives, g has Lipschitz continuous partial derivatives and h is linear, then either the sequence $\{\mathbf{x}^i\}$ terminates at a stationary point or every accumulation point $\bar{\mathbf{x}}$ is stationary, that is there exists no feasible direction

$\mathbf{p}$ at $\bar{\mathbf{x}}$ satisfying $\nabla f(\bar{\mathbf{x}})\mathbf{p} < 0$, $\nabla g_j(\bar{\mathbf{x}})\mathbf{p} < 0, j \in \{j | g_j(\bar{\mathbf{x}}) = 0\}$ and $\nabla h(\bar{\mathbf{x}})\mathbf{p} = 0$. If in addition f and g are convex on R^n and there exists some $\tilde{\mathbf{x}}$ such that $g(\tilde{\mathbf{x}}) < 0$ and $h(\tilde{\mathbf{x}}) = 0$ then $\bar{\mathbf{x}}$ solves Problem (1). ∎

We consider next a gradient projection algorithm which is useful for linearly constrained problems. The algorithm we present here is a variation of the Levitin-Polyak algorithm [Levitin and Polyak, 1966] which in our version here includes provisions for considering only a subset of the constraints and also provisions for introducing a matrix which can play the role of the inverse of the Hessian of the Lagrangean function or an approximation thereof.

6.6 Gradient Projection Algorithm [Levitin and Polyak, 1966]

Start with any $\mathbf{x}^0 \in X = \{\mathbf{x} | g(\mathbf{x}) \leqq 0,\ h(\mathbf{x}) = 0\}$, where g is convex and h is linear, and some fixed number $\epsilon^0 > 0$. Having $\mathbf{x}^i$, ϵ^i determine $\mathbf{x}^{i+1}$, ϵ^{i+1} as follows. Solve the quadratic programming problem

$$\underset{\mathbf{y} \in X^i}{\text{minimize}}\ \|\mathbf{x}^i - H(\mathbf{x}^i)\,\nabla f(\mathbf{x}^i) - \mathbf{y}\|^2_{H(\mathbf{x}^i)^{-1}}$$

where $\|\mathbf{z}\|^2_H = \mathbf{z}H\mathbf{z}$, $H(\mathbf{x}^i)$ is any continuous symmetric, positive definite matrix and $X^i = \{\mathbf{x} | g_j(\mathbf{x}) \leqq 0,\ j \in I(\mathbf{x}^i, \epsilon^i),\ h(\mathbf{x}) = 0\}$, $I(\mathbf{x}^i, \epsilon^i) = \{j | -\epsilon^i \leqq g_j(\mathbf{x}^i) \leqq 0\}$. Denote the solution of this quadratic program by $\mathbf{y}^i$. If $\mathbf{y}^i = \mathbf{x}^i$ stop, else take $\epsilon^{i+1} \geqq \hat{\epsilon} > 0$, where $\hat{\epsilon}$ is an arbitrary positive number. Set $\mathbf{p}^i = \nu^i(\mathbf{y}^i - \mathbf{x}^i)$ where $\nu^i = \max\ \{1, \frac{1}{2}, \frac{1}{4}, \ldots\}$ such that $\mathbf{x}^i + \mu\mathbf{p}^i \in X$ for all $\mu \in [0, 1]$. Determine $\mathbf{x}^{i+1} = \mathbf{x}^i + \lambda^i\mathbf{p}^i$ such that $f(\mathbf{x}^i + \lambda^i\mathbf{p}^i) = \underset{0 \leqq \lambda \leqq 1}{\text{minimum}}\ f(\mathbf{x}^i + \lambda\mathbf{p}^i)$ or $\lambda^i = \max\ \{1, \frac{1}{2}, \frac{1}{4}, \ldots\}$ such that $f(\mathbf{x}^i) - f(\mathbf{x}^i + \lambda^i\mathbf{p}^i) \geqq -\frac{1}{4}\nabla f(\mathbf{x}^i)\mathbf{p}^i$. If f is convex and has continuous first partial derivatives on R^n, g has Lipschitz continuous gradients on R^n and there exists an $\tilde{\mathbf{x}} \in X$ such that $h(\tilde{\mathbf{x}}) = 0$ and $g(\tilde{\mathbf{x}}) < 0$ and $M_1\|\mathbf{z}\|^2 \leqq \mathbf{z}H(\mathbf{x}^i)\mathbf{z} \leqq M_2\|\mathbf{z}\|^2$ for all i, all $\mathbf{z} \in R^n$ and some $M_2 \geqq M_1 > 0$, then either the sequence $\{\mathbf{x}^i\}$ terminates at a solution of Problem (1) or every accumulation point solves Problem (1). ∎

We observe that most of the work in the above algorithm is contained in solving a quadratic program for determining $\mathbf{y}^i$. For linearly constrained problems this can be quickly performed by principal pivoting or related methods [Lemke, 1962; Cottle and Dantzig, 1968] for which efficient computer codes are available [Teorey, 1972].

We terminate by giving a Newton algorithm for nonlinearly constrained problems for which local quadratic convergence can be established. The algorithm was originally proposed by Wilson [1963] and its quadratic convergence rate was established by Robinson [1974]. See Robinson [1972] for a related algorithm.

6.7 Newton Algorithm for Nonlinearly Constrained Problems [Wilson, 1963; Robinson, 1974]

Start with any $(\mathbf{x}^0, \mathbf{u}^0, \mathbf{v}^0) \in R^n \times R^m \times R^k$. Having $(\mathbf{x}^i, \mathbf{u}^i, \mathbf{v}^i)$ determine $(\mathbf{x}^{i+1}, \mathbf{u}^{i+1}, \mathbf{v}^{i+1})$ to be the closest solution to $(\mathbf{x}^i, \mathbf{u}^i, \mathbf{v}^i)$ of the following linearly constrained quadratic programming problem

$$\min_{\mathbf{p}} \nabla f(\mathbf{x}^1)\mathbf{p} + \tfrac{1}{2}\mathbf{p}\nabla_{11}L(\mathbf{x}^i, \mathbf{u}^i, \mathbf{v}^i)\mathbf{p}$$

subject to

$$g(\mathbf{x}^i) + \nabla g(\mathbf{x}^i)\mathbf{p} \leqq 0$$

$$h(\mathbf{x}^i) + \nabla h(\mathbf{x}^i)\mathbf{p} = 0$$

where L is the Lagrangean defined in Eqs. (5). Call the solution $\mathbf{p}^i$, the optimal Lagrange multipliers $\mathbf{u}^{i+1}$, $\mathbf{v}^{i+1}$, and set $\mathbf{x}^{i+1} = \mathbf{x}^i + \mathbf{p}^i$. If $(\mathbf{x}^0, \mathbf{u}^0, \mathbf{v}^0)$ is sufficiently close to a point $(\bar{\mathbf{x}}, \bar{\mathbf{u}}, \bar{\mathbf{v}})$ which satisfies the second order sufficiency condition of Section 2.3, and at which strict complementarity holds, that is $\bar{u}_i > 0$ for $g_i(\bar{\mathbf{x}}) = 0$, and $\nabla h_j(\bar{\mathbf{x}})$, $j = 1, \ldots, k$ and $\nabla g_i(\bar{\mathbf{x}})$ for $i \in \{i \mid g_i(\bar{\mathbf{x}}) = 0\}$ are linearly independent, and f, g and h are twice continuously differentiable around $\bar{\mathbf{x}}$, then the sequence $\{\mathbf{x}^i, \mathbf{u}^i, \mathbf{v}^i\}$ converges quadratically to $(\bar{\mathbf{x}}, \bar{\mathbf{u}}, \bar{\mathbf{v}})$, that is

$$\|(\mathbf{x}^i, \mathbf{u}^i, \mathbf{v}^i) - (\bar{\mathbf{x}}, \bar{\mathbf{u}}, \bar{\mathbf{v}})\| \leqq \sigma(\tfrac{1}{2})^{2^i}$$

where σ is some constant. ∎

REFERENCES

1. Arrow, K. J., F. J. Gould, and S. M. Howe, "A General Saddle Point Result for Constrained Optimization," *Math. Prog.*, **5**: 225–234 (1973).
2. Avriel, M., *Nonlinear Programming Analysis and Methods*, Prentice Hall, Englewood Cliffs, New Jersey (1976).
3. Bertsekas, D. P., "Multiplier Methods: A Survey," Automatica **12**: 133–145 (1976).
4. Blum, E. and W. Oettli, *Mathematische Optiemierung-Grundlagen und Verfahren*, Springer-Verlag, Berlin (1975). (Contains an updated bibliography of Reference 26.)
5. Broyden, C. G., J. E. Dennis, Jr., and J. J. Moré, "On the Local and Superlinear Convergence of Quasi-Newton Methods," *J. Inst. Maths. Applics.*, **12**: 223–245 (1973).
6. Buys, J. D., "Dual Algorithms for Constrained Optimization Problems," Doctorate Dissertation, University of Leiden (June 1972).
7. Cohen, A., "Rate of Convergence of Several Conjugate Gradient Algorithms," *SIAM J. Numer. Anal* **9**: 248–259 (1972).
8. Cottle, R. W. and G. B. Dantzig, "Complementary Pivot Theory of Mathematical Programming," *J. Linear Algebra Applic.* **1**: 103–125 (1968).
9. Danilin, Y. M., "Estimation of the Efficiency of an Absolute-Minimum-Finding Algorithm," *USSR Computational Math. and Mathematical Physics* (English Translation) **11**: 261–267 (1971).

10. Dantzig, G. B., *Linear Programming and Extensions*, Princeton University Press, Princeton, New Jersey (1963).
11. Dennis, J. E., Jr. and J. J. Moré: "Quasi-Newton Methods, Motivation and Theory," SIAM Review **19**, 46–89 (1977).
12. —— and A. F. Veinott, (eds.), *Math. of the Dec. Sci.*, Parts I and II, Amer. Math. Soc., Providence, Rhode Island (1968).
13. Evans, J. P., F. J. Gould, and J. W. Tolle, "Exact Penaly Functions in Nonlinear Programming," *Math. Prog.* **4**: 72–97 (1973).
14. Fiacco, A. V. and G. P. McCormick, *Nonlinear Programming: Sequential Unconstrained Minimization Techniques*, Wiley, New York (1968).
15. Fletcher, R., "An Exact Penalty Function for Nonlinear Programming with Inequalities," *Math. Prog.*, **5**: 129–150 (1973).
16. —— and M. J. D. Powell, "A Rapidly Convergent Descent Method for Minimization," *Computer J.* **6**: 163–168 (1963).
17. —— and C. M. Reeves, "Function Minimization by Conjugate Gradients," *Computer J.* **7**: 149–154 (1964).
18. Fox, R. L., *Optimization Methods for Engineering Design,* Addison-Wesley, Reading, Massachusetts (1971).
19. Garcia Palomares, U. M. and O. L. Mangasarian, "Superlinearly Convergent Quasi-Newton Algorithms for Nonlinearly Constrained Problems," Math. Prog. 11, 1–13 (1976).
20. Han, S.-P., "Penalty Lagrangean Methods Via a Quasi-Newton Approach," Department of Computer Science, Cornell University, Ithaca, Report TR 75-252 (1976).
21. Hestenes, M. R., *Optimization Theory the Finite Dimensional Case*, John Wiley, New York (1975).
22. Howe, S., "New Conditions for Exactness for a Simple Penalty Function," *SIAM J. Control*, **11**: 378–381 (1973).
23. John, F., "Extremum Problems with Inequalities as Subsidiary Conditions," in K. O. Friedrichs, O. E. Neugebauer & J. J. Stoker (eds.), *Studies and Essays: Courant Anniversary Volume*, 187–204, Interscience, New York (1948).
24. Kowalik, J. and M. R. Osborne, *Methods for Unconstrained Optimization Problems*, Elsevier, New York (1968).
25. Kuhn, H. W. and A. W. Tucker, "Nonlinear Programming" in J. Neyman (ed.), *Proceedings of the Second Berkeley Symposium in Mathematical Statistics and Probability*, 481–492, University of California Press, Berkeley, California (1951).
26. Künzi, H. P. and W. Oettli, "Nichtlineare Optiemierung: Neuere Verfahren Bibliographie," Lecture Notes in Operations Research and Mathematical Systems No. 16, Springer, Berlin (1969). (Most comprehensive bibliography on nonlinear programming up to 1969.)
27. Lemke, C. E., "A Method of Solution for Quadratic Programs," *Management Sci.* **8**: 442–455 (1972).
28. Levitin, E. S. and B. T. Polyak, "Constrained Minimization Methods," *USSR Computational Math. and Mathematical Physics* (English Translation) **6**: 1–50 (1966).
29. Lootsma, F. A., "Hessian Matrices of Penalty Functions for Solving Constrained Optimization Problems," Philips Res. Report #24, 322–331 (1969).
30. Lootsma, F. A. (ed.), *Numerical Methods for Non-linear Optimization*, Academic Press, London (1972).
31. Luenberger, D. G., *Introduction to Linear and Nonlinear Programming*, Addison-Wesley, Reading, Massachusetts (1973).
32. McCormick, G. P. and K. Ritter, "Alternate Proofs of the Convergence Properties

of the Conjugate Gradient Method," *J. Optimization Theory and Applic.*, **13:** 497–518 (1974).

33. —— and ——, "Methods of Conjugate Directions Versus Quasi-Newton Methods," *Math. Prog.* **3:** 101–116 (1972).
34. Mangasarian, O. L., *Nonlinear Programming*, McGraw-Hill, New York (1969).
35. ——, "Techniques of Optimization," *J. of Eng. for Ind.* **94,** Series **B, No. 2:** 365–372 (1972).
36. ——, "Unconstrained Lagrangeans in Nonlinear Programming," SIAM J. Control, **13:** 772–791 (1975a).
37. Mangasarian, O. L., "Unconstrained Methods in Nonlinear Programming," in, *Nonlinear Programming*, Volume **IX** SIAM-AMS Proceedings, American Math. Soc., Providence, Rhode Island, 169–184 (1975b).
38. Mangasarian, O. L., R. R. Meyer and S. M. Robinson, *Nonlinear Programming 2*, Academic Press. New York (1975).
39. —— and J. Ponstein, "Minmax and Duality in Nonlinear Programming," *J. Math. Anal. and Appl.* **11:** 504-518 (1965).
40. Murray, W., "Analytical Expressions for the Eigenvalues and Eigenvectors of the Hessian Matrices of Barrier and Penalty Functions," *J. Optimization Theory and Applic.*, **7:** 189–196 (1971).
41. Ortega, J. M. and W. C. Rheinboldt, *Iterative Solution of Nonlinear Equations in Several Variables*, Academic Press, New York (1970).
42. Ostrowski, A., *Solution of Equations and Systems of Equations*, Academic Press, New York (1966) (Second Edition).
43. Pietrzykowski, T., "An Exact Potential Method for Constrained Maxima," *SIAM J. Numer. Anal.* **6:** 299–304 (1969).
44. Polak, E. and G. Ribière, "Note sur la Convergence de Méthodes de Directions Conjuguées," Rev. Fr. Inform. Rech. Opér. **16-R1:** 35–43 (1969).
45. ——, *Computational Methods in Optimization: A Unified Approach*, Academic Press, New York (1971).
46. Polyak, B. T., "Minimization of Non-Smooth Functionals," *USSR Computational Math. and Mathematical Physics* (English Translation) **9:** 14–29 (1969a).
47. ——, "The Method of Conjugate Gradients in Extremum Problems," *USSR Computational Math. and Mathematical Physics* (English Translation) **9:** 94–112 (1969b).
48. Powell, M. J. D., "On the Convergence of the Variable Metric Algorithm," *J. Inst. of Maths. and Its Appl.* **7:** 21–36 (1971).
49. Powell, M. J. D., "Algorithms for Nonlinear Constraints that Use LaGrangean Functions," Department of Appl. Math. and Theor. Phys., Cambridge University, Cambridge (1976).
50. Robinson, S. M., "A Quadratically-Convergent Algorithm for General Nonlinear Programming Problems," Math. Prog. **3:** 145–156 (1972).
51. ——, "Perturbed Kuhn-Tucker Points and Rates of Convergence for a Class of Nonlinear Programming Algorithms," *Math. Prog.*, **7:** 1-16 (1974).
52. Rockafellar, R. T., "Convex Analysis," Princeton University Press, Princeton, New Jersey (1970).
53. ——, "New Applications of Duality in Convex Programming," Proceedings of the Fourth Conference on Probability, Brasov, Romania (1971).
54. ——, "A Dual Approach to Solving Nonlinear Programming Problems by Unconstrained Optimization," *Math. Prog.*, **5:** 354–373 (1973a).
55. ——, "The Multiplier Method of Hestenes and Powell Applied to Convex Programming," *J. Optimization Theory and Applic.*, **12:** 555–562 (1973b).

56. ——, "Augmented Lagrange Multiplier Functions and Duality in Nonconvex Programming," SIAM J. Control, **12:** 268–285 (1974).
57. Shampine, L. F. and R. C. Allen, Jr., "Numerical Computing: An Introduction," Saunders, Philadelphia (1973).
58. Stark, R. M. and R. L. Nichols, *Mathematical Foundations for Design-Civil Engineering Systems*, McGraw-Hill, New York (1972).
59. Tapia, R. A., "Diagonalized Multiplier Methods and Quasi-Newton Methods for Constrained Optimization," Department of Math. Sciences, Rice University, Houston (1976).
60. Teorey, T., "QUADPR, Quadratic Programming Subroutine," University of Wisconsin, Madison Academic Computing Center (June 1972).
61. Wilde, D. J., *Optimum Seeking Methods*, Prentice-Hall, Englewood Cliffs, New Jersey (1964).
62. Wilson, R. B., "A Simplicial Method for Convex Programming," Ph.D. Dissertation, Harvard University (1963).
63. Wolfe, P., "A Duality Theorem for Nonlinear Programming," *Quart. of Appl. Math.* **19:** 239–244 (1961).
64. Zangwill, W. I., "Nonlinear Programming via Penalty Functions," *Management Sci.* **13:** 344–358 (1967).
65. ——, *Nonlinear Programming: A Unified Approach*, Prentice-Hall, Englewood Cliffs, New Jersey (1969).
66. Zoutendijk, G., *Mathematical Programming Methods*, North-Holland, Amsterdam (1976).
67. ——, *Methods of Feasible Directions*, Elsevier, Amsterdam (1960).
68. ——, "Nonlinear Programming, Computational Methods," 37–86, in J. Abadie (ed.), *Integer and Nonlinear Programming*, North Holland, Amsterdam (1970).
69. ——, *Mathematical Programming Methods*, North Holland, Amsterdam (1976).

The research for this chapter was supported by NSF Grant GJ35292.

II-7

LARGE SCALE PROGRAMMING

Leon S. Lasdon
Case Western Reserve University

1. INTRODUCTION

One of the major reasons for the extensive use of mathematical programming today is the availability of computer codes which can solve large problems. Solution is achieved by exploiting problem structure. Large linear programs (LPs) almost always have special structure. The constraint matrix is usually quite sparse (most elements are zero) and, in many cases, the nonzero elements are often arranged in an ordered way, for example in blocks along the main diagonal except for a few rows or columns. Large nonlinear programs (NLPs) usually are also sparse. In addition, they often contain a high percentage of linear terms, and the nonlinear terms may have additional structure, e.g., separable.

Approaches to solving large mathematical programs may be divided into two classes: direct methods, and decomposition or partitioning techniques. Direct methods specialize an existing algorithm to a particular class of problems. These are most common in LP, where the basic tool is the simplex method (SM). Here the main computational problem is the manipulation of the inverse of the basis. In the case of special matrix structure, the necessary operations may often be performed while storing a matrix of reduced size. Algorithms of this type are discussed in Sections 2 and 3.

Decomposition methods break the original system up into subsystems, each with a smaller, independent subproblem. Since the subsystems interact, solving the subproblems will not, in general, yield the correct solution. The multilevel approach [Mesarovic, 1970] proposes that one account for the interactions by defining one or more "second level" subsystems which influence, in some way, the original subsystems, defined to be on the first level. The goal of the second level is to coordinate the actions of first level units so that the solution of the original problem is obtained. All large organizations operate in this way. Decomposition algorithms are discussed in Sections 4 and 5.

Throughout this chapter, the reader is assumed to be familiar with the material on LP in Chapter II-1.

2. SOLVING LARGE LP'S BY THE REVISED SIMPLEX METHOD (RSM)

Commercial codes are available today which can solve very large LPs. Most large computer companies and some other firms market these systems. Some of them can accommodate LPs of 8000 to 16,000 rows if sufficient core storage is available. If the model has the generalized upper bounding (GUB) structure (see Section 3) even larger problems can be solved—a 50,000 row problem of this type was solved recently by Management Science Systems, Inc. of Rockville, Maryland, using their MPS III mathematical programming system (see Hirshfeld [1972]). A problem with more than 5000 rows is large by any standard and, since LP models usually have more columns than rows, the number of matrix positions in such problems is often in the range 10^6 to 10^8. Solution of such problems is made possible by the fact that most of these positions are filled with zeros. Nonzero element densities of 0.5% or less are common for large problems.

Most LP models are not this large. The majority of commercial applications generate models with from 500 to 1500 rows, although such problems may contain several thousand columns. To solve these and larger problems, special solution and data management procedures have been developed. The remainder of this section deals with some of the solution techniques. An excellent survey of modern LP code characteristics, including data management, can be found in Orchard-Hays [1974], from which most of the statistics above were taken.

All modern commercial LP codes use the RSM. Most of them maintain the basis inverse, $\mathbf{B}^{-1}$, as a product of elementary matrices; $\mathbf{B}^{-1} = \mathbf{E}_k \mathbf{E}_{k-1} \cdots \mathbf{E}_1$ where each elementary matrix $\mathbf{E}_i$ differs from the identity matrix in only one column. This representation is called the product form of the inverse.

An important property of elementary matrices is that they can be stored in a computer memory by recording only the elements of the nonunit vector column and its position in the matrix (in practice, only the nonzero elements and their row positions need be stored). These columns are often called "eta vectors." Since the inverse is now not available explicitly, all computations involving it require a sequence of matrix multiplications. We consider these computations in their order of occurrence in the SM.

Evaluating the Simplex Multipliers. Let $\mathbf{c}_B$ be the vector of objective coefficients of the basic variables, ordered in the same way as the columns of the basis, $\mathbf{B}$. Then the simplex multipliers are given by

$$\boldsymbol{\pi} = \mathbf{c}_B \mathbf{B}^{-1} \tag{1}$$

so, if $\mathbf{B}^{-1}$ is given in product form, we must evaluate the matrix product

$$\boldsymbol{\pi} = (\cdots((\mathbf{c}_B \mathbf{E}_k)\mathbf{E}_{k-1})\cdots)\mathbf{E}_1 \tag{2}$$

The operations are carried out as indicated by the parentheses, i.e., first evaluate the row vector $\mathbf{c}_B \mathbf{E}_k$, then $(\mathbf{c}_B \mathbf{E}_k)\mathbf{E}_{k-1}$, etc. Each of these requires the multiplication of an elementary column matrix on the left by a row vector, say $\mathbf{v}$. In each such multiplication, the only component of $\mathbf{v}$ that changes is the one in the eta position, this being equal to the product of $\mathbf{v}$ with the eta column. Thus, computation of $\boldsymbol{\pi}$ when the product form contains k elementary matrices requires the evaluation of k scalar products.

Computing the Transformed Column, $\overline{\mathbf{P}}_s$. The vector $\overline{\mathbf{P}}_s$ is given by

$$\overline{\mathbf{P}}_s = \mathbf{B}^{-1}\mathbf{P}_s \tag{3}$$

$$\overline{\mathbf{P}}_s = \mathbf{E}_k(\cdots(\mathbf{E}_2(\mathbf{E}_1\mathbf{P}_s))\cdots) \tag{4}$$

Here the multiplications proceed in forward sequence, first $\mathbf{E}_1\mathbf{P}_s$, then $\mathbf{E}_2(\mathbf{E}_1\mathbf{P}_s)$, etc. Each operation requires the evaluation of a product of the form $\mathbf{E}\mathbf{v}$, with $\mathbf{v}$ a column vector. These are computed as follows.

$$\mathbf{E}\mathbf{v} = (\alpha_1, \ldots, \alpha_{m+1})' \tag{5}$$

where

$$\alpha_i = \begin{cases} v_i + \eta_i v_r, & i = 1, \ldots, m+1, \quad i \neq r \\ v_r \eta_r, & i = r \end{cases} \tag{6}$$

and r is the index of the eta column. Thus evaluating $\mathbf{E}\mathbf{v}$ requires $m + 1$ multiplications and m additions.

Updating the Inverse. This updating requires only adding a new eta vector to the list currently in storage, the elements of this vector being derived from the current $\overline{\mathbf{P}}_s$.

Taking Advantage of Sparsity. The product form of the inverse offers significant computational advantages in solving large problems. These derive from the fact that large LPs (i.e., with more than 100 rows) are almost always sparse. Efficient inversion routines have been developed which ensure that the eta vectors inherit this sparsity. Since only nonzero eta elements are stored, storage requirements are reduced, and a larger portion of the eta file can be kept in fast access (core) memory. The remainder must be kept in slower access memory, either disk or drum. Transferral of information from these devices to core memory is currently a "bottleneck" operation, significantly slower than arithmetic speeds. If the eta vectors are kept sparse, such transferrals will be needed less often and they will take less time. Sparse eta vectors also lead to faster computations of $\boldsymbol{\pi}$ in (1) and $\overline{\mathbf{P}}_s$ in (3). This is because the multiplications and additions need only be done when both operands are nonzero.

2.1 Efficient Inversion Algorithms

Efficient algorithms for computing $\mathbf{B}^{-1}$ in product form are based on the fact that, although the basis inverse is unique, its representation as a product of elementary matrices is not. Thus a representation can be sought which has certain desirable features, e.g., is sparse. The details of modern inversion algorithms are too complex to be given here; see Lasdon [1970a] and Hellerman [1971] for a more complete discussion. The basic ideas, however, are fairly simple. In selecting pivot elements, a prime consideration is to minimize the number of new nonzero elements created by the pivot. To do this, define the row count as the number of nonzero elements a row has in admissible columns, and similarly for the column count. Initially, all rows and columns are admissible. Since pivoting adds a multiple of the pivot row to other rows, pivot rows with low row counts will generate few new nonzero elements. In fact, a row with row count of one will generate no new nonzeros. If such a row can be found, it and the column containing the nonzero element are marked inadmissible, and the row and column counts are decreased to reflect their removal. Then a search is made for another row count of one. A similar procedure can be carried out looking for columns with column counts of one. Doing this locates a triangular subsection of the matrix; in many practical cases, the basis is almost completely triangular. The remaining portion (the "kernel") requires more careful treatment. The reader is referred to the references given above.

2.2 LU Decomposition

The LU decomposition of a nonsingular matrix $\mathbf{B}$ is [Bartels, 1969]: $\mathbf{B} = \mathbf{LU}$; where $\mathbf{L}$ and $\mathbf{U}$ are, respectively, nonsingular lower and upper triangular matrices. The inverse is then given by $\mathbf{B}^{-1} = \mathbf{U}^{-1}\mathbf{L}^{-1}$. Inversion routines based on the ideas described earlier yield $\mathbf{B}^{-1}$ in this form (to within a permutation of the rows) by giving the product form of $\mathbf{U}^{-1}$ and $\mathbf{L}^{-1}$. While the eta columns in this product form are usually quite sparse immediately after inversion, subsequent simplex iterations usually produce eta vectors of increasing density. This causes the eta file to quickly exceed core storage, and increases computation time. A modification which significantly eases this problem is described by Forrest [1972]. Instead of merging the eta files for $\mathbf{U}^{-1}$ and $\mathbf{L}^{-1}$ as in a standard product form code, these files are maintained and updated separately. When a new column enters the basis, each of these files is updated to yield $\mathbf{U}^{-1}$ and $\mathbf{L}^{-1}$ for the new basis. Details of the updating may be found in the reference above.

The **LU** decomposition approach has been incorporated into the UMPIRE mathematical programming system, marketed in the United States by Computer Sciences Corporation. Results quoted by Forrest [1972] show a reduction in the growth of new nonzero elements by about 90%, a reduction in the total length of the eta file by 60-70%, and an increase in simplex iterations per hour of about 40%, all in comparison with a standard product form code. Because of statistics such as these it is likely that future LP codes will incorporate these ideas.

2.3 "Supersparsity"

An idea originated by Kalan [1971] enables much larger problems to be solved all in core than was possible previously. It is based on the fact that the number of different nonzero elements in a typical matrix is usually much less than the total number of nonzeros. The value one is particularly common. This can be exploited by storing only the unique values, and maintaining a pointer in all matrix positions containing the same unique value which points to the computer core address containing that value. The pointers can be stored in a fraction of a computer word–perhaps in only two 8-bit bytes, rather than in the 4 bytes required to store a matrix element in a single precision word. Examples in [Kalan, 1971] suggest that the number of unique nonzero elements in LP matrices arising in practice is of the same order of magnitude as the number of columns, and is often less than the number of columns. Hence great economies in storage are possible using this scheme.

Even further economies are possible if another of Kalan's ideas is used. Recall that the eta vectors which represent the basis inverse are formed from the vectors $\overline{\mathbf{P}}_s$ defined in Eq. (3), using the formulas

$$\eta_i = \begin{cases} -\alpha_i/\alpha_r, & i \neq r \\ 1/\alpha_r, & i = r \end{cases}$$

where the α_i are elements of $\overline{\mathbf{P}}_s$, and row r is the pivot row. These eta vectors are used only in the computations of Eqs. (2) ($\boldsymbol{\pi}$) and (4) ($\overline{\mathbf{P}}_s$), and these computations may be coded so that the divisions by α_r and the sign reversals are incorporated in them. Hence the vectors $\overline{\mathbf{P}}_s$ can be stored and used to represent the basis inverse. As noted in Section 2.1, major portions of LP bases are triangular, e.g., those columns $\mathbf{P}_i$ not located in the "kernel." For such columns, $\mathbf{P}_i$ and $\overline{\mathbf{P}}_i$ are identical, so these columns can be stored using pointers to point to positions within the original coefficient matrix. In fact, as shown by Hellerman [1971], most kernel columns of the inverse can also be stored in this way. Thus the inverse may be represented using only a small number of nonzero elements not contained in the original coefficient matrix.

2.4 Multiple Pricing

The fact that the relative costs $\bar{c}_j$ must be computed separately in the RSM yields a great deal of flexibility. In product form codes, computation time depends largely on the number of times the complete problem data $(\mathbf{A}, \mathbf{b}, \mathbf{c})$ must be consulted. This is certainly true when the data is kept in auxiliary storage, since it must then be transferred to core each time. Let each referral to original problem data be termed a "pass." The number of passes can be reduced by the following tactic, called multiple pricing or suboptimization. Compute the multipliers $\boldsymbol{\pi}$, and, searching only through a subset of the nonbasic columns, find those with the k most negative reduced costs, $k > 1$. Transform these columns, and form a restricted problem (in core) involving only the current basic variables and these k columns. Apply the standard SM to this problem, again in core. When the restricted problem is solved, begin another pass.

Solving the restricted problem requires no referrals to the original data, and can yield large decreases in objective value. The number of passes, hence overall solution time, can be significantly reduced. In the current IBM MPSX-370 linear programming code, k is an integer between 1 and 9. Too high a value for k can slow convergence by wasting time on columns which are relatively unprofitable.

3. GENERALIZED UPPER BOUNDING

Generalized Upper Bounding (GUB) is an efficient specialization of the SM for LPs with the following structure

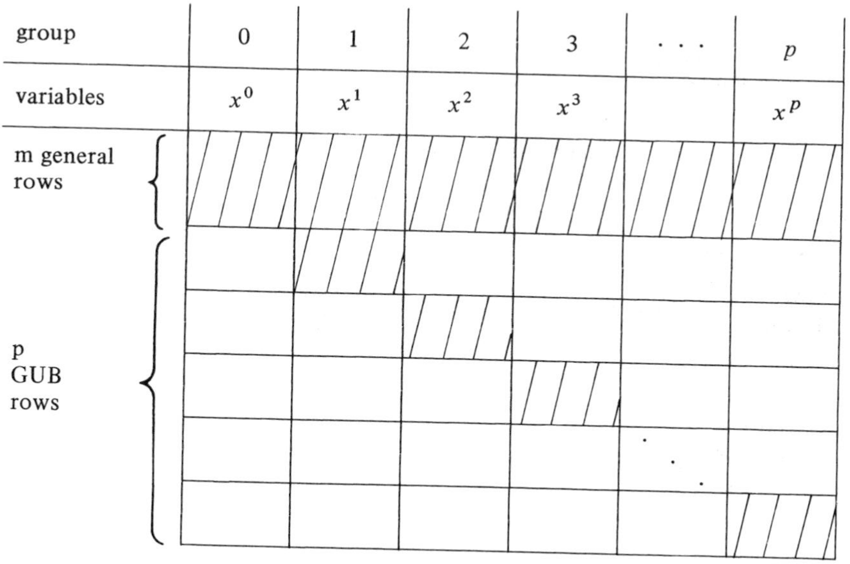
group
0
1
2
3
. . .
p
variables
x^0
x^1
x^2
x^3
x^p
m general rows
p GUB rows

There are m constraints of arbitrary structure and p constraints, called GUB rows, which contain no variables in common. The set of variables associated with each GUB row is called a group. The coefficients of the GUB rows are arbitrary and the relation between a GUB row and its right hand side may be =, $\leqslant$, $\geqslant$, or range ($\leqslant a, \geqslant b$). The GUB rows are often shown as having all coefficients equal to plus or minus one. This can be achieved by scaling the variables.

Almost all LP models contain some GUB rows and, in many, the majority of rows are of this type. Material balance equations, which have the form 111 . . . 1 -1-1-1 . . . -1 = 0; can be taken as GUB rows. These are quite common in LP models, and are often used to define new variables in terms of variables previously defined. Equations of the form 111 . . . 1 $\{\substack{=\\ \leqslant}\}$ b; can arise from convexity constraints in a Dantzig-Wolfe master program (see Section 5) or in the λ-form of separable programming [Hadley, 1964]. These have the equality relation and $b = 1$. Constraints which require that the total amount of a product manufactured or shipped either satisfy a certain demand or not exceed a specified supply also have this structure. Hence transportation, generalized transportation, and transshipment problems are GUB problems, where the GUB rows may be taken as either the supply or the demand rows. In many transportation problems, the number of destinations (customers or distribution centers) is much greater than the number of origins (factories or factory warehouses). Such problems have a majority of GUB rows. Many LPs include distribution activities, so these statements apply to general LP models as well.

GUB solves such problems while maintaining a "working basis" of dimension $m \times m$. This is a substantial saving when p is large compared to m. All the quantities needed to carry out an iteration of the SM, e.g., the values of the basic variables, simplex multipliers, and the representation of the incoming column in terms of the basic columns, are derived from the corresponding quantities associated with the working basis. The details of the algorithm will not be given here. Derivations may be found in Lasdon [1970b] and Dantzig [1967]. Information on how GUB can reduce storage requirements and solution time is given in Orchard-Hays [1974]. In Hirshfeld [1972], the MPS III GUB code of Management Science Systems, Inc., Rockville, Maryland (1974 version) is compared with the MPSX LP code of IBM. Results showed that, if $\frac{1}{2}$ of the rows are GUB rows, MPS III solved problems in about $\frac{1}{3}$ the time of MPSX, while if 80 to 90% of the rows are GUB rows, the ratio of solution times is about $\frac{1}{10}$. Experience on specific problems is given. Most commercial LP codes are now available with GUB, either as part of the package or as an enhancement that can be leased at extra cost.

In the remainder of this section, we formulate a variety of problems that contain GUB rows. These formulations are of interest in themselves, since they include many practical problems, and they also serve to illustrate the wide applicability of GUB.

3.1 Capacity Constrained Resource Allocation

The multi-item scheduling problems formulated in Manne [1958] and Dzielinski [1965] may be imbedded in the following class of resource allocation problems. Let there be I activities, indexed by i, and a single resource to be allocated to these activities in each of T time periods, indexed by t. Let x_{it} be the level of activity i in time period t and define

$$\mathbf{X}_i = (x_{i1}, \ldots, x_{iT}), \qquad i = 1, \ldots, I \tag{7}$$

Associated with each vector $\mathbf{X}_i$ is a cost, $c_i(\mathbf{X}_i)$. Activity i uses an amount $y_{it}(\mathbf{X}_i)$ of the resource in period t, the resource availability in that time period being b_t. Define

$$\mathbf{Y}_i(\mathbf{X}_i) = (y_{i1}(\mathbf{X}_i), \ldots, y_{iT}(\mathbf{X}_i)) \tag{8}$$

and

$$\mathbf{b} = (b_1, \ldots, b_T) \tag{9}$$

Each activity has its own technological constraints, symbolized by

$$\mathbf{X}_i \in S_i, \qquad i = 1, \ldots, I \tag{10}$$

The problem of optimal allocation is to

$$\text{minimize} \sum_{i=1}^{I} c_i(\mathbf{X}_i) \tag{11}$$

subject to

$$\sum_{i=1}^{I} \mathbf{Y}_i(\mathbf{X}_i) \leqslant \mathbf{b} \tag{12}$$

and

$$\mathbf{X}_i \in S_i, \qquad i = 1, \ldots, I. \tag{13}$$

In the problems of Manne [1958] and Dzielinski [1965], x_{it} is the quantity of item i produced in time period t, i.e., the lot size, S_i is the set of nonnegative production schedules for item i, which, for given demands, yield nonnegative inventory levels, $c_i(\mathbf{X}_i)$ is the sum of setup plus inventory costs over time for item i, and the resource is labor. In the latter reference, there may be a number of different resources, e.g., labor classes, and their availabilities are decision variables, with associated costs of hiring and firing. For simplicity, these alternatives are not considered here, although their incorporation poses no real difficulty.

Assume, now, that for each i the set of elements of S_i which need be considered as candidates for optimality in Problems (11)-(13) is finite, with the jth candidate denoted by X_{ij}. The set of all such candidates is denoted by V_i. This assumption is valid in Dzielinski [1965] by virtue of Mannes dominance theorem [Manne, 1958]. In the problem of Section 3.2, the S_i are finite to begin with. Assume further that $I > T$. Under these assumptions, an approximate solution to Problems (11)-(13) may be obtained by solving the following LP:

$$\text{minimize} \sum_{i,j} c_{ij}\theta_{ij} \tag{14}$$

subject to

$$\sum_{i,j} Y_{ij}\theta_{ij} \leqslant b \tag{15}$$

$$\sum_{j} \theta_{ij} = 1, \qquad i = 1, \ldots, I, \quad \theta_{ij} \geqslant 0 \tag{16}$$

where

$$c_{ij} = c_i(X_{ij}), \qquad Y_{ij} = Y_i(X_{ij})$$

If the θ_{ij} are restricted to be integers, the optimal solution of Problems (11)-(13) results. For the Problems (14)-(15) all b.f.s.'s have the following property [Lasdon, 1970c]: the number of indices i for which exactly one θ_{ij} is positive (and hence one) is at least $I - T$. Thus Problems (14)-(16) provide a good approximate solution to Problems (11)-(13) when the number of items, I, is substantially greater than the number of time periods, T. In this case, GUB can be used to advantage, since the I constraints (Eq. (16)) are GUB rows.

3.2 A Multi-Item Scheduling Problem

A specialization of the model of the previous sections may be found in Lasdon and Terjung [1971]. This involves the production of I items over T time periods, with a specified number of machines available to produce these items. Demands for each item in each time period are assumed known. Costs are: (a) inventory holding and storage costs and (b) setup costs. Setups occur when a given machine is changed from the production of one item to the production of another. We assume that any machine can, if suitably set up, produce any of the items, and that the setup cost is independent of which two items are involved in the changeover. A machine is set up to produce an item by installing in the machine a piece of equipment particular to the item (e.g., dies). The problem is to allocate the machines to the items so that the sum of inventory and setup costs over all items is minimized.

This problem fits the formulation Eqs. (11)-(13), quite nicely. The variables x_{it} are the number of machines used to produce item i in period t, while b_t is the number of machines available. The function $\mathbf{Y}_i(\mathbf{X}_i)$ is simply $\mathbf{X}_i$. The cost c_i is

$$c_i(\mathbf{X}_i) = p_s \sum_{t=1}^{T} (x_{it} - x_{i,t-1})_+ + \sum_{t=1}^{T} \gamma_{it}(v_{it}) \tag{17}$$

where the first term is the setup cost, p_s is the relative cost of a setup, the second term is the inventory cost, and v_{it} is the inventory level of item i in period t, based on the forecasted values of future demand. The function $(x)_+$ equals x if $x > 0$ and zero if $x \leqslant 0$. The functions γ_{it} represent holding costs for $v_{it} > 0$ and shortage costs for $v_{it} < 0$, and may have any convenient functional form. Finally, the set S_i is the set of all vectors $\mathbf{X}_i$ whose components x_{it} are nonnegative integers satisfying the constraints that (a) they be less than or equal to the number of dies available for item i and (b) that the inventory levels v_{it} lie between given upper and lower bounds.

For this problem, the LP, Eqs. (14)-(17), assumes the form

$$\text{minimize } \sum_{i,j} c_{ij}\theta_{ij} \tag{18}$$

subject to

$$\sum_{i,j} X_{ij}\theta_{ij} \leqslant b \tag{19}$$

$$\sum_{j} \theta_{ij} = 1, \qquad \text{all } i, \quad \theta_{ij} \geqslant 0 \tag{20}$$

Solution of this model is considered in Section 4.

3.3 Production and Distribution Problems

Other GUB models are described in Hirshfeld [1970]. One which appears often in practice has the form: maximize u_1; subject to

$$u_i \quad + \sum_{j=1}^{n_0} a_j^i x_j + \sum_{p=1}^{P} \sum_{k=1}^{n_p} a_{kp}^i x_{kp} = b_i, \qquad i = 1, \ldots, m$$

$$\sum_{k=1}^{n_p} x_{kp} \qquad = g_p, \qquad p = 1, \ldots, P$$

Logical variables	raw material production activities	order filling activities

where b_i = amount of resource i available; g_p = customer demand for product p; x_{kp} = amount of customer p's demand produced by the kth order filling activity. Different indices k could represent alternate ways of production at one plant, or production at different plants. The objective is generally cost minimization. Since P is often much larger than m, GUB has a significant advantage in solving such problems.

Extension of the above to two or more plants and time periods leads to truly large problems. The gross features of such a model extending over two time periods are described by Lasdon [1974]. The activities are raw material acquisition, production, shipments to warehouses, shipments to customers, and storage. Constraints include limited raw material availability, production resources, and storage capacity for raw materials at plants and for products at warehouses. There are also raw material balance equations, which relate raw material acquisition, production, and raw material storage. Some acquisition activities may produce products which are sent directly to warehouses, e.g., production of field trimmed lumber at a location where timber is felled. Production balance equations relate production and shipments to warehouses and customers. Warehouse balance equations relate amounts shipped to and stored at warehouses, and customer shipments.

The GUB rows require satisfaction of customer demands, and of limited storage capacities at plants and warehouses. Additional GUB rows may be present in the production and raw material capacity constraints. According to Hirshfeld, problems of this form having up to 4000 rows have been solved. Integrated planning models of this kind have, in many cases, not been formulated previously because of their size. They comprise one of the most exciting application areas for GUB today.

3.4 Extensions of GUB

The GUB algorithm has been extended to problems having the structure

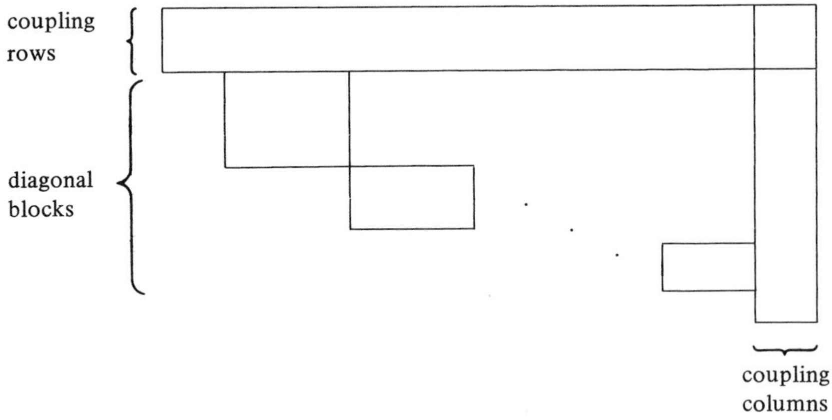

The blocks may represent activities of different plants or corporate divisions, or activities in different time periods. The coupling rows may express limitations on shared resources or demands which require production of more than one plant, while the coupling columns may result from inventory activities or from the shipment of goods from one plant to another. If there are no coupling columns, extended GUB solves such problems while maintaining only an m by m working basis inverse, and inverses from each of the blocks. As with GUB, the algorithm operates exactly as the primal SM would, but the basis inverse is maintained in compact form. Details are given by Lasdon [1970d]. If coupling columns are present, the working basis may be somewhat larger and the algorithm becomes more complicated–see Hartman [1970]. Dual forms of these algorithms have also been developed–see Lasdon [1970e], and Grigoriadis [1973]. As of 1974, to the author's knowledge, none of these algorithms have been implemented in a commercially available code. However, some development work is currently being done, and "extended GUB" algorithms may become available in the near future.

An alternative procedure for solving block-diagonal problems with coupling rows, the Dantzig-Wolfe decomposition principle, is described in Section 5.

4. COLUMN GENERATION

Consider a LP (whose objective is to be minimized) with columns $\mathbf{p}_j$ and cost coefficients c_j. Let $\mathbf{B}$ be a feasible basis for this problem, and let $\boldsymbol{\pi}$ be the vector of simplex multipliers associated with this basis. To improve the current b.f.s. we "price out" the nonbasic columns by forming their relative cost coefficients $\bar{c}_j = c_j - \boldsymbol{\pi}\mathbf{p}_j$. If a negative $\bar{c}_j$ can be found then, barring degeneracy, the current objective value can be reduced by introducing the associated column into the basis via a pivot transformation.

If there are many columns, i.e., from several thousands to several millions, then finding min $\bar{c}_j$ by computing each $\bar{c}_j$ and comparing may be tedious, if not impossible. Fortunately, in such large problems, the set of all columns generally has a well-defined structure, due to the structure of the real-world situation giving rise to the problem. This is almost always true, and fortunately so, since otherwise the task of gathering unordered numerical data to specify all the columns would be hopeless.

In general, then, let us assume that all columns, $\mathbf{p}_j$, are drawn from a set, S, which typically is the set of all $\mathbf{m}$-vectors satisfying some system of equations or inequalities. The column to enter the basis may then be chosen by solving the subproblem $\min_{\mathbf{p}_j \in S} c(\mathbf{p}_j) - \boldsymbol{\pi}\mathbf{p}_j$; where $c(\mathbf{p}_j) \equiv c_j$ is a given function of $\mathbf{p}_j$. Depending on the structure of S and the form of $c(\cdot)$, a variety of techniques may be used to solve this subproblem, e.g., LP, DP, etc. This approach is called column generation because, in solving the subproblem, only a small subset of columns in S are typically examined, and these are generated when needed. Thus none of the columns need be kept in computer storage, a definite advantage for large problems.

4.1 The Stock Cutting Problem

Consider the problem of cutting an unlimited number of pieces of stock of various lengths (for example, rolls of paper) so that at least n_i pieces of length l_i are furnished, $i = 1, \ldots, I$. The objective is to meet the demands, n_i, while minimizing the total number of rolls that must be cut. Since cutting each roll involves some waste, this keeps total waste at a low level.

Assume for simplicity, that all the pieces available for cutting have length l. If $l_i \leqslant l$, $i = 1, \ldots, I$, the problem has a solution. Define a cutting pattern as a particular way of cutting a length of stock, e.g., a_1 pieces of length l_1, a_2 pieces of length l_2, etc. A cutting pattern is thus uniquely determined by the vector $\mathbf{A} = (a_1 a_2, \ldots, a_I)$. There are a finite number of cutting patterns, although this number may be very large. The problem may be stated: specify the number of times each cutting pattern should be used so that all demands are met and the total number of rolls used is minimized.

Let j index the various cutting patterns and define a_{ij} = number of pieces of length l_i cut by pattern j; $\mathbf{p}_j = (a_{1j}, \ldots, a_{Ij})$, a vector describing the jth cutting pattern; x_j = number of times pattern j is used; $\mathbf{n} = (n_1, \ldots, n_I)$, a vector of demands for lengths $l_1 \cdots l_I$. Then the constraints that all demands must be met become $\sum_j \mathbf{p}_j x_j \geqslant \mathbf{n}$, $x_j \geqslant 0$, x_j integer. The objective function is: minimize $z = \sum_j x_j$; which minimizes the total number of pieces of length l cut.

The problem is very difficult to solve if the x_j must be integers, so this constraint is dropped. In many problems, especially those with high demands, the optimal fractional values of x_j are large enough so that little is lost in rounding to integers. However, solution is still difficult, since the number of columns $\mathbf{p}_j$ may be very large. For example, if the stock to be cut has length $l = 2000$ inches and there are demands for 40 different lengths from 20 to 80 inches, the number of possible patterns could easily exceed 10 to 100 million [Gilmore, 1963]. This, however, may be dealt with by pricing out the columns and defining suitable subproblems.

The relative cost coefficient for a nonbasic variable x_j is $\bar{c}_j = 1 - \sum_i \pi_i a_{ij}$; with the π_i simplex multipliers for the constraints. In order that a vector $\mathbf{A}$ describe a legitimate cutting pattern its coordinates must satisfy

$$a_i = \text{nonnegative integer}$$

$$\sum_{i=1}^{I} l_i a_i \leqslant l.$$

Thus the problem of minimizing $\bar{c}_j$ over all possible columns becomes that of maximizing $\sum_i \pi_i a_i$; subject to the above constraints. Problems of this form are called knapsack problems (KP) because of the following interpretation: a_i is the number of pieces of equipment of weight l_i and relative usefulness π_i to be carried on a camping trip in a knapsack which will hold at most a total weight l. Such problems may be solved efficiently by a number of algorithms, e.g., DP [Balinski, 1965]. Gilmore and Gomory describe an algorithm in [Gilmore, 1963] reported to be approximately five times faster than the standard DP recursion.

If the optimal knapsack value is v, then the simplex criterion for possible improvement, min $\bar{c}_j < 0$, becomes $v \leqslant 1$, and the corresponding pattern vector is formed and enters the basis. If $v \geqslant 1$ and if the reduced costs of the slack variables are nonnegative the current solution is optimal.

In [Gilmore, 1961] and [Gilmore, 1963] this formulation was successfully applied to a number of practical problems from the paper industry. Results are summarized in [Lasdon, 1970h]. Problems with up to 40 lengths, l_i, were solved, and minimal percentage wastes of one-half to one percent were achieved. In addition, some devices to speed computation were tested. One of these, the "median method," was derived to ease the following: in bringing the column with min $\bar{c}_j$ into the basis, one obtains maximum decrease of z per unit increase in x_j, but does not necessarily obtain the largest possible decrease in z. This is because x_j may be small, and the decrease in z is $\bar{c}_j x_j$. Often less negative $\bar{c}_j$ may lead to larger x_j. This requires too much computation to correct in general, but in this problem something could be done. In many stock cutting problems the demands n_i vary widely. Consider a cutting pattern containing both high and low demand lengths. The number of times this pattern may be used tends to be limited by the lowest demand, since otherwise this cutting pattern alone would exceed this demand. To permit large x_j and large changes in z, lengths were divided into a high and a low demand group (greater and less than the median demand). Every other pivot step, a KP was solved with the variables a_i for the low demand group set to zero. This tended to yield patterns with large x_j, and proved of much value.

In [Gilmore, 1963], this median method, with complete solution of the KP, (call this alternative (1)), was compared with the alternatives (2) median method but incomplete knapsack maximization, stopping with the first knapsack solution yielding $\bar{c}_j < 0$ and (3) same as (2) but no median method. The results were that (1) required moderately less computation time than (2), and much less computation time than (3) to find an optimal solution. Hence, in this case, finding min $\bar{c}_j$ is best, although this question has been discussed elsewhere (e.g., [Beale, 1965]) with varying conclusions. If a good approximation to min $\bar{c}_j$ can be found with significantly reduced effort, computation time can be reduced (see Section 4.2).

Stock cutting problems in two or more dimensions (cutting sheets or rectangles of stock) can also be posed as LPs with many columns, although the subproblems which generate the columns are harder to solve. Some two dimensional problems may be decomposed into a sequence of one dimensional knapsack solutions. For details, the reader is referred to [Gilmore, 1965].

4.2 Multi-Item Scheduling

Here we apply column generation to the multi-item scheduling problem of Section 3.2. The LP (18)-(20) has, for realistic problems, a tremendous number of columns, one for each possible production schedule for each item. Let **B** be a basis matrix for (18)-(20) and let $(\boldsymbol{\pi}_1, \boldsymbol{\pi}_2)$ be the simplex multipliers of this basis, with $\boldsymbol{\pi}_1$ associated with the constraints (Eq. (19)) and $\boldsymbol{\pi}_2$ with Eq. (20). Pricing out the column associated with θ_{ij}, the reduced cost coefficient is $\bar{c}_{ij} = c_{ij} - \boldsymbol{\pi}_1 \mathbf{X}_{ij} - \pi_{2i}$. To choose a column to enter the basis, we seek $\min \bar{c}_{ij} = \min_i \min_j \bar{c}_{ij}$. The inner minimization above may be accomplished by solving the subproblem:

$$\text{minimize} \quad c_i(\mathbf{X}_{ij}) - \boldsymbol{\pi}_1 \mathbf{X}_{ij};$$

or, since $\mathbf{X}_{ij}$ is an arbitrary element of the set S_i

$$\text{minimize} \quad c_i(\mathbf{X}_i) - \boldsymbol{\pi}_1 \mathbf{X}_i \tag{21}$$

subject to

$$\mathbf{X}_i \in S_i. \tag{22}$$

Note that these subproblems are single-item production scheduling problems, with a penalty term—$\boldsymbol{\pi}_1 \mathbf{X}_i$—for using the scarce resource of available machines. The vector—$\boldsymbol{\pi}_1$—contains the shadow prices for machine use in each of the T time periods. Each subproblem may be solved by DP with two state variables, x_{it} and v_{it}. Since the initial states x_{i0} are given, a forward recursion is used.

In [Lasdon, 1971], a number of multi-item scheduling test problems were solved. In solving them it was found that use of a full set of artificial variables in phase I led to very poor starting points for phase II. To avoid this, the single-item subproblems were first solved with $\boldsymbol{\pi}_1 = \mathbf{0}$. If these solutions satisfy the limitations on machine availability, constraints (19), they are optimal. If not, an initial b.f.s. is constructed using a single θ_{ij} for each of the subproblem solutions, plus T slack and artificial variables. The inverse of a basis so formed is easily found without numerical inversion, and the procedure leads to much better initial points for phase II.

Four test problems were solved by each of three methods. Method (1) is the Dantzig-Wolfe decomposition algorithm of Section 5. Method (2) is the column-generation approach with GUB in which, at each simplex iteration, the column yielding $\min_{i,j} \bar{c}_{ij}$ is generated and entered into the basis. That is, I DP subprob-

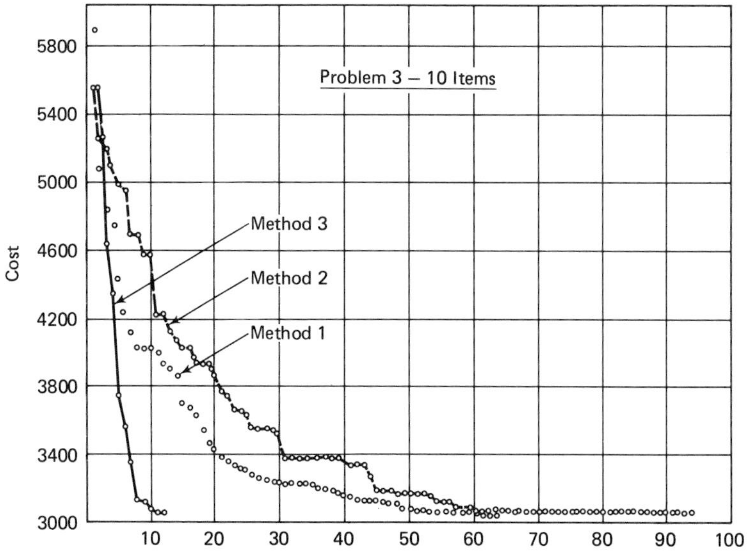

Fig. 1. Cost versus the number of iterations in Phase 2.

lems are solved, but only the "best" of the columns generated is used. In method (3), all I columns generated by the subproblems are taken as the non-basic columns of a "restricted master" LP, which has the current basic columns as its initial solution. A partial solution of this LP is obtained (all columns leaving the basis are dropped). In this method, many of the proposals generated by the subproblems may enter the basis before the subproblems are resolved. This is an application of the multiple pricing strategy of Section 2.4, in which the best column from each of I sections of the LP tableau is found, each containing the columns which represent schedules for a particular item.

Figure 1 shows a typical comparison of these three methods on a ten-item problem. Methods 1 and 2 both exhibit slow convergence near the optimum. Method 3 is far superior. Even though this method solves (perhaps partially) an LP at each iteration, while the other two do not, solution time is still approximately proportional to iteration count, because solving the restricted LP is much faster than solving the I subproblems.

A number of other ideas to shorten computations were also tested. One of these involves solving the subproblems by a DP algorithm with only one state variable, the other (the variable x_{it}) being fixed at its initial value x_{i0}. This is faster by factors of two or more, and often yields either optimal solutions or good approximations to them. It is useful as long as this or any other technique yields columns with negative reduced cost. Using this option until it met the optimality test, then switching to the correct, two-state variable algorithm, reduces running time by about a factor of two.

An extended version of the model described above now forms the core of a production scheduling and inventory control system currently being used by a major U.S. tire manufacturer in four of its plants. The extensions and computational experience are described in [Lasdon and Terjung, 1971].

5. THE DANTZIG-WOLFE DECOMPOSITION PRINCIPLE

This section describes an algorithm for solving LPs of the form

$$\text{minimize} \quad z = c_0 x_0 + c_1 \mathbf{x}_1 + c_2 \mathbf{x}_2 + \cdots + c_p \mathbf{x}_p \tag{23}$$

subject to

$$m \text{ coupling rows} \left\{ A_0 x_0 + A_1 \mathbf{x}_1 + A_2 \mathbf{x}_2 + \cdots + A_p \mathbf{x}_p = \mathbf{b} \right. \tag{24}$$

$$\begin{array}{r} p \text{ block} \\ \text{constraints} \\ \text{each block } \mathbf{B}_i \\ \text{has } m_i \\ \text{rows} \end{array} \left\{ \begin{array}{lll} \mathbf{B}_1 \mathbf{x}_1 & & = \mathbf{b}_1 \\ & \mathbf{B}_2 \mathbf{x}_2 & = \mathbf{b}_2 \\ & & \vdots \\ & & \mathbf{B}_p \mathbf{x}_p = \mathbf{b}_p \end{array} \right. \tag{25}$$

$$\mathbf{x}_1 \geqslant 0, \quad \mathbf{x}_2 \geqslant 0, \ldots, \quad \mathbf{x}_p \geqslant 0$$

For information on how such problems may arise, see Section 3.4 and [Lasdon, 1970f].

The dual of this problem has diagonal blocks and coupling columns. Since a solution to the dual of a LP is readily obtained if a (basic) solution to the primal is available, methods for solving problems with coupling rows can be applied to those with coupling columns and vice versa.

5.1 Decomposition Algorithm

Let $S_i = \{\mathbf{x}_i \mid \mathbf{B}_i \mathbf{x}_i = \mathbf{b}_i, \mathbf{x}_i \geqslant \mathbf{0}\}$ be the set of all feasible solutions to the ith block. Assume S_i is bounded and nonempty, and let $\mathbf{x}_i^j$ be the jth extreme point of S_i. Then any $\mathbf{x}_i$ in S_i may be written as a convex combination of the $\mathbf{x}_i^j$

$$\mathbf{x}_i = \sum_j \lambda_{ij} \mathbf{x}_i^j \tag{27}$$

where the weights λ_{ij} satisfy

$$\sum_j \lambda_{ij} = 1, \qquad \lambda_{ij} \geqslant 0 \tag{28}$$

For a proof of this result see [Lasdon, 1970g]. Substituting Eq. (27) into the objective and coupling constraints, Eqs. (23)-(24) and adding the convexity constraints, Eq. (28) transforms the LP Eqs. (23)-(25) into a new LP with variables λ_{ij}, called the master program

$$\text{minimize} \quad z = \sum_{i,j} (\mathbf{c}_i \mathbf{x}_i^j)\, \lambda_{ij} \tag{29}$$

subject to

$$\sum_{i,j} (\mathbf{A}_i \mathbf{x}_i^j)\, \lambda_{ij} = \mathbf{b} \tag{30}$$

$$\sum_j \lambda_{ij} = 1, \qquad i = 1, \ldots, p, \quad \lambda_{ij} \geqslant 0. \tag{31}$$

Solving this master program is completely equivalent to solving the original problem. Its solution yields optimal weights λ_{ij}, which are then substituted into Eq. (27) to yield optimal values for the vectors $\mathbf{x}_i$.

The master program has only $m + p$ rows, compared to the $m + \sum_{i=1}^{p} m_i$ rows of the original problem, a sizable saving if $\sum_i m_i$ is large. It also has one column for extreme point of each diagonal block, which will number in the hundreds of thousands or even millions for problems of any size. Rather than tabulate all these columns in advance, we use the column generation concept of Section 4, creating columns to enter the basis as they are needed. To see how this is done, consider the relative cost coefficient, $\bar{c}_{ij}$, for the variable λ_{ij}. Given a feasible basis $\mathbf{B}$ for the master program, let $\boldsymbol{\pi}$ be the simplex multipliers of this basis for the coupling rows, Eq. (30), and let π_i be the multiplier for the ith convexity row, Eq. (31). Then

$$\bar{c}_{ij} = \mathbf{c}_i \mathbf{x}_i^j - \boldsymbol{\pi} \mathbf{A}_i \mathbf{x}_i^j - \mu_i \tag{32}$$

To find a profitable column to enter the basis, we wish to find for each i

$$\min_j \bar{c}_{ij} = \min_j \, [(\mathbf{c}_i - \boldsymbol{\pi} \mathbf{A}_i)\, \mathbf{x}_i^j] - \mu_i \tag{33}$$

Recall that x_i^j is an extreme point of S_i, and note that the quantity being minimized in Eq. (33) is linear in x_i^j. Since a LP with bounded nonempty constraint set always has an optimal solution at an extreme point, the minimization in Eq. (33) may be accomplished by solving the subproblem

$$\text{minimize} \quad (\mathbf{c}_i - \boldsymbol{\pi} A_i)\, \mathbf{x}_i \tag{34}$$

subject to

$$\mathbf{B}_i \mathbf{x}_i = \mathbf{b}_i, \qquad \mathbf{x}_i \geqslant \mathbf{0} \tag{35}$$

To find the column yielding $\min \bar{c}_{ij}$ for a given i, solve this subproblem, obtaining a solution $\mathbf{x}_i^*$, and optimal objective value z_i^*. Then

$$\min_j \bar{c}_{ij} = z_i^* - \mu_i \tag{36}$$

If Eq. (36) is negative the column formed from x_i^* will (barring degeneracy), reduce the objective of the master program when entered into the basis. If, for each i, Eq. (33) is nonnegative, the current master program solution is optimal.

Summarizing, the Dantzig-Wolfe decomposition algorithm is an iterative procedure involving the master program Eqs. (29)-(31) and the subproblems Eqs. (34)-(35). Given an initial feasible basis, the master program sends the simplex multipliers $\boldsymbol{\pi}$ to the subproblems, which use them to form their objective functions. Solution of the subproblems yields new columns for the master program. Incorporating these into the master program basis yields a new basis and new simplex multipliers with which to repeat the procedure. Since this process is the simplex algorithm, then, if proper precautions are taken to avoid cycling, it will converge to an optimal solution in a finite number of iterations.

Note that, due to the convexity rows, the master program has GUB structure, and may be solved by the GUB algorithm of Section 3.

5.2 Economic Interpretation

This decomposition algorithm coordinates the subproblems by means of a pricing system. The simplex multipliers $-\boldsymbol{\pi}$ are "shadow prices" for the scarce resources. (See Section 5, Chapter II-1) If the objective is cost in dollars, π_i has units of dollars per unit of resource i. The subproblem objective, Eq. (34), is the sum of two terms: $c_i x_i$, which measures the direct cost to the subsystem of choosing activity levels x_i and $-\boldsymbol{\pi}\mathbf{A}_i\mathbf{x}_i$, which is the product of the price vector $-\boldsymbol{\pi}$ and the vector of resource amounts used, $\mathbf{A}_i\mathbf{x}_i$. This term represents a charge to the subsystem for using the scarce resources. By increasing the prices π_i for resources in short supply and reducing the prices for resources in excess supply, the master program causes the subproblems to create proposals which it can incorporate into an overall optimal plan.

5.3 Computations

Computational experience with the Dantzig-Wolfe decomposition algorithm has been mixed. Many investigators, e.g., Lasdon [1971] and Beale [1955], have reported slow convergence near the optimum. An example of this is given in Fig. (1) of Section 4.2. Others, e.g., Dzielinski [1965], have reported more favorable results. Behavior of the algorithm depends both on the problem being solved (in a largely unknown way) and on the solution strategy being used. Since the problem is one of column generation, the material in Section 4 applies. Many different strategies, combining partial or complete solution of the subproblems and solution of some or all subproblems in any one iteration, are possible. Based on the results of Sections 4.1 and 4.2, this author recommends obtaining at least near optimal solutions to the subproblems. The question of how many to solve at each cycle probably depends on data management considerations. If subproblem data is not stored in core memory, then bringing it into core will be time consuming; this argues for solution of fewer subproblems at each cycle, and for generation of columns corresponding to a number of near optimal solutions. If all data is stored in core, or if the subproblems have much data in common, then solution of all subproblems is probably preferable, with all columns generated used as nonbasic columns in a "restricted master" LP, which is solved completely. This approach was discussed in Section 4.3, and is an example of multiple pricing (see Section 2.4).

If all subproblems are solved at a given iteration, a lower bound on the optimal objective value is easily computed [Lasdon, 1970a, p. 163] $z^o \geqslant z_B + \sum_{i=1}^{p} \cdot (\min_j \bar{c}_{ij})$; where z^o and z_B are the optimal and current objective values respectively and $\min \bar{c}_{ij}$ is computed from Eq. (33). This bound may be used to terminate computations short of optimality.

As in any LP, fast convergence can depend heavily on having a good starting solution, which will generally be available if the problem is a variation on ones previously solved. If not, a reasonable starting procedure is to solve the subproblems with $\boldsymbol{\pi} = 0$. If these solutions satisfy the coupling constraints, they are optimal. Otherwise, use them, plus appropriate slack and artificial variables, in a phase I procedure. The extent to which the coupling constraints are violated by these "unconstrained optimal" solutions is a measure of how hard the problem will be to solve.

A good approximation to the optimal $\boldsymbol{\pi}$ values can also help in obtaining a good initial solution. Simply use them in the subproblem objectives, and use the solutions to form columns for an initial basis. It is interesting to note that, if the optimal $\boldsymbol{\pi}$ values were known exactly, it is possible to obtain an optimal solution to the master program without iteration. Simply solve the subproblems using the optimal $\boldsymbol{\pi}$ values and obtain all alternative optimal solutions (this is necessary, since any subproblem having two or more proposals in the optimal master program basis will have multiple optima). Then, solving the master program using only the relatively few columns so generated will yield its optimal solution.

5.4 Physical Interpretation of the Master Program

In many applications, the Dantzig-Wolfe master program has a direct interpretation as a meaningful alternative formulation of the problem. An example is the multicommodity network flow problem. As shown in [Tomlin, 1966], if the node-arc formulation of the problem (whose variables are the flows along each arc) is decomposed, the master program is the arc-chain formulation whose variables are the flows of each commodity on each chain from its source to its sink. Another example is the ship routing problem discussed in [Lasdon, 1973]. There, the variables of the original formulation are the number of trips each ship makes between each origin-destination pair. The variables of the master program are the number of trips each ship makes in traversing each simple cycle in the graph. In a problem discussed in [Jennergen, 1973] dealing with blending feedstock, the columns of the master are recipes for blends, the variables indicating how often each recipe is used.

5.5 Application to Nonlinear Subsystems

Consider the problem

$$\text{minimize} \sum_{i=1}^{p} f_i(\mathbf{x}_i)$$

subject to

$$\sum_{i=1}^{p} \mathbf{A}_i \mathbf{x}_i = b$$

$$\mathbf{x}_i \in S_i, \quad i = 1, \ldots, p$$

where f_i is a convex function of the vector x_i and S_i is a convex set. This is a nonlinear generalization of the LP Eqs. (23)-(25). Let $\{x_i^j\}$ be a set of "grid" points in S_i. Since S_i is a convex, all points of the form

$$\sum_j \lambda_{ij} x_i^j, \quad \sum_j \lambda_{ij} = 1, \quad \lambda_{ij} \geqslant 0 \tag{37}$$

are in S_i. The set of all such points, which is the convex hull of the set $\{x_i^j\}$, is called the inner linearization of S_i [Geoffrion, 1970]. An example is shown below

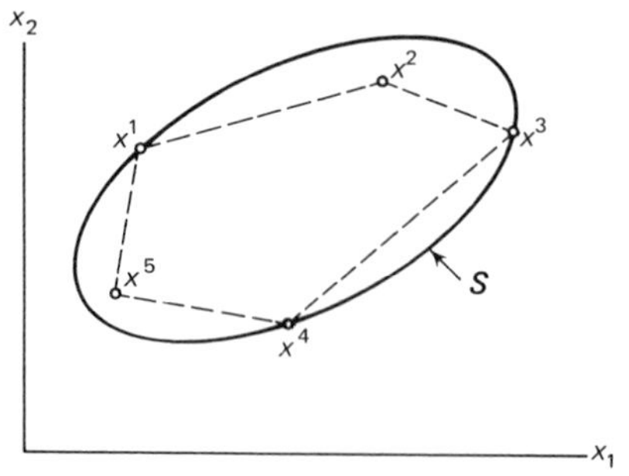

Inner linearization of a convex set.

A piecewise linear approximation to f_i over this inner linearization is [Lasdon, 1970],

$$f_i(\mathbf{x}_i) = \sum_j \lambda_{ij} f_i(x_i^j) \tag{38}$$

substituting Eqs. (37) and (38) into the original problem yields a linear master program exactly like Eqs. (29)-(34), with $f_i(x_i^j)$ replacing $\mathbf{c}_i\mathbf{x}_i^j$. This program can be solved by column generation. The subproblems are the nonlinear convex programs;

$$\text{minimize } f_i(\mathbf{x}_i) - \boldsymbol{\pi}\mathbf{A}_i\mathbf{x}_i$$

subject to

$$\mathbf{x}_i \in S_i$$

Solutions of these are used to generate columns for the master. The steps of the algorithm are precisely as in the linear case.

This nonlinear decomposition algorithm is not finitely convergent. This is because, unless S_i is polyhedral, no finite set of grid points can represent it exactly and, if f_i is not piecewise linear, Eq. (38) is only an approximation. It is proved in [Dantzig, 1963] that this algorithm will converge to an optimal solution as the number of iterations tends to infinity. Further, under the convexity assumptions, all intermediate solutions are feasible in the original problem. If some set S_i is not convex, intermediate solutions may not be feasible since the inner linearization of S_i may not lie inside S_i. Even if the final solution is feasible, it may be only a local, rather than global optimum. This may be the case also if some f_i is not convex.

A successful application of this procedure to a problem in water resources planning which does not satisfy the convexity assumptions is described in [Hall, 1970].

5.6 Current Status of Dantzig-Wolfe Decomposition

Interest in the Dantzig-Wolfe decomposition algorithm has declined steadily in the past six or seven years, after a peak in the mid-1960s. There are few, if any, commercial applications today and, of the few commercial codes that existed in the 1960s, none (to the author's knowledge) are now marketed. This situation is due in part to the erratic computational properties of the algorithm, and partly to the emergence of product form simplex and GUB codes capable of solving very large problems. In addition, the complexity of the system of computer programs needed to handle really large Dantzig-Wolfe models has hindered the use of this approach. The reader is referred to [Orchard-Hays, 1971] for a further discussion of these problems.

5.7 Acceleration via BOXSTEP

A procedure called BOXSTEP, recently developed by Marsten [1973] has improved the convergence properties of the Dantzig-Wolfe decomposition and related algorithms. Focusing on the dual of the master program Eqs. (29)-(31), BOXSTEP takes an initial simplex multiplier vector $\boldsymbol{\pi}_0$, and constrains the dual variables $\boldsymbol{\pi}$ to vary within a "box" (which can have sides of unequal length) centered at $\boldsymbol{\pi}_0$. The master program corresponding to this restricted dual has the same form as the original one, but now includes a slack and surplus variable in each row except the convexity rows. Solution of this modified master yields new $\boldsymbol{\lambda}^*, \boldsymbol{\pi}^*$. If $\boldsymbol{\pi}^*$ is interior to the box, this solution is optimal. If not, a new box (perhaps with sides of different length) is constructed centered at $\boldsymbol{\pi}^*$ and the procedure is repeated. Computational results show reductions in solution time by factors of roughly 1.5 to 2 over the standard Dantzig-Wolfe procedure (which corresponds to a single solution over a very large box). The best box size in these tests was about midway between the smallest and largest tried. Success of the procedure can probably be attributed to its damping of excessive fluctuations in the dual variables $\boldsymbol{\pi}$. The idea has general applicability, and can be profitably applied to a wide variety of algorithms.

6. LARGE SCALE NONLINEAR PROGRAMMING (NLP)

Currently, formulation and solution of large nonlinear models is much less widespread than is the use of linear models. However, advances are being made. Organizations which have used LP extensively are finding that, as mathematical programming is more widely accepted, situations requiring nonlinear models begin to occur. In the chemical industry, large nonlinear planning models have been used to study the question of allocating scarce raw materials to different product lines [Prabhakar, 1974]. The nonlinearities arise in characterizing the transformation of these raw materials into products. In the petroleum industry, nonlinear time-staged models have been used to study how to best exploit well fields which draw upon common pools of oil or gas. In product blending models, the variation of certain product properties (e.g., gasoline octane number) with the amount of certain additives (e.g., TEL lead) is nonlinear.

In this section, we discuss the two currently most popular algorithms for solving large NLPs. These are separable programming [Lasdon, 1970j] and approximation programming [Griffith and Stewart, 1961]. Both are based on linearization, in order to exploit existing LP technology.

6.1 Separable Programming

Separable programming, in its commercially available forms, applies to problems in which any nonlinear functions, f_i, which appear have the form $f_i(x_1, x_2, \ldots,$

$x_n) = \sum_{j=1}^{n} f_{ij}(x_j)$. Such functions are called separable. For each variable x_j which appears in a nonlinear function, a set of grid points $\{x_j^k\}_{k=1}^{n_j}$ is chosen. Then, each nonlinear function f_{ij} is approximated by a piecewise linear function with breaks at the grid points:

$$f_{ij} \doteq \sum_{k=1}^{n_j} \lambda_{jk} f_{ij}(x_j^k) \tag{39}$$

where

$$\sum_{k=1}^{n_j} \lambda_{jk} = 1, \qquad \lambda_{jk} \geqslant 0 \tag{40}$$

The idea is the same as was used in Section 5.5, and is shown graphically below in Fig. 2.

Replacing nonlinear f_{ij} by their approximations Eqs. (39), and adding the constraints, Eq. (40) converts a nonlinear separable program into a LP. In this program, the new variables λ_{jk} must satisfy the following condition: for each j, at most two λ_{jk} can be positive, and these must have adjacent k indices (i.e., k and $k + 1$). This ensures that linear interpolation occurs only between adjacent grid points, say x_j^2 and x_j^3 in Fig. 2, and not between x_j^1 and x_j^3. It is shown in (Lasdon, 1970j) that if each nonlinear f_{ij} is convex, there is an optimal solution to the approximating LP which has this property. In addition, the global optimum to the linearized problem will be found by solving the LP. Otherwise, special branch and bound procedures must be used, or a global optimum may not be found. Such procedures are described in [Forrest, 1974].

Separable programming is available as part of many commercial LP codes. It is an efficient algorithm for problems which are mostly linear and have convex separable nonlinearities. Available codes can solve very large problems of this kind, i.e., problems with thousands of rows and many thousands of columns.

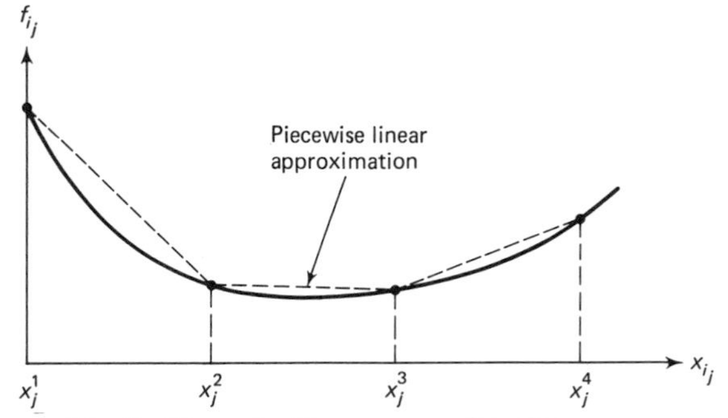

Fig. 2. Piecewise linear approximation.

6.2 Approximation Programming

Approximation programming [Griffith and Stewart, 1961] is an algorithm for solving NLPs which uses a LP code as a subroutine. It can deal with nonlinear functions of general form. Let the problem be

$$\text{minimize} \sum_{j=1}^{n} c_j x_j + g_0(y)$$

subject to

$$\sum_{j=1}^{n} a_{ij} x_j + g_i(y) = b_i, \qquad i = 1, m$$

The x_j are linear variables, $\mathbf{y}$ is an m-vector of nonlinear variables, and the g_i are nonlinear functions. All variables may have upper and lower bounds.

Assume an initial "base point" vector $\mathbf{y}_0$ is given. Each of the functions g_i is linearized about this point;

$$g_i(\mathbf{y}) \doteq g_i(\mathbf{y}_0) + \nabla g_i^T(\mathbf{y}_0)\, \Delta\mathbf{y} \tag{41}$$

where $\Delta\mathbf{y} = \mathbf{y} - \mathbf{y}_0$ and ∇g_i is the gradient vector of g_i. Replacing each g_i in the original problem by its approximation Eq. (41), reduces that problem to a LP. Of course, the approximation is accurate only for $\mathbf{y}$ close to $\mathbf{y}_0$, so upper and lower bounds on $\Delta\mathbf{y}$ must be imposed: $-\epsilon \leqslant \Delta\mathbf{y}_i \leqslant \epsilon$, $i = 1, m$. Then the LP created by replacing each g_i by its linearization is solved. The resulting values $\Delta\mathbf{y}^*$, are added to the initial base point $\mathbf{y}_0$ yielding a new base point, and the gradient vectors ∇g_i are recomputed at that point. The step-bound ϵ is reduced if necessary. The entire process is then repeated. The procedure is similar to the BOXSTEP algorithm of Section 5.6.

Geometrically, this process replaces the nonlinear problem by a linearized version, valid locally. This is solved, with the $\mathbf{y}$ variables restricted to lie in a hypercube of dimension 2ϵ, centered at the current base point. Often, the new point obtained may not be quite feasible, due to ϵ being too large. This can be corrected immediately by reducing ϵ at the new base point, or this reduction can be delayed until the terminal phase. In this phase, the current point is nearly optimal, and succeeding points oscillate about the optimum. This oscillation is damped by reducing ϵ until changes in the variables fall below some tolerance.

Few commercially available codes for approximation programming currently exist. However, there are a number of user developed proprietary codes [Busby, 1974]. Any potential user who has access to a LP code can develop an approximation programming code by constructing the logic needed to prepare the successive LP matrices, make use of the solution results, and adjust ϵ. The capabilities of the resulting code are limited only by the capacity of the LP routine, so very large problems can be solved. If the problem is mostly linear then efficient operation can be expected.

Most of the difficulties that arise in this procedure stem from the tolerance ϵ. The user must define a reasonable initial value, and the way ϵ is reduced affects the speed of convergence. Rather complex logic may be needed to make the method perform well on a variety of problems. Of course, any optimal point found may be only a local optimum, but this can occur with any algorithm.

Computational experience with approximation programming is reported in [Busby, 1974]. As successive LPs were solved, Busby found that, while the first LP might require many pivot steps, successive LPs took far fewer, with the number of pivots decreasing as iterations progressed. This is probably because only a small part of the problem was nonlinear, so initial LPs set the majority of variables at or near their optimal values, and later steps only made small modifications. Since Busby's work, other papers have discussed improvements in approximation programming designed to speed convergence. The reader is referred to [Beale, 1974] for further details.

7. FUTURE DEVELOPMENTS IN LARGE SCALE MATHEMATICAL PROGRAMMING

Current trends and new research projects indicate what some of the future developments will be in large scale mathematical programming. There will be continued improvement of LP and mixed integer programming (MIP) codes in terms of speed, size of problems that can be solved, and storage capacity required. Some of these improvements will be due to further implementation of the LU matrix decomposition and the supersparsity concept, discussed earlier. Other factors will be the development of improved branch and bound strategies for MIP problems, and improvements in computer hardware and systems software. In addition, the recent survey in [White, 1973] foresaw improvements in the control languages and data handling capabilities of LP systems. Included is the ability to use the system recursively in a "loop" as in Approximation Programming, (see Section 6) and to use it interactively through terminals. A system with the latter capability has been designed recently by W. Orchard-Hays and others at the Computer Research Center of the National Bureau of Economic Research, Cambridge, Massachusetts. To facilitate commonly occurring applications, systems which access data bases, build an LP matrix, solve the problem, and format a management-oriented solution report will be developed. All but the input and output will be transparent to the user.

One of the most notable recent specializations of LP and MIP technology is the work in [Glover, et al., 1974] on solving large network flow problems. Evidence given there shows that the SM, properly implemented to exploit the tree structure of the LP basis, can solve network problems with hundreds of thousands of nodes and/or arcs. Solution appears to be faster than with the most powerful network algorithms. Codes with these capabilities were constructed by a combination of computer science expertise (e.g., in choosing the data structures and list processing techniques to be used), and by proper choice and implementation of an algorithm, in this case, the simplex algorithm. Future advances in large scale mathematical programming codes, like past successes, will stem from the same factors.

Applications of nonlinear and mixed integer models should increase. A notable recent application of MIP in [Geoffrion, 1974], focusing on distribution system analysis and design, exploits the mathematical structure of the problem by employing Benders Decomposition algorithm. Problems of much larger size than can be attacked by general purpose codes are solved in this way. The capabilities of general purpose MIP codes, which have increased notably in recent years, will be further enhanced. These codes are now commercially available from most large computer vendors and are beginning to have a major impact in facilitating applications of MIP. In NLP, the pioneering work of Abadie on the Generalized Reduced Gradient algorithm [Abadie, 1970] indicates that this algorithm, properly implemented, may be capable of solving a wide variety of NLPs of significant size. Current research by the author [Lasdon, 1975] aims at exploring large scale implementations of this and other algorithms. In the next two to three years, codes capable of solving a wide variety of large NLPs should begin to become available.

Finally, in areas like MIP and NLP, where there is no single dominant solution algorithm, testing and comparison of the many proposed methods is essential to progress. To facilitate these activities, and to aid in the development of algorithms and related software, Dantzig has proposed the formation of Systems Optimization Laboratories [Dantzig, 1974], and has been instrumental in organizing the first of these at Stanford University. These laboratories will gather test problems and codes implementing algorithms, formulate performance criteria, and make public test results. Such testing is the experimental side of an activity, the development and implementation of algorithms, which requires both theory and experiment for its success. Work at such laboratories should play a significant role in advancing the state of the art in mathematical programming.

REFERENCES

1. Abadie, J., "Application of the GRG Algorithm to Optimal Control Problems," 191–211, in *Nonlinear and Integer Programming*, J. Abadie, Ed., North-Holland, Amsterdam (1974).
2. Balinski, M. L., "Integer Programming: Methods, Uses, Computation," *Management Sci.* **12:** 253–313 (1965).

3. Bartels, R. H. and Golub, G. H., "The Simplex Method of Linear Programming using LU Decomposition," *Communications ACM* **12:** 266-268, 275-278, (1969).
4. Beale, E. M. L., "A Conjugate Gradient Method of Approximation Programming," in *Optimization Methods*, R. W. Cottle and J. Krarup, Eds., English Universities Press, London (1974).
5. ——, P. A. B. Hughes, and R. E. Small, "Experiences in using a Decomposition Program," *Computer J.* **8:** 13-18 (1965).
6. Busby, B. "Techniques and Experience Solving Really Big Non-Linear Programs," in *Optimization Methods*, R. W. Cottle and J. Krarup, Eds., English Universities Press, London (1974).
7. Dantzig, G. B., *Linear Programming and Extensions*, Chaps. 22 and 24, Princeton University Press, Princeton, New Jersey (1963).
8. —— and R. M. Van Slyke, "Generalized Upper Bounding Techniques," *J. Computer System Sci.* **1:** 213-226 (1967).
9. ——, "On the Need for a Systems Optimization Laboratory," in *Optimization Methods for Resources Allocation,* R. W. Cottle and J. Krarup, Eds., English Universities Press, London (1974).
10. Dzielinski, B. P. and R. E. Gomory, "Optimal Programming of Lot Sizes, Inventory and Labor Allocations," *Management Sci.* **11:** 874-890 (1965).
11. Forrest, J. J. H. and J. A. Tomlin, "Updated Triangular Factors of the Basis to Maintain Sparsity in the Product Form Simplex Method," *Math. Prog.* **2:** 263-278 (1972).
12. ——, *et al*, "Practical Solution of Large Mixed Integer Programming Problems with Umpire," *Management Sci.* **20:** 736-774 (1974).
13. Geoffrion, A., "Elements of Large-Scale Mathematical Programming," *Management Sci.* **16:** 652-691 (1970).
14. —— and G. W. Graves, "Multicommodity Distribution Center Design by Benders Decomposition," *Management Sci.* **20:** 822-845 (1974).
15. Gilmore, P. C. and R. E. Gomory, "A Linear Programming Approach to the Cutting Stock Problem," *Operations Res.* **9:** 849-859 (1961).
16. —— and ——, "A Linear Programming Approach to the Cutting Stock Problem–Part II," *Operations Res.* **11:** 863-887 (1963).
17. —— and ——, "Multistage Cutting Stock Problems of Two or More Dimensions," *Operations Res.* **13:** 94-120 (1965).
18. Glover, F., D. Karney, and D. Klingman, "Implementation and Computational Study on Start Procedures and Basis Change Criteria for a Primal Network Code," *Networks* **20:** 191-212 (1974).
19. Griffith, R. E. and R. A. Stewart, "A Nonlinear Programming Technique for the Optimization of Continuous Processing Systems," *Management Sci.* **7:** 379-392 (1961).
20. Grigoriadis, M. D., "Unified Pivoting Procedures for Large Structured Systems and Programs," in *Decomposition of Large Scale Problems*, D. Himmelblau (Ed.), North-Holland/American Elsevier (1973).
21. Hadley, G., *Nonlinear and Dynamic Programming*, Chapter 4, Addison-Wesley, Reading, Massachusetts (1964).
22. Hall, W. A. and J. A. Dracup, *Water Resources Systems Engineering*, Chapter 7, McGraw-Hill, New York (1970).
23. Hartman, J. and L. S. Lasdon, "A Generalized Upper Bounding Method for Doubly Coupled Linear Programs," *Nav. Res. Log. Quart.* **17:** 411-429 (1970).
24. Hellerman, E. and D. Rarick, "Reinversion with the Preassigned Pivot Procedure," *Math. Prog.* **1:** 195-216 (1971).
25. Hirshfeld, David, "Mathematical Programming Development at Management Science

System, Inc.," Presented at SHARE 38, (March 1972). For copies, write to Management Science System, Inc., 121 Congressional Lane, Rockville, Maryland 20852.
26. Jennergen, P., "A Note on the Interpretation of the Extremal Problem of the Dantzig-Wolfe Decomposition Algorithm in a Particular Case," *Zeitschrift für Operations Res.* **17:** 69–73 (1973).
27. Kalan, James, "Aspects of Large-Scale In-Core Linear Programming," *ACM Proceedings of Annual Conference:* 304–313 (1971).
28. Lasdon, L. S., A. D. Waren, A. Jain, and M. Ratner, "Design and Testing of a Generalized Reduced Gradient Code for Nonlinear Optimization" Tech. Memo. No. 353, Operations Research Department, Case Western Reserve University (1975).
29. Lasdon, L. S., *Optimization Theory for Large Systems*, Sec. 6.2, Macmillan, New York (1970a).
30. ——, ibid, Sec. 6.4 (1970b).
31. ——, ibid. p. 173 (1970c).
32. ——, ibid, Sec. 6.5 (1970d).
33. ——, ibid, Chap. 5 (1970e).
34. ——, ibid, Sec. 2.5 (1970f).
35. ——, ibid, Chap. 3 (1970g).
36. ——, ibid, Sec. 4.1 (1970h).
37. ——, ibid, Sec. 4.4.2 (1970i)
38. ——, ibid, Sec. 4.4 (1970j).
39. Lasdon, L. S. and R. Terjung, "An Efficient Algorithm for Multi-Item Scheduling," *Operations Res.* **19:** 946–969 (1971).
40. Lasdon, L. S., "Decomposition of a Ship-Routing Problem," in *Decomposition of Large Scale Problems*, D. Himmelblau (Ed.), North-Holland/American Elsevier, (1973).
41. Lasdon, L. S., "Generalized Upper Bounding Methods in Production Scheduling and Distribution," in *Optimization Methods for Resource Allocation*, R. W. Cottle and J. Krarup, Eds., English Universities Press, London (1974).
42. Manne, A. S., "Programming of Economic Lot Sizes," *Management Sci.* **14:** 115–135 (1958).
43. Marsten, R. E., W. W. Hogan, and J. W. Blankenship, "The BOXSTEP Method for Large Scale Optimization," Working Paper No. 660-73, Alfred P. Sloan School of Management, Massachusetts Institute of Technology. Cambridge, Massachusetts (1973).
44. Mesarovic, M. D., D. Macko, and Y. Takahara, *Theory of Multi-Level Hierarchical Systems*, Academic Press, New York (1970).
45. Orchard-Hays, Wm., "On the Proper Use of a Powerful MPS," in *Optimization Methods for Resource Allocation*, R. W. Cottle and J. Krarup, Eds., English Universities Press, London (1974).
46. Prabhakar, T., "Large Scale Mathematical Programming: A Case Study," presented at ORSA-TIMS Joint National Meeting, Boston, Massachusetts (April 22–24, 1974).
47. Tomlin, J., "Minimum-Cost Multicommodity Network Flows," *Operations Res.* **14:** 45–51 (1966).
48. White, W., "A Status Report on Computing Algorithms for Mathematical Programming," *Computing Surveys* **5:** 135–166 (1973).

II-8

OPTIMAL CONTROL

Hans Sagan
North Carolina State University

1. STATEMENT OF PROBLEM

The theory of Optimal Control deals, in general, with systems the behavior pattern of which may be influenced (controlled) by parameters (controls) that may be chosen subject to certain restrictions. It is the aim of optimal control theory to establish a method for selecting these parameters such that a stated goal is achieved in an optimal manner, e.g., in minimum time, or with minimum fuel consumption, or with minimum waste, or at a maximum profit, etc.

Problems of this nature not only arise in modern technology, of which space technology is the most sophisticated and advanced application, but in a variety of situations that are associated with production processes, such as economic growth theories, production planning, cost studies, inventory analysis, and stock management, to mention a few examples. (See also [Adiri and Ben-Israel, 1966; Arrow, 1968; Eppen and Gould, 1968; Lee and Sheikh, 1969; McMasters, 1970; Sprzeuzkouski, 1967].)

In this chapter we shall only deal with systems, the state $(x_1(t), x_2(t), \ldots, x_n(t))$ at time t of which may be described by a system of n first order differential equations

$$\mathbf{x}' = \mathbf{f}(t, \mathbf{x}, \mathbf{u}(t)) \tag{1}$$

where $\mathbf{u}(t) = (u_1(t), \ldots, u_m(t))$ is the (vector) value of the *control* $\mathbf{u}$ at time t

and where **f** has the components $\phi_1, \phi_2, \ldots, \phi_n$. In general, practical considerations dictate that the values of the controls may not be chosen freely but are restricted to a given subset U of R^m:

$$\mathbf{u}(t) \in U \quad \text{for all} \quad t. \tag{2}$$

U is called the *control region.*

The problem is now to choose the controls **u**, subject to the restriction (2) in such a manner that the corresponding solution **x** of Eq. (1) (*trajectory*) transfers $\mathbf{x}(t)$ from a given *initial state*

$$\mathbf{x}(0) = \boldsymbol{\theta} \tag{3}$$

to a given *terminal state*

$$\mathbf{x}(T) = \mathbf{x}^T \tag{4}$$

at some, not necessarily specified, time $T > 0$ such that

$$\int_0^T \phi_0(t, \mathbf{x}(t), \mathbf{u}(t))\, dt \tag{5}$$

assumes the smallest (or largest) possible value. (Note that the special choice of the initial state does not amount to a loss of generality. Equation (3) may always be obtained by a translation of coordinates.)

A control for which (5) assumes the smallest (largest) value is called an *optimal control* and the corresponding trajectory **x** is called an *optimal trajectory*.

In the following sections we shall discuss a number of necessary and sufficient conditions for **u** to be an optimal control of a problem as stated above and related problems. We shall do this under certain regularity assumptions on **u**. We shall assume either that **u** is sectionally continuous throughout the interval during which it is effective, or, more generally, that it is bounded and measurable. We call a control *admissible* if $\mathbf{u}(t) \in U$ for all $t \in [0, T]$ and if **u** is either sectionally continuous or bounded and measurable. We call the system (1) *controllable* if there is an admissible control that transfers the initial state $\boldsymbol{\theta}$ into the terminal state $\mathbf{x}^T$. If the system is controllable, then, the trajectory from $\boldsymbol{\theta}$ to $\mathbf{x}^T$ is sectionally smooth if **u** is sectionally continuous and absolutely continuous (and almost everywhere differentiable) if **u** is bounded and measurable. In the first case, the state equations (1) are presumed to hold everywhere except where **u** has a jump discontinuity (which are the only discontinuities that can occur in a sectionally continuous function) and in the second case, Eq. (1) is presumed to hold almost everywhere.

To avoid extraneous complications, we shall assume throughout that ϕ_0 and the components $\phi_1, \phi_2, \ldots, \phi_n$ of **f** have continuous first order partial derivatives with respect to all variables.

If U is the entire R^m space or an open subset of R^m, then the problem (1)-(5), may be reformulated as a Lagrange problem. (See Section 2.2.)

The problem we have formulated in Eqs. (1)-(5) is a *nonautonomous optimal control problem of undetermined duration.* Two prominent special cases are the Time Optimal Control Problem (OCP) and the nonautonomous problem of fixed duration: If $\phi_0(t, \mathbf{x}, \mathbf{u}) \equiv 1$, then Eq. (1) becomes $T = \int_0^T dt$, i.e., the duration of the process is to be minimized. This is the *Time OCP.* If $\phi_1, \ldots, \phi_n$ do not explicitly depend on the time t, we have an autonomous time OCP.

Example 1: (One-dimensional soft landing): A unit mass moves along a straight line under the sole influence of an external force (control) u, its position and velocity (state) given by $(x(t), x'(t))$.

$$x'' = u(t)$$

is the equation of motion. To be found is a sectionally continuous control u with values $|u(t)| \leqslant 1$ such that the unit mass is transferred from the initial state x^0, x'^0 to the terminal state $(0, 0)$ in the shortest possible time. We let $x = x_1$, $x' = x_2$ and we see that this problem may be formulated as follows:

$$x_1' = x_2$$

$$x_2' = u$$

$x_1(0) = x^0, x_2(0) = x'^0, x_1(T) = 0, x_2(T) = 0$ where $T = \int_0^T dt$ has to be minimized. This is an autonomous Time OCP.

The nonautonomous OCP of Fixed Duration T_0 may be reformulated as an autonomous control problem of undetermined duration as follows: We introduce a new state variable x_{n+1} for t by means of

$$x_{n+1}' = 1, \quad x_{n+1}(0) = 0, \quad x_{n+1}(T) = T_0.$$

Then, the problem appears as the following autonomous problem in $n + 1$ state variables:

$$\mathbf{x}' = \mathbf{F}(x_{n+1}, \mathbf{x}, \mathbf{u}(t))$$

$$x_{n+1}' = 1$$

$\mathbf{x}(0) = \boldsymbol{\theta}, x_{n+1}(0) = 0, \mathbf{x}(T) = \mathbf{x}^T, x_{n+1}(T) = T_0.$ $\int_0^T \phi_0(x_{n+1}(t), \mathbf{x}(t), \mathbf{u}(t))\, dt$

has to be minimized. From a formal viewpoint, the terminal time appears to be free. It is, of course, fixed to be T_0 through $x_{n+1}(0) = 0, x_{n+1}(T) = T_0, x_{n+1}' = 1$.

Example 2: To be found is a sectionally continuous control u with value $u(t) \in (-\infty, \infty)$ such that

$$x_1' = u(t)$$
$$x_2' = tu(t)$$

and the initial state $(0, 0)$ is transported into the terminal state $x_1(1) = 0$, $x_2(1) = 1$ in such a manner that $\int_0^1 u^2(t)\, dt$ is as small as possible. This is a nonautonomous OCP of fixed duration. We let $x_3' = 1, x_3(0) = 0, x_3(T) = 1$ and obtain the autonomous OCP of undetermined duration

$$x_1' = u(t)$$
$$x_2' = x_3 u(t)$$
$$x_3' = 1$$

with the initial state $x_1(0) = 0, x_2(0) = 0, x_3(0) = 0$, the terminal state $x_1(T) = 0$, $x_2(T) = 1, x_3(T) = 1$ and $\int_0^T u^2(t)\, dt$ to be minimized.

The nonautonomous problem of undetermined duration may be transformed into an autonomous problem with a variable end point. This will be discussed in Section 2.3.

In the following sections, necessary and sufficient conditions for $\mathbf{u}$ to be optimal will be discussed. We shall not, however, deal with direct methods or programming methods. Some of these are treated elsewhere in this handbook. (See Chapters 1, 5, 6, and 7 of Part II, Chapter 9 of Part III, and Section 5 of this chapter.)

2. NECESSARY CONDITIONS

2.1 The Maximum Principle of Pontryagin

We consider an autonomous optimal control problem of undetermined duration

$$\mathbf{x}' = f(\mathbf{x}, \mathbf{u}(t)), \tag{6}$$

$$\mathbf{x}(0) = \boldsymbol{\theta}, \quad \mathbf{x}(T) = \mathbf{x}^T \tag{7}$$

where $\int_0^T \phi_0(\mathbf{x}(t), \mathbf{u}(t))\, dt$ is to be minimized by an admissible control with values $\mathbf{u}(t) \in U \subseteq R^m$. In order to state a necessary condition for $\mathbf{u}$ to be optimal in an efficient and concise manner, we consider the following (conjugate) system of linear first order differential equations for auxiliary variables $p_1, p_2, \ldots, p_n$:

$$p_i' = -\sum_{j=0}^{n} \frac{\partial \phi_j}{\partial x_i} (\mathbf{x}(t), \mathbf{u}(t))\, p_j, \qquad i = 1, 2, \ldots, n \tag{8}$$

and the *Hamiltonian* of the OCP

$$H(\mathbf{p}, \mathbf{x}, \mathbf{u}) = p_0 \phi_0(\mathbf{x}, \mathbf{u}) + \sum_{j=1}^{n} p_j \phi_j(\mathbf{x}, \mathbf{u}).$$

In terms of these entities, we may formulate a necessary condition for optimality, known as *Pontryagin's Maximum Principle*, as follows. ([Athans and Falb, 1965, p. 284; Halkin, 1967, p. 208; Lee and Markus, 1967, p. 254; Sagan, 1969, p. 289])

For the control $\mathbf{u}$ *and the corresponding trajectory* $\mathbf{x}$ *of the CP* (6) *and* (7) *to be optimal, it is necessary that there exists a solution* $\mathbf{p}$ *with values* $p_1(t), \ldots, p_n(t)$ *of the conjugate system,* Eq. (8), *and a constant* $p_0 \leqslant 0$ *such that* $(p_0, p_1(t), \ldots, p_n(t)) \neq \theta$ *and*

$$H(\mathbf{p}(t), \mathbf{x}(t), \mathbf{v}) \leqslant H(\mathbf{p}(t), \mathbf{x}(t), \mathbf{u}(t)) = 0 \tag{9}$$

for all vectors $\mathbf{v} \in U$ *at "each point"* $\mathbf{x}(t)$ *of the optimal trajectory* $\mathbf{x}$ *where the value of the control is* $\mathbf{u}(t)$. "Each point" in the above statement is to be understood as follows: If $\mathbf{u}$ is sectionally continuous, then Condition (9) has to hold at each point where $\mathbf{u}$ is continuous. If $\mathbf{u}$ is bounded and measurable, then Condition (9) has to hold almost everywhere. In the first case, $\mathbf{p}$ is continuous and has a sectionally continuous derivative where jump discontinuities can only occur where (at least one component of) $\mathbf{u}$ has a jump discontinuity. In the second case, $\mathbf{p}$ is absolutely continuous (and almost everywhere differentiable).

Example 3: (One-dimensional soft landing): For the case formulated in Example 1, the conjugate system, Eq. (8) has the form

$$p_1' = 0, \qquad p_2' = -p_1$$

with the solutions

$$p_1 = a, \qquad p_2 = -at + b.$$

The Hamiltonian appears as

$$H(\mathbf{p}, \mathbf{x}, u) = p_0 + a x_2 + (b - at) u.$$

Since $U = [-1, 1]$ it is clear that the Maximum Principle of Pontryagin yields

$$u = 1 \quad \text{if} \quad b - at > 0$$

and

$$u = -1 \quad \text{if} \quad b - at < 0.$$

As apparent from the above example, p_0 may be eliminated for the time optimal control problem. We have instead of Condition (9) that there has to be nontrivial solution $\mathbf{p}$ of

$$p_i' = -\sum_{j=1}^{n} \frac{\partial \phi_j}{\partial x_i} (\mathbf{x}(t), \mathbf{u}(t)) p_j, \qquad i = 1, 2, \ldots, n$$

such that with $p_0 \leqslant 0$,

$$\sum_{j=1}^{n} p_j \phi_j(\mathbf{x}(t), \mathbf{v}) \leqslant \sum_{j=1}^{n} p_j \phi_j(\mathbf{x}(t), \mathbf{u}(t)) = -p_0 \tag{10}$$

for all $\mathbf{v} \in U$ at "each point" of the optimal trajectory $\mathbf{x}$.

For the nonautonomous problem of fixed duration it follows directly from the Maximum Principle that there has to be a solution $\mathbf{p}$ of system (8) such that with a constant $p_0 \leqslant 0, (p_0, p_1(t), \ldots, p_n(t)) \neq (0, 0, \ldots, 0)$,

$$\sum_{j=0}^{n} p_j(t)\, \phi_j(t, \mathbf{x}(t), \mathbf{u}(t)) \geqslant \sum_{j=0}^{n} p_j(t)\, \phi_j(t, \mathbf{x}(t), \mathbf{v})$$

for all $\mathbf{v} \in U$ at "each point" $\mathbf{x}(t)$ of the optimal trajectory. (p_{n+1} arising from the new state variable $t = x_{n+1}$ is irrelevant.)

Example 4: For the problem in Example 2 we obtain $p_1' = p_2' = 0$ and hence, p_1, p_2 are constant. Consequently,

$$\sum_{j=0}^{2} p_j \phi_j(t, \mathbf{x}, u) = p_0 u^2 + (p_1 + p_2 t) u$$

where $p_0 \leqslant 0$. This function is maximized for $u = -\dfrac{1}{2p_0}(p_1 + p_2 t)$. With $p_0 = -\frac{1}{2}$, $p_1 = -6$, $p_2 = 12$ we obtain the trajectory $\mathbf{x}$ given by $x_1(t) = -6t + 6t^2$, $x_2(t) = -3t^2 + 4t^3$. We obtain $\displaystyle\int_0^1 u^2(t)\, dt = 12$. That this is actually the minimum will be seen in Section 4.2.

2.2 The Mayer Equations and the Weierstrass Condition

If the values of the optimal control $\mathbf{u}$ lie in the interior of U, or if U is an open subset of R^m, or even the entire R^m, then the OCP of Section 1 may be viewed as a Lagrange problem. Since any portion of an optimal control is an optimal control in its own right, the above also holds true for those portions of **u** whose values lie in the interior of U.

We formulate the Lagrange problem as follows: To be found is a vector function **y** with values $(y_1(t), y_2(t), \ldots, y_\mu(t))$ which satisfies the underdetermined system of $n < \mu$ first order differential equations

$$\mathbf{F}(t, \mathbf{y}, \mathbf{y}') = \mathbf{0} \tag{11}$$

where **F** has the components $(\Phi_1, \Phi_2, \ldots, \Phi_n)$, the initial conditions

$$\mathbf{y}(0) = \boldsymbol{\theta}, \tag{12}$$

the terminal conditions

$$\boldsymbol{\psi}(T, \mathbf{y}(T)) = \mathbf{0} \tag{13}$$

at some time $T > 0$, where $\boldsymbol{\psi}$ has the components $\psi_1, \psi_2, \ldots, \psi_k$, whereby $k \leqslant \mu$, and is such that

$$\int_0^T \Phi_0(t, \mathbf{y}(t), \mathbf{y}'(t))\, dt \tag{14}$$

assumes the smallest possible value.

We assume that Φ_0, the components of **F**, and the components of $\boldsymbol{\psi}$ have continuous partial derivatives with respect to all variables. We also assume that

$$\operatorname{rank}\left(\frac{\partial \psi_j}{\partial y_i}\right) = k.$$

Then, $\boldsymbol{\psi}(t, \mathbf{y}) = 0$ defines *a* $\mu + 1 - k$ dimensional manifold in $(t, y_1, \ldots, y_\mu)$-space. In particular, if Eq. (13) has the special form $y_i(T) = y_i^T$ where y_i^T are given, $i = 1, 2, \ldots, \mu$, then Eq. (13) represents a 1-dimensional manifold in $(t, y_1, \ldots, y_\mu)$-space. (Fixed endpoint, undetermined duration.) If T is also given, then Eq. (13) represents a 0-dimensional manifold (point).

If we substitute in the OCP (1), (3), (4), (5) (without the restriction $\mathbf{u}(t) \in U$)

$$x_i = y_i, \quad i = 1, 2, \ldots, n; \qquad u_j = y_{j+n}, \quad j = 1, 2, \ldots, \mu - n = m,$$
$$\mathbf{f} - \mathbf{y}' = \mathbf{F}, \quad \mathbf{y}(T) - \mathbf{y}^T = \boldsymbol{\psi}(T, \mathbf{y}(T)), \quad k = \mu, \tag{15}$$

we obtain instead of the problem (1), (3), (4), (5):

$$\mathbf{F}(t, \mathbf{y}, \mathbf{y}', y'_{n+1}, \ldots, y'_\mu) = 0,$$
$$\mathbf{y}(0) = \mathbf{0}, \quad \boldsymbol{\psi}(T, \mathbf{y}(T)) = \mathbf{0}$$

and $\int_0^T \phi_0(t, \mathbf{y}(t), y'_{n+1}(t), \ldots, y'_\mu(t))\, dt$ is to be minimized. This is indeed a

Lagrange problem if we add the initial conditions $y_{n+1}(0) = \cdots = y_\mu(0) = 0$. (These conditions may be added without penalty because only $u_j(t) = y'_{j+n}(t)$ is of interest.)

The following conditions are necessary for $\mathbf{y}$ to be a solution of the Lagrange problem: (see [Bliss, 1946, pp. 202, 223; McShane, 1940, p. 24; Sagan, 1969, pp. 334, 366]).

If rank $\dfrac{\partial \phi_j}{\partial y_i}(t, \mathbf{y}(t), \mathbf{y}'(t)) = n$ *for all points of the optimal trajectory* $\mathbf{y}(t)$, *then there exists a constant* λ_0 *and a vector valued function* $\boldsymbol{\lambda}$ *with values* $(\lambda_1(t), \ldots, \lambda_n(t))$, $(\lambda_0, \lambda_1(t), \ldots, \lambda_n(t)) \neq (0, 0, \ldots, 0)$ (*Lagrange Multipliers*) such that with

$$h(t, \mathbf{y}, \mathbf{y}', \boldsymbol{\lambda}) = \sum_{j=0}^{n} \lambda_j \Phi_j(t, \mathbf{y}, \mathbf{y}')$$

the Mayer equations

$$\frac{d}{dt} h_{\mathbf{y}'}(t, \mathbf{y}(t), \mathbf{y}'(t), \boldsymbol{\lambda}(t)) = h_{\mathbf{y}}(t, \mathbf{y}(t), \mathbf{y}'(t), \boldsymbol{\lambda}(t)) \tag{16}$$

hold and there is a vector

$$(\nu_1, \nu_2, \ldots, \nu_n)$$

with

$$(\lambda_0, \nu_1, \nu_2, \ldots, \nu_n) \neq (0, 0, \ldots, 0)$$

such that the transversality conditions

$$\sum_{j=1}^{k} \nu_j \psi_{jt}(T, \mathbf{y}(T)) = \lambda_0 \phi_0(T, \mathbf{y}(T), \mathbf{y}'(T)) - \sum_{j=1}^{\mu} h_{y'_j}(T, \mathbf{y}(T), \mathbf{y}'(T), \boldsymbol{\lambda}(T))\, y'_j(T) \tag{17}$$

and

$$\sum_{j=1}^{k} \nu_j \psi_{jy_i}(T, \mathbf{y}(T)) = h_{y'_i}(T, \mathbf{y}(T), \mathbf{y}'(T)), \qquad i = 1, 2, \ldots, \mu \tag{18}$$

are satisfied at the terminal time T. (Analogous conditions hold when there is an initial manifold.)

If $\mathbf{y}$ is continuous and has a sectionally continuous derivative, then $\boldsymbol{\lambda}$ is sectionally continuous and Eq. (16) has to hold wherever $\mathbf{y}'$ is continuous. At every jump discontinuity $(t_0, \mathbf{y}(t_0))$ of $\mathbf{y}'$ (corner of the trajectory) the corner conditions

$$h_{\mathbf{y}'}(t_0, \mathbf{y}(t_0), \mathbf{y}'(t_0 - 0), \boldsymbol{\lambda}(t_0 - 0)) = h_{\mathbf{y}'}(t_0, \mathbf{y}(t_0), \mathbf{y}'(t_0 + 0), \boldsymbol{\lambda}(t_0 + 0))$$
$$\left(h - \sum_{i=1}^{\mu} y_i' h_{y_i'}\right)(t_0 - 0) = \left(h - \sum_{i=1}^{\mu} y_i' h_{y_i'}\right)(t_0 + 0) \tag{19}$$

have to hold. [Bliss, 1946, p. 202].

If $\mathbf{y}'$ is bounded and measurable, then $\mathbf{y}$ is absolutely continuous, $\boldsymbol{\lambda}$ is bounded and measurable and continuous wherever $\mathbf{y}'$ is continuous. Equations (16) have to hold almost everywhere.

In addition to Eqs. (16) through (19), the Weierstrass condition

$$\lambda_0(\Phi_0(t, \mathbf{y}, \boldsymbol{\xi}) - \Phi_0(t, \mathbf{y}, \mathbf{y}')) - \sum_{i=1}^{\mu} (\xi_i - y_i') h_{y_i'}(t, \mathbf{y}, \mathbf{y}', \boldsymbol{\lambda}) \geqslant 0 \tag{20}$$

with $\lambda_0 \geqslant 0$ has to hold for every lineal element $(t, \mathbf{y}, \mathbf{y}')$ of the optimal trajectory where $\mathbf{y}'$ is continuous, for all lineal elements $(t, \mathbf{y}, \boldsymbol{\xi})$ for which $\mathbf{F}(t, \mathbf{y}, \boldsymbol{\xi}) = 0$ [McShane, 1940, p. 24].

Example 5: In Example 2, the control region U is the entire real line. Hence, we may reformulate this problem as a Lagrange problem by setting $x_1 = y_1$, $x_2 = y_2, u = y_3'$. Then, the constraining equations appear as

$$y_1' - y_3' = 0$$
$$y_2' - t y_3' = 0,$$

the boundary conditions as $y_1(0) = y_2(0) = y_3(0) = 0$, $y_1(1) = 0$, $y_2(1) = 1$. $y_3(1)$ is free and $\int_0^1 y_3'^2(t)\, dt$ has to be minimized. With

$$h(t, \mathbf{y}, \mathbf{y}', \boldsymbol{\lambda}) = \lambda_0 y_3'^2 + \lambda_1(y_1' - y_3') + \lambda_2(y_2' - t y_3')$$

we have $h_{y_1} = h_{y_2} = h_{y_3} = 0$, $h_{y_1'} = \lambda_1$, $h_{y_2'} = \lambda_2$, $h_{y_3'} = 2\lambda_0 y_3' - \lambda_1 - t\lambda_2$ and the Mayer equations (16) yield

$$\lambda_1 = \text{constant}, \quad \lambda_2 = \text{constant}, \quad 2\lambda_0 y_3' - \lambda_1 - t\lambda_2 = \text{constant}.$$

From Eq. (18), $\nu_1 = \lambda_1, \nu_2 = \lambda_2, 2\lambda_0 y_3'(1) - \lambda_1 - \lambda_3 = 0$. Hence, $h_{y_3'} = 2\lambda_0 y_3' - \lambda_1 - t\lambda_2 = 0$ for all $t \in [0, 1]$. Hence, $y_3' = \dfrac{1}{2\lambda_0}(\lambda_1 + t\lambda_2)$. With $\lambda_0 = 1$ we obtain from the constraining equations and the boundary conditions $\lambda_1 = -12$, $\lambda_2 = 24$ and we obtain, as in Example 4, the trajectory $y_1(t) = -6t + 6t^2$, $y_2(t) = -3t^2 + 4t^3$. The Weierstrass condition (20) reads $(\xi_3 - y_3')^2 \geqslant 0$ and is obviously satisfied for all $\xi_3 \in (-\infty, \infty)$.

The Mayer Eqs. (16) and the Weierstrass condition (20), for the OCP (1) through (5) with an open control region may be derived from Pontryagin's maximum principle that is stated in Section 2.1. [Pontryagin, et al., 1962, p. 240; Sagan, 1969, p. 316]. Conversely, one obtains with the notation (15), for the problem (1) through (5) with an open control region from Eqs. (16), (17), (18), (20), that conditions (8) and (9) have to hold and that, in addition,

$$H_{u_j}(\mathbf{p}(t), \mathbf{x}(t), \mathbf{u}(t)) = 0, \qquad j = 1, 2, \ldots, m$$

have to hold along the optimal trajectory.

2.3 Optimal Control Problems with a Variable Endpoint

In the OCP (6) and (7), we replace the terminal condition in Eq. (7) by the new condition that the phase point $\mathbf{x}(t)$ be transferred into a *terminal manifold* that is defined by

$$\boldsymbol{\psi}(\mathbf{x}) = \mathbf{0} \tag{21}$$

where $\boldsymbol{\psi}$ has the components $\psi_1, \psi_2, \ldots, \psi_k$, $k < n$, where the partial derivatives of the ψ_j are continuous and where rank $\left(\dfrac{\partial \psi_j}{\partial x_j}\right) = k$.

Then, in addition to the conditions which are listed in Section 8.2.1, *the vector* $(p_1(T), p_2(T), \ldots, p_n(T))$ *has to be orthogonal to the terminal manifold* (21) *at the point where the terminal manifold is reached by* $\mathbf{x}(t)$ [Pontryagin et al., 1962, p. 45]. The nonautonomous OCP of unspecified duration may be considered as an autonomous optimal control problem with a variable endpoint: We let $t = x_{n+1}$. Then $x'_{n+1} = 1, x_{n+1}(0) = 0$ and we have

$$\mathbf{x}' = \mathbf{f}(x_{n+1}, \mathbf{x}, \mathbf{u}(t))$$

$$x'_{n+1} = 1$$

with the initial conditions $\mathbf{x}(0) = \mathbf{0}$, $x_{n+1}(0) = 0$ and the terminal condition that the endpoint lies on the manifold $\mathbf{x} = \mathbf{x}^T$ which is a one dimensional manifold in $(x_1, x_2, \ldots, x_{n+1})$-space to which $(0, 0, \ldots, 0, 1) \in R^{n+1}$ is a tangent vector. With $f_{n+1}(x_{n+1}, x, u) = 1$ we obtain from the maximum principle that

$$p_0\phi_0(x_{n+1}, \mathbf{x}, \mathbf{u}) + \cdots + p_n\phi_n(x_{n+1}, \mathbf{x}, \mathbf{u}) + p_{n+1}$$

as a function of $\mathbf{u}$ has to assume the maximum zero at each point of the optimal trajectory and from the transversality condition $(p_1(T), p_2(T), \ldots, p_n(T), p_{n+1}(T)) \cdot (0, 0, \ldots, 0, 1) = 0$ we obtain that $p_{n+1}(T) = 0$, that is, we have to have in the original notation of the nonautonomous problem that

$$p_0(T)\,\phi_0(T, \mathbf{x}(T), \mathbf{u}(T)) + \cdots + p_n(T)\,\phi_n(T), \mathbf{x}(T), \mathbf{u}(T)) = 0.$$

3. SYNTHESIS

The problem of actually finding a control that satisfies the necessary conditions that have been stated in Section 2 is difficult and has to be broken down into special cases. Here, we shall only deal with two cases. First we deal with the simplest case about which a great deal of knowledge is available, namely the linear time OCP with a compact convex polyhedron as control region. Secondly, we shall deal with nonlinear control problems with a compact and convex control region that may be transformed into a Lagrange problem. Then, the synthesis is reduced to solving boundary value problems of differential equations.

3.1 The Linear Time Optimal Control Problem

Let U denote a compact convex polyhedron in R^m and let $\mathbf{A}$, $\mathbf{B}$ denote constant $n \times n$ and $n \times m$ matrices, respectively. To be found is a vector valued control $\mathbf{u}$ with values $(u_1(t), \ldots, u_m(t)) \in U$ such that

$$\mathbf{x}' = \mathbf{Ax} + \mathbf{Bu}(t), \quad \mathbf{x}(0) = \mathbf{0}, \quad \mathbf{x}(T) = \mathbf{x}^T \tag{22}$$

and $T = \int_0^T dt$ assumes the smallest possible value. (See also Example 1.)

If $\mathbf{A}$, $\mathbf{B}$, U are such that for every position vector $\mathbf{e}$ representing the direction of an edge of U, the n vectors $\mathbf{Be}, \mathbf{ABe}, \ldots, \mathbf{A}^{n-1}\mathbf{Be}$ are linearly independent, then the Eqs. (8), which read in this case

$$\mathbf{p}' = -\mathbf{A}^t\mathbf{p},$$

($\mathbf{A}^t$ is the transpose of $\mathbf{A}$) have nontrivial solutions none of the components of which vanish on any interval and the maximum condition (10) determines for each such solution a unique control $\mathbf{u}$. These controls are sectionally constant and their values between jump discontinuities are represented by a vertex of U. This is known as the *Bang-Bang Principle.* [Pontryagin, et al, 1962, p. 115; Sagan, 1969, p. 310]. Controls such as these are called *Bang-Bang Controls.*

If U is a right parallelepiped and if all eigenvalues of $\mathbf{A}$ are real, then there are at most $n - 1$ switches from one constant control to another. [Pontryagin, et al, 1962, p. 120; Sagan, 1969, p. 314].

Example 6: In Example 1, we have $\mathbf{A} = \begin{pmatrix} 0 & 1 \\ 0 & 0 \end{pmatrix}$, $\mathbf{B} = \begin{pmatrix} 0 \\ 1 \end{pmatrix}$, $U = [-1, 1]$. Hence, $\mathbf{e} = (1)$ and $\mathbf{Be} = \begin{pmatrix} 0 \\ 1 \end{pmatrix}(1) = \begin{pmatrix} 0 \\ 1 \end{pmatrix}$, $\mathbf{ABe} = \begin{pmatrix} 1 \\ 0 \end{pmatrix}$ are linearly independent. The eigenvalues $\lambda_1 = \lambda_2 = 0$ are real. The vertices of U are -1 and 1. Hence (10) determines the values $u = 1$, $u = -1$ of the control uniquely and there is at most $n - 1 = 1$ switch possible.

With the initial condition $x_1(0) = 2, x_2(0) = 2$, we have to start with the control $u = -1$ along the trajectory $x_1 = -\frac{t^2}{2} + 2t + 2$, $x_2 = -t + 2$ until the point $x_1 = 2, x_2 = -2$ is reached. Then, the control is to be switched to $u = 1$ and the trajectory $x_1 = \frac{t^2}{2} - 6t + 18$, $x_2 = t - 6$ leads to $(0, 0)$ after a total time of $T = 6$. (See Fig. 1.)

3.2 Nonlinear Optimal Control Problems with a Convex Compact Polyhedron as Control Region

If the control region U is a compact convex polyhedron in R^m with vertices $\mathbf{w}_0, \mathbf{w}_1, \ldots, \mathbf{w}_k$, then, the OCP (1) through (5) may be transformed into an equivalent Lagrange problem by means of the following transformation:

$$\mathbf{u} = \boldsymbol{\psi}(z') \equiv \begin{cases} \mathbf{w}_0 + \dfrac{\sin^2 \frac{\pi}{2} \sqrt{z_1'^2 + \cdots + z_k'^2}}{z_1'^2 + \cdots + z_k'^2} \sum_{j=1}^{k} (z_i'^2)(\mathbf{w}_i - \mathbf{w}_0) & \text{for } \mathbf{z}' \neq 0 \\ \mathbf{0} \text{ for } \mathbf{z}' = \theta. \end{cases} \tag{23}$$

This continuous transformation maps R^k onto U and also maps the closed unit sphere in R^k with center at $\boldsymbol{\theta}$ onto U. By a lemma of Filippov [1963] there is

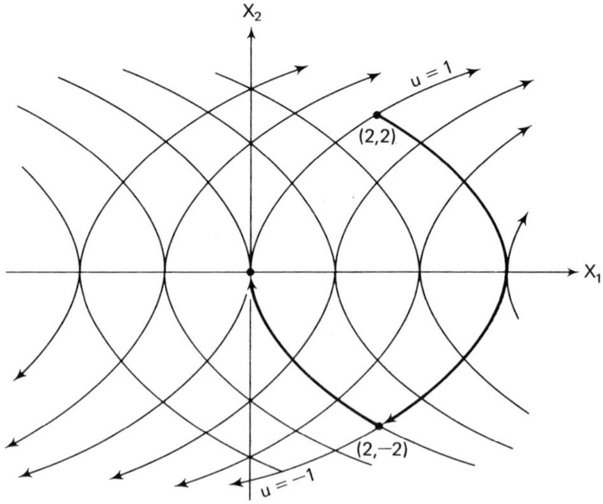

Fig. 1.

for every bounded measurable function $\mathbf{u}$ on $[0, T]$ a bounded measurable function $\mathbf{z}'$ on $[0, T]$ such that $\mathbf{u}(t) = \boldsymbol{\psi}(\mathbf{z}'(t))$. Since $\boldsymbol{\psi}$ is continuous and bounded, there also is for every bounded measurable $\mathbf{z}'$ on $[0, T]$ a bounded measurable $\mathbf{u}$ on $[0, T]$ such that $\mathbf{u}(t) = \boldsymbol{\psi}(\mathbf{z}'(t))$. Hence, the following Lagrange problem is equivalent [Park, 1970; Sagan, 1971] to the OCP (1) through (5):

To be found is a vector valued function $\mathbf{x}$ in R^n and a vector valued function $\mathbf{z}'$ in R^k such that

$$\begin{gathered} \mathbf{f}(t, \mathbf{x}, \boldsymbol{\psi}(\mathbf{z}')) - \mathbf{x}' = 0 \\ \mathbf{x}(0) = \boldsymbol{\theta}, \quad \mathbf{z}(0) = \boldsymbol{\theta}, \quad \mathbf{x}(T) = \mathbf{x}^T \end{gathered} \tag{24}$$

and

$$\int_0^T \phi_0(t, \mathbf{x}(t), \boldsymbol{\psi}(\mathbf{z}'(t))\, dt$$

assumes the smallest possible value. We have

$$h(t, \mathbf{x}, \mathbf{x}', \mathbf{z}', \boldsymbol{\lambda}) = \lambda_0 \phi_0(t, \mathbf{x}, \boldsymbol{\psi}(\mathbf{z}')) + \sum_{i=1}^{n} \lambda_i(\phi_i(t, \mathbf{x}, \boldsymbol{\psi}(\mathbf{z}')) - x_i')$$

and obtain from the Mayer Eqs. (16)

$$\begin{gathered} \lambda_i'(t) = -h_{x_i}(t, \mathbf{x}(t), \mathbf{x}'(t), \mathbf{z}'(t), \boldsymbol{\lambda}(t)), \qquad i = 1, 2, \ldots, n, \\ \frac{d}{dt} h_{z_l'}(t, \mathbf{x}(t), \mathbf{x}'(t), \mathbf{z}'(t), \boldsymbol{\lambda}(t)) = \frac{d}{dt}\left(\sum_{i=0}^{n} \sum_{j=1}^{m} \lambda_i \phi_{iu_j} \frac{\partial \psi_j}{\partial z_l'}\right) = 0, \qquad l = 1, 2, \ldots, k. \end{gathered} \tag{25}$$

Since T and $\mathbf{z}'(T)$ are free, we obtain from the transversality conditions (18) that

$$h_{z_l'}(T, \mathbf{x}(T), \mathbf{x}'(T), \mathbf{z}'(T), \boldsymbol{\lambda}(T)) = 0$$

and hence in conjunction with Eqs. (25)

$$h_{z_l'}(t, \mathbf{x}(t), \mathbf{x}'(t), \mathbf{z}'(t), \boldsymbol{\lambda}(t)) = \sum_{i=0}^{n} \sum_{j=1}^{m} \lambda_i \phi_{iu_j}(t, \mathbf{x}(t), \boldsymbol{\psi}(\mathbf{z}'(t))) \frac{\partial \psi_j}{\partial z_l'} (\mathbf{z}'(t)) = 0 \tag{26}$$

for all $t \in [0, T]$, and, from Eq. (17), that

$$\lambda_0 \phi_0(T, \mathbf{x}(T), \boldsymbol{\psi}(\mathbf{z}'(T)) + \sum_{j=1}^{n} \lambda_j(T)\, x_j'(T) = 0. \tag{27}$$

The Weierstrass Condition (20) reads, in view of Eqs. (25),

$$\lambda_0(\phi_0(t, \mathbf{x}(t), \boldsymbol{\psi}(\zeta)) - \phi_0(t, \mathbf{x}(t), \boldsymbol{\psi}(\mathbf{z}'(t))) + \sum_{j=1}^{n} (\xi_i - x_i'(t))\, \lambda_i(t) \geqslant 0 \tag{28}$$

for all lineal elements $(t, \mathbf{x}, \mathbf{x}', \mathbf{z}')$ of the optimal trajectory and all $\boldsymbol{\zeta}$ and all $\boldsymbol{\xi} = \mathbf{f}(t, \mathbf{x}, \boldsymbol{\psi}(\boldsymbol{\zeta}))$.

Hence, the problem of finding candidates for optimal controls reduces to the problem of solving the boundary value problem, Eqs. (24) and (25) in such a manner that (27) and (28) are satisfied.

Example 7: In Example 1, the control region is the compact convex polyhedron $[-1, 1]$ in R^1 with vertices $w_0 = -1$, $w_1 = 1$. We obtain for the transformation (23) with $u = 1$

$$u = \psi(z') = -1 + \left(\sin^2 \frac{\pi}{2} z'\right)(2z') = -\cos \pi z'.$$

Hence, the problem in Example 1 may be formulated as the following Lagrange problem

$$x_1' = x_2$$

$$x_2' = -\cos \pi z'$$

$x_1(0) = x^0$, $x_2(0) = x'^0$, $z(0) = 0$, $x_1(T) = 0$, $x_2(T) = 0$ with T to be minimized. With

$$h = \lambda_0 + \lambda_1(x_2 - x_1') - \lambda_2(\cos \pi z' + x_2')$$

we obtain from Eq. (25)

$$\lambda_1' = 0, \quad \lambda_2' = \lambda_1,$$

and from Eq. (26)

$$h_{z'} = \lambda_2 \pi \sin \pi z' = 0.$$

Hence, $\lambda_1 = a$, $\lambda_2 = at + b$ and $(at + b)\pi \sin \pi z' = 0$. From Eq. (17),

$$\lambda_0 + \lambda_1(T)x_1'(T) + \lambda_2(T)x_2'(T) = 0.$$

Hence, either $a = b = 0$ but then $\lambda_0 = \lambda_1 = \lambda_2 = 0$ which is not admissible, or else, $\sin \pi z' = 0$, i.e., $z' = 0, \pm 1, \pm 2, \ldots$. This yields $u = \pm 1$ and we are back to Example 6 where we obtained the trajectory $x_1 = -\dfrac{t^2}{2} + 2t + 2$, $x_2 = -t + 2$ on $[0, 4]$ and $x_1 = \dfrac{t^2}{2} - 6t + 18$, $x_2 = t - 6$ on $[4, 6]$. At $t = 4$ when z' is switched from 0 to 1, the corner conditions (19) have to hold: λ_1, λ_2, $\lambda_0 + \lambda_1 x_2 - \lambda_2 \cos \pi z'$ have to remain continuous when t passes from $4 - 0$ to $4 + 0$. Since λ_0, λ_1 are constant, since x_2 remains continuous, this implies $\lambda_2(4) = 0$, i.e.,

$$4a + b = 0.$$

From Eq. (17), with $\lambda_0 = 1$,

$$1 + (6a + b) = 0.$$

Hence, $a = -\frac{1}{2}$, $b = 2$ and we have

$$\lambda_0 = 1, \quad \lambda_1 = -\frac{1}{2}, \quad \lambda_2 = -\frac{t}{2} + 2.$$

The Weierstrass Condition (28) becomes

$$\left(-\frac{t}{2} + 2\right)(-\cos \pi\xi_3 + \cos \pi z') \geqslant 0$$

for all ξ_3. This is indeed satisfied because on $[0, 4]$ we have $z' = 0$ and $-\cos \pi\xi_3 + 1 \geqslant 0$, $-\frac{t}{2} + 2 \geqslant 0$ and in $[4, 6]$ we have $z' = 1$ and hence, $-\cos \pi\xi_3 - 1 \leqslant 0$, $-\frac{t}{2} + 2 \leqslant 0$.

The method of this section is not restricted to compact convex polyhedra as control regions. Whenever the control region U is compact and there is a continuous function $\boldsymbol{\psi}$ from some Cartesian space R^l onto U such that a compact subset of R^l is already mapped onto U, then Filippov's lemma applies and $\boldsymbol{\psi}$ may be utilized to transform the OCP into an equivalent Lagrange problem [Park, 1970].

4. SUFFICIENT CONDITIONS

A variety of sufficient conditions for a control to be optimal have been established over the past decade. (See, for example, [Boltyanskii, 1966; Lee, 1963; Mangasarian, 1966].) Most are technically very complicated. Here, we shall only discuss three cases, pertaining to the linear time OCP, to an OCP of fixed duration that is linear in the state variables, and the Lagrange problem of fixed duration.

4.1 The Linear Time Optimal Control Problem

Let $\mathbf{A}$, $\mathbf{B}$ represent constant $n \times n$ and $n \times m$ matrices, respectively, and consider the time OCP

$$\mathbf{x}' = \mathbf{A}\mathbf{x} + \mathbf{B}\mathbf{u}$$

$$\mathbf{x}(0) = \boldsymbol{\theta}, \quad \mathbf{x}(T) = \mathbf{x}^T$$

where T is to be minimized. (See also Section 3.1.)

If $U = \{\mathbf{u} \in E^m \big| |u_j| \leqslant 1\}$, the following simple sufficient condition holds:

If there is a Bang-Bang control **u** *which transfers the state* $\boldsymbol{\theta}$ *into the state* $\mathbf{x}^T$ *in time T and if*

$$\text{rank } (\mathbf{B}, \mathbf{AB}, \ldots, \mathbf{A}^{n-1}\mathbf{B}) = n,$$

then **u** *is the optimal control.* [Hermes and LaSalle, 1969, pp. 72, 74].

When **A**, **B** are matrix functions of t, this sufficient condition may be generalized. [Hermes and LaSalle, 1969, pp. 72–80].

Example 8: We have seen in Example 6 that there is a Bang-Bang control for the problem in Example 1. We have also seen in Example 6 that rank $(\mathbf{B}, \mathbf{AB}) = 2$. Hence, the above sufficient condition is applicable and the control found in Example 6 is indeed optimal.

4.2 Optimal Control Problems that are Linear in the State Variables

We consider the OCP (1) through (5) with the provision that T is fixed and that ϕ_0, **f** have the special structure $\phi_0(t, \mathbf{x}, \mathbf{u}) = a_{01}(t)x_1 + \cdots + a_{0n}(t)x_n + \psi_0(t, u)$, $\mathbf{f} = \mathbf{A}(t)\mathbf{x} + \boldsymbol{\psi}(t, \mathbf{u})$ where $\mathbf{A}(t)$ is an $n \times n$ matrix function of t and where ψ_0 and $\boldsymbol{\psi}$ are assumed to be continuous in t and **u**. The problem now reads: To be found is a control **u** with values $\mathbf{u}(t) \in U \subseteq R^m$ such that

$$\begin{aligned} \mathbf{x}' &= \mathbf{A}(t)\mathbf{x} + \boldsymbol{\psi}(t, \mathbf{u}(t)), \\ \mathbf{x}(0) &= \boldsymbol{\theta}, \quad \mathbf{x}(T) = \mathbf{x}^T \end{aligned} \tag{29}$$

for *fixed* $T > 0$ and

$$\int_0^T (a_{01}(t)x_1(t) + \cdots + a_{0n}(t)x_n(t) + \psi_0(t, \mathbf{u}(t)))\, dt$$

assumes the smallest possible value.

The maximum principle, somewhat modified, yields a sufficient condition for **u** to be optimal:

If **u**, **x** *are control and corresponding trajectory for which* Eqs. (6), (7), (8), *and the appropriate maximum condition are satisfied with* $p_0 = -1$, *for all* $\mathbf{v} \in U$ *then* **u** *is the optimal control and* **x** *the optimal trajectory* [Sagan, 1969].

In this particular case, Eq. (8) has the form

$$\mathbf{p}' = -\mathbf{A}^t\mathbf{p} \tag{30}$$

and, with $p_0 = -1$,

$$H(\mathbf{p}, \mathbf{x}, \mathbf{u}) = -\sum_{i=1}^{n} a_{0i}x_i - \psi_0(t, \mathbf{u}) + \mathbf{A}\mathbf{x}\mathbf{p} + \boldsymbol{\psi}(t, \mathbf{u})\mathbf{p}. \tag{31}$$

Hence, the above condition may be stated as follows: *If* $\mathbf{u}, \mathbf{x}, \mathbf{p}$ *satisfy* Eqs. (29) *and* (30) *and if*

$$-\psi_0(t, \mathbf{u}) + \sum_{j=1}^{n} \psi_j(t, \mathbf{u}) p_j \geqslant -\psi_0(t, \mathbf{v}) + \sum_{j=1}^{n} \psi_j(t, \mathbf{v}) p_j$$

for all $\mathbf{v} \in U$ *at each point of the trajectory, then* $\mathbf{u}$ *is the optimal control.*

Example 9: The problem in Example 2 is linear in the state variables; as a matter of fact, the state variables do not even appear explicitly in the constraining equations and the integrand. Hence, the control that was found in Example 4 is the optimal control.

4.3 Field Theory

We consider a Lagrange problem (see also Section 2.2) of fixed duration and with fixed endpoints. We shall formulate a sufficient condition for a trajectory to be optimal. Such a condition is then applicable to OCP that may be formulated or transformed into such Lagrange problems.

Suppose that $\mathbf{y}$ has a continuous derivative, is a solution of the Mayer equations and satisfies the Weierstrass condition of a Lagrange problem

$$\mathbf{F}(t, \mathbf{y}, \mathbf{y}') = \mathbf{0}, \quad \mathbf{y}(0) = \boldsymbol{\theta}, \quad \mathbf{y}(T) = \mathbf{y}^T \tag{32}$$

where T is fixed and where

$$\int_0^T \Phi_0(t, \mathbf{y}(t), \mathbf{y}'(t))\, dt \tag{33}$$

is to be minimized.

We say that $\mathbf{y}$ is embeddable in a field if there exists in some open set Ω in $(t, \mathbf{y})$-space which contains the trajectory $\{(t, \mathbf{y}(t)) | 0 \leqslant t \leqslant T\}$, a vector valued function $\boldsymbol{\chi}$ with values $\chi_i(t, y)$, $i = 1, 2, \ldots, \mu$, and continuous partial derivatives such that

$$\mathbf{y}'(t) = \boldsymbol{\chi}(t, \mathbf{y}(t)), \tag{34}$$

and a continuous vector valued function $\boldsymbol{\lambda}$ with values $\lambda_j(t, \mathbf{y}), j = 1, 2, \ldots, n$, such that the solutions of $\mathbf{y}' = \boldsymbol{\chi}(t, \mathbf{y})$ satisfy

$$\frac{d}{dt} g_{\mathbf{y}'}(t, \mathbf{y}(t), \boldsymbol{\chi}(t, \mathbf{y}(t)), \boldsymbol{\lambda}(t, \mathbf{y}(t))) = g_{\mathbf{y}}(t, \mathbf{y}(t), \boldsymbol{\chi}(t, \mathbf{y}(t)), \boldsymbol{\lambda}(t, \mathbf{y}(t))) \tag{35}$$

where

$$g(t, \mathbf{y}, \boldsymbol{\chi}, \boldsymbol{\lambda}) = \Phi_0(t, \mathbf{y}, \boldsymbol{\chi}) + \sum_{j=1}^{n} \lambda_j(t, \mathbf{y})\, \Phi_j(t, \mathbf{y}, \boldsymbol{\chi}),$$

that

$$\frac{\partial}{\partial y_i} g_{y'_k}(t, \mathbf{y}, \boldsymbol{\chi}(t, \mathbf{y}), \boldsymbol{\lambda}(t, \mathbf{y})) = \frac{\partial}{\partial y_k} g_{y'_i}(t, \mathbf{y}, \boldsymbol{\chi}(t, \mathbf{y}), \boldsymbol{\lambda}(t, \mathbf{y})) \tag{36}$$

and $\mathbf{F}(t, \mathbf{y}, \boldsymbol{\chi}(t, \mathbf{y})) = \mathbf{0}$ for all $(t, \mathbf{y}) \in \Omega$ [Sagan, 1969, p. 275].

If some of the terminal coordinates of $\mathbf{y}$, say $y_{k_1}, \ldots, y_{k_l}$ are free, the transversality conditions

$$g_{y'_{k_j}}(T, \mathbf{y}(T), \boldsymbol{\chi}(T, \mathbf{y}(T)), \boldsymbol{\lambda}(T, \mathbf{y}(T))) = 0, \quad j = 1, 2, \ldots, l, \tag{37}$$

also have to hold at the terminal time T.

Example 10: In Example 5 we formulated the problem of Example 2 as a Lagrange problem of fixed duration with one free coordinate:

$$y'_1 - y'_3 = 0$$

$$y'_2 - ty'_3 = 0$$

$y_1(0) = y_2(0) = y_3(0) = 0, y_1(1) = 0, y_2(1) = 1, \int_0^1 y_3'^2 \, dt$ is to be minimized. In Example 5, we obtained the trajectory $y_1 = y_3 = -6t + 6t^2, y_2 = -3t^2 + 4t^3$. The three parameter family of trajectories $y_1 = -6t + 6t^2 + a, y_2 = -3t^2 + 4t^3 + b, y_3 = -6t + 6t^2 + c$ also satisfies the Mayer equations, the constraining equations and covers the $(t, \mathbf{y})$-space simply, i.e., a, b, c are uniquely determined by (t, y_1, y_2, y_3). Thus, with every point in $(t, \mathbf{y})$-space there is associated a unique tangent vector to the trajectory that passes through this point:

$$\chi_1(t, \mathbf{y}) = -6 + 12t, \quad \chi_2(t, y) = -6t + 12t^2, \quad \chi_3(t, y) = -6 + 12t.$$

As in Example 5, we take $\lambda_1 = -12, \lambda_2 = 24$. We observe that the trajectory is a solution of Eq. (34), namely

$$y'_1 = -6 + 12t, \quad y'_2 = -6t + 12t^2, \quad y'_3 = -6 + 12t.$$

With $g = y_3'^2 + \lambda_1(y'_1 - y'_3) + \lambda_2(y'_2 - ty'_3)$ we have $g_{y'_1} = \lambda_1$, $g_{y'_2} = \lambda_2$, $g_{y'_3} = 2y'_3 - \lambda_1 - \lambda_2 t, g_{y_1} = g_{y_2} = g_{y_3} = 0$ and hence, Eq. (35) becomes

$$\frac{d}{dt}(\lambda_1) = 0, \quad \frac{d}{dt}(\lambda_2) = 0, \quad \frac{d}{dt}(\chi_3 - \lambda_1 - \lambda_2 t) = 0$$

which is obviously satisfied for the above choices of $\boldsymbol{\lambda}, \boldsymbol{\chi}$. Equations (36) and (37) for $k_j = 3$ are trivially satisfied. Hence, the trajectory is embeddable in a field. Ω is the entire $(t, \mathbf{y})$-space.

If $\mathbf{y}$ *is embeddable in a field and if*

$$g(t, \mathbf{y}, \boldsymbol{\xi}, \boldsymbol{\lambda}(t, y)) - g(t, \mathbf{y}, \boldsymbol{\chi}(t, \mathbf{y}), \boldsymbol{\lambda}(t, \mathbf{y})) + \sum_{i=1}^{n} (\chi_i(t, \mathbf{y}) - \xi_i) g_{y_i'}(t, \mathbf{y}, \boldsymbol{\chi}(t, \mathbf{y}), \boldsymbol{\lambda}(t, \mathbf{y})) \geqslant 0 \quad (38)$$

for all $(t, \mathbf{y}) \in \Omega$ *and all vectors* $\boldsymbol{\xi}$ *for which* $\mathbf{F}(t, \mathbf{y}, \boldsymbol{\xi}) = \mathbf{0}$, *then* $\mathbf{y}$ *is the solution of the Lagrange problem*, Eqs. (32) *and* (33) *relative to all other trajectories that satisfy the boundary conditions and lie in* Ω [Sagan, 1969, p. 275].

Example 11: We have seen in Example 10 that the trajectory of the problem in Example 2 is embeddable in a field. As in Example 5, we obtain for (38)

$$(\xi_3 - \chi_3(t, y))^2 \geqslant 0$$

which is obviously satisfied for all ξ_3. Hence, the trajectory that was obtained in Example 5 is indeed the solution of the problem.

5. CONCLUDING REMARKS

In very general terms, an OCP may be formulated as follows: Given a (function) space X, a function F: $X \to R$, and a subset Y of X. To be found is that element $\mathbf{x}_0 \in Y$ for which $F(\mathbf{x}_0) \leqslant F(\mathbf{x})$ for all $\mathbf{x} \in Y$. For example, in the OCP that was formulated in (1) through (5), X is the space of all (sectionally smooth, or absolutely continuous) functions from R into R^n, F is the integral in (5), and Y is the solution space of (1), (3), and (4) subject to the constraint (2).

To obtain meaningful and tractable necessary and sufficient conditions, algorithms for the solution of the problem, and, most important from the mathematicians point of view, a proof of the existence of a solution, X, Y, and F in the above formulation have to be specified so that the problem becomes amenable to mathematical analysis. One such choice has been made in this chapter; others are possible.

Once necessary and/or sufficient conditions are formulated analytically, the problem of synthesis arises, i.e., of finding candidates that satisfy these conditions. With few exceptions, only simple problems that rarely reflect reality with sufficient accuracy, or contrived problems, admit analytic solutions (in a closed form). For more complicated problems, numerical algorithms have to be devised. For example, a two-point boundary value problem arises from an application of the necessary conditions to the Lagrange Problem, or an application of Pontryagin's maximum principle to an optimal control problem. (The latter is somewhat more complicated by the presence of the constrained control vector $\mathbf{u}$). One may then proceed to apply numerical techniques to the solution of such boundary value problems without regard to the source from which they arose. (See, for example [Armstrong, 1967; Canon, Cullum and Polak, 1970; Kirk,

1970].) Alternate methods for developing algorithms for the computation of a solution may be put under the general heading "Direct Methods." These methods of which the various "descent methods" are typical, bypass the necessary (and sufficient) conditions and go directly for the minimum by iterations that decrease the value of the function that is to be minimized at every step. For example (see [Luenberger, 1969]), if F is a quadratic function

$$F(\mathbf{x}) = (\mathbf{x}, Q\mathbf{x}) - 2(\mathbf{b}, \mathbf{x})$$

on a Hilbert space X where Q is a self-adjoint positive definite operator on X, $\mathbf{b}$ is a fixed element in X, and (,) denotes the dot product in X, then, starting with any element $\mathbf{x}_1 \in X$, the iteration

$$\mathbf{x}_{n+1} = \mathbf{x}_n + \frac{\|\mathbf{b} - Q\mathbf{x}_n\|^2}{(\mathbf{b} - Q\mathbf{x}_n, Q\mathbf{b} - Q^2\mathbf{x}_n)}$$

generates a sequence $\{\mathbf{x}_n\}$ which converges in norm to an element $\mathbf{x}_0 \in X$ for which F assumes its minimum value. (See also [Hestenes, 1960; Horwitz and Sarachik, 1968, 1969; Lasdon, Miller and Waren, 1967; Lee and Sheikh, 1969; Nashed, 1970; Powell, 1970; Rosen, 1961; Sinnot and Luenberger, 1967; Straeter, 1971; Tokumaru, Adachi and Goto, 1970].) Various "programming methods" for the solution of optimal control problems are discussed elsewhere in this handbook. (Chapters II-1, 5, 6, 7 and Chapter III-9)

From the standpoint of the mathematician, the search for sufficient conditions and for proofs of the existence of a solution seem of primary concern. From the standpoint of the applications, the synthesis problem is very much in the foreground. Here, the direct methods seem most promising. In addition to providing an algorithm that can be handled by computers, they lead in many instances to a constructive proof of the existence of a solution.

REFERENCES

1. Adiri, I. and A. Ben-Israel, "An Extension and Solution of Arrow-Karlin Type Production Models by the Pontryagin Maximum Principle," *Cahiers du Centre d'Etudes de Recherche Opérationnelle* 8: 147–158 (1966).
2. Armstrong, E. S., "An Algorithm for the Iterative Solution of a Class of Two-Point Boundary Value Problems Occuring in Optimal Control Theory," Ph.D. Dissertation, North Carolina State University (1967).
3. Arrow, K. J., "Applications of Control Theory to Economic Growth," *Math. of the Dec. Sci.* Part II, Amer. Math. Soc. 85–119 (1968).
4. Athans, M. and P. L. Falb, *Optimal Control*, McGraw-Hill, New York (1965).
5. Bliss, G. A., *Lectures on the Calculus of Variations*, The University of Chicago Press, Chicago (1946).
6. Boltyanskii, V. G., "Sufficient Conditions for Optimality and the Justification of the Dynamic Programming Methods," *SIAM J. Control* 1: 326–361 (1966).

7. Canon, M. D., Clifton D. Cullum, Jr., and Elijah Polak, *Theory of Optimal Control and Mathematical Programming*, McGraw-Hill, New York (1970).
8. Eppen, C. D. and F. J. Gould, "A Lagrangian Application to Production Models," *Operations Res.* **16:** 819–829 (1968).
9. Filippov, A. F., "On Certain Questions in the Theory of Optimal Control," *SIAM J. Control* **1:** 76–84 (1963).
10. Halkin, H., "Mathematical Foundations of System Optimization," *Topics in Optimization*, Academic Press, New York (1967).
11. Hermes, H. and J. P. LaSalle, *Functional Analysis and Time Optimal Control*, Academic Press, New York (1969).
12. Hestenes, M. R., "Multiplier and Gradient Methods," *J. Optimization Theory and Applic.* **4:** 303–320 (1969).
13. Horwitz, L. B. and P. E. Sarachik, "Davidon's Method in Hilbert Space," *SIAM J. Appl. Math.* **16:** 676–695 (1968).
14. —— and ——, "A Survey of Two Recent Iterative Techniques for Computing Optimal Control Signals," *Proc. of the 10th Joint Automatic Control Conference*, Boulder, Colorado, pp. 50–51 (1969).
15. Kirk, Donald E., *Optimal Control Theory, An Introduction*, Prentice Hall, Englewood Cliffs, New Jersey (1970).
16. Lasdon, L. S., S. K. Miller, and A. D. Waren, "The Conjugate Gradient Method for Optimal Control Problems," *IEEE Trans. Auto. Control.* AC-**12(3):** 132–138 (1967).
17. Lee, E. B. and L. Markus, *Foundations of Optimal Control Theory*, Wiley & Sons, New York (1967).
18. Lee, E. B., "A Sufficient Condition in the Theory of Optimal Control," *SIAM J. Control* **1:** 241–245 (1963).
19. Lee, E. S. and M. A. Sheikh, "Optimal Production Planning by a Gradient Technique," *Management Sci.* **16:** 109–117 (1969).
20. Luenberger, D. G., *Optimization by Vector Space Methods*, Wiley & Sons, New York (1969).
21. Mangasarian, O. L., "Sufficient Conditions for the Optimal Control of Nonlinear Systems," *SIAM J. Control* **4:** 139–152 (1966).
22. McMasters, A. W., "Optimal Control in Determining Inventory Models," Nav. Postgrad. School, Document No. 55MG0031A (March 1970).
23. McShane, E. J., "Necessary Conditions in Generalized Curve Problems of the Calculus of Variations," *Duke J. Math.* **7:** 1–27 (1940).
24. Nashed, M. Z., "Steepest Descent for Singular Linear Operator Equations," *SIAM J. Numer. Anal.* **7:** 358–363 (1970).
25. Park, S. K., "On the Equivalence of Optimal Control Problems and the Transformation of Optimal Control Problems into Lagrange Problems," Ph.D. Dissertation, North Carolina State University (1970).
26. Powell, M. J. D., "A Survey of Numerical Methods for Nonconstrained Optimization," *SIAM Rev.* **12:** 79–97 (1970).
27. Pontryagin, L. S., V. G. Boltyanskii, R. V. Gramkrelidze, and R. V. Mishchenko, *The Mathematical Theory of Optimal Processes*, Interscience-Wiley & Sons, New York (1962).
28. Rosen, J. B., "The Gradient Projector Method for Nonlinear Programming, II, Nonlinear Constraints," *SIAM J. Appl. Math.* **9:** 514–532 (1961).
29. Sagan, H., *Introduction to the Calculus of Variations*, McGraw-Hill, New York (1969).

30. ——, "Calculus of Variations and Optimal Control Theory," *J. Franklin Institute* **291**: 305–313 (1971).
31. Sinnot, J. F., Jr. and D. G. Luenberger, "Solutions of Optimal Control Problems by the Method of Conjugate Gradients," 1967 Joint Automatic Control Conference, 566–573.
32. Sprzeuzkouski, Y., "A Problem in Optimal Stock Management," *J. Optimization Theory and Applic.* **1**: 232–241 (1967).
33. Straeter, T. S., "On the Extension of the Davidon-Broyden Class of Rank One, Quasi-Newton Minimization Methods to an Infinite Dimensional Hilbert Space with Applications to Optimal Control Problems," Ph.D. Dissertation, North Carolina State University (1971).
34. Tokumaru, H., N. Adachi, and K. Goto, "Davidon's Method for Minimization Problems in Hilbert Space with an Application to Control Problems," *SIAM J. Control* **8**: 163–179 (1970).

SECTION III

Methodology of OR: Stochastic Models

III-1

STOCHASTIC PROCESSES

Walter L. Smith
University of North Carolina

1. INTRODUCTION

A *stochastic* or *random process* is, strictly speaking, merely an indexed family of random variables. Such a definition may suit the pure mathematician interested in developing abstract theorems, but in a handbook of this type, aimed at readers who wish to use theoretical results in actual problems in the world about us, an alternative approach is surely desired. Most stochastic processes which have been examined in detail, and about which useful results have been obtained, are presented by way of a mathematical model. Let us therefore begin this chapter by examining a few such models.

Example 1: The simple random walk. Let $X_1, X_2, \ldots$ be an infinite sequence of random variables which are mutually independent and have the same probability distribution:

$$\left.\begin{aligned} \Pr\{X_j = -1\} &= q > 0, \\ \Pr\{X_j = +1\} &= p > 0, \end{aligned}\right\} \quad \text{for } j = 1, 2, 3, \ldots$$

where p and q are constants such that $p + q = 1$. Such a sequence of random variables might arise in the following way. Two players, Quentin and Peter, play a game of chance. The winner pays the loser \$1. The probability Peter wins a game is p, for Quentin the probability of winning is q. They play a sequence of independent games. If S_n is the amount by which Peter's capital has changed, after playing n games, then

$$S_n = X_1 + X_2 + \cdots + X_n. \tag{1}$$

The sequence $S_0 = 0$, $S_1, S_2, \ldots$ is called a *simple random walk;* the adjective *simple* telling us that the "steps" of the walk, that is the quantities X_j, can be only ± 1. For all its simplicity, the simple random walk has been the object of a great deal of research and many profound and surprising things are known about it. It provides a simple "model" of a variety of real-world phenomena, with varying degrees of verisimilitude. One application is to the study of the motion of a "hole" in a crystalline molecular structure.

Example 2: Recurrent events. Suppose we watch the above simple random walk and say the event ϵ occurs whenever $S_n = 0$, i.e., whenever the net change in Peter's capital is zero. Then it is plain, intuitively, that every time ϵ occurs the process is returning to the same condition as that in which it started. The probability distributions affecting the time until the next occurrence of ϵ are identical to those governing the time up to the first occurrence of ϵ after the game began. This particular example of a *recurrent event* ϵ is typical of a general class of stochastic processes, a class of inestimable value in analyzing more complicated processes which arise in OR, queuing theory, industrial replacement theory, and many other areas.

Example 3: Markov chains. Consider a minibus with seats for 6 passengers and no standing room. It makes a circular tour of a small city picking up and discharging passengers. If the bus approaches a busstop with $r (0 \leqslant r \leqslant 6)$ passengers aboard, let p_{rs} be the probability that after that stop there will be s passengers aboard. Thus p_{52} is the probability that, given the bus leaves one stop with 5 passengers aboard, it leaves the next stop with 2 aboard. Let us assume that the successive changes in the number of passengers aboard are *independent.* What we mean by this remark is as follows. Suppose, for example, that the bus approaches a stop with 3 passengers. Then if X be the number aboard on leaving the stop, X is a random variable such that $\Pr\{X = j\} = p_{3j}$, $j = 0, 1, 2, \ldots, 6$, and X is independent of all previous experience of the bus *except* for the fact that there are, in this example, 3 aboard. The fact that this "3" affects X is, of course, reflected by the dependence of the so-called *transition probabilities* p_{3j} on the number "3." If X_n is the number of passengers aboard after n stops, then $X_1, X_2, \ldots$ is called a *Markov Chain.* It is, indeed, called a Markov Chain with 7 states, because X_n is restricted always to one of the 7 possible values $0, 1, 2, \ldots, 6$. We shall see later that it is possible to have Markov chains with an infinite number of states. Markov chains arise in a wide range of problems in OR and infinite ones are of special importance in the theory of queues.

The 3 examples just discussed are examples of stochastic processes in *discrete time.* That is, we can imagine the time axis marked at the instants $0, 1, 2, 3, \ldots$, and the process develops in relation to these discrete time instants. For example, in the simple random walk one supposes the successive steps in the walk take place at multiples of some fixed, convenient, time unit. Realism demands in many cases that the mathematical model allow development of the process in *continuous time.* A few examples of such processes follow.

Example 4: The Poisson Process. This name is for a model of the way certain events A, say, occur on a continuous time scale; indeed, it is what the OR analyst means by "events occurring randomly in time." Let $N(a, b]$ denote the (random) number of these events to occur in the time interval $(a, b]$. The fact that we "close" the interval to the right is really no more than pedagogy, since we shall see that the probability of an event A occurring at a specified time instant b is 0. Let $\lambda > 0$ be a constant, called the ***intensity*** of the process; λ has the dimension of $[\text{time}]^{-1}$. Then for any small $h > 0$ we suppose:

(P1) $\Pr\{N(t, t+h] = 1\} = \lambda h + o(h)$;
(P2) $\Pr\{N(t, t+h] \geqslant 2\} = o(h)$;
(P3) the random variable $N(t, t+h]$ is, for all $h > 0$, independent of occurrences of A prior to t, and even precisely at t.

To amplify (P3) a little, it means, in particular, that the distribution of $N(t, t+h]$ is the same whether or not A occurs at the instant t. An easy deduction from the assumptions is

(P4) $\Pr\{N(t, t+h] = 0\} = 1 - \lambda h + o(h)$.

We shall see later that two important properties of the Poisson distribution are:

(P5) For any $T \geqslant 0$ and any time t, $N(t, t+T)$ has a Poisson distribution with mean λT; thus λ is the mean number of events A per unit of time;
(P6) The time intervals separating successive occurrences of A are independent random variables with the exponential p.d.f. $\lambda e^{-\lambda x}, x \geqslant 0$.

The Poisson process is used as a model for the random arrival of customers in queuing problems, for the random breakdown of machines and computers, for the occurrence of accidents in factories, and many other similar applications.

Example 5: Renewal Processes. Imagine an item in use in an industrial context, say, which is subject to failure and prompt replacement from time to time. The simplest example to think of is the humble lightbulb, but others will spring to mind, depending on one's practical background. Let the lifetime of successive items be $X_1, X_2, \ldots$, supposing these X_j to be independent and identically distributed random variables with the same p.d.f. $f(x)$, say. Of course, $f(x) \equiv 0$ for $x < 0$. Let us also write $F(x) = \int_0^x f(y)\,dy$ for $\Pr\{X_j \leqslant x\}$, and let $N(x)$ be the number of replacements or *renewals* to occur in $(0,x]$. The *renewal function* is $H(x) = \mathcal{E}N(x)$, the expected number of renewals to occur in the time interval $(0,x]$. It can be shown that

$$H(x) = F(x) + \int_0^x H(x - z)\, f(z)\, dz,$$

this being the *integral equation of renewal theory*. The *renewal density* is $h(x) = H'(x)$ and it satisfies the *renewal density equation*

$$h(x) = f(x) + \int_0^x h(x - z)\, f(z)\, dz.$$

It can be shown that $h(x) \cdot \delta x$ is, to the first order of small quantities, the probability of a renewal occurring in the time interval $(x, x + \delta x)$, provided $h(x)$ is continuous in that interval. A graph of $h(x)$ also serves to highlight the points in time when renewals are more and less likely to occur.

A stochastic process curiously different from all those we have so far discussed is the *renewal age* process $Y(x)$ which gives the age of the item in use at time x. A graph of an actually realized $Y(x)$ is a jagged saw-tooth affair with abrupt drops to zero at the renewal instants and inclines of unit slope. The renewal age is, in some contexts, also called the *backward delay*, since it measures backwards in time from x to the immediately preceding renewal instant. Similarly one has the *forward delay* $Z(x)$, say, which measures the time from x to the next following renewal instant.

The astute reader will see that renewal processes are the continuous time analogue of recurrent event processes. They have great value in analyzing more complex processes, apart from their more immediately obvious applications to problems of industrial replacement and other, similar, replacement problems.

Example 6: Brownian motion, or, sometimes the *Wiener process*. The idea for this process arose from observations by an English botanist Brown; but Wiener was the first to discuss it with mathematical rigor. Indeed, although the process is useful in discussing applied problems, a correct mathematical treatment calls for very sophisticated mathematical tools, beyond the range of this chapter. This should not deter us from using Brownian motion as a model (e.g., for stock prices) when it seems appropriate. Indeed, except when one examines Brownian motion under a high-powered microscope, as it were, one's intuition is a reasonably safe guide.

Let us write $W(t)$ for the coordinate of the "Brownian particle" at time t and, for ease, suppose $W(0) = 0$. $\mathcal{E}[W(t)] = 0$ for all t. Let $0 < t_1 < t_2 < \cdots < t_n$, say. Then a basic property of the process is that $W(t_1)$, $W(t_2) - W(t_1), \ldots,$ $W(t_n) - W(t_{n-1})$ are independent Gaussian variables, the variance of $W(t_j) -$

$W(t_{j-1})$ being $(t_j - t_{j-1})$. A graph of this process made by observing it at extremely close equi-spaced time instants and connecting the resulting points on the graph linearly, presents an appearance similar to that of stock prices, or the humidity trace made on the humidity-measuring devices one sees in libraries, or the trace made by a seismograph in the absence of serious earth tremors. With a suitable transformation, $W(t)$ may model fairly well the tracking errors in guiding a rocket from the ground. There are many other such possible applications.

It can be proved that, with probability one, $W(t)$ is a continuous function of t. Unfortunately, it can also be proved that if one examines a track of $W(t)$ over any finite time interval, then, with probability one there is not one time instant t at which $W(t)$ has a differential coefficient. This latter fact bothers physicists who wish to use $W(t)$ as a model for the diffusion of particles (a frequent application of $W(t)$, by the way) since it implies impossibly rapid changes of momentum, only possible if the particle were to have zero mass or if the particle were responding to forces of infinite magnitude. Nevertheless, as we have already hinted, if one doesn't examine $W(t)$ too closely it will happily model a variety of interesting real-world processes in their grosser aspects.

Our object in this section has been to display to the reader a few of the more important stochastic processes used in the literature of OR. In the remainder of this chapter we shall present formulae for a number of specific processes; due to limitations of space we shall adopt a more succinct style. However, before we leave this introductory section, we must comment on the important notion of *stationarity*.

By way of illustration, consider a system which can exist in only two "states" or "conditions," A or B, say. If the system is in state A at time t, let there be a probability $\alpha\delta t + o(\delta t)$ that the system will flip instantaneously into B during $(t, t + \delta t)$, independently of all previous history of the process. If the process is in state B let the corresponding probability be $\beta\delta t + o(\delta t)$. We suppose $\alpha > 0$ and $\beta > 0$ are constants. Then if $p_A(t)$ and $p_B(t)$ are the probabilities of being in states A and B, respectively, at time t, one can show

$$\frac{dp_A}{dt} = -\alpha p_A(t) + \beta p_B(t)$$
$$\frac{dp_B}{dt} = \alpha p_A(t) - \beta p_B(t) \tag{2}$$

These equations have the solution (using $p_A(t) + p_B(t) = 1$, for all t)

$$p_A(t) = \frac{\beta}{\alpha + \beta}\,[1 - e^{-(\alpha+\beta)t}] + p_A(0)\,e^{-(\alpha+\beta)t}$$
$$p_B(t) = \frac{\alpha}{\alpha + \beta}\,[1 - e^{-(\alpha+\beta)t}] + p_B(0)\,e^{-(\alpha+\beta)t} \tag{3}$$

We draw certain observations from these equations.

(i) As $t \to \infty$,

$$p_A(t) \longrightarrow \frac{\beta}{\alpha + \beta} = \pi_A, \quad \text{say;}$$

$$p_B(t) \longrightarrow \frac{\alpha}{\alpha + \beta} = \pi_B, \quad \text{say.}$$

(ii) If $p_A(0) = \pi_A$ and $p_B(0) = \pi_B$, then $p_A(t) = \pi_A$ and $p_B(t) = \pi_B$, for all $t > 0$.

(iii) If $a = 1/\alpha$, $b = 1/\beta$, then a and b are the average lengths of sojourns by the system in A and B respectively. Then

$$\pi_A = \frac{a}{a + b}$$

$$\pi_B = \frac{b}{a + b}$$

(iv) The quantities π_A and π_B can be discovered from the linear equations one gets from (Eqs. (2)) by setting the time derivatives equal to zero, coupled with the extra requirement $\pi_A + \pi_B = 1$. Note that (Eqs. (2)) lead in this way to the redundant system

$$\begin{aligned} 0 &= -\alpha\pi_A + \beta\pi_B \\ 0 &= \alpha\pi_A - \beta\pi_B \end{aligned} \tag{4}$$

The distribution (π_A, π_B) is called the *stationary* distribution of the system; the reason is given in (iii). Whatever the initial distribution over the states (at time $t = 0$), (i) shows that as time passes the distribution approaches more and more closely to the stationary one. Thus, if we were discussing the operation of such a system in the real world, and if it had been "running" an indefinite, but presumably long, time, then the stationary distribution would be the appropriate distribution with which to describe the process. Finally, (iii) and (iv) give quick ways of determining the stationary distribution. The method (iii) depends on being able to calculate the average duration of a *cycle* in the process, in this case easily seen to be $a + b$; this method is often too difficult to apply. The method (iv) is essentially based on the logic that if a system has the stationary distribution, then the possible changes in $(t, t + \delta t)$ must have zero net effect. This basic idea can be applied to a wide range of quite complicated models and often successfully leads to the required stationary distribution.

It should be realized that all the ideas we have thus developed by considering this easily discussed two-state process apply with only obvious changes to a wide gamut of processes arising in OR.

A final observation is of considerable practical importance. It can be shown from the strong law of large numbers that if such a process is observed for a very long time T, then π_A is approximately the proportion of T during which the system is in state A. The approximation gets better and better, as $T \to \infty$. Thus we have an operational interpretation of a stationary distribution which applies generally and is of prime practical importance.

It is as well that the stationary distribution of a process is so informative, since the so-called *transient* distribution, exemplified by (Eqs. (3)) for the relatively easy two-state process, is usually impossible to determine. In many situations where the transient distributions are thus intractable, the stationary distribution can be calculated, or at least moments of it can be determined.

The stochastic processes to which we have so far introduced the reader, and the ones we shall mainly discuss in what follows, are defined by equations, or a "model," which give the rules by which the process changes as time passes. Another approach, not so much used in OR except for the important *stationary processes*, is to define the process by specifying certain overall gross characteristics which may not give any clue as to the instant-by-instant behavior of the process. The important class, just mentioned, of *stationary processes* will be described briefly in the final section of this chapter.

2. RANDOM WALKS

If $X_1, X_2, \ldots$ are real-valued, identically distributed, mutually independent random variables, let $S_o = 0$, $S_n = X_1 + X_2 + \cdots + X_n$, for $n = 1, 2, \ldots$, etc. Then $\{S_n\}$ is a *random walk*. If $\Pr\{X_j = +1\} = p$ and $\Pr\{X_j = -1\} = q$, where $p + q = 1$, we have a *simple random walk*.

If $\mathcal{E} X_1 = \mu_1$ and $\operatorname{Var} X_1 = \sigma^2$ are both finite (the usual case in applications) then S_n is asymptotically normal and, for real $y_1 < y_2$,

$$\Pr\{y_1 \leqslant S_n \leqslant y_2\} \simeq (2\pi\sigma^2 n)^{-1/2} \int_{y_1}^{y_2} \exp\left(-\frac{(x - n\mu)^2}{2n\sigma^2}\right) dx$$

This result follows from the famous Central Limit Theorem. Even without a finite variance it is true that $n^{-1} S_n \to \mu_1$, as $n \to \infty$, with probability one. This is the strong law of large numbers. Thus if $\mu_1 > 0$, say, one can assert, for any $\epsilon > 0$, that $S_n > (\mu_1 - \epsilon)n$ for *all* n greater than some random integer $N(\epsilon)$ whose distribution, of course, depends on the specific distribution of the X's and on ϵ. What is true is the statement $\Pr\{N(\epsilon) < \infty\} = 1$. Similarly $S_n < (\mu_1 + \epsilon)n$ for all sufficiently large n. If, however, σ^2 is finite, one can strengthen the strong law to the statement that, for every $\epsilon > 0$,

$$\sum_{n=1}^{\infty} \Pr\left\{\left|\frac{S_n}{n} - \mu_1\right| > \epsilon\right\} < \infty \tag{5}$$

This result, and many similar but more general ones are given in various published articles on "complete convergence" of partial sums.

A stopping rule defines a random integer T by means of a sequence of functions of real variables $\phi_1(x_1)$, $\phi_2(x_1, x_2)$, $\phi_3(x_1, x_2, x_3)$, . . . , etc. We imagine ourselves *sampling* the X's from an infinite population. If we find X_1 has value x_1', say, then we conduct a random trial (independent of all else) with probability of "success" $\phi_1(x_1')$. If this trial is a "success" we sample for X_2, but otherwise we stop sampling and $T = 1$. If we sample X_2 and find $X_2 = x_2'$, say, then we decide whether or not to continue sampling by conducting a further independent "trial" with probability of success $\phi_2(x_1', x_2')$; if this trial gives a "fail" then $T = 2$. It should be clear how this process continues. In most applications the functions ϕ_j have only two possible values: 0 or 1; this is where it is decided to stop sampling at a given stage, if experience of the walk up to that stage is of a certain kind, otherwise the walk continues. Indeed the most common of all stopping rules is based on two real numbers a and b, say, and the walk stops as soon as $S_n \leqslant -a$ or $S_n \geqslant +b$. Notice that a stopping rule may not base a decision to stop at stage n on future values of the X's; in applications such a rule would imply an impossible ability to foretell the future.

In addition, for a stopping rule to be *proper* we must have $\Pr\{T < \infty\} = 1$. In some problems it can be tedious, or difficult, to verify that a stopping rule is proper. However, if $\sigma^2 < \infty$, and the rule is of the type "$S_n \leqslant -a$ or $S_n \geqslant +b$" then it is proper *even if* $\mu_1 = 0$. This fact can be most helpful in practical problems.

Let us now suppose T is a proper stopping rule. Then *Wald's Equation* states that, quite generally,

$$\mathcal{E} S_T = \mu_1 \mathcal{E} T \tag{6}$$

and, in a variety of circumstances, one can even state that

$$\mathcal{E}(S_T - T\mu_1)^2 = \sigma^2 \mathcal{E} T. \tag{7}$$

A sufficient condition for the validity of the second Eq. (7) is that the X's be bounded random variables and that the stopping rule makes T the first integer j for which $|S_j|$ exceeds a given finite constant.

Wald's Eq. (6) is useful in disproving various beguiling but invalid popular arguments. For instance, in a given family, let $X_j = +1$ if a birth is a girl and $X_j = -1$ if a birth is a boy. For simplicity of argument we shall ignore multiple births. Let $\Pr\{X_j = +1\} = p$ and $\Pr\{X_j = -1\} = q$, $p + q = 1$. Then Wald's Eq. (6) shows that no proper stopping rule, however complicated it may be, can affect the overall ratio q/p of boys to girls in a population. It has been (wrongly) urged that some family plans, such as deciding to keep having children until a boy is born, might affect the overall ratio. Similarly one can see that no system of gambling in a sequence of independent fair gambles can hope to do better than any other, however naive, system.

If the X's have a p.d.f. $f(x)$ then, in many cases, the moment generating function (m.g.f.)

$$M(\theta) = \mathcal{E}e^{\theta X} = \int_{-\infty}^{+\infty} e^{\theta x} f(x)\, dx \tag{8}$$

will exist for all real θ in some real interval: $\alpha \leqslant \theta \leqslant \beta$. It usually happens that $M(\theta) \uparrow \infty$ as $\theta \downarrow \alpha$ and as $\theta \uparrow \beta$. We also see that $M(0) = 1$ and $M'(0) = \mu_1$, and that, provided $\mu_1 \neq 0$, there will be an interval for θ in which $M(\theta) \geqslant 1$. If we call this interval I then for all $\theta \in I$ one can claim

$$\mathcal{E}\left\{\frac{e^{\theta S_T}}{|M(\theta)|^T}\right\} = 1. \tag{9}$$

This is Wald's Fundamental Identity. It is difficult, rigorously, to extract information from it, but it is of some use, nonetheless, for suggesting results and for leading to approximations. For example, Eqs. (6) and (7) can be "obtained" by differentiating Eq. (9) with respect to θ twice, and then setting $\theta = 0$. As another practical illustration consider the following. Let the stopping rule be of the type "$S_n \leqslant -a$ or $S_n \geqslant b$," usually referred to as stopping when the walk crosses a *barrier*. Let P_a be the probability that the walk stops because $S_n \leqslant -a$ and P_b be the probability that the walk stops because $S_n \geqslant b$. Assume further that the X's are small relative to a and b. Then, if $S_T \leqslant -a$, not too great an error is committed if we write $S_T = -a$; similarly if $S_T \geqslant b$. Let us, further, write θ^* for the unique θ-value distinct from 0 at which $M(\theta^*) = 1$ (a picture will show there is usually such a θ^*). Then Eq. (9) gives that

$$P_a e^{-a\theta^*} + P_b e^{b\theta^*} \simeq 1$$

since we must have $P_a + P_b = 1$ we discover, for instance, that

$$P_a \simeq \frac{1 - e^{b\theta^*}}{e^{-a\theta^*} - e^{b\theta^*}}. \tag{10}$$

It may be shown that $\theta^* > 0$ if $\mu_1 < 0$ and that $\theta^* < 0$ if $\mu_1 > 0$. One can often solve a problem for which $\mu_1 = 0$ by a limiting procedure.

In the last twenty years a number of identities concerned with the random walk have been discovered which are associated with the names of Spitzer and Sparre-Anderson. So far they have found only limited application in OR. We give here just one example, due to Spitzer. Let $M_n = \max(0, S_1, S_2, \ldots, S_n)$ for $n = 1, 2, \ldots$ and set $M_o = 0$. Let $\psi_n(\theta) = e^{i\theta M_n}$ be the characteristic function of M_n. Let $S_n^+ = S_n$ if $S_n \geqslant 0$, $S_n^+ = 0$ if $S_n < 0$, and let $\chi_n(\theta)$ be the characteristic function of S_n^+. Then, for every ρ such that $0 < \rho < 1$,

$$\exp \sum_{n=1}^{\infty} \frac{\rho^n}{n} \chi_n(\theta) = \sum_{n=0}^{\infty} \rho^n \psi_n(\theta) \tag{11}$$

and

$$\exp \sum_{n=1}^{\infty} \frac{\rho^n}{n} \Pr\{S_n \leqslant 0\} = \sum_{n=0}^{\infty} \rho^n \Pr\{M_n = 0\}.$$

3. THE SIMPLE RANDOM WALK

This special case of the random walk is sufficiently important to warrant separate discussion.

Two absorbing barriers. Recall that $S_o = 0$. Suppose that integers $a > 0$ and $b > 0$ are given and that the walk will stop when either $S_n = -a$ or $S_n = b$. Let $P(b, -a)$ be the probability that the walk will stop at the "upper" barrier, i.e., that $S_T = b$. Plainly

$$P(b, -a) = pP(b - 1, -(a + 1)) + qP(b + 1, -(a - 1)).$$

Indeed, if j is any integer, $-a < j < b$, then

$$P(b - j, -(a + j)) = pP(b - j - 1, -(a + j + 1)) + qP(b - j + 1, -(a + j - 1)).$$

If we set

$$u_j = P(b - j, -(a + j))$$

we are faced with a set of recurrence equations

$$u_j = pu_{j+1} + qu_{j-1} \qquad -a < j < b,$$

with the boundary conditions $u_{-a} = 0$, $u_b = 1$. The solution to this problem depends on whether $p \neq q$. Suppose first, therefore, that $p \neq q$. We note that $u_o = P(b, -a)$, and find

$$P(b, a) = \frac{(q/p)^a - 1}{(q/p)^{(a+b)} - 1}. \tag{12}$$

On the other hand, if $q = p = \frac{1}{2}$, then one can show that

$$P(b, a) = \frac{a}{b + a} \tag{13}$$

The latter result shows, in particular, that if two players A and B with capitals $\$a$ and $\$b$ respectively play a series of independent *fair* ($p = q$) games until one player is bankrupt, then their chances of final success are in the ratio of their capitals, or

$$\frac{\Pr\{A \text{ is bankrupt}\}}{\Pr\{B \text{ is bankrupt}\}} = \frac{b}{a}.$$

One can also write $d(b, a)$ for the expected numbers of (not necessarily fair) games to be played before bankruptcy, i.e., the expected number of steps taken by the walk until a barrier is crossed. It can be shown that when $p \neq q$,

$$d(b,a) = \frac{a + b - b(p/q)^a - a(q/p)^b}{(q-p)\{(p/q)^a - (q/p)^b\}} \tag{14}$$

However, if $p = q = \frac{1}{2}$, then one has the very simple result

$$d(b,a) = ab. \tag{15}$$

One absorbing barrier. Once again we have $S_o = 0$ but now the walk is stopped iff $S_n = b$ (>0). We shall see that this stopping rule may be improper. Let $P(b)$ be the probability that the walk does stop at the barrier at b. Then a little reflection will show that for every integer $b \geqslant 1$ we must have

$$P(b) = \{P(1)\}^b. \tag{16}$$

But for $b \geqslant 1$

$$P(b) = pP(b-1) + qP(b+1).$$

Thus, using Eq. (16), we have

$$P(1) = q\{P(1)\}^2 + p.$$

This quadratic equation for $P(1)$ leads to the equation

$$(qP(1) - p)(P(1) - 1) = 0.$$

When $p = q = \frac{1}{2}$ we have a unique solution $P(1) = 1$, so in this case $P(b) = 1$ for all b. When $p > q$ we can rule out the possibility that $P(1) = p/q$ since $p/q > 1$, an impossibility for a probability. Thus, in this case also, $P(b) = 1$ for all b. When $p < q$ we are in a quandary since p/q and 1 are both possible values for a probability. However, in this case we note that by the strong law of large numbers $n^{-1} S_n \to p - q < 0$, as $n \to \infty$. Thus, if b is large enough, there is plainly a positive probability that S_n never assumes the value b. Hence we must have $P(1) = p/q < 1$, and $P(b) = (p/q)^b$, which decreases to 0 as $b \to \infty$. Thus in the one case $p < q$, we have an *improper* stopping rule; otherwise it is *proper*.

Let us suppose $p \geqslant q$, and write $d(b)$ for the expected number of stops before stopping at the barrier. It should be evident that $d(b) = bd(1)$, for all $b \geqslant 1$. Further, for $b \geqslant 1$,

$$d(b) = 1 + pd(b-1) + qd(b+1),$$

with the boundary condition $d(0) = 0$. We are thus led to the equation

$$bd(1) = 1 + \{b - p + q\}\, d(1),$$

which requires that

$$(p - q)\, d(1) = 1.$$

If $p > q$ we discover that

$$d(1) = \frac{1}{p - q}.$$

If $p = q = \frac{1}{2}$ the only possibility is that $d(1) = \infty$. This is, indeed, correct, although we can hardly claim to have proved it here. A proof can, however, be obtained from the theory of recurrent events.

4. RECURRENT EVENTS

The importance and usefulness of this kind of stochastic process was first recognized and the theory developed by Feller. We imagine an event A to happen at times $S_0, S_1, S_2, \ldots$, where $S_n = X_0 + X_1 + \cdots + X_n$ for $n = 0, 1, 2, \ldots$. We also suppose the X's to be independent random variables, all multiples of some fixed "period" $\omega > 0$. For simplicity, and with no loss of generality, it is usual to take $\omega = 1$. The important assumption is that $X_1, X_2, \ldots$, etc., are identically distributed, and we shall set

$$f_j = \Pr\{X_n = j\}, \quad j = 1, 2, \ldots. \tag{17}$$

Much of the theory is developed for the case $X_0 = 0$, when there is necessarily an occurrence of A at the time origin. This special case is what is always meant by a *recurrent event process.* The more general situation, in which X_0 has some arbitrary distribution, is called a *delayed* recurrent event process. *We shall restrict this section to the less general process.*

Let u_n be the probability that A occurs at time n, and let N_n be the number of occurrences of A in the time interval $[0, n]$. Thus $u_n = \Pr\{N_n > N_{n-1}\}$. It is easy to show that (notice $u_0 = 1$), for example,

$$\mathcal{E}N_n = 1 + u_1 + u_2 + \cdots + u_n = U_n, \text{ say,} \tag{18}$$

and that, if $\mu_1 = \mathcal{E}X_j < \infty$, then

$$\mathcal{E}N_n \sim \frac{n}{\mu_1}, \quad \text{as } n \to \infty. \tag{19}$$

The quantity μ_1 is called the *mean recurrence time* of A, and A is said to be *null* if $\mu_1 = \infty$.

If the X's happen (with probability 1) to be multiples of some integer greater than unity then the recurrent event process is said to be *periodic*, otherwise it is called *aperiodic.* It is easy to see how, by a change of time scale, one can convert a periodic process to an aperiodic one. Thus we shall proceed on the assumption that we have an aperiodic process, with no loss of generality. In that case we have the crucial result that

$$u_n \longrightarrow \frac{1}{\mu_1}, \qquad \text{as} \quad n \longrightarrow \infty. \tag{20}$$

This limit holds even if $\mu_1 = \infty$, in which case $u_n \longrightarrow 0$ (one interprets μ_1^{-1}, in the case $\mu_1 = \infty$, as 0!). A useful consequence of Eq. (20) in applying this theory to various OR problems is that if $\{a_n\}$ is any sequence of real constants such that $\sum_0^\infty |a_n| < \infty$, then

$$\sum_{j=0}^{n} u_j a_{n-j} \longrightarrow \frac{1}{\mu_1} \sum_{j=0}^{\infty} a_j, \qquad \text{as} \quad n \longrightarrow \infty.$$

Here again one must take $\mu_1^{-1} = 0$ if $\mu_1 = \infty$.

Suppose we introduce generating functions of the dummy variable $\zeta, 0 < \zeta < 1$,

$$F(\zeta) = \sum_1^\infty f_n \zeta^n$$

$$U(\zeta) = \sum_0^\infty u_n \zeta^n.$$

The following relation, for $n = 1, 2, \ldots$, is easily proved:

$$u_n = f_n + f_{n-1} u_1 + \cdots + f_1 u_{n-1}, \tag{21}$$

and from it one can quickly discover

$$F(\zeta) = \frac{U(\zeta) - 1}{U(\zeta)}, \tag{22}$$

$$U(\zeta) = \frac{1}{1 - F(\zeta)}. \tag{23}$$

Let us write $\sum_1^\infty f_n = f$. Some recurrent events of interest are such that $f < 1$. Such events are called *transient*, otherwise they are *persistent* (i.e., when $f = 1$). It is possible from Eq. (22) to show that A is transient iff $\sum_0^\infty u_n < \infty$, and that, when this is so,

$$f = 1 - \frac{1}{\sum_0^\infty u_n}. \tag{24}$$

This last equation is useful in settling the matter of persistence or transience for many fairly complicated processes.

If $\mu_2 = \mathcal{E} X_n^2 < \infty$, let us set $\sigma^2 = \mu_2 - \mu_1^2$. Then it can be shown that

$$\operatorname{Var} N_n \sim \frac{\sigma^2}{\mu_1^3} n, \qquad \text{as } n \longrightarrow \infty \tag{25}$$

and that, for example,

$$\frac{N_n - n/\mu_1}{\sigma n^{1/2} \mu_1^{-3/2}} = \tilde{N}_n \tag{26}$$

has, asymptotically as $n \longrightarrow \infty$, a standardized normal distribution:

$$\Pr\{\tilde{N}_n \leqslant x\} \longrightarrow \frac{1}{\sqrt{(2\pi)}} \int_{-\infty}^{x} e^{-1/2y^2}\, dy, \qquad \text{as } n \longrightarrow \infty, \tag{27}$$

for each fixed x. The latter "Central Limit Theorem for Recurrent Events" is of considerable applied value.

When $\mu_2 < \infty$ one can also obtain more "refined" results concerning the u_n. As examples we give two results.

$$\sum_0^\infty \left| u_n - \frac{1}{\mu_1} \right| < \infty. \tag{28}$$

$$U_n = \frac{n+1}{\mu_1} + \frac{\mu_2}{2\mu_1^2} + o(1), \qquad \text{as } n \longrightarrow \infty. \tag{29}$$

These results, and Eq. (25), are not easy to prove. For their proofs and for many more elaborate results, one must refer to the specialized literature.

5. MARKOV CHAINS

Suppose we are studying a system which can exist at any given moment in one, and only one, of a sequence of possible *states*, called, say, $\mathcal{S}_0, \mathcal{S}_1, \mathcal{S}_2, \ldots$. There may be a finite or an infinite number of these states. Suppose that every unit of time the system can instantaneously move from its present state to another one. Suppose further that, given it is in $\mathcal{S}_i$, the probability it moves to $\mathcal{S}_j$ is p_{ij}, and that the selection of the next state of the system is independent of all previous history of the process except for the fact that it is presently in $\mathcal{S}_i$. Plainly such a set-up is entirely defined by the *transition matrix* $[p_{ij}]$, with the properties

$$p_{ij} \geqslant 0 \qquad \text{all } (i, j) \tag{30}$$

$$\sum_{j=0}^{\infty} p_{ij} \leqslant 1 \qquad \text{all } i. \tag{31}$$

If one has a strict inequality in Eq. (31) the process is said to be *dishonest*, otherwise it is *honest*. Although Markov Chains arise very often indeed in OR it is extremely rare that a dishonest one appears. For this reason we shall, for the remainder of this section, assume we are discussing an *honest* process.

Let $p_{ij}(n)$ be the probability that, given the system was in $\mathcal{S}_i$ at time zero, it is in $\mathcal{S}_j$ at time n. In many applications the calculation of the various $p_{ij}(n)$ is desirable. When the number of states is finite, this calculation is not too difficult, unless the number of states is large. For, if we set $[p_{ij}] = \mathbf{P}$, say, then

$$[p_{ij}(n)] = \mathbf{P}^n. \tag{32}$$

It is possible to simplify Eq. (32) even further if one is prepared to discover the eigenvalues and eigenvectors of the matrix $\mathbf{P}$. Let its eigenvalues be $\lambda_1, \lambda_2, \ldots, \lambda_N$, where N is the number of states (so that $\mathbf{P}$ is $N \times N$). Note that, unfortunately, these eigenvalues are often complex valued. For simplicity, let us assume these λ's to be distinct. Let $\underset{\sim}{\mathbf{y}}_j$ be the $(1 \times N)$ row vector associated with λ_j:

$$\underset{\sim}{\mathbf{y}}_j \mathbf{P} = \lambda_j \underset{\sim}{\mathbf{y}}_j. \tag{33}$$

One can normalize $\underset{\sim}{\mathbf{y}}_j$ by dividing it by any element of largest modulus, so that the resulting row vector contains at least one unit coordinate and all the others are no greater than unity in modulus. Let $\underset{\sim}{\boldsymbol{\eta}}_j$ be the $(1 \times N)$ row vector $\{0, 0, \ldots, 0, 1, 0, \ldots, 0\}$ with zeros in all coordinates except for a unit in position j. Then it is possible to find constants $c_1, c_2, \ldots, c_N$, say, such that

$$\underset{\sim}{\boldsymbol{\eta}}_i = c_1 \underset{\sim}{\mathbf{y}}_1 + c_2 \underset{\sim}{\mathbf{y}}_2 + \cdots + c_N \underset{\sim}{\mathbf{y}}_N. \tag{34}$$

Let us write $\underset{\sim}{\mathbf{p}}_i(n)$ for the row vector $\{p_{i1}(n), p_{i2}(n), \ldots, p_{iN}(n)\}$. Then it follows easily from Eqs. (33) and (34) that

$$\underset{\sim}{\mathbf{p}}_i(n) = c_1 \lambda_1^n \underset{\sim}{\mathbf{y}}_1 + c_2 \lambda_2^n \underset{\sim}{\mathbf{y}}_2 + \cdots + c_N \lambda_N^n \underset{\sim}{\mathbf{y}}_N \tag{35}$$

This formula has computational advantages over Eq. (32) in some situations.

A set of states $\mathcal{C}$, say, is said to be *closed* if there is no $\mathcal{S}_i$ in $\mathcal{C}$ and $\mathcal{S}_j$ outside $\mathcal{C}$ such that $p_{ij} > 0$. Thus if the system gets into a state in a closed set $\mathcal{C}$ it can never again leave $\mathcal{C}$. If $\mathcal{C}$ consists of a single state that state is called an *absorbing* state.

A state $\mathcal{S}_i$, say, is called *persistent* if, given the system is in $\mathcal{S}_i$, the probability is one that the system will return to $\mathcal{S}_i$ in a finite time. Thus, if $\mathcal{S}_i$ is persistent, *then with probability one* it either does not occur at all or it occurs an infinite number of times.

We say $\mathcal{S}_j$ is *accessible* to $\mathcal{S}_i$ if there is an integer n such that $p_{ij}(n) > 0$. We say $\mathcal{S}_i$ and $\mathcal{S}_j$ are *mutually* accessible if $\mathcal{S}_j$ is accessible to $\mathcal{S}_i$ and $\mathcal{S}_i$ is accessible to $\mathcal{S}_j$. If $\mathcal{C}$ is a closed set of states such that all pairs of states in $\mathcal{C}$ are mutually accessible then we say $\mathcal{C}$ is *irreducible*. Let $\mathcal{C}(\mathcal{S}_i)$ represent the set of states accessible to $\mathcal{S}_i$. Then, if $\mathcal{S}_i$ is a *persistent* state, $\mathcal{C}(\mathcal{S}_i)$ is an irreducible closed set of persistent states. If $\mathcal{S}_j$ is a state in $\mathcal{C}(\mathcal{S}_i)$ then $\mathcal{C}(\mathcal{S}_j)$ and $\mathcal{C}(\mathcal{S}_i)$ are identical.

We can associate with a state $\mathcal{S}_j$, say, a recurrent event A_j. Every time the system enters $\mathcal{S}_j$ we say the event A_j occurs; it should not be difficult to see that the intervals separating occurrences of A_j are independent and identically distributed random variables. Plainly $\mathcal{S}_j$ is persistent iff A_j is persistent. If A_j is persistent and $\mu_1^{(j)}$ is the mean recurrence time of A_j then $\mu_1^{(j)}$ is also called the mean recurrence time of $\mathcal{S}_j$; $\mathcal{S}_j$ is *positive* if $\mu_1^{(j)} < \infty$ and $\mathcal{S}_j$ is *null* if $\mu_1^{(j)} = \infty$. If A_j is *transient* then so is $\mathcal{S}_j$. Every state in the chain is of a specific *type*, either positive, persistent null, or transient.

In many problems the events A_j are periodic and no change of time scale is convenient, or can be applied without an element of artificiality (since the interval between successive transitions between states is a natural time unit). If A_j is periodic with period ω_j then the same is said of $\mathcal{S}_j$.

A most remarkable theorem states that if $\mathcal{S}_j$ is persistent, then all states in $\mathcal{C}(\mathcal{S}_j)$ are of the same type and the same period. Thus the states of an arbitrary Markov Chain can be divided into transient states and persistent states, and the persistent states can be associated, in a unique way, each with a particular irreducible closed set of persistent states of the same type and period.

One class of problems relates to a system which starts in a transient state $\mathcal{S}_t$, for example. What is the probability the system will ever be "trapped" in an irreducible closed set of persistent states (assuming at least one such set exists)? If g_t is the required probability then

$$g_t = \sum_{s \in T} p_{ts} g_s + \sum_{s \in P} p_{ts}. \tag{36}$$

In this equation the first summation is over all s such that $\mathcal{S}_s$ is transient, the second over s such that $\mathcal{S}_s$ is persistent. Thus, by allowing t to take on all values such that $\mathcal{S}_t$ is transient, Eq. (36) provides a set of linear equations for the unknown probabilities g_t, g_s, etc. However, it can be shown that if the chain is finite (i.e., has only a finite number of states) then the system will enter a persistent state ultimately, with probability 1. In this case, then, every $g_t = 1$. It should be remarked, however, that for some infinite chains there may be a positive probability that the system will remain forever in transient states.

In most applications to OR one can restrict discussion to the behaviour of the system in a chain which is itself an irreducible closed set, briefly called an *irreducible chain*. To determine the type and periodicity of all states in the chain it is enough to examine any one convenient state.

Let us now suppose we have established that a chain is irreducible and aperiodic (i.e., no state is periodic). Then as $n \longrightarrow \infty$, for every fixed (i, j),

$$p_{ij}(n) \longrightarrow \frac{1}{\mu_1^{(j)}} = u_j, \tag{37}$$

for example. Notice that if one state $\mathcal{S}_j$, say, is null, then all states are null and $u_j = 0$ for all j. To discover the $\{u_j\}$ and determine whether or not the states are null or positive one usually tackles the so-called stationarity equations:

$$y_j = \sum_{i=0}^{N-1} y_i p_{ij}, \quad j = 0, 1, 2, \ldots \tag{38}$$

In these equations $(N - 1)$ is taken as infinity, of course, if there are infinitely many states. If one can find nonzero y's such that Eqs. (38) hold and also $\sum_0^{N-1} |y_j| < \infty$, then one may conclude that the states are all positive, and

$$u_j = \frac{y_j}{\sum_0^{N-1} y_j}. \tag{39}$$

It is known that when the states are all positive then one must have $\sum_0^{N-1} u_j = 1$, and this normalization is the reason for Eq. (39). Thus the numbers $\{u_j\}$ provide a probability distribution over the states. On the other hand, if one can show that every solution to Eqs. (38) is either null (all zeros) or such that $\sum_0^{N-1} |y_j| = \infty$, then one can infer that all states of the chain are null.

Indeed Eq. (39) holds whether the chain is irreducible or not, but, for this brief discussion we shall continue to assume irreducibility. In that case we can say that if the chain has period ω (an integer!) then there are exactly ω eigenvalues on the unit circle, including the one at unity, and they are given by the expressions

$$\exp \frac{2k\pi i}{\omega}, \quad k = 0, 1, 2, \ldots, \omega - 1.$$

The remaining eigenvalues (if any) lie strictly within the unit circle.

Thus, for a finite *aperiodic* irreducible chain we may assume $\lambda_1 = 1$ and that $|\lambda_j| < 1$ for $j = 2, 3, \ldots, N$. It is then apparent from Eq. (35) that

$$\underset{\sim}{p}_i(n) \longrightarrow c_1 \underset{\sim}{y}_1, \quad \text{as } n \longrightarrow \infty, \tag{40}$$

and that this convergence is geometrically fast. Thus, for the finite aperiodic chain, we have an alternative (and more informative, in view of the information on the rapidity of convergence) proof of convergence to a stationary distribution.

Clearly one can apply results from recurrent event theory to Markov chains. For instance, under suitable conditions, one can show that the number of returns to a state $\mathcal{S}_j$, say, has, asymptotically, a normal distribution. Some of the computations that arise in such applications can be very tedious, however.

6. MARTINGALES

Although *martingales* do not so far seem to have played an important role in OR work, their theory has been extensively developed in the literature of probability theory. Martingales provide, on occasion, a powerful theoretical tool, and they will doubtless find increasing use by those engaged in OR.

Let $Y_1, Y_2, \ldots$ be an infinite sequence of random variables such that $\mathcal{E}|Y_j| < \infty$ for all $j = 1, 2, \ldots$. The sequence is called a martingale if

$$\mathcal{E}\{Y_{n+1}|Y_1, Y_2, \ldots, Y_n\} = Y_n, \tag{41}$$

for $n = 1, 2, \ldots$. The condition (41) is very general, in that it merely requires that the expected value of Y_{n+1}, conditional upon knowing all "earlier" values of the Y's, shall equal Y_n. There is no mention of independence or of the random variables being identically distributed.

A simple example of a martingale is provided by a gambler who spends successive evenings in a variety of gambling activities. We merely make the assumption that all these activities are "fair," in the sense that if he starts an evening with $\$Y_n$ then he "expects" to end the evening with the same sum. Alas, few real gambles are fair in this sense.

An important result about martingales concerns *optional stopping*. Suppose we consider a martingale $Y_1, Y_2, \ldots$, and use it to determine a *stopping epoch* N as follows. We assume we provide ourselves with an infinite sequence of (measurable) functions $\phi_1(y_1), \phi_2(y_1, y_2), \phi_3(y_1, y_2, y_3), \ldots$, etc., of real valued variables, such that

$$0 \leqslant \phi_n(y_1, y_2, \ldots, y_n) \leqslant 1$$

for all $n, y_1, y_2, \ldots, y_n$. This is all very much as we described in the random walk section. We observe Y_1 and then perform a random trial, independent of all else, with probability of success $\phi_1(Y_1)$. If this trial is a failure then $N = 1$. If this trial is a success we then observe Y_2 and perform a further independent random trial with probability of success $\phi_2(Y_1, Y_2)$. A failure here fixes $N = 2$, and so on. We can then define a new sequence $Z_1, Z_2, \ldots$, etc. by the rule that

$$\begin{aligned} Z_n &= Z_N \quad \text{if} \quad n \geqslant N \\ &= Y_n \quad \text{if} \quad n < N. \end{aligned}$$

It can be proved that the Z-sequence is also a martingale; it was derived from the Y-martingale by *optional stopping.*

This result is frequently useful in giving a shortcut to the solution of quite messy problems. As a very simple illustration, consider a particle performing a simple random walk. Let its coordinate after n steps be $S_n = X_1 + X_2 + \cdots + X_n$ $(S_0 = 0)$, where the X's are independent and identically distributed: $P\{X_j = +1\} = p, P\{X_j = -1\} = q, p + q = 1$. Then if we set $Y_n = (q/p)^{S_n}$ it can be verified that Y_n is a martingale. Suppose our "stopping rule" is such that, for all j,

$$\phi(y_1, y_2, \ldots, y_j) = 0 \quad \text{if} \quad y_j = -a \quad \text{or} \quad +b$$
$$= 1 \quad \text{otherwise.}$$

This corresponds to our previous discussion in Section 3 in which the walk stops when it reaches barriers at $-a$ or $+b$. Now it is clear that Z_n is, ultimately, either $(q/p)^{-a}$, with probability α, say, or $(q/p)^b$, with probability $(1 - \alpha)$. Thus

$$\mathcal{E} Z_n \longrightarrow \alpha(q/p)^{-a} + (1 - \alpha)\,(q/p)^b.$$

But $\mathcal{E} Z_n = \mathcal{E} Z_0 = 1$, for all n. Thus we are led to an equation from which α is easily determined (and found to agree with our earlier results in Section 3).

Another maneuver with a martingale involves *optional sampling.* We discuss a very easy case. Suppose the stopping epoch N is as given above, but that $\Pr\{N < \infty\} = 1$. Then the random quantity Y_N is obtained from the martingale $\{Y_n\}$ by optional sampling, and under quite general conditions $\mathcal{E} Y_N = \mathcal{E} Y_0$.

This result on optional sampling can be used to derive a wide range of interesting results. For example, let $X_1, X_2, \ldots$ be independent and identically distributed and have a moment generating function $\phi(\theta) = \mathcal{E} e^{\theta X_j}$, where θ is real and $\phi(\theta) < \infty$ for $-\alpha < \theta < \beta$ (α and β being nonnegative constants.) Let $S_n = X_1 + X_2 + \cdots + X_n$, as usual, and let N be a stopping rule as described in Section 2. Then $Y_n = e^{\theta S_n} \{\phi(\theta)\}^{-n}$ is a martingale such that $\mathcal{E} Y_n = 1$ for all n. Thus $\mathcal{E} e^{\theta S_N} \{\phi(\theta)\}^{-N} = 1$, by the result on optional stopping; we thus have the famous Wald's Fundamental Identity, Eq. (9). Unfortunately the verification of the technical conditions justifying this and other applications of the optional sampling result can be quite difficult.

If the martingale is such that

$$\mathcal{E} |Y_n| < C < \infty$$

for all n, where C is a constant, then Doob showed the existence of a random variable Y such that $Y_n \longrightarrow Y$ as $n \longrightarrow \infty$, with probability one. Furthermore $\mathcal{E} Y_n = \mathcal{E} Y$ for all n. This is one version of the *Martingale Convergence Theorem*, a powerful tool in research. There is no space for us to explore its implications in this chapter, unfortunately.

7. RENEWAL PROCESSES

As we have seen in the introduction, these processes form the continuous time analogue of the recurrent event processes on the "discrete" time scale. We let $\{X_n\}$ be an infinite sequence of independent and identically distributed nonnegative random variables, with distribution function $F(x) = \Pr\{X_n \leqslant x\}$ and moments $\mu_1 = \mathcal{E}X_j$, $\mu_2 = \mathcal{E}X_j^2$, etc. We assume an event called a *renewal* occurs at times $0, S_1, S_2, \ldots, S_n, \ldots$ etc. where

$$S_n = X_1 + X_2 + \cdots + X_n, \qquad n = 1, 2, \ldots$$

We further write $N(x)$ for the number of renewals in the time interval $(0, x]$. Then $H(x) = N(x)$, the expected number of renewals by time x, is called the *renewal function.* It is known that $H(x)$ satisfies the integral equation

$$H(x) = F(x) + \int_0^x H(x - z)\, F(dz), \tag{42}$$

which arises in many problems in OR.

For simplicitiy in this introductory exposition we shall assume $F(x)$ to be absolutely continuous, with a p.d.f. $f(x)$:

$$F(x) = \int_0^x f(y)\, dy. \tag{43}$$

The reader interested in weird set-ups must turn to the specialist literature.

The rather superficial *Elementary Renewal Theorem* states that

$$H(x) \sim \frac{x}{\mu_1} \quad \text{as} \quad x \longrightarrow \infty. \tag{44}$$

The much more profound *Blackwell's Theorem* states that, for every fixed $c > 0$,

$$H(x + c) - H(x) \longrightarrow \frac{c}{\mu_1}, \qquad \text{as} \quad x \longrightarrow \infty, \tag{45}$$

with the rubric that μ_1^{-1} is interpreted as zero if $\mu_1 = \infty$.

A theorem essentially equivalent to Eq. (45) but in a more usable form is the *Key Renewal Theorem* which states that for a variety of absolutely integrable functions $k(x)$, as $x \longrightarrow \infty$,

$$\int_0^x k(x - z)\, H(dz) \longrightarrow \frac{1}{\mu_1} \int_0^\infty k(z)\, dz. \tag{46}$$

It is not simple to delineate the class of functions $k(x)$ for which Eq. (46) holds, but for the present section in which we are supposing $F(x)$ to be absolutely continuous, the following is a useful guide: $k(x)$ must be a bounded function which tends to zero as $x \longrightarrow \infty$ and $\int_0^\infty |k(x)|\, dx < \infty$.

When sufficiently high moments of the X's are finite one can make statements about the cumulants of $N(x)$. If $n \geqslant 1$ and $p \geqslant 0$ are integers and $\mu_{n+p+1} < \infty$ then there are constants a_n and b_n such that $k_n(x)$, the nth cumulant of $N(x)$ is given by

$$k_n(x) = a_n x + b_n + \frac{\lambda(x)}{(1+x)^p}. \tag{47}$$

In Eq. (47), a_n is a function of $\mu_1, \mu_2, \ldots, \mu_n$ and b_n is a function of $\mu_1, \mu_2, \ldots, \mu_{n+1}$; $\lambda(x)$ is a function of bounded variation which tends to 0 as $x \longrightarrow \infty$. If one has only $\mu_n < \infty$, it is still true that

$$k_n(x) \sim a_n x \qquad \text{as } x \longrightarrow \infty. \tag{48}$$

Rather important special cases of these results are the following, which both require $\mu_2 < \infty$.

$$H(x) = \frac{x}{\mu_1} + \frac{\mu_2}{2\mu_1^2} - 1 + o(1), \qquad x \longrightarrow \infty, \tag{49}$$

$$\operatorname{Var} N(x) \sim \frac{\mu_2 - \mu_1^2}{\mu_1^3} x, \qquad x \longrightarrow \infty. \tag{50}$$

The first of these results, Eq. (49), is sometimes called the *second renewal theorem.* When $\mu_2 < \infty$, we have a result which parallels one for recurrent events, namely that

$$\frac{N(x) - x/\mu_1}{\sigma x^{1/2} \mu_1^{-3/2}}$$

is asymptotically $N(0, 1)$ as $x \longrightarrow \infty$. Here, of course, $\sigma^2 = \mu_2 - \mu_1^2$ as usual.

If for real $s > 0$, we write

$$\phi(s) = \int_0^\infty e^{-sx} f(x)\, dx$$

for the Laplace Transform of $f(x)$ then it should be apparent that $\phi(s) \longrightarrow 0$ as $s \longrightarrow \infty$. Now it is obvious that $\mathcal{E} e^{-sS_n} = \{\phi(s)\}^n$, so that for any $x > 0$ we have $e^{-sx} \Pr\{S_n \leqslant x\} \leqslant \{\phi(s)\}^n$. But $S_n \leqslant x$ iff $N(x) \geqslant n$. Thus $\Pr\{N(x) \geqslant n\} \leqslant e^{sx}\{\phi(s)\}^n$, and *à fortiori* $\mathrm{P}\{N(x) = n\} \leqslant e^{sx}\{\phi(s)\}^n$. Since $\phi(s)$ can be made as small as we wish by taking s sufficiently large, we see that the tail of the p.d. of $N(x)$ tends to 0 faster than any geometric series. Consequently $\mathcal{E} e^{\theta N(x)} < \infty$ for any $\theta < 0$, however large, and, in particular, all moments of $N(x)$ are finite.

A great deal indeed is known about renewal processes and the renewal function $H(x)$ in particular. Much has been done to obtain simple approximations and bounds for $H(x)$, usually derived by means of the integral equation of renewal theory. A simple example due to Feller is as follows. If $B(x)$ is any function $\geqslant F(x)$ and if $A(x)$ is the solution to

$$A(x) = B(x) + \int_0^x A(x - z)\, F(dz) \tag{51}$$

then $A(x) \geqslant H(x)$. A similar $B(x) \leqslant F(x)$ leads to an $A(x) \leqslant H(x)$. Feller suggests putting $A(x) = \mu_1^{-1} x + C$ and determining a minimum value C_1 for C so that the resulting $B(t) \geqslant F(t)$.

It might be commented that Eqs. (51) and (42) do have unique solutions bounded in every finite interval (provided, in the case of Eq. (51), that $B(x)$ is of bounded total variation, and it would be stupid to make it otherwise).

8. CUMULATIVE PROCESSES

There are a number of general results concerning so-called *cumulative processes* which have wide applicability in OR. To explain these we must explain first what we mean by a *regenerative process* (not to be confused with the very much more general process given the same name by J. F. C. Kingman). Let us suppose we are interested in a stochastic process which, as a function of time, t, is represented by $X(t)$. Notice that $X(t)$ may be real-valued, but in many applied problems it may be vector-valued. Let $\mathfrak{X}$ represent the space in which $X(t)$ takes values. By a "tour" of $\mathfrak{X}$ we mean an ordered pair $\mathfrak{I} = \{X, x(t)\}$ in which X is a real nonnegative number the duration of the tour, and $x(t)$ is a function defined for all $0 \leqslant t < X$ and taking values on $\mathfrak{X}$. Now let $\mathfrak{I}_1$, $\mathfrak{I}_2, \ldots$, be an infinite sequence of independent and identically distributed tours. We assume that in any application one may have in mind it is clear that an appropriate probability measure on an appropriate space is possible; such topics cannot be given discussion in this article. In any case, $X_1, X_2, \ldots$ gives a renewal process and, in familiar notation, we can define a stochastic process $X(t)$ for all $t \geqslant 0$ by writing

$$X(t) = x_{N(t)+1}(t - S_{N(t)}), \tag{52}$$

taking $S_0 = 0$. What this means is that we sample a tour and get $\mathfrak{I}_1$, say; thus over the time period $(0, X_1)$ we have $X(t) = x_1(t)$. When we reach the time $t = X_1$ we sample a fresh tour and get $\mathfrak{I}_2 = \{X_2, x_2(t)\}$, say. Thus over the time interval $(X_1, X_1 + X_2)$ we put $X(t) = x_2(t - X_1)$. It is clear how this construction proceeds. On inspection, many processes used in OR are of this regenerative type; one has only to discover the instants when a fresh tour begins, called regeneration points, and at these instants, the past history of the process loses relevance as far as future development is concerned.

Under very general conditions the instantaneous p.d. of a process of this regenerative type tends, as $t \longrightarrow \infty$, to a limiting distribution for the process.

A special, but important, example of a regenerative process is the *Semi-Markov process*, concerning which there is now an enormous literature. For this process we have a sequence (possibly finite) of states $\mathcal{S}_0, \mathcal{S}_1, \ldots$ and a transition matrix $[\mathbf{p}_{ij}]$ of the sort we have already met in dealing with Markov Chains. However, there is also a matrix of proper d.f.'s $[\boldsymbol{\Omega}_{ij}]$. The process proceeds from state to state like a Markov chain, but instead of resting in states for a unit of time, the system remains there for a random period called the *sojourn* or the *wait*. If it is in $\mathcal{S}_i$ and the next state is to be $\mathcal{S}_j$, then it waits in $\mathcal{S}_i$ for a period of time which has a d.f. $\boldsymbol{\Omega}_{ij}$; this wait is to be independent of all other aspects of the development of the process. Provided $[\mathbf{p}_{ij}]$ refers to an irreducible chain and not all the $\boldsymbol{\Omega}_{ij}$ put their unit mass of probability at 0, the Semi-Markov process develops in a "reasonable" way, with finitely many state-transitions in a unit of time (with probability one), and the process *will* have a limit distribution over the states as $t \longrightarrow \infty$.

Suppose now that $X(t)$ is regenerative, in the sense of this present treatment, and let $X_1, X_2, \ldots$ be the associated renewal process (duration of successive tours). Let us write $S_n = X_1 + X_2 + \cdots + X_n$, as usual, and consider a process $W(t)$ with the following properties:

(C1) $W(S_1) - W(0)$, $W(S_2) - W(S_1)$, $W(S_3) - W(S_2), \ldots$ is a sequence of independent, identically distributed, random variables.

(C2) $W(t)$ is, with probability one, of bounded variation in every finite t-interval.

(C3) If we define as associated *variation* process

$$\widetilde{W}(t) = \int_0^t |W(dt)| \tag{53}$$

then $\widetilde{W}(t)$ also satisfies (C1).

Such processes are widespread; typically they are nondecreasing and the conditions are easy to verify (in this case $\widetilde{W} \equiv W$).

For simplicity, assume $W(0) = 0$. Then let us set $\kappa_r = \mathcal{E}\{W(S_1)\}^r$, and when the moment exists, $\tilde{\kappa}_r = \mathcal{E}\{\widetilde{W}(S_1)\}^r$, and we note that $\tilde{\kappa}_r < \infty$ implies $\kappa_r < \infty$. Let $\mu_r = \mathcal{E}X_j^r$ as usual. Then if $\mu_1 < \infty$ and $\tilde{\kappa}_1 < \infty$ it follows that $W(t)/t \longrightarrow \kappa_1/\mu_1$ as $t \longrightarrow \infty$, with probability one. Also, under the same conditions $\mathcal{E}W(t)/t \longrightarrow \kappa_1/\mu_1$. If $\mu_2 < \infty$ and $\tilde{\kappa}_2 < \infty$ and we set $\sigma_1^2 = \mu_2 - \mu_1^2$ and $\sigma_2^2 = \kappa_2 - \kappa_1^2$, and ρ for the correlation between X_1 and $W(S_1)$, then

$$\operatorname{Var} W(t) \sim \mu_1^{-1} t\{\sigma_2^2 - 2\rho\sigma_1\sigma_2(\kappa_1/\mu_1) + \sigma_1^2(\kappa_1/\mu_1)^2\}, t \longrightarrow \infty.$$

One also has: if $\tilde{\kappa}_2 < \infty$ and $\mu_1 < \infty$, then

$$\frac{W(t) - \kappa_1 N(t)}{\sigma_2 (t/\mu_1)^{1/2}} \tag{54}$$

is asymptotically $N(0, 1)$ as $t \longrightarrow \infty$. If, however, $\mu_2 < \infty$ one has a more convenient result:

$$\frac{W(t) - \kappa_1 t \mu_1^{-1}}{(\gamma t/\mu_1)^{1/2}} \tag{55}$$

is asymptotically $N(0, 1)$ as $t \longrightarrow \infty$, where

$$\gamma^2 = \sigma_2^2 - 2\rho\sigma_1\sigma_2(\kappa_1/\mu_1) + \sigma_1^2(\kappa_1/\mu_1)^2 .$$

There are multivariate versions of these results as well.

9. BRANCHING PROCESSES

This kind of process is quite different from all that we have discussed so far. We start with a p.g.f. $\phi(s)$ of an integer-valued random variable

$$\phi(s) = \sum_0^\infty p_n s^n, \qquad 0 \leqslant s \leqslant 1,$$

where $p_j \geqslant 0$, all $j = 0, 1, 2, \ldots$, and $\sum_0^\infty p_j = 1$. Suppose in "generation" zero, g_0, there are Z_0 objects which we shall call "particles." Each particle will be replaced by a random number in generation one, g_1; the random number has a distribution described by $\phi(s)$ and the "family sizes" stemming from the distinct particles are independent r.v.'s. Thus the total size of g_1 is Z_1, say, where Z_1 has a p.g.f. $\{\phi(s)\}^{Z_0}$. In the same way, the Z_1 particles of g_1 are each replaced in g_2 by Z_1 "families" of independent sizes, but all governed by the p.g.f. $\phi(s)$. Thus Z_2, the size of g_2, has in turn a p.g.f. $\{\phi(\phi(s))\}^{Z_0}$. It should be clear how this model develops. It has been used to study many applied phenomena, such as the decay of family surnames, the spread of rumours and mutations in genetics, the development of avalanches, and the development of various atomic processes. There is a considerable literature concerning this subject and we must be content here with giving just a few basic results.

The original, classical question concerning the branching process was whether or not it would ultimately die out (become "extinct"). The crucial parameter for answering this question is μ_1, the mean number of offspring from a single parent particle:

$$\mu_1 = \sum_1^\infty n p_n .$$

If $\mu_1 \leqslant 1$, then, with probability one, the process will indeed become extinct. If, however, $\mu > 1$ then the process will become extinct with probability ζ^{Z_0}, where ζ is the unique real such that $0 < \zeta < 1$ and $\zeta = \phi(\zeta)$.

10. GENERALIZED BIRTH-AND-DEATH PROCESSES

These processes are special examples of Markov Chains in continuous time (the Markov Chains, of Section 5 develop in "discrete" time since we suppose transitions occur every unit of time). Birth-and-Death processes have something in common with Branching Processes.

Suppose we are given two sequences of nonnegative constants: $\alpha_0, \alpha_1, \alpha_2, \ldots$, and $\beta_1, \beta_2, \beta_3, \ldots$. Suppose that at any time t the process is of "size" $X(t)$. Typically, we are dealing with a colony of particles (animate or otherwise) and $X(t)$ is the size of the colony at time t. If $X(t) = n$, an integer, suppose that in the infinitesimal time interval $(t, t + \delta t)$ only two changes in $X(t)$ are possible:

$$X(t) \longrightarrow n + 1 \quad \text{with probability} \quad \alpha_n \delta t + o(\delta t)$$

$$X(t) \longrightarrow n - 1 \quad \text{with probability} \quad \beta_n \delta t + o(\delta t).$$

If $n = 0$, the latter transition is to be disallowed, since we cannot tolerate a negative number in our colony. Suppose further that what happens in $(t, t + \delta t)$ is to be independent of the whole history of the process up to time t, except for the fact that $X(t) = n$. This latter assumption is the so-called Markov property of the process.

If $p_n(t) = \Pr\{X(t) = n\}$ then one can show that for $n \geqslant 1$

$$\frac{dp_n(t)}{dt} = \alpha_{n-1} p_{n-1}(t) - (\alpha_n + \beta_n) p_n(t) + \beta_{n+1} p_{n+1}(t), \tag{56}$$

and

$$\frac{dp_0(t)}{dt} = -\alpha_0 p_0(t) + \beta_1 p_1(t) \tag{57}$$

It is, in general, impossible to write down a solution to this infinite system of equations. However, in various special cases of interest, progress is possible. We list a few examples.

(a) *Birth-Death* In this we have $\alpha_n = n\alpha$, $\beta_n = n\beta$; for some finite constants $\alpha > 0, \beta > 0$. One can introduce a p.g.f.

$$\Pi(s, t) = \sum_0^\infty s^n p_n(t), \qquad 0 \leqslant s \leqslant 1,$$

and reduce the system of Eqs. (56) and (57) to the single partial differential equation

$$\frac{\partial \Pi}{\partial t} = (\alpha s - \beta)(s - 1) \frac{\partial \Pi}{\partial s} \tag{58}$$

This partial differential equation is a special case of the Lagrange type of partial differential equation; such equations occur frequently in dealing with generalized birth-death processes; there are standard methods of attacking these equations, given in textbooks on differential equations, but, unfortunately, they are not always successful. The present case is a happy exception. If the population starts at $t = 0$ and $\alpha \neq \beta$ with m particles, then

$$\Pi(s,t) = \left(\frac{e^{-(\alpha-\beta)t}(\alpha s - \beta) - \beta(s-1)}{e^{-(\alpha-\beta)t}(\alpha s - \beta) - \alpha(s-1)} \right)^m \tag{59}$$

A great deal of information can be gleaned from this equation. For example, if $\alpha > \beta$, then $\Pi(s,t) \longrightarrow (\beta/\alpha)^m$ as $t \longrightarrow \infty$; this shows that when $\alpha > \beta$ there is a probability $(\beta/\alpha)^m$ of the population becoming extinct (since $(\beta/\alpha)^m$ is the coefficient of "s^0" in the limiting degenerate p.g.f.). Since the limit contains no other terms, in particular none involving powers of s, one concludes that the population has a probability $1 - (\beta/\alpha)^m$ of becoming arbitrarily large as $t \longrightarrow \infty$.

If $\alpha = \beta$ one has the special result

$$\Pi(s,t) = \left(\frac{s + \alpha t(1-s)}{1 + \alpha t(1-s)} \right)^m \tag{60}$$

and note that in this case $\Pi(s,t) \longrightarrow 1$ as $t \longrightarrow \infty$. Thus, when $\alpha = \beta$ the population will ultimately become extinct (zero population size), with probability one. It may be verified from Eq. (59) that the same thing happens if $\alpha < \beta$.

(b) *Immigration-Death* In this case we have (for finite constants $\alpha > 0$, $\beta > 0$): $\alpha_n = \alpha$, $n = 0, 1, 2, \ldots$; $\beta_n = n\beta$, for all $n = 1, 2, \ldots$. One is led to the equation

$$\frac{\partial \Pi}{\partial t} = \alpha(s-1)\,\Pi - \beta(s-1)\,\frac{\partial \Pi}{\partial s} \tag{61}$$

If we again suppose $\Pi(s, 0) = s^m$, we find

$$\Pi(s,t) = [1 + e^{-\beta t}(s-1)]^m \, e^{(\alpha/\beta)(s-1)(1-e^{-\beta t})} \tag{62}$$

From this it is clear that as $t \longrightarrow \infty$, $\Pi(s,t) \longrightarrow e^{(\alpha/\beta)(s-1)}$, the p.g.f. of the familiar Poisson distribution with mean (α/β). Thus the size of a population developing as an Immigration-Death process may be taken as having a Poisson distribution if one is considering a time remote from the initial instant.

(c) *Immigration-Emigration* Here we have $\alpha_n = \alpha$, $n = 0, 1, \ldots$; $\beta_n = \beta$, $n = 1, 2, \ldots$. One is led to the equation

$$\frac{\partial \Pi}{\partial t} = \left[\alpha(s-1) + \beta\left(\frac{1}{s} - 1\right) \right] \Pi - \beta\left(\frac{1}{s} - 1\right) p_0(t) \tag{63}$$

It will be seen that the (unknown) probability $p_0(t)$ appears on the right, and provides an entirely novel problem not covered by textbook discussions of the

Lagrange equation. Various ingenious methods have been developed to solve Eq. (63) but they are far too involved to be given here. Since Eq. (63) describes the transient behaviour of a simple kind of queue, it is discussed and solved in various texts on queueing theory. We have considered this case to show that quite simple assumptions about the $\{\alpha_n\}$ and $\{\beta_n\}$ can lead to truly difficult mathematical problems.

Even when the generalized birth-death process appears to be thus intractable, it is always possible to calculate the *stationary* distribution (or the *limit* distribution, as $t \longrightarrow \infty$), if it exists. First calculate the numbers

$$r_1 = \frac{\beta_1}{\alpha_0}, \quad r_2 = \frac{\beta_1\beta_2}{\alpha_0\alpha_1}, \quad r_3 = \frac{\beta_1\beta_2\beta_3}{\alpha_0\alpha_1\alpha_2}, \tag{64}$$

and so on. If $S = 1 + \sum_1^\infty r_n$ diverges, there is no stationary distribution. If S converges, the stationary distribution is given by

$$\pi_0 = \frac{1}{S}; \quad \pi_n = \frac{r_n}{S}, \qquad n = 1, 2, \ldots. \tag{65}$$

(where we have written π_n for the stationary probability that the population shall have size n).

11. TIME SERIES AND STATIONARY PROCESSES

This is a highly important area of modern research activity, the results of which have found many applications in a variety of fields. However, one suspects these ideas have had insufficient use in OR. Unlike all the stochastic processes we have discussed so far, which are studied by means of a mathematical model which, as it were, generates successive values of the stochastic process, the study of stationary processes typically begins with certain "global" assumptions.

The stationary process will be denoted $\{X(t)\}$ in *continuous time*, $-\infty < t < \infty$, or $\{X_n\}$ in *discrete time*, where n is restricted to integer values, $-\infty < n < \infty$. In much of the literature a stationary process in discrete time is called a *time series*. For simplicity we shall restrict the discussion of this section to time series only; there are rather analogous results for the continuous time processes, although in some instances they call for greater mathematical subtlety.

The sequence $\{X_n\}$ is *stationary in the strict sense* if the following conditions hold:

(S1) For every finite integer $k > 0$, every set of k integers $(n_1, n_2, \ldots n_k)$ and every set of k reals $(x_1, x_2, \ldots, x_k)$,

$$P\{X_{n_1+l} \leqslant x_1, X_{n_2+l} \leqslant x_2, \ldots, X_{n_k+l} \leqslant x_k\}$$

is independent of the integer l, $-\infty < l < \infty$.

Although many processes in OR can reasonably be regarded as stationary in the strict sense, it is a broader class of processes which has received most attention in the literature and which provides us with the most powerful research tools. This is the class of *second-order* stationary processes, satisfying the following condition (weaker than (S1)):

(S2) (a) $\mathcal{E}X_n$ and $\mathcal{E}(X_n)^2$ exist for all n's and are independent of n.
(b) If $\mu = \mathcal{E}X_n$, the product moment

$$\mathcal{E}(X_{n_1} - \mu)(X_{n_2} - \mu)$$

is a function of $|n_1 - n_2|$ only.

In discussing such processes it is convenient to arrange, by a suitable scale change, that $\mu = 0$ and that $\mathcal{E}(X_n)^2 = 1$. We shall then write $\mathcal{E}X_{n_1}X_{n_2} = \rho(n_1 - n_2)$, and call $\rho(.)$ the *autocorrelation* function. Clearly $\rho(0) = 1$ and $\rho(-h) = \rho(h)$.

If it is known (or assumed!) that every finite collection of the $\{X_n\}$ has a multivariate Gaussian distribution we shall call the process $\{X_n\}$ a *gaussian* one. Since the aforementioned multivariate distributions are fully determined by the means of the $\{X_n\}$ and their variance-covariance matrix, it should be clear that a second-order stationary gaussian process is actually a strictly stationary one.

Suppose now that $\{X_n\}$ is a real-valued second order stationary process. An important and surprising result, the so-called Wiener-Khinchine Theorem, is that there exists a distribution function $F(.)$, say, on the interval $[0, \pi)$ such that

$$\rho(n) = \int_0^{\pi} (\cos n\lambda)\, F(d\lambda), \tag{66}$$

for $n = 0, \pm 1, \pm 2, \ldots$ Thus the values of the autocorrelation function are necessarily Fourier coefficients of a *spectral distribution* $F(.)$. The converse to this statement is also part of the theorem: if $F(.)$ is any distribution function on $[0, \pi)$ then there exists a real-valued stationary (second order) process whose autocorrelation function is given by Eq. (66).

At points λ where $F(.)$ is continuous, one has

$$F(\lambda) = \frac{2\lambda}{\pi} + \frac{2}{\pi} \sum_1^{\infty} \rho(n) \frac{\sin n\lambda}{n} \tag{67}$$

In many problems $F(\lambda) = \int_0^{\lambda} f(w)\, dw$, and the p.d.f. $f(w)$ is called the *spectral density*. In a formal way, one has, from Eq. (67), the result

$$f(w) = \frac{2}{\pi} + \frac{2}{\pi} \sum_1^{\infty} \rho(n) \cos nw \tag{68}$$

but this series may not be convergent.

To understand the significance of the spectral distribution we must consider some concepts which call for rather sophisticated mathematical tools to be rigorously presented. Even so, a heuristic discussion may be helpful.

Suppose $Y(\lambda)$ to be a possibly complex-valued, stochastic process depending on a "time" parameter λ, $-\pi \leqslant \lambda \leqslant \pi$. Suppose that for every choice of $-\pi \leqslant \lambda_1 < \lambda_2 \leqslant \lambda_3 < \lambda_4 \leqslant \pi$, the two quantities $Y(\lambda_4) - Y(\lambda_3)$, $Y(\lambda_2) - Y(\lambda_1)$ are uncorrelated variables with zero expectations and finite variances. Since these quantities are possibly complex valued, we must adopt a somewhat different definition of variance and product moment. If Z is a complex-valued r.v. of zero expectation we shall mean by its variance the number $\mathcal{E}|Z|^2$. In a similar way, if Z_1 and Z_2 are two such variables, then there are two possible product-moments, one the complex conjugate of the other, given by $\langle Z_1, Z_2 \rangle = \mathcal{E} Z_1 \overline{Z}_2$ and $\langle Z_2, Z_1 \rangle = \mathcal{E} \overline{Z}_1 Z_2$. To say that Z_1 and Z_2 are uncorrelated is to imply that these product-moments vanish. Subject to these ideas then, the process $Y(\lambda)$ is called a process with *orthogonal increments.* If $\varphi(\lambda)$ is any continuous function of λ on $[-\pi, \pi]$, it is possible, by a suitable limiting argument based on approximating sums, to define an integral

$$\int_{-\pi}^{+\pi} \varphi(\lambda)\, dY(\lambda)$$

Then, if $\{X_n\}$ is a second-order stationary process, it has been proved that there exists a process $Y(\lambda)$ with orthogonal increments such that

$$X_n = \int_{-\pi}^{+\pi} e^{in\lambda}\, dY(\lambda), \tag{69}$$

for all integer values of n. Moreover if we write $G(\lambda) = \text{Var}\,\{Y(\lambda) - Y(0)\}$ then $G(\lambda) + G(-\lambda) = F(\lambda)$, $0 \leqslant \lambda \leqslant \pi$, where $F(.)$ is the spectral distribution function of the process.

Suppose $F(\lambda)$ has a jump discontinuity at λ^*, say. Then

$$\mathcal{E}|Y(\lambda^* + 0) - Y(\lambda^* - 0)|^2 + \mathcal{E}|Y(-\lambda^* + 0) - Y(-\lambda^* - 0)|^2 > 0$$

showing that $Y(\lambda)$ will, with a positive probability, also have a jump discontinuity at $\pm\lambda^*$. This would give rise in the integral (69) to a term

$$e^{\pm in\lambda^*}\{Y(\pm\lambda^* + 0) - Y(\pm\lambda^* - 0)\},$$

a pure sinusoidal oscillation of frequency $\dfrac{\lambda^*}{2n}$. Thus, if $F(\lambda)$ has a jump at λ^* then with a positive probability $\{X_n\}$ involves a pure sinusoidal oscillation of frequency $\dfrac{\lambda^*}{2\pi}$ in its composition. In a similar way one can see that even if $F(\lambda)$ does not have a jump, the composition of $\{X_n\}$ attaches, on the average, a greater weight to oscillatory elements $e^{\pm in\lambda}$ for λ-values where $F(\lambda)$ is increasing more rapidly than otherwise. When there exists a spectral density function, it is in the neighborhood of its peaks that $F(\lambda)$ will be most rapidly increasing.

One way by which time-series analysts have sought for "hidden" frequencies in time series data has been to estimate $F(\lambda)$, often through the use of *periodogram analysis.* However, it has been realized that the classical approach to this problem has serious flaws and quite an elaborate theory has been developed involving the notion of "*spectral windows*". The discussion of these ideas would carry us too far afield for this introductory exposition.

Autoregressive Processes

The stationary processes known as "autoregressive" are of such considerable importance in applied work that they deserve at least a brief special discussion. Contrary to our remarks at the opening of this section, these processes can be generated sequentially by a mathematical model. The autoregressive scheme of order k involves the recurrence relation

$$X_n = a_1 X_{n-1} + a_2 X_{n-2} + \cdots + a_k X_{n-k} + Z_n \tag{70}$$

where the $\{Z_n\}$ are *iid* and, for each n, Z_n is independent of $X_{n-1}, X_{n-2}, \ldots,$ and so on. In Eq. (70) the a_j's are constants and, as is usual in applications, we may assume them to be real. However, these constants must satisfy suitable conditions if Eq. (70) is to be satisfied by a stationary process.

Let

$$P(x) = a_k x^k + a_{k-1} x^{k-1} + \cdots + a_1 x - 1 \tag{71}$$

have zeros $\lambda_1, \lambda_2, \ldots, \lambda_k$ and, for simplicity, let us suppose these zeros to be distinct. Then it is necessary that $|\lambda_j| > 1$ for $j = 1, 2, \ldots, k$. One can then write

$$X_n = \sum_{j=1}^{k} \frac{1}{\lambda_j P'(\lambda_j)} \left\{ Z_n + \frac{Z_{n-1}}{\lambda_j} + \frac{Z_{n-2}}{\lambda_j^2} + \cdots \right\}, \tag{72}$$

an equation which displays X_n as an infinite linear combination of $Z_n, Z_{n-1}, Z_{n-2}, \ldots,$ and so on.

As is usual, we shall assume that $\mathcal{E} Z_n = 0$, which implies that $\mathcal{E} X_n = 0$ for all n. If one then also assumes that $\sigma^2 = \mathcal{E}(Z_n)^2 < \infty$, it is possible to calculate the variance of X_n from Eq. (72), but the general result is messy. Nor is it easy to relate the condition $|\lambda_j| > 1$, all j, which ensures that our scheme generates a stationary process, to usable conditions on the constants $\{a_j\}$, except for the special cases $k = 1$ (trivial!) and $k = 2$. Even the case $k = 2$ is involved, and we must refer the interested reader to a curious diagram given in texts on this subject [Box and Jenkins, 1970].

In the special case when $\{X_n\}$ is autoregressive of order one, it is easy to find that $\lambda_1 = 1/a_1$, so we must have $|a_1| < 1$. One then finds that

$$\text{Var } X_n = \frac{\sigma^2}{1 - a_1^2} \tag{73}$$

and that the autocorrelation function $\mathscr{E} X_n X_{n-m}/\text{Var } X_n$ is given by

$$\rho(m) = (a_1)^m. \tag{74}$$

The autoregressive scheme of order two has been much used in applied work and has had some success in describing a variety of phenomena. One can show that

$$\text{Var } X_n = \frac{\lambda_1^2 \lambda_2^2 (1 + \lambda_1 \lambda_2)\, \sigma^2}{(\lambda_1 \lambda_2 - 1)(\lambda_1^2 - 1)(\lambda_2^2 - 1)} \tag{75}$$

and that the autocorrelation function is given by

$$p(m) = \frac{1}{(\lambda_1 \lambda_2 + 1)(\lambda_2 - \lambda_1)} \left\{ \frac{\lambda_2^2 - 1}{\lambda_1^{m+1}} - \frac{\lambda_1^2 - 1}{\lambda_2^{m+1}} \right\}. \tag{76}$$

Thus, when λ_1 and λ_2 are real, the autocorrelation function is a linear combination of two decaying geometric series. If, however, λ_1 and λ_2 are complex conjugates, and if we write $\lambda_1 = re^{i\gamma}$, $\lambda_2 = re^{-i\gamma}$, where $0 < r$ and $0 < \gamma < \pi$, then Eq. (75) yields

$$\text{Var } X_n = \frac{r^4(1 + r^2)}{(r^2 - 1)(r^4 - 2r^2 \cos \gamma + 1)}. \tag{77}$$

In the same circumstances of complex λ_1 and λ_2 we find

$$\rho(m) = \frac{1}{r^m} \frac{\sin (k\gamma + \beta)}{\sin \beta} \tag{78}$$

where

$$\tan \beta = \left(\frac{r^2 + 1}{r^2 - 1} \right) \tan \gamma.$$

Moving Average Processes

Once more let $\{Z_n\}$ be an infinite sequence $(-\infty < n < +\infty)$ of *iid* variables with zero means and finite variances equal to σ^2. Let $b_0, b_1, \ldots, b_k$ be finite real constants and define

$$X_n = b_0 Z_n + b_1 Z_{n-1} + \cdots + b_k Z_{n-k}. \tag{79}$$

This defines $\{X_n\}$ as a moving average of order $(k + 1)$, and it is necessarily stationary, whatever the values of the b's. One obtains easily that

$$\text{Var } X_n = \sigma^2 (b_0^2 + b_1^2 + \cdots + b_k^2) \tag{80}$$

and that, for $0 \leqslant m \leqslant k$,

$$\rho(m) = \frac{b_0 b_m + b_1 b_{m+1} + \cdots + b_{k-m} b_k}{b_0^2 + b_1^2 + \cdots + b_k^2} \tag{81}$$

It is also clear that $\rho(m)$ is zero whenever $m > k$. This suggests that a moving average scheme is inappropriate in circumstances where behavior of a system at a given time has after-effects which persist for a very long while.

General Comments

The purpose of this section on stationary processes has merely been to expose a few basic ideas from what is now an enormously explored subject. Much is known about estimating spectra in both the discrete and the continuous time cases, and also about estimating and testing hypotheses for the autoregressive and other models. A line of enquiry of wide ramifications is that concerned with the extrapolation and interpolation of stationary processes. The reader must turn to specialized texts for information on these subjects.

REFERENCES AND FURTHER READING

We give below a selection of books which will have most immediate appeal to the reader who is interested more in OR applications than in mathematical generalities and niceties. For general reading, we suggest the following, which have chapters on most, or all, of the topics we have covered:

1. Bartlett, M. S., *An Introduction to Stochastic Processes*, Cambridge University Press, London (1955).
2. Cox, D. R. and H. Miller, *The Theory of Stochastic Processes*, Wiley, New York (1965).
3. Feller, W., *An Introduction to Probability Theory and its Applications, Volume 1*, 2nd. ed.. Wiley, New York (1975).
4. Parzen, E., *Stochastic Processes*, Holden-Day, San Francisco (1962).
5. Ross, S. M., *Applied Probability Models With Optimisation Applications*, Holden-Day, San Francisco (1970).
6. Takacs, L., *Stochastic Processes: Problems and Solutions*, Methuen, London (1960).

The little book by Takacs is mainly a collection of problems for the reader, including solutions, but it contains useful summaries of main features of the relevant theory. More specialized topics will be found, discussed in a reasonably elementary way, in the following:

7. Cox, D. R., *Renewal Theory*, Methuen, London (1962).
8. Cox, D. R. and W. L. Smith, *Queues*, Methuen, London (1961).
9. Kemeny, J. G. and J. L. Snell, *Finite Markov Chains*, Van Nostrand Reinhold, New York (1960).

For more information on the theory and practice of time series and stationary processes, see:

10. Box, G. E. P. and G. M. Jenkins, *Time Series Analysis: Forecasting and Control*, Holden-Day, San Francisco (1970).
11. Whittle, P., *Prediction and Regulation*, English Universities Press, London (1963).

If one would pursue the theory of random walk and, especially, the identities of the Spitzer-Sparre-Anderson type, then the following is an excellent first step:

12. Spitzer, F., *Principles of the Random Walk*, Van Nostrand Reinhold, New York (1964).

III-2

THEORY OF QUEUES

U. Narayan Bhat*
Southern Methodist University

1. INTRODUCTION

A "queue" is a waiting line of units demanding service at a service facility (counter); the unit demanding service is called the "customer" and the device at which or the person by whom it gets served is known as the "server." This terminology is used in a wide context. Here are a few realistic examples of this customer-server mechanism.

(a) Vehicles demanding service arrive at a garage and, depending on the number of employees, one or more vehicles may be repaired at a time.
(b) Patients arrive at a doctor's clinic for treatment. Even if some appointment system exists, due to the emergency service rendered, there is a random element present in the arrival scheme and there is a possibility of a waiting-line formation.
(c) In a telephone exchange, incoming calls are the customers who demand service in the form of telephone conversations.
(d) Passengers demanding tickets queue up in front of a ticket counter.

It is possible to give numerous examples of this type, where a queue situation

*Work on this chapter was partially supported by NSF grant GK-19537 and ONR grant N0014-72-A-0296-003. Revised May, 1974.

exists in various forms. As suggested by the above problems, some of these situations differ from each other in several details. However, it is not difficult to see that all of them have certain common basic characteristics.

(a) *Input process:* If the occurrence of arrivals and offer of service are strictly according to schedule, a queue can be avoided. But in practice this is not so and in most cases arrivals are controlled by external factors. Therefore, the best that can be done is to represent the input process in terms of random variables. Some of the factors needed for the complete specification of an input process are: the source of arrivals, the type of arrivals and the inter-arrival times.

(b) *Service mechanism:* The uncertainties involved in the service mechanism are the number of servers, the number of customers getting served at any time, and the duration and mode of service. In problems of Network Flows and Job-Shop Scheduling, one has to deal with more than one queue (server) in series and/or in parallel. Again, random variable representations for these characteristics seem to be essential.

(c) *Queue discipline:* All other factors regarding the rules of conduct of the queue can be pooled under this heading. One of these is the rule followed by the server in taking the customers in service. In this context, the rules such as "first-come, first-served" (FCFS), "last-come, first-served" (LCFS), and "random selection for service" (RS) are self-explanatory. In many situations "priority" disciplines need to be introduced, so as to make the system more realistic. Some of the other factors that may be included here are based on the customer behavior, such as balking, reneging and jockeying.

Queueing theory embodies studies made on systems with the above characteristics and provides information on their various aspects as well as methodologies and techniques developed in deriving them. It is the intention of this chapter to give an overview of the growth of queueing theory over the last six and a half decades. The major aim is to draw a global picture, emphasizing only the significant aspects. No attempt will be made to give a complete bibliography on the subject. The references cited herein are merely directive in that the interested reader would be able to compile his own bibliography from them without much effort.

A few words on the arrangement of topics. In order to keep our focus on queueing systems, significant results are presented without mentioning how they can be derived. Analysis techniques are recounted in Section 7. Technical terms such as "Markovian" have been introduced earlier without definition so as to avoid distraction from the major theme. Definitions for these terms can be found in the pages on analysis techniques.

2. PROBLEMS, TERMINOLOGIES AND NOTATIONS

A grid-type categorization of queueing theory is possible based on problem nature and application area. Three classes of problems may be identified: (1) behavioral problems, (2) statistical problems, and (3) operational problems. There are several application areas. Telephone, transportation, computer, health, and service systems are some of them. In each of these areas different types of problems arise.

(a) Behavioral Problems

The study of behavioral problems is aimed at understanding the system behavior through mathematical models idealized to varied degrees of realism. Major characteristics investigated are the following:

$Q(t)$, *queue length at time t:* Number of customers in the system at time t (some authors prefer to define $Q(t)$ as the number actually waiting).

Q_n, *queue length at the nth time epoch:* The nth discrete time epoch is characterized by an event such as an arrival or a departure of a customer.

$W(t)$, *virtual waiting time at time t:* The time a customer has to wait for his service if he is to arrive at time t.

W_n, *waiting time of the nth customer.*

T_i, *busy-period initiated by i customers:* Starting with i customers in the system at time 0, the length of time the server or the system remains continuously busy. When $i = 1$ (or 0, just before an arrival), it is commonly identified as the "busy period."

I_n, *nth idle period:* The length of time the server or the system remains continuously idle for the nth time. It should be noted that idle and busy periods alternate in queueing systems.

In addition to the above, various modifications of these characteristics such as *throughput time* (total time spent by the customer in the system), *busy cycle* (sum of two adjacent busy and idle periods), and *server utilization* (fraction of time the server is busy) have also been used in queueing theory investigations. Because of the assumptions of randomness in the input process and/or service mechanism, $Q(t)$, Q_n, $W(t)$, and W_n are stochastic processes (family of random variables indexed by a parameter) with respective state and parameter spaces and T_i and I_n are r.v.'s. Distribution properties and moments of these stochastic processes and r.v.'s are major targets for a behavioral study.

It should be noted that the queue length is independent of queue discipline provided the server remains working as long as there are customers to be served in the system, that service is given to completion when a customer enters service, and that the queue discipline is not of a dynamic type as in some priority cases. However, waiting time is very much a product of queue discipline. When the queue discipline is FCFS in a single server system, virtual waiting time is in fact the service load of the server.

Many real life systems exhibit some sort of stable behavior in the long run. In terms of system characteristics, this translates into the properties of the processes $\{Q(t)\}$ and $\{W(t)\}$ as $t \longrightarrow \infty$ and $\{Q_n\}$ and $\{W_n\}$ as $n \longrightarrow \infty$. For convenience we shall denote $Q(\infty) = Q$ and $W(\infty) = W$ and retain Q_∞ and W_∞ for the latter. When these processes exhibit stable behavior (which is not a function of time) they are said to be in steady state or in equilibrium state. Conditions under which systems attain steady state are of considerable interest.

In practice, system performance indices given by simple measures are more useful than complex distributions and moment formulae. Many of these would depend on the nature of the system and objectives of analysis. Nevertheless, the most used performance measure is the server utilization given by the traffic intensity $\rho = \dfrac{\text{Effective arrival rate}}{\text{Effective service rate}}$.

(b) Statistical Problems

Statistical investigation is an integral part of building a mathematical model for a real system. A model can exist by itself; but relating it to the system at hand is done by a statistical study of empirical data, estimation of parameters, and tests of relevant hypotheses.

System parameters are essentially the parameters occurring in the arrival process and the service mechanism, or some functions of these. To be specific, let customers $C_1, C_2, \ldots$ arrive at time epochs $t_1, t_2, \ldots$ respectively. The time interval $U_n = t_n - t_{n-1}$ is known as the inter-arrival time between customers C_{n-1} and C_n and let V_n be the service time of the customer C_n. (In case customers arrive in groups, necessary modifications need to be made to these definitions in addition to defining the group size distribution.) Let $A(x) = \Pr\{U_n \leqslant x\}$ $(x \geqslant 0)$ and $B(x) = \Pr\{V_n \leqslant x\}$ $(x \geqslant 0)$. The dependence of $A(x)$ and $B(x)$ on n is not represented notationally for the sake of convenience. The system parameters are then the parameters of $A(x)$, $B(x)$, other distributions such as group size, and physical characteristics such as the number of servers, the number of queues, waiting room capacity, etc. Statistical problems of the queueing system are therefore statistical problems related to these parameters of the basic processes.

(c) Operational Problems

Problems inherent in the operation of real life systems bring queueing theory under OR. Naturally, some of these problems are statistical in nature. Others are related to the design, control, and measurement of effectiveness of such systems. Thus, one can distinguish between descriptive and normative approaches to operational problems in queueing systems. In the descriptive approach, system description given by the behavioral measures is used in making decisions for system operation. On the other hand, in the normative approach, norms are set for effective system operation by way of mathematical modeling. For instance, based on the cost and physical restrictions on the system, 'best' arrival or service rates can be set so as to optimize a suitable objective function.

Next we shall identify some of the areas where queueing theory has actually found useful applications.

3. APPLICATION AREAS

As any other area of applied mathematics or OR, queueing theory has its origin in practical problems. Historically, Johannsen's "Waiting Times and Number of Calls" (an article published in 1907 and reprinted in *Post Office Electrical Engineers Journal*, London, 1910) seems to be the first paper on the subject. But the method used in this paper is not mathematically exact and therefore, from the point of view of exact treatment, the paper of historic importance is A. K. Erlang's "The Theory of Probabilities and Telephone Conversations" (*Nyt tidsskrift for Matematik*, **B**, **20**, 1909, p. 33). The origin of queueing theory is therefore in telecommunications systems. Even to this day it has continued to be the dominant area of application and the contributions made by the telecommunication researchers to queueing theory are considerable.

In discussing the application of queueing theory in OR, Morse [1967] gives a classification of papers and books published up to the year 1960 by field of application. It is significant to note that of the grand total of 753 papers and books found in the bibliography in Saaty [1961], 486 are in applications and 267 in general theory. Among the different areas of applications, telecommunication systems command 222 articles, transportation systems (road, rail and air) 125 articles, maintenance and service systems 53 articles, and the remaining 86 articles are spread over areas such as inventories, production, health, hydrostorage and physics. Even though this classification is not up-to-date, it is highly significant in maintaining our perspective over the development of queueing theory. After 1960, another field has emerged as having the same potential as telecommunication systems in terms of application. This is the area of computer systems.

For a field of investigation to maintain its vigor, it is essential that the developments in theory go hand in hand with sophistications in applications. That is why these application areas are so important for the growth of queueing theory.

In telecommunication systems, pioneering work of A. K. Erlang [Brockmeyer *et al*, 1948] has been continued by researchers such as C. D. Crommelin, C. Palm, A. E. Vaulot, P. J. Burke, V. Beneš, R. I. Wilkinson, J. Riordan and others. The area has also benefited by the strong theoretical investigations carried out by researchers such as F. Pollaczek, A. Khintchine and L. Takács. Two major journals that carry important papers on queueing theory in telecommunication systems are *The Bell System Technical Journal* and *Ericsson Technics*. For a bibliography of articles in this area, the reader is referred to these journals and proceedings of the triennial International Teletraffic Congress as well as books by Syski [1960], Riordan [1962], Beneš [1965] and Cooper [1972].

Queueing models of transportation systems have been gaining sophistication over the last few years. It should be noted that many times transportation models involve other stochastic and deterministic models as well. In the case of road traffic this is well illustrated in Haight [1963]. Nevertheless, queueing theory has remained one of the essential tools for the study of transportation systems. Articles in this area can be found in the journals on road traffic research such as *Transportation Science*, books by Haight [1963] and Lee [1966], and other journals in OR.

With the sophistication of computer systems, development of mathematical models of their congestion problems is inevitable. Several articles have appeared in journals such as *Journal of the Association for the Computing Machinery, Communications of the Association for the Computing Machinery*, and *SIAM Journal on Computers*, on the application of queueing results and techniques in the congestion analysis of computer systems.

Maintenance and service systems are also common examples of queueing systems. They occur under varied situations such as servicing of machines and reliability systems. Articles on queueing applications in these and other miscellaneous areas can be found either in area journals or in journals carrying OR articles of general interest.

It is worthwhile to point out the distinction between the nature of work in theoretical developments in queueing and their applications. In the former, one would be interested in the general structure and a mathematical solution. In the latter, the general structures need to be translated into simple physical structures and the mathematical solutions need to be transformed into useful results. These results are therefore either numerical in nature or in forms convenient for computations.

Having given a general overview of the nature of problems and problem areas of queueing theory, we shall concentrate on discussing some of the significant developments that have taken place over the past six and a half decades. These developments in different queueing systems will be identified with reference to the three classes of problems and application areas described above.

In discussing various systems, it is convenient to use some notation. The widely used notation due to Kendall [1953] represents a queueing system in terms of its three major characteristics:

Arrival Process/Service Time Distribution/Number of Servers.

Letter notations are used for various distributions. Common notations are: M for Poisson (exponential, both with Markovian properties), D for Deterministic, E_k for k-Erlangian (gamma with integer parameter k), G for general (arbitrary), and *GI* for General Independent (recurrent). Various modifications for this three-element representation have appeared in the literature, with the objective of a complete and realistic representation of the system. However, in our discussion we shall restrict ourselves to the 3-element notation and describe other characteristics of the system when necessary.

Thus, by a queueing system $M/D/s$ we denote an s-server queueing system in which arrival of customers is in a Poisson process and the service time is a constant (deterministic).

4. BEHAVIORAL ANALYSIS

Poisson distribution has a special place in queueing theory. It was originally obtained by S. D. Poisson in 1837 in his treatise on Probability Theory. Its importance in representing telephone traffic was established by Erlang in his paper, referred to earlier. The 'memoryless' property of the related negative exponential distribution simplifies the investigation considerably. Thus, realism and convenience have made queueing theory's dependence on Poisson distribution rather heavy. This will reflect in the discussion given below as well.

For an historical account of the growth of queueing theory, the reader is referred to Bhat [1969]. In tracing the development of results it would be clear that in the analysis of queueing systems, the initial emphasis has been mostly on their equilibrium (steady state) behavior. This is natural because of the simple nature of steady-state results and their use in applications. However, to develop the finer points of the system behavior, an appeal to the transient behavior is unavoidable. Normally, even in simple systems, transient behavior can be investigated only through heavy analysis and sophisticated mathematical techniques.

The concept of statistical equilibrium of stochastic processes is an extension of the ergodic principle developed in connection with the application of statistics to physical problems. Erlang (cf. Brockmeyer et al [1948]) exploited this basic principle to derive meaningful results for problems in the theory of telephone traffic. According to this principle, under certain conditions, if the system is operated for an infinite length of time, the influence of the initial state disappears and the system reaches a situation for which the absolute state distribution is independent of time (stationary). In systems with a finite number of states, the condition for equilibrium is that they belong to a single irreducible class (communicating set of states). But in queueing systems with infinitely many states, most of the time the condition that the traffic intensity ρ be $\leqslant 1$ forms the basis for statistical equilibrium. (It should be noted that in systems of complex type this ρ might have to be defined accordingly.)

In the field of telecommunications, the traffic intensity ρ which turns out to be the fraction of time a server is busy, has been accepted as the international traffic unit called *erlang* (in recognition of the contributions of A. K. Erlang to the theory of telephone traffic; also see Syski [1960], pp. 186–190).

The inadequacy of the equilibrium theory was noted by Pollaczek [1934] in understanding the behavior of underlying stochastic processes of queueing systems. Contributions made by Pollaczek and others in this direction have provided several useful results in addition to making queueing theory a significant part of applied mathematics and probability.

In the rest of this discussion we shall recount the significant developments in queueing theory based on system types in the order: single server systems, multiserver systems and other variations. Unless stated otherwise we shall assume the conditions for statistical equilibrium exist for the systems considered.

4.1 The Queue M/M/1

The single server queue with Poisson arrivals and exponential service has been used more often than any other system in queueing theory. Let λ and μ be the arrival and service rates, respectively. Clearly, the traffic intensity $\rho = \frac{\lambda}{\mu}$.

The queue $M/M/1$ can be derived as special cases of systems $M/G/1$, $GI/M/1$, $GI/G/1$ and their multiserver and other variations. Thus, the first investigations of the equilibrium behavior of $M/M/1$ can be deduced from those of $M/M/s$ due to Erlang (cf. Brockmeyer et al (1948)) and Molina [1927]. Let $\pi_j = \Pr\{Q = j\}$, $j = 0, 1, 2, \ldots$. We have

$$\pi_j = (1 - \rho)\rho^j \qquad j = 0, 1, 2, \ldots \tag{1}$$

$$E[Q] = \frac{\rho}{1 - \rho} \quad \text{and} \quad \text{Var}\,[Q] = \frac{\rho}{(1 - \rho)^2}. \tag{2}$$

The method used in deriving these limiting results is based on the 'interconnection formula' of Erlang, which was identified later as an example of Chapman-Kolmogorov equations for Markov processes. In the equilibrium state they have also been called the balance of state equations (cf. Bhat (1972)).

When the queue discipline is FCFS, noting that the waiting time of a customer is equivalent to the service load of the server, one gets

$$F(x) = \Pr\{W \leqslant x\} = 1 - \rho e^{-\mu(1-\rho)x} \tag{3}$$

$$E[W] = \frac{\rho}{\mu(1 - \rho)} \quad \text{and} \quad \text{Var}\,[W] = \frac{\rho(2 - \rho)}{\mu^2(1 - \rho)^2}. \tag{4}$$

Two relations, obvious from (2) and (4) are

$$\frac{1}{\mu} E[Q] = E[W] \quad \text{and} \quad E[Q] = \lambda E\left[W + \frac{1}{\mu}\right]. \tag{5}$$

Of these, the first is true only when the service times are exponential and the second relation is true under very general conditions.

Let

$$P_{ij}(t) = \Pr\{Q(t) = j \mid Q(0) = i\}. \tag{6}$$

Then we get

$$P_{i0}(t) = \frac{1}{\mu t} e^{-(\lambda+\mu)t} \sum_{r=i+1}^{\infty} r\rho^{r/2} I_{-r}(2\sqrt{\lambda\mu}\, t) \tag{7}$$

$$\begin{aligned} P_{ij}(t) = e^{-(\lambda+\mu)t} \Bigg[& \rho^{(j-i)/2} I_{j-i}(2\sqrt{\lambda\mu}\, t) \\ & + \rho^{(j-i-1)/2} I_{j+i+1}(2\sqrt{\lambda\mu}\, t) \\ & + (1-\rho)\rho^{j} \sum_{k=j+i+2}^{\infty} \rho^{-k/2} I_k(2\sqrt{\lambda\mu}\, t) \Bigg] \qquad j = 1, 2, \ldots \end{aligned} \tag{8}$$

where $I_j(x)$ is the modified Bessel function defined by

$$I_j(x) = \sum_{n=0}^{\infty} \frac{(x/2)^{2n+j}}{n!(n+j)!} \tag{9}$$

(Clarke [1956], Bailey [1954], Ledermann and Reuter [1954], Champernowne [1956], Conolly [1958a]). For a discussion of the methods used in their derivation see Prabhu [1965]. Expressing the transition probability $P_{ij}(t)$ by means of trigonometric functions, the auto-correlation function $\psi(t)$ of the queue-length $Q(t)$ has been obtained by Morse [1955] as

$$\psi(t) = \frac{\lambda^2}{(\mu-\lambda)^2} + (\mu-\lambda)\frac{\lambda\mu}{\pi}\int_0^{2\pi} \frac{\sin^2\theta e^{-\omega t}}{\omega^3}\, d\theta \tag{10}$$

where $\omega = \mu + \lambda - 2\sqrt{\lambda\mu}\cos\theta$. The function $\psi(t)$ has the frequency spectrum

$$W(f) = 4\lambda\mu\left(\frac{\mu-\lambda}{\pi}\right)\int_0^{2\pi} \frac{\sin^2\theta\, d\theta}{\omega^2(\omega^2 + 4\pi^2 f^2)}. \tag{11}$$

The speed with which the distribution of $Q(t)$ approaches its limiting value $\{\pi_j\}_{j=0}^{\infty}$ is given by its relaxation time $t \simeq 2\lambda/(\mu-\lambda)^2$. (Also, see Cohen [1969]).

Further, the following asymptotic (t large) results derived by Prabhu [1969] are significant in understanding the transient behavior of the queue $M/M/1$ $\left[o(t)\right.$ is such that $\left.\lim \frac{o(t)}{t} = 0\right]$.

	$\rho < 1$	$\rho = 1$	$\rho > 1$
$E[Q(t)]$	$\dfrac{\lambda}{\mu - \lambda} + o(1)$	$2\sqrt{\dfrac{\lambda t}{\pi}} + o(\sqrt{t})$	$(\lambda - \mu)t + o(1)$
$\text{Var}\,[Q(t)]$	$\dfrac{\lambda\mu}{(\mu - \lambda)^2} + o(1)$	$2\lambda t\left(1 - \dfrac{2}{\pi}\right) + o(t)$	$(\lambda + \mu)t + o(t)$

(12)

and when $\rho = 1$

$$\Pr\left\{\frac{Q(t)}{\sqrt{2\lambda t}} \leqslant x\right\} \to \int_{-x}^{x} \frac{1}{\sqrt{2\pi}}\, e^{-y^2/2}\, dy \tag{13}$$

and when $\rho > 1$

$$\Pr\left\{\frac{Q(t) - (\lambda - \mu)t}{\sqrt{(\lambda + \mu)t}} \leqslant x\right\} \to \int_{-\infty}^{x} \frac{1}{\sqrt{2\pi}}\, e^{-y^2/2}\, dy \tag{14}$$

Similar results for $W(t)$ can be found in Prabhu [1969].

The busy period distribution has also attracted considerable attention in this system. An explicit expression for the probability density function $g_i(t)$ of T_i can be given as

$$g_i(t) = \frac{i}{t}\, \rho^{-i/2} e^{-(\lambda+\mu)t} I_i(2\sqrt{\lambda\mu}\, t) \tag{15}$$

(Palm [1943], Kendall [1951], Bailey [1956] and Prabhu [1960]).

When the queue discipline is LCFS, the waiting time has the distribution given by (15). For the waiting time distribution, when the queue discipline is RS the reader is referred to Palm [1957] and Riordan [1962].

Under statistical equilibrium the departure process is also Poisson with the same parameter as the arrival process (Burke [1956], Reich [1957, 1965]).

4.2 The Queue M/G/1

In many real systems assumption of a Poisson process for arrivals is more natural than the exponential assumption for the service time distribution. Also, due to the development of some powerful analysis techniques, a considerable amount of useful information can be derived even when only one of the arrival or service processes is Poisson. Thus the queue $M/G/1$, in which customers arrive in a Poisson process and get service from a single server with a general service time distribution, has been extensively analyzed over the last four decades.

Erlang's original work (cf. Brockmeyer *et al* [1948]) allows only constant and exponential service times. Initial investigation on general service time distributions are due to Pollaczek [1930] and Khintchine [1932]. In an $M/G/1$ queue let $F(x)$ be the distribution function of $W(\equiv W(\infty))$ and define $\Phi(\theta) = \int_0^\infty e^{-\theta x} \cdot dF(x)$, $Re(\theta) > 0$, as the Laplace-Stieltjes transform of $F(x)$. The Pollaczek-Khintchine formula gives

$$\Phi(\theta) = \frac{(1 - \rho)\theta}{\theta - \lambda + \lambda\psi(\theta)}$$

where λ is the arrival rate and $\psi(\theta)$ is the Laplace-Stieltjes transform of the service time distribution. Let V be the random variable representing the service times. We get

$$E[W] = \frac{\lambda E[V^2]}{2(1 - \rho)} \tag{16}$$

For more information on waiting times, Takács' [1955] integro-differential equation for their distribution can be used. Let

$$F(x_0; x, t) = \Pr\{W(t) \leqslant x \mid W(0) = x_0\}, \qquad (t > 0; x, x_0 \geqslant 0).$$

Then Takács [1955] obtains $[F(x_0; x, t) \equiv F(x, t)]$

$$\frac{\partial F(x,t)}{\partial t} - \frac{\partial F(x,t)}{\partial x} = -\lambda F(x,t) + \lambda \int_0^x F(x - v, t)\, dB(v) \tag{17}$$

where $B(x)$ is assumed to be the service time distribution. For solutions of this equation and other related results, the reader is referred to Takács [1962], Prabhu [1965] and Bhat [1965].

Although analytical results were available for the queue length process through the efforts of Pollaczek, it was not until the early fifties that these results were made available for general use by simpler means. The method of imbedded Markov chain of Kendall [1951], which identifies the departure points in the system as regeneration points for the process and treats queue length at these points as a Markov chain, has opened up a new direction in the study of semi-Markovian systems. Writing down the transition probability matrix of the imbedded Markov chain, the probability generating function $\Pi^*(z)$ of the limiting distribution of the queue length process $\{Q_n\}$ is obtained as

$$\Pi^*(z) = E[z^{Q_\infty}] = \frac{(1 - \rho)(1 - z)K(z)}{K(z) - z} \tag{18}$$

where $K(z)$ is the probability generating function of the number of customers arriving during a service period. From Eq. (18), it follows

$$E[Q_\infty] = \rho + \frac{\lambda^2 E[V^2]}{2(1-\rho)}. \tag{19}$$

Using combinatorial methods the limiting distribution $\{\pi_j^*\}$ has been explicitly obtained by Prabhu and Bhat [1963b] as

$$\pi_0^* = 1 - \rho$$

$$\pi_j^* = (1-\rho)\left[\sum_0^\infty k_{n+j-1}^{(n)} - \sum_0^\infty k_{n+j}^{(n)}\right] \qquad j = 1, 2, \ldots \tag{20}$$

where $\sum_{j=0}^{\infty} k_j^{(n)} z^j = [K(z)]^n$. For an extensive combinatorial treatment of the process $\{Q_n\}$ the reader is referred also to Takács [1967].

Although it is not true in general, in the queue $M/G/1$, the limiting distributions of Q_n and $Q(t)$ are the same. The transient behavior of the process Q_n and $Q(t)$ has been given by several authors, including Cox [1955], Gaver [1959], Keilson and Kooharian [1960], Takács [1961, 1962], Prabhu and Bhat [1963a, b], Prabhu [1965], Bhat [1964a, 1968b] and others.

In particular, the busy period distribution $dG_i(t)$ of T_i can be explicitly obtained as

$$dG_i(t) = \sum_{n=i}^{\infty} \frac{i}{n} e^{-\lambda t} \frac{(\lambda t)^{n-i}}{(n-i)!} dB_n(t) \tag{21}$$

where $B_n(x)$ is the n-fold convolution of $B(x)$ with itself, with $B_n(0) = 1$ if $n = 0$ and $= 0$ otherwise (Prabhu and Bhat [1963a]). Further

$$E[T_i] = \frac{iE[V]}{1-\rho} \tag{22}$$

The busy period distribution of the queue $M/G/1$ when the queue discipline is FCFS is also its waiting time distribution when the queue discipline is LCFS. For RS, queue discipline limiting behavior has been investigated by Kingman [1962]. For other results in special cases the reader is referred to Riordan [1962] and Saaty [1961] for references.

Apart from $M/M/1$, the systems $M/D/1$ and $M/E_k/1$ are other important special cases of the queue $M/G/1$ which have attracted some attention. References are given in the books cited in the chapter.

4.3 The Queue GI/M/1

Results available for this queue are similar to those for the queue $M/G/1$. Kendall's [1953] imbedded Markov chain approach yields the limiting distribution of the queue length Q_n (now defined at arrival epochs). It is obtained as

$$\pi_j^* = (1 - \zeta)\,\zeta^j \qquad j = 0, 1, 2, \ldots \tag{23}$$

where ζ is the least positive root of the functional equation $\omega = K(\omega)$, where $K(z)$ is the p.g.f. of the number of possible services during an inter-arrival time.

In the queue $GI/M/1$, the limiting distributions of Q_n and $Q(t)$ are different. Writing Pr $\{Q(\infty) = j\} = \pi_j$, we get

$$\pi_0 = 1 - \rho$$

$$\pi_j = \rho(1 - \zeta)\,\zeta^j \qquad j = 1, 2, 3, \ldots \tag{24}$$

(cf. Conolly [1958b] and Bhat [1964a, 1968b]).

The transient behavior of the process $\{Q_n\}$ and $\{Q(t)\}$ has been given by several authors including Conolly [1958b], Takács [1960, 1962], Prabhu and Bhat [1963b], Bhat [1964a, 1967, 1968b] and others. In particular, the busy period distribution $g(t)$ of T_1 can be given as

$$g(t) = \sum_n e^{-\mu t} \frac{\mu^n t^{n-2}}{(n-1)!} \int_0^t (t - \tau)[1 - A(t - \tau)]\, dA_{n-1}(\tau) \tag{25}$$

where mean service time is $1/\mu$ and inter-arrival time distribution is $A(t)$. (Conolly [1959], Takács [1960], Bhat [1964a, 1968b].) Further,

$$E[T_1] = \frac{1}{\mu(1 - \zeta)} \tag{26}$$

Because of exponential service waiting time distribution in the queue $GI/M/1$ can be directly derived. A related significant result is a theorem derived by Smith [1953] which states that the limiting waiting time distribution in $GI/M/1$ is exponential whatever be the inter-arrival time distribution.

Apart from $M/M/1$, $D/M/1$ and $E_k/M/1$, there are other important special cases of the queue $GI/M/1$. General references given at the end of the chapter provide sufficient indication of material on these systems.

4.4 The Queue GI/G/1

Let $A(x)$ and $B(x)$ be the inter-arrival and service time distributions, respectively, in the single server queue $GI/G/1$. As defined earlier, let W_n be the waiting time of the nth customer C_n and $X_n = V_n - U_n$ where V_n is the service time of C_n and U_n is the inter-arrival time between C_{n-1} and C_n. The process $\{W_n\}$ is Markovian and it has been extensively studied by several authors such as Pollaczek ([1952, 1957, 1965]; Pollaczek considered this queue as early as 1930), Lindley [1952], Spitzer [1956], Kemperman [1961], Kingman [1962b, 1966], Takács [1962, 1963], Prabhu [1965] and others. Let $F(x) = \Pr\{W_\infty \leqslant x\}$, and $K(x) =$

$\Pr\{X_n \leqslant x\}$. Then Lindley [1952] has shown that it satisfies the integral equation

$$F(x) = -\int_{0-}^{\infty} F(y)\, dK(x-y) \qquad (x \geqslant 0) \tag{27}$$

In special cases this equation may be solved to derive exact distributions. For $F(x)$ in $D/E_k/1$ and $E_k/D/1$ see Prabhu [1962]. For $F_n(x) = \Pr\{W_n \leqslant x | W = 0\}$, expressing W_n as the maximum of a partial sum process, Spitzer [1956] has obtained the result (also see, Pollaczek [1957]):

$$\sum_0^\infty z^n \int_{0-}^{\infty} e^{\theta x}\, dF_n(x) = \exp\left[\sum_1^\infty \frac{z^n}{n} \Pr\{S_n \leqslant 0\} + \sum_1^\infty \frac{z^n}{n} \int_{0+}^{\infty} e^{\theta x}\, dK_n(x)\right]$$

$$\cdot\, [|z| < 1,\ Re(\theta) < 0] \tag{28}$$

where $S_n = X_1 + X_2 \cdots + X_n$ and $K_n(x)$ is the n-fold convolution for $K(x)$ with itself. The relationship between the $\{W(t)\}$ and $\{W_n\}$ processes has been investigated by Takács [1963, 1967]. For busy period distributions the readers are referred to Kingman [1962b], Rice [1962] and Prabhu [1965].

For applied operations researchers, analysis of the system $GI/G/1$ by itself may not be attractive. However, such heavy analysis results in establishing general structures of systems, as well as simple results to represent them. Four such results are significant.

(1) The result $E[Q] = \lambda E[W + V]$, which has been known as Little's formula ([1961], also Jewell [1967]). This result has been found to hold in many situations more general than $GI/G/1$, such as multi-server queues and priority queues (for such systems, averaging function should reflect the complexity of the situations; see Stidham [1972].)

(2) Heavy traffic approximation to the waiting time distribution given by Kingman [1961, 1962c, 1965]. He has shown that when the traffic intensity is close to 1, under the usual assumptions of independence, the waiting time distribution is approximately negative exponential with mean

$$\frac{1}{2}\left[\frac{\text{inter-arrival time variance + service time variance}}{\text{mean inter-arrival time} - \text{mean service time}}\right] \tag{29}$$

if the denominator of expression (29) is small compared with the square root of the numerator.

(3) Bounds for $E[W]$ as derived by Kingman [1962c] and Marshall [1968]. Kingman has shown that

$$E[W] \leqslant \frac{\text{Inter-arrival time variance + service time variance}}{2(\text{mean inter-arrival time})\,(1-\rho)} \tag{30}$$

and Marshall [1968] provides a lower bound by showing that

$$E[W] \geqslant l \tag{31}$$

where l is the unique solution of the equation

$$x = \int_{-x}^{\infty} [1 - K(u)]\, du, \qquad x \geqslant 0$$

when $\rho < 1$.

(4) Functional limit theorems and weak convergence theorems which establish the asymptotic properties of the waiting time behavior for different values of ρ. For a bibliography see Iglehart and Whitt [1970] and Whitt [1973].

4.5 Multi-Server Queues

When the service time distribution is not exponential, multi-server queues are hard to analyze. In the general case $GI/G/s$, although many efforts have been made (Pollaczek [1953], Kiefer and Wolfowitz [1955]), few useful results have emerged. There has been better success in special cases such as $M/D/s$, $GI/M/s$ and $M/M/s$. Erlang's original results (cf. Brockmeyer et al [1948]) include waiting time results in statistical equilibrium for $M/D/s$ where $s = 1$, 2 and 3. A more elegant treatment of this problem in the general case has been later provided by Crommelin [1932].

For the queue $GI/M/s$, the imbedded Markov chain (queue length at arrival epochs) analysis is due to Kendall [1953]. He gives equilibrium distribution of the queue length process $\{Q_n\}$. More recently, Bhat [1968a] has given the transient behavior of the queue length process at departure epochs. Methods have also been given by Bhat [1973] to derive numerical results for the busy period, and transient and equilibrium behavior of the $GI/M/s$ under a finite queue restriction.

The original investigation of the queue $M/M/s$ is due to Erlang (cf. Brockmeyer et al [1948]) and Molina [1927]. Let λ and μ be the arrival and service rates and $\rho = \lambda/s\mu$. The limiting queue length distribution $\{\pi_j\}$ can be given as

$$\pi_j = \begin{cases} \dfrac{(s\rho)^j}{j!}\,\pi_0 & (0 \leqslant j \leqslant s) \\[2ex] \dfrac{(s\rho)^j}{s^{j-s}s!}\,\pi_0 & (j \geqslant s) \end{cases} \tag{32}$$

where

$$\pi_0 = \left[\sum_{0}^{s-1} \frac{(s\rho)^j}{j!} + \frac{(s\rho)}{s!}(1 - \rho)^{-1}\right]^{-1}.$$

Also,

$$E[Q] = s\rho + \frac{\rho\pi_s}{(1-\rho)^2}. \tag{33}$$

For the waiting time W one gets

$$F(0) = \Pr\{W = 0\} = \pi_0 \sum_0^{s-1} \frac{(s\rho)^j}{j!}$$

$$f(x)\,dx = \Pr\{x < W \leqslant x + dx\} \tag{34}$$

$$= s\mu\pi_s e^{-x(s\mu-\lambda)}\,dx \qquad 0 < x < \infty$$

and

$$E[W] = \frac{\pi_s}{s\mu(1-\rho)^2}. \tag{35}$$

The behavior of $Q(t)$ in finite time has been given by Saaty [1960]. As in $M/M/1$, the departure process in the limit has also been found to be Poisson (Burke [1956], Reich [1965].) For other investigations on this system the reader is referred to other books and bibliographies cited below.

4.6 Finite Queues

In the queueing systems considered so far we have assumed that the state space of the queue length process $Q(t)$ is countably infinite. In the real world we see mostly systems in which $Q(t)$ has a finite limit. Of course, from a practical viewpoint, a large limit, though finite, is as good as being infinite. But systems such as a telephone switchboard do not belong to this class. Therefore, we shall review some results that are pertinent to this class of systems.

Finite queues can be purely loss systems or loss and delay systems. In a loss system, customers arriving when all the servers are busy are denied service and are lost to the system. In a loss and delay system, such customers wait provided the number in system does not exceed a finite number (finite waiting room).

First consider the case in which the arrivals are in a Poisson process with rate λ and service times are negative exponential with mean $1/\mu$. Let the number of servers be s. Let $\{\pi_j\}$ be the limiting distribution of the number of customers in the system. For the loss system we get the result due to Erlang

$$\pi_j = \frac{\frac{1}{j!}\rho^j}{\sum_{k=0}^{s} \frac{1}{k!}\rho^k} \qquad j = 0, 1, 2, \ldots, s \tag{36}$$

where $\rho = \dfrac{\lambda}{\mu}$. (cf. Brockmeyer et al [1948].) In particular, π_s, the probability of blocking (probability of losing a customer) is known as *Erlang's loss formula.* This formula has been proved to be quite general by many authors. For a discussion and a complete proof see Takács [1969].

In the above system, suppose the source of arrivals is finite and of size N. Let λ be the constant, such that an idle source at time t will demand service between $(t, t + \Delta t)$ with probability $\lambda \Delta t + o(\Delta t)$ $\left[o(\Delta t) \text{ such that } \dfrac{o(\Delta t)}{\Delta t} \longrightarrow 0 \text{ as } \Delta t \longrightarrow 0\right]$. Then the limiting distribution $\{\pi_j\}$ can be obtained as

$$\pi_j = \frac{\binom{N}{j} \rho^j}{\sum_{k=0}^{s} \binom{N}{k} \rho^k} \qquad j = 0, 1, 2, \ldots, s \tag{37}$$

This expression is referred to as the *Engset* distribution. The proportion of lost customers L_c, (the probability that an arriving customer will be denied service) is given by

$$L_c = \frac{\binom{N-1}{s} \rho^s}{\sum_{j=0}^{s} \binom{N-1}{j} \rho^j}. \tag{38}$$

The expression (38) is known as the *Engset loss formula* (also *Engset-O'Dell formula*; cf. Syski [1960], Riordan [1962]).

Suppose waiting is allowed in the finite source problem given above. The resulting system is the well known machine-interference model of Palm [1947]. Then we get

$$\begin{aligned} \pi_j &= \binom{N}{j} \rho^j \pi_0 && 0 \leqslant j \leqslant s \\ &= \binom{N}{j} \frac{j!}{s!\, s^{j-s}} \rho^j \pi_0 && s \leqslant j \leqslant N \end{aligned} \tag{39}$$

where

$$\pi_0 = \left[\sum_{j=0}^{s-1} \binom{N}{j} \rho^j + \sum_{j=s}^{N} \binom{N}{j} \frac{j!}{s!\, s^{j-s}} \rho^j\right]^{-1} \tag{40}$$

(cf. Feller [1968]). When $N = \infty$, results corresponding to Eqs. (39) and (40) are obtained by replacing $\binom{N}{j}$ by $1/j!$, results due to Erlang and Jensen (cf. Brockmeyer et al [1948], Syski [1960]).

Consider the finite queue $M/M/1$ with a finite limit of N for the number of customers in the system (loss and delay system). The limiting distribution $\{\pi_j\}$ of $Q(t)$ is given by

$$\pi_j = \frac{(1 - \rho)\rho^j}{1 - \rho^{N+1}} \qquad j = 0, 1, 2, \ldots, N \tag{41}$$

When the inter-arrival time or the service time distribution has a general form, the resulting expressions are not elegant. For limiting distributions of finite queue $M/G/1$ see Keilson [1966] and Cohen [1969], for $GI/M/1$ see Keilson [1966], for $M/G/1$ with finite source of customers see Takács [1962] and Bhat and Nance [1971], and for $GI/M/s$ loss system see Takács [1962] (cf. Syski [1960]).

When the state space is not large, in the case of $M/G/1$ or $GI/M/s$ (or $G/M/s$ where dependence of the inter-arrival time distribution on the state of the system is allowed), analysis based on a semi-Markovian model and the imbedded Markov chain is computationally rewarding. Bhat [1973] gives such an efficient methodology for the analysis of two classes of finite queues (1) $M/G/1$ with finite source of customers and (2) $G/M/s$ with finite limit on the number in system (loss or loss and delay system). As demonstrated in this paper, several results of practical interest in these systems can be easily computed using the fundamental matrix (see Kemeny and Snell [1970] and Bhat [1972] for definition and treating state zero as absorbing) of the corresponding transition probability matrix.

Major references for finite queues are Syski [1960], Riordan [1962] and Cohen [1969].

4.7 Other Queueing Systems

The queueing systems discussed above have simple queue disciplines and structures. However, many of the systems encountered in the real world are more complex than these. Since it is impossible to discuss every one of them, we would like to indicate some references from which readers will be able to extract articles on systems of their interest.

In section 1 we have listed the three basic characteristics of a queueing system. Corresponding to each characteristic a host of system variates may be identified.

(a) *Input Process:* Finite output source instead of an input source of unlimited size, customer arrival in groups, customers denied of service mill around, more than one type of arrivals, customer arrivals in correlated streams, input process is dependent on the state of the system, scheduled but inexact arrivals, etc.

(b) *Service Mechanism:* Finite waiting room, a moving single server offering service to stationary customers, service offered continuously even when no customer is present, service offered in quanta of constant length, service offered by a series of customers (tandem queue), waiting room between servers may be limited or unlimited, servers are located in parallel, no waiting allowed (loss system), number of servers varies depending on the state of the system, servers work as a pool, servers have specific functions and these functions are not interchangeable, a network of queues consisting of servers operating in series and in parallel, etc.

(c) *Queue Discipline* (in addition to the three mentioned earlier): Disciplines incorporating customer behavior such as balking, impatience and jockeying; priority disciplines and mixtures of disciplines. Under priority disciplines a large number of variations can be noted: Exogenous (state-independent) such as head-of-the-line, pre-emptive resume, pre-emptive identical, shortest processing time first, longest processing time first, alternating priority, feed back disciplines such as round robin and discretionary priority; Endogenous (state-dependent) such as dynamic priority based on waiting, bribery, congestion, etc.

Clearly all possible combinations of these as well as dependencies between these can be visualized. If one looks at the literature, it is clear that most of the problems can be solved only under Markovian assumptions. The following reference list along with recent journal articles may be used for developing bibliographies of one's interest: Doig [1957], Morse [1958], Khintchine [1960], Syski [1960], Cox and Smith [1961], Saaty [1961, 1966], LeGall [1962], Riordan [1962], Takács [1962, 1967], Beneš [1963, 1965], Prabhu [1965], Lee [1966], Conway, *et al* [1967], Jaiswal [1968], Bhat [1969], Cohen [1969], Cooper [1972], and Gross and Harris [1974].

5. STATISTICAL ANALYSIS

In the formulation of the queueing model, one starts with the identification of its elements and their properties. The structure and system discipline are easily formulated through observations, but the determination of the form and properties of the input and service processes is done with the help of statistical techniques. Four major steps can be identified in this procedure:

(1) *Collection of Data:* Initially, decision has to be made on the nature of data needed for analysis. In this context it is to be noted that the required data form depends largely on the proposed model itself. Thus it would be safer to assume as little of the model form as possible in laying out data collection procedure. There are two major aspects: (a) nature of observations and (b) sample size.

The nature of observations also depends on how they will be used in the model. For instance, in an $M/M/1$ queue, traffic intensity can be estimated as the ratio of the estimates of arrival, and service rates which are characteristics of system elements. Alternately, noting that the traffic intensity provides the utilization factor of the system, one can use the empirical utilization factor (fraction of time the system is being used) as its estimate. Evidently, the first method is more precise and useful. Methods are available to develop confidence intervals for the traffic intensity in this approach [Lilliefors (1966)]. An additional problem would be the process of actually recording observations. How long should the system be observed—for a specified length of time or until a specified number of customers arrive? If the arrival process is Poisson, it can be shown that the second alternative is more advantageous in determining an optimum sample size than the first [Birnbaum (1954)]. Therefore, the best guideline is to make the best use of the information available in the system through practice. To derive maximum benefit, frequent revision of the experimental design may be needed at early stages.

A similar problem exists regarding sample size. Most of the discussion on this topic in the literature is parametric [Mace (1964)], an exception being the use of Chebyshev's inequality. Based on this result, regardless of the distribution the population mean can be estimated within a range of one half the standard deviation around it with 98% confidence with a sample size of 200. When distribution forms are known with the same sample size, much better results are obtained.

(2) *Tests for Stationarity in Time:* Because of the complexities in the analysis of non-stationary processes in queueing systems, there are very few papers that assume non-stationarity. However, many real systems show non-stationary trends during some time intervals. Cyclical trends in customer behavior are quite common. One simple way of using queueing results that has been derived based on stability conditions to non-stationary processes is to divide time into stationary periods. Statistical tests may be employed to do this division. Since no parametric forms are assumed initially, non-parametric tests are particularly useful. One such test is Putter's [1955] modification of the Wilcoxon Two-Sample Rank Test which takes into account ties that may occur in discrete observations (also see Moore [1972]).

(3) *Tests for Independence:* One of the assumptions that simplify analysis of queueing systems relates to the independence of arrival times and/or service times. Appropriate tests of independence may be employed. In many cases the correlation structure of the processes can be determined by treating data as a time series (see literature on Time Series Analysis for a bibliography on this technique). Tests may also be made for specific dependence structures such as Markov chains. Interested readers may refer to the treatment of such topics given in Cox and Lewis [1966], Billingsley [1961] and Lee *et al* [1970], and other books on statistical theory. Billingsley has developed the maximum likeli-

hood theory for Markov processes which is a common feature in many of the simpler queueing models.

(4) *Tests for Specific Distributions:* This involves the estimation and tests of hypothesis regarding specific parameters and forms of distribution. It is advantageous to start with simpler distributions such as Poisson, since analysis under such assumptions is considerably simpler. Standard curve fitting techniques may be employed along with goodness of fit χ^2-tests. In the case of the Poisson process, we may use either the number of arrivals and service in constant intervals of time or inter-arrival times and service times. But in other distributions such as uniform, normal, and Erlangian, only inter-arrival and service times may be used. As in all statistical procedures, availability of data and resources should be the guiding factor in selecting these tests.

While testing for the Poisson process of events (arrivals or service completions are the events; or the exponentiality of inter-occurrence times) several options are available. Important among them are: (a) curve-fitting with a goodness of fit test, (b) an F test based on mean normalized spacings, (c) the Kolmogorov-Smirnov test, (d) the Anderson-Darling test and (e) a uniform distribution test. The first four are standard tests whose descriptions can be found in books on statistical inference. (Also see Gross and Harris [1974].) The last alternative uses the property of the Poisson distribution, associating it with the uniform distribution. If $(T_1, T_2, \ldots, T_n)$ are the time epochs when events occur in a Poisson process during $(0, T)$, then the sample $(T_1, T_2, \ldots, T_n)$ can be considered an ordered sample of size n from a uniform distribution in $(0, T)$. Consequently, if $S_n = \sum_{i=1}^{n} T_i$, $E[S_n] = nT/2$ and $\text{Var}\,[S_n] = nT^2/12$. A standardized normal test now follows, appealing to the central limit theorem.

The need for one or more of these statistical procedures has been demonstrated in queueing theory in the studies reported by Erlang (cf. Brockmeyer et al [1948]), Molina [1927], Fry [1928], Bailey [1952, 1955], Edie [1956], to mention only a few. To find more of these studies one has to go to the literature on queueing theory applications.

The problem of identification of the appropriate model assumes the availability of such models. When no available model fits the situation, new models need to be developed or to be identified for the first time. The Erlangian distribution is such an example. The probability density function $b(x)$ of this distribution can be given in the form

$$b(x) = e^{-k\mu x} \frac{(k\mu)^k}{(k-1)!} x^{k-1} \qquad (x > 0). \tag{42}$$

The Erlangian distribution represents a family of distributions with a broad range of properties. When $k = 1$ it reduces to an exponential distribution and when $k \longrightarrow \infty$ to the deterministic case. In addition, $b(x)$ given above also represents the distribution of the sum of k independent and identically distributed exponential random variables each with mean $\frac{1}{k\mu}$. This property has been gainfully exploited in the analysis of systems with Erlangian arrivals and/or service times. A direct generalization of this distribution is the one investigated by Luchak [1956] who has shown the wider applicability of his weighted-sum-Erlangian model. In general it is derived from Eq. (42) by treating k as an independent random variable with distribution $\{p_k\}_{k=1}^{\infty}$. Then we get

$$b(x) = \sum_{k=1}^{\infty} p_k e^{-k\mu x} \frac{(k\mu)^k}{(k-1)!} x^{k-1} \qquad (x > 0) \tag{43}$$

Morse's [1958] characterization of the hyper-exponential distribution is also an attempt in identifying the proper distribution based on the properties of available data. Suppose customers choose between services at two different rates $2p_1\mu$ and $2p_2\mu$ with probabilities p_1 and p_2 $(=1 - p_1)$ respectively. The resulting service time density function $b(x)$ can then be given as

$$b(x) = 2p_1^2\mu e^{-2p_1\mu x} + 2p_2^2\mu e^{-2p_2\mu x} \qquad (x > 0) \tag{44}$$

By varying the values of p_1 in the range $(0, \frac{1}{2})$, this can represent different distributions with variances in the range $\left(\frac{1}{\mu^2}, \infty\right)$. A direct generalization of the form suggested by Morse can be given as

$$b(x) = \sum_{i=1}^{M} p_i \mu_i e^{-\mu_i x} \tag{45}$$

where

$$\sum_{i=1}^{M} p_i = 1 \quad \text{and} \quad \sum_{i=1}^{M} (p_i/\mu_i) = \frac{1}{\mu}.$$

For a discussion of the statistical properties of the Erlangian as well as the hyper-exponential distribution, the reader is referred to Morse [1958].

Another aspect of statistical analysis of queueing systems is the employment of special techniques that incorporate the structural characteristics of the system. For instance, Clarke [1957] gives the maximum likelihood estimates for the parameters (arrival rate λ and service rate μ) of the queue $M/M/1$, which is in statistical equilibrium. Beneš [1957] has given a sufficient set of statistics for the queue $M/M/\infty$ and Wolff [1965] has derived likelihood ratio tests and maximum likelihood estimators for simple queueing models. Other papers and books that may be of interest are Cox [1965], Harris [1973], and Gross and Harris [1974].

6. OPERATIONAL ANALYSIS

In queueing theory literature the descriptive approach to the operational analysis has been predominant. Evidence to this fact can be found in literature on telecommunication systems, computer systems, transportation systems, maintenance and service systems, etc. For instance, Erlang's paper (cf. Brockmeyer *et al* [1948]) "On the Rational Determination of the Number of Circuits" deals with determining the optimum number of channels so as to reduce the probability of loss to the system. Bailey's [1952] simulation procedure to achieve a better appointment system in hospitals, Brigham's [1955] determination of the optimum number of clerks to be assigned to the tool crib counters, and Edie's [1956] study of traffic delays at toll booths are other significant examples. A few other significant investigations are also mentioned below, introducing the corresponding normative approach.

In maintenance and service systems, measures of performance are used as guides for improving system efficiency (cf. Cox and Smith [1961], Benson and Cox [1951, [1952]). In Bhat and Rao [1972] properties of system characteristics such as queue length and busy period are used to specify control parameters for the dynamic regulation of the traffic intensity in queueing systems $M/G/1$ and $GI/M/1$.

Application area literature provides many more examples of this descriptive approach to operational analysis. The major emphasis in this procedure is to look for the "best" value for the decision parameter based on system performance (cf. Cox and Smith [1961], Lee [1966], Wagner [1969]).

In the solution of complex operational problems, simulation has been a useful tool. The function of simulation is diagnostic rather than remedial. As long as this limitation is understood by the practitioner, it can be effectively used in improving the system. The reader is referred to the chapter on simulation for a bibliography in this area.

In a normative approach, optimum values of characteristics or parameters are set, based on physical or cost restrictions to the system. For example, optimum values for the waiting room size, number of servers, mode of service, traffic intensity, arrival rate, service rate, etc. can be determined based on costs related to delay, quality of service and return to the management. Over the last few years many significant problems in this area have been considered. The nature of results obtained in these studies are indicated below, categorizing them in terms of problem types.

(1) Simple Cost Models

In these models, cost functions are developed based on results derived through a behavioral analysis. For example, consider the mean waiting time $E[W]$ of Eq.

(16). Specializing this result for a k-Erlangian distribution [Eq. (42)] we get

$$E[W] = \rho \frac{\left(1 + \frac{1}{k}\right)}{2\mu(1 - \rho)} \tag{46}$$

where $\rho = \frac{\lambda}{\mu}$. Clearly $E[W]$ is the smallest when $k \longrightarrow \infty$ (constant service) and the largest when $k = 1$ (exponential service). An analogous result can also be established for the dual system $E_k/M/1$ (see Fischer [1974]).

Morse's [1958] analysis of the multi-server system $M/M/s$ provides simple problems of this nature as well. One of the significant results states that when the traffic intensity $(\lambda/s\mu)$ and the arrival rate are held constant, mean queue length and waiting time are minimized when $s = 1$. Further, if C_s is the cost per server per unit time and C_w is the cost of waiting per unit time for each customer, in a single server system $M/M/1$, he has shown that the system cost is minimized if the service rate μ is given by

$$\mu^* = \lambda + \sqrt{\frac{\lambda C_w}{C_s}} \tag{47}$$

Problems of this type can also be found in Hillier and Lieberman [1967], Conway, Maxwell and Miller [1967], Wagner [1969] and Bhat [1972]. With the same cost structure as above Bhat [1972, p. 237] has shown that in a department store with s checkout counters, when the arrivals are Poisson with rate λ, and b_1 and b_2 are the first and second moments of the service time distribution (general) the optimum value of s that minimizes the total system cost is given by

$$s^* = b_1 + \sqrt{\frac{\lambda b_2 C_w}{2C_s}} \tag{48}$$

(2) Varying Service Rates

For an effective operation of a queueing system, control of either the arrival or the service rate is essential. Normally, the system can exercise control over only the service rate. This can be done either by increasing the number of servers or by increasing the rate of service through other means such as automation, etc. One of the significant earlier papers on this approach is by Moder and Phillips [1962] in which the number of customers in a queue $M/M/s$ is varied as follows: Starting from a minimum number of s servers, additional servers are brought in every time the number of waiting customers goes beyond a pre-assigned number N. The maximum number of servers allowed is S. The added servers are taken off as and when the number of waiting customers falls below another pre-assigned quantity. Even though the analysis provided here is behavioral, the measures of effectiveness are good guides for the selection of parameters for the system. A modification of this model has been given by Yadin and Naor [1967] where again a descriptive analysis provides clues for operational purposes. Yadin and Naor employ a variational service policy in a queue $M/M/1$ as follows. Suppose $\{\mu_0, \mu_1, \ldots, \mu_k, \ldots\}$ be a sequence of feasible service rates such that $\mu_0 = 0$ and $\mu_{k+1} > \mu_k$. Also consider two sequences of integers $\{R_1, R_2, \ldots, R_k, \ldots\}$ and $\{S_0, S_1, S_2, \ldots, S_k, \ldots\}$ such that $R_{k+1} > R_k$, $S_{k+1} > S_k$, $R_{k+1} > S_k$, $S_0 = 0$. The service policy is as follows: Whenever queue size reaches a value R_k (from below) and service rate is μ_{k-1}, it is increased to μ_k; whenever queue size drops to a value S_k (from above) and service rate is μ_{k+1}, it is decreased to μ_k.

Optimality of service policies of this type in an $M/M/1$ queue has been established by Crabill [1969, 1972]. Using a general cost rate $C(i)$ dependent on the state of the system (i) and a cost rate r_i associated with each of the possible service rates, Crabill establishes the following optimal policy. Let λ be the constant arrival rate and $\{\mu_i, i = 1, 2, \ldots, k\}$ be the set of possible service rates. Then, if $C(i)$ is nondecreasing and approaches ∞ as $i \longrightarrow \infty$, $0 < \mu_1 < \mu_2 < \cdots < \mu_k$, $0 \leqslant r_1 < r_2 < \cdots < r_k$, $\lambda < \mu_k$ and $\sum_{i=0}^{\infty} C(i)\,(\lambda/\mu_k) < \infty$ then the optimal stationary policy is given by the specification of $k+1$ numbers $0 = d_1 \leqslant d_2 \leqslant \cdots \leqslant d_k \leqslant d_{k+1} = \infty$ with the interpretation that service rate μ_j is used in states $d_j \leqslant i < d_{j+1}$.

(3) Server On-Off Policies

In the investigations for optimal operating policies for queueing systems, Heyman's [1968] paper is a watershed. Until 1968 the operational investigations of queueing systems had concentrated mainly on deriving optimal parameter values based on simple cost functions or comparisons of behavioral results. Yadin and Naor's [1963] results on a queueing system $M/G/1$ with a removable service station when the queue length drops to zero is one such example. Heyman's investigations refine this model further. He considers the optimality of the operating policy: turn the server on when n customers are present and then turn it off when the system is empty. His cost structure includes a server start-up cost, a server shut-down cost, a cost per unit time when the server is turned on and a holding cost per unit time spent in the system for each customer. He derives a closed form expression for the optimal value of n for the undiscounted, infinite horizon problem. For finite horizon problems, dynamic programming recursion relations are established to find the optimal policy.

As a natural extension of this problem, Sobel [1969] considers the optimality of the following (M, m) operating policy for a $GI/G/1$ queue under a more general cost structure in the undiscounted infinite horizon case. If the queue length is m or less, then do not provide service until the queue length reaches M, whereupon service should begin and continue until the queue length drops to m again. Clearly $m = 0$ is the case considered by Heyman [1968]. Balachandran [1973] gives the workload analogue of the Hyman-Yadin-Naor result. Other extensions of these inventory type on-off policies have come from Blackburn [1972] who incorporates balking and reneging, and Deb and Serfozo [1972] who consider a bulk service scheme in which minimal group size for service is the point of attention.

(4) Design Considerations

As evidenced by the different areas of literature in queueing theory applications, system designers have gained most of their information from descriptive models. For a wide variety of simple cost models, the reader is referred to Hillier and Lieberman [1967]. There have been normative models only in a very few cases. Two such efforts are given below.

It is an intuitive feeling that it would be more efficient to use a team of servers than to use servers individually, even though the combined service rates are the same in both cases. This follows from the fact that in the former case, servers would be idle when no customer is in the system, whereas in the latter this is not so. Morse's [1958] conclusions on the $M/M/s$ system support this principle. However, it is to be noted that the optimality of the team approach is very much dependent on cost considerations and server characteristics. This aspect has been considered in much detail by Stidham [1970] and Brumelle [1971]. Using the long-run expected average cost per unit time as the optimality criterion, and a fairly general cost structure, Stidham establishes the superiority of the team approach in a wide variety of queueing systems in the $G/E_k/s$ class. Brumelle's extension is to $M/G/s$ queueing systems.

Evans [1971] uses a different approach and aims at deriving an optimal transition rate matrix that would optimize a cost function dependent on the steady state probabilities of the system. His investigations of the derivatives of the objective function lead him to gradient algorithms for finding locally optimum rates.

(5) Priority Queues

Priority queues present interesting decision problems which are also hard to handle. Priority rules are essential for job scheduling. For an extensive discussion of the use of behavioral analysis in deriving improved systems, the reader is referred to Conway, *et al* [1967]. One of the significant results is the superiority of the queue discipline, which makes use of the information on the length of service. It is commonly known that if specific information on the length of service for the arriving customer is not available, average characteristics such as mean queue length and mean waiting time remain unaltered under a broad class of queue disciplines. Generally, priority queue disciplines are based on additional information on customer demands. Phipps [1956] has shown that if lengths of service demanded by the customers are known, the shortest processing time discipline (customer with the shortest service time is served first) minimizes the overall mean queue length and waiting time (non-preemptive case). When the queue discipline is of the preemptive type (higher priority customer preempts low priority service) the analogous situation has been shown to be the "shortest remaining processing time" discipline by Schrage [1968] (also see Schrage and Miller [1966]).

A simple but significant result in the assignment of priorities has been established by Brosh and Naor [1963]. If there are N Poisson arrival classes with mean service times b_i $(i = 1, 2, \ldots, N)$ and waiting costs h_i $(i = 1, 2, \ldots, N)$ respectively, then they show that the optimal ordering is achieved by arranging the ratios b_i/h_i in an ascending order (class with min b_i/h_i has the highest priority).

Another class of problems relates to the purchase of priorities by the customers (also known as the bribing situation). Investigating this problem in a $M/G/1$ queue both with and without preemption Kleinrock [1967] relates it to the "impatience" factor among customers and shows that the only condition necessary for an optimum payment function is that it be montonically increasing with the impatience factor. Defining a payment policy as stable if it does not pay an individual customer to deviate from it if everyone else uses it, Balachandran [1972] considers the stability of different optimal policies with regard to the queue $M/M/1$.

The above are only some of the significant problems and results considered in the operational analysis of queueing systems. Because of the Markovian structure of queueing problems of practical interest, the development of the theory of Markov decision processes and the optimization of queues have occurred simultaneously, deriving mutual benefit from their growth. For an extensive bibliography, the readers are referred to recent survey type articles by Prabhu and Stidham [1973], Sobel [1973] and Crabill, Gross and Magazine [1974].

7. THEORETICAL ANALYSIS TECHNIQUES

In the last three parts of this chapter, an overview of queueing theory was presented from a systems perspective. Being an area of applied probability and mathematics, contributions in queueing theory are possible from two distinct classes of researchers: (1) those who are interested only in the theoretical development of the subject and (2) those who are interested only in solving real life problems. In between, there are many theoreticians who understand applications and many practitioners who realize the need and comprehend the power of theoretical work. From the point of the development of queueing theory as a whole, contributions of theoreticians are as important as those of others who try to solve system problems. In this section we present the highlights of theoretical developments in analysis techniques; in the next, we discuss efforts that have been made in applying them.

Queueing theory has its theoretical base in Probability and Stochastic Processes. During the last four decades, developments in queueing theory and the theory of stochastic processes have gone on simultaneously. Often it is hard to separate one from the other. By the richness in structural varieties of basic stochastic processes, queueing theory has made substantial contributions to the development of the theory of stochastic processes. Common processes used in the analysis of queueing systems are Markov and renewal processes. Markovian queues (systems with Poisson arrivals and exponential service) are excellent examples of birth and death processes, and the virtual waiting time process in the queue $M/G/1$ is a mixed type Markov process in which changes of state occur continuously as well as in jumps. When the system is not Markovian, it is possible to identify renewal points in the basic process (e.g., arrival epochs in the queue $GI/M/1$ are renewal points). Thus, renewal theory has become a convenient tool in queueing analysis. For an account of these processes, the reader is referred to the chapter on Stochastic Processes in the *Handbook* as well as other standard books on the subject.

Theoretical developments in queueing theory also involve the identification and analysis of basic processes using concepts and results from the theory of stochastic processes, as well as mathematics in general. Some of the significant developments of this kind are recounted below. We shall start by giving definitions of some of the technical terms we use later.

Stochastic process (SP): A collection of random variables that are indexed by a parameter such as time and space. *State-space:* Set of values assumed by the process; *parameter space:* Set of values assumed by the index parameter.

Markov process: Consider a SP $X(t)$ with continuous state and parameter space. Let $(t_0, t_1, \ldots, t_n, t)$, $t_0 < t_1 < t_2 < \cdots < t_n < t$ be a finite (or countably infinite) set of points in the parameter space. Then $X(t)$ is called a Markov process if

$$\Pr\{X(t) \leqslant x | X(t_n) = x_n,\ X(t_{n-1}) = x_{n-1}, \ldots, X(t_0) = x_0\}$$
$$= \Pr\{X(t) \leqslant x | X(t_n) = x_n\}$$

i.e., if the conditional distribution of $X(t)$ for given values of $X(t_0), X(t_1), \ldots, X(t_n)$ depends only on $X(t_n)$, which is the most recent value of the process.

A Markov process with a discrete parameter space will be called a *Markov chain* (some authors identify discrete state space Markov processes as Markov chains.) Most of the Markov chains encountered in practice also have a discrete state space. Let $\{X_n, n = 0, 1, 2, \ldots\}$ be such a chain and

$$P_{ij}^{(m,m+n)} = \Pr\{X_{m+n} = j \mid X_m = i\}$$

If

$$P_{ij}^{(m,m+n)} = P_{ij}^{(0,n)} (\equiv P_{ij}^{(n)}),$$

for all m, the Markov chain is said to be *time-homogeneous.* The matrix whose elements are $P_{ij} (\equiv P_{ij}^{(1)})$ is known as the transition probability matrix and it completely defines the Markov chain.

Semi-Markov process: Consider a SP $X(t)$ with discrete state space and continuous parameter space. Let $(t_0, t_1, \ldots, t_n, \ldots)$ be a discrete set of points in the parameter space. Further, let $X(t)$ be such that $\{X(t_n), n = 0, 1, 2, \ldots\}$ be a Markov chain as defined above with transition probabilities $P_{ij}, i, j \in S$ (S-state space). Define a random variable, Y_{ij}, to represent the time needed for the transition $i \longrightarrow j$ of the Markov chain $\{X(t_n)\}$. Let $F_{ij}(t) = \Pr\{Y_{ij} \leqslant t\}$ be its distribution function. Also let $Q_{ij}(t)$ be the joint conditional probability that, given the process occupies state i at a transition epoch, it will be in state j at the following transition epoch, and the amount of time taken for this transition is less than or equal to t. Clearly we have

$$Q_{ij}(t) = P_{ij} F_{ij}(t).$$

Processes of this type are called semi-Markov processes. [See Pyke (1961, Neuts [1973], Cinlar [1969].)

Renewal process: Let $t_0, t_1, t_2, \ldots, t_{n-1}, t_n, \ldots$ be the epochs of time certain events occur. Let $X_n = t_n - t_{n-1}, n = 1, 2, \ldots$ be independent and identically distributed random variables. Thus, we have a process that 'renews' itself at these points and therefore $\{X_n\}$ is known as a renewal process. Let $N(t)$ be the number of renewals in time t, i.e. $N(t) = \max\{n \mid X_1 + X_2 \cdots + X_n \leqslant t\}$. Now $\{N(t), t \geqslant 0\}$ is known as the renewal counting process.

Laplace-Stieltjes transform: Let $F(t)$ be a real valued function; then we define the Laplace-Stieltjes transform of $F(t)$ as

$$\int_0^\infty e^{-st}\, dF(t) \qquad Re(s) > 0.$$

If $F(t)$ is absolutely continuous, writing $dF(t) = f(t)\,dt$, we get the Laplace transform

$$\int_0^\infty e^{-st} f(t)\, dt \qquad Re(s) > 0.$$

Generating function (Z-transform): Let $\{a_n\}_{n=0}^\infty$ be a sequence of real numbers. If

$$A(z) = \sum_{n=0}^{\infty} a_n z^n$$

exists, then $A(z)$ is called the generating function of the sequence $\{a_n\}_{n=0}^{\infty}$. In particular, when $\{a_n\}_{n=0}^{\infty}$ is a probability distribution we have the probability generating function.

Significant analysis techniques now follow.

(a) Birth and Death Process

When arrivals have Poisson characteristics and service times are exponential, the resulting queueing process is Markovian. Further, it has the characteristics of a special class of Markov process commonly known as the birth and death processes.

Arrivals (births): Let the number of customers in the system at time t be n. During the following infinitesimal interval $(t, t + \Delta t]$ let the probability of occurrence of one new arrival be $\lambda_n \Delta t + o(\Delta t)$, no new arrival be $1 - \lambda_n \Delta t + o(\Delta t)$ and more than one new arrival be $o(\Delta t)$ where $o(\Delta t)$ is such that $o(\Delta t)/\Delta t \longrightarrow 0$ as $\Delta t \longrightarrow 0$.

Service: If the number of customers in the system at time t is n, let $\mu_n \Delta t + o(\Delta t)$ be the probability of one service completion during $(t, t + \Delta t]$. Clearly, the probability of no service completion during that interval is $1 - \mu_n \Delta t + o(\Delta t)$ and the probability of more than one service completion is $o(\Delta t)$.

Further we shall assume that arrival and service completion epochs are independent of the most recent corresponding epoch. Also, they are dependent mutually only through the number of customers in the system. To be realistic we assume $\mu_0 = 0$ and $\lambda_0 > 0$.

Under these conditions the queue length process (number of customers in the system) is a Markov process. Let $Q(t)$ be the number of customers in the system at time t and define

$$P_{ij}(t) = \Pr\{Q(t) = j \mid Q(0) = i\}.$$

Writing down probabilities of transitions between $(0, t]$ and $(t, t + \Delta t]$, we can derive the difference-differential equations

$$\begin{aligned} P'_{i0}(t) &= -\lambda_0 P_{i0}(t) + \mu_1 P_{i1}(t) \\ P'_{ij}(t) &= -(\lambda_j + \mu_j) P_{ij}(t) + \lambda_{j-1} P_{ij-1}(t) \\ &\quad + \mu_{j+1} P_{ij+1}(t) \end{aligned} \tag{49}$$

With the initial conditions

$$P_{ij}(0) = \begin{cases} 1 & \text{if } j = i \\ 0 & \text{if } j \neq i. \end{cases}$$

Except for a few simple cases, solution of this set of equations is formidable. Even under the simple assumptions of the queue $M/M/1$, one has to make use of generating functions and Laplace transforms. For complete solutions for the transient behavior using equations of this type for the systems $M/M/1$ and $M/M/s$, the reader is referred to Saaty [1961]. (Also, Riordan [1962], Gross and Harris [1974].) The resulting expressions for $M/M/1$ are given by Eqs. (7)-(9).

As $t \longrightarrow \infty$, when the limiting distribution exists, the balance of state equations may be written down setting $\lim_{t\to\infty} P'_{ij}(t) = 0$ in Eqs. (49) above or by directly considering the possible transitions in and out of a state. Let $\lim_{t\to\infty} P_{ij}(t) = \pi_j$. These equations are

$$\lambda_0 \pi_0 = \mu_1 \pi_1$$

$$(\lambda_j + \mu_j)\pi_j = \lambda_{j-1}\pi_{j-1} + \mu_{j+1}\pi_{j+1} \qquad j > 0 \tag{50}$$

$$\sum_{j=0}^{\infty} \pi_j = 1.$$

These equations can be solved recursively to give

$$\pi_0 = \left[1 + \sum_{n=1}^{\infty} \frac{\lambda_0\lambda_1 \cdots \lambda_{n-1}}{\mu_1\mu_2 \cdots \mu_n}\right]^{-1} \tag{51}$$

$$\pi_j = \frac{\lambda_0\lambda_1 \cdots \lambda_{j-1}}{\mu_1\mu_2 \cdots \mu_j}\pi_0 \qquad (j > 0). \tag{52}$$

Clearly, the limiting distribution exists only if the denominator on the right hand side of Eq. (51) is finite.

In queueing systems with group arrivals and/or group service, balance of state equations of the type Eq. (50) cannot be solved recursively. Then a generating function approach is necessary. For instance, consider a queue $M/M/1$ with arrivals in groups of size G whose distribution is given by $\{g_k\}$. Let $\gamma(z) = \sum_{j=1}^{\infty} \cdot$ $g_j z^j (|z| \leqslant 1)$ be its probability generating function. Then $\Pi(z) = \sum_{j=0}^{\infty} \pi_j z^j$, the probability generating function of the limiting distribution is given by

$$\Pi(z) = \frac{\mu(1-\rho)(1-z)}{\mu(1-z) - \lambda z[1-\gamma(z)]} \qquad (|z| \leqslant 1)$$

For specific forms of $\gamma(z)$, $\Pi(z)$ can be inverted to give $\{\pi_j\}$.

(b) Supplementary Variable

For a system to be Markovian it is essential that the basic process completely specifies the state of the system at the given time and that this information be sufficient to describe the future development of the process. Thus, if the queue length $Q(t)$ is non-Markovian by itself, along with it other processes or variables can be defined to make the set Markovian. For instance, let $R(t)$ be the time since the last arrival and $S(t)$ be the time since the start of the current service if one is in progress at time t. Then clearly the vector process $\{Q(t), R(t), S(t)\}$ provides sufficient information in a $GI/G/1$ queue to describe its future development. Because of the Markovian property of the exponential distribution, the corresponding vector processes for $M/G/1$ and $GI/M/1$ are $\{Q(t), S(t)\}$ and $\{Q(t), R(t)\}$ respectively. When the general distribution is Erlangian $R(t)$ and $S(t)$ can be replaced by the number of exponential phases that have elapsed after the previous corresponding event (arrival or start of service). (See [Luchak, 1956] for alternate method.) For the queue $M/G/1$, Cox [1955] has used this method to analyze the queue length behavior at an arbitrary time point when the service time distribution is continuous. Let $B(x)$ be its distribution function and $\mu(x)$ be its hazard function defined as

$$\mu(x)\,dx = \frac{dB(x)}{1 - B(x)}$$

Further, let $P_j(t, s)$ be the joint probability and the density function that at time t there are j customers in the system and that the expended service time of the one at service be s. Using λ as the arrival rate and from the same arguments as in the birth and death model, the following differential equations may be obtained in steady state (corresponding steady state notations are used).

$$0 = -\lambda\pi_0 + \int_0^\infty \pi_1(s)\,\mu(s)\,ds$$

$$\frac{\partial\pi_1(s)}{\partial s} = -(\lambda + \mu(s))\,\pi_1(s) \tag{53}$$

$$\frac{\partial\pi_j(s)}{\partial s} = -(\lambda + \mu(s))\,\pi_j(s) + \lambda\pi_{j-1}(s) \qquad (j > 1)$$

Also

$$\pi_j(0) = \int_0^\infty \pi_{j+1}(s)\,\mu(s)\,ds + \delta_{1j}\lambda\pi_0$$

where $\delta_{1j} = 1$ if $j = 1$ and $= 0$ otherwise. Solutions to these equations can be obtained with the help of generating functions.

Jaiswal [1968] has used this method extensively in the study of priority queues. Keilson and Kooharian [1960] also use supplementary variables in their analysis of the queue $M/G/1$.

(c) Takács Integro-Differential Equation

The integro-differential equation presented in Eq. (17) is obtained by noting that the virtual waiting time process $W(t)$ in the queue $M/G/1$ is a mixed type Markov process with changes of state occurring in jumps as well as in continuous time [Takács, 1955]. Waiting time results obtained from this equation can be converted into queue length results as done in Prabhu [1965].

(d) Imbedded Markov Chain

As noted in (2) above, in the queue $M/G/1$ the vector process $\{Q(t), S(t)\}$ is Markovian. Now let $t_0, t_1, t_2, \ldots$ be the time epochs at which $S(t_n) = 0$ ($n = 0, 1, 2, \ldots$). Clearly these time epochs are departure points from the system. As a result $\{Q(t_n)\}$ is a Markov chain and it is called the imbedded (or embedded) Markov chain of the queue $M/G/1$. If X_n is the number of customers arriving during the nth service time with $\Pr\{X_n = j\} = k_j$ we have the relation

$$Q_{n+1} = \max\,[X_{n+1}, Q_n - 1 + X_{n+1}]. \tag{54}$$

The transition probability matrix of this Markov chain can be obtained as

$$P = \begin{array}{c|ccccccc} \nearrow & 0 & 1 & 2 & 3 & \cdot & \cdot & \cdot \\ \hline 0 & k_0 & k_1 & k_2 & k_3 & \cdot & \cdot & \cdot \\ 1 & k_0 & k_1 & k_2 & k_3 & \cdot & \cdot & \cdot \\ 2 & \cdot & k_0 & k_1 & k_2 & \cdot & \cdot & \cdot \\ \cdot & \cdot & \cdot & k_0 & k_1 & \cdot & \cdot & \cdot \\ \cdot & \cdot & \cdot & \cdot & \cdot & \cdot & \cdot & \cdot \\ \cdot & \cdot & \cdot & \cdot & \cdot & \cdot & \cdot & \cdot \end{array}$$

In the queue $GI/M/1$ queue length at arrival epochs is an imbedded Markov chain. In this queue, if we denote the queue length just before the nth arrival as Q_n and the number of possible services during the nth arrival interval as X_n, we get the relation

$$Q_{n+1} = \max\,[0, Q_n + 1 - X_{n+1}] \tag{55}$$

Now writing $\sum_{r=j+1}^{\infty} k_r = \alpha_j$, the transition probability matrix of the Markov chain $\{Q_n\}$ can be obtained as

↗	0	1	2	3	4	· · ·
0	α_0	k_0	0	0	0	· · ·
1	α_1	k_1	k_0	0	0	· · ·
$P = 2$	α_2	k_2	k_1	k_0	0	· · ·
.	.	.	.	.	.	. . .
.	.	.	.	.	.	. . .

Properties of the queue length process $\{Q_n\}$ can be now readily derived through standard techniques. As noted earlier, the method of imbedded Markov chains in queueing theory is due to Kendall [1951, 1953]. Further use of these Markov chains have been made by Prabhu and Bhat [1963b], Bhat [1964b] and Takács [1967].

(e) Semi-Markovian Analysis

With the imbedded Markov chain structure, the queue length process in a wide variety of queueing systems with Poisson arrivals can be identified as a Semi-Markov process, as defined earlier. Extensive investigations have been carried out in this analysis technique and the reader is referred to papers by Neuts [1966, 1971] and others (see [Cheong *et al*, 1973] for a bibliography).

(f) Renewal Theoretic Approach

In queueing processes it is easy to identify convenient renewal points and renewal periods. For instance, in a $GI/G/1$ queue the epochs of commencement of busy periods are renewal points and the busy cycles are renewal periods. Thus, if the distribution of the renewal period is available, the transition distributions of the basic processes can be developed using well known results in renewal theory. This method has been very widely used in deriving transforms as well as explicit results for the queue behavior in systems $M/G/1$ and $GI/M/1$ (Gaver [1959]; Takács [1962]; Bhat [1964a, 1967, 1968b]).

(g) Combinatorial Methods

The Markov process $\{W_n\}$ (waiting time of the nth customer C_n) in the queue $GI/G/1$ has inspired several combinatorial methods in its analysis. Let V_n be the service time of C_n, and U_n be the inter-arrival time between C_{n-1} and C_n. Then we have

$$W_n = \max [0, W_{n-1} + V_n - U_n] \tag{56}$$

which yields the Lindley integral Eq. (27). Writing $X_n = V_n - U_n$ and $S_n = X_1 + X_2 + \cdots + X_n$ we can represent ($W_0 \equiv 0$).

$$W_n \sim \max (0, S_1, S_2, \ldots, S_n). \tag{57}$$

where $\sim$ has been used to denote equality in distribution. The partial sum process (57) is one of the significant aspects of the fluctuation theory of random variables, advances in which are due to F. Spitzer, W. Feller, S. Andersen, J. H. B. Kemperman, L. Takács, N. U. Prabhu and others (for a bibliography see Prabhu [1965] and Takács [1967].)

It should be noted that with proper initial conditions and suitably defining the variables, recurrence relations (54) and (55) yield expressions in the form

$$M/G/1: \; Q_n \sim X_n + \max (0, S_1, S_2, \ldots, S_n)$$

$$GI/M/1: \; Q_n \sim \max (0, S_1, S_2, \ldots, S_n)$$

These combinatorial forms have been used by Prabhu and Bhat [1963b], Bhat [1964b] and Takács [1967] in the imbedded Markov chain analysis of queueing systems.

The recurrence relation (56) is also the basis for the heavy traffic and other approximations in queueing theory (Kingman [1961, 1962c], Marshall [1968], Iglehart and Whitt [1970]). Kingman [1966] has used it to provide an algebraic structure for the representation and analysis of general queueing systems. Weak convergence and functional limit theorems providing the general properties of queueing processes under different conditions are also founded on relations of this type (Iglehart and Whitt [1970], Whitt [1973]).

(h) Pollaczek Method

One of the major contributors to queueing theory is F. Pollaczek [1934, 1953, 1957, 1965]. He considered waiting time problems as early as 1930 and has continued to make fundamental contributions to the complete analysis of single server as well as multiserver queues with general arrival and service times. His approach is highly analytical, and therefore few operations researchers have the fullest appreciation of his methods and results. His method is also based on the relation (56) for the single server queues and its analogue for the multiserver queues. In his basic approach, the determination of the Laplace-Stieltjes transform of W_n (i.e. $E[e^{-\theta W_n}]$) is reduced to the problem of solving a system of simultaneous integral equations (or a single integral equation in the single server case) using complex variable techniques (also see Cohen [1969]).

(i) Diffusion Approximation

Process approximation is one way of deriving simple approximate results. Under heavy traffic assumptions a reasonably approximate process can be obtained by considering the queueing process as a diffusion process (a class of Markov processes which change states continually in such a way that the time averages of the mean and variance of displacement in an infinitesimal interval of time is finite) with corresponding infinitesimal first and second moments. As shown in Gaver [1968], for the waiting time process $W(t)$ in the queue $M/G/1$ (λ-arrival rate; V-service time) the infinitesimal mean and variance are given by

$$\mu = \lambda E(V) - 1$$

$$\sigma^2 = \lambda E[V^2].$$

Using these parameters a proper approximating diffusion process can be identified. (Also, see Iglehart [1965], Fischer [1971].)

Given above are but a few of the significant theoretical developments in queueing analysis. For other techniques the readers are referred to books and bibliographies in queueing theory. In addition, we may also mention the new area of Markov decision processes which has been the basis for many control problems mentioned earlier. For a bibliography, the reader is referred to Ross [1970] and Derman [1970] and the chapter on Dynamic Programming in the *Handbook*.

8. COMPUTATIONAL PROBLEMS

In an area of applied mathematics, usefulness of theoretical results is directly related to the degree of ease with which they can be numerically evaluated. In many areas like physics, theoretical results are accepted only after experimental substantiation. In view of this, it is worthwhile to investigate the extent to which computational problems have been handled in queueing theory.

Computational problems arise in the following situations: (a) empirical data analysis, (b) tables and graphs for system characteristics, (c) numerical evaluation of formulae, (d) numerical solutions of system equations, and (e) simulation. Literature on these different problems are scattered over a wide variety of journals, most of them in application areas.

Many new developments in queueing theory have been inspired through the study of empirical data. Erlang's and others' work in telephone traffic theory, queueing theory applications to computer systems analysis, and queueing applications in transportation science are all examples in which model development has occurred after a need has been detected. In an attempt to make queueing theory results meaningful, tables have been developed for some queueing systems. Peck and Hazelwood's [1958] tables for the queue $M/M/s$ with finite waiting room, queueing tables for determining system manning and related support requirements by Purvis, McLaughlin and Mallory [1964], as well as tables for transition probabilities and busy period distributions in queues $M/M/1$, $M/D/1$, $D/M/1$, $M/E_k/1$ and $E_k/M/1$ developed by Bhat and Sahin [1969], are examples of such investigations.

Success in the numerical evaluation of the formulae depends on their form and nature. These in turn depend on the objectives of the author. Naturally, the results derived by theoreticians are often not in computationally feasible forms—unless the final result is simple. But there are many researchers who have made efforts to interpret these results to the practitioner and many who have tried to solve problems, with computations in mind. For simple evaluations of formulae in addition to the literature that has appeared in application areas of queueing theory mentioned in Section 3 the reader may refer to textbooks on OR such as Hillier and Lieberman [1967] and Wagner [1969] as well as Morse [1958]. Numerical inversion of Laplace transforms is a useful tool in the evaluation of complex formulae. Considerable work has been done in making this tool efficient in the context of functions that appear in queueing theory. See papers by Gaver [1966], Stehfest [1970] and Dubner and Abate [1968] for information in this area. Bhat and Nance [1971] have developed a methodology of analysis for the queue $M/G/1$ with a finite source of customers, which exploits the system structure to develop results that are computationally convenient. This method has been further extended by Bhat [1973] for the analysis of the finite queue $G/M/s$ as well.

An alternate method to derive numerical results is to solve the system equations numerically. The papers of Luchak [1956], Leese and Boyd [1966], Neuts [1973a], Klimko and Neuts [1973], Neuts and Heimann [1973] and Bagchi and Templeton [1972] are examples of this approach. Of these, the first two authors have concentrated on the queue $M/M/1$ and its variations. A comparative study of different techniques has been given by Leese and Boyd [1966]. The group led by M. F. Neuts has given the numerical solution for the discrete time finite queue $M/G/1$, based on recursive relations for transition probabilities. Bagchi and Templeton [1972] have numerically analyzed a bulk queue with a finite waiting room, starting from Kingman's [1966] algebraic relations.

In some problems a mixture of numerical evaluation of formulae and the numerical analysis of system equations is much more effective. This has been demonstrated by Moore [1972] in developing an analysis technique for a cyclically non-stationary queueing system.

Simulation of queueing systems is common while dealing with complex systems. A discussion on simulation and its role in system solution can be found in the chapter on Simulation. Oftentimes, simulation results lead the way to theoretical results. Although it is true that simulation results are dependent on parameter values and a large number of results need to be analyzed to arrive at general conclusions, this may be the only way of deriving information because of system complexities. Thus, the role of simulation would be to supplement theoretical results wherever needed. In spite of its heavy use, reported investigations on queueing system simulation are few. Systems Analysis books such as McMillan and Gonzalez [1968] describe the method at an introductory level. Some of the specific problems that arise in queueing system simulation have been investigated by Mitchell [1973], Fishman [1974] and others. Also, recent investigations carried out by A. B. Pritsker and his group of researchers on Graphical Evaluation and Review Technique (GERT) and the GASP IV simulation language promise to have great potential in queueing simulations. For a description of their contributions, the readers are referred to Pritsker [1974] and Pritsker and Phillips [1972].

9. SIGNIFICANT TRENDS

Looking at the literature on queueing theory, the following trends may be observed:

(a) *Basic Processes:* The objective seems to be a better understanding of the properties of basic processes of queueing systems. Contributions in this area are essential for maintaining the methodological strength of queueing theory, though benefits to OR may be indirect. Investigations on the Wiener-Hopf representations in queues by Prabhu [1973], combinatorial properties by Takács [1973], the convexity and monotonicity of queueing distributions by Keilson [1973], the Markov renewal branching processes by Neuts [1973b] and the general theory of Markov renewal processes by Cinlar [1969] are examples of this trend.

(b) *Limit Properties:* Exploration of the asymptotic and limiting behavior of the underlying processes is the objective. Functional limit theorems derived by D. Iglehart, W. Whitt and others (cf. [Whitt, 1973]) have the potential for use in the solution of major operational problems as well.

(c) *Approximations:* In the process of simplifying queueing theory results, process approximation seems to be more fruitful than approximating the results. Gaver's [1968] diffusion approximation and Newell's [1971] fluid approximation results are evidence to this statement. From the point of view of the application of queueing theory, the potential of results is immense in this direction [Moore, 1972; Gaver and Shedler, 1973].

(d) *Queueing Networks:* With the emergence of computer and communications networks, congestion problems related to queueing networks have taken added significance. Major contributions in this area in the context of job shop scheduling has been reported in Conway, Maxwell and Miller [1967]. Recent papers of Disney [1973], Wallace [1973] and Evans [1973] are indicative of the efforts continuing in this area.

(e) *Applying Queueing Theory:* It is being increasingly realized that if queueing theory has to remain a part of OR–its system orientation and applicability qualifies it to be so–it should not lose its relevance to real problems.

Thus it is necessary that the problems solved are real and immediate, even though abstract techniques and concepts are used. The papers by D. P. Gaver [Gaver and Shedler 1973] in which approximations are used to derive meaningful results, and the computational methodology developed by Bhat [1973] in the solution of finite queues $M/G/1$ and $G/M/s$, are in this direction. Some of the investigations carried out by Harris [1973] are in the same spirit as well.

(f) *Decision Problems:* Because of simplicity and ease of application, simple cost models will always be popular. Theoretical developments in Markov decision processes should pave the way for the solution of some of the harder design problems as well as the establishment of general structural properties for the design and control of queueing systems.

Finally, it is encouraging to note that over the last few years the computer systems area has been added to the list of application areas of queueing theory. Besides, in the context of sophisticated communication systems, there is resurgent interest in queueing analysis as well.

10. CONCLUSION

In this chapter we have given an overview of queueing theory as it has developed over the last six and a half decades. With more than fifteen hundred articles available, it is not possible to give a review of all the major results in the area. The aim, therefore, has been to indicate, rather than to describe what has been done on specific topics; only major topics have been covered. Moreover an effort has been made to retain an historical perspective and be objective in presentation. Nevertheless, we are aware that the picture perceived may vary from one reader to another. It is our hope that what is perceived is not too distorted to be effective.

REFERENCES

1. Bagchi, T. J. and J. G. C. Templeton, *Numerical Methods in Markov Chains and Bulk Queues*, Springer-Verlag, Berlin (1972).
2. Bailey, N. T. J., "Study of Queues and Appointment Systems in Out-Patient Departments with Special Reference to Waiting times," *J. Roy. Stat. Soc.* **B14:** 185–199 (1952).
3. ——, "A Continuous Time Treatment of a Simple Queue Using Generating Functions," *J. Roy. Stat. Soc.* **B16:** 288–291 (1954).
4. ——, "A Note on Equalizing the Mean Waiting Time of Successive Customers in a Finite Queue," *J. Roy. Stat. Soc.* **B17:** 262–263 (1955).
5. Balachandran, K. R., "Parametric Priority Rules: An Approach to Optimization in Priority Queues," *Operations Res.* **18:** 526–540 (1970).
6. ——, "Purchasing Priorities in Queues," *Management Sci.* **18:** 319–326 (1972).
7. ——, "Control Policies for a Single Server System," *Management Sci.* **19:** 1013–1018 (1973).

8. Beneš, V. W., "A Sufficient Set of Statistics for a Simple Telephone Exchange Model," *Bell Syst. Tech. J.* **36:** 939-964 (1957).
9. ——, *General Stochastic Processes in the Theory of Queues*, Addison-Wesley, Reading, Massachusetts (1963).
10. ——, *Mathematical Theory of Connecting Networks and Telephone Traffic*, Academic Press, New York (1965).
11. Benson, F. and D. R. Cox, "The Productivity of Machines Requiring Attention at Random Intervals," *J. Roy. Stat. Soc.* **B13:** 65-82 (1951); **B14:** 200-219 (1952).
12. Bhat, U. N., "Some Simple Bulk Queueing Systems," Ph.D. Dissertation, Department of Math., University of Western Australia (1964a).
13. ——, "Imbedded Markov Chain Analysis of Single Server Bulk Queues," *J. Aust. Math. Soc.* **4(2):** 244-263 (1964b).
14. ——, "On a Stochastic Process Occurring in Queueing Systems," *J. Appl. Prob.* **2(2):** 467-469 (1965).
15. ——, "Some Explicit Results for the Queue GI/M/1 with Group Service," *Sankhya* **A29:** 199-206 (1967).
16. ——, "Transient Behavior of Multi-Server Queues with Recurrent Input and Exponential Service Times," *J. Appl. Prob.* **5(1):** 158-168 (1968a).
17. ——, *A Study of the Queueing Systems M/G/1 and GI/M/1*, Springer-Verlag, Berlin (1968b).
18. ——, "Sixty Years of Queueing Theory," *Management Sci.* **15(6):** **B**-280-**B**-294 (1969).
19. ——, *Elements of Applied Stochastic Processes*, John Wiley & Sons, New York (1972).
20. ——, "Some Problems in Finite Queues," *Proc. of Conf. on Math. Methods in Queueing Theory*, (ed. A. B. Clarke), Western Michigan University (1973).
21. —— and R. E. Nance, "Busy Period Analysis of a Time-Sharing System Modeled as a Semi-Markov Process," *J. ACM* **18:** 221-238 (1971).
22. —— and I. Sahin, "Transient Behavior of Queueing Systems M/D/1, $M/E_k/1$, D/M/1 and $E_k/M/1$," Tech Memo. #135, Department of Operations Research, Case Western Reserve University, Cleveland, Ohio (1969).
23. —— and S. Subba Rao, "A Statistical Technique for the Control of Traffic Intensity in the Queueing Systems M/G/1 and GI/M/1," *Operations Res.* **20:** 955-966 (1972).
24. Billingsley, P., *Statistical Inference for Markov Processes*, University of Chicago Press, Chicago (1961).
25. Birnbaum, A., "Statistical Methods for Poisson Processes and Exponential Populations," *J. Amer. Stat. Assn.* **49:** 254-266 (1954).
26. Blackburn, J. D., "Optimal Control of a Single Server Queue with Balking and Reneging," *Management Sci.* **19:** 297-313 (1972).
27. Brigham, G., "On a Congestion Problem in an Aircraft Factory," *J. Operations Res. Soc. Amer.* **3:** 412-428 (1955).
28. Brockmeyer, E., H. L. Halstrom, and A. Jensen, *The Life and Works of A. K. Erlang*, *Trans. of the Danish Acad. Sci.* **No. 2** (1948).
29. Brosh, I. and P. Naor, "On Optimal Disciplines in Priority Queueing," *Bull. Int. Stat. Inst.* **40(2):** 593-607 (1963).
30. Brumelle, S. L., "Some Inequalities for Parallel-Server Queues," *Operations Res.* **19:** 402-413 (1971).
31. Burke, P. J., "The Output of a Queueing System," *Operations Res.* **4:** 699-704 (1956).
32. Champernowne, D. G., "An Elementary Method of the Solution of the Queueing Problem with a Single Server and a Constant Parameter," *J. Roy. Stat. Soc.* **B18:** 125-128 (1956).

33. Cheong, C. K., J. H. A. deSmit, and J. L. Teugels, "Bibliography on Semi-Markov Processes," CORE Discussion Paper, #7310, Center for Operations Research and Econometrics, Universite Catholique de Louvain, Brussels, Belgium (1973).
34. Cinlar, E., "Markov Renewal Theory," *Adv. Appl. Prob.* **1**: 123–187 (1969).
35. Clarke, A. B., "A Waiting Time Process of Markov Type," *Ann. Math. Stat.* **27**: 452–459 (1956).
36. ——, "Maximum Likelihood Estimates in a Simple Queue," *Ann. Math. Stat.* **28**: 1036–1040 (1957).
37. Cohen, J., *The Single Server Queue*, American Elsevier, New York (1969).
38. Conolly, B. W., "A Difference Equation Technique Applied to the Simple Queue," *J. Roy. Stat. Soc.* **B20**: 165-167 (1958a).
39. ——, "A Difference Equation Technique Applied to the Simple Queue with Arbitrary Arrival Interval Distributions," *J. Roy. Stat. Soc.* **B20**: 167–175 (1958b).
40. ——, "The Busy Period in Relation to the Queueing Process GI/M/1," *Biometrika* **46**: 246–251 (1959).
41. Conway, R. W., W. L. Maxwell, and L. W. Miller, *Theory of Scheduling*, Addison-Wesley, Reading, Massachusetts (1967).
42. Cooper, R. B., *Introduction to Queueing Theory*, Macmillan, New York (1972).
43. Cox, D. R., "The Analysis of Non-Markovian Stochastic Processes by the Inclusion of Supplementary Variables," *Proc. Camb. Phil. Soc.* **51**: 433–441 (1955).
44. ——, "Some Problems of Statistical Analysis Connected with Congestion," *Proc. Symp. on Congestion Theory* (eds. W. L. Smith and W. E. Wilkinson) University of North Carolina, Chapel Hill, North Carolina (1965).
45. —— and P. A. W. Lewis, *The Statistical Analysis of Series of Events*, Metheun and Co., London (1966).
46. —— and W. L. Smith, *Queues*, Metheun and Co., London (1961).
47. Crabill, T. B., "Optimal Control of a Queue with Variable Service Rates," Ph.D. Dissertation, Department of Operations Research, Cornell University (1968).
48. ——, "Optimal Control of Service Facility with Variable Exponential Service Times and Constant Arrival Rate," *Management Sci.* **18**: 560–566 (1972).
49. ——, D. Gross, and M. Magazine, "A Survey of Research on Optimal Design and Control of Queues," *Operations Res.* **22** (to appear 1974).
50. Crommelin, C. D., "Delay Probability Formulae When Holding Times are Constant," *P.O. Elect. Eng. J.* **25**: 41–50 (1932).
51. Deb, R. K. and R. F. Serfozo, "Optimal Control of Batch Service Queues," *Adv. Appl. Prob.* **5(2)**: 340–361 (1973).
52. Derman, C., *Finite State Markovian Decision Processes*, Academic Press, New York (1970).
53. Disney, R. L. "Some Topics in Queueing Network Theory," *Proc. Conf. on Math. Methods in Queueing Theory* (ed. A. B. Clarke) Western Michigan University (1973).
54. Doig, A., "A Bibliography on the Theory of Queues," *Biometrika* **44**: 490–514 (1957).
55. Dubner, H. and J. Abate, "Numerical Inversion of Laplace Transforms by Relating Them to the Finite Fourier Cosine Transform," *J. ACM* **15**: 115–123 (1968).
56. Edie, L. C., "Traffic Delays at Toll Booths," *Operations Res.* **4**: 107–138 (1956).
57. Etschmaier, M., "Discretionary Priority Processes," Tech. Memo. #60, Operations Research Group, Case Institute of Technology (1966).
58. Evans, R. V., "Problems and Changes in the Stable Behavior of a Class of Markov Chains," *J. Appl. Prob.* **8**: 543–550 (1971).

59. ——, "Assembly Operations," Faculty Working Papers, College of Commerce and Bus. Adm., University of Illinois at Urbana-Champaign (April 4, 1973).
60. Feller, W., *An Introduction to Probability Theory and its Applications* (3rd ed.), John Wiley & Sons, New York (1968).
61. Fischer, M. J., "On Two Problems in Alternating Queues," Ph.D. Dissertation Southern Methodist University (1971).
62. ——, "The Waiting Time in the $E_k/M/1$ Queueing System," *Operations Res.* **22:** 898-902 (1974).
63. Fishman, G. S., "Estimation in Multiserver Queueing Simulations," *Operations Res.* **22** (1974).
64. Fry, T. C., *Probability and its Engineering Uses*, Van Nostrand Reinhold, New York (1928).
65. Gaver, D. P. Jr., "Imbedded Markov Chain Analysis of a Waiting Line Process in Continuous Time," *Ann. Math. Stat.* **30:** 698-720 (1959).
66. ——, "Observing Stochastic Processes and Approximate Transform Inversion," *Operations Res.* **14:** 444-459 (1966).
67. ——, "Diffusion Approximations and Models for Certain Congestion Problems," *J. Appl. Prob.* **5:** 607-623 (1968).
68. —— and G. S. Shedler, "Processor Utilization in Multi-programming Systems via Diffusion Approximations," *Operations Res.* **21:** 569-576 (1973).
69. Gross, D. and C. M. Harris, *Fundamentals of Queueing Theory*, John Wiley and Sons, New York (1974).
70. Haight, F. A., *Mathematical Theories of Traffic Flow*, Academic Press, New York (1963).
71. Harris, C. M., "Some New Results in the Statistical Analysis of Queues," *Proc. Conf. on Math. Methods in Queueing Theory* (ed. A. B. Clarke), Western Michigan University (1973).
72. Heyman, D. P., "Optimal Operating Policies for M/G/1 Queueing Systems," *Operations Res.* **16:** 362-382 (1968).
73. Hillier, F. S. and G. J. Lieberman, *Introduction to Operations Research*, Holden-Day, San Francisco (1967).
74. Iglehart, D. L., "Limiting Diffusion Approximations for the Many Server Queue and the Repairman Problem," *J. Appl. Prob.* **2:** 429-441 (1965).
75. —— and W. Whitt, "Multiple Channel Queues in Heavy Traffic II," *Adv. Appl. Prob.* **2(2):** 355-369 (1970).
76. Jaiswal, N. K., *Priority Queues*, Academic Press, New York (1968).
77. Jewell, W., "A Simple Proof of: $L = \lambda W$," *Operations Res.* **15:** 1109-1116 (1967).
78. Keilson, J., "The Ergodic Queue Length Distribution for Queueing Systems with Finite Capacity," *J. Roy. Stat. Soc.* **B28:** 190-201 (1966).
79. ——, "Convexity and Complete Monotonicity in Queueing Distribution, and Associated Limit Behavior," *Proc. Conf. on Math. Methods on Queueing Theory* (ed. A. B. Clarke), Western Michigan University (1973).
80. —— and A. Kooharian, "On Time Dependent Queueing Processes," *Ann. Math. Stat.* **31:** 104-112 (1960).
81. Kendall, D. G., "Some Problems in the Theory of Queues," *J. Roy. Stat. Soc.* **B13:** 151-185 (1951).
82. ——, "Stochastic Processes Occurring in the Theory of Queue and Their Analysis by the Method of Imbedded Markov Chains," *Ann. Math. Stat.* **24:** 338-354 (1953).
83. Kemeny, J. G. and J. L. Snell, *Finite Markov Chains*, Van Nostrand Reinhold, New York (1960).

84. Kemperman, J. H. B., *The Passage Problem for a Stationary Markov Chain*, University of Chicago Press, Chicago (1961).
85. Khintchine, A., "Mathematisches über die Erwartung von einen öffentlicher Schalter," *Sbornik* **40:** 2 (1935).
86. ——, *Mathematical Methods in the Theory of Queueing*, Charles Griffin, London (1960).
87. Kiefer, J. and J. Wolfowitz, "On the Theory of Queues with Many Servers," *Trans. Am. Math. Soc.* **78:** 1–18 (1955).
88. Kingman, J. F. C., "The Single Server Queue in Heavy Traffic," *Proc. Camb. Phil. Soc.* **57:** 902–904 (1961).
89. ——, "On Queues in which Customers are Served in Random Order," *Proc. Camb. Phil. Soc.* **58:** 79–91 (1962a).
90. ——, "The Use of Spitzer's Identity in the Investigation of the Busy Period and Other Quantities in the Queue GI/G/1," *J. Aust. Math. Soc.* **2:** 345–356 (1962b).
91. ——, "On Queues in Heavy Traffic," *J. Roy. Stat. Soc.* **B24:** 383–392 (1962c).
92. ——, "The Heavy Traffic Approximation in the Theory of Queues," *Proc. Symp. on Congestion Theory* (eds. W. L. Smith and W. E. Wilkinson), University of North Carolina Press, Chapel Hill (1965).
93. ——, "On the Algebra of Queues," *J. Appl. Prob.* **3:** 285–326 (1966).
94. Kleinrock, L., "Optimal Bribing for Queue Position," *Operations Res.* **15:** 304–318 (1967).
95. Klimko, E.M. and M.F. Neuts, "The Single Server Queue in Discrete Time–Numerical Analysis II and III," *Nav. Res. Log. Quart.* **20:** 297–304 (1973).
96. Ledermann, W. and G. E. Reuter, "Spectral Theory for the Differential Equations of Simple Birth and Death Processes," *Phil. Trans. Roy. Soc. Lond.* **A246:** 321–369 (1954).
97. Lee, A. M., *Applied Queueing Theory*, St. Martin's Press, New York (1966).
98. Lee, T. C., G. G. Judge, and A. Zellner, *Estimating the Parameters of the Markov Probability Model from Aggregate Time Series Data*, North Holland, Amsterdam (1970).
99. Leese, E. L. and D. W. Boyd, "Numerical Methods of Determining the Transient Behavior of Queues with Variable Arrival Rates," *J. Canadian Operations Res. Soc.* **4(1):** 1–13 (1966).
100. LeGall, P., *Les Systémes Avec au Sans Attente et Les Processus Stochastiques*, Tome 1, Dunod, Paris (1962).
101. Lilliefors, H. W., "Some Confidence Intervals for Queues," *Operations Res.* **14(4):** 723–727 (1966).
102. Lindley, D. V., "The Theory of Queues with a Single Server," *Proc. Camb. Phil. Soc.* **48:** 277–289 (1952).
103. Little, J. D. C., "A Proof of the Queueing Formula $L = \lambda W$," *Operations Res.* **9:** 383–387 (1961).
104. Luchak, G., "The Solution of the Single Channel Queueing Equation Characterized by a Time-Dependent Poisson Distributed Arrival Rate and a General Class of Holding Times," *Operations Res.* **4:** 711–732 (1956).
105. Mace, Arthur E., *Sample Size Determination*, Van Nostrand Reinhold, New York (1964).
106. Marshall, K. T., "Some Inequalities in Queueing," "Bounds for Some Generalizations of the GI/G/1 Queues," *Operations Res.* **16:** 651–665, 841–848 (1968).
107. McMillan, C. and R. F. Gonzales, *Systems Analysis: A Computer Approach to Decision Models*, Richard D. Irwin, Homewood, Illinois (1968).

108. Mitchell, W., "Variance Reduction by Antithetic Variates in GI/G/1 Queueing Simulations," *Operations Res.* **21** (1973).
109. Moder, J. J. and C. R. Phillips, Jr., "Queueing with Fixed and Variable Channels," *Operations Res.* **10:** 218-231 (1962).
110. Molina, E. C., "Application of the Theory of Probability to Telephone Trunking Problems," *Bell. Syst. Tech. J.* **6:** 461-494 (1926).
111. Moore, S. C., "Approximate Techniques for Non-Stationary Queues," Ph.D. Dissertation, Southern Methodist University, Dallas, Texas (1972).
112. Morse, P. M., "Stochastic Properties of Waiting Lines," *J. Operations Res. Soc. Amer.* **3:** 255-261 (1955).
113. ——, *Queues Inventories and Maintenance*, John Wiley & Sons, New York (1958).
114. ——, "The Application of Queueing Theory in Operations Research," *Queueing Theory: Recent Developments and Applications*, American Elsevier, New York (1967).
115. Neuts, M. F., "The Single Server Queue with Poisson Input and Semi-Markov Service Times," *J. Appl. Prob.* **3:** 202-230 (1966).
116. ——, "A Queue Subject to Extraneous Phase Changes," *Adv. Appl. Prob.* **3:** 78-119 (1971).
117. ——, "The Single Server Queue in Discrete Time–Numerical Analysis I," *Nav. Res. Log. Quart.* **20:** 305-319 (1973a).
118. ——, "Markov Renewal Branching Processes in Queueing Theory," *Proc. Conf. on Math. Methods in Queueing Theory* (ed. A. B. Clarke), Western Michigan University (1973b).
119. —— and D. Heimann, "The Single Server Que in Discrete Time–Numerical Analysis IV," *Nav. Res. Log. Quart.* **20:** 735-766 (1973).
120. Newell, G. F., *Applications of Queueing Theory*, Chapman and Hall, London (1971).
121. Oliver, R. M. and G. Pestalozzi, "On a Problem of Optimum Priority Classification," *J. Indust. Appl. Math.* **13(3):** 580-591 (1965).
122. Palm, C., "Intensitätsschwankungen im Fernsprechverkehr," *Ericsson Technics* **44:** 1-89 (1943).
123. ——, "The Distribution of Repairmen in Servicing Automatic Machines" (in Swedish), *Indust. Nord.* **75:** 75-90, 90-94, 119-123 (1947).
124. ——, "Waiting Times with Random Served Queue," *Tele* **1:** 1-107 (English ed.) (1957).
125. Peck, L. G. and R. N. Hazelwood, *Finite Queueing Tables*, John Wiley & Sons, New York (1958).
126. Phipps, T. E. Jr., "Machine Repair as a Priority Waiting Line Problem," *Operations Res.* **4:** 76-85 (1956).
127. Pollaczek, F., "Uber das Warteproblem," *Math. Z.* **38:** 492-537 (1934).
128. ——, "Sur une Généralisation de la Théorie des Attentes," *C. R. Acad. Sci. Paris* **236:** 578-580 (1953).
129. ——, *Problèms Stochastiques Posés par le Phénomene de Formation d'une Queue d'Attente à un Guichet et par des Phénoménes Apparentés*, Gauthiers Villars, Paris (1957) (see reference for 1930).
130. ——, "Concerning an Analytic Method for the Treatment of Queueing Problems," *Proc. Symp. on Congestion Theory*, (eds. W. L. Smith and W. E. Wilkinson) University of North Carolina Press, Chapel Hill (1965).
131. Prabhu, N. U., "Some Results for the Queue with Poisson Arrivals," *J. Roy. Stat. Soc.* **22:** 104-107 (1960).
132. ——, "Elementary Methods for Some Waiting Time Problems," *Operations Res.* **10:** 559-566 (1962).

133. ——, *Queues and Inventories*, John Wiley & Sons, New York (1965).
134. ——, "The Simple Queue in Non-Equilibrium," *Opsearch* **6(2):** 118–128 (1969).
135. ——, "Wiener-Hopf Techniques in Queueing Theory," *Proc. Conf. on Math. Methods in Queueing Theory* (ed. A. B. Clarke), Western Michigan University (1973).
136. —— and U. N. Bhat, "Further Results for the Queue with Poisson Arrivals," *Operations Res.* **11:** 380–386 (1963a).
137. —— and U. N. Bhat, "Some First Passage Problems and Their Applications to Queues," *Sankhya* **A25:** 281–292 (1963b).
138. —— and S. Stidham, Jr., "Optimal Control of Queueing Systems," *Proc. Conf. on Math. Methods in Queueing Theory* (ed. A. B. Clarke), Western Michigan University (1973).
139. Pritsker, A. A. B., *The Gasp IV Simulation Language*, John Wiley and Sons, New York (1974).
140. —— and D. T. Phillips, "GERT Network Analysis of Complex Queueing Systems," Research Memo. #72-1, School of Industrial Engineering, Purdue University, Lafayette, Indiana (1972).
141. Purvis, R. E., R. L. McLaughlin, and W. K. Mallory, *Queueing Tables for Determining System Manning and Related Support Requirements*, Behavioral Sciences Lab. Air Force Systems Comm., Wright Patterson Air Force Base, Ohio (1964).
142. Putter, J., "The Treatment of Ties in Some Nonparametric Tests," *Ann. Math. Stat.* **26:** 268–386 (1955).
143. Pyke, R. A., "Markov Renewal Processes: Definitions and Preliminary Properties," "Markov Renewal Processes with Finitely Many States," *Ann. Math. Stat.* **32:** 1231–1242, 1243–1259 (1961).
144. Reich, E., "Waiting Times When Queues are in Tandem," *Ann. Math. Stat.* **28:** 768–773 (1957).
145. ——, "Departure Processes," *Proc. Symp. on Congestion Theory* (eds. W. L. Smith and W. E. Wilkinson) University of North Carolina Press, Chapel Hill (1965).
146. Rice, S. O., "Single Server Systems–II, Busy Periods," *Bell Syst. Tech. J.* **41:** 279–310 (1962).
147. Riordan, J., *Stochastic Service Systems*, John Wiley & Sons, New York (1962).
148. Ross, S. M., *Applied Probability Models with Optimization Applications*, Holden-Day, San Francisco (1970).
149. Saaty, T. L., "Time Dependent Solution of Many Server Poisson Queue," *Operations Res.* **8:** 755–772 (1960).
150. ——, *Elements of Queueing Theory*, McGraw-Hill, New York (1961).
151. ——, "Seven More Years of Queueing Theory: A Lament and a Bibliography," *Nav. Res. Log. Quart.* **13:** 447–476 (1966).
152. Schrage, L., "A Proof of the Optimality of the Shortest Remaining Processing Time Discipline," *Operations Res.* **16:** 687–690 (1968).
153. —— and L. W. Miller, "The Queue M/G/1 with Shortest Remaining Processing Time Discipline," *Operations Res.* **14:** 670–684 (1966).
154. Smith, W. L., "On the Distribution of Queueing Times," *Proc. Camb. Phil. Soc.* **49:** 449–461 (1953).
155. Sobel, M. J., "Optimal Average-Cost Policy for a Queue with Start-up and Shut-down Costs," *Operations Res.* **17:** 145–162 (1969).
156. ——, "Optimal Operation in Queues," *Proc. Conf. on Math Methods in Queueing Theory* (ed. A. B. Clarke), Western Michigan University (1973).
157. Spitzer, F., "A Combinatorial Lemma and its Applications to Probability Theory," *Trans. Am. Math. Soc.* **82:** 323–339 (1956).

158. Stehfest, H., "Algorithm 368: Numerical Inversion of Laplace Transforms," *Communications ACM* **13:** 47-49 (1970).
159. Stidham, S., Jr., "On the Optimality of Single Server Queueing Systems," *Operations Res.* **18:** 708-732 (1970).
160. ——, "L = λW: A Discounted Analogue and a New Proof," *Operations Res.* **20:** 1115-1126 (1972).
161. Syski, R., *Introduction to Congestion Theory in Telephone Systems*, Oliver and Boyd, London (1960).
162. Takács, L., "Investigation of Waiting Time Problems by Reduction to Markov Processes," *Acta Math. Acad. Sci. Hungar.* **6:** 101-129 (1955).
163. ——, "Transient Behavior of a Single Server Queueing Process with Recurrent Input and Exponentially Distributed Service Times," *Operations Res.* **8:** 231-245 (1960).
164. ——, "The Transient Behavior of a Single Server Queueing Process with Poisson input," *Proc. Fourth Berkeley Symp. on Math. Stat. and Prob.*, 535-567, University of California Press, Berkeley, California (1961).
165. ——, *Introduction to the Theory of Queues*, Oxford University Press, New York (1962).
166. ——, "The Limiting Distribution of the Virtual Waiting Time and the Queue Size for a Single Server Queue with Recurrent Input and General Service Times," *Sankhya* **A25:** 91-100 (1963).
167. ——, *Combinatorial Methods in the Theory of Stochastic Processes*, John Wiley & Sons, New York (1967).
168. ——, "On Erlang's Formula," *Ann. Math. Stat.* **40:** 71-78 (1969).
169. ——, "Occupation Time Problems in the Theory of Queues," *Proc. Conf. on Math. Methods in Queueing Theory* (ed. A. B. Clarke), Western Michigan University (1973).
170. Wagner, H. M., *Principles of Operations Research*, Prentice Hall, Englewood Cliffs, New Jersey (1969).
171. Wallace, V. L., "Algebraic Techniques for Numerical Solution of Queueing Networks," *Proc. Conf. on Math. Methods in Queueing Theory* (ed. A. B. Clarke), Western Michigan University (1973).
172. Whitt, W., "Recent Research on Queues in Heavy Traffic," *Proc. Conf. on Math. Methods in Queueing Theory* (ed. A. B. Clarke), Western Michigan University (1973).
173. Wolff, R. W., "Problems of Statistical Inference for Birth and Death Queueing Models," *Operations Res.* **13:** 343-357 (1965).
174. Yadin, M. and P. Naor, "On Queueing Systems with a Removable Server," *Operations Res.* **14:** 393-405 (1963).
175. —— and ——, "On Queueing Systems with Variable Service Capacities," *Nav. Res. Log. Quart.* **14:** 43-54 (1967).

III-3

VALUE THEORY

Peter C. Fishburn
The Pennsylvania State University

1. INTRODUCTION

Research on the design, operation and management of purposive systems almost inevitably involves the needs, goals and desires of those who manage or are affected by such systems. Hence, consideration of human values is basic to the theory and practice of OR.

The purpose of this chapter is to set forth some theories of coherent value structures that seem most relevant to modern decision theory and the practice of OR. In consideration of decision makers and those engaged in helping them in their decision-making activities, we are motivated by the desire to provide theoretical foundations for procedures that can be used to clarify and measure preferences and which enable such preferences to be represented quantitatively in ways that will be useful for decision analysis.

In view of this it may be noted that "value" is being used in two senses. The first, and more fundamental, is the qualitative or comparative sense, characterized by statements such as "I value this more than that" or "I prefer x to y." The second sense is a quantitative or numerical sense which is designed to reflect the comparative mode. Generally speaking, a numerical representation of values is a convenient quantitative expression of the basic qualitative preference relation. To keep these two senses in perspective, we shall use "preference" for the qualitative or comparative mode and "utility" for quantitative or numerical representations of preferences. Thus, as discussed in this chapter, *value theory is the theory of preferences and utilities.*

1.1 Brief Historical Sketch

The advent of modern preference and utility theory began in the early eighteenth century when several mathematicians, interested in the emerging probability calculus and its application to games of chance and insurance, challenged the maxim that prudent individuals faced with risky decisions affecting their wealth ought to take the decision which maximizes their expected wealth or monetary return. For example, it was argued that a person of very modest means may sensibly prefer an outright gift of nine thousand ducats to an even-chance gamble (depending on the outcome of a coin toss) which pays either nothing or twenty thousand ducats. As an alternative to maximizing expected monetary return, Gabriel Cramer and then Daniel Bernoulli [1738] proposed maximization of the expected value of the utility of money. It was further suggested that, for use in computing expectations, the utility of wealth would (for many people) increase as wealth increases with the rate of increase decreasing with increasing wealth. Figure 1 pictures this so-called law of diminishing marginal utility: as wealth increases, the addition of one more unit of wealth produces a smaller increase in utility.

Although the basic expected utility idea of Cramer and Bernoulli was not totally ignored, the use of utility in risky or uncertain decision situations under-

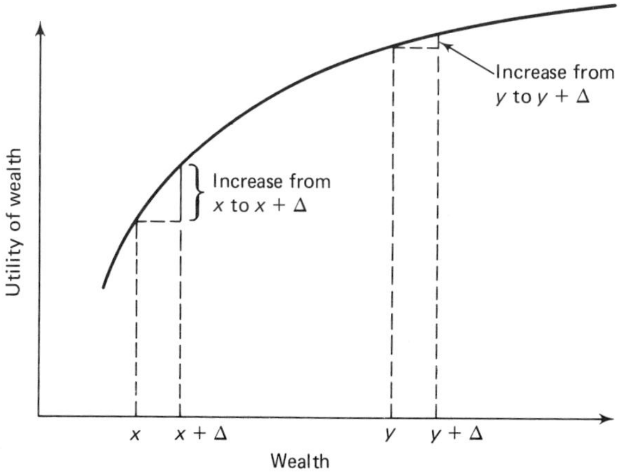

Fig. 1. Diminishing marginal utility.

went no noteworthy advance until the young philosopher and mathematician, Frank P. Ramsey [1931], outlined an axiom system for subjective expected utility, nearly two centuries after Cramer and Bernoulli presented their ideas. We shall return to this momentarily.

Meanwhile, economists, working with nonrisky consumption possibilities in the theory of consumer demand, developed their own utility theory with a diminishing marginal utility aspect. To illustrate this, let $(x_1, x_2, \ldots, x_n)$ denote a commodity bundle which provides amount x_1 of the first commodity (or good or service), amount x_2 of the second commodity, and so forth. During the 1870's, Jevons, Menger, and Walras computed an individual's total satisfaction derived from $(x_1, x_2, \ldots, x_n)$ by the additive utility form $u_1(x_1) + \cdots + u_n(x_n)$ wherein the utility u_i of the ith commodity depends only on the quantity x_i of that commodity. Moreover, they assumed that each u_i increased at a decreasing rate as x_i increased, thus applying the diminishing marginal utility notion to each commodity separately. Later in the nineteenth century and early in the twentieth century, several other prominent economists, including Edgeworth, Fisher, Pareto, and Slutsky, argued for the replacement of the additive form by the more general utility function $u(x_1, x_2, \ldots, x_n)$ on the grounds that the latter allows interdependencies (including complementarities and substitutabilities) among commodities and, under suitable restrictions, enables derivations of the important aspects of the static theory of consumer demand which had previously been obtained under the additive form.

Soon thereafter, Ragnar Frisch [1926] made an important advance by presenting axioms for preferences and comparisons of preference differences which were intended to provide a basis for deriving a quantitative measure of preference in the economic sense. The idea of basing utility on axioms for preferences was further solidified by the works of Herman Wold [1943-44] and Gerard Debreu [1959]. Interestingly, a viable axiomatization for the additive utility form used by Jevons and others did not appear until quite recently [Debreu, 1960].

During this period, economic theory was enlivened by the axiomatization of utility for risky decisions developed by John von Neumann and Oskar Morgenstern [1944]. Their axioms for preference between risky alternatives, which take outcome probabilities (however interpreted) as given, placed the Cramer-Bernoulli notion of expected utility on a rigorous foundation. Although von Neumann and Morgenstern were anticipated to some extent by Ramsey [1931], who sought to enable derivation of both utility and probability from preference axioms, Ramsey went largely unnoticed until his outline was cited by Leonard J. Savage [1954], who achieved the first rigorous axiomatization of subjective expected utility (wherein both utility and probability measures are derived from the preference axioms).

1.2 Preview

Although the situations discussed above exhibit certain structural features, preference theory in its barest form presumes only two primitives. The first is a non-empty set, which is usually interpreted as a set of decision alternatives, strategies, or courses of action. In many cases this set contains alternatives that may be infeasible, either because of the difficulty of identifying all feasible alternatives in a simple way or because certain infeasible alternatives may help in measuring or scaling utilities.

The second primitive is a binary preference or preference-or-indifference relation on the alternative set. After discussing basic aspects of binary relations, the next section shows that under rather mild restrictions it is purely a matter of personal taste whether one adopts "preference" or "preference-or-indifference" as the primitive relation. In this chapter "preference" will be used as the primitive, with "indifference" and "preference-or-indifference" defined therefrom. The section then discusses aspects of ordering relations, including transitivity, and goes on to present basic ideas in utility theory which depend only on our two primitive notions and on axioms or assumptions which might apply to the structure of preferences.

Later sections consider specific structures for the alternatives. The third section views this set as a set of probability distributions defined on a set of consequences or on a set of pure strategies. Two axiomatizations for linear utility (i.e., expected utility) are reviewed in this context. One of these is similar to the von Neumann and Morgenstern axiomatization [1944] of the Cramer-Bernoulli expected utility notion. The other is a weaker (more general) system of axioms designed to accommodate certain aspects of psychological reality, including nontransitive indifference. The section concludes with a brief review of key notions in the theory of the utility of wealth, including certainty equivalence and risk aversion.

The fourth section focuses on alternatives or consequences which are characterized by a number of specific criteria, factors, commodities, or attributes. We shall examine notions of preference independence among factors or attributes which lead to special forms for utility, such as the lexicographic or hierarchical model and the additive model $u(x_1, x_2, \ldots, x_n) = u_1(x_1) + u_2(x_2) + \cdots + u_n(x_n)$. Additive and related forms for utilities of multiple-attribute consequences in the risky decision setting are also mentioned.

The chapter concludes with remarks on subjective expected utility theory, where axioms for preferences on uncertain decision alternatives lead to utilities for consequences and probabilities for uncertain events. Without going into axiomatic details, we review the approaches of Ramsey [1931] and Savage [1954] to see how they differ and what they require in addition to the expected utility theory of von Neumann and Morgenstern.

2. PREFERENCES AND UTILITIES

Since binary relations are fundamental in the study of preference theory, we begin with a few facts about binary relations.

A binary relation R on a non-empty set X is a subset of the product set $X \times X = \{(x,y)\colon x \text{ and } y \text{ in } X\}$ of all ordered pairs of elements in X. We write xRy (x stands in the relation R to y) to mean that (x,y) is in R; similarly *not* (xRy) will mean that (x,y) is not in R, or that x does not stand in the relation R to y.

Eight potential properties of binary relations are listed in four two-element groups as follows. The defining expressions are meant to apply to all x, y and z in X.

reflexivity: xRx
irreflexivity: *not* (xRx)

symmetry: if xRy then yRx
asymmetry: if xRy then *not* (yRx)

transitivity: if xRy and yRz then xRz
negative transitivity: if *not* (xRy) and *not* (yRz) then *not* (xRz)

connectedness: xRy or yRx
weak connectedness: if $x \neq y$ then xRy or yRx.

These terms are standard except for the last two. Connectedness is often referred to as strong connectedness or completeness; weak connectedness is also referred to as completeness, connectedness or connectivity. The terminology specified above will be used here.

The two properties in the first group are contraries (both cannot hold simultaneously), but this is not true of the latter three groups. For example, asymmetry and negative transitivity imply transitivity, connectedness implies weak connectedness, and both symmetry and asymmetry hold if R is empty. If R is not empty, then symmetry and asymmetry are contraries.

When X is the set of all living people: "is taller than" is irreflexive, asymmetric, transitive, and negatively transitive; "is as old as" is reflexive, transitive, negatively transitive, and connected; "is the sister of (with at least one parent in common)" is symmetric (why not transitive?); and "knows the name of," accounting for amnesia, satisfies none of the eight properties.

Transitive binary relations are called orders or ordering relations. Unfortunately, the terminology of ordering relations is not uniform. For example, a relation which is asymmetric, transitive and weakly connected (as in "greater than" on the set of real numbers) is variously referred to as a linear order, strict order, strong order, simple order, total order, complete order, connected order, and chain. Some of these terms are also used for orders with other defining properties. Hence, when speaking of a certain type of order, it is essential to note its defining properties.

2.1 Preference and Indifference

The primitive binary relation on X that is used in preference theory is either taken to be a preference-or-indifference relation $\succsim$ (read $x \succsim y$ as "x is preferred or indifferent to y" or "y is not preferred to x") or a preference relation $\succ$ (read $x \succ y$ as "x is preferred to y"). The former has predominated in the literature, but recently several authors have adopted the latter approach.

When $\succsim$ is taken as primitive, relations of preference ($\succ$) and indifference ($\sim$) are defined from it as follows:

$$x \succ y \quad \text{if and only if} \quad x \succsim y \quad \text{and } not \quad (y \succsim x) \tag{1}$$

$$x \sim y \quad \text{if and only if} \quad x \succsim y \quad \text{and} \quad y \succsim x.$$

When $\succ$ is taken as primitive, relations of indifference and preference-or-indifference are defined from *it* as follows:

$$x \sim y \quad \text{iff} \quad not \quad (x \succ y) \quad \text{and } not \quad (y \succ x)$$

$$x \succsim y \quad \text{iff} \quad x \succ y \quad \text{or} \quad (not\,(x \succ y) \quad \text{and } not \quad (y \succ x)). \tag{2}$$

Connections between these two approaches are explored in Chapter 3 in Fishburn [1972b], and in certain cases they are equivalent. In particular, if $\succ$ is defined from $\succsim$ by (1), and if this definition of $\succ$ is inserted in the right side of (2), and $\succsim'$ is defined by the right side of (2), then $\succsim' = \succsim$ iff $\succsim$ is connected. Going the other way, if $\succsim$ is defined from $\succ$ by (2), and if this definition of $\succsim$ is inserted in the right side of (1), and $\succ$ is defined by the right side of (1), then $\succ' = \succ$ iff $\succ$ is asymmetric.

In point of fact, when $\succ$ is taken as primitive, it seems eminently reasonable to presume that it is asymmetric, for otherwise we allow the possibility that, simultaneously, x is preferred to y *and* y is preferred to x. Likewise, when $\succsim$ is taken as primitive, it seems reasonable to presume that it is connected, for otherwise we allow the possibility that, simultaneously, x is not considered as desirable as y *and* y is not considered as desirable as x.

Henceforth we assume that, regardless of whether $\succsim$ or $\succ$ is taken as primitive, $\succsim$ is connected and $\succ$ is asymmetric. As we have seen above, it is then only a matter of taste whether one adopts $\succsim$ or $\succ$ as the primitive relation. Since my preference is to work with $\succ$ as primitive, I shall use the latter approach, defining indifference as the absence of a definite preference, as in the line preceding (2), with $\succsim$ defined as in (2): $x \succsim y$ iff $x \succ y$ or $x \sim y$. With $\succ$ asymmetric (and hence irreflexive), it follows that indifference is reflexive ($x \sim x$); $\sim$ is symmetric by definition.

2.2 Transitivity

The preference relation $\succ$ on X is transitive if, whenever x is preferred to y and y is preferred to z, it is true also that x is preferred to z. On the surface, this seems like a reasonable property and we shall presume that it holds in much of what follows. Transitivity fails if $(x \succ y, y \succ z, x \sim z)$ or $(x \succ y, y \succ z, z \succ x)$ for some x, y and z in X.

Despite the apparent reasonableness of transitive preferences, enough examples and evidence have been given (e.g., Davidson, et al. [1955], Weinstein [1968], Tversky [1969]) to suggest that reasonable people may have intransitive preferences in some situations. The alternatives used to illustrate this generally involve several criteria or attributes, as in the following case of three academic job offers:

(a) x: an assistant professorship at Big Name University at $15,000 salary
(b) y: an associate professorship at State University at $18,000 salary
(c) z: a full professorship at Little-Known College at $21,000 salary.

Reasoning that the difference in prestige of Big Name University over State University outweighs the one-rank advantage and the $3,000 salary difference, the candidate prefers x to y; for a similar reason he prefers y to z; however, in comparing x and z he feels that the rank and salary differences are now enough to outweigh the name prestige consideration and hence he prefers z to x. In this case his preferences are cyclic since $x \succ y, y \succ z$ and $z \succ x$.

The problem for a theory of choice that is posed by this example is that the binary preferences provide no clue as to what might be chosen from $\{x, y, z\}$ since each alternative is less preferred than some other alternative. That is, there is no maximal-preference alternative. Hence theories of choice that can account for cyclic preferences (Tversky [1972], Schwartz [1972]) must be "richer" than the theories discussed in this chapter.

The indifference relation $\sim$ on X is transitive if, whenever x is indifferent to y and y is indifferent to z, it is true also that x is indifferent to z. It is not transitive, or intransitive, if there are x, y and z in X for which $x \sim y, y \sim z$ and $x \succ z$. Although many examples of intransitive indifference use several criteria or attributes, unidimensional examples also demonstrate the phenomenon. This can be seen by employing the discriminatory threshold with insignificant or non-noticeable differences, as in Luce's [1956] coffee example where grains of sugar are added one by one to an individual's cup of coffee. We would expect indifference between x and $x + 1$ grains for x from say 0 to 5000, but would not expect indifference between $x = 0$ and $x = 5000$.

When preferences are not cyclic and indifference is not presumed to be transitive, every non-empty finite subset of X has a maximal-preference alternative, one that is not less preferred than some other alternative in the subset. Hence numerical representations of preferences, which have $u(x)$ [utility of x] greater than $u(y)$ when $x \succ y$, can identify maximal-preference alternatives in such cases. Surveys of preference theory with intransitive indifference are presented by Roberts [1970] and Fishburn [1970a].

As done elsewhere (Fishburn [1970a, 1970b, 1972b]) I shall refer to $\prec$ as a *weak order* when both $\succ$ and $\sim$ are transitive. Equivalently, $\succ$ is a weak order when it is negatively transitive (and asymmetric, as assumed earlier). Since negative transitivity says that either $x \succ z$ or $z \succ y$ when $x \succ y$, it says that there will be a "noticeable" preference between x and z or between y and z when x is not indifferent to y, and it is this aspect which leads to the transitivity of indifference. When $\succ$ is a weak order, $\succsim$ as defined by (2) is transitive and connected. Traditionally, a transitive and connected relation $\succsim$ has been called a weak order or complete preorder. Thus my use of weak order for $\succ$ is tantamount to its traditional usage for $\succsim$.

We assume in this paragraph that $\succ$ is a weak order. Then, since $\sim$ is transitive, it is an equivalence (transitive, symmetric, reflexive) and hence can be used to partition or divide X into equivalence classes or indifference classes. These classes are non-empty subsets of X: if A and B are two such classes and x is in A and y is in B then $x \sim y$ if and only if $A = B$, and if $x \succ y$ then $x' \succ y'$ for every x' in A and every y' in B. An illustration of indifference classes in a two-commodity or two-attribute context is shown in Fig. 2. The indifference classes are connected curves, with indifference between any two points on the same curve and with preference increasing as one moves away from the origin.

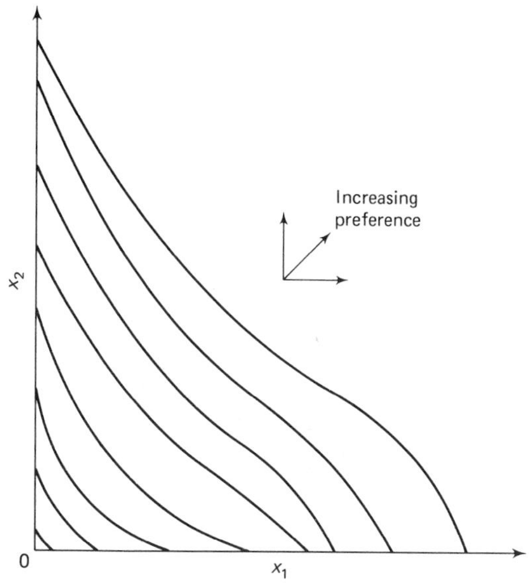

Fig. 2. An indifferent map.

Because these curves have negative slopes, a decrease in x_1 requires an increase in x_2 to maintain indifference. Such curves are also referred to as trade-off curves and indifference loci. In higher dimensions we would speak of indifference surfaces or trade-off surfaces. Economists refer to the system of all such indifference loci as an indifference map, and frequently assume that these loci are convex to the origin as is true of the curves closest to the origin in Fig. 2.

2.3 Utilities

Let u be a function from X into the real numbers. We shall say that u is a *utility function* for a preference relation $\succ$ on X if $u(x) > u(y)$ whenever $x \succ y$, and that u is a *complete utility function* for $\succ$ on X if, for all x and y in $X, u(x) > u(y)$ iff $x \succ y$. When a complete utility function u exists for $\succ$ on X, which can happen only if $\succ$ is a weak order, we have $x \sim y$ if and only if $u(x) = u(y)$ so that the indifference classes in X are identified by the subsets of alternatives with equal utilities. Hence, in this case the indifference classes are also referred to as isoutility contours. Proofs of assertions about utility functions in this section are available in Fishburn [1970b].

The set X is countable if it is finite or if its elements can be placed in one-to-one correspondence with the positive integers. Suppose X is countable. Then there exists a utility function for $\succ$ on X iff $\succ$ is acyclic ($x_1 \succ x_2, x_2 \succ x_3, \ldots, x_{m-1} \succ x_m, x_m \succ x_1$ for no $x_1, x_2, \ldots, x_m$ in X); and there exists a complete utility function for $\succ$ on X iff $\succ$ is a weak order. When $\succ$ is a weak order then, regardless of the cardinality or "size" of X (countable or uncountable), a utility function exists for $\succ$ on X if and only if a complete utility function exists for $\succ$ on X.

The set X is uncountable if it is infinite and not countable. I am not presently aware of a set of conditions for $\succ$ on uncountable X that are necessary and sufficient for the existence of a utility function for $\succ$ on X. On the other hand, a *complete* utility function exists for $\succ$ on X iff $\succ$ on X is a weak order *and* there is a *countable* subset of X which is $\succ$ order-dense in X. This order-denseness condition, which dates from Cantor [1895], says there is a *countable* subset Y of X such that for every x and z in X for which $x \succ z$ there is a y in Y that is either indifferent to one of x and z or else satisfies $x \succ y \succ z$. When this holds and $\succ$ is a weak order, u is first defined on an appropriate countable subset of X and then extended to all of X with limit theorems.

When $\succ$ on X is a weak order, and the foregoing countable order-denseness condition fails, then the set of real numbers is not rich enough to provide a complete utility function for $\succ$ on X. In a manner of speaking, there are not enough real numbers to go around. A prime example of this is the natural lexicographic order on the set E^2 of all ordered pairs of real numbers (two-dimensional Euclidean space), defined by $(x_1, x_2) \succ (y_1, y_2)$ iff $x_1 > y_1$ or ($x_1 = y_1$ and

$x_2 > y_2$). In this example $\succ$ is a linear order with no indifference between distinct elements and each indifference class consisting of a single point. The countable order-denseness condition fails since no countable subset of E^2 is $\succ$ order-dense in E^2. This does not however rule out some form of numerical representation for $\succ$ on E^2. For example with u_1 and u_2 defined on E^2 by $u_1(x) = x_1$ and $u_2(x) = x_2$ when $x = (x_1, x_2)$, it is trivially true that $x \succ y$ iff $u_1(x) > u_1(y)$ or $[u_1(x) = u_1(y)$ and $u_2(x) > u_2(y)]$. This is a simple case of a two-dimensional lexicographic utility representation, or a representation with two-dimensional utility vectors $(u_1(x), u_2(x))$. Lexicographic utilities are discussed in some detail by Chipman [1960] and Fishburn [1974a].

Given that u is a complete utility function for $\succ$ on X, v also is a complete utility function for $\succ$ on X iff for all x and y in X, $v(x) > v(y)$ if and only if $u(x) > u(y)$. If $X = \{x, y, z\}$, $x \succ y \succ z$, $\{u(x) = 100, u(y) = 99, u(z) = 0\}$ and $\{v(x) = 100, v(y) = 1, v(z) = 0\}$, then both u and v are utility functions for $\succ$ on X. The fact that y has a utility of 99 in one case and a utility of 1 in the other case has no particular significance.

When indifference is not transitive, u and v need not be monotonically related as in the preceding paragraph for both to be utility functions. An example is $X = \{x, y, z\}$, $x \sim y$, $y \sim z$, $x \succ z$, $\{u(x) = 1, u(y) = 2, u(z) = 0\}$ and $\{v(x) = 1, v(y) = -1, v(z) = 0\}$.

In concluding this section, we note that for specific applications, especially those which entail a utility-maximization operation, a certain amount of analytical convenience can result when the utility function satisfies special conditions. An example is the continuity or upper semi-continuity of u [Debreu, 1964; Fishburn, 1970b, 1972b]. Other conditions which are tailored to specific structural characteristics of the alternatives are pursued in the remainder of this chapter.

3. EXPECTED UTILITY THEORY

Throughout this section, $\succ$ is a binary relation of preference on the set P of all simple probability distributions $p, q, \ldots$ on a non-empty set X. The elements in X may be pure strategies or alternatives or they may be outcomes or consequences of risky decision alternatives whose probabilities for the consequences are described by certain of the distributions in P.

A *simple* probability distribution p is one which has $p(x) > 0$ for at most a finite number of x in X, with the sum of the $p(x)$ values equal to 1. Nonsimple distributions [Fishburn, 1970b] will not be considered here. Depending in part on context, the distributions in P are often referred to as wagers, gambles, lotteries, risky alternatives, mixed strategies, and randomized strategies. For any two distributions p and q in P and any real number α between 0 and 1, $\alpha p + (1 - \alpha)q$ is the direct linear combination of p and q. Thus if $r = \alpha p + (1 - \alpha)q$

then $r(x) = \alpha p(x) + (1 - \alpha)\, q(x)$ for each x in X. If p and q are in P and $0 \leqslant \alpha \leqslant 1$ then $\alpha p + (1 - \alpha)\, q$ is in P also.

Thus, suppose that elements in X are monetary amounts, that $p(\$0) = .3$, $p(\$10) = .2$, and $p(\$20) = .5$; $q(\$7) = .7$ and $q(\$10) = .3$; and $\alpha = \frac{1}{2}$. Then, with $r = \alpha p + (1 - \alpha) q = (\frac{1}{2})p + (\frac{1}{2})q$, $r(\$0) = .15$, $r(\$7) = .35$, $r(\$10) = .25$ and $r(\$20) = .25$.

3.1 Linear Utility Functions

According to prior definitions, a real-valued function u on P is a utility function for $\succ$ on P if $u(p) > u(q)$ whenever $p \succ q$, and a complete utility function for $\succ$ on P if, for all p and q in P, $u(p) > u(q)$ iff $p \succ q$. Since P is uncountable when X has more than one element, the remarks of section 2.3 for uncountable sets apply to u on P.

In the present context the structure of P gives rise to a special property for u which is known as linearity. The *linearity property* is defined by

$$u(\alpha p + (1 - \alpha)\, q) = \alpha u(p) + (1 - \alpha)\, u(q), \tag{3}$$

for all α between 0 and 1 and for all p and q in P. When this holds for a utility function u for $\succ$ on P, we shall call u a *linear utility function.* Similarly, if u is a complete utility function which satisfies (3) then u is a *complete linear utility function.*

The importance of linearity can be seen by defining the *auxiliary function* v on X from u on P by

$$v(x) = u(p) \quad \text{when} \quad p(x) = 1. \tag{4}$$

If we take $x \succ' y$ iff $p \succ q$ when $p(x) = q(y) = 1$, then v is a utility function for $\succ'$ on X when u is a utility function for $\succ$ on P. With $x_1, x_2, \ldots, x_n$ distinct elements in X and $p(x_1) + p(x_2) + \cdots + p(x_n) = 1$, repeated use of (3) under definition (4) gives

$$u(p) = p(x_1)\, v(x_1) + p(x_2)\, v(x_2) + \cdots + p(x_n)\, v(x_n). \tag{5}$$

This says that the utility of p, given (3), equals the expected value of the auxiliary function v on X with respect to the p.d. p on X. Referring to $v(x)$ as the utility of "outcome" x, (5) says the utility of a risky alternative equals the expected utility for the outcomes which might arise under that alternative. Hence the phrase "expected utility."

The importance of (5) stems from its convenience in scaling and computing utilities. If v on X is scaled or estimated in a manner that is consistent with linearity and (4) then $u(p)$ can be computed as in (5) for any p in P. If $\succ$ on P is a weak order and $x \succ y \succ z$ and u is a complete linear utility function, then any one of $v(x)$, $v(y)$ and $v(z)$ can be uniquely determined relative to the other two by identifying the value of α at which y is indifferent to a gamble giving x

with probability α and z with probability $1 - \alpha$. If α^* is this value of α, then $v(y) = \alpha^* v(x) + (1 - \alpha^*) v(z)$.

For example, if $x \succ y \succ z$ and we set $v(x) = 1$ and $v(z) = 0$ then $v(y) = \alpha^*$ when y is indifferent to the α^* gamble. This is illustrated in Fig. 3. The point α^* can be "determined" by interrogation about preference between y and gambles between x and z as represented in the figure. Needless to say, psychological realities may make it rather difficult to locate a precise α^* at which indifference holds with y either preferred to the α gamble or conversely for every $\alpha \neq \alpha^*$.

In the following several pages we shall use u to denote a utility function (linear or otherwise) on P, and let v denote an auxiliary utility function on X which is defined in the manner of (4). The relation $\succ'$ on X is defined after (4).

Before going into axioms for linear or expected utility we shall note a few facts about linear and nonlinear utility functions. Suppose first that u is a complete linear utility function for $\succ$ on P. Then u^* also is a complete linear utility function for $\succ$ on P iff there are real numbers b and c with $b > 0$ such that $u^*(p) = bu(p) + c$ for all p in P. In this event u^* and u are said to be related by an affine transformation or by a positive (or increasing) linear transformation, and $v^*(x) = bv(x) + c$ for all x in X. The auxiliary utility functions v^* and v are also said to be related by an increasing linear transformation, and such a function is sometimes referred to as a "cardinal utility function," as "unique up to an origin and a scale unit," or as "measured on an interval scale." These expressions simply mean: (a) if x and y are two elements in X for which $x \succ' y$, then $v(x)$ and $v(y)$ can be any two numbers which satisfy $v(x) > v(y)$, and (b) given $v(x)$ and $v(y)$, $v(z)$ is uniquely determined for each z in X according to the type of equation derived from indifference, based on (3) and (4), that was presented in the paragraph after (5). Given any such v on X, the corresponding complete linear u on P can be fully recovered or computed in the manner of (5).

It is important to note that a linear utility function u on P depends only on the "ordinal" preference relation $\succ$ on P, and great caution should be exercised in interpreting such a u or its auxiliary v as a measure of preference intensity (Luce and Raiffa [1957] section 2.6). If u is a complete linear utility function for $\succ$ on P and u^* has $u^*(p) > u^*(q)$ iff $u(p) > u(q)$, then u^* is a complete utility function for $\succ$ on P. This u^* will not be linear unless it is related to u by

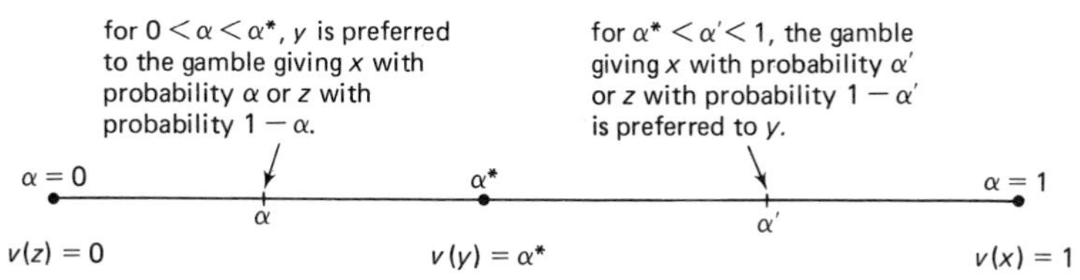
for $0 < \alpha < \alpha^*$, y is preferred to the gamble giving x with probability α or z with probability $1 - \alpha$.
for $\alpha^* < \alpha' < 1$, the gamble giving x with probability α' or z with probability $1 - \alpha'$ is preferred to y.
$\alpha = 0$
α
α^*
α'
$\alpha = 1$
$v(z) = 0$
$v(y) = \alpha^*$
$v(x) = 1$

Fig. 3. $x > y > z$.

an affine transformation, and if u^* is not linear then computation by expectation from v^* as in (5) will not be valid. Nevertheless, v^* remains a legitimate complete utility function for $\succ'$ on X.

It may of course be true that $\succ$ on P admits the existence of a complete utility function (iff $\succ$ on P is a weak order and some countable subset of P is $\succ$ order-dense in P) without giving rise to any complete *linear* utility function. When this is true, we can still speak about maximizing utility even though (5) cannot be used to compute u from v by expectations.

The foregoing remarks apply in modified form to (incomplete) utility functions for $\succ$ on P. If u is a linear utility function for $\succ$ on P then u^* is also a linear utility function for $\succ$ on P if u^* is related to u by an affine transformation. However, if $\succ$ on P is not a weak order (but is acyclic), then two linear utility functions u and u^* for $\succ$ on P need not be related by an affine transformation. For example, if $X = \{x, y, z\}$ and $p \succ q$ if and only if $p(x) > q(x)$ and $p(y) > q(y)$, then $\succ$ on P is transitive but is not a weak order since indifference is not transitive. Let $\{v(x) = 1, v(y) = v(z) = 0\}$, $\{v^*(y) = 1, v^*(x) = v^*(z) = 0\}$, and let u and u^* be defined on P from v and v^* respectively by (5). Then u and u^* are linear utility functions for $\succ$ on P which are not related by an affine transformation.

3.2 Axioms for Linear Utility

We shall now examine axioms or conditions for $\succ$ on P which imply the existence of a linear utility function for $\succ$ on P. The first set, $\{A1, A2, A3\}$, due to Fishburn [1972a], gives axioms which are sufficient for the existence of a linear utility function for $\succ$ on P. The second set, $\{B1, B2, B3\}$, due to Jensen [1967], gives axioms which are necessary and sufficient for the existence of a complete linear utility function for $\succ$ on P. In each case X is any non-empty set: it need not be finite or countable. The axioms do not imply that utilities are bounded, although boundedness usually results when similar axioms are applied to nonsimple probability distributions.

As noted in the introduction, the original axiomatization for complete linear utility was presented by von Neumann and Morgenstern [1944] and hence a complete linear u or its auxiliary v on X is often referred to as a von Neumann-Morgenstern utility function. The term "Bernoullian utilities" is also used for this because of the early contribution by Daniel Bernoulli [1738].

Each axiom applies to all p, q, r and s in P and, in the case of $A2$ or $B2$, to all α strictly between 0 and 1.

$A1$. *$\succ$ on P is irreflexive;*

$A2$. *If $0 < \alpha < 1$ and $p \succ q$ and $r \succ s$, then $\alpha p + (1 - \alpha)r \succ \alpha q + (1 - \alpha)s$;*

$A3$. *If $p \succ q$ and $r \succ s$, then $\alpha p + (1 - \alpha)s \succ \alpha q + (1 - \alpha)r$ for some α strictly between 0 and 1.*

*B*1. $\succ$ *on P is a weak order;*
*B*2. *If* $0 < \alpha < 1$ *and* $p \succ q$, *then* $\alpha p + (1 - \alpha) r \succ \alpha q + (1 - \alpha) r$;
*B*3. *If* $p \succ q$ *and* $q \succ r$, *then* $\alpha p + (1 - \alpha) r \succ q$ *and* $q \succ \beta p + (1 - \beta) r$ *for some* α *and* β *strictly between* 0 *and* 1.

Axioms *A*1 and *B*1 have been discussed previously. (*A*1 and *A*2 imply that $\succ$ is acyclic.)

Axioms *A*2 and *B*2 are variously referred to as independence, additivity, sure-thing, or linearity conditions. The linear aspect of u, as in (3), derives primarily from these axioms. The rationale for them is usually based on the probabilistically legitimate (but sometimes psychologically debatable) interpretation of "implementing" $\alpha p + (1 - \alpha) r$ by first selecting p or r with respective selection probabilities of α and $1 - \alpha$ and then carrying through the one of p and r thus selected. To illustrate *A*2 in this fashion consider the accompanying display

	α	$1 - \alpha$
A	p	r
B	q	s

where you choose row *A* or *B*, a neutral observer chooses a column according to the probabilities α and $1 - \alpha$, and you then "receive" the one of p, q, r and s determined by the row and column choices. If you prefer p to q and prefer r to s then, since the first row strictly dominates the second row in a preference sense, it is suggested that you will (or ought to) choose *A* over *B* regardless of the value of α. Since *A* and *B* are characterizations of $\alpha p + (1 - \alpha) r$ and $\alpha q + (1 - \alpha) s$, we thus have: if $p \succ q$ and $r \succ s$, then $\alpha p + (1 - \alpha) r \succ \alpha q + (1 - \alpha) s$.

A similar defense of *B*2 replaces s with r in the above matrix, with $\alpha > 0$. If $p \succ q$ then (since $r \sim r$) it seems reasonable to suppose or suggest that *A* will be chosen over *B* or that $\alpha p + (1 - \alpha) r \succ \alpha q + (1 - \alpha) r$. From a psychological viewpoint, one weakness of *B*2 is its disregard of threshold phenomena. If α is very nearly zero then the individual may not really care about or be able to perceive the difference between *A* and *B* and may therefore be indifferent as to which he chooses. This criticism does not apply to *A*2 since both $p \succ q$ and $r \succ s$ in its hypotheses.

Examples can also be given to challenge the reasonableness of *B*2 (and of *A*2) on somewhat different grounds. A very lucid discussion of this along with other salient points will be found in section 5.6 of Savage [1954].

Axioms *A*3 and *B*3, which are often referred to as Archimedean axioms or continuity conditions, complete our two axiom sets. Their technical function, in conjunction with the other axioms, is to ensure the existence of real-valued utility functions and in this regard they perform a service that is similar to the countable order-denseness condition of section 2.3. Lexicographic complete linear utilities, involving utility vectors such as $(u_1(p), \ldots, u_n(p))$, arise

(Hausner [1954], Chipman [1960, 1971], Fishburn [1971a]) when the Archimedean axiom $B3$ is deleted.

Axiom $A3$ is stronger than $B3$ since it implies $B3$. The apparent reasonableness of these axioms can be seen by taking α near to 1 in $A3$, and by taking α near to 1 and β near to 0 in $B3$.

3.3 On the Utility of Wealth

Because X is frequently presumed to be a set of monetary amounts in discussions of expected utility theory, we conclude this section with a few remarks for this context. We shall let $x = 0$ denote present wealth with values in X increments to present wealth. Axioms $B1$, $B2$, and $B3$ are assumed to hold, u is a complete linear utility function for $\succ$ on P, v is the auxiliary function on X defined by (4), and v is assumed to increase in x.

The three concepts of certainty equivalent, minimum selling price, and maximum buying price for a gamble p on X are often encountered in this context. Presuming that v is continuous (Grandmont [1972], Foldes [1972]), these are defined as follows. The certainty equivalent $c(p)$ of p is the value of x at which the individual is indifferent between receiving p and receiving x; hence it is given by $u(p) = v(c(p))$. The minimum selling price $s(p)$ of p is the least value of x he would sell p for if he had received p as a "gift" and thus had title to it. Since his utility with p is $u(p)$ and his utility is $v(x)$ if he trades p for x, $u(p) = v(s(p))$, so that $s(p) = c(p)$. Thus the certainty equivalent and minimum selling price are the same.

On the other hand, the maximum buying price $b(p)$ of p is the most he would pay (with zero transaction cost) from his present resources to gain title to p. If he pays x for p then, with p_x defined by $p_x(y - x) = p(y)$ for all y in Y, his utility after the transaction is $u(p_x)$. Since his utility prior to the transaction is $v(0)$, $v(0) = u(p_{b(p)})$. There is no assurance that $b(p) = s(p)$ unless v is linear in x (risk-neutral). In addition, $s(p)$ and $b(p)$ can be negative as well as positive or zero. For example, if $b(p) < 0$ then he would require payment of a "sweetener" in the amount of $-b(p)$ or larger before he would accept the "unfavorable" gamble p. Similarly, if $s(p) < 0$, he will give up cash in the amount of $-s(p)$ or smaller to be rid of p.

If p is a generally favorable gamble, there need be no inconsistencies in the following types of behavior: you would pay up to \$300 to obtain title to p, but, had you been given p at no cost, you would sell it for as little as \$250; you would pay up to \$1000 to get p but, if you purchased p for say \$980, you would be unwilling to pay more than \$850 for a second gamble that is a copy of p.

A number of authors (e.g. Friedman and Savage, [1948], Markowitz [1952],

Archibald [1959], Yaari [1965], Hakansson, [1970]) attempt to rationalize or explain individual actions, such as gambling and buying insurance, using curvature characteristics of v. In this connection, v is said to be risk-averse (see Fig. 1), risk-neutral or risk-seeking on an interval of the line if respectively it is strictly concave on the interval $[x \neq y$ and $0 < \alpha < 1$ imply $\alpha v(x) + (1 - \alpha) v(y) < v(\alpha x + (1 - \alpha) y)]$, linear on the interval $[\alpha v(x) + (1 - \alpha) v(y) = v(\alpha x + (1 - \alpha) y)]$ or strictly convex on the interval $[\alpha v(x) + (1 - \alpha) v(y) > v(\alpha x + (1 - \alpha) y)]$. If v is continuous on the interval, it is risk-averse iff $c(p) < \alpha x + (1 - \alpha) y$ whenever $p(x) = \alpha$, $p(y) = 1 - \alpha$, $0 < \alpha < 1$ and $x \neq y$ with x and y in the interval, and if v is twice differentiable, it is risk-averse on the interval iff $v''(x) < 0$ for all x in the interior of the interval. Pratt [1964] and Arrow [1965] examine $-v''(x)/v'(x)$ as a measure of local risk aversion. Similar remarks apply to risk-seeking with $c(p) > \alpha x + (1 - \alpha) y$ or $v''(x) > 0$.

A given v may of course be risk-seeking on one interval and risk-averse on another. In Fig. 4, v is risk-seeking on $[0, x]$ and risk-averse on $[x, y]$. It is risk-neutral on $[x - b(p), 0]$. With $p(x) = p(y) = \frac{1}{2}$, the certainty equivalent $c(p)$ and maximum buying price $b(p)$ of p are illustrated by the figure.

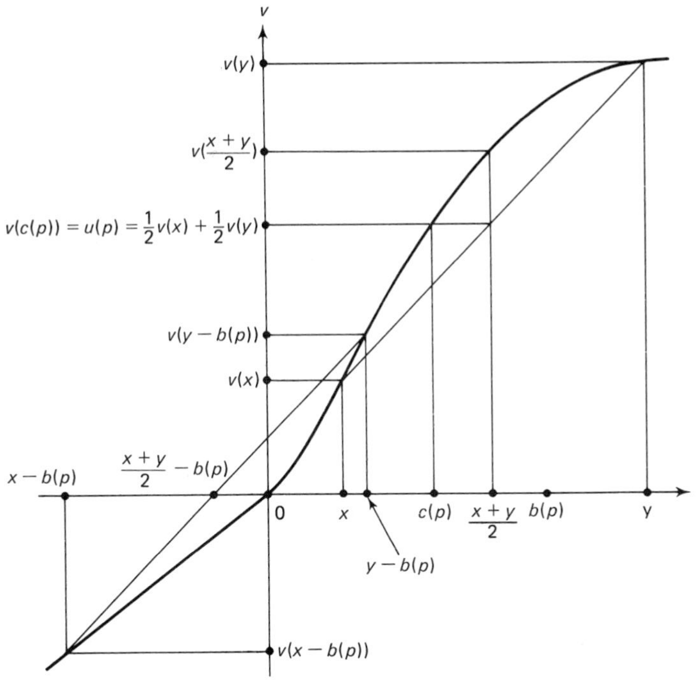

Fig. 4. An auxiliary utility function. $p(x) = p(y) = \frac{1}{2}$.

4. MULTIPLE ATTRIBUTE VALUE THEORY

Except in the simplest situations, decision alternatives or consequences are judged on the basis of a number of criteria, factors, objectives or attributes (MacCrimmon [1973]). In this section we shall therefore examine some aspects of preferences and utilities when the alternatives or consequences in X can be represented as n-tuples $x = (x_1, x_2, \ldots, x_n)$ with x_i in the set X_i for $i = 1, 2, \ldots, n$. Each X_i is a set of levels or values of a particular factor or attribute. The several X_i may refer to factors in a given time period (net profit, gross sales, market share, etc.) or to similar factors over successive time periods (net profit this year, net profit next year, etc.).

Thus we view X as a subset of the product set $X_1 \times X_2 \times \cdots \times X_n$. Superscripts will identify n-tuples in X, as $x^1 = (x_1^1, x_2^1, \ldots, x_n^1)$ and $x^2 = (x_1^2, x_2^2, \ldots, x_n^2)$. The preference relation $\succ$ will apply either to X, as in section 2, or to the set P of simple probability distributions on X, as in section 3.

4.1 An Independence Condition

Most of the theory considered in this section depends on some notion of preference independence among factors or attributes. A simple independence condition will be discussed first. Later in this section we shall present more complex independence conditions.

We suppose here that $X = X_1 \times X_2 \times \cdots \times X_n$ and that $\succ$ on X is a weak order. By fixing the levels of $X_2, \ldots, X_n$ at $x_2^0, \ldots, x_n^0$, a conditional weak order $\succ_1^0$ on X_1 is defined from $\succ$ on X by $x_1 \succ_1^0 y_1$ iff $(x_1, x_2^0, \ldots, x_n^0) \succ (y_1, x_2^0, \ldots, x_n^0)$. If the fixed levels of $X_2, \ldots, X_n$ are now changed, another conditional weak order can be defined on X_1 in a similar manner. The independence condition under consideration asserts that any two such conditional weak orders on X_1 are identical. Moreover, this will be true for each X_i when we consider various combinations of fixed levels of $X_1, \ldots, X_{i-1}, X_{i+1}, \ldots, X_n$. In summary, the condition asserts that

$$(x_1, \ldots, a_i, \ldots, x_n) \succ (x_1, \ldots, b_i, \ldots, x_n)$$
$$\text{iff} \quad (y_1, \ldots, a_i, \ldots, y_n) \succ (y_1, \ldots, b_i, \ldots, y_n)$$

whenever i is in $\{1, \ldots, n\}$ and the four n-tuples are in X.

Given this simple independence condition, we can drop explicit mention of the conditioning $n - 1$ tuple since the conditional order on X_i does not depend on it, and write $\succ_1, \succ_2, \ldots, \succ_n$ for the induced weak orders thus defined on $X_1, X_2, \ldots, X_n$.

It may of course be true that the independence condition is false, thus signifying some degree of preference interdependence among the factors. Although the interdependent case may predominate in reality, the independent case has been studied more extensively. Some theory of interdependent preferences is discussed by Fisher [1892] and Fishburn [1972c].

Perhaps the simplest preference model which uses the independence condition and involves all of the induced orders $\succ_1, \succ_2, \ldots, \succ_n$ is the completely noncompensatory lexicographic model wherein there is a strict dominance order on the factors. Supposing that X_1 is the most important factor, X_2 is the next most important factor, and so forth, this model has $(x_1, x_2, \ldots, x_n) \succ (y_1, y_2, \ldots, y_n)$ iff $x_1 \succ_1 y_1$ or $(x_1 \sim_1 y_1$ and $x_2 \succ_2 y_2)$ or $(x_1 \sim_1 y_1, x_2 \sim_2 y_2, x_3 \succ_3 y_3)$ or ... or $(x_i \sim_i y_i$ for all $i < n$, and $x_n \succ_n y_n)$. A survey of this and related lexicographic models is presented by Fishburn [1974a]. Although certain situations may be amenable to lexicographic analyses, situations which involve compensatory aspects or trade-offs among the factors are probably of greater practical interest and we shall therefore concentrate on these in the remainder of this section. Because of their analytical tractability, additive utility models will receive primary consideration.

4.2 Additive Utilities

Given a non-empty subset X of $X_1 \times X_2 \times \cdots \times X_n$ and a preference relation $\succ$ on X, a function u from X into the real numbers is an *additive utility function* for $\succ$ on X iff it is a utility function and there are real-valued functions $u_1, u_2, \ldots, u_n$ on $X_1, X_2, \ldots, X_n$ respectively such that, for all $x = (x_1, \ldots, x_n)$ in X,

$$u(x_1, x_2, \ldots, x_n) = u_1(x_1) + u_2(x_2) + \cdots + u_n(x_n). \tag{6}$$

Similarly, u is a *complete additive utility function* for $\succ$ on X if it is a complete utility function and there are u_i which satisfy (6).

To express the independence conditions which are needed to ensure additive utilities we define $(x^1, \ldots, x^m) \cong (y^1, \ldots, y^m)$ iff m is a positive integer greater than 1, each of $x^1, \ldots, x^m, y^1, \ldots, y^m$ is in X, and, for each i from 1 to n, $x_i^1, x_i^2, \ldots, x_i^m$ is a rearrangement (permutation) of $y_i^1, y_i^2, \ldots, y_i^m$. If (6) holds and $(x^1, \ldots, x^m) \cong (y^1, \ldots, y^m)$ then, as seen by substitution from (6) and cancellation of identical u_i terms, $u(x^1) + \cdots + u(x^m) = u(y^1) + \cdots + u(y^m)$. Hence, given $(x^1, \ldots, x^m) \cong (y^1, \ldots, y^m)$, if u is an additive utility function for $\succ$ on X then we cannot have $x^k \succ y^k$ for $k = 1, \ldots, m$, and if u is a complete additive utility function for $\succ$ on X then it cannot be true that $x^k \succsim y^k$ for $k = 1, \ldots, m$ and $x^k \succ y^k$ for some k.

Suppose that X is finite. Then, as proved in Adams [1965] or Fishburn [1970b], there exists an additive utility function for $\succ$ on X iff whenever $(x^1, \ldots, x^m) \cong (y^1, \ldots, y^m)$ it is false that $x^k \succ y^k$ for every k from 1 to m. Similarly (Fishburn [1970b]), there exists a complete additive utility function for $\succ$ on X iff whenever $(x^1, \ldots, x^m) \cong (y^1, \ldots, y^m)$ it is false that $x^k \succsim y^k$ for every k from 1 to m and $x^k \succ y^k$ for some k. As may be readily proved, the first order-independence condition with $\cong$ implies that $\succ$ is acyclic, and the second $\cong$ condition implies that $\succ$ is a weak order.

The foregoing order-independence conditions are also necessary (but not sufficient) for additive or complete additive utilities when X is infinite. However, the principal developments to date on additivity with infinite X (Debreu [1960], Luce and Tukey [1964], Krantz, et al. [1971]) all presume rather strong structure for X, such as each X_i a continuum (or something close to this) and $X = X_1 \times X_2 \times \cdots \times X_n$, and that $\succ$ on X is a weak order. As a result of this, they require less formidable looking independence or cancellation conditions. A typical condition which suffices for $n = 2$ (in the presence of various structural assumptions) is the $m = 3$ condition: if $(x^1, x^2, x^3) \cong (y^1, y^2, y^3)$ then it is false that $x^1 \succsim y^1, x^2 \succsim y^2, x^3 \succsim y^3$ and $x^k \succ y^k$ for some k in $\{1, 2, 3\}$. For $n > 2$ the $m = 2$ condition suffices: if $(x^1, x^2) \cong (y^1, y^2)$, or $\{x_i^1, x_i^2\} = \{y_i^1, y_i^2\}$ for $i = 1, \ldots, n$, then it is false that $x^1 \succsim y^1, x^2 \succsim y^2$ and $x^k \succ y^k$ for some k in $\{1, 2\}$.

Because of the strong structural properties employed in the theories of the preceding paragraph, different complete additive utility representations for a particular $\succ$ on X for these theories are related by similar affine transformations. That is, if u is a complete additive utility function for $\succ$ on X with $u_1, \ldots, u_n$ satisfying (6), then u^* with associated functions $u_1^*, \ldots, u_n^*$ for (6) is also a complete additive utility function for $\succ$ on X iff there are real numbers $b, c_1, \ldots, c_n$ with $b > 0$ such that $u^*(x) = bu(x) + c_1 + \cdots + c_n$ for all x in X and, for each i from 1 to n ($\geqslant 2$), $u_i^*(x_i) = bu_i(x_i) + c_i$ for all x_i in X_i.

As might be expected, this essential uniqueness of the u_i functions is very convenient in scaling or estimating these functions, as was so lucidly pointed out by Irving Fisher [1892]. In cases where X is finite or does not possess "nice" structure, the same type of uniqueness will not generally hold and different estimation techniques may be needed. Estimation methods for both situations are discussed by Fishburn [1967].

4.3 Additive and Other Linear Utilities

We now turn to the context where $\succ$ is a preference relation on the set P of simple probability distributions on a subset X of a product set $X_1 \times X_2 \times \cdots \times X_n$. For a given p in P we shall let p_i be the marginal distribution of p on X_i. Thus, if $p(x_1, x_2, x_3) = .3$ and $p(y_1, y_2, x_3) = .7$ with $x_1 \neq y_1$ and $x_2 \neq y_2$ then $p_1(x_1) = p_2(x_2) = .3, p_1(y_1) = p_2(y_2) = .7$ and $p_3(x_3) = 1$.

Since virtually all the special work done in this context has presumed that $\succ$ on P is a weak order, we shall consider only complete linear utility functions. Axioms $B1, B2$ and $B3$ (section 3.2) are assumed to hold.

A real-valued function u on P is a *complete additive linear utility function* for $\succ$ on P iff it is a complete linear utility function for $\succ$ on P (section 3.1) and, with v on X its auxiliary function defined by (4), there are real-valued functions $v_1, v_2, \ldots, v_n$ on $X_1, X_2, \ldots, X_n$ respectively such that, for all x in X,

$$v(x_1, x_2, \ldots, x_n) = v_1(x_1) + v_2(x_2) + \cdots + v_n(x_n). \tag{7}$$

When this holds and $u_i(p_i)$ is defined as the expected value of v_i with respect to the probability distribution p_i on X_i, then $u(p) = u_1(p_1) + u_2(p_2) + \cdots + u_n(p_n)$ for all p in P.

As noted by Fishburn [1971b], a complete additive linear utility function exists for $\succ$ on P iff $p \sim q$ whenever $p_i = q_i$ for $i = 1, \ldots, n$. This is another form of independence condition; it asserts that the individual will be indifferent between p and q whenever the marginal of p on X_i equals the marginal of q on X_i for $i = 1, \ldots, n$. If $X = X_1 \times X_2 \times \cdots \times X_n$ then [Fishburn, 1965; Pollak, 1967] a weaker condition involving only 50-50 gambles suffices. It says that if $p(x) = p(y) = q(z) = q(w) = \frac{1}{2}$ and $\{x_i, y_i\} = \{z_i, w_i\}$ for $i = 1, \ldots, n$ then $p \sim q$.

Other special forms for v on X are implied by less demanding independence conditions as shown for example by Pollak [1967], Keeney [1968, 1971, 1972] and Fishburn [1974b]. We illustrate these with $X = X_1 \times X_2$. For a fixed x_2 in X_2, define the conditional order $\succ_{x_2}$ on the distributions $a, b, \ldots$ on X_1 by $a \succ_{x_2} b$ if and only if $p \succ q$ when $p_1 = a$, $q_1 = b$ and $p_2(x_2) = q_2(x_2) = 1$. Similarly, with r and s distributions on X_2, $r \succ_{x_1} s$ iff $p \succ q$ when $p_2 = r, q_2 = s$ and $p_1(x_1) = q_1(x_1) = 1$. As shown by Keeney and Pollak: if $\succ_{x_2}$ is identical to $\succ_{y_2}$ for all x_2 and y_2 in X_2, then v can be written in the form $v(x_1, x_2) = v_2(x_2) + v_1(x_1) f_2(x_2)$; if $\succ_{x_1}$ is identical to $\succ_{y_1}$ for all x_1 and y_1 in X_1, then v can be written in the form $v(x_1, x_2) = v_1(x_1) + v_2(x_2) f_1(x_1)$; and if both $\succ_{x_2} = \succ_{y_2}$ for all x_2 and y_2, and $\succ_{x_1} = \succ_{y_1}$ for all x_1 and y_1, then v can either be written additively as in (7) or else (after an appropriate affine transformation) it can be written multiplicatively as $v(x_1, x_2) = v_1(x_1)\, v_2(x_2)$. A somewhat more complex independence condition is used by Fishburn [1974b] to derive the form $v(x_1, x_2) = v_1(x_1) + v_2(x_2) + f_1(x_1) f_2(x_2)$.

Methods of scaling or estimating the several single-factor functions used in these special forms are discussed by Fishburn [1967], Raiffa [1969] and Keeney [1971, 1972].

5. SUBJECTIVE PROBABILITY AND EXPECTED UTILITY

According to Savage [1954, p. 3], personalistic or subjectivistic views of the meaning of probability "hold that probability measures the confidence that a particular individual has in the truth of a particular proposition, for example, the proposition that it will rain tomorrow. These views postulate that the individual concerned is in some ways 'reasonable,' but they do not deny the possibility that two reasonable individuals faced with the same evidence may have different degrees of confidence in the truth of the same proposition." In concluding this chapter, we comment briefly on preference theories for decision making under uncertainty, in which subjective probabilities (for the various consequences of courses of action) as well as utilities, arise from the axioms of preference to combine in an expected utility model.

Two principal formulations have been suggested as bases for subjective expected utility theory. The first (Savage [1954]) takes consequences and states of the world as basic, and views an act or course of action as a function which assigns a consequence in X to each state of the world in S. The state that "obtains" or is the "true state" is not known by the decision maker when he makes his decision, and it is assumed that the states are independent of the acts in the sense that the selected act will not influence the state that obtains. We use $f(s)$ to denote the consequence assigned to state s by act f. F is the set of acts. In the finite-states model, with $S = \{s_1, s_2, \ldots, s_n\}$, there is a simple probability distribution P^* on S along with a utility function u on F and its auxiliary v on X. $P^*(s_i)$ is the decision maker's subjective probability for state s_i, and $v(x)$ is his utility for consequence x. Assuming that $\succ$ on F is a weak order, the model has $u(f) > u(g)$ iff $f \succ g$, for any f and g in F, with

$$u(f) = P^*(s_1)\, v(f(s_1)) + P^*(s_2)\, v(f(s_2)) + \cdots + P^*(s_n)\, v(f(s_n)) \tag{8}$$

for each act f in F.

The second formulation (Fishburn [1964]) views the set F of acts and the set X of consequences as basic. States of the world are not explicitly defined. The finite-consequences model, with $X = \{x_1, x_2, \ldots, x_m\}$, involves u on F and v on X along with a probability distribution p_f on X for each f in F. As before, $v(x)$ is the decision maker's utility for consequence x; we interpret $p_f(x)$ as his subjective probability for the proposition "if I do f then x will be the resultant consequence." Assuming that $\succ$ on F is a weak order, the model has $u(f) > u(g)$ iff $f \succ g$, with

$$u(f) = p_f(x_1)\, v(x_1) + p_f(x_2)\, v(x_2) + \cdots + p_f(x_m)\, v(x_m). \tag{9}$$

Although these two models seem rather different, they are proposed in the same spirit and, in a sense discussed at greater length in Chapter 12 in Fishburn [1970b], they are isomorphic.

5.1 Axioms and Measurement

With the exception of theories by Luce and Krantz [1971], Krantz, *et al.* [1971] and Balch and Fishburn [1973], axiomatizations of subjective expected utility have concentrated on the first formulation given above, and I shall focus on it in concluding this chapter.

The most elegant formal theory under the first formulation is due to Savage [1954]; summaries are provided by Luce and Raiffa [1957] and Luce and Suppes [1965], and a complete account is presented by Fishburn [1970b]. Savage's theory was preceded by Ramsey's outline [1931], which was fleshed out by Suppes [1956], and succeeded by a number of other axiom systems, including those by Anscombe and Aumann [1963], Pratt, *et al.* [1964] and Fishburn [1970b]. Since the approaches of Savage and of Ramsey illustrate the basic ideas of these theories, I shall concentrate on these two. Later axiomatizations have been designed, in part, to avoid some potentially objectionable structural presumptions of the earlier theories.

Ramsey's approach uses an "ethically neutral proposition" (or something tantamount to an event E with probability $\frac{1}{2}$) to measure utilities of consequences by a successive bisection procedure which, for full generality, requires X to be infinite: if the elements in X are monetary amounts (with more preferred to less) and if $x > z$, one determines a y between x and z such that y with certainty is indifferent to (x if E occurs or z if E does not occur). Then $v(y) = \frac{1}{2} v(x) + \frac{1}{2} v(z)$. (Some other theories have presumed a full range of "extraneous scaling probabilities" (Fishburn [1970b]) which allow X to be finite in obtaining v unique up to an affine transformation.) Then v on X is used to measure probabilities for P^*: if A is an event (subset of S) and if x, y and z with $v(x) > v(y) > v(z)$ are such that y with certainty is indifferent to (x if A obtains or z if A does not obtain), then $P^*(A)$ is determined by $v(y) = P^*(A)\, v(x) + [1 - P^*(A)]\, v(z)$.

Savage's approach reverses the measurement procedure. He derives P^* first, on the basis of his axioms for $\succ$ on F, using a form of bisection procedure which requires S to be infinite: if x is preferred to y and the individual is indifferent between (x if A or y if not A) and (y if A or x if not A), then $P^*(A)\, v(x) + [1 - P^*(A)]\, v(y) = P^*(A)\, v(y) + [1 - P^*(A)]\, v(x)$ gives $P^*(A) = \frac{1}{2}$, regardless of the particular values of $v(x)$ and $v(y)$ so long as $v(x) \neq v(y)$. A general format for this is presented in the following diagram where B is a subevent of event A, and A-B denotes the event "A occurs but B doesn't occur."

	B	A-B	not A
Option 1	x	y	x
Option 2	y	x	x

If x is not indifferent to y but Option 1 $\sim$ Option 2, then direct calculation from the subjective expected utility model gives $P^*(B) = \frac{1}{2} P^*(A)$.

Having obtained a unique P^*, v on X is then obtained with the aid of P^*: if x is preferred to y which in turn is preferred to z, and if A is an event which makes y with certainty indifferent to (x if A or z if not A), then $v(x)$, $v(y)$ and $v(z)$ are related by $v(y) = P^*(A)\, v(x) + [1 - P^*(A)]\, v(z)$. In fact, as Savage notes, his axioms imply that P^* leads to a set of induced measures p_f on X for the various f in F which possess the structure used in the von Neumann-Morgenstern [1944] expected utility theory (section 3.2). Hence, given P^*, the existence of an appropriate v on X follows from the earlier theory.

Apart from a number of structural conditions, which I shall not discuss, the main new axiom in these theories that is not employed as such in the theories of section 3, is a form of independence-regularity for events and consequences. From the Ramsey approach, this guarantees that if $v(x) > v(y) > v(z)$, $v(x') > v(y') > v(z')$, if $[v(y) - v(z)] / [v(x) - v(z)] = [v(y') - v(z')] / [v(x') - v(z')]$ and if y is indifferent to (x if A or z if not A), then y' is indifferent to (x' if A or z' if not A). Then $P^*(A)$ is unambiguously defined by the ratio of v differences. For the Savage viewpoint, it guarantees that if $P^*(A) = P^*(B)$, if x is preferred to y is preferred to z, and if y is indifferent to (x if A or z if not A), then y is indifferent to (x if B or z if not B). Then the ratio $[v(y) - v(z)]/[v(x) - v(z)]$ is unambiguously defined as the value of $P^*(A)$.

Additional information on methods of estimating subjective probabilities is available in Winkler [1967a, 1967b], Raiffa [1968] and Savage [1971].

6. CONCLUDING REMARKS

This chapter has sought to explain the basic ideas used in theories of preferences and utilities. Many relevant topics have been mentioned only briefly or not at all. For example, there is a rapidly growing literature–mostly in economics and mathematical psychology–in which 'preference' as a primitive notion is replaced by 'choice' as primitive. In the latter case, the theory begins with a choice function, either deterministic or probabilistic, defined on subsets of alternatives, rather than with a preference relation on the alternatives.

Moreover, very little has been said here about the use of preference and utility theory in the analysis of real problems. Two areas in which the explicit use of the theory may be advisable are (1) multiattribute or multiple criterion problems, and (2) decision making under uncertainty. Both have received widespread attention in recent years from research workers who are interested in putting the theory to practical use. The next chapter in this Handbook illustrates the use of subjective expected utility theory in decision making under uncertainty.

REFERENCES

1. Adams, E. W., "Elements of a Theory of Inexact Measurement," *Phil. Sci.* **32,** 205-228 (1965).
2. Anscombe, F. J. and R. J. Aumann, "A Definition of Subjective Probability," *Ann. of Math. Stat.* **34:** 199-205 (1963).
3. Archibald, G. C., "Utility, Risk, and Linearity," *J. Pol. Econ.* **67:** 437-450 (1959).
4. Arrow, K. J., *Aspects of the Theory of Risk-Bearing*, Yrjö Jahnssonin Säätiö, Helsinki (1965).
5. Balch, M. and P. C. Fishburn, "Subjective Expected Utility for Conditional Primitives," in M. Balch, D. McFadden and S. Y. Wu (Eds.), *Essays on Economic Behaviour Under Uncertainty*, North-Holland, Amsterdam (1973).
6. Bernoulli, D., "Specimen theoriae novae de mensura sortis," *Commentarii Academiae Scientiarum Imperialis Petropolitanae* **5:** 175-192 (1738); Translated by L. Sommer, *Econometrica* **22:** 23-36 (1954).
7. Cantor, G., "Beiträge zur Begründung der transfiniten Mengenlehre," *Mathematische Annalen* **46:** 481-512 (1895); Translated with notes by P. E. B. Jourdain in *Contributions to the Founding of the Theory of Transfinite Numbers*, Dover, New York (1915).
8. Chipman, J. S., "The Foundations of Utility," *Econometrica* **28:** 193-224 (1960).
9. ——, "Non-Archimedean Behavior Under Risk: An Elementary Analysis–With Application to the Theory of Assets," in J. S. Chipman, L. Hurwicz, M. K. Richter and H. F. Sonnenschein (Eds.), *Preferences, Utility, and Demand*, Harcourt Brace Jovanovich, New York (1971).
10. Davidson, D., J. C. C. McKinsey, and P. Suppes, "Outlines of a Formal Theory of Value, I," *Phil. Sci.* **22:** 140-160 (1955).
11. Debreu, G., *Theory of Value: An Axiomatic Analysis of Economic Equilibrium*, Wiley, New York (1959).

12. ——, "Topological Methods in Cardinal Utility Theory," in K. J. Arrow, S. Karlin and P. Suppes (Eds.), *Mathematical Methods in the Social Sciences, 1959*, Stanford University Press, Stanford (1960).
13. ——, "Continuity Properties of Paretian Utility," *Int. Econ. Rev.* **5:** 285–293 (1964).
14. Fishburn, P. C., *Decision and Value Theory*, Wiley, New York (1964).
15. ——, "Independence in Utility Theory with Whole Product Sets," *Operations Res.* **13:** 28–45 (1965).
16. ——, "Methods of Estimating Additive Utilities," *Management Sci.* **13:** 435–453 (1967).
17. ——, "Intransitive Indifference in Preference Theory: A Survey," *Operations Res.* **18:** 207–228 (1970a).
18. ——, *Utility Theory for Decision Making*, Wiley, New York (1970b).
19. ——, "A Study of Lexicographic Expected Utility," *Management Sci.* **17:** 672–678 (1971a).
20. ——, "Additive Representations of Real-Valued Functions on Subsets of Product Sets," *J. Math. Psych.* **8:** 382–388 (1971b).
21. ——, "Alternative Axiomatizations of One-Way Expected Utility," *Ann. Math. Stat.* **43:** 1648–1651 (1972a).
22. ——, *Mathematics of Decision Theory*, Mouton, The Hague (1972b).
23. ——, "Interdependent Preferences on Finite Sets," *J. Math. Psych.* **9:** 225–236 (1972c).
24. ——, "Lexicographic Orders, Utilities and Decision Rules: A Survey," *Management Sci.* **20:** 1442–1471 (1974a).
25. ——, "Von Neumann-Morgenstern Utility Functions on Two Attributes," *Operations Res.* **22:** 35–45 (1974b).
26. Fisher, I., "Mathematical Investigations in the Theory of Values and Prices," *Trans. of the Conn. Acad. of Arts and Sci.* **9:** 1–124 (1892); Augustus M. Kelley, New York (1965).
27. Foldes, L., "Expected Utility and Continuity," *Rev. Econ. Studies* **39:** 407–421 (1972).
28. Friedman, M. and L. J. Savage, "The Utility Analysis of Choices Involving Risk," *J. Pol. Econ.* **56:** 279–304 (1948).
29. Frisch, R., "Sur un problème d'économie pure," *Norsk Matematisk Forenings Skrifter* **1(16):** 1–40 (1926); English translation in J. S. Chipman, L. Hurwicz, M. K. Richter and H. F. Sonnenschein (Eds.), *Preferences, Utility, and Demand*, 386–423, Harcourt Brace Jovanovich, New York (1971).
30. Grandmont, J.-M., "Continuity Properties of a von Neumann-Morgenstern Utility," *J. Econ. Theory* **4:** 45–57 (1972).
31. Hakansson, N. H., "Friedman-Savage Utility Functions Consistent with Risk Aversion," *Quart. J. Econ.* **84:** 472–487 (1970).
32. Hausner, M., "Multidimensional Utilities," in R. M. Thrall, C. H. Coombs and R. L. Davis (Eds.), *Decision Processes*, Wiley, New York (1954).
33. Jensen, N. E., "An Introduction to Bernoullian Utility Theory. I. Utility Functions," *Swedish J. Econ.* **69:** 163–183 (1967).
34. Keeney, R. L., "Quasi-Separable Utility Functions," *Nav. Res. Log. Quart.* **15:** 551–565 (1968).
35. ——, "Utility Independence and Preference for Multiattributed Consequences," *Operations Res.* **19:** 875–893 (1971).
36. ——, "Utility Functions for Multiattributed Consequences," *Management Sci.* **18:** 276–287 (1972).
37. Krantz, D. H., R. D. Luce, P. Suppes, and A. Tversky, *Foundations of Measurement, Vol. 1*, Academic Press, New York (1971).

38. Luce, R. D., "Semiorders and a Theory of Utility Discrimination," *Econometrica* **24:** 178-191 (1956).
39. —— and D. H. Krantz, "Conditional Expected Utility," *Econometrica* **39:** 253-271 (1971).
40. —— and H. Raiffa, *Games and Decisions*, Wiley, New York (1957).
41. —— and P. Suppes, "Preference, Utility, and Subjective Probability," in R. D. Luce, R. R. Bush and E. Galanter (Eds.), *Handbook of Mathematical Psychology, Vol. III*, Wiley, New York (1965).
42. —— and J. W. Tukey, "Simultaneous Conjoint Measurement: A New Type of Fundamental Measurement," *J. Math. Psych.* **1:** 1-27 (1964).
43. MacCrimmon, K. R., "An Overview of Multiple Objective Decision Making," in J. L. Cochrane and M. Zeleny (Eds.), *Multiple Criteria Decision Making*, University of South Carolina Press, Columbia, South Carolina (1973).
44. Markowitz, H., "The Utility of Wealth," *J. Pol. Econ.* **60:** 151-158 (1952).
45. Pollak, R. A., "Additive von Neumann-Morgenstern Utility Functions," *Econometrica* **35:** 485-494 (1967).
46. Pratt, J. W., "Risk Aversion in the Small and in the Large," *Econometrica* **32:** 122-136 (1964).
47. ——, H. Raiffa, and R. Schlaifer, "The Foundations of Decision Under Uncertainty: An Elementary Exposition," *J. Amer. Stat. Assoc.* **59:** 353-375 (1964).
48. Raiffa, H., *Decision Analysis: Introductory Lectures on Choices Under Uncertainty*, Addison-Wesley, Reading, Massachusetts (1968).
49. ——, "Preferences for Multi-Attributed Alternatives," Memorandum RM-5868-DOT RC, The RAND Corporation, Santa Monica, California (1969).
50. Ramsey, F. P., "Truth and Probability," in F. P. Ramsey, *The Foundations of Mathematics and Other Logical Essays*, Harcourt, Brace and Co., New York (1931). Reprinted in H. E. Kyburg and H. E. Smokler (Eds.), *Studies in Subjective Probability*, Wiley, New York (1964).
51. Roberts, F. S., "On Nontransitive Indifference," *J. Math. Psych.* **7:** 243-258 (1970).
52. Savage, L. J., *The Foundations of Statistics*, Wiley, New York (1954); second edition, Dover, New York (1972).
53. ——, "Elicitation of Personal Probabilities and Expectations," *J. Amer. Stat. Assoc.* **66:** 783-801 (1971).
54. Schwartz, T., "Rationality and the Myth of the Maximum," *Noûs* **6:** 97-117 (1972).
55. Suppes, P., "The Role of Subjective Probability and Utility in Decision-Making," *Proc. of the Third Berkeley Symp. on Math. Stat. and Probab., 1954-1955* **5:** 61-73 (1956).
56. Tversky, A., "Intransitivity of Preferences," *Psych. Rev.* **76:** 31-48 (1969).
57. ——, "Elimination by Aspects: A Theory of Choice," *Psych. Rev.* **79:** 281-299 (1972).
58. von Neumann, J. and O. Morgenstern, "Theory of Games and Economic Behavior," Princeton University Press, Princeton, New Jersey (1944).
59. Weinstein, A. A., "Individual Preference Intransitivity," *Southern Econ. J.* **34:** 335-343 (1968).
60. Winkler, R. L., "The Assessment of Prior Distributions in Bayesian Analysis," *J. Amer. Stat. Assoc.* **62:** 776-800 (1967a).
61. ——, "The Quantification of Judgment: Some Methodological Suggestions," *J. Amer. Stat. Assoc.* **62:** 1105-1120 (1967b).
62. Wold, H. O. A., "A Synthesis of Pure Demand Analysis. I, II, III," *Skandinavisk Aktuarietidskrift* **26:** 85-118, 220-263 (1943); **27:** 69-120 (1944).
63. Yaari, M. E., "Convexity in the Theory of Choice Under Risk," *Quart. J. Econ.* **79:** 278-290 (1965).

III-4

DECISION ANALYSIS*

Ralph L. Keeney
Woodward-Clyde Consultants

1. INTRODUCTION

1.1 What is Decision Analysis?

Decision analysis (DA) is a set of concepts and systematic procedures for rationally analyzing decision problems involving uncertainty. The objective is to improve the decision-making process. The logic of DA is provided by the set of axioms discussed in Section 2. If a decision-maker accepts these axioms as being appropriate for guiding his decisions, he should follow the procedures of DA and its resulting implications in his decision-making. In other words, a decision-maker must either violate the axioms of DA or act in accord with the procedures of DA.

DA is based on the assumption that the attractiveness of alternatives *should* depend on two factors:

1. the decision-maker's judgment about the likelihoods of the various possible consequences which may occur if a particular alternative decision is chosen, and
2. the decision-maker's preferences for each of these possible consequences.

*This work was supported in part by The Office of Naval Research under Contract N00014-67-A-0204-0056. It was written while the author was affiliated with the M.I.T. Operations Research Center during 1973–74. Consequently, references to contributions since that time are not included.

Both of these factors are formally incorporated in a DA of a problem. To do this, we will need to quantify the judgmental likelihoods, using subjective probability, and the preferences, using utility theory. The spirit of DA is to divide and conquer. The methodology requires one to work on the different complexities separately and then to combine the parts into an overall model for making decisions.

For discussion purposes, it is convenient to distinguish four steps of DA:

1. *Structuring the problem* includes generation of alternative courses of action. An appropriate set of objectives and their associated measures of effectiveness, to indicate the degree to which these objectives might be achieved by various alternatives, must be specified. For each alternative, the possible consequences are described in terms of the measures of effectiveness. Furthermore, the chronology of the problem, including options for collecting sample information, should be indicated.
2. *Describing likelihoods of the possible consequences* of each alternative requires that the uncertainties associated with alternative decisions be quantified by using a probability distribution. With this step, the probability of each possible consequence resulting from any particular decision is specified.
3. *Assigning preferences to the possible consequences* in terms of their utility. Here the tradeoffs among the various measures of effectiveness, if there are more than one, and the decision-makers attitudes toward the consequences and uncertainties are quantified.
4. *Rationally synthesizing the information* from the first three steps to decide which of the proposed alternatives is preferred. Sensitivity analysis is also included in this step.

These steps are simply the core of a "common sense" approach to decision-making. The distinguishing feature of a DA is the degree of formalization in each of the steps.

1.2 The Role of Decision Analysis

DA provides a normative theory which prescribes how a decision-maker should behave in order to be consistent with his judgments and preferences. It does not provide a method for describing how, in fact, individuals do behave. It is an aid to the decision-maker in that it provides a methodology for making complex decisions involving important subjective elements, but it is not a substitute for the decision-maker himself. Specifically, as a problem increases in complexity, one's ability to informally process all relevant information in a manner consistent with one's judgments and preferences decreases. In such a situation decision analysis has advantages over other analytical approaches in that it formally includes these more subjective aspects of a problem. Although the effort necessary to do a first DA can be substantial, it is of the same order as any kind of analysis in a complex situation. Initial decision analyses must be considered somewhat exploratory. "However, if documented for scrutiny by others, these attempts serve well as a basis for comment and critical review, modification, and improvement," (Keeney and Raiffa [1972]).

1.3 Problems Addressed by Decision Analysis

There are many characteristics of "typical" decision problems which DA may help to clarify and analyze:

1. *Multiple Objectives.* For most complex problems, there are many objectives which concern the decision-maker. These objectives will nearly always be conflicting in that the further achievement of one can only occur at the expense of another. Thus, the decision maker is inevitably concerned with tradeoffs among competing objectives.
2. *Impacts Over Time.* All of the important consequences of a problem do not occur at the same instant in time, nor does each aspect occur only at one, and only one, point in time. For example, the monetary consequences of a new product venture may continue to be significant for many years.
3. *Many Intangibles.* Considerations like good will, prestige, excitement, fun, pain, and political effects are examples of some very important intangibles that contribute to a problem's complexity.
4. *Uncertainty.* As previously mentioned, at the time a decision-maker must select an alternative, it is unlikely that the consequences will be known for each of the alternatives. This is especially true in light of the three characteristics previously described.
5. *Possibilities for Sample Information.* Often, one can acquire sample information to help decide which alternative should be chosen. For instance, it may be possible to conduct a market survey to evaluate a new product's potential, to perform medical tests to help diagnose a disease and its subsequent treatment, or to collect information from a seismic survey to help decide whether or not to drill for oil on a particular parcel of land. However, this information may be expensive, both in terms of time and cost, in addition to not being completely reliable.
6. *Dynamic Decision Aspects.* The problem might not end immediately after an alternative is chosen but might require that another critical decision be made in the next few years. The current alternative chosen may "close the door" to some of the possible actions and "open it wider" for others. It is important to recognize these dynamic aspects of the problem and the future flexibility that a current decision may afford the decision-maker.

7. *Group Considerations.* A chosen alternative may have impacts on many different groups, particularly in government decision-making. Clearly, any knowledge that would help the decision maker anticipate such impacts would be useful.
8. *Multiple Decision Makers.* The responsibility for selecting an alternative often falls on a group of individuals rather than on one individual. In fact, for certain problems, the responsibilities for the decision-making function in a certain sphere may not be clearly specified.

Many important decision problems do not possess all of the above complications. But often, enough are present to make the problem tough. DA allows us to address each of these considerations independently and provides a further framework for consistently integrating the information into a "best" course of action.

1.4 History of Decision Analysis

It is difficult to trace DA from its beginning to the present because of the evolutionary nature of both its content and its name. The foundations of DA are the intertwined concepts of subjective probability and utility, and Ramsey [1931] was the first to suggest a theory of decision-making based on these two ideas.* On the uncertainty side, DeFinetti [1937] contributed greatly to the structure of subjective probability. Modern utility theory for decision-making under uncertainty was developed, independently, by von Neumann and Morgenstern [1944]. They postulated a set of axioms similar to those in the next section (using only objective probabilities) and demonstrated that a utility could be assigned to each consequence in a manner such that a decision-maker should always choose the alternative with the highest expected utility, in order to act in accord with the axioms. This result is often referred to as the expected utility hypothesis.

Wald [1950], in his classic work on statistical decision problems, used theorems of game theory to prove certain results in statistical decision theory. Although he did not use utility theory, using an expected-loss criterion instead, it was only a minor modification to introduce utility into the Wald framework. This work highlighted a critical problem, namely, how to account for informal information about the states of the world in his model. The school of statisticians and decision theorists, including J. Marschak, H. Chernoff, and H. Rubin, advocated the use of judgmental probability as one method of tackling the statistical decision problems proposed by Wald. The pioneering work of Black-

*For a historical discussion of earlier development of subjective probability and utility theory, see Fellner [1965].

well and Girshick [1954] contributed to the integration of utilities and subjective probabilities into a coherent program for handling these problems. Then Savage [1954], in a major contribution, provided a rigorous philosophical foundation and axiomatic framework for the approach.

Once the theory was developed, many individuals began applying it to mathematically well-structured problems involving uncertainties and possibilities for sampling or experimentation. These results, building on the previous work of others, formed a body of results known as Bayesian or statistical decision theory (Schlaifer [1959], Raiffa and Schlaifer [1961], Pratt, *et al.* [1965]). When in the early 1960's, these same individuals and their associates, mainly at the Harvard Business School, began using these theories on real business problems involving uncertainties, whether or not sampling and experimentation were possible, an adjective was added to give us applied statistical decision theory. However, as it became more apparent that applied statistical decision theory was relevant to broad classes of complex decision problems (see Schlaifer [1969]) it also became apparent that in an applications-oriented society, it would be much better to have a more application-oriented name, hence the term decision analysis (DA) appeared in the literature (Howard [1966]).

Over the past twenty-five years, the contributions of many people concerned with the behavioral aspects of decision-making have had a significant impact on normative DA. Mosteller and Nogee [1951], Friedman and Savage [1952], Edwards [1954], and Davidson *et al.* [1957] made early contributions to the assessment of preferences and judgments. Two excellent reviews of this work are Slovic and Lichtenstein [1971] and Fischer and Edwards [1973].

Procedures have been developed to better account for specific characteristics of decision problems mentioned in the previous subsection. Examples include work by Pratt [1964] and Schlaifer [1969] on assessing utility functions, Winkler [1967], Edwards [1968], Schlaifer [1969], and Tversky and Kahneman [1973] for assigning subjective probabilities, Arrow [1951, 1963] and Harsanyi [1957] on group decision problems, Fishburn [1964, 1965, 1974a], Pollak [1967], Raiffa [1969] and Keeney [1968, 1971] on multiattribute preferences, Koopmans [1960], Lancaster [1963], and Meyer [1969] on preferences over time, and numerous contributions of people in system analysis, simulation, and computer sciences to develop better probabilistic models.

Along with the theoretical developments, there have been substantial improvements in the art of DA. Better software systems have been developed for dealing with the computational aspects of large decision analyses (Rousseau and Matheson [1967], Schlaifer [1971]), and procedures for doing "approximate" decision analyses, thus saving time and effort, have been developed (Howard [1971], Hammond [1974]). Perhaps more important, the number of reported applications is rapidly increasing, as indicated in the following section.

1.5 Applications of Decision Analysis

Some of the first decision analyses of important problems were in the oil and gas industry (Grayson [1960], Kaufman [1963]). However, for proprietary reasons, many of the completed decision analyses do not appear in the published literature. Fortunately, the essence of some of these analyses do appear in the form of "fictitious" analyses or case studies. Magee [1964a, 1964b] describes applications to capital investment decisions and Howard [1966] discusses a product introduction. A number of cases, representing experiences of the early 1960's, are found with analyses in Schlaifer [1968]. A more recent paper by Brown [1970] and a book by Newman [1971] review the contributions of DA through the 1960's.

Matheson [1969] summarizes three applications of DA: the introduction of a new product, the unmanned exploration of Mars by the US, and the possible introduction of nuclear power into the national power system of Mexico. The later study is discussed in more detail in a report by the Stanford Research Institute [1968]. Brown [1971] discussed specific applications of DA in three private corporations for problems such as acquisitions and mergers, corporate investments, and product planning. Bernhardt [1972] describes a disappointing experience with the use of DA and indicates some pitfalls to be avoided.

In the past few years, there have been a few more published decision analyses of problems faced by segments of government. These include the possibility of seeding hurricanes threatening the coast of the United States (Howard *et al.* [1972]) and metropolitan airport development in Mexico City (de Neufville and Keeney [1972]).

2. THE AXIOMS OF DECISION ANALYSIS

In this section, the axiomatic foundations of DA are stated. The principle that one should choose from the alternative courses of action in a manner that maximizes expected utility follows from these axioms. If one accepts the axioms as reasonable for a particular problem, then one's judgments and preferences must be quantified as specified in Axioms 4 and 5 below, in order to render the theory operational. Procedures for such assessments are discussed in Sections 4 and 5.

Before stating the axioms of DA, we must define our notation. A *simple lottery*, written $L(x_1, p, x_2)$ is a probabilistic event characterized by two possible consequences, which will be designated by x_1 and x_2, and their respective probabilities of occurrence, designated by p and $1 - p$. The symbols $\succ$, $\sim$, and $\succeq$ will be read "is preferred to," "is indifferent to," and "is either preferred to or indifferent to," respectively. Thus, $x_1 \sim L(x_2, p, x_3)$ says that x_1 is indifferent to the lottery which yields either x_2 with probability p or x_3

with probability $1 - p$. Let us now formally state a set of axioms for DA, which are only slightly modified from the formulation of Pratt *et al.* [1965].

Axiom 1: *Existence of Relative Preferences.* For every pair of consequences x_1 and x_2, the decision maker will have preferences such that either $x_1 \sim x_2, x_1 \succ x_2$, or $x_2 \succ x_1$.

Axiom 2: *Transitivity.* For any lotteries L_1, L_2, and L_3, the following hold:
(a) $L_1 \sim L_2$ and $L_2 \sim L_3$ implies that $L_1 \sim L_3$
(b) $L_1 \succ L_2$ and $L_2 \sim L_3$ implies that $L_1 \succ L_3$, etc.

Since a consequence can be interpreted as a degenerate lottery (i.e., $p = 1$), axioms 1 and 2 together imply that the decision maker has a ranking of the relative desirability of the various possible consequences. They do not say that he can articulate this, nor do they require that this ranking be stationary over time. Let us designate as x° a consequence which is not preferred to any of the other consequences for a problem, and as x^* a consequence which is at least as preferred as each of the other consequences. Therefore, one possibility is that x° and x^* designate the least and most preferred consequences, although they may represent hypothetical consequences such that $x^* \succ x$ and $x \succ x^\circ$, for all possible x. We now continue with the axioms.

Axiom 3: *Comparison of Simple Lotteries.* If, for the decision-maker $x_1 \succ x_2$, then
(a) $L_1(x_1, p_1, x_2) \succ L_2(x_1, p_2, x_2)$ if $p_1 > p_2$,
(b) $L_1(x_1, p_1, x_2) \sim L_2(x_1, p_2, x_2)$ if $p_1 = p_2$.

Axiom 4: *Quantification of Preferences.* For each possible consequence x, the decision-maker can specify a number $\pi(x)$, where $0 \leq \pi(x) \leq 1$, such that $x \sim L(x^*, \pi(x), x^\circ)$.

Axioms 3 and 4, taken together, establish a measure of the relative desirability of the various consequences to the decision-maker. The $\pi(x)$ value, or indifference probability, as it is called, is that measure.

Axiom 5: *Quantification of Judgmental Uncertainties.* For each possible event E which may affect the eventual consequence of a decision, the decision-maker can specify a number $P(E)$, where $0 \leqslant P(E) \leqslant 1$, such that he is indifferent between $L(x^*, P(E), x^\circ)$ and the situation where he receives x^* if event E occurs and x° if E does not occur.

It may be possible to make a large sample survey to obtain reasonable estimates for the probabilities of various events. However, as we have indicated previously, in many important problems this may not be the case. Axiom 5 provides a mechanism for obtaining the necessary judgmental probabilities in both of these situations. The probabilities $P(E)$ obey the axioms of probability theory so all the results of that area can be applied in analyzing problems.

Axiom 6: Substitutability. If a decision problem is modified by replacing one consequence or lottery by another consequence or lottery which the decision-maker finds indifferent to the first, then he should be indifferent to both the old and the modified decision problems.

Axiom 7: Equivalence of Conditional and Unconditional Preferences. Let L_1 and L_2 designate lotteries which are possible only if event E occurs. After it is known whether or not E occurred, the decision maker must have the same preferences between L_1 and L_2 as he had before it was known whether E occurred.

As indicated, the measure $\pi(x)$ in Axiom 4 indicates the relative preferences for x. Clearly, since the standards x° and x^* for measuring $\pi(x)$ are somewhat arbitrary, different π functions may be assessed for a specific decision-maker in a particular situation. However, to be consistent with these seven axioms, all possible functions must be positive linear transformations of each other. Any positive linear transformation of π of the form

$$u(x) = a + b\,\pi(x), \qquad b > 0, \tag{1}$$

is referred to as a utility scale for consequences x. The quantity $u(x)$ is said to be the utility of consequence x. If one accepts the above axioms one *should* always choose alternatives that maximize expected utility. There are no alternative procedures for making decisions consistent with these axioms.

Since maximizing expected utility is equivalent to maximizing the expected value of π in Eq. (1), the arbitrary choice of x^* and x° has no influence on the actual decision chosen. Utility provides a relative scale analogous to the temperature scales, and two scales which are positive linear transformations of each other are identical for decision-making purposes.

3. THE METHODOLOGY OF DECISION ANALYSIS

The methodology for analyzing a decision problem using DA is summarized in this section. Essentially, we are illustrating the fourth step of DA outlined in Section 1, assuming the problem has been structured and judgmental probabilities and utilities have been assessed. The development closely follows similar material in Pratt *et al.* [1965], Howard [1968], and Tribus [1969], which may be referred to for slightly different treatments.

Before proceeding, one must outline the problem. The decision-maker has some decisions which must be made; the desirability of each depends on the "states of the world." For instance, the desirability of drilling or not drilling for oil depends on whether "oil is present" or "oil is not present." To gain information about the true states of the world, it is possible for the decision-maker to conduct a number of different experiments. Each experiment has a monetary cost. As an eventual result of the experimentation and subsequent decisions, consequences of interest to the decision-maker, which depend on the state of the world, occur. However, at the time of decision-making, there is uncertainty as to which consequence will eventually result. Hence, we want our methodology to help answer the following questions:

(a) With no experimentation, which decision is best?
(b) Should the decision maker experiment, and if so, which experiment is best?
(c) What is the maximum that should be paid for a particular experiment?
(d) What is the maximum the decision-maker should pay for any amount of experimental information?

A graphical display of a structured decision problem is given by the decision tree in Fig. 1. To illustrate our notation, let us look at a typical branch of the tree. Beginning on the left, first the decision maker must choose an experiment e_r costing c_r or no experiment e_0 for no cost c_0. Conditional on this choice, an outcome o_t is observed. The conditional probability distribution, p_r, of the various outcomes given e_r describes the likelihoods of these outcomes. Once this outcome is known, another decision d_i must be chosen. Conditional on this, the likelihoods that state of the world s_j prevails is given by the condi-

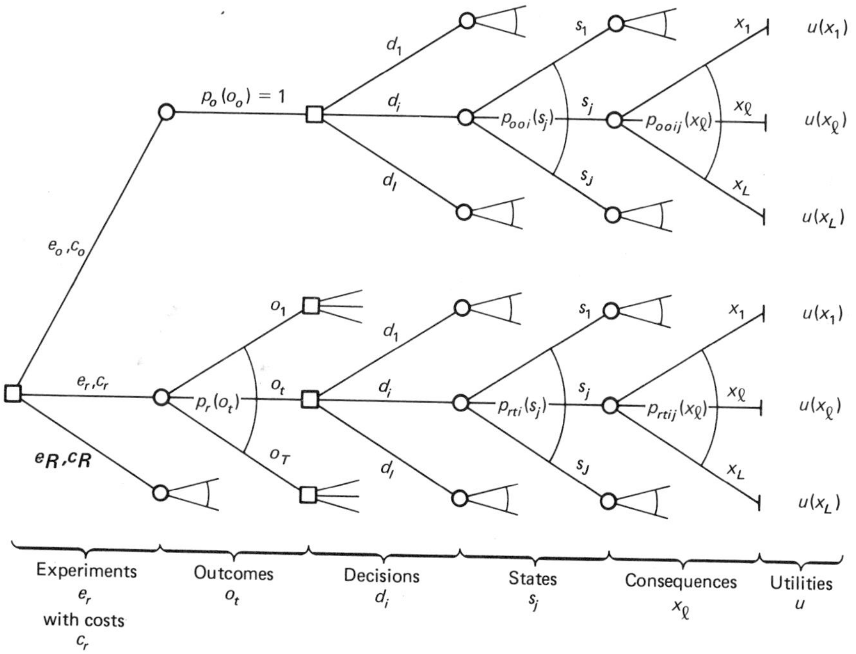

Fig. 1. Section of a decision tree.

tional probability distribution p_{rti}, where the r refers to the experiment, t to its outcome, and i to the decision. Finally, conditional on all that went on before, a consequence x occurs. The probability of the various consequences is quantified with the conditional probability distribution p_{rtij}, where j refers to the state of the world. The relative desirability of the possible consequences is given by the utility function $u(x)$.

Although the notation is cumbersome, it is a simple matter to analyze such a decision tree. Notice there are only two types of *nodes* in Fig. 1: decision nodes, designated by the boxes, and chance nodes, designated by the circles. Beginning at the right of the figure, one can work backward through the tree, using the principle that expected utility should be maximized. At any chance node, one uses the probability distribution originating at that node to calculate the expected utility associated with the node. At any decision node, one selects the alternative that leads to the highest expected utility and assigns this utility to the decision node.

3.1 Analyzing the General Decision Problem

Let us analyze the tree in Fig. 1 to illustrate the method. Here we will use the notation $\bar{u}_{rtij}$, for instance, to denote the expected utility of selecting experiment e_r, observing outcome o_t, choosing decision d_i, and having state s_j prevail. Similarly $\bar{u}_{rt}$ will designate the expected utility of choosing experiment e_r and observing o_t. In terms of this notation, clearly $\bar{u}_{rtijl}$ is $u(x_l)$ as given by the utility function u. Then

$$\bar{u}_{rtij} = \int_x u(x_l)\, p_{rtij}(x_l) \tag{2}$$

where $\int_x$ designates summation for discrete problems and integration for continuous problems with respect to x. Similarly, the expected utility of choosing e_r, observing o_t, and selecting d_i is

$$\bar{u}_{rti} = \int_s \bar{u}_{rtij}\, p_{rti}(s_j). \tag{3}$$

At the decision node, one selects the decision d_i leading to the highest expected utility. Hence

$$\bar{u}_{tr} = \max_{d_i} \bar{u}_{rti}. \tag{4}$$

Backing up one more stage, the expected utility of choosing experiment e_r is given by

$$\bar{u}_r = \int_0 \bar{u}_{rt}\, p_r(o_t). \tag{5}$$

Thus the best experiment e_{r*} is that with the highest expected utility, which is given by

$$\bar{u}_{r*} = \max_{e_r} \bar{u}_r.$$

Once r^* is chosen and some o_t occurs, the optimal decision is then d_{i*} defined by

$$\bar{u}_{r*ti*} \equiv \max_{d_i} \bar{u}_{r*ti}.$$

The desired result of a DA is a complete decision strategy, indicating the option that should be selected at each decision node. This is conceptually easy to obtain if the axioms of DA are followed. Any decision problem can be structured into sequences of decision and chance nodes. Hence, by using the procedures described above—calculating expected utilities at chance nodes and selecting to maximize expected utility at decision nodes—a problem with as many stages as necessary can be analyzed.

3.2 Selecting a Decision Strategy

Let us now return to answer the four questions posed at the beginning of this section.

1. The Optimal Strategy with No Experimentation. The expected utility of initial experiment e_r, observing outcome o_t, and selecting decision d_i is $\bar{u}_{rti}$ as given by Eq. (3). The optimal strategy with no experimentation is the decision d_i which maximizes $\bar{u}_{rti}$ when $r = 0$. Recall e_0 designates "no experiment" and we can label $t = 0$ to indicate "no information gained." Hence, $\bar{u}_{00i}$ is by definition the expected utility of no experiment and selecting decision d_i. The optimal decision with no experimentation is d_i^* defined by

$$\bar{u}_{00i*} \equiv \max_{d_i} \bar{u}_{00i}. \tag{6}$$

Note that by definition, $u_0 = \bar{u}_{00i*}$.

2. Selecting an Experiment. From Eq. (5), the optimal experiment is e_{r*} defined by

$$\bar{u}_{r*} \equiv \max_{e_r} \bar{u}_r. \tag{7}$$

If $r^* = 0$, then e_0 is the optimum strategy and it is best not to experiment.

3. The Expected Value of Sample Information. Recall that a cost c_r was associated with each experiment e_r. This represented the cost of conducting the experiment and processing the information. An important question is: how much money is e_r worth? If the only option to experiment was e_r, at cost c_r, then one should select this option if the expected utility of e_r is greater than the expected utility of no experiment e_0. That is if $\bar{u}_r > \bar{u}_0$, the experiment e_r is worth the cost c_r. As the cost c_r of the experiment e_r monotonically increases from zero, the expected utility $\bar{u}_r$ decreases. This can be seen from Eq. (2) because the probabilities of greater costs, encoded in $p_{rtij}(x)$, increase when c_r increases. This lower expected utility is carried through Eq. (3) and Eq. (4) to $\bar{u}_r$ in Eq. (5). For some cost, call it c_r^*, of experiment e_r,

$$\bar{u}_r = \bar{u}_0. \tag{8}$$

This cost c_r^* is called the expected value of experiment e_r. For any $c_r < c_r^*$, it would be better to choose experiment e_r than not to experiment. Similarly, if $c_r > c_r^*$, the decision maker should prefer not experimenting rather than experiment e_r.

4. The Expected Value of Perfect Information. It is often computationally difficult to calculate the expected value of sample information. Our interest in the sample information is that it provides knowledge about the likelihoods of various possible consequences.

If experiment e_r provided insight only on the state of the world s_j and if we could determine that it would only be worth \$10,000 to know the true value of s_j, then it would be clear that experiment e_r could be worth no more than \$10,000. It is sometimes computationally rather simple to determine such an expected value of perfect information and use it to rule out some possible experiments.

To be a bit more concrete, recall the oil drilling example at the beginning of this section. The states of the world might be categorized as "oil is present" or "oil is not present." Experiments could be conducted to provide information about the presence of oil. However, in general, their information is not perfect. If one could determine the maximum amount one would pay for a knowledge of which state of the world prevails, then clearly it would not be reasonable to pay more than this to obtain sample information.

Suppose we can conduct an experiment e_R which will give us perfect information for a cost c_R. This experiment will indicate which state s_j prevails. If state s_j prevails, the optimal decision, label it $d_{i^*(j)}$, is given by

$$\bar{u}_{i^*(j)} = \max_{d_i} \bar{\bar{u}}_{i(j)}, \tag{9}$$

where $\bar{\bar{u}}_{i(j)}$ designates the expected utility of decision d_i, given state s_j prevails. Since we are assuming no sample information is taken, $\bar{\bar{u}}_{i(j)}$ equals $\bar{u}_{00ij}$. The probability distribution $p_{00i}(s_j)$ indicates the likelihood that state s_j will be found to prevail, assuming e_R has been conducted. Thus, the expected utility of obtaining the perfect information is

$$\bar{u}_R = \int_S \bar{\bar{u}}_{i^*(j)}\, p_{00i}(s_j). \tag{10}$$

As was the case with sample information, as the cost c_R of the perfect information increases, its expected utility decreases. For some cost c_{R^*}, the expected utility of the perfect information equals the expected utility of no information. That is

$$\bar{u}_{R^*} = \bar{u}_0. \tag{11}$$

The cost c_{R^*} is the expected value of perfect information. It represents the maximum amount one should pay for perfect information, and hence, it is an upper bound on the amount one should pay for any sample information.

In complex problems, the state of the world may be characterized in terms of many descriptors. That is, such a description may be multidimensional. Using ideas analogous to those above, one can determine the expected value of perfect information for any one or more dimensions.

3.3 The Certainty Equivalent

It is difficult to interpret utility directly, both because of the arbitrariness of scale and because it represents an aggregation of the decision-makers preferences over several measures of effectiveness. When the decision maker wishes to make a meaningful intuitive comparison of two alternatives with expected utilities u_1 and u_2 respectively, it is necessary to return to the consequences. A certainty equivalent of an alternative with utility u_i is any consequence x_i such that

$$u(x_i) = u_i. \tag{12}$$

Thus, if x_1 and x_2 are certainty equivalents for alternatives 1 and 2, respectively, a comparison of x_1 and x_2 should provide some meaning to their relative impact. Going further, if x_1 and x_2 are chosen to be identical on all measures but the first, which may be selected to be cost, the differences in cost of the two certainty equivalents might give a clearer picture of the degree to which one is preferred.

4. QUANTIFICATION OF JUDGMENTAL UNCERTAINTIES

The judgmental probability $p(E)$ of an event E is defined by the fifth axiom of DA in Section 2. It indicates the decision-maker's degree of belief in whether an event will occur and is based on his willingness to act upon this belief. A decision-maker may generate his subjective probabilities for various possible events from a number of sources. These include a knowledge of physical phenomena, empirical data, the output of models relating various factors, and the judgment of various individuals including himself, particularly specialists in the field of concern.

4.1 Judgmental Probability Based on Physical Phenomena

In some situations, one would reason that all of the possible events of an experiment are equally likely. Therefore, if there are N possible events, the probability of each is $1/N$. Based on such reasoning, we usually assign probabilities of $\frac{1}{2}$ and $\frac{1}{6}$ to the occurrence of heads on the flip of a fair coin or the occurrence of a "six" on the roll of a fair die. Such probabilities, which can be verified by exhaustive experiments, are often referred to as objective probabilities. Most individuals would be in agreement on these probabilities. By definition, they are also subjective probabilities if one believes in them and is willing to act accordingly.

4.2 Judgmental Probability Based on Data and Models

If data exists concerning the possible occurrence of events of interest, it can be used in assigning judgmental probabilities. Let $E_1, E_2, \ldots, E_n$ be a set of mutually exclusive and collectively exhaustive events. Then if we have observed N occurrences of either event E_1 or E_2 or ... or E_n and if N_i of these occurrences were event E_i, then we might assign a probability to E_i equal to N_i/N. For example, if 10,000 of the most recent 25,000 fire alarms in a city were false, then one may wish to assign 0.4 to the probability that an alarm is false. The manner for combining such data with judgmental assessments is addressed in Section 4.5.

In some situations the data may be more detailed. One might build an analytical or simulation model to relate various input variables to important output variables. With the model, data on the probabilities of occurrences of the input variables can be used to generate probabilities of desired output variables. The theory of derived probability distributions is employed in the case of analytical models (Parzen [1960], Drake [1967]), and Monte Carlo techniques are used with simulation (Gaver [1974], Gordon [1974]).

4.3 Assessing the Probability of a Discrete Event

Especially in strategic one-of-a-kind decisions, there is often little historical data to help obtain the probabilities of relevant events. Judgmental assessments must be made for either the input variables to a model or directly for the quantities of interest. To illustrate the procedure, let us suppose E is the event of interest and $p(E)$ is its judgmental probability, which is as yet unspecified.

First, as shown in Fig. 2, set up two lotteries, $L_1 = (x^*, p, x^\circ)$ and L_2 which yields either x^* if E occurs or x° if E does not occur, where x^* is chosen to be preferable to x°. Then, for a specified value of p, ask the decision-maker which lottery is preferred or if they are indifferent. If L_1 is preferred, reduce p and repeat the question; if L_2 is preferred, increase p and repeat. After a few iter-

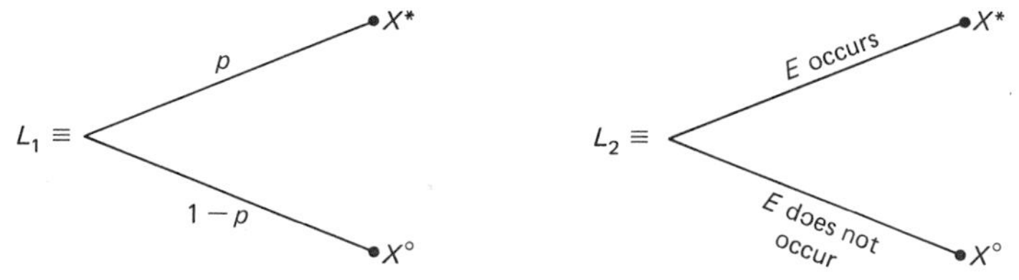

Fig. 2. Quantifying the judgmental probability of a discrete event.

ations, the value of p, call it p', should be found such that L_1 is indifferent to L_2. The decision-maker's judgmental probability for event E is p'. If E_i, $i = 1, 2, \ldots, n$ are a set of mutually exclusive and collectively exhaustive events, then $\sum_i p(E_i)$ equals one for consistency. In practice one should check this and revise estimates if it is not true. Raiffa [1968] has an interesting discussion of these aspects.

4.4 Judgmental Assessment of a Probability Distribution

The most common approach for assessing a probability distribution over quantities which take on a continuum of values is called the fractile method. With this approach, one solicits a few points on the cumulative probability distribution function of the quantity of interest and then "fits" a curve to these points.

Suppose we wish to obtain a probability distribution for the quantity X, where small x will designate specific amounts of X. For instance, X may be "profits" and then x may be \$100,000. First one tries to assess the "0.5 fractile," the amount $x_{.5}$ such that the probability X is less than $x_{.5}$ is 0.5. One asks the decision-maker (or a designated individual), "For what amount x is it equally likely that X will be more or less than this amount?" The answer, which might be arrived at using the converging idea indicated in the previous subsection, is $x_{.5}$. Next we would ask "Given in fact that X is less than $x_{.5}$, what amount x divides the interval $[-\infty, x_{.5}]$ into equally likely parts?" The response is $x_{.25}$, the 0.25 fractile. Of course, it follows that the probability X is less than $x_{.25}$ should be 0.25. Similarly $x_{.75}$ is obtained. Finally we try to assess $x_{.01}$ and $x_{.99}$ by asking, for instance, "What value of x would you select such that the probability that X will be less than this value is 0.01?" The answer is $x_{.01}$.

Continuing in this fashion, we can obtain more values x_k such that the probability P that $X \leqslant x_k$ is k. That is,

$$P(X \leqslant x_k) = k. \tag{13}$$

The points (x_k, k) may be plotted on a graph, as illustrated in Fig. 3, and a smooth curve connecting them will be the judgmental cumulative probability

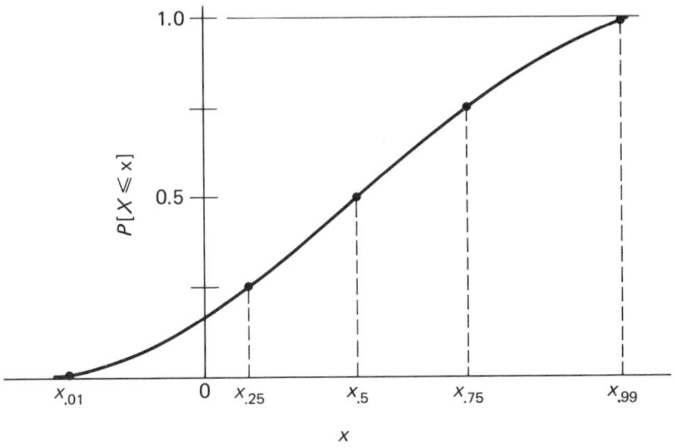

Fig. 3. A judgmental cumulative probability distribution.

distribution function for X. The derivative of this is the judgmental probability density function.

4.5 Combining Judgmental Assessments and Sample Information

Often it may be important to combine judgmental assessments with relevant data. Bayes' theorem is a relationship which allows us to revise probabilistic assessments to incorporate new information which has become available. To begin, note that all of our probabilistic assessments are encoded by either a probability mass function $p(E)$, for the case of discrete events, or a probability density function $f(x)$, when continuous consequences are involved.

For the discrete case, Bayes' theorem is

$$p'(E) = P(E|S) = \frac{P(S|E)\,p(E)}{\sum_E P(S|E)\,p(E)}, \tag{14}$$

where S designates sample information (i.e., data), so $P(E|S)$ means the probability of E, given S, and $P(S|E)$ is the probability of S, given E. The function $p(E)$ and $p'(E)$ are referred to respectively as the prior probability mass function and the posterior probability mass function.

Analogously for continuous problems, Bayes' theorem is

$$f'(x) = \frac{f_x(S|x)\,f(x)}{\int_x f_x(S|x)\,f(x)\,dx}, \tag{15}$$

where $f_x(S|x)$ designates the probability density for sample information S given

x, $f'(x)$ is the posterior probability density function given S, and $f(x)$ is the prior probability density function. The next section suggests methods for simplifying the implementation of Eqs. (14) and (15).

4.6 Practical Considerations in Assessing Judgmental Probabilities

Since the judgmental probability assessments of an individual are not always logically consistent on the first try, the analyst must check for internal inconsistencies and point them out to the individual concerned (see Raiffa [1968] and Schlaifer [1969]). Recent work by Tversky and Kahneman [1973] has indicated that people systematically employ a number of heuristic biases in their assessment of uncertain quantities. A knowledge of these biases is a first step in developing procedures to avoid them. Finally, when one relies on the judgment of "experts," it is important to promote their openness and honesty. This has led to the development of reward functions or "scoring rules" to calibrate such assessors (Winkler [1969]).

An operational difficulty with judgmental probability assessments is that the results can be tedious to use directly. Fortunately, some of the results of statistical decision theory greatly simplify both the assessment process and the ensuing analysis. The basic idea is to select $p(E)$ or $f(x)$ from particular families of probability functions that are easy to work with.

Let us illustrate this with $f(x)$ although the ideas are relevant to $p(E)$ also. It would be nice if $f(x)$ were a member of a family of probability densities with only a few parameters, which we will designate by $\boldsymbol{\lambda}$. Thus, one can write $f(x/\boldsymbol{\lambda})$. Then only $\boldsymbol{\lambda}$ needs to be assessed to completely specify f. For instance, a member of the normal probability family is completely specified from the mean and variance. It is generally much easier to estimate these two parameters than to assess a complete cumulative probability distribution as discussed in Section 4.4. If the family is rich enough in the sense that a wide range of judgments can be reasonably expressed by some member of that family, it is probably not a gross error to initially assume that the judgmental uncertainties can be modeled with a member of the family.

The other advantage of selecting a member of a particular family is that it might make updating via Bayes' theorem relatively simple. For instance, for certain families and certain sampling techniques, the posterior probability density $f'(x)$ in Eq. (15) will be a member of the same family as the prior probability density $f(x)$. That is, these densities could be written as $f(x \mid \boldsymbol{\lambda}')$ and $f(x \mid \boldsymbol{\lambda})$ respectively. Furthermore, one can find $f'(x)$ by simply updating $\boldsymbol{\lambda}$ in a simple manner, depending on the sample data, to yield $\boldsymbol{\lambda}'$. A discussion of relevant considerations, as well as details of many specific cases, is found in Pratt *et al.* [1965].

5. ASSESSING UTILITIES

This section assumes there is a single measure of effectiveness X over which the decision-makers' preferences are to be assessed. Our problem is to assign a utility $u(x)$ to each possible consequence $x_1, x_2, \ldots$. If the set of consequences is discrete, one could directly assess their utilities by determining the $\pi(x)$ indifference probabilities defined by Axiom 4. However, since the number of possible consequences is usually large, it is necessary (and easier) to assess a utility function $u(x)$. A method for this is illustrated in this section.

For discussion purposes, a procedure for assessing utility functions might be divided into five steps:

1. preliminaries to actual assessment,
2. specifying the relevant qualitative characteristics,
3. specifying quantitative restrictions,
4. choosing a utility function,
5. checking for consistency.

5.1 Preliminaries to Actual Assessment

Assessing utility functions is perhaps more of an art than it is a science. The success one has in such attempts is closely linked with the analyst's ability to communicate with the decision-maker–to indicate the importance of this process, to enlist his support, and to make him feel comfortable with the assessment procedure.

Before the assessment of a utility function, the concept of DA should be discussed. It should be made clear to the decision-maker that the preferences of interest are his–that they represent his subjective feelings–and that there are no objectively correct preferences. At any time, if the decision maker feels uncomfortable with any of the information he has offered about his subjective feelings, it is perfectly all right–in fact, necessary for a correct analysis–for him to change his mind. This is one of the purposes of DA–to require the decision-maker to reflect on his preferences and, it is hoped, to straighten them out in his own mind.

5.2 Specifying the Relevant Qualitative Characteristics

The qualitative characteristics we are interested in are monotonicity and attitudes toward risk. To ascertain whether a monotonicity condition is appropriate is quite simple. One asks the decision-maker which is preferred between x_1 and x_2, where $x_2 > x_1$. Probably you, the assessor, would expect a certain answer to this question based on your own understanding of the consequences. If x_2 is preferred, you would tend to think preferences are monotonically increasing in attribute X. You would then just ask whether more of the attribute is always preferred to less of it.

Let us suppose preferences are monotonically increasing in X, as we expect the case to be with profits, for example. Then, one is said to be *risk averse* if, for all values of x_1 and x_2, the amount $(x_1 + x_2)/2$ is preferred to the lottery $L_1(x_1, \frac{1}{2}, x_2)$ yielding either x_1 or x_2 with equal probability. Notice that $(x_1 + x_2)/2$ is the expected value of L (as opposed to its expected utility). In addition, one is said to be *risk prone* (*risk neutral*) if the lottery L_1 is preferred to (is indifferent to) the amount $(x_1 + x_2)/2$ for all values of x_1 and x_2. These risk characteristics are useful in restricting the shape and the utility function illustrated in Fig. 4. A utility function is concave, convex, or linear, respectively, if the decision maker is risk averse, risk prone, or risk neutral.

To verify these risk properties, one might divide the possible domain of X into four equal segments with consequences designated x_0, x_1, x_2, x_3, and x_4. Then the decision-maker would be asked his preferences between the lotteries $L(x_i, \frac{1}{2}, x_j)$, $i = 0, 1, 2, 3$; $j = 1, 2, 3, 4$; $j > i$, and their respective expected values $(x_i + x_j)/2$. If all responses were consistent with one of the risk attitudes, it would be appropriate to assume this attitude prevailed.

There are more sophisticated risk properties which require the concept of the certainty equivalent. The *certainty equivalent* for a lottery $L(x_1, p, x_2)$ is the amount $\hat{x}$ which the decision-maker finds indifferent to L. The *risk premium* is defined as the expected value minus the certainty equivalent.

Suppose one is risk averse, and $\hat{x}$ and r are the certainty equivalent and risk premium, respectively, for the lottery $L(x_1, \frac{1}{2}, x_1 + h)$ where h is a positive amount. Then, clearly, $r = (x_1 + h/2) - \hat{x}$. One is said to be *constantly risk averse* if the risk premium for L does not depend on the value of x_1. In this case, if x_1 is increased by an increment k, then so must the certainty equivalent increase by the same amount k. As shown by Pratt [1964], if constant

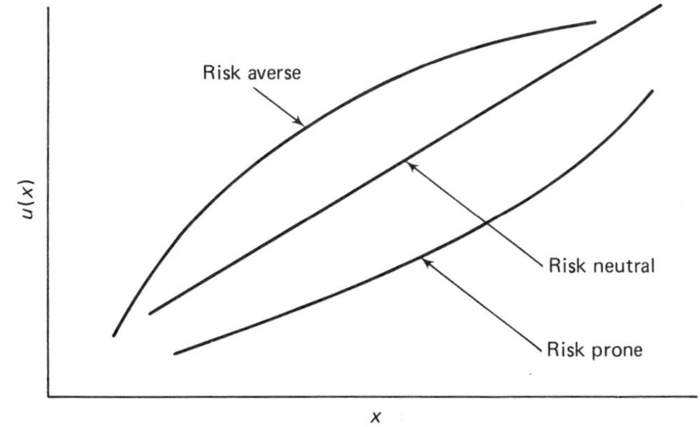

Fig. 4. Risk attitudes.

risk aversion obtains, the utility function must be of the form

$$u(x) = a + b(-e^{-cx}), \quad b > 0, \tag{16}$$

where a and b are the arbitrarily set scaling constants.

If, for the above lottery, the risk premium decreases (increases) as x_1 is increased, one is said to be *decreasingly risk averse* (*increasingly risk averse*). Pratt [1964] also discusses classes of utility functions possessing these types of risk attitudes. By exploiting the decision-maker's basic attitudes toward risk, one can completely characterize an individual's preferences by assessing a few parameters as indicated by Eq. (16).

5.3 Specifying Quantitative Restrictions

Specifying quantitative restrictions means determining a few points on the decision-maker's utility curve. Let us choose x^* and x°, as in Axiom 4, such that x^* is at least as preferred as each of the consequences which, in turn, is at least as preferred as x°. Then we can arbitrarily assign utilities to these two consequences for reference, subject to the condition that $u(x^*) > u(x^\circ)$. Next we wish to obtain a value of x (call it x_1) such that the decision-maker is indifferent between the consequence x_1 and the lottery $L_1(x^*, \frac{1}{2}, x^\circ)$. Then, because their utilities must be equal, we assign

$$u(x_1) = \tfrac{1}{2}\, u(x^*) + \tfrac{1}{2}\, u(x^\circ). \tag{17}$$

This gives us a third point on the utility graph, as illustrated in Fig. 5. Similarly, by assessing the decision-maker's certainty equivalents x_2 and x_3 for the lotteries $L_2(x^*, \frac{1}{2}, x_1)$ and $L_3(x_1, \frac{1}{2}, x^\circ)$, respectively, we obtain the utilities of two more points

$$u(x_2) = \tfrac{1}{2}\, u(x^*) + \tfrac{1}{2}\, u(x_1) \tag{18}$$

and

$$u(x_3) = \tfrac{1}{2}\, u(x_1) + \tfrac{1}{2}\, u(x^\circ). \tag{19}$$

Using this technique, we can always obtain the utility of a third consequence from the known utilities of two other consequences.

An important question is "how does one get the certainty equivalents?" This requires an interactive procedure, where the decision maker must make a series of choices between the specified lottery and specified consequences. For instance, we would choose an amount x_a and ask whether the decision-maker preferred x_a for certain or the lottery L_1. Regardless of which is preferred, it should be possible to identify whether x should be increased or decreased to find the desired certainty equivalent x_1. Suppose it was obvious that the true x_1 would be greater than x_a. We would select an x_b such that $x_b > x_a$ and ask whether x_b or L_1 is preferred. Based on this response, again we should know whether x should be increased or decreased. One continues in this manner, progressively "converging" to x_1, the consequence indifferent to L_1.

Schlaifer [1969] makes two important pragmatic points to keep in mind in assigning utilities to consequences. First, the consequences used in the questioning must be meaningful to the decision-maker. Second, the spread of the consequences in the simple lotteries must be large enough to be meaningfully different. If these conditions are not satisfied, the decision-maker's responses are of little use in specifying his preferences.

5.4 Choosing a Utility Function

Once the qualitative characteristics are determined, we hope to be able to select a parametric family of utility functions which satisfies these properties. Let us designate such a family of utility functions as $u(x/\boldsymbol{\lambda})$, where $\boldsymbol{\lambda}$ represents the parameters. Then the choice of a specific utility function is reduced to selecting the parameter values. This is simpler and more consistent than specifying a complete utility function, and allows one to do sensitivity analysis without unnecessary computation. We would generally expect three parameters to be sufficient in most situations, since a wide range of risk characteristics can be modeled with three or less parameters.

Using this form and the previously assessed parts on the utility curve, we can use (17), for example, to see

$$u(x_1 \,|\, \boldsymbol{\lambda}) = \tfrac{1}{2}\, u(x^* \,|\, \boldsymbol{\lambda}) + \tfrac{1}{2}\, u(x^\circ \,|\, \boldsymbol{\lambda}), \tag{20}$$

which is one equation with the number of unknowns equal to the number of parameters. Using assessed certainty equivalents, we generate the same number of equations as unknowns and solve them for the parameters to obtain the utility function as indicated in Figure 5.

Meyer and Pratt [1968] developed a procedure for checking the internal consistency of the combined set of qualitative and quantitative restrictions placed on the utility function. Using such ideas, Schlaifer [1971] has a series of computer programs for choosing a utility function which is consistent with the decision-maker's risk attitudes and empirically assessed preferences.

5.5 Checking for Consistency

There are many different consistency checks which can be used to detect "errors" in the decision-maker's utility function. By an error, we mean the utility function we have assessed for him does not adequately represent his true preferences. Separate ways to ascertain whether certain qualitative characteristics, such as risk aversion, hold for a particular individual, can be used as a check on each

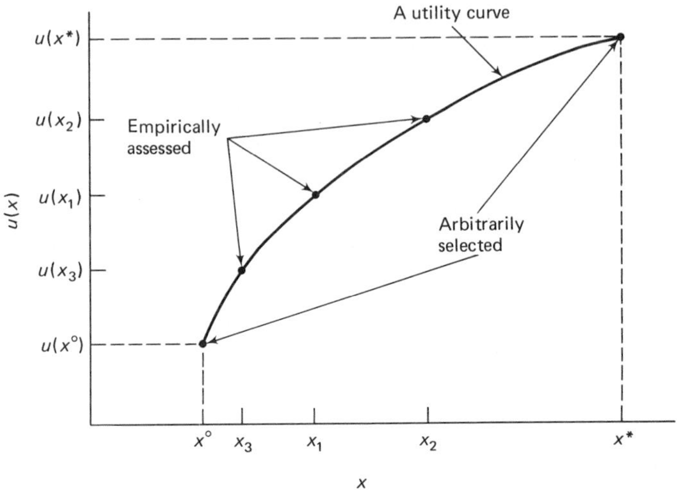

Fig. 5. A utility function.

other. One generally useful check involves asking the decision-maker his preference between any lottery and any consequence, or between two lotteries. In both cases, the expected utility of the preferred situation as calculated from his utility function must be greater in order to be consistent. Whenever the analyst feels uncomfortable about any aspect of the decision-maker's utility function, it would be useful to check this aspect and make any appropriate adjustments.

One of the most common and important errors made in assessing utility functions involves fitting the parameters using certainty equivalents of lotteries whose spread is too narrow. For instance, suppose the decision-maker says his certainty equivalent for the lottery $L(200, \frac{1}{2}, 0)$ is 80, and that a constantly risk-averse utility function is specified from this. Then, if we extrapolate to find the certainty equivalent implied by the resulting utility function for the lottery $L(1000, \frac{1}{2}, 0)$ it will often be much less than what the decision-maker would empirically assess. The utility function might imply the certainty equivalent is 250, whereas the decision-maker would state it should be more like 400. To avoid this problem, the parameters should be fit using lotteries with realistically wide spreads for the problem at hand.

6. ADVANCED ISSUES IN DECISION ANALYSIS

Three very important problems often faced by the decision analyst are what I will refer to as the multiattribute problem, the time preferences problem, and the group decision problem. Under certain conditions, each of these problems can be modeled by considering the consequences as being represented by N-tuples

$\mathbf{x} = (x_1, x_2, \ldots, x_N)$, where x_n denotes an arbitrary level of attribute (measure of effectiveness) X_n. As in other cases, if the axioms of DA are appropriate, it follows that one should choose alternatives to maximize expected utility. The added complexity occurs in trying to generate the required judgmental probability distributions for each alternative (which in the general case are N-variable probability density functions) and the utility function $u(x)$ over the N attributes.

Often one would construct a computer model to assist in assigning probabilities to the consequences of each alternative (see Howard [1968]), or it might be necessary to empirically assess these using techniques similar to the single dimensional case covered in Section 4. (See, for example, Keeney [1973a].) Because the formalization of the preference structure is more unique to DA than to probabilistic analysis, let us briefly survey this work.

6.1 The Multiattribute Problem

If possible, one would like to break down the direct assessment of preferences over the N-attributes into smaller problems in which assessments can be made over subsets of the N-attributes, and then put together. For instance, it would be convenient if the additive formulation

$$u(\mathbf{x}) = \sum_{n=1}^{N} k_n u_n(x_n), \tag{21}$$

where u_n is a utility function over attribute X_n and k_n is a scaling constant, were appropriate. More generally, we want to find a simple function f such that

$$u(\mathbf{x}) = f[u_1(x_1),\ u_2(x_2), \ldots, u_N(x_N)], \tag{22}$$

in order to reduce the preference assessment to a manageable task.

The usual procedure is to make various independent assumptions which imply a particular functional form of f. Then, of course, in any specific problem, the assumptions must first be verified. An elementary discussion of the three major types of assumptions used in these situations is found in Keeney [1973b]. MacCrimmon [1973] and Section 4 of the preceding chapter by Fishburn [1977] survey many of the main results and provide excellent bibliographies of contributions in the area. A few very recent developments are found in Boyd [1973], Fishburn [1974], Fischer [1973], Huber [1973], Keeney [1974], and Krantz *et al.* [1971].

6.2 Preferences Over Time

The basic question concerning preferences over time asks how the utility of a consequence $\mathbf{x}^{t_0}$ at time t_0 (say the present) relates to the utility of $\mathbf{x}^{t_i}$ at some other time t_i in the future. If one denotes by $\mathbf{x}^t = (x_1^t, x_2^t, \ldots, x_N^t)$ the consequence at time t, then assuming it is appropriate to discretize time periods, a complete consequence might be designated as $\mathbf{x} = (\mathbf{x}^1, \mathbf{x}^2, \ldots, \mathbf{x}^t)$. The objective is to assess a utility function $u(\mathbf{x})$.

A very special case of time preferences is that in which $\mathbf{x}^t$ designates only monetary consequences. In this situation, it may be appropriate to use discounting to obtain net present values that may serve as the evaluation measure. There is, at most, little justification for discounting attributes other than monetary ones, and Meyer [1969] indicates the justification is weak even in this case.

If one treats the formulation of discrete time preferences as a multiattribute problem, the results referenced in the proceeding section might be directly applicable. Meyer [1969] used such an approach in addressing the problem of time preferences when $N = 1$, namely, X_1^t was consumption in time period t. Bell [1974] used similar assumptions in looking at the single period case. Using a different approach, Lancaster [1963] analyzed single period time preferences, and Koopmans [1960], Koopmans *et al.* [1964], and Pollard [1969] studied the multiple period case. They avoided uncertainty explicitly and utilized stationary assumptions to derive a net present value for each possible consequence in the future. One can then assess a utility function for the current time that incorporates the decision-maker's attitudes toward risk.

6.3 Group Decision Problems

In the case of multiple decision-makers, it may be helpful for each of the individuals in the decision-making group to make his own analysis. Comparison of these individuals analyses will indicate differences and concurrences among the group members. For instance, there may be agreement on the possible impacts of the different alternatives, but disagreement on what values to assign to them. The identification of such differences should contribute toward elevating discussion to a constructive level. The model itself can be a mechanism for identifying "better solutions," in that it provides a methodology for examining proposed compromise solutions and indicating areas in which they may be weak. As pointed out by Raiffa [1968], the axioms of DA are not so appealing for group decisions. Nevertheless, in certain situations they may be appropriate. By interpreting attribute X_n from the multiattribute problem as an indicator of the preferences of the nth individual of the group, Harsanyi [1955] and Keeney and Kirkwood [1973] have developed group utility functions that aggregate the individual's utility functions.

Many extremely interesting attempts have been made to aggregate individuals' preferences into a group preference. Perhaps the best known is Arrow [1951, 1963]. He proves that there is no general procedure for obtaining a group ranking of alternatives from individual group members' rankings that is consistent with five "reasonable assumptions." Fleming [1952] and Fishburn [1969] have each postulated conditions that imply ordinal group utility functions (ranking of the consequences to the group) can be written as the sum of the ordinal utility functions of the group members. The impact of uncertainty and attitudes toward risk were considered by Nash [1950] in suggesting arbitration solutions. One of the fundamental difficulties in group decision-making concerns the interpersonal comparison of preferences (Luce and Raiffa [1957]). Recently, Sen [1970] has indicated that some useful results for group decision-making can be obtained without complete interpersonal comparison of utility. Spetzler [1968] presents an interesting attempt to obtain an actual corporate utility function from a group.

7. THE FUTURE

Many of the specific techniques of DA are currently developed to the degree that they capture most of the complexities of complicated problems. To be sure, better methodological procedures concerning multiattribute preferences, group effects, assessments of information, software systems, etc. will continue to be produced. The challenge now is to successfully apply the theory to worthwhile problems and to disseminate these experiences to provide improvement in the art of application. If this is done, DA has the potential to significantly improve our decision-making process.*

REFERENCES

1. Arrow, K. J., *Social Choice and Individual Values*, Wiley, New York, (1951); 2nd Edition (1963).
2. Bell, D. E., "Evaluating Time Streams of Income," *Omega* **2**: 691–699 (1974).
3. Bernhardt, K. L., "American Auto Inc.: Case Study of a False Start in PDA," Marketing Science Institute (1972).
4. Blackwell, D. and M. A. Girshick, *Theory of Games and Statistical Decisions*, Wiley, New York (1954).
5. Boyd, D., "Interactive Preference Assessment for Decisions with Multi-Attribute Outcomes," Fourth Research Conference on Subjective Probability, Utility, and Decision Making, Rome, Italy (1973).
6. Brown, R. V., "Do Managers Find Decision Theory Useful?," *Harvard Bus. Rev.* **48**: 78–89 (1970).
7. ——, "Marketing Applications of Personalist Decision Analysis," Marketing Science Institute (1971).
8. Davidson, D., P. Suppes, and S. Siegel, *Decision Making: An Experimental Approach*, Stanford University Press, Stanford, California (1957).
9. DeFinetti, B., "La prévision: ses lois logiques, ses sources subjectives," *Annales de*

*The comments by Alvin W. Drake, Lisa Greenbaum, and Craig W. Kirkwood on earlier drafts of this paper were very helpful.

l'Institut Henri Poincare **7**: 1–68 (1937); English translation by H. E. Kyburg, Jr., in H. E. Kyburg, Jr. and H. E. Smokler, (eds.), *Studies in Subjective Probability*, Wiley, New York (1964).
10. de Neufville, R. and R. L. Keeney, "Use of Decision Analysis in Airport Development for Mexico City," in *Analysis of Public Systems*, Drake, A. W., Keeney, R. L., and Morse, P. M. (eds.), M.I.T. Press, Cambridge, Massachusetts (1972).
11. Drake, A. W., *Fundamentals of Applied Probability Theory*, McGraw-Hill, New York (1967).
12. Edwards, W., "The Theory of Decision Making," *Psychological Bull.* **51**: 380–417 (1954).
13. ——, "Conservatism in Human Information Processing," in *Formal Representations of Human Judgment*, B. Klein-Muntz, (ed.), Wiley, New York (1968).
14. Fellner, W., *Probability and Profit: A Study of Economic Behavior Along Bayesian Lines*, Richard D. Irwin, Homewood, Illinois (1965).
15. Fischer, G. W., and W. Edwards, "Technological Aids for Inference, Evaluation, and Decision Making: A Review of Research and Experience," Engineering Psychology Laboratory, University of Michigan (1973).
16. Fischer, G. W., "Multidimensional Utility Models for Riskless and Risky Decision Making: Theory and Experimental Application," Duke University, Durham, North Carolina (1973).
17. Fishburn, P. C., *Decision and Value Theory*, Wiley, New York (1964).
18. ——, "Independence in Utility Theory With Whole Product Sets," *Operations Res.* **13**: 28–45 (1965).
19. ——, "Preferences, Summation, and Social Welfare Functions," *Management Sci.* **16**: 179–186 (1969).
20. ——, "Von Neumann-Morgenstern Utility Functions on Two Attributes," *Operations Res.* **22**: 35–45 (1974).
21. ——, "Value Theory," Chapter 3, Section III in this volume.
22. Fleming, M., "A Cardinal Concept of Welfare," *Quart. J. Econ.* **66**: 366–384 (1952).
23. Friedman, M. and L. J. Savage, "The Expected-Utility Hypothesis and the Measurability of Utility," *J. Pol. Econ.* **60**: 463–474 (1952).
24. Gaver, D. P., "Simulation: Theory," Chapter 7, Section III in this volume.
25. Gordon G., "Simulation: Computation," Chapter 8, Section III in this volume.
26. Grayson, C. J., *Decision Under Uncertainty: Drilling Decisions by Oil and Gas Operators*, Division of Research, Harvard Business School, Boston, Massachusetts, (1960).
27. Hammond, J. S., "Simplifying the Choice Between Uncertain Prospects With Nonlinear Utility," *Management Sci.* (1974).
28. Harsanyi, J. C., "Cardinal Welfare Individualistic Ethics, and Interpersonal Comparisons of Utility," *J. Pol. Econ.* **63**: 309–321 (1955).
29. Howard, R. A., "Decision Analysis: Applied Decision Theory," *Proc. Fourth Int. Conf. on Operational Res.*, Boston, Massachusetts (1966).
30. ——, "The Foundations of Decision Analysis," *IEEE Systems Sci. and Cybernetics* **SSC-4**: 211–219 (1968).
31. ——, "Proximal Decision Analysis," *Management Sci.* **17**: 507–541 (1971).
32. ——, J. E. Matheson, and D. W. North, "The Decision to Seed Hurricanes," *Sci.* **176**: 1191–1202 (1972).
33. Huber, G. P., "Development of Multi-Attribute Utility Models: A Review of Field and Field-Like Studies," University of Wisconsin, Madison, Wisconsin (1973).
34. Kaufman, G. M., *Statistical Decision and Related Techniques in Oil and Gas Exploration*, Prentice-Hall, Englewood Cliffs, New Jersey (1963).

35. Keeney, R. L., "Quasi-Separable Utility Functions," *Nav. Res. Log. Quart.* **15:** 551–565 (1968).
36. ——, "Utility Independence and Preference for Multiattributed Consequences," *Operations Res.* **19:** 875–893 (1971).
37. ——, "A Decision Analysis with Multiple Objectives: The Mexico City Airport," *Bell J. Economics Management Sci.* **4:** 101–117 (1973a).
38. ——, "Concepts of Independence in Multiattribute Utility Theory," in *Multiple Criterion Decision Making*, J. Cochrane and M. Zeleny, (eds.) University of South Carolina Press, Columbia, South Carolina (1973b).
39. ——, "Multiplicative Utility Functions," *Operations Res.* **22:** 22–34 (1974).
40. ——, and C. W. Kirkwood, "Group Decision Making Using Cardinal Social Welfare Functions," Technical Report 83, Operations Research Center, M.I.T. (1973).
41. ——, and H. Raiffa, "A Critique of Formal Analysis in Public Decision Making," in *Analysis of Public Systems*, Drake, A. W., R. L. Keeney, and P. M. Morse, editors, M.I.T. Press, Cambridge, Massachusetts (1972).
42. Koopmans, T. C., "Stationary Ordinal Utility and Impatience," *Econometrica* **28, No. 2:** 287–309 (1960).
43. ——, P. A. Diamond, and R. E. Williamson, "Stationary Utility and Time Perspective," *Econometrica* **32, Nos. 1-2:** 82–100 (1964).
44. Krantz, D. H., R. D. Luce, P. Suppes, and A. Tversky, *Foundations of Measurement, Vol. 1*, Academic Press, New York (1971).
45. Lancaster, K. J., "An Axiomatic Theory of Consumer Time Preference," *Int. Econ. Rev.* **4:** 221–231 (1963).
46. Luce R. D. and H. Raiffa, *Games and Decisions*, Wiley, New York (1957).
47. MacCrimmon, K. R., "An Overview of Multiple Objective Decision Making," in *Multiple Criteria Decision Making*, J. L. Cochrane and M. Zeleny, editors, University of South Carolina Press, Columbia, South Carolina (1973).
48. Magee, J. F., "Decision Trees for Decision Making," *Harvard Bus. Rev.* **42, No. 4:** 126–138 (1964a).
49. ——, "How to Use Decision Trees in Capital Investment," *Harvard Bus. Rev.* **42, No. 5:** 79–96 (1964b).
50. Matheson, J. E., "Decision Analysis Practice: Examples and Insights," *Proc. Fifth Int. Conf. on Operational Res.*, Venice, Italy (1969).
51. Meyer, R. E., "On the Relationship Among the Utility of Assets, the Utility of Consumption and Investment Strategy in an Uncertain But Time Invariant World," *Proc. Fifth Int. Conf. on Operational Res.*, Venice, Italy (1969).
52. —— and J. W. Pratt, "The Consistent Assessment and Fairing of Preference Functions," *IEEE Systems Sci. and Cybernetics* **SSC-4, No. 3:** 270–278 (1968).
53. Mosteller, F. and P. Nogee, "An Experimental Measurement of Utility," *J. Pol. Econ.* **59:** 371–404 (1951).
54. Nash, J. F., "The Bargaining Problem," *Econometrica* **18:** 155–162 (1950).
55. Newman, J. W., *Management Applications of Decision Theory*, Harper and Row, New York (1971).
56. Parzen, E., *Modern Probability Theory and Its Applications,* Wiley, New York, (1960).
57. Pollak, R. A., "Additive von Neumann-Morgenstern Utility Functions," *Econometrica* **35:** 485–494 (1967).
58. Pollard, A. B., "A Normative Model for Joint Time/Risk Preference Decision Problems," Stanford Research Institute (1969).
59. Pratt, J. W., "Risk Aversion in the Small and in the Large," *Econometrica* **32:** 122–136 (1964).

60. ——, H. Raiffa, and R. Schlaifer, *Introduction to Statistical Decision Theory*, McGraw-Hill, New York (1965).
61. Raiffa, H., *Decision Analysis: Introductory Lectures on Choices Under Uncertainty,* Addison-Wesley, Reading, Massachusetts (1968).
62. ——, "Preferences for Multi-Attributed Alternatives," Memorandum RM-5868-DOT RC, the RAND Corporation, Santa Monica, California (1969).
63. —— and R. O. Schlaifer, *Applied Statistical Decision Theory*, Harvard Business School, Division of Research, Boston, Massachusetts (1961).
64. Ramsey, F. P., "Truth and Probability," in *The Foundations of Mathematics and Other Logical Essays,* by F. P. Ramsey; Harcourt, Brace, and Co., New York, (1931). Reprinted in *Studies in Subjective Probability,* H. E. Kyburg and H. E. Smokler (eds.), Wiley, New York (1964).
65. Rousseau, W. R. and J. E. Matheson, "Computer Programs for Decision Analysis," Stanford Research Institute (1967).
66. Savage, L. J., *The Foundations of Statistics,* Wiley, New York, (1954); Second Edition, Dover, New York (1972).
67. Schlaifer, R. O., *Probability and Statistics for Business Decisions*, McGraw-Hill, New York (1959).
68. ——, *Manual of Cases on Decision Under Uncertainty With Analyses and Teaching Notes*, McGraw-Hill, New York (1968).
69. ——, *Analysis of Decisions Under Uncertainty*, McGraw-Hill, New York, (1969).
70. ——, *Computer Programs for Elementary Decision Analysis*, Division of Research, Harvard Business School (1971).
71. Sen, A., "Interpersonal Aggregation and Partial Comparability," *Econometrica* **30:** 393-409 (1970).
72. Slovic, P. and S. Lichtenstein, "Comparison of Bayesian and Regression Approaches to the Study of Information Processing in Judgment," *Organizational Behav. and Human Per.* **6:** 649–744 (1971).
73. Spetzler, C. S., "The Development of a Corporate Risk Policy for Capital Investment Decision," *IEEE Systems Sci. and Cybernetics* **SSC-4:** 279–300 (1968).
74. Stanford Research Institute, "Decision Analysis of Nuclear Plants in Electrical Systems Expansion," Report on Project 6496, Menlo Park, California (1968).
75. Tribus, M., *Rational Descriptions, Decisions and Designs*, Pergamon Press, New York, (1969).
76. Tversky, A. and D. Kahneman, "Judgment Under Uncertainty: Heuristics and Biases," The Hebrew University, Jerusalem, Israel (1973).
77. von Neumann, J., and O. Morgenstern, *Theory of Games and Economic Behavior*, Princeton University Press, Princeton, New Jersey (1944).
78. Wald, A., *Statistical Decision Functions*, Wiley, New York (1950).
79. Winkler, R. L., "The Quantification of Judgment: Some Methodological Suggestions," *J. Amer. Stat. Assoc.* **62:** 1105–1120 (1967).
80. ——, "Scaring Rules and the Evaluation of Probability Assessors," *J. Amer. Stat. Assoc.* **64:** 1073-1078 (1969).

III-5

GAME THEORY AND GAMING

Guillermo Owen
Rice University

HISTORICAL INTRODUCTION

The theory of Games was first given a systematic development by von Neumann and Morgenstern [1944], though several of its ideas had appeared as early as the 1920s. This original development considered mainly economic applications, which treated economic conflict as the most easily quantifiable. During the Second World War, and shortly thereafter, game theory was given substantial consideration by the military, which saw in this a mathematical treatment of strategic concepts. Since then, economic considerations have again become dominant. Nevertheless, considerable work is underway with a view towards applications in other social sciences, mainly psychology, which studies the mechanics of bargaining and negotiation, and political science, which studies coalitional behavior in political power systems.

1. EXTENSIVE AND NORMAL FORMS

The extensive form of an n-person game gives, in logical order, the several possible moves in a game. Each move is assigned either to a player (personal move) or to chance (random move). At a personal move, the options available to the player and the information given to him are made explicit. At a random move, a probability distribution is specified. Finally, at each terminal position of the game, a payoff or outcome can be expressed by a vector $(p_1, \ldots, p_n)$, where p_i represents the utility to player i of the given outcome.

Generally, the extensive form is represented by a game tree with a distinguished node (the initial position). Each node represents a position of the game; each arc, a move. Information is indicated by the use of *information sets:* essentially, two positions belong to the same information set if the same player must move at each position and he cannot distinguish between them.

A *strategy* is a rule which tells a player what to do, i.e., which alternative to choose, at each information set. If a player has k information sets, with $j_1, j_2, \ldots, j_k$ alternatives, respectively, at these, then he has a total of $j_1 j_2 \ldots j_k$ strategies for the game.

If strategies $\sigma_1, \sigma_2, \ldots, \sigma_n$ are designated for the n players, then the outcome of the game is determined except for chance moves. Since the probabilities at chance moves are well defined, it follows that the expected payoff for each player (for this choice of strategies) is also well defined. The *normal form* of the game is the function which assigns the vector of expected payoffs to each n-tuple of strategies.

The *normal form* of the game, then, is a function which assigns, to each n-tuple $(\sigma_1, \sigma_2, \ldots, \sigma_n)$ of strategies, an n-vector $(p_1, p_2, \ldots, p_n)$ of payoffs. In this context, p_i is the payoff to player i if the given n-tuple of strategies is used.

An n-tuple $(\sigma_1, \sigma_2, \ldots, \sigma_n)$ of strategies is said to be an *equilibrium n-tuple*, if, for every player i, and for every strategy s_i of player i,

$$p_i(\sigma_1, \sigma_2, \ldots, \sigma_i, \ldots, \sigma_n) \geqslant p_i(\sigma_1, \sigma_2, \ldots, s_i, \ldots, \sigma_n). \tag{1}$$

In other words, if an n-tuple of strategies is in equilibrium, then none of the players can gain by a unilateral change of strategies. Unfortunately, most games fail to have equilibrium n-tuples. The only case in which the existence of an equilibrium n-tuple can be guaranteed is the case of *perfect information:* if, in a finite game, every player knows at every one of his moves everything that has been done up to that point, then the game will have at least one equilibrium n-tuple.

Example 1: As an example, let us take the following very rudimentary form of poker. At the start of the game, each player places one unit in the pot. A deck (containing m high and n low cards) is shuffled, and one of these cards is given to P_1. Seeing this card, P_1 can now either pass or bet an amount a.

If P_1 passes, the game terminates immediately; P_1 wins one unit with a high card, and loses one with a low card. In case P_1 bets, P_2 (in ignorance of P_1's card) must decide whether to call the bet, or fold.

If P_2 folds, then P_1 wins one unit. If P_2 calls, there is a showdown, with P_1 winning $1 + a$ units with a high card, and losing $1 + a$ with a low card.

Figure 1 shows the extensive form (tree) for this game. The vertices, A through K, are the positions of the game. A is a chance move, B and C belong to P_1, while E and F belong to P_2. The remaining vertices are *terminal* vertices, and a payoff vector, representing the two players' winnings, is assigned to each.

P_1 has two information sets–the two vertices B and C. On the other hand, P_2 has only one information set–holding both vertices E and F, as he cannot distinguish between them. (We recall that P_1 makes his bet knowing the outcome of the chance move, but P_2 must call or fold in ignorance of this.)

Since P_1 has two information sets, and two choices (bet or pass) at each, he has $2 \cdot 2 = 4$ strategies, which we may label BB (always bet), BP (bet only on high), PB (bet only on low), and PP (always pass). His opponent has only one information set, and two choices there, so he has two strategies, namely C (call) or F (fold).

For each choice of strategies, we may compute the expected payoff. Thus if P_1 chooses BB (always bet) and P_2 chooses C, there is a probability $p = m/(m+n)$ that P_1 will win $1 + a$ units, and $1 - p$ that P_1 will lose $1 - a$. Thus P_1's expected winnings are $(2p - 1)(1 + a)$. A table of P_1's expected winnings can then be written as

$$\begin{array}{c} \\ BB \\ BP \\ PB \\ PP \end{array} \begin{array}{c} \begin{array}{cc} \quad C \quad & \quad F \quad \end{array} \\ \begin{pmatrix} (2p-1)(1+a) & 1 \\ 2p-1+ap & 2p-1 \\ (2p-1)a+p-1 & 1 \\ 2p-1 & 2p-1 \end{pmatrix} \end{array}$$

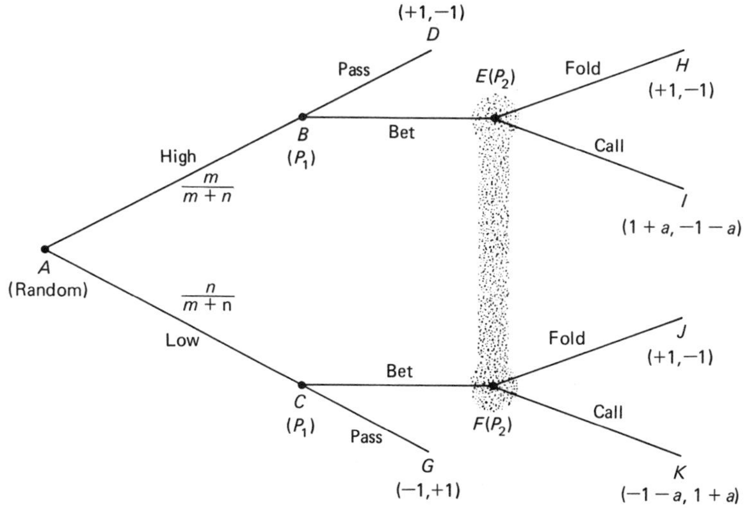

Fig. 1. Extensive form (tree) for a rudimentary form of poker.

Clearly P_2's expected winnings are the negative of this. This is the *normal form* of the game.

2. ZERO-SUM TWO-PERSON GAMES

2.1 Introduction

In a zero-sum game, the sum of the payoffs for any outcome is zero. When $n = 2$, this means that the payoff vector will always have the form $(a, -a)$, where a is the payoff to player I, and consequently, $-a$ is the payoff to II. This means in effect that we can dispense with the second component and represent the payoff by a single number, a. It will be understood that this is the amount won by I, and lost by II; i.e., II pays this amount to I. (A negative amount represents, of course, a gain for II.)

Equilibrium pairs are defined, here, just as in the more general n-person case above. The fact that the payoff is represented by a single number (rather than a vector) allows a somewhat simpler definition.

Definition. *Let* $(S_1, S_2; P)$ *be a two-person zero-sum game. Then the strategies* $\sigma^* \in S_1, \tau^* \in S_2$ *are in equilibrium if*

$$P(\sigma^*, \tau) \geqslant P(\sigma^*, \tau^*) \geqslant P(\sigma, \tau^*) \tag{2}$$

for all $\sigma \in S_1, \tau \in S_2$. *An equilibrium pair is also known as a* saddle-point.

There is, of course, no guarantee that a game has any saddle-points. Assuming that more than one exists, the following theorem is of interest.

THEOREM 1. Let (σ, τ) and (σ', τ') be saddle-points. Then (σ, τ') and (σ', τ) are also saddle-points, and moreover,

$$P(\sigma, \tau) = P(\sigma', \tau').$$

This theorem is best summarized by saying that saddle-points are interchangeable and equivalent. Note that this does not generalize to other games, i.e., it is not true for nonzero-sum games or for 3-person games.

2.2 Matrix Games

If the strategy sets S_1, S_2 are finite, then the normal form can be represented by a matrix, $\mathbf{A} = (a_{ij})$, where the rows represent strategies for I, the columns are strategies for II, and a_{ij} is the payoff (from II to I) if I chooses the ith row, and II the jth column. (This is the accepted convention: the row-chooser maximizes, while the column-chooser minimizes, the payoff.)

A saddle-point now is any entry a_{kl} such that

$$a_{il} \leqslant a_{kl} \leqslant a_{kj} \tag{3}$$

for any other i and j. Thus a saddle-point is simultaneously the smallest entry in its row, and the largest entry in its column.

We can check for existence of a saddle-point by seeing whether any entry a_{kl} satisfies Eq. (3). An alternative method is based on defining the *minorant value* V_{I} and *majorant value* V_{II} for the game matrix $\mathbf{A} = (a_{ij})$ by

$$V_{\mathrm{I}} = \max_i \min_j a_{ij} \tag{4}$$

$$V_{\mathrm{II}} = \min_j \max_i a_{ij} \tag{5}$$

It is easy to see that $V_{\mathrm{I}} \leqslant V_{\mathrm{II}}$ in all cases.

THEOREM 2. Let a_{kl} be a saddle-point for the game **A**. Then $V_{\mathrm{I}} = V_{\mathrm{II}} = a_{kl}$. Conversely, if $V_{\mathrm{I}} = V_{\mathrm{II}}$, then there is a saddle-point a_{kl}.

The theorem tells us that we can look for a saddle-point by merely checking whether $V_{\mathrm{I}} = V_{\mathrm{II}}$. If so, it is generally easy to find the saddle-point, as it will be at the intersection of the row and column which give the maximum (max) and minimum (min), respectively.

Mixed Strategies. Most matrix games lack saddle-points. This generally makes it important for a player to prevent his adversary from guessing the strategy which he will use. The usual way of accomplishing this is to use a *mixed strategy*. Essentially, a mixed strategy (for a given player) is a scheme for choosing a pure strategy at random. Mathematically, it is described as a probability distribution over the player's strategy set.

Definition. *Let* $\mathbf{A} = (a_{ij})$ *be an* $m \times n$ *matrix game. Then a mixed strategy for* I *is a vector* $\mathbf{x} = (x_1, \ldots, x_m)$ *satisfying*

$$x_i \geqslant 0 \qquad i = 1, \ldots, m \tag{6}$$

$$\sum_{i=1}^{m} x_i = 1 \tag{7}$$

while a mixed strategy for II *is a vector* $\mathbf{y} = (y_1, \ldots, y_n)$ *such that*

$$y_j \geqslant 0 \qquad j = 1, \ldots, n \tag{8}$$

$$\sum_{j=1}^{n} y_j = 1. \tag{9}$$

Essentially, the meaning is that I, when using the mixed strategy **x**, employs some random mechanism which assigns probability x_i to the ith row. Similarly, II, using **y**, assigns probability y_j to the jth column. These two randomization schemes will be assumed independent, so that the probability that I chooses i, while II chooses j, is $x_i y_j$. In that case, there will be a payoff of a_{ij}. Summing over all i and j, we find that the expected payoff is

$$\sum\sum a_{ij}x_iy_j$$

or, in matrix notation, $\mathbf{x}^t\mathbf{A}\mathbf{y}$.

It is now possible to define saddle-points in terms of mixed strategies: the pair $(\mathbf{x}^*, \mathbf{y}^*)$ is a saddle-point if

$$\mathbf{x}^t\mathbf{A}\mathbf{y}^* \leqslant \mathbf{x}^{*t}\mathbf{A}\mathbf{y}^* \leqslant \mathbf{x}^*\mathbf{A}\mathbf{y}^t \tag{10}$$

for any $\mathbf{x} \in \mathbf{X}, \mathbf{y} \in \mathbf{Y}$, where $\mathbf{X}$ and $\mathbf{Y}$ are the two sets of mixed strategies.

THEOREM 3. Every matrix game has at least one saddle-point in mixed strategies.

This theorem is frequently given in the following form:

MINIMAX THEOREM. For any matrix game $\mathbf{A}$

$$\min_{\mathbf{y}\in\mathbf{Y}} \max_{\mathbf{x}\in\mathbf{X}} \mathbf{x}^t\mathbf{A}\mathbf{y} = \max_{\mathbf{x}\in\mathbf{X}} \min_{\mathbf{y}\in\mathbf{Y}} \mathbf{x}^t\mathbf{A}\mathbf{y}. \tag{11}$$

The common value of these two is known as the value of the game, V.

Definition. *An optimal strategy is any strategy which (in expectation) guarantees the value of the game, i.e.,* $\mathbf{x}^*$ *is optimal for* I *if*

$$\min_{\mathbf{y}\in\mathbf{Y}} \mathbf{x}^{*t}\,\mathbf{A}\mathbf{y} = V \tag{12}$$

and $\mathbf{y}^*$ *is optimal for* II *if*

$$\max_{\mathbf{x}\in\mathbf{X}} \mathbf{x}^t\mathbf{A}\mathbf{y}^* = V. \tag{13}$$

In this case it will also be true that

$$\max_i \left\{\sum a_{ij}y_j^*\right\} = \min_j \left\{\sum a_{ij}x_i^*\right\} = V. \tag{14}$$

The minimax theorem guarantees the existence of at least one optimal strategy for each player. It is easy to see that any pair of optimal strategies is in equilibrium, and conversely, if $(\mathbf{x}^*, \mathbf{y}^*)$ is a saddle-point; then $\mathbf{x}^*$ and $\mathbf{y}^*$ are optimal.

2.3 Computation of Optimal Strategies

Generally speaking, the computation of optimal strategies (the solution of a game) is easy for small games but becomes quite complicated as the number of strategies increases. Several methods are recommended.

Saddle-points: The simplest method is to look for a saddle-point in pure strategies. If such a saddle-point exists, the two pure strategies which give it are optimal.

Domination: One common method of reducing the size of a game deals with row and column domination. Briefly speaking, we say the kth row of matrix A dominates the ith row if

$$a_{ij} \leqslant a_{kj} \qquad \text{for all} \quad j \tag{15}$$

$$a_{ij} < a_{kj} \qquad \text{for at least one} \quad j. \tag{16}$$

Similarly, the lth column dominates the jth column if

$$a_{il} \leqslant a_{ij} \qquad \text{for all} \quad i \tag{17}$$

$$a_{il} < a_{ij} \qquad \text{for at least one} \quad i. \tag{18}$$

The interpretation of domination is that the dominating strategy is never worse, and sometimes better, than the dominated strategy. It follows that there is no need to use a dominated strategy. In fact, optimal mixed strategies which assign probability zero to a dominated row or column will always exist, and the game can be solved without regard to such rows and columns. This frequently allows us to reduce the size of the matrix.

Example 2: In the game with matrix

$$\begin{pmatrix} 5 & 2 & 1 \\ 2 & 1 & 3 \\ 3 & 6 & 4 \end{pmatrix}$$

the third row dominates the second. Deletion of the second row give us

$$\begin{pmatrix} 5 & 2 & 1 \\ 3 & 6 & 4 \end{pmatrix}$$

and, for this reduced matrix, the third column dominates the second. This will give us

$$\begin{pmatrix} 5 & 1 \\ 3 & 4 \end{pmatrix}.$$

If a solution to this game can be obtained, it can then be extended to a solution of the original game by simply assigning probability zero to the deleted row and column.

Simple procedures for solving 2×2, $2 \times n$ and $m \times 2$ games can be found in the text by Williams [1954]. General procedures, required to solve larger games, will be considered below.

Fictitious Play: For larger games, several methods have been suggested. We recommend two of these; one is the method of *fictitious play*.

Essentially, fictitious play consists of simulating many plays of the game, choosing at each play that pure strategy which is best against the opponent's observed distribution. The empirical distributions thus obtained will be optimal in the limit.

More precisely, we define two sequences of vectors $\{\mathbf{X}^q\}$, $\{\mathbf{Y}^q\}$, as follows:

$$X_i^0 = 0 \qquad i = 1, \ldots, m \tag{19}$$

$$Y_j^0 = 0 \qquad j = 1, \ldots, n. \tag{20}$$

Inductively, assume $\mathbf{X}^{q-1}$ and $\mathbf{Y}^{q-1}$ have been chosen. Define

$$k(q) = \text{that } i \text{ which maximizes } \sum_j a_{ij} Y_j^{q-1}$$

$$l(q) = \text{that } j \text{ which minimizes } \sum_i a_{ij} X_j^{q-1}$$

where, if there are ties for max or min, *any one* of the maximizing or minimizing values may be chosen.

Then

$$X_i^q = \begin{cases} X_i^{q-1} & \text{if } i \neq k(q) \quad (21) \\ X_i^{q-1} + 1 & \text{if } i = k(q) \quad (22) \end{cases}$$

$$Y_j^q = \begin{cases} Y_j^{q-1} & \text{if } j \neq l(q) \\ Y_j^{q-1} + 1 & \text{if } j = l(q). \end{cases} \tag{23}$$

The two sequences of vectors then define strategies $\mathbf{x}^q$, $\mathbf{y}^q$ by

$$\mathbf{x}^q = \frac{1}{q} \mathbf{X}^q \qquad \mathbf{y}^q = \frac{1}{q} \mathbf{Y}^q. \tag{24}$$

It is easy to see that, for $q \geqslant 1$, $\mathbf{x}^q$ and $\mathbf{y}^q$ will be strategies. There is no guarantee that $\{\mathbf{x}^q\}$ or $\{\mathbf{y}^q\}$ converges, but accumulation points will (by compactness) exist.

THEOREM 4. If $\mathbf{x}^*$ and $\mathbf{y}^*$ are any accumulation points of the sequences $\{\mathbf{x}^q\}$ and $\{\mathbf{y}^q\}$, then $\mathbf{x}^*$ and $\mathbf{y}^*$ are optimal strategies.

This method generally requires a large number of iterations, but the iterations are relatively simple. Several modifications exist, e.g., we might let $\mathbf{Y}^q$ depend on $\mathbf{X}^q$ rather than $\mathbf{X}^{q-1}$.

Linear Programming: The other recommended method for solving matrix games is linear programming. Generally, the optimal strategies $\mathbf{x}^*$ and $\mathbf{y}^*$ will be solutions of the two linear programs

$$\text{Maximize } \lambda \text{ subject to} \tag{25}$$

$$\sum_i a_{ij} x_i - \lambda \geqslant 0 \qquad j = 1, \ldots, n \tag{26}$$

$$\sum_i x_i = 1 \tag{27}$$

$$x_i \geqslant 0 \quad i = 1, \ldots, m. \tag{28}$$

and

$$\text{Minimize } \mu \text{ subject to} \tag{29}$$

$$\sum_j a_{ij} y_j - \mu \leqslant 0 \quad i = 1, \ldots, m \tag{30}$$

$$\sum_i y_j = 1 \tag{31}$$

$$y_j \geqslant 0 \quad j = 1, \ldots, n. \tag{32}$$

These two are feasible, mutually dual linear programs. By duality theory, the max of λ will equal the min of μ; their common value is the value of the game.

2.4 Constrained Games

An interesting case occurs when there is some extraneous constraint on the mixed strategies, so that not all mixed strategies are permissible. In this case we may find ourselves with a payoff function of the form

$$f(\mathbf{x}, \mathbf{y}) = \mathbf{x}^t\mathbf{C} + \mathbf{b}^t\mathbf{y} - \mathbf{x}^t\mathbf{A}\mathbf{y} \tag{33}$$

and strategy sets **X**, **Y** defined by the matrix inequalities

$$\mathbf{x}^t\mathbf{D} \leqslant \mathbf{e}^t \qquad \mathbf{F}\mathbf{y} \geqslant \mathbf{g} \tag{34}$$

$$\mathbf{x} \geqslant 0 \qquad \mathbf{y} \geqslant 0. \tag{35}$$

Example 3: As a trivial example, we might consider the case of a baseball pitcher who has to choose between throwing his curve and his fast ball. Generally, any combination of pitches is permissible, and so any mixed strategy (x_1, x_2) can be used. Suppose, however, that his arm is slightly sore; the trainer might tell him not to use his curve more than 70% of the time. This will introduce a constraint, $x_1 \leqslant 0.7$ which must be satisfied by his strategy.

Example 4: As a less trivial example, let us consider a game in which the payoff is not a single number, but a vector (a_{ij}, b_{ij}). In a battle, say, a_{ij} might be the probability of capturing a strong point, and b_{ij} the number of casualties suffered. In that case, a commander may be given instructions to "maximize the probability of capturing the strong point, subject to losing (in expectation) not more than 1000 men." Thus the constraint

$$\mathbf{x}^t\mathbf{B} \leqslant (1000, 1000, \ldots, 1000)$$

would limit the possible mixed strategies for that commander.

Again, we can determine minorant and majorant values

$$V_{\mathrm{I}} = \max_{\mathbf{x}\in\mathbf{X}} \min_{\mathbf{y}\in\mathbf{Y}} f(\mathbf{x}, \mathbf{y}) \tag{36}$$

$$V_{\mathrm{II}} = \min_{\mathbf{y}\in\mathbf{Y}} \max_{\mathbf{x}\in\mathbf{X}} f(\mathbf{x}, \mathbf{y}). \tag{37}$$

There is no guarantee that the values V_{I} and V_{II} exist, since the sets $\mathbf{X}$ and $\mathbf{Y}$ need not be compact. If, however, either one exists, then so will the other, and they will be equal. In particular, this will happen if both $\mathbf{X}$ and $\mathbf{Y}$ are non-empty and bounded. (Boundedness is not, however, a necessary condition.)

The optimal constrained strategies, $\mathbf{x}$ and $\mathbf{y}$, can be obtained by solving the linear programs

$$\max \quad \mathbf{x}^t\mathbf{C} + \mathbf{u}^t\mathbf{g} \tag{38}$$

subject to

$$\mathbf{x}^t\mathbf{A} + \mathbf{u}^t\mathbf{F} \leqslant \mathbf{b}^t \tag{39}$$

$$\mathbf{x}^t\mathbf{D} \leqslant \mathbf{e}^t \tag{40}$$

$$\mathbf{x}, \mathbf{u} \geqslant 0 \tag{41}$$

and

$$\text{Minimize} \quad \mathbf{b}^t\mathbf{y} + \mathbf{e}^t\mathbf{v} \tag{42}$$

subject to

$$\mathbf{A}\mathbf{y} + \mathbf{D}\mathbf{v} \geqslant \mathbf{C} \tag{43}$$

$$\mathbf{F}\mathbf{y} \geqslant \mathbf{g} \tag{44}$$

$$\mathbf{y}, \mathbf{v} \geqslant 0. \tag{45}$$

It may be seen that these are mutually dual programs. Their common value will be the value of the constrained game.

2.5 Infinite Games

A much more complicated situation arises when the sets of pure strategies for a game are infinite. The consequent loss of compactness generally means that the minimax theorem will not hold. This happens, e.g., in the case of games where the pure strategy sets are denumerable.

Games on the Square. An interesting case occurs when the pure strategy sets are isomorphic to the unit interval $[0, 1]$. The normal form is then a function defined over the unit square, giving rise to the name *game on the square.* The general representation is then $A(x, y)$, where x and y vary over $0 \leqslant x \leqslant 1$, $0 \leqslant y \leqslant 1$.

Example 5: Suppose two competing companies, C_1 and C_2, wish to apportion their advertising budgets between cities A and B. Assuming a fixed total amount, a typical strategy for C_1 is to apportion a fraction x $(0 \leqslant x \leqslant 1)$ to A, and the remaining fraction, $1 - x$, to B. Similarly, a strategy for C_2 is to apportion a fraction y $(0 \leqslant y \leqslant 1)$ to A, and the remainder, $1 - y$ to B.

As payoff, we will choose C_1's share of the total business in the two cities (the total business may be assumed fixed to preserve the zero-sum property of the game). If so, then it is clear that the payoff should be some function–probably continuous–of the two strategy variables, x and y. For example, suppose there is total business of a and b dollars at A and B respectively, and assume that, at each city, the business is divided in direct proportion to the advertising there. If so, C_1's share would be

$$A(x, y) = \frac{ad_1 x}{d_1 x + d_2 y} + \frac{bd_1(1 - x)}{d_1(1 - x) + d_2(1 - y)}$$

where d_1 and d_2 are the companies' advertising budgets.

For these games, we can define mixed strategies as probability distributions, F, G, over the unit interval. The expected payoffs are defined in the usual manner by Stieltjes integrals:

$$E[F, y] = \int_0^1 A(x, y)\, dF(x) \tag{46}$$

$$E[x, G] = \int_0^1 A(x, y)\, dG(y) \tag{47}$$

$$E[F, G] = \int_0^1 \int_0^1 A(x, y)\, dF(x)\, dG(y). \tag{48}$$

With these, we can define minorant and majorant values:

$$V_{\mathrm{I}} = \sup_F \inf_y E[F, y] \tag{49}$$

$$V_{\mathrm{II}} = \inf_G \sup_x E[x, G]\,. \tag{50}$$

In general, it is not permissible to replace inf and sup by min and max, nor are V_{I} and V_{II} equal. There are, however, important cases when this can be done.

THEOREM 5. Let $A(x,y)$ be continuous on the square $0 \leqslant x \leqslant 1$, $0 \leqslant y \leqslant 1$. Then

$$V_{\mathrm{I}} = \max_F \min_y E[F, y] \tag{51}$$

$$V_{\mathrm{II}} = \min_G \max_x E[x, G] \tag{52}$$

and, moreover, $V_{\mathrm{I}} = V_{\mathrm{II}}$.

Unfortunately, no analytic methods exist for solving such games; the only known method is to approximate the continuous game by finite games, i.e., matrices $\mathbf{A}^{(n)} = (a_{ij}^{(n)})$, defined by

$$a_{ij}^{(n)} = A\left(\frac{i}{n}, \frac{j}{n}\right) \qquad \begin{array}{l} i = 1, \ldots, n \\ j = 1, \ldots, n. \end{array} \tag{53}$$

For each n, this gives an $n \times n$ matrix game. If $\mathbf{r}^{(n)} = (r_1^{(n)}, \ldots, r_n^{(n)})$ is a strategy for I in $\mathbf{A}^{(n)}$, this can be used to define a strategy $F^{(n)}$ for the continuous game by

$$F^{(n)}(x) = \sum_{i=1}^{[nx]} r_i^{(n)}. \tag{54}$$

Similarly, a strategy $\mathbf{s}^{(n)}$ for II will define a strategy $G^{(n)}$ for the continuous game. Then

THEOREM 6. If the game $\mathbf{A}^{(n)}$ has value v_n, and optimal strategies $\mathbf{r}^{(n)}$ and $\mathbf{s}^{(n)}$, then the sequence v_n converges to a limit V, and the sequence $F^{(n)}$ and $G^{(n)}$ will each have at least one accumulation point F^* and G^*. The limit V will be the value of the continuous game A, and F^*, G^* will be optimal strategies for A.

Games of Timing. An important class of games on the square have a payoff which is discontinuous on the diagonal. More precisely, they have the form

$$A(x, y) = \begin{cases} K(x, y) & \text{if } 0 \leqslant x < y \leqslant 1 \\ L(x, y) & 0 \leqslant y < x \leqslant 1 \\ \varphi(x) & x = y \end{cases} \tag{55}$$

where K and L have continuous second-order derivatives on $0 \leqslant x \leqslant y \leqslant 1$ and $0 \leqslant y \leqslant x \leqslant 1$ respectively, and φ is continuous on $0 \leqslant x \leqslant 1$. The discontinuity of the payoff function means that optimal strategies need not exist. On the other hand, this discontinuity will frequently make an analytic computation possible.

Example 6: Two duelists, D_1 and D_2, each carrying a gun with one bullet, approach each other. They start at time 0 and will reach each other (unless one is first hit) at time 1. Each man may fire when he wishes. If one hits the other, the duel is immediately over, and the one who fired successfully is the winner. If both miss, or if they hit each other simultaneously, the duel is considered a stand-off.

If D_1 chooses to fire at time x, and D_2 at time y, with $x < y$, then D_1 will win with probability p_x, and lose with probability $(1 - p_x)q_y$, where p_x and q_y are the two players' accuracy functions (i.e., a shot by D_1 at time x will be successful with probability p_x, one by D_2 at time y will be successful with probability q_y). Thus the expected payoff is $p_x - q_y + p_x q_y$. On the other hand, if $x > y$, then the expected payoff will be $p_x - q_y - p_x q_y$ (note the difference in sign). Finally, if $x = y$, the expected payoff is $p_x - q_x$. Thus

$$A(x,y) = \begin{cases} p_x - q_y + p_x q_y & \text{if } x < y \\ p_x - q_x & \text{if } x = y \\ p_x - q_y - p_x q_y & \text{if } x > y. \end{cases}$$

Briefly speaking, a wide class of these games has optimal strategies which take the form of a jump α at 0, a density f which is positive inside an interval $c \leqslant x \leqslant 1$, and another jump β at 1. (This is the most general form, and, depending on special cases, any one or two of these three parts may vanish.) The optimal F for player I, represented by

$$F = \{\alpha \mathrm{I}_0, f_c, \beta \mathrm{I}_1\}$$

will satisfy the equation

$$\{L(y,y) - K(y,y\} f(y) - \int_a^y K_2(x,y) f(x)\, dx - \int_y^1 L_2(x,y) f(x)\, dx$$
$$= \alpha K_2(0,y) + \beta L_2(1,y) \quad (56)$$

for all $y, a \leqslant y \leqslant 1$. (Here, the subscripts denote partial differentiation.)

Similarly, the optimal strategy G for player II will have the form

$$G = \{\gamma \mathrm{I}_0, g_c, \delta \mathrm{I}_1\}$$

and satisfy the equation

$$\{K(x,x) - L(x,x\} g(x) - \int_a^x L_1(x,y) g(y)\, dy - \int_x^1 K_1(x,y) g(y)\, dy$$
$$= \gamma L_1(x,0) + \delta K_1(x,1). \quad (57)$$

Additionally, F and G must satisfy the usual conditions, namely that they be strategies and that they guarantee the value v of the game. Together, this will give rise to a set of conditions on $\alpha, \beta, \gamma, \delta, c, v, f$, and g which may or may not be easy to solve.

It should be pointed out that not all games with kernel of the type discussed above have solutions of this type. A sufficient condition is that both $K(x,y)$

and $L(x, y)$ be strictly increasing in x, and strictly decreasing in y, that $\varphi(0)$ lie between $K(0,0)$ and $L(0,0)$ and $\varphi(1)$ lie between $K(1,1)$ and $L(1,1)$. (This condition is not, however, necessary.)

2.6 Multi-Stage Games

A multi-stage game is one in which, at fixed intervals, both players are given perfect information. Each of these intervals marks a stage of the game. The importance of this is that such games can be simplified by the use of dynamic programming techniques.

Generally speaking, we can represent such games by a number of *game elements* $\Gamma_1, \Gamma_2, \ldots, \Gamma_p$, each of which is an $m_k \times n_k$ "matrix"

$$\Gamma_k = (\alpha_{ij}^k)$$

whose entries are not, however, simple payoffs; rather they take the form

$$\alpha_{ij}^k = a_{ij}^k + \sum q_{ij}^{kl} \Gamma_l. \tag{58}$$

where a_{ij}^k is a payoff, and the q_{ij}^{kl} are transition probabilities. Thus, if, at time t, the game is in element Γ_k, and the players choose row i and column j, then there will be a payoff a_{ij}^k, plus a probability q_{ij}^{kl} of transition to game element Γ_l at time $t + 1$. This means that

$$q_{ij}^{kl} \geqslant 0; \qquad \sum_{l=1}^{p} q_{ij}^{kl} \leqslant 1. \tag{59}$$

Games of Exhaustion. The simplest case occurs when a game is to terminate after (at most) some finite number of stages. In this case, we can rank the game elements according to the maximal number of remaining stages, and it is clear that transition is possible only to game elements of lower rank, i.e., $q_{ij}^{kl} > 0$ only if Γ_l is of lower rank than Γ_k.

Example 7. Women and Cats versus Mice and Men. In this game, team 1 consists of m_1 women and m_2 cats; team 2 of n_1 mice and n_2 men. At each stage, each team selects one of its members, and one of the two members thus chosen is eliminated, according to the rule that a woman eliminates a man, who eliminates a cat, who eliminates a mouse, who eliminates a woman. The game can be represented by elements $\Gamma(m_1, m_2; n_1, n_2)$, where m_1, m_2, n_1, n_2 are positive integers. Then

$$\Gamma(m_1, m_2; n_1, n_2) = \begin{pmatrix} \Gamma(m_1 - 1, m_2; n_1, n_2) & \Gamma(m_1, m_2; n_1, n_2 - 1) \\ \Gamma(m_1, m_2; n_1 - 1, n_2) & \Gamma(m_1, m_2 - 1; n_1, n_2) \end{pmatrix}$$

The game terminates as soon as one of the four components is equal to zero; the corresponding team has then lost. Since one member is eliminated at each stage, the game will certainly terminate after at most $m_1 + m_2 + n_1 + n_2 - 3$ stages, where m_1, m_2, n_1, n_2 are the original sizes of the two teams.

In this case, we can define

$$v_k = \text{val}\,(\mathbf{B}^k) \tag{60}$$

where $\mathbf{B}^k = (b_{ij}^k)$ is the matrix with entries

$$b_{ij}^k = a_{ij}^k + \sum_{l=1}^{p} q_{ij}^{kl} v_l. \tag{61}$$

This will define a value vector, $(v_1, \ldots, v_p)$ inductively, by induction on the rank of the $\mathbf{\Gamma}_k$. The optimal strategies for the game element $\mathbf{\Gamma}_k$ will be exactly those for the matrix game $\mathbf{B}^k$.

Stochastic Games. These games are characterized by the condition

$$\sum_{l=1}^{p} q_{ij}^{kl} < 1 \tag{62}$$

which states that, at each stage, there is a positive probability of termination. This guarantees that no matter what strategies are chosen, there is at most a probability s^n (where $s < 1$ is a preassigned number) that the game will continue after n time-periods. A consequence is that the payoff will always have finite expectation.

Example 8: Two gamblers, G_1 and G_2, play continually the game with matrix

$$\begin{pmatrix} -1 & 1 \\ 1 & -1 \end{pmatrix}.$$

The gamblers start with 10 units between them, and agree to stop play whenever one of them is wiped out. Additionally, after each play of the game, a fair coin is tossed. If the coin lands heads up, the game will terminate even if neither player is wiped out.

Let $\mathbf{\Gamma}_k$ $(1 \leqslant k \leqslant 9)$ be the game element which occurs when G_1 has k units. Then we can represent this by

$$\mathbf{\Gamma}_k = \begin{pmatrix} -1 + \frac{1}{2}\,\mathbf{\Gamma}_{k-1} & 1 + \frac{1}{2}\,\mathbf{\Gamma}_{k+1} \\ 1 + \frac{1}{2}\,\mathbf{\Gamma}_{k+1} & -1 + \frac{1}{2}\,\mathbf{\Gamma}_{k-1} \end{pmatrix}$$

with the understanding that $\mathbf{\Gamma}_0$ and $\mathbf{\Gamma}_{10}$ both represent termination.

The value vector $\mathbf{V} = (v_1, \ldots, v_p)$ must once again satisfy the equation (60)–(61). Essentially, we can define it as a fixed point of the transformation

$$T(w_1, \ldots, w_p) = (w_1', \ldots, w_p') \tag{63}$$

where

$$w_k' = \text{val}\,[\mathbf{B}^k(\mathbf{w})] \tag{64}$$

and

$$\mathbf{B}^k(\mathbf{w}) = \left(a_{ij}^k + \sum_{l=1}^{p} q_{ij}^{kl} w_l \right). \tag{65}$$

It can be shown that this mapping is a contraction in the l_∞ norm. Thus the mapping will have a unique fixed point which can be obtained by the method of successive approximations, i.e., it will be the limit of any sequence $\mathbf{w}, \mathbf{w}'$, $\mathbf{w}''$, . . . , where

$$\mathbf{w}^{n+1} = T(\mathbf{w}^{(n)}). \tag{66}$$

Recursive Games. These games differ from stochastic games in that the probability of termination (at a given stage) need not be positive. Thus, infinitely long games might have positive probability (depending on the strategies chosen). Because of this, a payoff a_∞ is specified in case of non-terminating play (*survival payoff*).

Generally speaking, the value equations (60)-(61) will have nonunique solutions. It is necessary to choose among these one which actually is attainable; this is usually one which is "close" to the survival payoff a_∞.

Example 9: A military commander is surrounded in a fort. He would like to make his way to friendly territory, which can be found some distance either to the East or to the West. Every night, therefore, he has the choice of attempting a sortie in either of these directions.

His opponent, in turn, may choose to guard either of the two roads. If a sortie is attempted, and the enemy is guarding that road, the army will be captured en masse. If the enemy is guarding the other road, then the sortie will be successful.

Finally, the commander has the option of staying inside the fort, in which case the game element is repeated.

The game may be represented by

$$\mathbf{\Gamma} = \begin{pmatrix} -1 & +1 \\ +1 & -1 \\ \Gamma & \Gamma \end{pmatrix}$$

where 1 is the utility of a successful sortie and -1 that of being captured en masse. For a game such as this, it is clear that a_∞ (the utility of indefinite extension) must be known to determine the optimal strategies. For if $a_\infty > 0$ (i.e., if something can be gained by staying in the fort) then the commander should choose row 3. If, on the other hand, $a_\infty < 0$, then he should choose rows 1 and 2 with probability $\frac{1}{2}$ each.

2.7 Differential Games

Differential games are, essentially, multi-stage games with continuous time. The transition from state to state is then described by means of differential equations. The usual assumption is that two players together control the motion of a particle in n-dimensional space. Thus, if the particle is in position $\mathbf{x} = (x_1, \ldots, x_n)$ at time t, its motion is given by

$$\frac{dx_i}{dt} = f_i(\mathbf{x};\boldsymbol{\varphi};\boldsymbol{\psi}) \qquad i = 1, \ldots, n \tag{67}$$

where $\boldsymbol{\varphi} = (\varphi_1, \ldots, \varphi_p)$ and $\boldsymbol{\psi} = (\psi_1, \ldots, \psi_q)$ are *control vectors* chosen by players I and II, respectively, and subject to constraints of the form

$$a_k \leqslant \varphi_k \leqslant b_k \qquad k = 1, \ldots, p \tag{68}$$

$$c_l \leqslant \psi_l \leqslant d_l \qquad l = 1, \ldots, q. \tag{69}$$

The game terminates when the vector $\mathbf{x}$ reaches some preassigned surface (the terminal surface). Two types of payoff are considered: an integral payoff, equal to the integral

$$\int_0^T K(\mathbf{x};\boldsymbol{\varphi};\boldsymbol{\psi})\, dt$$

of some function K from the beginning of the game at time 0 until its termination at time T; and a terminal payoff equal to some function G defined on the terminal surface C of the game. More generally, the total payoff may be expressed as a sum of these two.

Example 10: A pursuer (P_2) is trying to catch an evader (P_1) in the shortest possible time. Both P_1 and P_2 are moving inside a region; we may assume that their velocity is a function of their position inside the region. Each controls, at each moment of time, his direction of motion. Then, if (x_1, x_2) and (x_3, x_4) are their positions, we would have

$$\frac{dx_1}{dt} = u(x_1, x_2) \cos \varphi$$

$$\frac{dx_2}{dt} = u(x_1, x_2) \sin \varphi$$

$$\frac{dx_3}{dt} = w(x_3, x_4) \cos \psi$$

$$\frac{dx_4}{dt} = w(x_3, x_4) \sin \psi$$

where $u(x_1, x_2)$ and $w(x_3, x_4)$ are the two players' velocity functions. The game will terminate when they are close enough for capture to occur; generally, this will be whenever

$$(x_1 - x_3)^2 + (x_2 - x_4)^2 \leqslant \rho^2,$$

ρ being the capture distance. The payoff here is time to capture (which P_1 wants to maximize); it may be expressed as the integral of the function $K = 1$.

In a special case, the velocity u of the evader is zero everywhere. In this case, the problem reduces to an optimal control problem; namely, to bring the variable point (x_3, x_4) to a fixed point (x_1, x_2) in the shortest possible time. Generally, it is possible to view control problems as differential games in which one player is unable to act.

For games such as these, a strategy for player I is a rule for choosing the control vector $\boldsymbol{\varphi}$, as a function of $\mathbf{x}$. Similarly, a strategy for II will choose $\boldsymbol{\psi}$ as a function of $\mathbf{x}$.

A value–if it exists–will be a function of the initial state $\mathbf{x}_0$ of the game. We may define $P(\mathbf{x}_0; \boldsymbol{\varphi}; \boldsymbol{\psi})$ to be the total payoff, if the game starts in state $\mathbf{x}_0$ and the two players use the strategies $\boldsymbol{\varphi} = \varphi(\mathbf{x})$ and $\boldsymbol{\psi} = \psi(\mathbf{x})$, respectively.

We now define

$$V_{\mathrm{I}}(\mathbf{x}) = \max_{\varphi} \min_{\psi} P(\mathbf{x}; \boldsymbol{\varphi}; \boldsymbol{\psi}) \tag{70}$$

$$V_{\mathrm{II}}(\mathbf{x}) = \min_{\psi} \max_{\varphi} P(\mathbf{x}; \boldsymbol{\varphi}; \boldsymbol{\psi}). \tag{71}$$

These two functions, V_{I} and V_{II}, may or may not be equal. If equal we say that $V = V_{\mathrm{I}} = V_{\mathrm{II}}$ is the value function for the differential game.

A sufficient (but not necessary) condition for the existence of the value function $V(\mathbf{x})$ is that the integral payoff function K, and the vector control functions f_i, be separable into parts, independent of one players control, i.e.,

$$K(\mathbf{x}; \boldsymbol{\varphi}; \boldsymbol{\psi}) = K'(\mathbf{x}; \boldsymbol{\varphi}) + K''(\mathbf{x}; \boldsymbol{\psi}) \tag{72}$$

$$f_i(\mathbf{x}; \boldsymbol{\varphi}; \boldsymbol{\psi}) = f_i'(\mathbf{x}; \boldsymbol{\varphi}) + f_i''(\mathbf{x}; \boldsymbol{\psi}). \tag{73}$$

Assuming that the value function V exists, the strategies which give this value will be called optimal strategies. The optimal strategies $\hat{\boldsymbol{\varphi}}$ and $\hat{\boldsymbol{\psi}}$ and the value function will satisfy the equation

$$K(\mathbf{x}; \hat{\boldsymbol{\varphi}}(\mathbf{x}); \hat{\boldsymbol{\psi}}(\mathbf{x})) + \sum_{i=1}^{n} V_i(\mathbf{x}) = 0 \tag{74}$$

where

$$V_i = \frac{\partial V}{\partial x_i} \tag{75}$$

This equation (74) is known as the *main equation.*

In general, optimal play will cause the state $\mathbf{x}$ to move along a path which is at least piecewise smooth. This path will satisfy the differential equations

$$\begin{cases} \dfrac{dx_i}{dt} = f_i(\hat{\mathbf{x}};\boldsymbol{\varphi}(\mathbf{x});\hat{\boldsymbol{\psi}}(\mathbf{x})) \\ \dfrac{dV_i}{dt} = -K_j(\mathbf{x};\hat{\boldsymbol{\varphi}}(\mathbf{x});\hat{\boldsymbol{\psi}}(\mathbf{x})) - \sum_{i=1}^{n} V_i(\mathbf{x}) f_{ij}(\mathbf{x};\hat{\boldsymbol{\varphi}}(\mathbf{x});\hat{\boldsymbol{\psi}}(\mathbf{x})) \end{cases} \tag{76}$$

where

$$K_j = \partial K/\partial x_j, \qquad f_{ij} = \partial f_i/\partial x_j.$$

These are known as *path equations.*

To determine a solution to this system of differential equations, we note that each path must terminate on the surface C. Now for a point on C, the coordinates $(x_1, \ldots, x_n)$ are assumed known. Moreover, the value function V will coincide, on C, with the terminal payoff function G. This fact will allow us to calculate the partial derivative, V_j, on C. In fact, if C is parameterized by the $n - 1$ parameters $(s_1, \ldots, s_{n-1})$, we will have

$$\frac{\partial G}{\partial s_i} = \sum_{j=1}^{n} V_j \frac{\partial x_j}{\partial s_i} \tag{77}$$

and this gives us a system of $n - 1$ equations for $V_1, \ldots, V_n$. The main equation (74) gives us a system of n equations which can be solved for $V_1, \ldots, V_n$ at a point on C.

The system (76) of differential equations is thus determined by a set of terminal conditions (i.e., values of x_i and V_j at time T of termination). It is sometimes simpler to replace *forward time t* by *retrograde time*

$$\tau = T - t$$

since, in this form, the terminal conditions become *initial conditions* (i.e., conditions satisfied at $\tau = 0$).

Generally speaking, the equations given above will be valid, *except along certain lower-dimensional surfaces*, if the value function $V(\mathbf{x})$ exists. Several types of singular surfaces are distinguished:

(a) *Transition Surfaces.* On such surfaces the optimal control is discontinuous, giving rise to a non-smooth path.
(b) *Universal Surfaces.* Such surfaces are characterized by a merging of optimal paths.
(c) *Equivocal Surfaces.* From points on such surfaces, more than one path begins. This generally gives rise to a (momentary) randomization.
(d) *Barriers.* Such surfaces correspond to discontinuities of the value function

itself; in some pursuit games they serve to separate the space into the capture zone (where a pursuer can force capture) and the escape zone (where the pursued can avoid capture indefinitely).

Differential Games of Kind. A game of kind is one in which only a few payoffs are recognized (e.g., "win" and "loss") as opposed to those discussed above (games of degree) in which a continuum of payoffs are recognized. One possible technique for the solution of such games consists in embedding them in a game of degree, i.e., if only the payoffs "win" and "lose" are recognized, replace this payoff by a terminal function G which is positive for every "win" outcome and non-positive for every "loss." An alternative technique will attempt to construct the *barrier* which separates the *winning zone* (section of space where I can force a win) from the *losing zone* (section where II can force I's loss). This is usually done by looking for the normal vector

$$\boldsymbol{\nu} = (\nu_1, \ldots, \nu_n)$$

to the barrier surface. The fact is that ν will behave exactly as the gradient

$$\nabla \mathbf{V} = (V_1, \ldots, V_n)$$

behaves for games of degree, i.e., it will satisfy the same differential equation system.

3. TWO-PERSON NONZERO-SUM GAMES

3.1 Introduction

In two-person nonzero-sum games, a substantial difference in emphasis occurs because what is good for one player is not necessarily bad for the other player. Consequently, the two players are not acting entirely *against* each other and may actually be able to obtain an advantage in making their strategy known.

We distinguish two possibilities for these games: the non-cooperative case, where preplay communication, binding contracts, and correlated strategies are forbidden; and the cooperative case, where one or more of these are allowed.

3.2 Non-Cooperative Games

In these games we are given two payoff functions, $A(\sigma, \tau)$ and $B(\sigma, \tau)$ defined for all pairs of strategies (σ, τ), and corresponding to the payoffs for I and II respectively. If the strategy sets are finite, then A and B can be represented as matrices $\mathbf{A} = (a_{ij})$ and $\mathbf{B} = (b_{ij})$. The game is then said to be a bi-matrix game.

Most of the work for such games has centered on the question of equilibrium pairs. In general, equilibrium pairs of pure strategies need not exist. However, it has been shown that *every bi-matrix game has at least one equilibrium pair of mixed strategies.*

Unfortunately, equilibrium pairs for nonzero-sum games are not a totally satisfactory solution concept. The difficulties with this are best exemplified by two examples.

Example 11: A company, C_1, has a factory which may be used to produce either a cheap or an expensive grade of coffee. A second company, C_2, can produce either an expensive or a cheap coffee urn. The expensive coffee can be brewed in either urn, but the cheap coffee can only be brewed in the expensive urn.

If one company makes the expensive product, and the other the cheap product, then there will be sizeable sales, the company making the expensive item will have high profits, and the other will have reasonable profits. If both make the expensive product, then sales will be small and neither company will make any profits. If both make the cheap product, there will be no sales, and neither company will make profits.

This game could reasonably be represented by the two matrices:

$$\mathbf{A} = \begin{array}{c} \\ \sigma \\ \sigma' \end{array} \begin{array}{c} \tau \quad \tau' \\ \begin{pmatrix} 4 & 0 \\ 0 & 1 \end{pmatrix} \end{array} \qquad \mathbf{B} = \begin{array}{c} \\ \sigma \\ \sigma' \end{array} \begin{array}{c} \tau \quad \tau' \\ \begin{pmatrix} 1 & 0 \\ 0 & 4 \end{pmatrix} \end{array}$$

It may be seen that this game has the equilibrium pairs (σ, τ) and (σ', τ'). However, neither (σ, τ') nor (σ', τ) are in equilibrium; moreover, the payoffs at the two equilibrium points are distinct. Thus, some sort of pre-play communication (normally forbidden by the rules) would be useful in this game.

Example 12: (The Prisoner's Dilemma). Two prisoners are suspected of taking part in some crime. The district attorney talks to each of them in turn, offering each one clemency if he turns state's witness against his partner, and threatening to jail them both on some minor trumped-up charges if neither confesses. Each prisoner has the choice of two strategies: not confess (σ and τ) or to confess (σ' and τ'). A reasonable assignment of utilities would give the following matrices:

$$\mathbf{A} = \begin{array}{c} \\ \sigma \\ \sigma' \end{array} \begin{array}{c} \tau \quad \tau' \\ \begin{pmatrix} 5 & 0 \\ 10 & 1 \end{pmatrix} \end{array} \qquad \mathbf{B} = \begin{array}{c} \\ \sigma \\ \sigma' \end{array} \begin{array}{c} \tau \quad \tau' \\ \begin{pmatrix} 5 & 10 \\ 0 & 1 \end{pmatrix} \end{array}.$$

Here it may be seen that (σ', τ') is the only equilibrium pair. Unfortunately it may be seen that the non-equilibrium position (σ, τ) gives higher payoffs for both players than the "rational" equilibrium pair.

3.3 Cooperative Games

The point behind cooperative games is that both players can generally do better by acting together than separately; thus the value of cooperation. This cooperation must, of course, be paid for, thus giving rise to bargaining.

In the simplest case, it is assumed that the two players cannot affect each other unless they come to an agreement. Thus the game is defined by a subset S of Euclidean space, representing the (joint) payoffs which the two players can obtain by cooperation, and two numbers, u_0, v_0, representing the amount that each player can obtain without the other's cooperation. It is generally agreed that S should be closed and convex, and bounded above (in the sense that, for any (a, b), the set of all $(u, v) \in S$ with $u \geqslant a$, $v \geqslant b$ is bounded). In this case, a reasonable system of axioms (due to Nash) leads to the conclusion that the players "should" agree to obtain that point (u, v) in S which maximizes the product

$$(u - u_0)(v - v_0) \tag{78}$$

subject, of course, to $u \geqslant u_0$, $v \geqslant v_0$. This point (u^*, v^*) is known as the *Nash point*, and can be shown to be unique.

Example 13: Two men can, by working together, obtain a certain quantity, q, of some commodity. It is necessary to determine how they will divide this quantity.

Let us assume that the men have functions U and V for this commodity, i.e., a quantity x will give them utilities $U(x)$ and $V(x)$, respectively. Then, if the first man receives x units, the second will receive $q - x$, and then utilities will be $U(x)$ and $V(q - x)$ respectively. Thus, by cooperation they can obtain any point on the curve

$$u = U(x), \quad v = V(q - x), \quad 0 \leqslant x \leqslant q.$$

In case of no cooperation, then neither receives any of the good, and their utilities will be $U(0)$ and $V(0)$, respectively. Finally, by randomizations, any point in the convex hull of the curve and $(U(0), V(0))$ can be obtained. Thus the set S will be the convex hull of $(U(0), V(0))$ and the curve.

In the more general case, each player can affect the other even when no agreement is reached. Thus, the game will have a more complicated structure, consisting of two payoff functions $A(\sigma, \tau)$ and $B(\sigma, \tau)$, which will be obtained if no agreement can be reached (here σ and τ are strategies for the two players) and a set S similar to that discussed above. The idea then is that σ and τ are chosen as *threats*, to be used only if no agreement is reached. Then, with each player knowing the other's threat, bargaining can be conducted.

It stands to reason that the outcome of the bargaining will depend—to some extent at least—on the threats. It is suggested that if the threats σ and τ are made, the bargaining outcome should be that point (u^*, v^*) which maximizes the product

$$(u - A(\sigma, \tau))\,(v - B(\sigma, \tau)) \tag{79}$$

subject, of course, to

$$(u, v) \in S, u \geqslant A(\sigma, \tau), v \geqslant B(\sigma, \tau).$$

Looked at from this point of view, the point (u^*, v^*) is the logical outcome of the threat pair (σ, τ). It is then possible to define equilibrium pairs (σ, τ) in terms, not of the (threat) payoffs $A(\sigma, \tau)$, $B(\sigma, \tau)$, but rather in terms of the logical outcome (u^*, v^*). We can give a theorem about these terms.

THEOREM 7. If the strategy sets for both players are finite, then there will exist at least one equilibrium pair of *mixed* threat strategies. These are also known as optimal threat strategies.

This last theorem guarantees the existence, for finite games, of a value (u^*, v^*), and of optimal threats. The computation of these is, of course, quite complex, depending both on the payoff matrices $\mathbf{A}$ and $\mathbf{B}$, and on the set S.

The rule is that, if $\mathbf{x}^*$ and $\mathbf{y}^*$ are (mixed) threat strategies, and (u^*, v^*) a point of S, then a sufficient condition for $\mathbf{x}^*$, $\mathbf{y}^*$ to be optimal threat strategies, and (u^*, v^*) to be the value of the game is that, for some m, $\mathbf{x}^*$, $\mathbf{y}^*$ be optimal strategies for the matrix game

$$m\mathbf{A} - \mathbf{B},$$

that the line through (u^*, v^*) with slope m pass through $(\mathbf{x}^{*t}\mathbf{A}\mathbf{y}^*, \mathbf{x}^{*t}\mathbf{B}\mathbf{y}^*)$, and that the line through (u^*, v^*) with slope $-m$ lie entirely above and to the right of the set S.

4. n-PERSON GAMES

4.1 Definitions

For n-person games, as for two-person nonzero-sum games, a distinction is made between cooperative and non-cooperative games. For non-cooperative games, however, there is little difference between the n-person and two-person theories.

For cooperative n-person games, the emphasis is on the formation of coalitions rather than on the strategies chosen in the actual play. Thus such games are usually studied in their *characteristic function form.*

Essentially, the characteristic function tells us how much utility the members of a coalition can guarantee for themselves (if the coalition forms). It is assumed that this utility can be divided among the members of the coalition in any way desired. (This is the *side payments* condition.)

Mathematically, we can let $N = \{1, 2, \ldots, n\}$ be the set of players for an n-

person game. A *characteristic function* is then a function v, which assigns a real number $v(S)$ to each subset S of N, satisfying

$$v(\emptyset) = 0 \tag{80}$$

$$v(S \cup T) \geqslant v(S) + v(T) \quad \text{if} \quad S \cap T = \emptyset. \tag{81}$$

The second condition, known as *super-additivity*, is sometimes weakened to

$$v(S \cup \{i\}) \geqslant v(S) + v(\{i\}) \quad \text{if} \quad i \notin S. \tag{82}$$

We generally identify the game with the function v.

The elements of N are *players*, the non-empty subsets of N are *coalitions*.

An *imputation* (for the game v) is a vector $\mathbf{x} = (x_1, \ldots, x_n)$ such that

$$x_i \geqslant v(\{i\}) \quad \text{for all} \quad i \in N \tag{83}$$

$$\sum_{i \in N} x_i = v(N). \tag{84}$$

From the definition of a characteristic function, we see that

$$v(N) \geqslant \sum_{i \in N} v(\{i\}). \tag{85}$$

Now, if equality holds here, the game will have only one imputation, and is said to be *inessential* (i.e., there is no point in forming coalitions). If inequality holds, then the game is *essential*; there are an infinite number of imputations (in fact they form a simplex in n-space).

S-equivalence Normalization. Two games, u and v, are said to be S-equivalent if there exist a number $\alpha > 0$ and a vector $\boldsymbol{\beta} = (\beta_1, \ldots, \beta_n)$ such that for all $S \subset N$,

$$u(S) = \alpha\, v(S) + \sum_{i \in S} \beta_i. \tag{86}$$

All of the accepted solution concepts are preserved by S-equivalence. Thus, it suffices to study one game from each S-equivalence class.

A game v is in (0, 1) normalization if

$$v(\{i\}) = 0 \quad \text{for all} \quad i \in N \tag{87}$$

$$v(N) = 1 \tag{88}$$

Any essential game is S-equivalent to one (and only one) game in (0, 1) normalization. Thus, we will frequently confine ourselves to (0, 1) normalized games.

Example 14: (The Horse-trade Game). A man (1) owns a horse which he values at \$50.00. Two prospective buyers (2 and 3) value the horse at \$100.00 and

\$90.00, respectively. If we let utility correspond to money, we see that the first player has (by himself) utility equal to 50 units, while the others have none. However, increases in utility can be obtained by trading among the players. Specifically, 1 can sell the horse to either of the others, assuming that such a coalition (for trading purposes) can be solved. Thus, 1 and 2 together can obtain a total of 100 units; 1 and 3 can obtain 90 units. We have, then

$$V(\{1\}) = 50$$

$$V(\{2\}) = V(\{3\}) = V(\{2, 3\}) = 0$$

$$V(\{1, 3\}) = 90$$

$$V(\{1, 2\}) = V(\{1, 2, 3\}) = 100.$$

The imputations for this game will consist of all vectors (x_1, x_2, x_3), such that

$$x_1 + x_2 + x_3 = 100$$

$$x_1 \geqslant 50; \quad x_2 \geqslant 0; \quad x_3 \geqslant 0.$$

In (0, 1) normalization, this game will have the form

$$U(\{i\}) = 0 \qquad \text{for} \quad i = 1, 2, 3$$

$$U(\{2, 3\}) = 0$$

$$U(\{1, 3\}) = 0.8$$

$$U(\{1, 2\}) = U(\{1, 2, 3\}) = 1.$$

The imputations then are all vectors (x_1, x_2, x_3) with

$$x_1 + x_2 + x_3 = 1$$

$$x_i \geqslant 0.$$

Example 15: (The 5-person Voting Game). Consider a voting game with five players, in which player 1 (the strong player) has 3 votes, and each of the others has 1 vote. There is a total of 7 votes, with 4 needed for a majority. We shall assign characteristic function $v(S) = 1$ if S has at least 4 votes, and 0 otherwise. Thus

$$v(\{i\}) = 0 \qquad \text{for all} \quad i$$

$$v(S) = 0 \quad \text{if} \quad |S| = 2 \quad \text{or} \quad 3, \quad \text{and} \quad 1 \notin S$$

$$v(S) = 1 \quad \text{if} \quad |S| = 2 \quad \text{or} \quad 3, \quad \text{and} \quad 1 \in S$$

$$v(S) = 1 \quad \text{if} \quad |S| = 4 \quad \text{or} \quad 5.$$

This game is already in (0, 1) normalization. Its imputations are all vectors $(x_1, \ldots, x_5)$ with

$$x_1 + \ldots + x_5 = 1$$
$$x_i \geqslant 0.$$

4.2 Domination, the Core, Stable Sets

For a game v, we will say that an imputation, $\mathbf{x}$, *dominates* another imputation $\mathbf{y}$, with notation

$$\mathbf{x} \succ \mathbf{y}$$

if there exists a non-empty $S \subset N$ such that

$$x_i > y_i \quad \text{for all} \quad i \in S \tag{89}$$

$$\sum_{i \in S} x_i \leqslant v(S). \tag{90}$$

The *core* of a game is the set of all *undominated* imputations. (Unfortunately, wide classes of games have empty cores.)

A *stable set* (also known as a von Neumann-Morgenstern solution) is a set V of imputations such that:

a. No $\mathbf{x} \in V$ dominates another $\mathbf{y} \in V$.

b. If $\mathbf{z}$ is an imputation, $\mathbf{z} \notin V$, there is $\mathbf{x} \in V$ such that $\mathbf{x} \succ \mathbf{z}$.

Unfortunately, most games have a large number of stable sets; some, however, have no stable sets.

Generally, the core is a subset of every stable set. If the core itself is stable, it will be the *only* stable set.

Example 16: In the horse-trade game mentioned above, the core consists of all imputations $(x_1, x_2, 0)$, where

$$90 \leqslant x_1 \leqslant 100; \quad x_1 + x_2 = 100.$$

Thus, 2 buys the horse, paying at least \$90.00.

The core, here, is not a stable set. A typical stable set for this game consists of the core plus a "bargaining curve," consisting of imputations which correspond to the possibility that the two buyers might form a coalition to drive down the price of the horse.

Example 17: In the 5-person voting game mentioned above, the core is empty; there are many stable sets. One stable set consists of the five imputations

$$(\tfrac{3}{4}, \tfrac{1}{4}, 0, 0, 0)$$
$$(\tfrac{3}{4}, 0 \ \tfrac{1}{4}, 0, 0)$$
$$(\tfrac{3}{4}, 0 \ 0 \ \tfrac{1}{4}, 0)$$

$$\left(\tfrac{3}{4},\quad 0 \quad 0 \quad 0,\ \tfrac{1}{4}\right)$$
$$\left(0,\quad \tfrac{1}{4}\ \tfrac{1}{4},\ \tfrac{1}{4},\ \tfrac{1}{4}\right).$$

Additionally, there are four so-called discriminatory solutions, in which player 1 and one other split one unit in all possible ways, one discriminatory solution in which 2, 3, 4, and 5 split one unit in all possible ways, and many others too numerous to mention.

4.3 The Shapley Value

The Shapley Value is an *a priori* expectation of the amount a player may hope to gain by playing a game. Axiomatically, it is a mapping from the set of n-person games to the set of n-vectors (payoffs) which has the properties of: symmetry (if a game is symmetric its value must be symmetric); efficiency (the set of all players who can contribute at all to the game receives as much as the players can obtain); additivity (the value for the sum of two games is equal to the sum of the values). It can be shown that only one value satisfies these axioms. This is $\boldsymbol{\varphi}[v] = (\varphi_1, \ldots, \varphi_n)$ given by

$$\varphi_i[v] = \sum_{\substack{S \subset N \\ i \notin S}} \frac{(n-s-1)!s!}{n!} [v(S \cup \{i\}) - v(S)]. \tag{91}$$

where s and n are the number of players in S and N, respectively.

Example 18: In the horse-trade game discussed above the Shapley value is (81.7, 11.7, 6.7).

Example 19: In the five-player voting game above, the value is

$$(0.6, 0.1, 0.1, 0.1, 0.1).$$

For large games, the value as given above may be quite difficult to evaluate, even if the games have a reasonable structure (e.g., weighted voting games). In such cases, the alternative formula

$$\varphi_i[v] = \int_0^1 \frac{\partial f}{\partial x_i}(t, t, \ldots, t)\, dt \tag{92}$$

where

$$f(x_1, \ldots, x_n) = \sum_{S \subset N} \left\{ \prod_{j \in S} x_j \prod_{j \notin S} (1 - x_j) \right\} v(S) \tag{93}$$

may be of use. The function $f(x_1, \ldots, x_n)$, known as the *multilinear extension* of v, can usually be approximated by the use of probabilistic limit theorems.

4.4 The Bargaining Sets

The *Bargaining Set* represents a different approach to stability. In essence, it assumes that coalitions have been formed, and then looks for payoff vectors which will be stable in a special sense; namely, that no player can be threatened in a manner which will decrease his share of the payoff.

A *coalition structure*, $\mathcal{T} = \{T_1, \ldots, T_m\}$, is a partition of the player set N (i.e., a collection of disjoint sets whose union is N).

An *individually rational payoff configuration* (i.r.p.c.) is a pair $\langle \mathcal{T}, \mathbf{x} \rangle$ where $\mathcal{T}$ is a coalition structure, and $\mathbf{x} = (x_1, \ldots, x_n)$ is a vector satisfying

$$\sum_{i \in T_j} x_i = v(T_j) \qquad \text{for all} \quad T_j \in \mathcal{T} \tag{94}$$

$$x_i \geqslant v(\{i\}) \qquad \text{for all} \quad i \in N. \tag{95}$$

Finally, if $\mathcal{T}$ is a coalition structure, and $i \in N$, then the *partners of i in* $\mathcal{T}$ is the set T_j such that $i \in T_j \in \mathcal{T}$. We write this $P(i, \mathcal{T})$.

If $\langle \mathcal{T}, \mathbf{x} \rangle$ is an i.r.p.c., and k, l are partners in $\mathcal{T}$, then an objection of k against l is another i.r.p.c. $\langle \mathcal{U}, \mathbf{y} \rangle$ such that:

(a) If $i \in P(k, \mathcal{U})$, then $y_i > x_i$

(b) $l \notin P(k, \mathcal{U})$.

A counter-objection of l against k is a third i.r.p.c., $\langle \mathcal{V}, \mathbf{z} \rangle$, such that

(a) If $i \in P(l, \mathcal{V})$, then $z_i \geqslant x_i$

(b) If $i \in P(l, \mathcal{V}) \cap P(k, \mathcal{U})$ then $z_i \geqslant y_i$

(c) $k \notin P(l, \mathcal{V})$.

A *stable i.r.p.c.* is any i.r.p.c. such that for any objection of a k against an l, l has a counter objection.

The bargaining set $\mathcal{M}_1^{(i)}$ is the set of all stable i.r.p.c.'s. This set is non-empty in the strong sense that, for any $\mathcal{T}$, there exists at least one $\mathbf{x}$ such that $\langle \mathcal{T}, \mathbf{x} \rangle \in \mathcal{M}_1^{(i)}$.

Different bargaining sets can be obtained by modifying the types of objection; i.e., we might allow objections of one set of players against another set, or objections of one player against one who is not among his partners.

A closely related concept is the *kernel*. For any coalition S and any payoff vector $\mathbf{x}$, we define the excess of S in $\mathbf{x}$ by

$$e(S, \mathbf{x}) = v(S) - \sum_{i \in S} x_i. \tag{96}$$

Then, the *surplus of k against l* is

$$s_{kl}(\mathbf{x}) = \max_{\substack{T \\ k \in T \\ l \notin T}} e(T, \mathbf{x}). \tag{97}$$

We say that k *outweighs* l ($k \succ\succ l$) if

$$s_{kl}(\mathbf{x}) > s_{lk}(\mathbf{x}) \tag{98}$$

and

$$x_l > v(\{l\}). \tag{99}$$

We say also that k, l are in equilibrium ($k \sim l$) if *neither* $k \succ\succ l$ *nor* $l \succ\succ k$.

The *kernel* $\mathcal{K}$ is the set of all i.r.p.c.'s $\langle \mathcal{T}, \mathbf{x} \rangle$ such that any k and l which belong to the same $T_j \in \mathcal{T}$ are in equilibrium.

Once again, the kernel is non-empty in the sense that, for any $\mathcal{T}$, there is some $\mathbf{x}$ such that $\langle \mathcal{T}, \mathbf{x} \rangle \in \mathcal{K}$. Moreover, $\mathcal{K} \subset \mathfrak{M}_1^{(i)}$.

The *nucleolus* is a further solution concept related to the kernel. We may define the vector $\boldsymbol{\theta}(\mathbf{x})$ by

$$\boldsymbol{\theta}(\mathbf{x}) = (e(S_1, \mathbf{x}), e(S_2, \mathbf{x}), \ldots, e(S_{2n}, \mathbf{x})) \tag{100}$$

where $e(S_j, \mathbf{x})$ is the excess of S_j and the $S_1, S_2, \ldots, S_{2n}$ are all the subsets of N, arranged in order of decreasing excess:

$$e(S_1, \mathbf{x}) \geqslant e(S_2, \mathbf{x}) \geqslant \ldots \geqslant e(S_{2n}, \mathbf{x}). \tag{101}$$

We now order the set of $\boldsymbol{\theta}(\mathbf{x})$ by the lexicographic ordering. It can be proved that, in the set of imputations, there is a *unique* imputation, $\boldsymbol{v}$, for which $\boldsymbol{\theta}(\mathbf{x})$ is minimal in the lexicographic ordering. This $\boldsymbol{v}$ is known as the *nucleolus.*

If $\mathcal{T} = \{N\}$ is the coalition structure consisting only of the grand coalition, then the i.r.p.c. $\langle \mathcal{T}, \nu \rangle$ belongs to the kernel $\mathcal{K}$.

Example 20: In the horse-trade game mentioned above, suppose the coalition structure $\{\{1, 2\}, \{3\}\}$ forms. Then the bargaining set will contain all vectors $(x_1, x_2, 0)$ with

$$90 \leqslant x_1 \leqslant 100, \quad x_1 + x_2 = 100.$$

Thus, this coincides with the core. The kernel, however, contains only the vector (95, 5, 0). Moreover, (95, 5, 0) is the nucleolus.

Example 21: In the 5-person voting game, suppose the coalition structure $\{\{1, 2\}, \{3\}, \{4\}, \{5\}\}$ forms. Then the bargaining set consists of the vectors $(x_1, x_2, 0, 0, 0)$ where

$$0.5 \leqslant x_1 \leqslant 0.75, \quad x_1 + x_2 = 1$$

the kernel, however, contains only the vector (0.5, 0.5, 0, 0, 0).

The nucleolus is the vector $(\frac{3}{7}, \frac{1}{7}, \frac{1}{7}, \frac{1}{7}, \frac{1}{7})$.

It is quite complicated, in general, to compute all of the kernel or the bargaining set. Methods exist for obtaining at least one element.

A *demand function* is a set of n^2 lower semi-continuous functions d_{ij} (i, $j = 1, \ldots, n$) such that

$$0 \leqslant d_{ij}(x) \leqslant \min \{x_j, \max [\tfrac{1}{2}(s_{ij}(\mathbf{x}) - s_{ji}(\mathbf{x})), 0]\} \tag{102}$$

where s_{ij} is the surplus of i against j.

Let

$$\mathcal{B} = \{\mathbf{x} \,|\, d_{ij}(\mathbf{x}) = 0 \quad \forall i, j\} \tag{103}$$

be the bargaining set associated with d_{ij}. By a suitable choice of d_{ij}, $\mathcal{B}$ can be the kernel $\mathcal{K}$, the bargaining set $\mathfrak{M}_1^{(i)}$, or any one of many interesting sets.

Starting from an arbitrary imputation $\mathbf{x}^\circ$, we define a sequence $\{\mathbf{x}^t\}$ inductively by:

$$i(t), j(t) \text{ are such as to maximize } d_{ij}(\mathbf{x}^t)$$

$$x_{i(t)}^{t+1} = x_{i(t)}^t + d_{i(t),j(t)}(\mathbf{x}^t) \tag{104}$$

$$x_{j(t)}^{t+1} = x_{j(t)}^t - d_{i(t),j(t)}(\mathbf{x}^t) \tag{105}$$

$$x_k^{t+1} = x_k^t \qquad \text{for all other } k. \tag{106}$$

Then the sequence $\{\mathbf{x}^t\}$ will converge to a limit $\mathbf{x}^*$, and $\mathbf{x}^* \in \mathcal{B}$.

An alternative, related method uses only *continuous* demand functions $d_{ij}(\mathbf{x})$. Starting again from an arbitrary imputation $\mathbf{x}(0)$, define a system of differential equations

$$\frac{dx_i}{dt} = \sum_j (d_{ij}(\mathbf{x}) - d_{ji}(\mathbf{x})). \tag{107}$$

As $t \to \infty$, the system $\mathbf{x}(t)$ will converge to a limit $\mathbf{x}^*$. Once again, $\mathbf{x}^* \in \mathcal{B}$.

4.5 Games Without Side Payments

In the above (side payments) theory, it was assumed that a coalition could divide its winnings in any way desired. In a more general context this need not be so; only certain divisions are possible or permissible. This gives rise to the *no-side-payments* (NSP) theory.

In the NSP theory, the characteristic function v assigns to each coalition S, not a single number, but rather a set of points in n-dimensional space; namely, the set of those points $\mathbf{x}$ such that coalition S can guarantee, to all of its members, their share of $\mathbf{x}$.

Mathematically, we assume that we are given a compact convex subset K of n-dimensional space. A characteristic function is then a function v which assigns, to each $S \subset N$, a non-empty, closed, convex subset of n-space, satisfying:

(a) If $\mathbf{x} \in v(S)$, $y_i \leqslant x_i \; \forall i \in S$,
then $\mathbf{y} \in v(S)$

(b) $v(S) \cap v(T) \subset v(S \cup T)$
if $S \cap T = \phi$

(c) $\mathbf{y} \in v(N)$ iff $\exists \mathbf{x} \in K$
such that $y_i \leqslant x_i \quad \forall i \in N$.

Domination, for these games, is defined by saying that $\mathbf{x} \succ \mathbf{y}$ if there is a non-empty $S \subset N$ such that

$$x_i > y_i \quad \text{for all} \quad i \in S$$
$$\mathbf{x} \in v(S).$$

With this definition of domination, empty sets and the core are defined as for side-payment games.

Similarly, the concept of the bargaining set may be generalized to the NSP games. Unfortunately, the direct generalization of $\mathcal{M}_1^{(i)}$ need not be non-empty in the sense mentioned above. A somewhat weaker version, known as $\mathcal{M}_{1+}^{(i)}$ is, however, non-empty.

The Shapley value, kernel, and nucleolus are difficult to generalize; as yet no generally accepted method of doing so exists.

Example 22: Two players (1 and 2) can, by working together, produce 100 lbs. of a commodity which 1 values at \$1.00 per pound, and 2, at \$0.25 per pound. They have no money. A third player, 3, who has money, values the commodity at \$1.00 per pound.

Players 1 and 2, together, can divide the commodity in any way they wish. Thus they can obtain any point satisfying

$$u_1 + 4u_2 \leqslant 100$$
$$u_1 \leqslant 100$$
$$u_2 \leqslant 25.$$

Players 1 and 3, or 2 and 3, together, can obtain no profits. However, if all three cooperate, it becomes practical to sell part of the commodity to 3, at a price (presumably) somewhere between \$0.25 and \$1.00 per pound. Then the three players can obtain points satisfying

$$u_1 + u_2 + u_3 \leqslant 100$$
$$u_i + u_j \leqslant 100 \quad \text{for} \quad i \neq j$$
$$u_i \leqslant 100.$$

For this game, the core consists of all vectors (u_1, u_2, u_3) satisfying

$$u_1 + u_2 + u_3 = 100$$

$$u_1 + 4u_2 \geqslant 100$$
$$u_i \geqslant 0.$$

In case the 3-person coalition forms, the bargaining set will contain all imputations in the core. There is a lack of agreement as to the value; the values $(\frac{1}{2}, \frac{1}{2}, 0)$, $(\frac{2}{5}, \frac{2}{5}, \frac{1}{5})$ and (.518, .476, .006) have all been suggested.

4.6 Games for a Continuum of Players

A game for a continuum of players is defined as a σ-algebra $\mathfrak{A}$ of sets, (coalitions) together with a real-valued characteristic function v. The usual properties, *viz.*

$$v(\emptyset) = 0$$
$$v(S \cup T) \geqslant v(S) + v(T) \quad \text{if } S \cap T = \emptyset$$

are assumed to hold.

The usual ideas of domination, normalization, the core, and stable sets can be generalized to these games with a slight amount of care. Most of the work done for such games, however, has dealt with the Shapley value. (Using an axiomatic approach, the existence of this has been proved for a wide class of games; games exist, however, for which no "reasonable" value can be defined.)

Example 23: Consider a (very large) finite game, consisting of many traders, each holding a commodity bundle (i.e., a certain quantity of each of several commodities). Strictly speaking, the game is finite, and so can be analyzed according to the several concepts discussed above. From a practical point of view, this may, however, present an enormous task. It is therefore easier to represent the traders as points on a line; the commodity bundles can then be represented by densities on that line. The game then becomes (in effect) a game for a continuum of players.

5. GAMING

Gaming deals with the use of human beings to simulate the actual behavior of humans in situations of conflict of interest. In general, a strict mathematical analysis is not sought (although such analysis may be useful); rather, games are used for several other purposes.

Generally, it is recognized that a gaming exercise can have any one of several goals. These include:

1. Teaching and Training
2. Operations
3. Experimentation

4. Entertainment
5. Therapy.

We shall discuss these in some slight detail.

5.1 Teaching and Training

The most common use of gaming is for teaching purposes. As such, it is used at all levels, both in the schools (where it can be an adjunct to classwork) and in organizations, where the juniors are sometimes trained in their jobs by means of games. In general, the most valuable aspects of gaming, in this context, lie in the fact that it frequently motivates learners, and in that it teaches certain groups to relate to others (by encouraging them to play opposite roles).

An additional aspect of gaming here is its use for teaching theory. Unfortunately, it should be added that quite frequently the theory has been poorly developed. Thus, great care should be taken in the construction of games.

5.2 Operational Gaming

Another frequent application of gaming is for operational purposes. Essentially, a game is used to determine the likely outcomes of policies which may be chosen by the decision-makers. In this respect, it is usually important to use the decision-makers themselves, as far as is possible, in playing the game. It should also be noticed that quite frequently the outcome of the game is itself not as important as the decision processes which led to this outcome. Thus, lengthy briefing and debriefing sessions are normally a part of the exercise.

When using gaming for operational purposes, it should be noted that the makers of the game are usually able to introduce biases of varying degrees. Thus it is generally important to recognize the game-maker's biases before too much stock is placed on the outcome of the gaming exercise. (Conversely, a well-constructed game can be used to impress decision-makers with the value of certain policies.)

5.3 Experimentation

Gaming is also used for experimental purposes, both to test hypotheses as to human behavior, and to generate new hypotheses. Experimental gaming is also used for the study of artificial intelligence.

In developing artificial intelligence, some distinction should be made between the type of intelligence needed to solve problems and that which is needed for interpersonal relations. This distinction parallels the distinction between two-person zero-sum games (where no cooperation is of use) and other games where social cooperation is frequently useful and necessary.

5.4 Entertainment

Games are, of course, generally thought of as entertainment—though it may be questioned whether such games can be thought of as gaming exercises. In fact, however, there is only a thin line between these two applications of games, and, in evaluating a gaming exercise, the game director should, indeed, be aware of the possibility that what he considered an operational game was, in reality, treated by the participants as a type of entertainment.

5.5 Therapy

Games can also be used for therapeutic purposes; both psychodrama and transactional analysis show instances of this. Again, this is an application of games which should not, strictly speaking, be included under our general subject of gaming. Nevertheless, we include it here as a possible purpose of gaming exercises.

The reader is also referred to Chapter II-5 on Military Systems in the companion volume, *Handbook of Operations Research: Models and Applications*, where game theory, war gaming, and man-machine games are treated.

REFERENCES

For a popular introduction to the field, see Ref. 5 or 9. The original work that launched the field was Ref. 8. Refs. 1, 2, 3, and 7 below, are collections of research papers which serve to show the general advances in the field. For a critical discussion of the subject, see Ref. 4. A detailed mathematical development can best be obtained from Ref. 6.

1. Dresher, M., L. S. Shapley, and A. W. Tucker, (eds.), *Advances in Game Theory*, Annals of Mathematics Study No. 52, Princeton University Press, Princeton, New Jersey (1964).
2. ——, A. W. Tucker, and P. Wolfe, (eds.), *Contributions to the Theory of Games, III*, Annals of Mathematics Study No. 39, Princeton University Press, Princeton, New Jersey (1957).
3. Kuhn, H. W. and A. W. Tucker, (eds.), *Contributions to the Theory of Games, I, II*, Annals of Mathematics Studies No. 24, 28, Princeton University Press, Princeton, New Jersey (1950, 1953).
4. Luce, R. D. and H. Raiffa, *Games and Decisions*, Wiley & Sons, New York (1957).
5. McDonald, J., *Strategy in Poker, Business, and War*, W. W. Norton, New York (1950).
6. Owen, G., *Game Theory*, W. B. Saunders, Philadelphia, Pennsylvania (1968).
7. Tucker, A. W. and R. D. Luce, (eds.), *Contributions to the Theory of Games IV*, Annals of Mathematics Study No. 40, Princeton University Press, Princeton, New Jersey (1959).
8. von Neumann, J. and O. Morgenstern, *Theory of Games and Economic Behavior*, Princeton University Press, Princeton, New Jersey (1944, 1947, 1953).
9. Williams, J. D., *The Compleat Strategyst*, Wiley & Sons, New York (1954).

III-6

SEARCH THEORY*†

Philip M. Morse
Massachusetts Institute of Technology

INTRODUCTION

Being a part of a Handbook of Operations Research, this Chapter is addressed to the average worker in the field, not to the specialist in search theory. Results and conclusions are emphasized, rather than niceties of derivations (these can be found by going to the references). Procedural outlines and graphical aids are provided so that use can be made of the theory in planning actual searches. The aim has been to foster such use, and the hope is that interest will be aroused in developing more usable solutions for real search problems.

Search is an example of an operations research (OR) subject wherein theory and practice have diverged as they have developed. Search theory (ST), as a distinct subject of study, was begun during World War II†† in response to a very practical need for the efficient use of planes and ships to find enemy submarines.

*Support for the calculations reported in Section 5 has been provided by the U.S. Army Research Office (Durham) under Contract DAHCO4-70-C-0058.
†Submitted November 1973.
††"Preliminary Report on the Submarine Search Problem," by P. M. Morse, R. F. Rinehart and others, issued in May 1942, was the first Technical Report of the newly formed Anti-Submarine Warfare Operations Research Group, financed by the National Defense Research Committee and assigned to the Office of the Chief of Naval Operations, Admiral King. It covered parts of the material in Sections 2.3, 3.2 and 5.2 below. The contents of this and of many other studies by various members of the Group are reported in consolidated form in Koopman [1946].

The theory worked out then, rudimentary as it was, turned out to be of considerable help to the Navy in preparing search plans and procedures that were more effective than the earlier, more intuitive tactics. Since that time, the mathematical logic underlying the theory has been appreciably strengthened (see, for example, Dobbie [1968] and Pollock [1971]) and the range of suggested application has been conjecturally extended, but it is questionable whether many of the later, more elegant, extensions are in a form to be of much help to an operator carrying out an actual search, with its attendant urgencies and errors.

Part of the reason for the lack of advance in applications is the wide variety of situations implied in the word *search*. Aside from the basic probabilistic principles, there is little in common between the computational search for the maxima of a complex function of many variables, and the search for a lost child on the slope of a mountain or the search by the police for a fugitive who is continually changing his hiding place. If ST is to extend its range of applicability, many specific practical cases will have to be analyzed in detail, and usable solutions (even though they be approximate and inelegant) must be found for each case.

As pointed out by Pollock [1971] (see also Danskin [1962]) the term *search* has, at times, come to encompass not only the strategy of the operation of looking for a "lost" object or person (the target), but also the design and use of the detection equipment, and the question of what to do after the object has been found. In this chapter, the less inflated definition will be accepted: *search is the planning and carrying out of the process of looking for the target.* We assume that the characteristics of the detection equipment have been obtained; either directly, from operational experiments (as described in Section 2.3) or indirectly, from the combined use of the statistical theory of signal detection and decision theory. We then proceed to discuss how the equipment can be used in devising the strategy of actual search.

This concentration on the actual search process allows us to shorten the list of appropriate measures of effectiveness. In general, we assume the desideratum is to maximize the probability of finding the target, for a given expenditure of search effort. Occasionally, we assume the criterion is to minimize the expected time required to find the target; indeed, in many cases these two criteria require the same strategies. We do not consider other criteria, such as maximizing the amount of information gathered, as discussed by Mela [1961] and Dobbie [1968].

We will first treat the case of continuous search, because it has been studied in more detail. Here, the military applications are more numerous, though other search situations have been dealt with. Some space is given to consideration of the effect, on the structure of an optimal search, of false targets that often dilute an actual search. Later sections deal with the problem of the search of discrete sites, with potential applications to the prospecting for ore or oil, or the police search for evidence. Finally, the problem of the search for an active evader is touched on; here, the theoretical development is just beginning and the application to practice is yet to come. Details of these recent developments may be obtained from the papers, given in the bibliographies, of Enslow [1966], Dobbie [1968] and Pollock [1971].

1. FUNDAMENTAL CONCEPTS

We start with the operation basic to nearly all physical search: that of a person searching with his eyes over an area, to see whether he can recognize some object, symbol, or pattern (that we shall call the *target*) which he believes (or hopes) to be present somewhere in the area. Visual search displays nearly all the characteristics of more complicated search operations: the phenomenon of diminishing returns and the degree of improvement resulting from more orderly search patterns, for example. In addition, visual search is usually a component of more instrumented searches, in that the instruments–the radar or sonar screen, for instance–must be scanned visually.

1.1 Visual Search of an Area

The pertinent properties of the eyes in scanning an area, and the nature of the psychophysiological response are reviewed in Chapter 4 of Koopman [1946]. They form the basis of the following discussion.

The human eyes scan an area in a sequence of *fixations* in various directions (for about $\frac{1}{2}$ to $\frac{1}{4}$ second apiece) separated by rapid changes of eye direction; the eye does not "see" while the line of sight is moving. The detail seen per fixation drops off rapidly with angle away from the line of sight. Fine detail is perceived only by the fovea, the small central portion of the retina, subtending only a few degrees. Large objects, with a strong contrast, may be detected when 20° or more from the line of sight, but the central 2° to 5° are needed for fine detail.

These effects may be expressed in terms of a probability $\mu(\beta)$ that the searched-for target is recognized during a given fixation of the eyes, in a direction at angle β to the line to the target. Probability μ, of course, depends on β, but also on the illumination, the angular size and visual contrast of the target and, of course, on the state of the viewer's eyes. As noted, μ has a sharp maximum at $\beta = 0$, dropping rapidly to zero beyond $\beta \simeq 5^\circ$. The effective solid angle scanned for the target, per fixation, would then be the integral of μ over solid angle $d\Omega = d\alpha \sin\beta \, d\beta$,

$$\Gamma = \iint \mu(\beta)\, d\Omega$$

The value of Γ also depends on the nature of the target and on the conditions of illumination; it is a measure of the utility of a single glimpse in finding the target. In many cases this effective solid angle is small, of the order of 10 square degrees.

The magnitude of the search task also depends on the total solid angle Ω_s subtended, at the searcher's eyes, by the total area to be searched over. If, initially, the searcher has no idea of the position of the target in the solid angle Ω_s, and if the plane is oriented and illuminated so that Γ is independent of the direction to which the line of sight is pointed, when the chance of detecting the target in a single fixation, directed at random within Ω_s, will be constant, independent of direction (other cases will be considered later). This chance, called the *a priori glimpse probability*, the ratio between the effective solid angle scanned per fixation and the total solid angle to be scanned, $g = \Gamma/\Omega_s$, is the probability that the target will be recognized in a single, randomly pointed fixation.

When, as is usual in such visual searches, successive fixations are randomly directed, the probability that the object will be recognized in the nth fixation is $(1 - g)^{n-1}g$, the probability that it will still be undetected after the nth glimpse is $(1 - g)^n$ and the probability that it will be located by, or before, the nth fixation is

$$P_n = 1 - (1 - g)^n \tag{1}$$

Since g is usually considerably smaller than unity, and since searches of any importance involve hundreds of fixations (i.e., times of half a minute or more) this formula may be replaced by its asymptotic form

$$P_n = 1 - e^{-ng} \tag{2}$$

It is often useful to express this formula in terms of time t spent and total solid angle Ω_s to be searched. If ν is the frequency of eye fixations during the search, so that $n = \nu t$, we can write

$$P(\Phi) = 1 - e^{-\Phi}; \quad \Phi = E/\Omega_s; \quad E = \omega t \tag{3}$$

as the probability that the target will be detected in time t or sooner; where $\omega = \nu\Gamma$ is the *search rate*, in solid angle per unit time, E is the *total search effort*, in effective solid angle scanned in time t, and Φ is the *specific search effort* or *sighting potential* of the search.

We note the important property of diminishing returns, paramount in all search procedures. Doubling the search effort E does not double the probability of finding the target. Other search operations, discussed later, correspond to less simple relations between $P(\Phi)$ and Φ, but for all well-organized searches the probability $P(\Phi)$ is related to the specific search effort Φ by the following general properties (see discussion of Eq. 21)

$$\left.\begin{array}{l} P(\Phi) \text{ is a monotonically } \textit{increasing} \text{ function of } \Phi, \text{ and} \\ \quad P(0)=0;\, P(\Phi) \longrightarrow U \leqslant 1 \text{ as } \Phi \longrightarrow \infty; \text{ furthermore} \\ P'(\Phi) \equiv (dP/d\Phi) \text{ is a monotonically } \textit{decreasing} \text{ function} \\ \quad \text{of } \Phi \text{ and } P'(\Phi) \longrightarrow 0 \text{ as } \Phi \longrightarrow \infty \end{array}\right\} \quad (4)$$

The adjective "well-organized" implies that the properties of $P(\Phi)$, expressed in (4), are, in effect, a definition of what we mean by "well-organized" search. At any time during the expenditure of search effort we should, if possible, direct our next quantum of effort in that direction that promises the greatest results; that is, for which P' is greatest then. If we can do this at every instant of the search, we will have picked first the action for which P' is the largest (or at least not smaller than for any other action), and so on; P' will, as a result, be a monotonically decreasing function of Φ. (For further discussion see Koopman [1956b], de Guenin [1961] and Section 3.3 of this chapter). These properties of $P'(\Phi)$, summed up in the phrase "diminishing returns," usually imply that the most efficient search involves a very non-linear distribution of search effort, as will be seen in Section 3.3.

1.2 False Alarms, Non-random Scanning

Just now, however, we must return to an actual example of visual search, to see whether our assumption, inherent in Eq. (1), of the statistical independence of successive glimpse probabilities is (or can be made) valid, and whether the actual search rate ω is in practice equal to $\nu\Gamma$. For example, suppose a person is standing in front of a large bookcase, trying to find a particular book he believes is somewhere on the shelves. He first scans at random; then, out of the corner of his eye he may glimpse what seems to be the right title and he directs his next fixations there to check. Perhaps the follow-up shows he was in error, so he returns to random scanning. Next time his attention is caught he may have to come close, or even to take the book off the shelf, before he realizes this also is not the book he is looking for. Eventually, a glimpse, followed by a closer look, discovers the wanted book (if it is truly there).

Thus the actual process of visual search involves both random and correlated fixations. In addition, some of the "detections" prove to be false alarms that tend to dilute the rate of search and thus delay the eventual discovery. The best we can do at present is to assume these effects will not change the form of Eq. (3) but will reduce the magnitude of the search rate ω.

In fact, one can verify experimentally that the probability of finding a wanted book in a bookcase containing N books (N large) in time t is approximately given by the formula

$$P(\Phi) = 1 - e^{-\Phi}; \quad \Phi = \rho t/N \tag{5}$$

where ρ, the effective search rate in books per unit time, depends on the searcher, the degree of illumination and the physical characteristics of the book, and includes the effects of false alarms. In practice, this rate turns out to lie between 100 and 200 books per minute (see Morse [1970]) if the books are arranged at random on the shelves, so the *a priori* probability of the book's location is uniform throughout the bookcase. In this case, the deviations (following up false alarms) slow the search but do not seem to alter its generally random nature.

The formula of Eq. (5) is an exemplar of the relationship between the probability $P(\Phi)$ of discovery, and the specific search coverage $\Phi = E/A$, the ratio between search effort E and the area A to be covered. We note again the property of diminishing returns, characteristic of all P's satisfying (4); if effort E is doubled, Φ is doubled but P is not doubled (unless E is small). Probability P is not additive, but search coverage is additive. For this reason, Φ is often called the sighting potential (see Koopman [1956b]).

To measure the degree of inefficiency caused by this process of random fixation, we turn to the idealized situation of complete regularity of search. Suppose our eyes could be made to swing smoothly across area A and suppose the target would certainly be discovered if it came within a solid angle subtending a circular region R of diameter W on A, and would not be discovered if it were outside A (this assumption eliminates the effects of false targets). We could then try to cover area A efficiently by moving the line of sight so that region R sweeps out a regular, non-overlapping path, either in a spiral or a zigzag pattern, eventually covering all of A but never covering any area more than once.

If the target is equally likely to be anywhere in A, the probability that it will have been discovered by the time an area a of A had thus been searched over is

$$P(a) = \begin{cases} (a/A) & (a \leqslant A) \\ 1 & (a \geqslant A) \end{cases} \tag{6}$$

where $a > A$ means that some of A has to be searched over again. To compare this with Eq. (5), for random search, we note that the sighting potential in the present case is $\Phi = a/A$. Thus, the two curves for P start with the same initial value and slope at $\Phi = 0$ and both approach each other as $\Phi \longrightarrow \infty$. The greatest difference between the two curves is at $\Phi = 1$, where the probability for uniform coverage is 1.00, and that for random coverage is 0.63. As we shall see later, the results for any intermediate degree of regularity in search coverage give results intermediate between these two curves (see Fig. 8).

2. MOTION OF THE SEARCHER

We turn now to a different operational situation; that of an aircraft flying over the ocean, searching for a ship or surfaced submarine. The plane's altitude is h; it is flying a straight course at speed v, which is great enough so the ship may be considered to be at rest. Here again we must discuss the rate of search, but in this case the rate is determined by the speed of the plane, which sweeps out a "searched strip" as it flies along.

2.1 Visual Search

First consider the case of a visual observer, looking for the target ship. The most noticeable feature of a small ship, such as a submarine, is usually its wake, if it is moving. Thus, as he glances about, the observer's chance per glimpse of spotting it is roughly proportional to the solid angle the wake subtends at his eye, in addition to depending on the state of the sea and the transparency of the atmosphere. As indicated in Fig. 1, this solid angle is inversely proportional to $(r^2 + h^2)$ and proportional to $\cos\theta = h/(r^2 + h^2)^{1/2}$. In other words, his glimpse probability for spotting the target when it is a horizontal distance r from the searching plane is $g(r) = Ch/(r^2 + h^2)^{3/2}$ where the value of the constant C depends on the size of the ship plus wake, its contrast to the surrounding sea (i.e., on the state of the sea) and on the range of atmospheric visibility. For further details see Koopman [1946].

In a time dt, during which the plane will have moved a distance $dy = v\,dt$ in the y direction, the observer will have had time to make $\nu\,dt = (\nu/v)\,dy$ eye fixa-

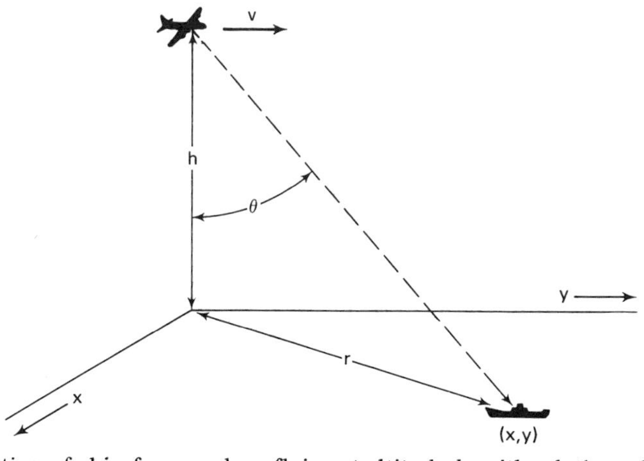

Fig. 1. Sighting of ship from a plane flying at altitude h, with relative velocity v in the y direction.

tions. Following the discussion of the previous section, the probability of *not* spotting the ship during time dt, when the ship is a horizontal distance r from the plane is $q(t) = \exp\,[-\nu Ch\,dt/(h^2 + r^2)^{3/2}]$ and the cumulative probability of not finding the ship, as the plane progresses on its search course, is the product of all the partial probabilities, $\cdots q(t - dt)\,q(t)\,q(t + dt)\,q(t + 2dt) \cdots$, for as long as the ship is within the solid angle searched over by the observer. Thus, the probability $p = 1 - [\cdots q(t - dt)\,q(t)\,q(t + dt) \cdots]$ of finding the ship during the passage of the search plane is given by the equation

$$p = 1 - e^{-F(x)}; \quad F(x) = \int \nu g(r)\,dt \tag{7}$$

where the integration is taken over the whole time during which the target is within the solid angle covered by the observer. The comments about visual search at the end of the previous section indicate that the effective value of the constant νC is rather less than laboratory measurements would predict; indeed, to be safe, its value must be measured under operational conditions, as will be discussed later. Nevertheless, the general form of Eq. (7) is valid.

The quantity $F(x)$ is, as mentioned previously, a sighting potential; its additive property is evidenced by its being an integral. If, later in the search, the plane's course brings it again within sighting range of the ship, the combined probability of detection would be obtained by adding the two values of F: $p = 1 - \exp\,(-F_1 - F_2)$. The individual F of Eq. (7) is a sum of all the infinitesimal sighting potentials accumulated as the plane passes by the target.

Returning to the formula for $g(r)$ for visual sighting, we can work out the visual sighting potential for a ship that is a perpendicular distance x (called the *lateral range*) from the plane's course. It is

$$F(x) = \frac{kh}{v} \int_{y_0}^{\infty} \frac{dy}{(h^2 + x^2 + y^2)^{3/2}} = \frac{kh}{v(h^2 + x^2)} \left[1 - \frac{y_0}{\sqrt{h^2 + x^2 + y_0^2}}\right] \tag{8}$$

where y_0 is the rearward limit of the observer's scanned area, as shown in Fig. 2. If the observer scans the entire forward half of the ocean, $y_0 = 0$, the formula simplifies and the resulting probability of detection of a ship at lateral range x, from a plane at altitude h, travelling on a straight course with speed v, is

$$p(x) = 1 - \exp\,[-kh/v(h^2 + x^2)] \simeq 1 - e^{-kh/vx^2} \quad (h \ll x) \tag{9}$$

which is plotted as curve *a* in Fig. 3.

In view of the discussion preceding Eq. (6), we see that the parameter k is likely to be rather smaller than νC. Nevertheless, k is determined by the contrast and size of the sought object, the atmospheric visibility and the observer's alertness, plus the degree to which his position in the plane hinders clear vision in all directions; (it may also depend on v if the plane is going very fast). The details of the methods of visual search are also important. For example, the use of

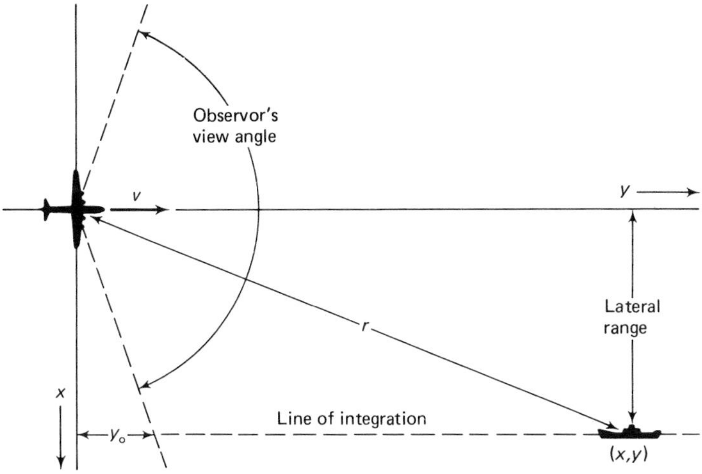

Fig. 2. Plan view of sighting.

binoculars may actually reduce the value of k, because such use reduces the frequency ν of fixations and also the size of the solid angle covered per fixation, even though it increases the probability of detection *if* the target is within the angle of view. Methods of measuring k under operational conditions will be discussed later.

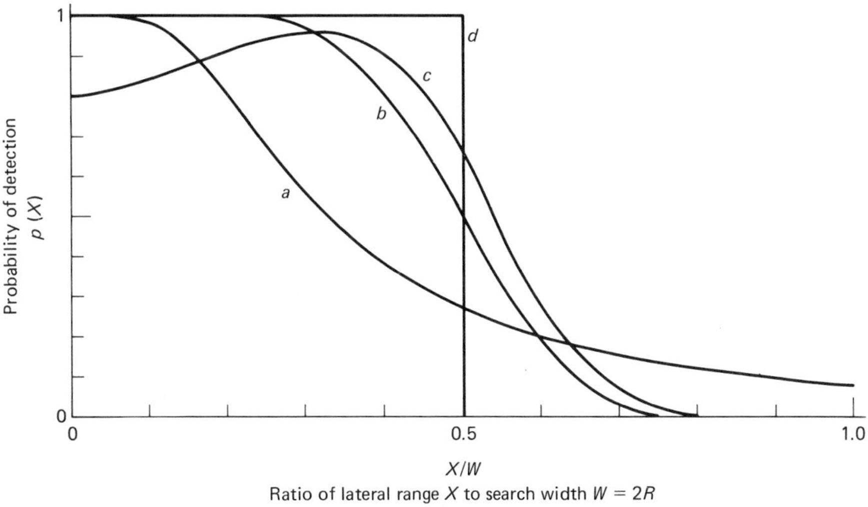

Fig. 3. Typical curves of probability of detection $p(x)$, as function of lateral range x. Curve a is for visual search from a plane, b for radar, c for radar with sea return and curve d is for idealized definite range law. All curves to scale $W = 2R$, as defined in Eq. 11.

2.2 Lateral Range Probabilities for Different Detection Devices

The *lateral range curve* for visual search from a plane, curve *a* of Fig. 3, is one example of various curves corresponding to various instruments used to detect the searched-for target. A lateral range curve embodies the details of the search effectiveness of the detection equipment that is carried at uniform velocity v along a straight path that happens to pass a distance x from the target. The shape of the curve is dependent on the nature of the target and the type of detection equipment involved. In the idealized case, where the object is not detected if it never comes within a definite range R of the observer, and certainly is seen if it comes within range R, the curve is the *definite range curve* marked *d* in Fig. 3.

In actual practice, the lateral range curve seldom approaches the definite range curve *d*; nearly always there is a range of uncertainty near the limit of detection. For example, a search radar sends out a succession of pulses as it swings its directional antenna around, and reflections from the target are received, and displayed as a "blip" on the scope, at a point corresponding to the position of the target with respect to the radar. Only when the blip appears nearly every scan, i.e., only when the *blip-scan ratio* approaches unity, can the observer be sure that an object is really detected. For further details, see Koopman [1946], Chapter 5. Basically, radar search is a two-level search: the radar producing blips on the screen and the observer searching the screen for persistent blips.

There are analytic methods (see, for example, Pollock [1971]) to balance between the chance of false alarm and the chance of overlooking the target, in terms of the blip-scan ratio. Usually the exigencies of the search, and the stress on the searcher, preclude the application of such niceties in actual practice. The degree of fatigue of the observer, for example, has been found to have a much larger effect on the results than any prescribed rule for blip-scan ratio; observer fatigue can at times reduce the effective range of detection to half the optimal range. Also, if the plane's speed is great enough, the observer may not have time to scan the scope thoroughly; P then will depend on v, as it does for visual search.

In any case, under reasonably good conditions, the lateral range curve for radar search would have the general shape shown in curve *b* of Fig. 3. No detection occurs when the lateral range x is some factor (50% in the curve shown) greater than the effective range R; perfect detection occurs if x is less than R by about the same factor. Under poor conditions, the curve may be more like curve *c* of Fig. 3. For example, the search plane may be flying over a rough sea, or over heavily wooded terrain, with a great number of false blips (sea or ground clutter) that tend to hide the true blip. In some cases the clutter is greatest in the forward direction, so the chance of detection is greatest for some intermediate value of x, as illustrated in curve *c* of Fig. 3. For further details see Koopman [1946], Chapter 5.

Most of the remarks made for radar search apply to the case of the use of sonar by a surface vessel searching for a submerged submarine (see Koopman [1946], Chapter 6). Instead of ground clutter, the so-called reverberation tends to hide the true blip; also, the signal tends to be lost when the vessel is nearly over the submarine. Therefore, except for the differences in distance scale, lateral range curves for sonar resemble curves *b* and *c* of Fig. 3.

Many other search situations correspond to the model discussed here. For example, the visual search from a helicopter for a lost child would probably conform roughly to curve *a* of Fig. 3, and thus to Eq. (9). If the person were lost in wooded territory, and the search had to be conducted on foot, the lateral range curve would more nearly correspond to *b* of Fig. 3, the visibility being sharply limited by the trees. On the other hand, if shouts were used to alert the lost one, the shape may be nearer curve *a*. When dogs are used, still another curve may be appropriate. For further discussion of these problems, see Kelley [1973].

The sighting potentials $F(x)$, for the four curves of probability $p(x)$, shown in Fig. 3, are displayed in Fig. 4. As mentioned before, these potentials are additive; if several observers are involved, either following along the same path or

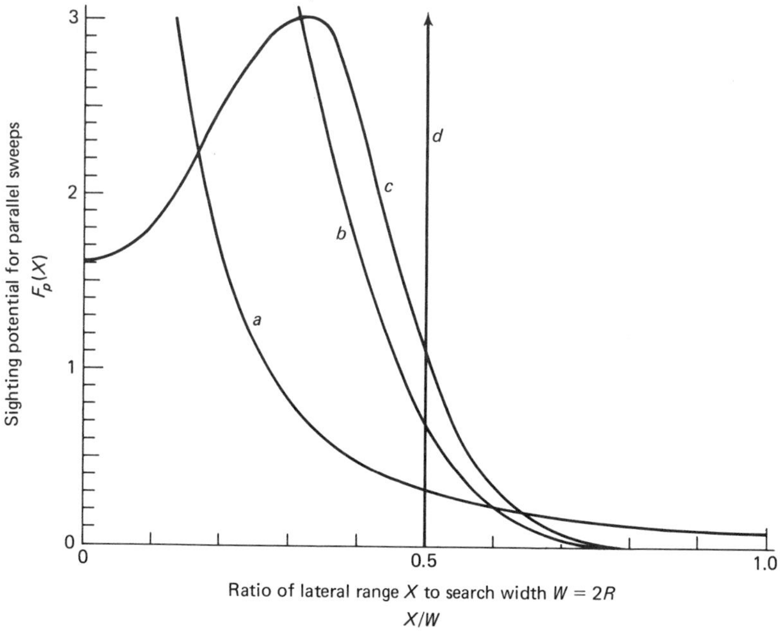

Fig. 4. Curves of sighting potential $F_p(x)$ for the typical probability curves of Fig. 3.

travelling in parallel paths, their potentials are to be added, to obtain the resultant probability of detection,

$$p(x) = 1 - \exp\left[-F_1(x) - F_2(x) - \cdots\right] \tag{10}$$

For example, if the search plane has n visual observers, or if n planes follow the same path, the k of Eqs. (8) and (9) is to be replaced by nk. Because the probabilities follow the law of diminishing returns, such duplication of effort is inefficient unless $F(x)$ for a single observer is less than about 0.7, or $p(x)$ less than about 0.5. Thus, additional sighting potential would be useful, in the visual case (curve a) for $|x| > 0.3\ W$.

2.3 Search Width and Its Measurement

The effective width of the path swept out by the searcher in his course is found by integrating the probability of detection over the lateral range x,

$$W = \int_{-\infty}^{\infty} p(x)\, dx = \int_{-\infty}^{\infty} \{1 - \exp\left[-F(x)\right]\}\, dx \tag{11}$$

where $F(x)$ is the sighting potential. The *search width* W is the most useful single measure of the effectiveness of a detection instrument that is carried by an observer moving in a continuous path over the area to be searched. As he moves, he can be reasonably certain to find the searched-for target if it comes within the swept path of width W, centered on his track. As one can see from Fig. 3, most search will not detect the target with certainty if it lies between $\frac{1}{2}W$ and $-\frac{1}{2}W$ of the path; but there is a compensating chance of finding it if it lies beyond $\pm\frac{1}{2}W$, so the effective width is W.

The effective search width for visual search from low altitude is, according to Eq. (9),

$$W \simeq \int_{-\infty}^{\infty} \left[1 - \exp(-kh/vx^2)\right] dx = 2\left[x(1 - e^{-kh/vx^2})\right]_0^\infty$$

$$+ 2\int_0^\infty (2kh/vx^2)\, e^{-kh/vx^2}\, dx = 2\sqrt{\pi kh/v} \qquad (\text{for } h < W/10) \tag{12}$$

(Note the difference with Eq. 29 of Koopman [1956b]; we assume the observer looks in the forward half circle, instead of all around.) For higher altitudes, an approximate formula is

$$W \simeq 2\sqrt{\pi kh/v}\, \exp(-hv/4k) \tag{13}$$

We note that the width increases with altitude up to $h \simeq (2k/v)$, above which visibility begins to reduce the chance of spotting the target, even when below the plane. We note also that increasing the speed of the search plane reduces the search width, since increasing the speed of the plane shortens the time during which any given area is scanned. As was noted before, if n independent observers traverse the same track, the k in the square root is replaced by nk.

Each of the curves of Fig. 3 and Fig. 4 have the abscissa scaled to the effective search width. The curve for the usual radar and sonar search (b in Figs. 3 and 4) is much closer to the idealized definite range curve d, than is the visual search curve a; the fringe of low probability for curve b does not extend very far beyond $x = W/2$, and over the range $0 < x < W/2$ the chance of detecting the target is nearly unity. In this case, it would be a nearly complete waste of effort for another radar or sonar vehicle to repeat the same path (unless the seeing is poor, as with curve c).

We have noted earlier that the ability of an observer, with his vehicle and equipment, to detect some target, depends on so many variables that, in practice, it is well nigh impossible to predict this ability from laboratory measurements. Thus, if it is important to conserve search effort (and for this one needs to know the value of W), the only safe procedure is to *measure* W under conditions closely approximating those in actual search. It was found, in World War II, that the usual search width W for radar planes searching for German submarines was one half to one third the value, based on laboratory measurements, claimed by the radar manufacturer. This is not surprising when one compares the results of tests on an optimally tuned radar, operated by an expert, with the results using a radar that had seen heavy service, operated by a tired radar operator. If the manufacturer's claims had been used in planning, there would have been large "holes" in the search plans. In addition to these differences between laboratory and practice, there is the effect of "false alarms" and the pauses to verify questionable detections (discussed in Sections 1 and 4) which serve to dilute the search effort by amounts that can usually only be determined experimentally.

If a target simulating the real target is easy to construct, the measurement can be carried out as follows. Lay out a band of width D, at least 3 times the best estimate of the search width W and of length L at least 10 times D, with a well-marked, straight search course down its middle. Now place T simulated targets, more or less uniformly distributed over the whole area LD, but not so regularly spaced that it would be possible to deduce the regularity. If one wishes to measure $p(x)$ as well as W, the distance from the search path to each target should be measured and recorded. An observer is then sent along the search path and required to note the position of each target he observes during his passage. After checking his records and removing the "false alarms," if it turns out he has spotted n of the T targets then an estimate of the search width is nD/T. If n is larger than $\frac{1}{2}T$, then the band width D was chosen too small; D should be doubled, the targets redistributed uniformly over the new band, and the experiment run over again.

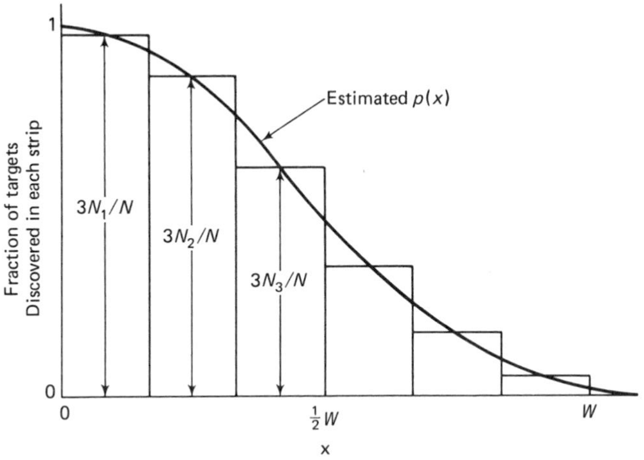

Fig. 5. Block diagram, illustrating experimental determination of lateral range curve, $p(x)$.

If the number n of true targets spotted is less than about 20, statistical fluctuations will preclude accuracy in the result. In this case a number m of independent observers should be run through the course, making sure each is ignorant of the location of the targets or of the findings of other observers. When the total number $N = \sum n$ of targets spotted by all m observers reaches a value of 100 or more, the resulting ratio (ND/mT) will be a reasonably accurate estimate of the search width W.

If one can persist long enough for N to reach values of 500 to 1000, and if the lateral range of each target has been measured, then a rough estimate of the lateral range curve of Fig. 3 can be constructed. One divides the N spotted targets (counting each target as many times as it has been spotted, as before) into those within $W/6$ on either side of the search path (suppose there are N_1 of these), those with lateral range between $\pm(W/6)$ and $\pm(W/3)$ (N_2 of those), those with lateral range between $\pm(W/3)$ and $\pm(W/2)$ (N_3 of these) and so on until all the N have been counted. One can then construct a block diagram, as shown in Fig. 5, with the height of the ith block equal to $(3N_i/N)$, which will be a rough estimate of the lateral range curve, as shown in Fig. 5 by the solid line. The accuracy of the result depends, in part, on the uniform distribution of the initial placing of targets; there should be a roughly equal number in each of the strips parallel to the path.

3. SEARCH OF AN AREA

The usual search operation involves the covering of an area to find some target presumed present. In this section we assume there is no initial guess as to the object's whereabouts, so one has to assume it is equally likely to be anywhere in the area. In accord with the discussion following Eq. (5), and dealt with further in Section 3.3, the best way of applying our search effort, in this case, is to distribute it as evenly over the whole area as is operationally possible. Details of the derivation of many of the equations given in this section may be found in Koopman [1956b].

3.1 Parallel Sweeps

If the area to be searched is considerably larger than can be covered by a stationary inspection or by a single sweep through it, the best way of insuring uniform coverage is by a sequence of parallel sweeps, spaced a distance S apart. This may be accomplished by a spiral path or by the zigzag course of a single observer, as shown in Fig. 6, or else by a number of observers following parallel courses interspaced a distance S. Depending on the time and degree of effort available, n

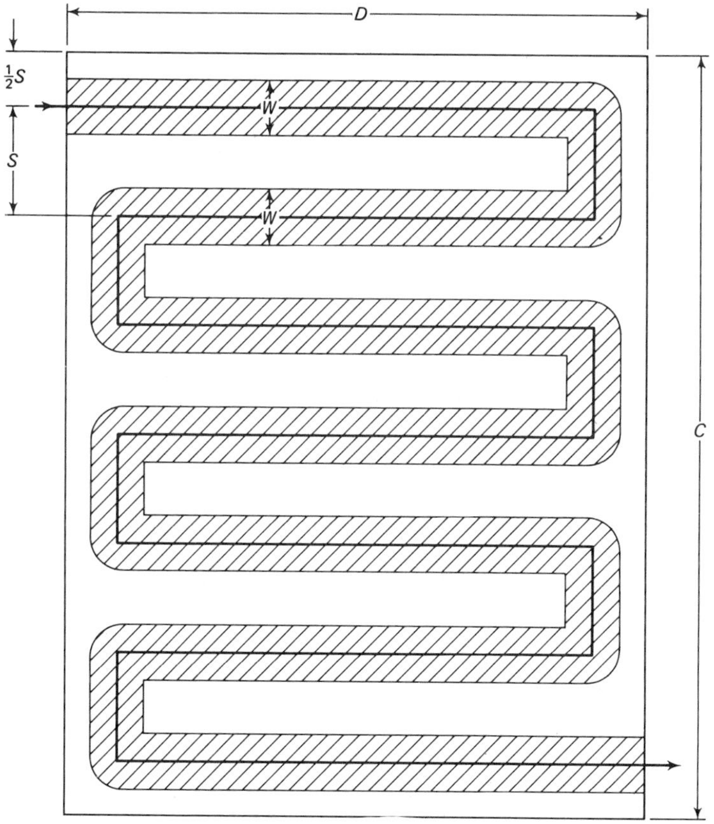

Fig. 6. Parallel sweeps, of search width W, spaced a distance S apart, providing uniform coverage of area $A = CD$.

parallel courses can be afforded, each of length D, spaced $S = C/n$ apart, thus amounting to a total path length $L = nD$. From the previous section we have measured an effective search width W, so that $WL = nDW = A(W/S)$ is the area effectively searched (or the *total search effort*), $A = CD$ being the area to be searched and $WL/A = W/S$ being the *fractional search coverage* (or *specific search effort*, or *total sighting potential*). If the dimensions C and D of the area are considerably larger than W, n and thus L can be considered to be continuous variables. Also, if the area A is not rectangular, as shown in Fig. 6, but is sufficiently large and compact in shape, a spiral pattern or one of parallel sweeps can be laid out that produce essentially the same uniform coverage and the same fractional coverage for the same total search effort WL.

To predict the probability of finding the target during such a coverage, we must add the sighting potentials F of Fig. 4, for the parallel sweeps as shown in Fig. 7. We have (if A is large enough)

$$p_p(x) = 1 - \exp\,[-F_p(x)]$$

$$F_p(x) = \sum_{n=-n_0}^{n_0+1} F(|x - nS|); \qquad \text{see Fig. 7} \tag{14}$$

for the probability of detection if the target has a lateral range x from one of the paths. The formulas represent the fact that each parallel sweep contributes its share to the total sighting potential F_p. The limiting value n_0 is the integer such that $F(x)$ becomes negligible for $|x|$ between $n_0 S$ and $(n_0 + 1)S$; usually F is such that n_0 is small. Thus, in practice we need not consider "edge effects" for the sweeps next to the edges of the area. If these edge effects are neglected, both F_p and p_p are periodic functions of x with period S.

Let the distance of the searched-for target from edge D be z. If the target is equally likely to be anywhere in A, it is equally likely for z to have any value between 0 and $nS = C$. Thus, the probability that the object will be found by the end of the n sweeps is an integral of the periodic function p_p over the whole width C, divided by C,

$$P(\Phi) = \frac{1}{nS}\int_0^{ns} p_p\left(z - \frac{1}{2}S\right) dz = \frac{1}{nS}\int_{-\frac{1}{2}S}^{(n-\frac{1}{2})S} p_p(x)\,dx = \frac{1}{S}\int_0^S p_p(x)\,dx$$

$$= \frac{1}{S}\int_0^S \{1 - \exp\,[-F_p(x)]\}\,dx; \qquad \Phi = \frac{W}{S} = \frac{WL}{A} \tag{15}$$

The integration can be carried out analytically for the visual search case of Eq. (8). The result (when h is small enough so that $F \simeq kh/vx^2$) is

$$P(\Phi) = \operatorname{erf}\left(\frac{\pi}{S}\sqrt{\frac{kh}{v}}\right) = \operatorname{erf}\left(\tfrac{1}{2}\sqrt{\pi}\,\Phi\right) \tag{16}$$

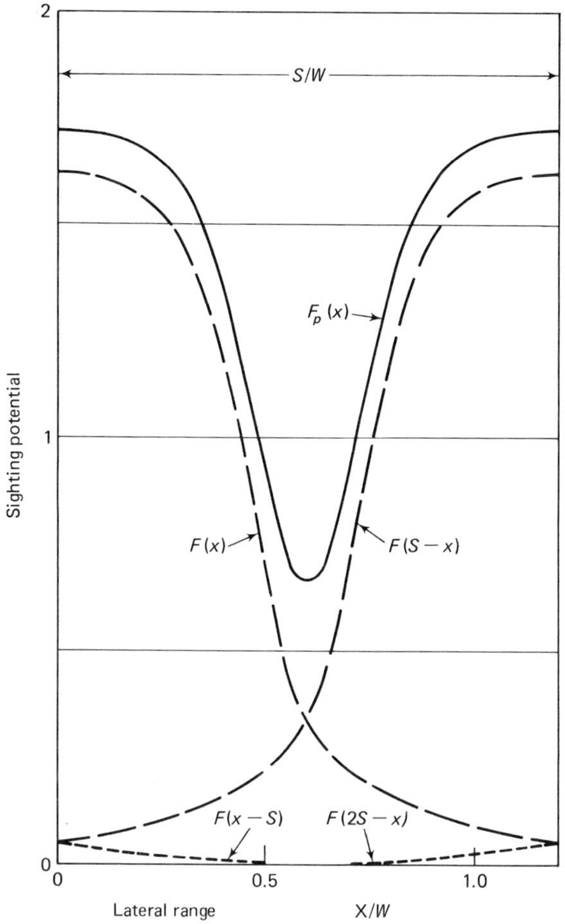

Fig. 7. Sighting potential $F_p(x)$ for parallel sweeps a distance S apart.

where $\mathrm{erf}\,(u) = (2/\sqrt{\pi}) \int_0^u e^{-t^2}\, dt$ is the well-known error function. Details of the calculation may be found in Koopman [1956b] (note the misprint in his Eq. 45). Other cases may be calculated numerically, once the appropriate sighting potential $F(x)$ has been determined by measuring $p(x)$ operationally and computing $F(x) = \ln\,[1 - p(x)]$, then calculating F_p and p_p and, finally, integrating p_p/S numerically from $x = 0$ to $x = S$.

The curves for $P(\Phi)$, as functions of the fractional search coverage $\Phi = WL/A$, are shown in Fig. 8, for parallel sweeps of equipment exhibiting the different detection capabilities displayed in the lateral range curves of Fig. 3. All of them show a decided diminution of value when $\Phi = W/S = WL/A$ becomes smaller

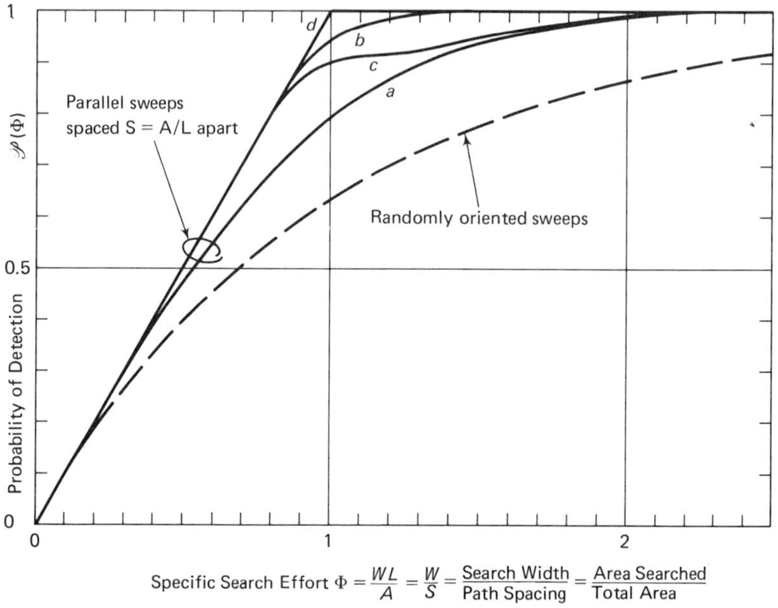

Fig. 8. Probability of detection $\mathcal{P}(\Phi)$ for parallel sweeps a distance S apart, as function of the search coverage W/S, for the curves of Fig. 3. Lower curve is for randomly uniform coverage.

than unity, but a substantial diminishment of additional returns when Φ becomes larger than unity. Also the curves a, b and c are not greatly different from the limiting curve d, for the definite range law. The implications of these properties, when the *a priori* probability of presence of the target is *not* uniform throughout A, will be discussed in the next section.

Curve b, for radar search under good conditions, is nearly identical with the definite range curve d. In both cases, an increase of specific search effort Φ greater than unity produces practically no additional sightings. If, however, too optimistic a value of W is used, one may erroneously think $W/S > 1$ and that no further effort is needed.

Curve c, for radar under difficult conditions of sea or ground return, is an interesting case because of the peaks in $F(x)$ and $p(x)$ for $|x| > 0$ (see Figs. 3 and 4). This results in a curve for $P(\Phi)$ that nearly flattens out when the peaks of $F(x)$ and $F(S - x)$ coincide, and then rises again slowly as S is further decreased (or $\Phi = W/S$ is further increased). Thus $P'(\Phi) = dP/d\Phi$ has a minimum value and then rises again to a subsidiary maximum as Φ is increased further, before dropping asymptotically to zero. Thus, this curve does not meet the requirements of Eq. (4) for a well-organized search. As will be indicated later, this makes it difficult to optimize the search effort. Luckily, the conditions giving rise to curve c do not arise in practice very often.

3.2 Randomly Distributed Sweeps

In actual searches, it is often quite difficult to traverse the precisely parallel, equally-spaced tracks assumed in the previous section. In fact, unless all the tracks are laid out *and checked* during execution, by accurate visual or radar triangulation, it is unlikely that the optimistic calculations of detection probability, indicated in curves a to d of Fig. 8, can be achieved. It is much more likely that the results will correspond more nearly to an assumption that the path or paths cover area A more or less uniformly but are randomly oriented. To be more precise, the likelier model is that of search paths made up of a number of straight segments (as sketched in Fig. 9a) of total length L within A, with the position and orientation of one segment independent of the position and orientation of any other segment that is separated from the first by several intermediate pieces.

To analyze this case, we examine the length ΔL of search track, as shown in Fig. 9b. If the target is equally likely to be anywhere in A, and if the search track is randomly located (in the sense of the previous paragraph), then the target is equally likely to be anywhere in relation to the element of track ΔL. If the detection equipment has a definite range $\frac{1}{2}W$, as indicated by curve d of Fig. 3, the chance of detection while traversing ΔL is the area of the shaded

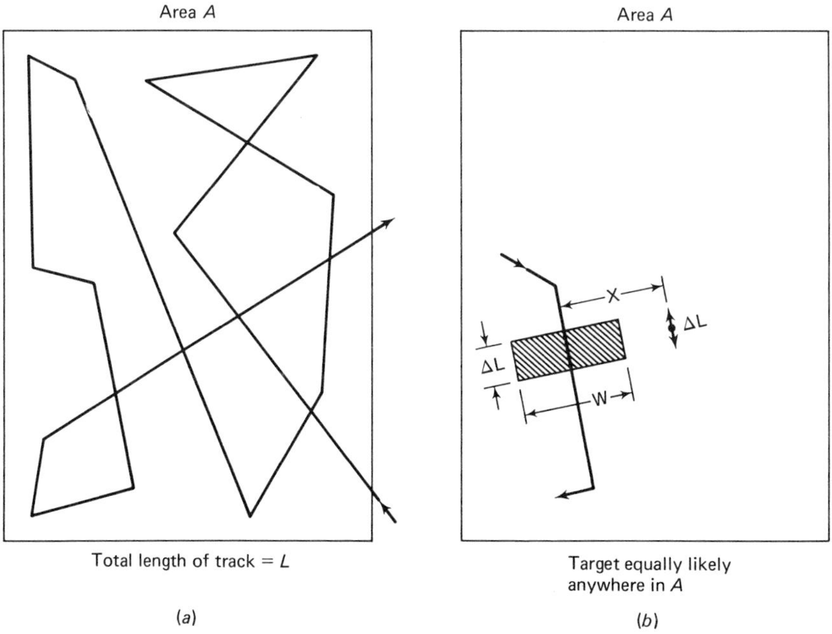

Fig. 9. Randomly oriented sweeps to cover A mo:: :or less randomly.

rectangle of Fig. 9b; $W\Delta L$, divided by A. The result is the same for any lateral range curve; the probability the target is in the elementary area $dx\Delta L$, a distance x from the track, is $dx\Delta L/A$. Thus, the chance of detection during ΔL by equipment having the lateral range probability $p(x)$ is

$$P = (\Delta L/A) \int_{-\infty}^{\infty} p(x)\, dx = (W\Delta L/A) \tag{17}$$

according to the definition of search width W, given in Eq. (11).

The argument now proceeds as did that of Section 1, and reaches a similar result. The chance of *not* finding the target while traversing the element ΔL is $[1 - (W\Delta L/A)]$ and the chance of not finding it in a sequence of n elements is $[1 - (W\Delta L/A)]^n$. Since there are $n = L/\Delta L$ such elements in the total track traversed in the search, the chance of *finding* the target during the search is

$$P(\Phi) = 1 - \left[1 - \frac{W\Delta L}{A}\right]^{L/\Delta L} \xrightarrow[\Delta L \to \infty]{} 1 - e^{-\Phi} \tag{18}$$

where $\Phi = (WL/A)$ is (as previously) the effective search potential or specific search effort. The curve for this probability is shown in Fig. 8, along with the curves for the parallel sweeps of the previous section.

Thus, as soon as random deflections disorganize to any extent a parallel search pattern, no matter what the detection equipment, the probability of success reduces to the same exponential dependence on search effort as was found in Section 1 (Eq. 5) for the simplest sort of visual search. Of course, the constants involved, expressed in terms of W and L, differ in value from the ω and t of Eq. (3), depending on the nature of the detection equipment and its carrier. Nevertheless, the similarity in form of the resulting equation for $P(\Phi)$ means we can develop procedures for opt allocation of search effort that are almost completely independent of the nature of the search, as long as it involves covering an area.

A glance at Fig. 8 shows that parallel sweeps should be used whenever possible, but one should be sure that the paths are accurately parallel and equally spaced, or one runs the danger of overestimating the search effectiveness. Finally, it should be realized that covering an area *uniformly*, even with randomly oriented sweeps, requires a fair amount of planning and path control.

3.3 Miscellaneous Examples

Isbell [1957] and Gluss [1961] have discussed a very different "search" problem, where the target is very large and the searcher is blind and must find the target by moving around until he bumps into it. For example, the "lost at sea" problem assumes one is in a dense fog and knows exactly how far from shore he is but has no idea in what direction it is. The problem is to devise a path that either minimizes the maximum (max) distance traveled (Isbell [1957]), or minimizes the statistical expectation of the distance to be travelled (Gluss [1961]).

Search for other large objects have also received attention. For example, Gluss [1961b] has worked out the optimal path for finding (by touching) a circle of known radius and distance away, but of unknown direction. The result could also be useful in trying to find a point target a known distance L away, direction unknown, by use of detection equipment with known definite range R for the target ($L > R$). However, these exercises are of limited utility in practice because of the assumption of precise knowledge of target distance, and the solutions are quite sensitive to these assumptions.

Other problems, discussed by Bellman and Dreyfus [1962] and, for example, Heyman [1968], involve the "search" for maxima (or zeros) of a function of many variables by means of dynamic (or linear) programming. A survey of this work would lead us too far afield from the practical problems surveyed in this chapter.

4. OPTIMAL ALLOCATION OF SEARCH EFFORT

If nothing is known as to the position of the target except that it is inside area A, the optimal procedure is to distribute the available search effort uniformly over A. This is easily verified if one considers the search coverage $E_j = WL_j$ to be a function of each subarea A_j in A. The probability of finding the target in A_j is the product of the probability A_j/A that the target is in A_j, times the probability $P(\phi_j)$, ($\phi_j = E_j/A_j$), that it would be found *if* it were in A_j, so the total probability of success is $P(\phi) = \sum (A_j/A)\, P(\phi_j)$. If the coverage is made nonuniform by making ϕ_i somewhat greater (by an amount $\Delta\phi$, say) than the average potential $\phi = WL/A$ and, in consequence, making E_i/A_i for another equal subarea $A_i = A_j$ less by the same amount $\Delta\phi$ then, because $P(\phi)$ is subject to the law of diminishing returns, the total probability $P(\phi)$ will be reduced for all the cases so far discussed. Since $P(\phi + \Delta\phi) - P(\phi) < P(\phi) - P(\phi - \Delta\phi)$, the total probability will be diminished by the negative amount $(A_i/A)[P(\phi + \Delta\phi) + P(\phi - \Delta\phi) - 2P(\phi)]$.

4.1 The Effect of Some Knowledge of the Target's Whereabouts

Now suppose something *is* known about the target's location, so that its *a priori* probability of presence varies from region to region within A. We deal first with the rather impractical general case, when the *a priori probability density* $g(r)$, of its being at the point indicated by the vector r, is known to vary from point to point within A. Since $g(r)$ is a probability density

$$\iint_A g(r)\, dA = 1. \tag{19}$$

If the density of search coverage $\phi(r) = \lim_{A_j \to 0} (WL_j/A_j) = d\Phi/dA$ at point r also may differ from point to point in A, the probability $\mathcal{P}(\Phi)$ of detecting the target, during the expenditure of a given search effort

$$\Phi A = \iint_A \phi(r)\, dA = WL \tag{20}$$

throughout A, is the integral of the product of the probability $g(r)\, dA$ of target presence in dA and the probability $P[\phi(r)]$ that the target is found if it is in dA,

$$\mathcal{P}(\Phi) = \iint_A g(r)\, P[\phi(r)]\, dA. \tag{21}$$

Suppose two distributions of search density (each adding up to the same total coverage Φ) are compared; one being $\phi(r)$ and the other $\phi(r) + \delta\phi(r)$, differing from ϕ by the relatively small amount $\delta\phi$ (such that $\iint \delta\phi\, dA = 0$ so that the the integral of both ϕ's over A equals the same ΦA). The difference in total probability of detection $\mathcal{P}$ will be

$$\begin{aligned} \Delta\mathcal{P} &= \iint_A g(r)[P(\phi) + \delta\phi P'(\phi) - P(\phi)]\, dA \\ &= \iint_A \delta\phi g(r)\, P'[\phi(r)]\, dA \end{aligned} \tag{22}$$

where $P'(\phi) = dP/d\phi$. The distribution of search effort $\phi(r)$ will yield the maximum probability of detection $\mathcal{P}(\Phi)$ when $\Delta\mathcal{P} = 0$. And the only way $\Delta\mathcal{P}$ can be zero, for *any* choice of $\delta\phi$ (as long as $\delta\phi$ is small and $\iint \delta\phi\, dA = 0$) is for the product $g(r)\, P'[\phi(r)]$ to be a constant, G, independent of r.

Of course, this optimal distribution ϕ must satisfy Eq. (20), in that the integral of ϕ over A must equal the specified total search effort $WL = \Phi A$. The requirement, arrived at in the last paragraph, that $P'(r) = G/g(r)$ if $\mathcal{P}$ is to be max, may involve an inconsistency; for the curves of Fig. 8 show that the max value of $P'(\phi)$ is unity (when $\phi = 0$), no matter which curve is used. Now if, for any value of r, the *a priori* probability density of presence of the target is less than the value of the constant G, the requirement that $P' = G/g$ cannot be satisfied, so this region must have zero coverage. No region in A, for which $G/g > 1$, can be covered by the search, if it is to be optimal; any effort would more effectively be used in an area where $G/g < 1$. Thus, the properties of the search operation outlined in (5), prescribe a highly discriminatory search plan, if search effort is not limitless. Details of the derivation of this formula, and proof that the resulting $\mathcal{P}$ is a max, not minimum (min), are given in de Guenin [1961] and Dobbie [1963].

More explicitly, the procedure for computing the search coverage $\phi(r)$ that maximizes the probability $\mathcal{P}(\Phi)$ of detection of the target for a specified total search effort $\Phi A = WL$, is a two-phase one:

(1) The appropriate value of the constant $G = g(r)\, P'[\phi(r)]$ may exclude some portions of area A; those for which $G/g(r) > 1$. In this excluded area A_e the search density is to be zero. In the searched area $A_s = A - A_e$ the density of search $\phi(r)$ must be such that $P'[\phi(r)] = G/g(r)$, which in A_s is everywhere less than or equal to unity.

(2) In addition, G must satisfy the requirement that the integral of the search density ϕ, as specified in (1) over the searched area A_s, be equal to the specified search effort $\Phi A = WL$.

These requirements can be more compactly stated in terms of the inverse function of $1/P'(\phi) = g/G$. Call it $f(g/G) = \phi$, so that $1/P'[f(g/G)] = g/G$, and $f[1/P'(\phi)] = \phi$. Then, to maximize the probability of detection in an area A, within which the *a priori* probability density of presence of the target at r is $g(r)$, for a given total search effort, defined as $WL = \Phi A$, we find a value of G such that

$$\iint_{A_s} f[g(r)/G]\; dA = \Phi A, \text{ with the integration over the portion of}$$

area A_s within which $g(r)/G \geqslant 1$. Then the optimal search density at r is $f[g(r)/G]$ in A_s and zero in $A_e = A - A_s$, where $g/G < 1$. The resulting maximal probability of detection is then **(23)**

$$\mathcal{P}(\Phi) = \iint_{A_s} g(r)\, P\{f[g(r)/G]\}\; dA \tag{23}$$

Curves of $f(1/P')$, for the cases shown in Fig. 8, are plotted in Fig. 10.

One limitation of this procedure comes from the assumption that $P'(\phi)$ has a single-valued inverse function f. This is the case for curves a, b and d and the random coverage curve of Fig. 8. However, curve c does not have a single valued inverse because its P' is not a monotonically decreasing function of ϕ. As long as g/G does not rise above about 15 over the whole of A, we can ignore the complication, but if the available search effort is large enough so that $g/G > 20$

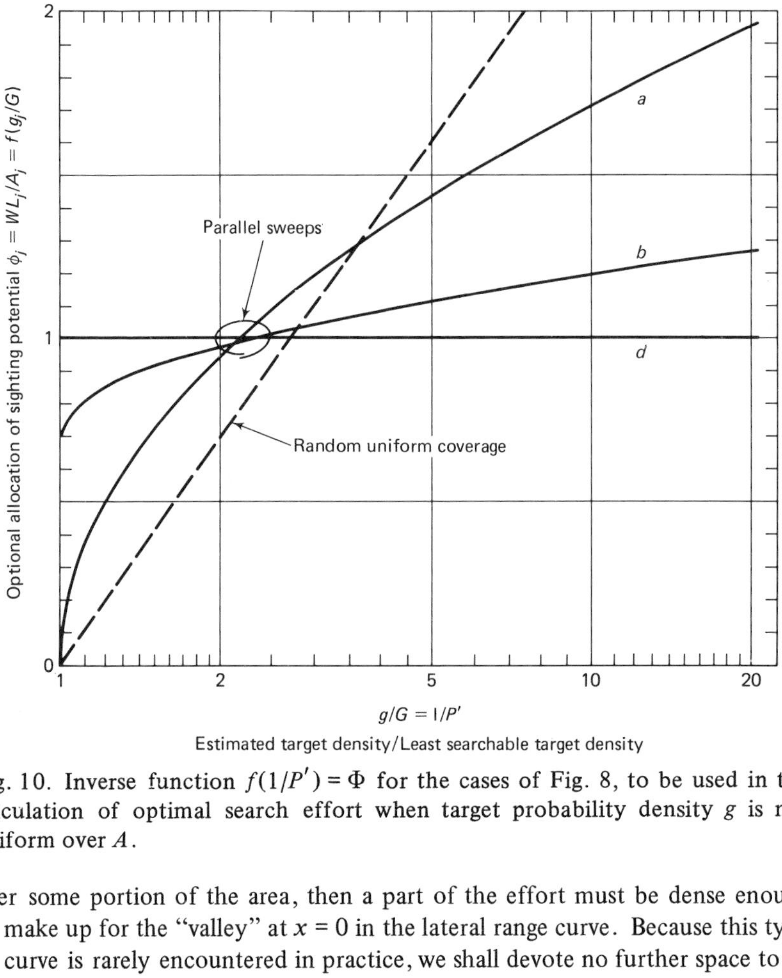

Fig. 10. Inverse function $f(1/P') = \Phi$ for the cases of Fig. 8, to be used in the calculation of optimal search effort when target probability density g is not uniform over A.

over some portion of the area, then a part of the effort must be dense enough to make up for the "valley" at $x = 0$ in the lateral range curve. Because this type of curve is rarely encountered in practice, we shall devote no further space to its idiosyncrasies.

Even with "normal" inverse functions $\phi = f(1/P')$, which are single-valued functions of $1/P'$, the features of procedure (23) do not correspond to intuitive allocations of search effort. The fact that regions of low *a priori* probability of presence should be avoided entirely is due to the fact that the maximum value of P' is unity, which occurs for $\phi = 0$. As long as the value of target density $g(r)$ in some region is larger than the value of g elsewhere, it is best to concentrate on the high-g region until the search there has reduced the Baysian, *a posteriori* target probability density to a value equal to the g for the next most likely region. And, if the search effort is limited, some low-g areas will have to be left out entirely. In fact, the process of optimal search may be restated in terms of a sequence of decisions as to where the next quantum of search effort can be most productively used (see Charnes and Cooper [1958] and Dobbie [1968], for example).

When false targets (call them ghosts) are present as well as the single target looked for, the analysis becomes much more complicated, and only a few cases have been worked out in detail. The results depend strongly on the number and nature of the ghosts and on the search strategy regarding them. The ghosts may be caused by sporadic malfunctioning of the detection equipment (among which may be included some of the radar ground and sea clutter and the reverberation in sonar equipment), in which the delay required to establish the contact as false may be quite short. Or the ghost may be a definite object (such as a sunken wreck or a "second-time-round" echo from an islet) that would take some time to verify as a ghost but, once verified, could be mapped so reverification would not be needed. Or the ghost could be mobile (as with a friendly ship or a whale) that would require reverification each time a contact was made.

Many strategies could be devised for dealing with these false targets. In regions where the ghosts are chiefly of the reverberation type, one might decide to limit the effort spent on any individual contact to a time somewhat longer than the average time needed to verify that the contact is really a false contact. An optimal search plan has been worked out by Stone and Stanshine [1972] for a specialized case of this kind of search strategy. The results show the greatly increased complexity of calculations required to reduce the theory to practice. One is tempted to assume that the effect of such ghosts is to dilute the search effort required, without the ghosts, by a factor proportional to the estimated ghost density.

When the ghosts are actual targets, though false ones, the searcher may be forced to follow up each new contact for as long as it takes to determine whether it is true or false. Here also the resulting formulas (Stone, *et al.* [1972]) are quite difficult to apply. In the cases where the ghosts are stationary and mappable, a sequential procedure has been worked out by Dobbie [1973]. An example of this procedure, for the simplest possible situation, will be given in the next subsection.

It should be noted that in many of the cases involving false targets, the more feasible criterion for optimal search strategy appears to be the minimization of total effort (including that used to verify that a contact is a ghost) expected to be used to find the target, rather than the maximization of the detection probability for a given search effort. Indeed, in some cases, the two criteria may lead to different strategies (see Dobbie [1973]).

4.2 Applying the Formula

Using procedures (23), in all their generality, has disadvantages. First, it is seldom that one's *a priori* knowledge of the whereabouts of the target is good enough to enable one to specify target density $g(r)$ in detail over all of A. Often, we know only that it is within A; then the search coverage should be uniform over A. In some cases we can divide A into two subareas, with the target being rather more likely in one than in the other; in only a few cases is our *a priori* knowledge more detailed than this. It is thus useful to work out simple procedures to solve (23) for the two subarea case.

Here the probability density $g(r)$ is uniform within each of the subareas A_1 and A_2 (so the search density ϕ is uniform within each subarea) but g_1 differs from g_2 (so ϕ_1 will differ from ϕ_2). We can then reduce (23) to dimensionless terms by using as parameters and unknowns the following:

Ratios of areas; $\alpha_j = A_j/A$; $\alpha_1 + \alpha_2 = 1$

Probability that the target is in a subarea; $\gamma_j = A_j g_j = A\alpha_j g_j$; $\gamma_1 + \gamma_2 = 1$

Minimum searchworthy probability of presence; $\lambda = AG$

Optimal specific search coverage of a subarea; (24)

$$\Phi_j = \alpha_j \phi_j = WL_j/A = \alpha_j f(g_j/G) = \alpha_j f(\gamma_j/\alpha_j \lambda)$$

$$\Phi_1 + \Phi_2 = \Phi = WL/A$$

Optimal probability of finding target in a subarea;

$$\mathcal{P}_j = \gamma_j P f(\gamma_j/\alpha_j \lambda); \quad \mathcal{P}(\Phi) = \mathcal{P}_1 + \mathcal{P}_2$$

The values of Φ_j and $(\mathcal{P}_j/\lambda)$, as functions of γ_j/λ are displayed in nomogram form in Figs. 11 to 14, for the cases of visual search in parallel sweeps and for random coverage, any detection means. The specific formulas for the two cases shown are obtained by referring to Eqs. (16) and (18);

For parallel sweeps, visual sighting

$$P(\phi) = \text{erf}\left(\tfrac{1}{2}\sqrt{\pi}\,\phi\right); \quad P'(\phi) = \exp\left(\frac{1}{2}\,\frac{\pi}{4}\,\phi^2\right)$$

$$f(1/P') = (2/\sqrt{\pi})\sqrt{\ln(1/P')} = \phi \tag{25}$$

For uniform coverage of random sweeps per subarea

$$P(\phi) = 1 - e^{-\phi}; \quad P'(\phi) = e^{-\phi}$$

$$f(1/P') = \ln(1/P') = \phi$$

These are the functions used to compute the scales of Figs. 11 to 14.

The left-hand half of each chart corresponds to the smaller subarea, which we call A_1; the right-hand half goes with A_2. The first charts (Figs. 11 or 13) serve to determine λ, given the total search effort $WL = A\Phi$ that can be expended. Suppose we have guessed that the target has a chance γ_1 of being in subarea $A_1 = \alpha_1 A$ of the area A to be searched, and that it has a corresponding chance $\gamma_2 = 1 - \gamma_1$ of being in the subarea making up the rest of $A, A_2 = \alpha_2 A$. We first choose the pair of columns corresponding to the relative sizes of the subareas, given by the values of α_1 and $\alpha_2 = 1 - \alpha_1$.

Next we determine the ratio γ_2/γ_1 of the probabilities of presence in the two subareas. The γ_j/λ scales are logarithmic, so moving a line between the columns parallel to itself preserves the ratio of the γ's. For each values of γ_j/λ on the scale to the left of each column, there is a corresponding value of Φ_j on the scale to the right. We slide the line parallel to itself until the two values, Φ_1 and Φ_2, picked out at the two ends of the line, add to equal $\Phi = WL/A$, the prescribed specific search effort.

An example is shown in Fig. 11, in which we have guessed that the target has a probability $\gamma_1 = 0.4$ of being in the small subarea $A_1 = 0.2A$ and, therefore, that the chance of its being in the remaining $A_2 = 0.8A$ is $\gamma_2 = 0.6$. We also have decided that we can only spend a total effort $WL = 0.5A$ on the search. The ratio of the γ's is 1 to 1.5, so we set a ruler on $\gamma_1/\lambda = 1$ on the $\alpha_1 = \frac{1}{5}$ column and on $\gamma_2/\lambda = 1.5$ on the $\alpha_2 = \frac{4}{5}$ column and move it parallel to itself until the sum of the corresponding Φ's equals 0.5. This occurs at the two ends of the line a, for $\gamma_1/\lambda = 0.58$, $\Phi_1 = 0.235$ and $\gamma_2/\lambda = 0.87$, $\Phi_2 = 0.265$. Thus we must spend nearly half (0.47) of our search effort in the smaller area A_1. Note that if the available search effort were less than $0.26A$, the right-hand end of the parallel line would come above the top of the right-hand column, indicating that Φ_2 must be zero and that A_1 gets all the search effort, even though the chance of finding the target in A_2 is 1.5 times the chance of finding it in A_1. With such a small available effort, it is better to spend it all in the smaller area, where the probability *density* is greater.

Since we assumed γ_1 to be 0.4, λ must then be $(0.4/0.58) = 0.69$. To check, we divide $\gamma_2 = 0.6$ by 0.87 and again get 0.69. To find the predicted probability of detection, we turn to Fig. 12 and draw the same line, between $\gamma_1/\lambda = 0.58$ and $\gamma_2/\lambda = 0.87$, between the same two columns. The probability scales on these columns show that $\mathcal{P}_1/\lambda = 0.5$ and $\mathcal{P}_2/\lambda = 0.3$. Having already found that $\lambda = 0.69$, we determine that the chance $\mathcal{P}_1$ of finding the target in A_1 is 0.34 and that of finding it in A_2 is $\mathcal{P}_2 = 0.21$, with a total chance of finding the target as 0.55.

This example was for visual search using parallel sweeps. Figs. 13 and 14 are for the more usual case of uniform coverage of each subarea by randomly oriented sweeps, and any form of detection equipment (the only effect the equipment has on the results is in its determination of the sweep width W).

From these nomograms, one can work up curves for any particular case fairly quickly. As examples, Fig. 15 shows two pairs, to compare parallel, visual sweeps with random sweeps, for two different sets of α's and γ's. In the first case, the two to the left, we have a large difference in areas, $\alpha_1 = 0.2$ and $\alpha_2 = 0.8$, and a lesser difference in probabilities of presence, $\gamma_1 = 0.4$ and $\gamma_2 = 0.6$ (so the probability density of presence $g_1 = \gamma_1/\alpha_1 = 2$ in A_1 is larger than $g_2 = 0.75$). Thus, the search starts in A_1, though not much effort is needed there before it begins to be worthwhile to begin searching in the larger A_2. The

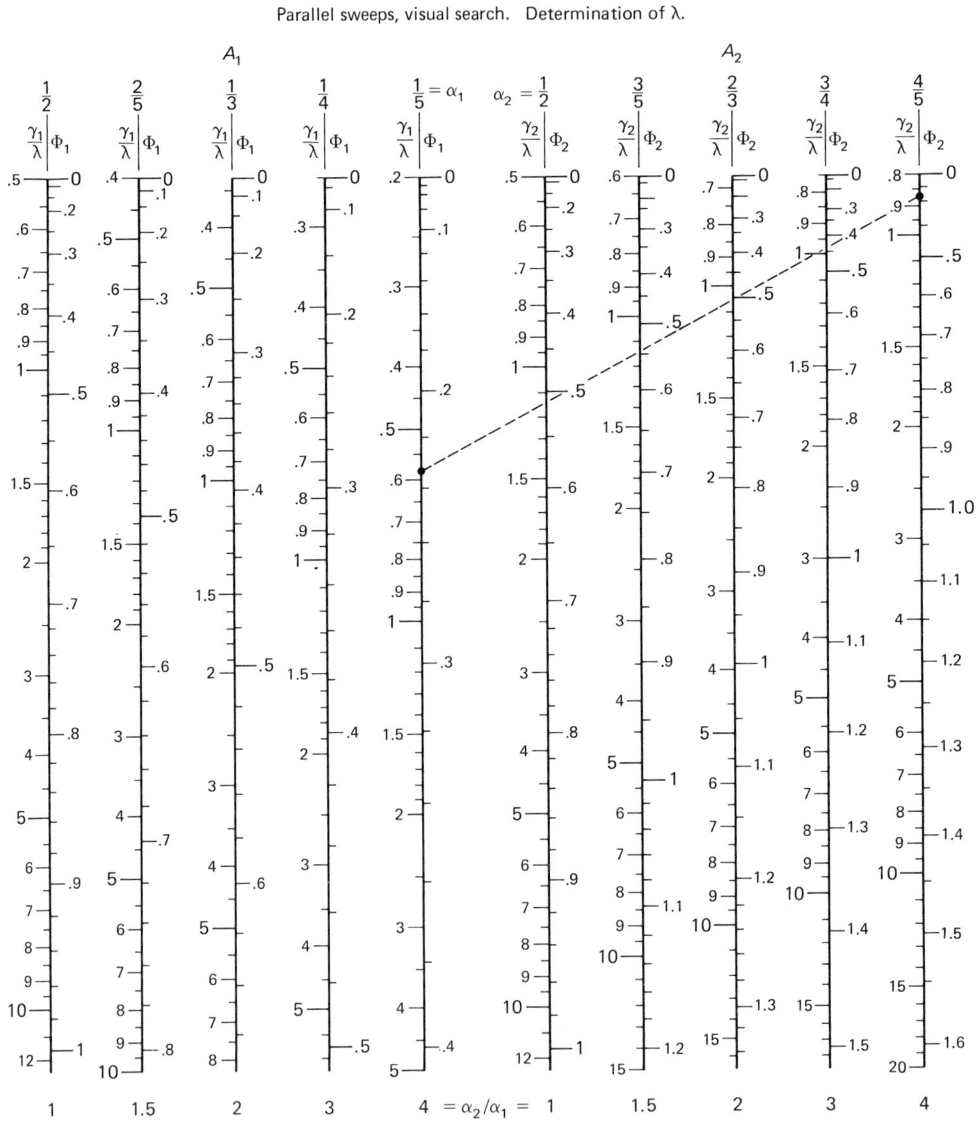

Fig. 11. Nomogram for calculation of optimal allocation of Φ between two areas, for curve *a* of Figs. 8 and 10.

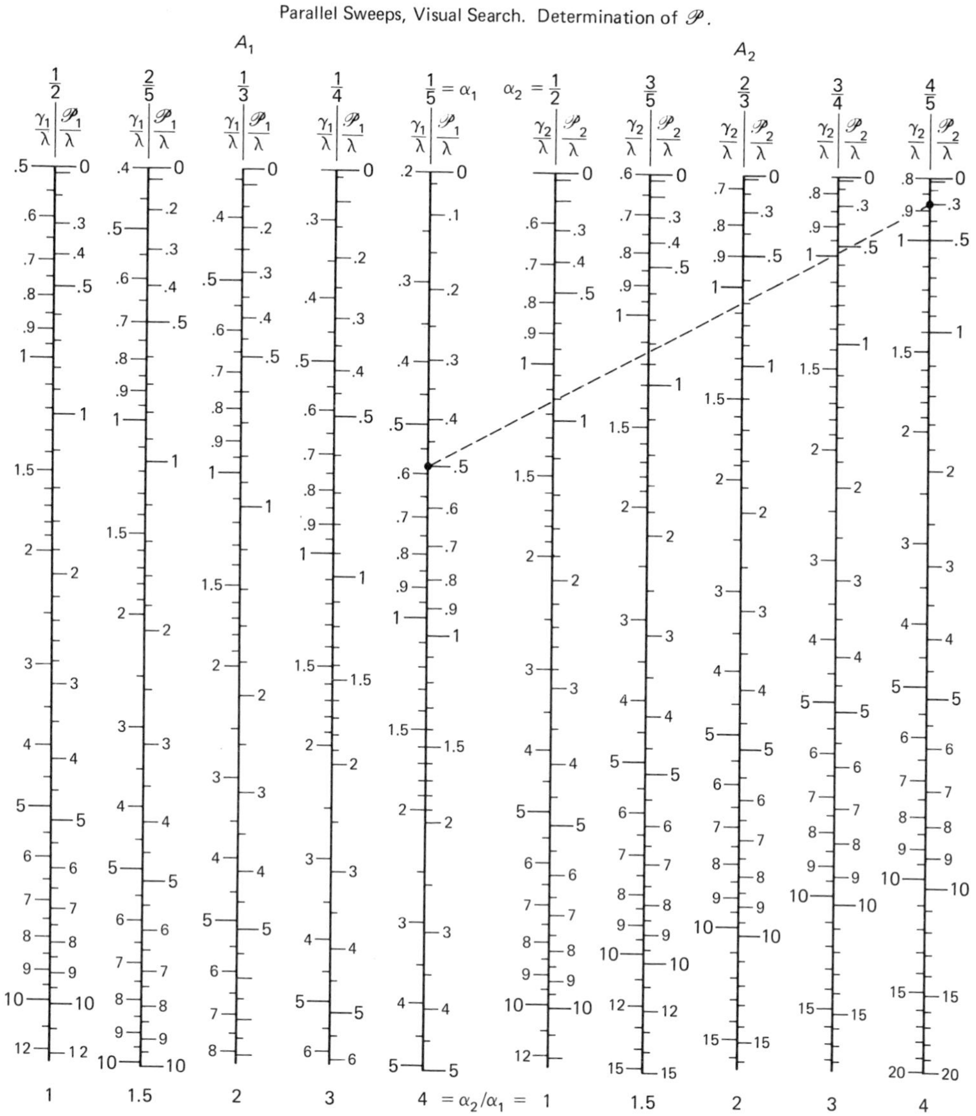

Fig. 12. Nomogram to be used with Fig. 11.

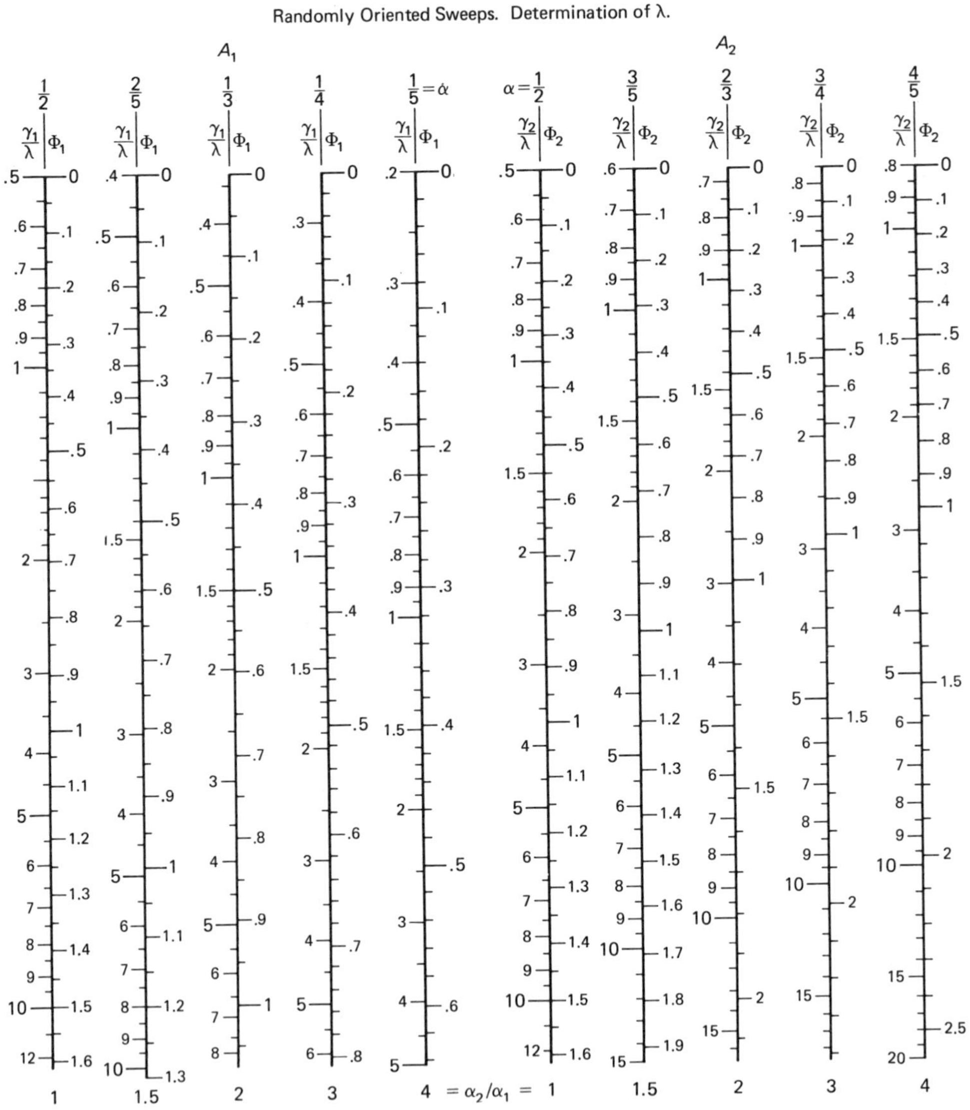

Fig. 13. Nomogram for calculation of optimal allocation of Φ between two areas, for uniform, randomly oriented sweeps.

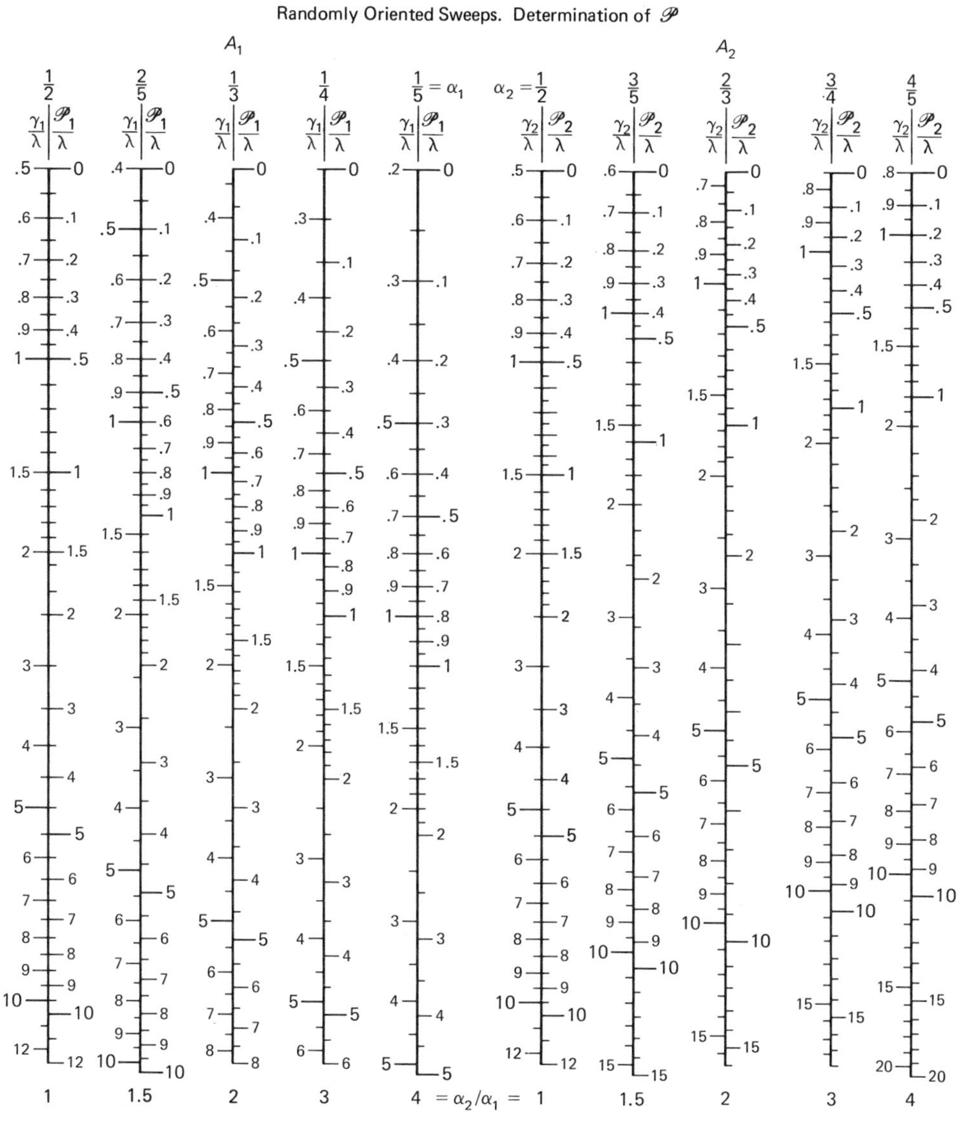

Fig. 14. Nomogram to be used with Fig. 13.

right-hand pair of curves are for somewhat more equal subareas, but a 2 to 1 ratio of probability of presence ($\alpha_1 = 0.4, \gamma_1 = 0.67; \alpha_2 = 0.6, \gamma_2 = 0.33$).

Note that the lower set of curves, for random sweeps display a quite similar pattern to the upper set, for parallel visual sweeps, but that the probability of success for the same search effort is about 15 percent smaller for the random sweep cases. The right-hand pair of curves, for the more nearly equal areas, shows that the less likely area is not touched until WL equals nearly $A/2$, but that by the time available effort has reached $3A/2$, the search effort in the two areas is nearly equal; though the probability of detection in A_2 is still considerably smaller than that in A_1, further search in A_1 would not improve matters.

When the *a priori* estimates of the target's presence are detailed enough to require the separation of A into more than two subareas, a computational procedure to use with a minicomputer or a log-log slide rule can be developed for the case of random sweeps. Referring to Eqs. (23), (24) and (25), proceed as follows:

1. Having divided area A into N subareas, with area fractions $\alpha_j = A_j/A$ and target presence probabilities γ assigned to each, one rank-orders the areas in descending order of $\gamma_j/\alpha_j = g_jA$, starting with the subarea having the largest γ/α as A_1, and so on, so that $\gamma_{j-1}/\alpha_{j-1} \geqslant \gamma_j/\alpha_j$. We then compute and tabulate the two sets of limits,

$$K_n = \sum_{j=1}^{n} \alpha_j \ln(\gamma_j/\alpha_j) \qquad (n = 1, 2, 3, \ldots, N)$$

$$L_n = K_n - \left[\sum_{j=1}^{n} \alpha_j\right] \ln(\gamma_{n+1}/\alpha_{n+1})$$

   Limits L_n form a monotonically increasing function of n.

2. When the total available specific search effort $\Phi = WL/A$ is less than $L_1 = \alpha_1 \ln(\gamma_1\alpha_2/\gamma_2\alpha_1)$, search should be concentrated solely in subarea A_1. The probability of detection of the target (in the only searched A_1) is

$$\mathcal{P} = \gamma_1(1 - e^{-\Phi/\alpha_1}) = \gamma_1(1 - e^{-WL/A_1})$$

3. When $L_{n-1} < \Phi = WL/A < L_n$, the search is to be in the subareas $A_1, A_2, \ldots, A_n$ only, with the search effort in A_j

$$A\Phi_j = A\alpha_j \left[\ln\left(\frac{\gamma_j}{\alpha_j}\right) + \left(\frac{\Phi - K_n}{\alpha_1 + \alpha_2 \cdots + \alpha_n}\right)\right] \qquad (j = 1, 2, \ldots, n)$$

   This results from the equation $\Phi = K_n - (\alpha_1 + \cdots + \alpha_n) \ln \lambda$ so that $\lambda = \exp[(K_2 - \Phi)/(\alpha_1 + \cdots + \alpha_n)]$. Therefore, we have

$$\sum_{j=1}^{n} \Phi_j = K_n + \Phi - K_n = \Phi$$

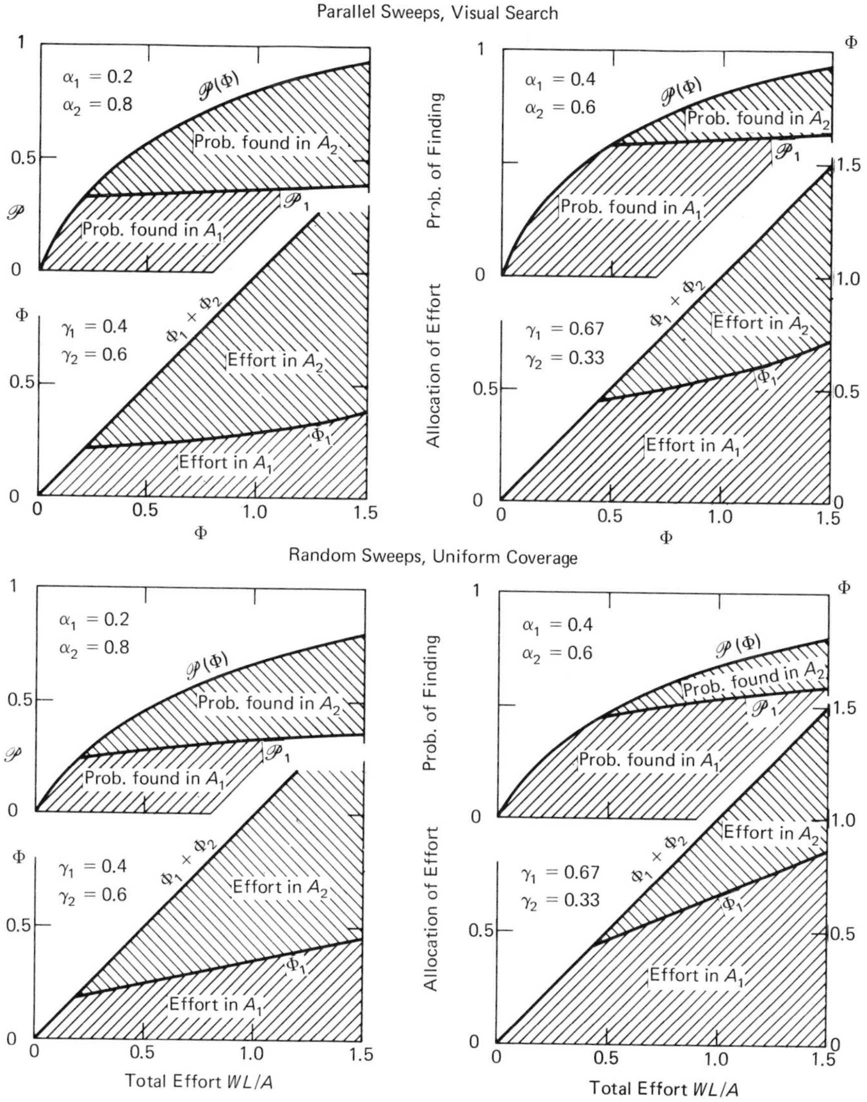

Fig. 15. Examples of use of Figs. 11 to 14.

The probability that the target will be discovered in A_j during the search is then

$$\mathcal{P}_j = \gamma_j - \alpha_j\lambda = \gamma_j - \alpha_j \exp\left[\frac{K_n - \Phi}{\alpha_1 + \cdots + \alpha_n}\right] \quad \text{so that}$$

$$\mathcal{P} = \sum_{j=1}^{n} (\gamma_j - \alpha_j\lambda)$$

4. When Φ is greater than L_N, the largest of the L's of Eq. (26), then all subareas of A are to be searched, with individual efforts given by

$$A\Phi_j = WL_j = A\alpha_j[\ln(\gamma_j/\alpha_j) + \Phi - K_N] \tag{26}$$

which results from the equation $\lambda = \exp(K_N - \Phi)$. The probability that the target will be discovered in A_j is

$$\mathcal{P}_j = \gamma_j - \alpha_j\lambda = \gamma_j - \alpha_j \exp(K_N - \Phi) \quad \text{so that}$$

$$\mathcal{P} = 1 - \exp(K_N - \Phi)$$

Note that $K_N \leqslant 0$ and that $K_N = 0$ only when all ratios $\gamma_j/\alpha_j = g_jA$ are equal and thus all equal to 1. Note also that if the search effort were to be distributed uniformly (random orientation) over the entire area A, the probability of detection would be $1 - \exp(-\Phi)$. Therefore, when $K_N < 0$ (i.e., when the probability densities of presence of the target, $g_j = \gamma_j/\alpha_j$, are *not* all equal) the probability of success $\mathcal{P}$ is increased if the search effort is allocated according to Eqs. (26). For another kind of application, see Morse [1970].

It can be shown (see Dobbie [1963]) that this allocation produces a $\mathcal{P}$ that is the largest achievable for a given Φ; likewise that the Φ, distributed according to the formulas, is the smallest effort that can achieve the resulting $\mathcal{P}$.

One example of the results is shown in Fig. 16, for three subareas. The least likely area A_3 is neglected until the search coverage WL becomes greater than $(\frac{3}{4})A$. The dashed line shows the probability of success if the search effort had been spread evenly over A. One would have to increase Φ by 20% to get an equal $\mathcal{P}$.

An example of the effect of false targets has been worked out by Dobbie [1973], for the very simple case of two areas and only one stationary false target. Since this, almost the simplest of search allocation problems involving false targets, gives rise to operating rules that would be difficult to follow in the heat of an actual search, it may be questioned whether precise analysis of more complex situations would be more an admirable mathematical exercise than a practical aid in actual searches. One can hope that approximate solutions can be developed that will be simpler to carry out in practice.

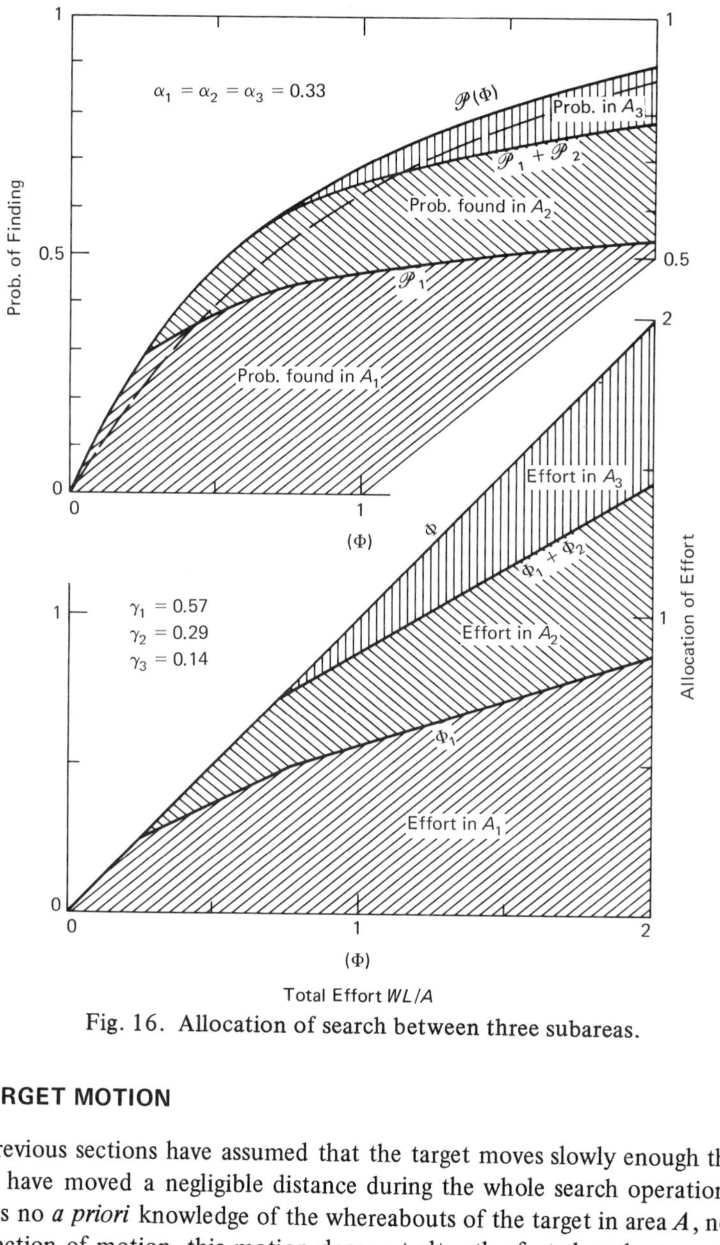

Fig. 16. Allocation of search between three subareas.

5. TARGET MOTION

The previous sections have assumed that the target moves slowly enough that it would have moved a negligible distance during the whole search operation. If there is no *a priori* knowledge of the whereabouts of the target in area A, nor of its direction of motion, this motion does not alter the fact that the target may be anywhere in A (assuming it cannot leave A). Thus, the best procedure still is to provide uniform coverage of A. If the target can leave A, the area to be searched will have to be increased in size as the search proceeds. If this increase is a small fraction of A, it makes little difference in the organization of the search or in its outcome. On the other hand, if the increase is equal to or greater than A by the time A has been searched over and if the target has not been found by then, it is unlikely that further search will be able to keep up with the expanding area of presence.

5.1 Target Position and Motion Unknown

To justify these statements, it is convenient to use the differential equation governing the probability P of finding the target. The searcher, as in previous sections, is assumed to move with velocity v and to have a search width W. Referring to Fig. 9b, the increase in the probability $P(L)$ of having found the target, after a search path of length L, is equal to the increase in the area of coverage $da = Wvdt$, divided by the area q, within which the target is likely to be, and multiplied by the probability $1 - P$ that the target is not yet found;

$$dP = (1 - P)(W/q)\,dL = (1 - P)(da/q) \tag{27}$$

where $a = WL$ is the area already searched over by the time the path has reached length L.

If the target is confined within the area A and if, initially, it can be anywhere inside A, then target motion will not change its probability density of presence, which will be $(1/q)$ at any instant. If, in addition, the search is random-uniform, then the area q in Eq. (27) will be practically equal to A (as long as W^2 is small compared to A); possible target motion within a confined area A cannot change its probability density of presence. The equation and its solution are then

$$\frac{dP}{P - 1} = -\frac{W}{A}\,dL; P(a) = 1 - e^{-WL/A} = 1 - e^{-a/A} \tag{28}$$

identical with Eq. (18).

On the other hand, if the target can cross the perimeter of the area A, then the area of possible presence, q in Eq. (27), increases with time. In this section, we suppose the target is not aware of the searcher and that its motion is randomly oriented. If it happened to be on the perimeter of A, in only half the cases would its motion take it outside A, and the average distance it would penetrate beyond A in time dt would be

$$(udt/2\pi)\int_0^{\pi} \sin\theta\, d\theta = (u/\pi)\,dt = (u/\pi v)\,dL = (u/\pi vW)\,da$$

where u is the estimated mean target speed of target motion, v is the speed of the searcher, and W is his search width. This "leakage" produces a gradual enlargement of the area of presence of the target, over the initial value A, as though the various possible positions of the target were molecules in a gas, with mean speed u. The gas expands with a mean velocity (u/π) normal to the boundary. In fact, the expected enlargement of the area is

$$dq = \frac{u}{\pi} s\,dt = \frac{us}{\pi v W}\,da$$

where s is the length of the perimeter of q. If the initial area A is circular or square, s is equal to the perimeter S of A times $\sqrt{q/A}$. Even if the length of A is twice its width, the formula $s \simeq S\sqrt{q/A}$ is approximately correct as long as q is less than twice A.

Therefore, the area of presence of the target q, after area a has been searched over in a random-uniform manner, is approximately equal to the solution of the differential equation

$$\frac{dq}{\sqrt{q}} = 2\gamma \frac{da}{\sqrt{A}} \text{ or } q = A\left(1 + \gamma\frac{a}{A}\right)^2 \text{ where } \gamma = \frac{uS}{2\pi v W}$$

Inserting this into Eq. (27) we obtain the probability $P(a)$ of detection of the target after random-uniform search effort $WL = a$ of an area initially of magnitude A, when the target is initially anywhere within A and has an estimated, randomly directed speed u (and is not confined within A)

$$P(a) \simeq 1 - \exp\left[\frac{-a/A}{1 + \gamma(a/A)}\right]; a = WL \tag{29}$$

This differs from Eq. (28) by the term in the denominator of the exponential, resulting from the "leakage" of the moving target into the region outside A. It is a valid approximation as long as factor $\gamma = (u/2\pi v)(S/W)$ is small, which assumes that ratio (u/v) of estimated average target speed to searcher speed is no larger than the ratio (W/S) of search width to perimeter of A. In fact if $\gamma \simeq 1$, $P(a)$ ceases to increase soon after a becomes equal to A, after which area q expands faster than the search can catch up. However, if (W/S) for a single searcher is smaller than u/v, γ can be reduced in value by employing more than one searcher. For m independent searchers, each following a uniform-random path, W in the formula is changed to mW and thus γ is changed to (γ/m).

To see what degradation is produced by this possible "leakage" of the target outside initial area A, we tabulate $P(A)$, the probability of detection after a total area $mWL = A$ has been searched over, for different values of γ.

TABLE 1.

γ	0	0.1	0.2	0.3	0.4	0.5
$P(A)$	0.632	0.597	0.565	0.537	0.510	0.487
a_1/A	1.000	1.111	1.250	1.429	1.667	2.000

The third line measures the area $a_1 = mWL_1$ that must be searched over in order that the probability of detection $P(a_1)$ equal the value 0.632 for $\gamma = 0$ and $a = A$. Further increase of a beyond a_1 of course produces further increases of $P(a)$, but these further gains are made at the cost of disproportionately large efforts. The gain in $P(A)$ by dividing the search efforts among m searchers comes in the fact that γ becomes γ/m, because each searcher needs to search only area A/m (provided the m paths, between them, cover A uniformly) and

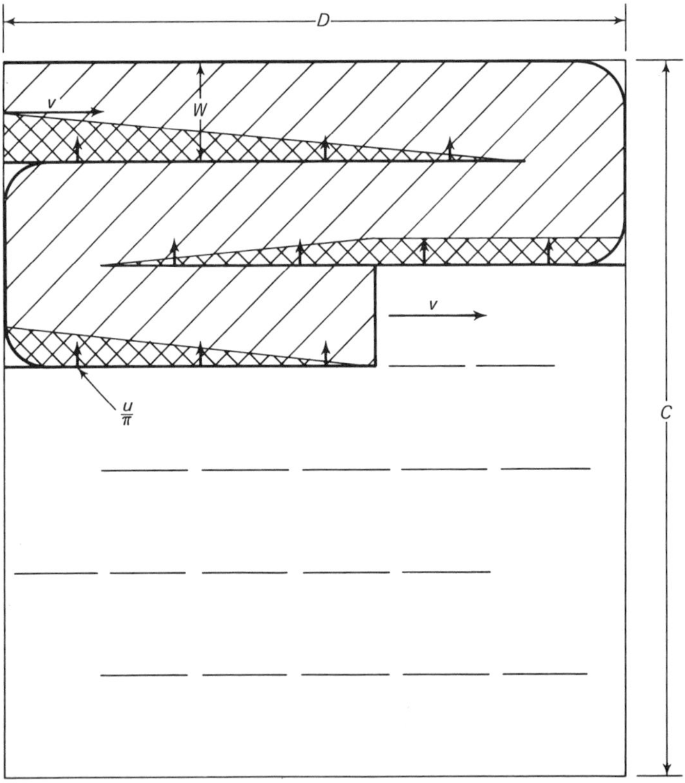

Fig. 17. Tight search coverage of area $A = CD$. Shaded area is a, the portion completely searched if target is at rest. If target has average speed u in a random direction it can leak back into cross-hatched area b. Area of possible presence of target is thus $A - a + b$, if target cannot cross perimeter of A.

the search is completed in $(1/m)$th the time, so the target has less time to "leak out."

An exact analysis of target motion on a regularly patterned search (such as the parallel sweeps of Fig. 6) has not yet been worked out. For comparison, as an opposite limit from the random-uniform case just presented, we can look at the idealized case of using definite-range equipment in parallel sweeps spaced $S = W$ apart, so as to leave no unsearched area between sweeps. If the target is at rest somewhere within A, the probability of detection by the time the path length has reached $L = a/W$ is given by Eq. (6) and by curve d of Fig. 8 ($P = a/A$).

First, we assume the target is in motion, with a randomly directed average speed u, but that it is confined to motion within the initial area A. In this case, the only way the target can "leak out" is into the area, a, that was assumed to have been completely swept. Examination of Fig. 17 indicates that when the area is completely swept, so that $a \equiv LW = A$, the regions where the target could have leaked back (the cross-hatched areas) have an area

$$q(A) = \frac{nu}{\pi v} D^2 = \frac{uD}{\pi v W} A \text{ since } n = \frac{C}{W} \text{ and } A = CD$$

within which the target may still reside, unfound (we assume it takes n parallel sweeps to completely cover A).

This leaked-back area is approximately proportional to the swept area so that, at the stage when area a has been swept (as shown in Fig. 17), the area within which the target may still be (if it has not yet been discovered) is

$$q(a) = A - (1 - \mu)a \text{ where } \mu = \frac{u}{\pi v}\frac{D}{W}$$

Finally, inserting this into Eq. (27) results in

$$\frac{dP}{1 - P} = \frac{da}{A - (1 - \mu)a} \text{ or } P(a) = 1 - \left[1 - (1 - \mu)\frac{a}{A}\right]^{1/(1-\mu)} \tag{30}$$

for the case where the target is constrained to move inside A.

The probability of detection when $a = A$ (when the search would have been complete if there were no target motion) is not unity but

$$P(A) = 1 - \mu^{1/(1-\mu)}$$

This is tabulated for a few values of μ;

TABLE 2.

μ	0	0.05	0.10	0.15	0.20	0.25
$P(A)$	1.000	0.957	0.923	0.893	0.866	0.843

As with the random case, the analysis is valid when constant $\mu = (u/\pi v)(D/W)$ is small. Better results can be achieved by using m searchers, in which case each searcher needs to cover only area A/m and constant μ becomes $(u/\pi v)(D/mW)$. In an actual search, the detection will not have the sharp cut-off of the definite range curve d of Fig. 3, nor will the sweeps be the perfect pattern of Fig. 17. Therefore, the actual probability of detection for $WL = A$ will be somewhere between the $P(A)$ of Table 2 and the $1 - e^{-1} = 0.632$ of Eq. (28) for random coverage. The difference between these limits is less when a is less than or is greater than A.

If the target is not prevented from crossing the perimeter of A, the bottom side of A (as shown in Fig. 17) will be penetrated and the increase in searchable area, because of this side, when $a = A$, is D times the effective velocity u/π of leakage, times the duration $T = nD/v = A/vW$ of the search. This also increases linearly as the search progresses, so this addition to the area of q also is $(uD/\pi vW)a = \mu a$. The leakage out of each of the sides C of A is a stepwise approximation to a triangle with vertex at the upper corner and base, down a distance $C(a/A)$ from the top, of width $(u/\pi vW)a$, plus a rectangle of width $(u/\pi vW)a$ beyond the rest of side C. The added area on both sides, when (a/A) of the search has been completed, is thus $\nu[2 - (a/A)]\,a$, where $\nu = (uC/\pi vW)$. Therefore, when the searched area is $a = WL$, the area within which the target may yet be is

$$q \simeq A - a(1 - 2\gamma) - (\nu/A)a^2$$

where $\gamma = \mu + \nu = (u/\pi vW)\ (C + D) = (u/2\pi v)\ (S/W)$, S being the perimeter of A, as in Eq. (29).

The probability of discovering the target after area a has been searched over by the "ideal" coverage of Fig. 17, is the solution of Eq. (27) with this new value of q inserted. It is

$$P(a) = 1 - \lambda\left\{\frac{1 - \lambda[1 - 2\gamma + 2\nu(a/A)]}{1 + \lambda[1 - 2\gamma + 2\nu(a/A)]}\ \frac{1 + \lambda(1 - 2\gamma)}{1 - \lambda(1 - 2\gamma)}\right\}^{\lambda} \tag{31}$$

where $\lambda = 1/\sqrt{1 - 4\mu + 4\gamma^2}$. To measure the effect of this leakage, we tabulate P when A is a square (when $\gamma = 2\mu = 2\nu$) and when $a = A$, for different values of γ;

TABLE 3.

γ	0	0.1	0.2	0.3	0.4	0.5
$P(A)$	1.000	0.878	0.785	0.718	0.680	0.667

Comparison with Table 2, for the case when the target is kept inside A (for $\gamma = 2\mu$) shows that leakage over the perimeter of A produces a considerable reduction in the probability of detection. Of course, if m searchers are used, moving accurately in line abreast, W becomes mW and γ becomes γ/m. If one has enough manpower, the search can be completed quickly enough so the effect of target motion can be minimized.

Of course, Table 3 is for the perfect coverage of A implied in Fig. 17. If the lateral range curve differs from d of Fig. 3 and/or the sweeps are not exact, the detection probability $P(A)$ will approach the lower limit for random coverage, given in Table 1.

Other patterns of parallel sweeps, with definite range equipment, will result in slightly different values of the upper limit of $P(A)$, but the difference will not be large. For example, the approximate analysis for a path that covers the perimeter first and then spirals in to the center yields results similar to those of Table 3, but with $\gamma \simeq (3uS/8\pi vW)$, roughly three quarters of the γ for Eq. (31). Covering the perimeter of A first is some improvement, but the leakage into the swept path still occurs. In any case, these results are for the ideal case of definite range, perfectly aligned, parallel sweeps. It is safer to predict probabilities nearer those of Table 1, for random-uniform sweeps.

5.2 Crossover Barrier

When the target motion is not randomly oriented, the search problem differs again. Only two specific cases have been analyzed sufficiently to yield results of practical utility. The simplest case of this sort is when the direction and magnitude of the target's motion is known, but its position is not.

Suppose an aerial search is to discover a ship that must pass through an ocean strait, of navigable width D, as shown in Fig. 18a. If the ship is known to have a speed u as it passes through the strait, we can analyze the search path most easily by transforming to a coordinate system moving with the ship, as shown in Fig. 18b. In these coordinates, the most efficient search path will be series of parallel sweeps that transform back to coordinates at rest with respect to the ocean, as the angular figure 8 shown in Fig. 18a. Note that the short, end legs are in a direction opposed to that of the target.

If this path is to close on itself, if the barrier patrol is to keep up with the motion of the target, the spacing S between parallel sweeps in co-moving coordinates must be related to the width of the strait, to the speed u of the target and to the speed v of the search plane. The time $T = 2D/v$ that it takes the plane to go across and back (we assume u/v is small enough so the length of the diagonal leg in Fig. 18a is nearly equal to D; if not, correction can be made) must equal the length of time $T = 2S/u$ for the co-moving coordinates to move downward by two sweep spacings. Thus, spacing S and the resulting sighting potential Φ are given by the formulas

$$S = D(u/v); \quad \Phi = W/S = (Wv/Du) \tag{32}$$

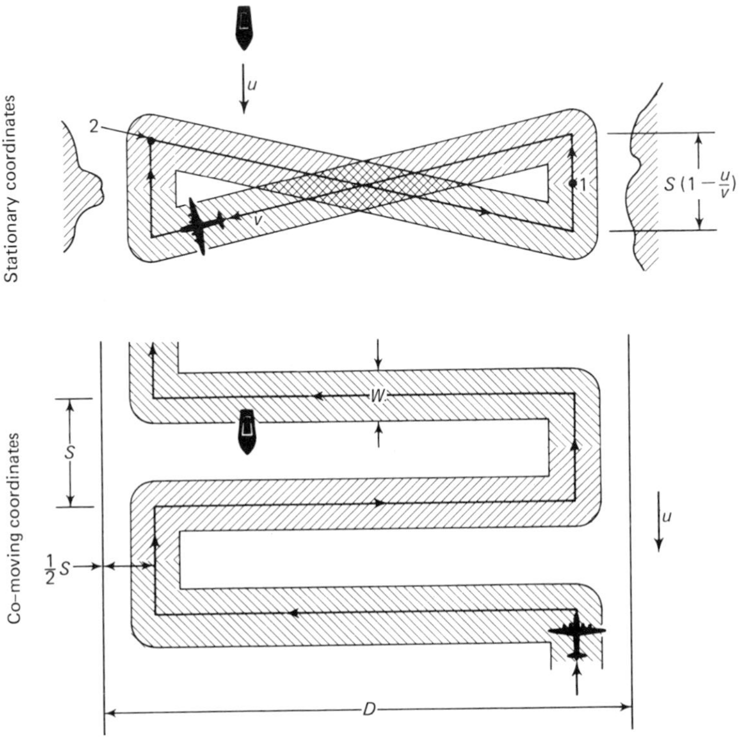

Fig. 18. A cross-over barrier patrol to catch a ship passing through an ocean strait.

This path, translated back to stationary coordinates, as shown in Fig. 18a, is called a *crossover barrier patrol.*

If it is not known where, along the line D across the strait, the target is to pass, nor is it known, within a time $T = 2D/v$, when it is to pass, then the whereabouts of the target may be anywhere within an area $2SD$ in co-moving coordinates. Thus, *if* the barrier patrol is in operation when the target passes through the strait, the probability of detection is the probability $P(\Phi)$ that has been given in Eqs. (16) or (18) or shown in Fig. 8, for parallel sweeps. There is a more complete discussion of this problem in Chapter 7 of Koopman [1946].

If Φ, as given in Eq. (32), is less than $\frac{1}{2}$, i.e., if the ratio W/D is less than half the ratio u/v, between target speed and search plane speed, the probability P of detection will not be satisfactorily large. Several search planes should then be used, if possible, either flying parallel courses a distance S/n apart (if n planes are used) or spaced in sequence along the same course, spaced in time. For example, if two planes are to be flown in sequence, the second plane should be started at point 2 in Fig. 18a when the first plane is at point 1, halfway up the opposite vertical leg; in this manner, the second plane's sweeps would come half way between those of the first plane, in co-moving coordinates. If the multiple sweeps are carefully flown, so that the n parallel sweeps are equally spaced in comoving coordinates, the effective sighting potential would be nWv/Du, and this value could be used as Φ to determine the probability $P(\Phi)$ of detection.

Barrier patrols are useful in many other military, police and life saving operations.

5.3 Retiring Search Sweeps

Another situation, not infrequently encountered, arises when the target is located exactly, at some instant, but the search is not able to start until a time T_0 later. One has to assume that the target has moved during that time and, if the target's maximum velocity u is known and if there is no indication of the direction of its motion, at T_0 it could be anywhere within a circle of radius uT_0. As the search progresses, this circle of presence continues to expand; so the search path, if possible, should be an expanding spiral, trying to cover this increasing area.

If the search effort is to be limited to the value $E(T) = WvT$, it must be within that part of the circle, of radius $R(T) = u(T_0 + T)$, that the allocation rules of Eqs. (23) say should be searched. In most cases, when it is not known whether the target's actual speed is its maximum speed u, or zero, or something in between, the point of maximum probability of presence of the target would be at the origin, where the target had originally been spotted. Therefore, the search would begin at the center and spiral outward, with spacing between the arms prescribed by the density $\phi = W/S$ determined by Eqs. (23).

The analysis of this operation is still more "intrinisic" than that for a stationary target. We shall go through it using the formulas for random sweeps; partly because it is the only case for which the answers can be analytic, and partly because it is unlikely that careful interpath spacing can be maintained in a spiral search, so that it is safer to assume the less optimistic formulas. We consider the case at time T, when the allocated search effort WvT has been used up and the radius of the circle of presence of the target is $u(T_0 + T)$. Looking back on the search, which started at the center at $t = 0$ and spiralled out as the spiral passed through the radius $r < R(T)$, and effort $E(t) = Wvt$ has already been used up, the *a priori* estimate of the probability density of presence of the target there would then have been $g(r)$, which can be estimated for each value of r and T out to the value at which the search ends.

If the area of presence is not a circle, it is more convenient, and leads to easier generalization, to change variables from radius to area. The area of presence $A(t)$ at time t after the start of the search and the area $q(t)$ inside the circle of radius r (the area already searched over by time t) are given by the formulas

$$A(t) = \pi u^2 (T_0 + t)^2; \quad q(t) = \pi r^2$$

Time during search can be measured in terms of search effort $E(t) = Wvt$ so that these variables can be expressed in terms of dimensionless quantities

$$\begin{gathered} A(t) = \alpha(1 + z)^2; \quad z = (t/T_0) = E(t)/\beta; \quad q(t) = \alpha x \\ \alpha = A(0) = \pi u^2 T_0^2; \quad \beta = WvT_0 \end{gathered} \tag{33}$$

Thus, α is the area of presence of the target at the start of the search and β is the area that could have been searched with density $\phi = 1$ during the time T_0 (which we can call the *delay time*). The interrelation between these quantities must be given in terms of the rules of search given in (23), only now they must include the fact that the probability density of presence $g(r)$ refers to the time t at which the plane was searching at the distance r from the origin.

Before we start the analysis, however, some salient points should be noted. When the search ends at time T, the search effort WvT has been expended. But by this time the area of presence of the target has become $\pi u^2 (T_0 + T)^2$. Therefore, by the end of the search, the mean sighting potential $\Phi = E/A$ has become $[WvT/\pi u^2 (T_0 + T)^2]$. This quantity increases with T for a while, but it reaches a maximum at $T = T_0$ and thereafter declines. Its maximum value at $T = T_0$ is $\Phi_m = (W/4\pi u T_0)(v/u)$, inversely proportional to T_0, a product of a ratio of areas and a ratio of velocities of target and searcher. This has two consequences: first, the sooner one can start the search, the more efficient is the search coverage; second, the first part of the search, during a time equal to the delay time T_0, is by far the most effective part of the search. Further search, beyond $T = T_0$, is chasing a widening circle of presence that has already gone too far to catch up with.

Returning to procedure (23), we first have to decide on a reasonable form for the probability of presence $g(r)$, at the instant of time t when the search has reached r and the area of presence has reached $A(t)$. Since we do not know the actual speed or course of the target beyond its maximum speed u, we might assume an average distribution and let

$$g(r) = (2/A)[1 - (\pi r^2/A)] = (2/A)[1 - (q/A)]$$

with its maximum at $r = 0$, tapering off to zero at $q = A$. Since A is a function of t and therefore of z, g is a function of z. But since $q = \alpha x$ also is a function of search effort $z\beta$, we can say that A, g, and z are all functions of x. Their interrelations are given by (33).

We require that the density g, times $P'(\phi)$, the derivative of the probability density of sighting, a function of the density of search ϕ there, must equal a constant G or, if it cannot, ϕ must be zero. In the case of random sweeps, this leads to the equation

$$\phi = \ln (g/G) = \ln (2/AG) + \ln [1 - (q/A)] \tag{34}$$

$$\text{if } \phi \text{ is positive, otherwise } \phi = 0$$

But ϕ, the density of search, is the derivative of E with respect to q, and the whole equation can be written as a differential equation in terms of the variables defined in Eqs. (33)

$$z'(x) \equiv \frac{dz}{dx} = k \left\{ C - \ln (1+z)^2 + \ln \left[1 - \frac{x}{(1+z)^2} \right] \right\} \tag{35}$$

$$\text{where } k = \frac{\alpha}{\beta} = \frac{\pi u^2 T_0^2}{W v T_0}; \quad C = \ln (2/\alpha G)$$

This equation may be integrated numerically, for different values of k and C, out to $x = x_m$, where z' goes to zero. The value of z at that point, z_m, times $\beta = WvT_0$, is equal to the total search effort $E(T)$ expended; the value of x_m, times $\pi u^2 T_0^2 = \alpha$, is equal to the total area searched, $Q = \pi (r_m)^2$, and the value of $z'(x)$ times $1/k$ is equal to the density of search ϕ at the radius $r = \sqrt{\alpha x/\pi}$. In other words

$z'(x)$ goes to zero at $x = x_m$, where $z = z_m$
Total search effort $E_m = \beta z_m = WvT_0 z_m$
Total area searched $Q = \pi r_m^2 = \alpha x_m = \pi u^2 T_0^2 x_m$
Search density at $r = \sqrt{\alpha x/\pi} < r_m$, is

$$\phi \equiv W/S = (1/k) z'(x) = (WvT_0/\pi u^2 T_0^2)(dz/dx) \tag{36}$$

Probability density of presence of target at time and place of search

$$g(x) = \frac{2/\alpha}{(1+z)^2} \left[1 - \frac{x}{(1+z)^2} \right]$$

The probability of success in the whole search is then

$$\mathcal{P} = \int_0^Q (1 - e^{-\phi}) g\,dq = \alpha G \int_0^{x_m} (e^{\phi} - 1)\,dx = 2e^{-C} \int_0^{x_m} (e^{z'/k} - 1)\,dx \tag{37}$$

which also can be evaluated numerically.

A few examples of the results are shown in Figs. 19 and 20. Two values of the parameter $k = \alpha/\beta = (\pi u T_0/W)(u/v)$ were used, 1 and 2. Since α is the area of presence of the target at the instant the search starts and β is the area that could have been searched effectively ($\phi = 1$) in the delay time T_0, $k = 1$ represents

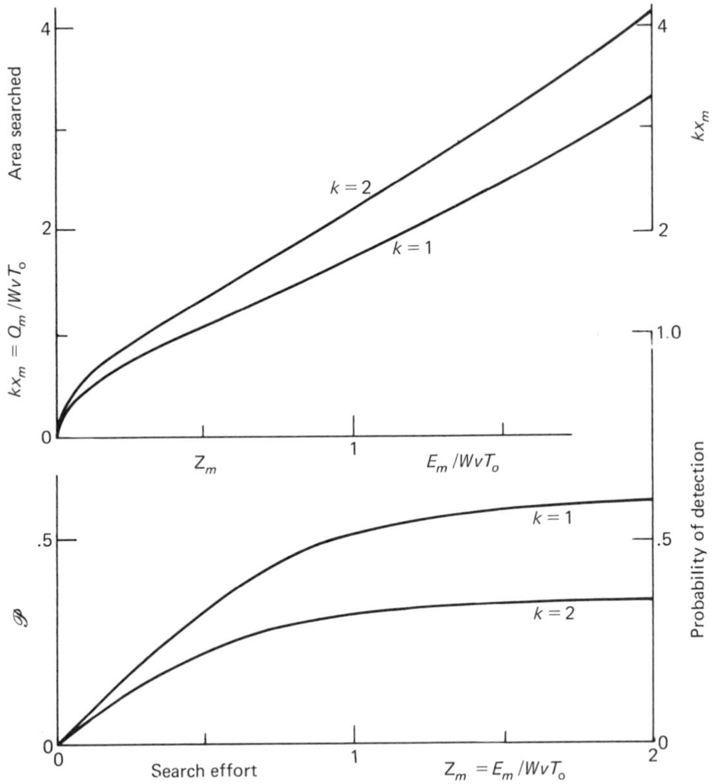

Fig. 19. Curves for determination of searched area Q and probability of detection $\mathcal{P}$ as functions of total search effort $E = WvT$, for the retiring search spiral of Eq. (35).

cases where the search started before the target could get very far away from the origin. Case $k = 2$ represents searches where the target got more of a start, and the searcher had less chance of catching up.

We note that the probability of detection for $k = 1$ is nearly twice that for $k = 2$, and that neither probability increases much after E_m becomes larger than WvT_0, the area searched in time $t = T_0$. After covering the central region, the area covered, Q, rises slowly as search effort E is increased, but then begins to rise faster as the quadratically increasing area of presence increases faster than the search can keep up. More area has to be covered for the $k = 2$ case than for $k = 1$, which means that it has to be covered less densely and thus the probability of detection suffers.

Fig. 20 shows typical curves of search density ϕ for the same two values of k, but for specific values of C and thus of z_m. As expected, ϕ is greatest at the beginning of the search, near the origin, where the target was spotted. It has to cover a greater area for $k = 2$ than for $k = 1$ because the area of presence is always greater in the $k = 2$ case. The dashed lines are proportional to the probability of presence $g(x)$ at the time the search reaches $x = \pi r^2/\alpha$. This quantity is not yet zero when the search ends, at $x = x_m$, because the area of presence extends beyond the area searched, as required by (33). Thus, the results more or less bear out our preconceptions; though it is doubtful that intuition would have advised cutting off as early as $t = T_0$ or would have insisted on such a high concentration of search density close to the origin, as is evidenced by Fig. 20.

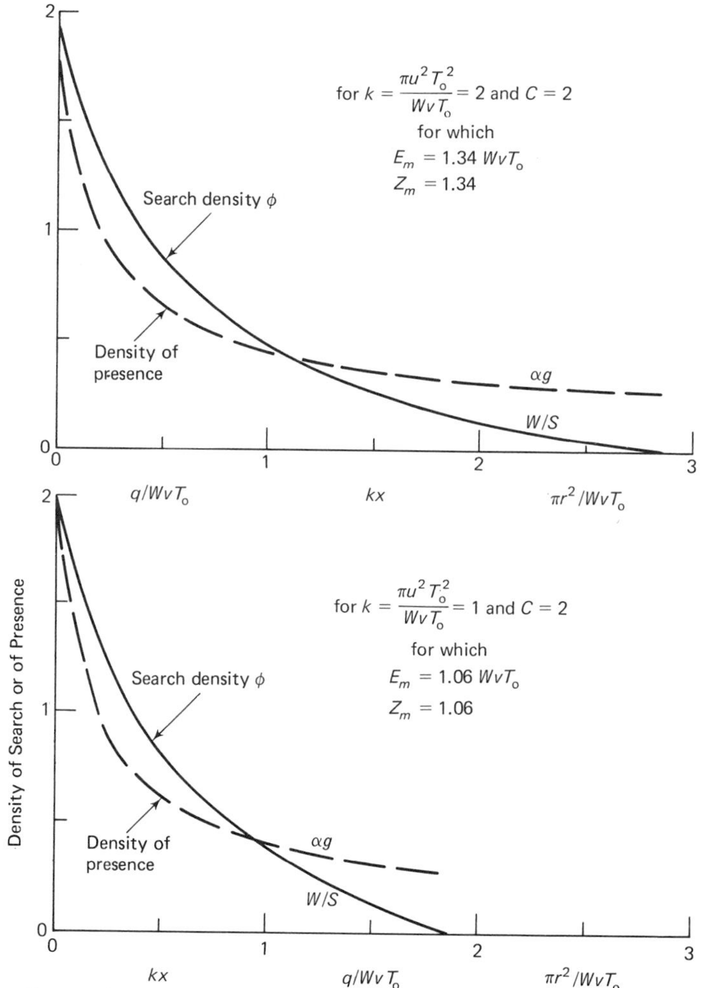

Fig. 20. Curves for search density ϕ as a function of area q already covered, for two values of C and k. Dashed line is proportional to density of presence, $g(q)$, at time of search.

Another approach to a related problem, using game theory, has been discussed by Danskin [1968].

6. SEARCH OF DISCRETE SITES

There are operational situations that can be more easily modeled in terms of the search of discrete sites (boxes, in more mathematical jargon). The individual sites may themselves be separated areas, or have more complicated structure. All we need to know is the relationship between the effort expended in search at a site and the probability of discovery of the searched-for object. Here, the "target" may not be a unique object that may be in one site or another but not in both; it may be in several sites simultaneously. So the probabilities of presence γ may not have to add up to unity. For example, the search may be to locate the failure in a complex piece of equipment; more than one failure may be present. An interesting example of this sort of search problem is the strategy of search for ores or oil. Other examples of equal complication are those connected with police search. All we can do in this section is to report a few simple models, in the hope that they may be of more use than no model at all, or than a model too complex to put to practical use.

From one point of view, these discrete site-search problems are simpler than the area search problems we have been discussing earlier. We did not treat them first because the area-search problem is the classical search problem, and, to date, of more practical utility.

6.1 An Analogue of Area Search

The discrete analogue of the classical allocation of search effort, given in Eqs. (23) to (31) for the area case, is the following one:

There are N sites, the probability of presence of the target in the jth site is γ_j, where $0 \leqslant \gamma_j \leqslant 1$ but $\sum \gamma_j$ is not necessarily unity. We rank-order the sites in a decreasing order of probability, so that $\gamma_j \geqslant \gamma_{j+1}$. The probability that a target is discovered in site j, if it is present, is related to a quantity we shall call the search effort ϕ_j in j by a function $P(\phi)$, that satisfies the specifications given in (5) and is the same function for every site. We wish to distribute the search effort $E = \sum \phi_j$ over the N sites so as to maximize the sum of the probabilities $\gamma_j P(\phi_j)$. See Charnes and Cooper [1958] for details.

This is actually a simpler problem than that of Eqs. (23) to (26) since, in the present case, the only parameters to evaluate are the γ's, instead of the γ's and α's of Eq. (24). The added complication may be achieved by assuming the search effort has different powers in different sites, so that the probability of detection in site j is $P(\alpha_j \phi_j)$ instead of $P(\phi_j)$. In this case the problem is completely parallel to that of Section 4. Because of the simplicity of the results and the wide range of applicability of the formulas, we will go into details only for the case of the exponential formula

$$P(u) = 1 - e^{-u}$$

Assuming equal searchability of each site (i.e., that $\alpha_j = 1$ for each site) our problem is to

$$\text{Maximize} \quad \mathcal{P}(E) = \sum_{j=1}^{N} \gamma_j (1 - e^{-\phi_j})$$

subject to the requirement $\sum_{j=1}^{N} \phi_j = E$. The standard procedure is to minimize

$$J(E) = \sum_{j=1}^{N} [\gamma_j e^{-\phi_j} + \lambda\phi_j] \tag{38}$$

with parameter λ to be adjusted so that the sum of the ϕ's equals E. The process of solution is as follows:

1. Compute the sequence $\ln(1/\gamma_j)$, increasing with j. Also compute the partial sums $K_n = \sum_{j=1}^{n} \ln(1/\gamma_j)$ and the sequence $L_n = (1/n) K_n - \ln(1/\gamma_n)$, that also increases with n.
2. The minimization is accomplished by setting the derivative of $J(E)$ with respect to ϕ_j equal to zero. Thus $\lambda = \gamma_j e^{-\phi_j}$. The requirement that $\sum \phi_j = E$ leads to the formula $\ln \lambda = -(1/n)(K_n + E)$ and thus to the elimination of λ from the formulas for ϕ_j and $\mathcal{P}_j$.
3. When $L_1 = 0 \leqslant E \leqslant L_2$ site 1 only is searched (the site with the largest value of probability of presence γ). Then $\phi_j = E$ for $j = 1$ and 0 for $j > 1$ and $\mathcal{P} = \gamma_1(1 - e^{-E})$.

   When $L_n \leqslant E \leqslant L_{n+1}$, only the most probable n sites are searched, and

$$\begin{aligned} \phi_j &= (1/n)(K_n + E) - \ln(1/\gamma_j) \quad \text{if} \quad j \leqslant n, = 0 \text{ if } \quad j > n \\ \mathcal{P} &= \sum_{j=1}^{n} \mathcal{P}_j; \quad \mathcal{P}_j = \gamma_j - \exp[-(1/n)(K_n + E)] \quad \text{if} \quad j \leqslant n \end{aligned} \tag{39}$$

   When $L_N < E$, all N sites are searched and

$$\phi_j = (1/N)(K_N + E) - \ln(1/\gamma_j); \quad \mathcal{P}_j = \gamma_j - \exp[-(1/N)(K_N + E)]$$

$$E = \sum_{j=1}^{N} \phi_j; \quad \mathcal{P} = \sum_{j=1}^{N} \mathcal{P}_j$$

If, after expending effort E, the target is not yet found, and it is decided to spend an extra $\Delta E = E' - E$, recompute (39) using E' instead of E and add search efforts $\phi_j' - \phi_j$ to each site j. The author has prepared a nomograph to aid in solving Eq. 39 which gives two figure accuracy.

Solutions for other kinds of discrete search problems have been developed by Gluss [1959] for the allocation of effort in testing for failures in a complex electronic system. In this case, instead of a probability of detection depending on a continuous effort function, times are assumed for checking out each site and probabilities are given that the specified times will find the error. A dynamic programming technique is developed to determine the order in which the sites are to be searched so that expected total time is minimized.

6.2 Detection Errors

In most cases, when laying out a continuous search strategy in practice, we are forced, at present, to assume that the presence of false targets will not alter the structure of the theoretical models, aside from reducing the magnitude of some of the parameters. In the case of the search of discrete sites, the inclusion of false targets (or detection errors) again adds complexity to the analysis. In a few cases, however, one can simplify the assumptions sufficiently to produce usable solutions. These solutions may at least indicate the structure of yet another search operation, that of searching for oil or for ore. Here, the employment of a certain amount of search effort at a site may produce a positive or a negative indication. If the indication is positive, it is still possible that the desired oil or ore is, nevertheless, absent from the site. Likewise, there is a nonzero chance that a negative indication may be erroneous. A detailed study of the observer's process of deciding whether he has found the target, and how this affects the cost of both kinds of error, has been discussed by Pollock [1964] and others (see Pollock [1971] for a bibliography). Here, we need only take the results, to show how they modify the allocation of search effort. The example we use to illustrate our formulas is a simplified model of prospecting for oil or ore.

In looking for new sources of minerals, one first looks for possible sites for more detailed study, by searching for particular geological formations or other characteristics that have been present in previous successful strikes–including simple proximity to known sources. This preliminary exploration, partly in the field and partly from maps, yields estimates of the likelihood of striking "pay dirt" at a number of possible sites. From this list of *a priori* probabilities of presence of ore, one must lay out a strategy for the more expensive part of the prospecting operation. Of course one could blindly sink all further effort into the single highest rated site, but it might be better in the long run to utilize these *a priori* probabilities as fully as possible in deciding whether, and how, to go ahead. These estimates of the probability of presence of the mineral (which we can again call γ_j) at each possible site j will be changed as the operation progresses, but at the beginning, when the first plans are made, they are the only measure available.

At each likely site a survey must be made, using sonic or gravitational or magnetic or electrical equipment, to sharpen our estimate of the probability of presence of the mineral. The preliminary plan must decide how extensive such a survey should be. Again, the preliminary estimates of survey effort may be modified later, but the initial allocation of effort must be made on the basis of the *a priori* probabilities γ. By the end of the survey a decision must be made, whether to abandon further effort at that site or to commence excavation (or drilling), hopefully to obtain actual samples of the desired mineral.

The excavation or drilling is usually much more expensive than the instrumental survey, and one hopes that the survey has reduced the chance of an erroneous decision to excavate, with no ore to show for the digging. (An alternative analysis of this decision process is given by MacQueen and Miller [1960]).

It may be that the result of the survey measurements is to increase the chance of deciding to excavate. With no survey we may be disinclined to dig or drill; with a very extensive survey we would have reached a fairly precise estimate of the worth of excavation. At the time of the preliminary plans our best guess as to the likelihood of a decision to excavate at site j would be the *a priori* probability γ_j. Thus, one possible forecast of the results of the instrumental survey is that as the survey effort is increased from zero to some large value, the chance of our deciding to investigate would start from zero and approach the value γ_j asymptotically. In other words, this chance would depend on the effort ϕ_j expended on the survey, something like the function $\gamma_j(1 - e^{-\phi_j})$, with ϕ_j being proportional to the expenditure involved in making the survey at site j.

Unless the instruments used in the survey are perfect, a certain fraction of times the decision is made to excavate, it will have been a wrong decision and a lot more money would have been needlessly spent. The crucial question is: how does the fraction of "dry holes" to "strikes" depend on the amount of effort spent on the instrumental survey? Decision theory does not give us an unequivocal answer to this question. Indeed, the answer depends on the nature of the equipment used in the survey and on *how* it is used. All we can do here is to make a few reasonable guesses as to possibilities and work out models to correspond to them. In the end, the choice of model and the values of its parameters will have to be decided on the basis of operational experiments, just as was done for the model of search for a submarine by a plane. In view of the costs of mineral prospecting and the value of a "strike," such a series of measurements would seem to be a worth while investment.

At one end of the sequence of possibilities is to assume that the amount of effort expended on the instrumental survey changes the probability of reaching a decision to excavate but does not alter the ratio between success and failure if excavation is carried out. Put in terms of expected monetary costs and returns, this limiting model is:

A priori probability of presence of ore at site j, reached from the preliminary exploration, is γ_j, the only quantiative estimate available at the time of the initial planning.

Estimated returns from site j, if ore is present and discovered by excavation, is R_j.

Expected cost of excavation to "prove out" site j is D_j.

Expected cost of instrumental survey at j to help decide whether to excavate is C_j.

A priori probability that a decision will be made to excavate at j is $\gamma_j(1 - e^{-\beta C_j})$.

A priori probability that this decision will be correct, if made, is assumed in this model to be equal to γ_j, the *a priori* probability of presence of the ore. Until the instrumental survey is made, we have no information except γ_j and the estimated costs; we must use them in laying out our preliminary strategy.

Thus, the expected return from site j, if survey effort costing C_j were to be expended there, is

$$q_j = \gamma_j(\gamma_j R_j - D_j)(1 - e^{-\beta C_j})$$

In other words, the expected net return from site j, if excavation is decided, is $S_j = \gamma_j R_j - D_j$; there is a chance γ_j that the excavation succeeds, returning R_j, but a certainty that the excavation will cost an expected D_j. Thus, the variational problem representing this case is:

$$\begin{aligned} &\text{Maximize } Q = \sum_j [\gamma_j S_j(1 - e^{-\beta C_j}) - C_j] \\ &\text{Subject to the requirement that } \sum C_j = C \end{aligned} \tag{40}$$

This is quite similar to the Eqs. (38) for simple search of N sites, with βC_j substituted for ϕ_j and $S_j\gamma_j$ for γ_j. The solution also is quite similar;

Rank the sites in decreasing order of magnitude of $\gamma_j S_j$, then calculate the sequences $K_n = \sum_{j=1}^{n} \ln(\beta\gamma_j S_j)$ and $L_n = K_n - n \ln(\beta\gamma_n S_n)$.

When $L_1 = 0 < C < L_2$, only site 1 (with the largest γS) is to be considered. The survey at site 1 is planned to cost C and the expected return is

$$Q(C) = \gamma_1 S_1(1 - e^{-\beta C})$$

When $L_n < C < L_{n+1}$ (assume that $L_{N+1} \longrightarrow \infty$) then only the n most promising sites are surveyed, the survey cost allocation for site j being

$$\left.\begin{aligned} &C_j = \frac{1}{\beta}\left[\ln(\beta\gamma_j S_j) - \frac{1}{n} K_n\right] + \frac{1}{n} C \qquad (j \leqslant n) \\ &\text{and the expected return is} \\ &Q(C) = \sum_{j=1}^{n} \gamma_j S_j - \frac{n}{\beta} \exp\left[\frac{1}{n}(K_n - \beta C)\right] - C \end{aligned}\right\} \tag{41}$$

We can now adjust the survey cost C to produce the greatest return $Q(C)$, by setting the differential of Q with respect to C equal to zero. We find the value of n for which

$$\left.\begin{aligned} &Q_{\max}(n) = \sum_{j=1}^{n} \gamma_j S_j - \frac{1}{\beta}(K_n + n) \quad \text{is greatest} \\ &\text{The corresponding optimal survey cost allocation is then} \\ &C_{\max}(n) = K_n/\beta \quad \text{and} \quad C_j = (1/\beta)\ln(\beta\gamma_j S_j) \qquad (1 \leqslant j \leqslant n) \end{aligned}\right\} \tag{42}$$

The optimal value of C is for $n = N$ (all sites surveyed) unless $\beta\gamma_j S_j$ is less than unity for some site; in which case n is the largest value of j for which $\beta\gamma_j S_j > 1$.

To assume, as this model does, that the effect of the instrumental survey will have no effect on the ratio between success or failure of the excavation, but only on the chance of deciding to excavate, is perhaps the most pessimistic assumption to make. We see that it results in the rule that the sites with the largest values of $\gamma_j S_j$ should be surveyed first.

At an opposite extreme is the assumption that the probability of making a decision to excavate at site j is independent of the amount of survey effort put in at site j (i.e., it has the value γ_j for all values of C_j) but the probability that the excavation is successful increases, from γ_j for $C_j = 0$, asymptotically to unity as $C_j \longrightarrow \infty$. In other words, the expected probability of deciding to excavate site j is γ_j and the expected cost of such excavation is $\gamma_j D_j$, but the expected return from a possible successful excavation is $\gamma_j[1 - (1 - \gamma_j)\, e^{-\alpha C_j}]\, R_j$, increasing as C_j is increased. Each of the N sites chosen may be excavated; the detailed instrumental survey is used to improve the chance that the excavation is successful. This effect would be greater when γ_j is near $\frac{1}{2}$ than when γ_j is near unity (when a detailed survey may not be needed).

To be realistic, this model must represent a separation of the decision process into three steps instead of two (see Engel [1957] for another such model):

1. On the basis of map and field exploration a list of sites is chosen that have a good chance of containing the searched-for mineral.
2. An initial survey, using simple equipment costing C_0, is run on all chosen sites. On the basis of this survey, probabilities γ_j are assigned. It may be that some γ's are near enough unity to justify going ahead with the excavation. Also those sites turning out to have γ's less than some lower limit (presumably $\frac{1}{2}$ or even greater) will be discarded from the list.
3. On the basis of the solution of the variational problem, given below, some or all of the sites remaining may have further, more intensive surveys applied before the decision to excavate is made.

The variational problem is thus:

$$\left.\begin{aligned} &\text{Maximize} \quad Q = \sum \gamma_j[1 - (1 - \gamma_j)\, e^{-\alpha C_j}]\, R_j - C_j - \gamma_j D_j \\ &\text{subject to the requirement that} \quad \sum C_j = C \end{aligned}\right\} \tag{43}$$

and the procedure for solution is;

Rank the sites in descending order of $\gamma(1-\gamma)R$, with $\gamma_1(1-\gamma_1)R_1$ being the largest (if the R's are equal and if all the γ's are greater than $\frac{1}{2}$, the sites will be in *increasing* order of the γ's, the *smallest* γ being first).

Calculate the ascending sequences $K_n = \sum_{j=1}^{n} \ln\,[\alpha\gamma_j(1-\gamma_j)R_j]$ and $L_n = K_n - n\ln\,[\alpha\gamma_n(1-\gamma_n)R_n]$.

When $L_1 = 0 < C < L_2$, make the intensive survey only in site 1, which has the greatest uncertainty $\gamma_1(1-\gamma_1)R_1$ in expected return; decide on excavating the other sites on the basis of the γ's obtained from the initial survey (using some decision procedure that results in a probability γ_j of deciding to excavate site j).

The expected payoff is then

$$Q(C) = Q(0) + \gamma_1(1-\gamma_1)R_1(1-e^{-\alpha C})$$

$$Q(0) = \sum \gamma_j(\gamma_j R_j - D_j) - C_0$$

When $L_n < C < L_{n+1}$ (assume that $L_N \longrightarrow \infty$) only the first n sites are given a more detailed survey, the jth costing C_j; the rest are decided on the basis of the initial survey. The recommended costs C_j of the further survey, and the expected payoff of the plan are then

$$C_j = \frac{1}{\alpha}\left\{\ln\,[\alpha\gamma_j(1-\gamma_j)R_j] - \frac{1}{n}K_n\right\} + \frac{1}{n}C \qquad \text{for } j \leqslant n \tag{44}$$

$$Q(C) = Q(0) + \sum_{j=1}^{n}\left\{\gamma_j(1-\gamma_j)R_j - \frac{1}{\alpha}\exp\left[\frac{1}{n}K_n - \frac{\alpha}{n}C\right]\right\} - C$$

$$Q(0) = \sum_{j=1}^{n} \gamma_j(\gamma_j R_j - D_j) - C_0$$

As before, we can now determine the cost of the detailed survey allocation that will produce the greatest expected return. The result is, for the largest value of n for which $\alpha\gamma_n(1-\gamma_n)R_n$ is greater than unity,

$$C_{\max}(n) = (K_n/\alpha) \quad \text{and} \quad C_j = \frac{1}{\alpha}\ln\,[\alpha\gamma_j(1-\gamma_j)R_j] \tag{45}$$

$$Q_{\max}(n) = \sum_{j=1}^{n} \gamma_j(\gamma_j R_j - D_j) - \frac{1}{\alpha}(K_n + n) - C_0$$

An example of this solution is shown in Fig. 21.

Thus, the final results of these two alternative models are similar in some respects and contrasting in others. They both point to the importance of deter-

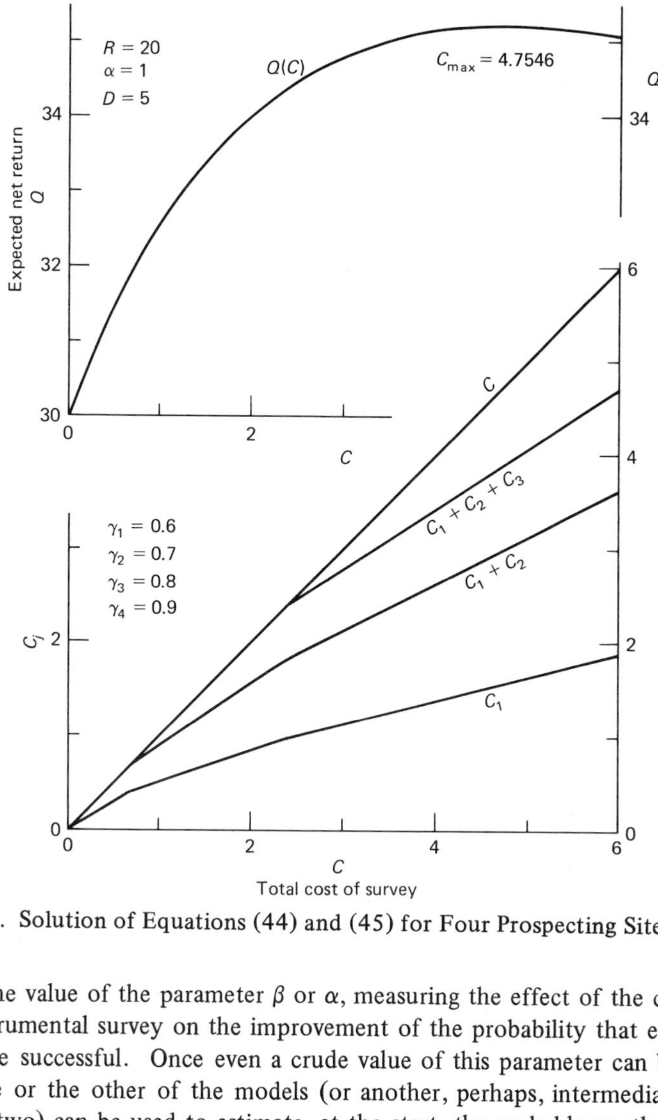

Fig. 21. Solution of Equations (44) and (45) for Four Prospecting Sites.

minining the value of the parameter β or α, measuring the effect of the cost C_j of the instrumental survey on the improvement of the probability that excavation will be successful. Once even a crude value of this parameter can be obtained, one or the other of the models (or another, perhaps, intermediate between the two) can be used to estimate, at the start, the probable worth of the campaign and an initial estimate of the allocation of effort that may be involved. These estimates will be altered as the search goes on, but at the beginning, the appropriate model, with the best estimates of the values of the γ's, R's, D's and of α or β, is the only way it will be possible to estimate, quantitatively, the projected campaign.

For example, both results show that a site j for which the *a priori* estimate of $\beta\gamma_j S_j$ or $\alpha\gamma_j(1 - \gamma_j)R_j$ is less than unity is probably not worth including in the campaign. It is better to reduce the number of sites to those that can all be covered by some amount of instrumental survey. The particular model that has been shown to be appropriate will then indicate which sites deserve more coverage than others.

As a final comment, the models discussed here may be useful in other than prospecting operations. For example, the process of testing a few samples from each manufactured production lot would be the preliminary exploration, determining γ; the more detailed "instrumental survey" might be the sampling of a larger fraction of the output. "Excavation" would be the testing, and repairing or discarding each defective unit. Decision "not to excavate" would correspond to deciding to scrap the batch without further testing. Analogues in police investigation also come to mind.

7. SEARCH FOR AN ACTIVE EVADER

Heretofore we have concentrated on the search for an object that either stays put or moves without relation to the details of the search path. A still more difficult task is the devising of search strategies for a target that is aware of the search and tries to evade. In fact, there are very few such solutions that are realistic enough to be of practical use. All of them, to date, utilize the Theory of Games (see Chapter 3-5), a theory not too productive of useful results as yet. Still, some of the results may qualitatively indicate the desired strategy.

As seems to have been the usual case in ST, a continuous, rather than a discrete example was first worked out. The example (see Morse and Kimball [1946] page 105) is an oversimplified model of an air patrol purposing to prevent a submarine from getting through a long strait of varying width, with the submarine able to submerge part but not all the time, and the cross-over barrier patrol having varying degrees of coverage. An alternative example is that of a patrol to prevent infiltration across a length L of the border of a country.

As with many game theory solutions, the strategies of both sides, the infiltrators (I) and the repulsive patrol (R), must vary their actions along the border; otherwise, the opposition will learn these actions and devise means of circumventing them. Only by continuously varying actions, according to a prescribed probability distribution, can the opponent be kept guessing. Suppose side I sends each infiltrator at random across the border with a probability density $\Psi(x)$ that he cross at point x $\left(\text{so that } \int_0^L \Psi(x)\,dx = 1\right)$. And suppose that side R places its patrol at random along x with a probability density $\phi(x)$ that the patrol covers x $\left(\text{here also, } \int_0^L \phi(x)\,dx = 1\right)$. And, finally, suppose that if a patrol happens to be covering x and an infiltrator happens to try crossing at x then, the probability that he will be prevented from crossing is $P(x)$. This probability will vary with x, depending on the terrain; in heavily wooded or mountainous country P would be small, for example. The expected fraction of infiltrators that are prevented from crossing the border will, in the long run, be

$$J = \int_0^L \phi(x)\, \Psi(x)\, P(x)\, dx \tag{46}$$

The problem for side I is to adjust the likelihood of crossing Ψ so that J is as small as possible; that for side R is to adjust the frequency of patrols ϕ so that J is as large as possible. To be safe, side I should arrange Ψ so that no action by R can make J larger, and side R should arrange ϕ so that no action by I can make J any smaller.

Taking side R first, note that in integral J, if the product ϕP is smaller, for some range of x, than it is elsewhere, then if side I finds this out, more infiltrators will be sent through the "weak" range of x, and J will be reduced in value. Therefore, the safe strategy for R is to make ϕ inversely proportional to $P(x)$ (heavy patrolling where P is small, light patrolling where P is large). To be more precise, side R should make

$$\phi(x) = [1/N(L)\, P(x)]\,; \quad N(L) = \int_0^L [1/P(x)]\, dx$$

in which case the fraction of infiltrators prevented from crossing is (47)

$$J(L) = [1/N(L)] \int_0^L \Psi(x)\, dx = [1/N(L)]$$

no matter what I does about the shape of $\Psi(x)$.

However, unless side I does the same thing with Ψ, side R could modify ϕ so as to increase J. For example, $\Psi(x)$ might be $[h/P(x)]$ over a smaller range L_h of L, for which $P(x) < H$ and be zero when $P(x) > H$. In this case

$$\Psi(x) = \begin{cases} [1/N(L_h)\, P(x)] & \text{over } L_h \\ 0 & \text{over the rest of } L \end{cases} \tag{48}$$

where $N(L_h) = \int_0^{L_h} (1/P)\, dx$. If side R stuck to the patrol density ϕ of Eq. (47), the value of J would still be $[1/N(L)]$, but if R learned of the change to the Ψ of Eq. (48), he can change ϕ to increase J. For example, he can make ϕ equal to the Ψ of Eq. (48), omitting any patrolling along $L - L_h$, where there is no infiltration. In that case $J(L_h)$ would equal $[1/N(L_h)]$, which is larger than $[1/N(L)]$ because L_h is smaller than L. Of course, if R continued to use this patrol density and side I learned of it, he could send infiltrators through the unpatrolled length $L - L_h$ without any loss.

Therefore, the safe strategy for both sides is to have both Ψ and ϕ equal the $\phi(x)$ of Eq. (47).

Finally, there should be mentioned the discrete cases involving a search for a conscious evader. The problem of a number of discrete sites, where the evader can hide and the searcher may look, seems to be a very difficult one to solve. A start at a solution has been made by Norris [1962] for the very simplified case where the search is conducted in a series of discrete "looks" into the different sites, with specified probabilities q_j of discovering the evader if he is in site j when that site is looked into. As with other game theory solutions, this requires a mixed strategy solution, with the evader moving from site to site, between looks of the searcher, with specified probabilities that he make the change, plus specified probabilities for being initially in the different sites. The searcher must also use a mixture of strategies, each of which consists of a series of looks at a specified sequence of sites.

The game is determined by allotting quanta of gains to the evader every time the searcher looks but does not find him and assigning costs every time he changes sites. Norris solved the case for two sites in some completeness. He found that if the cost of changing sites is larger than some limit, the best strategy for the evader is to choose a site initially, with a probability P of going to site 1 and $1 - P$ of going to site 2, and then staying put. These probabilities are determined by the relative magnitudes of the probabilities q_1 and q_2 of being discovered (which are presumed known to both sides). If the searcher assumes that the evader has hidden according to these safest probabilities, he then can look in one of the sites, thus changing the *a priori* probability P into an *a posteriori* probability (if his look does not find the evader). (See Pollock [1960] for further discussion). The desired sequences of looks are those which tend to keep these *a posteriori* probabilities oscillating within limits. The searcher must also use a mixture of these "good" sequences.

The same considerations enter into the game when the evader can move from one site to another between looks. When more than two sites are involved, the problem is considerably more complicated. Other aspects are treated by Neuts [1963].

Indeed, this part of the theory is not yet in shape to be useful in any real world situation. In fact as we said in the beginning, ST, in regard to practical applications, is still in an embryonic state.

8. APPLICATIONS

As indicated several times in this chapter, although much of the basic structure of search strategy has been elucidated in the literature, the specific solutions appropriate to a given application are, for the most part, yet to be worked out.

The search process enters into a surprisingly large number of our individual, as well as group, actions. We look for a book in the library or an item in a catalogue; searches are conducted for a lost child, a fugitive, a buried city or pocket of oil, an enemy submarine or infiltrating division, a faulty component in an ailing piece of equipment or an error in a manufacturing process. Each of these searches has its own physical, procedural and economic boundary conditions; each requires considerable study and experimentation before a workable search strategy can be devised for it. In only a few cases have they been studied, measured and analyzed in detail.

To date, most of the practice of search theory has been in the military field (see, for example, Koopman [1946] and the bibliographies of Enslow [1966] and Dobbie [1968]). Much of the detail of these applications is, of course, buried in secrecy. The nature of the search for a person lost in a wilderness, and a few applications of the theory have been reported by Kelley [1973]. Some applications in the search for flaws in equipment have been reported (see Gluss [1959] for example) and a few reports in the field of prospecting (see Engel, for example). A small amount of work has been reported (Larson [1972]) on the police search problem, particularly in regard to the allocation of patrol effort. Practical applications in many other fields are still lacking.

As for the development of theory, some interesting progress has recently been made in the analysis of the effects of false targets on search strategy (see Stone [1973] and Dobbie [1973]) and a little progress has been made into the immensely difficult problem of the search for a conscious evader. In general, however, one has the impression that the theory needs to be proved out by application in many more fields before further mathematical superstructure is added.

REFERENCES

1. Bellman, R. E. and S. E. Dreyfus, *Applied Dynamic Programming*, Chapter 4, Princeton University Press, Princeton, New Jersey (1962).
2. Charnes, A. and W. W. Cooper, "The Theory of Search, Optimum Distribution of Search Effort," *Management Sci.* **5:** 44–50 (1958).
3. Danskin, John M., "A Theory of Reconnaissance," *Operations Res.* **10:** 285–299 (1962).
4. ——. "A Helicopter vs. Submarine Search Game," *Operations Res.* **16:** 509 (1968).
5. de Guenin, J., "Optimum Distribution of Effort, an Extension of the Koopman Basic Theory," *Operations Res.* **9:** 1–7 (1961).
6. Dobbie, James M., "Search Theory, a Sequential Approach," *Nav. Res. Log. Quart.* **10:** 323–334 (1963).
7. ——, "A Survey of Search Theory," *Operations Res.* **16:** 525–537 (1968).
8. ——, "Search with False Contacts," *Operations Res.* **21:** 907–925 (1973).
9. Engel, J. H., "Use of Clustering in Mineralogical and other Surveys," *Proc. First Int. Conf. on Operations Res.*, 176–192 Oxford (1957).
10. Enslow, P. H. Jr., "A Bibliography of Search Theory and Reconnaissance Theory Literature," *Nav. Res. Log. Quart.* **13:** 177–202 (1966).

11. Gluss, Brian, "An Optimum Policy for Detecting a Fault in a Complex System," *Operations Res.* **7**: 468–477 (1959).
12. ——, "An Alternative Solution to the 'Lost at Sea' Problem," *Nav. Res. Log. Quart.* **8**: 117–121 (1961).
13. ——, "The Minimax Path in a Search for a Circle in a Plane," *Nav. Res. Log. Quart.* **8**: 357–360 (1961b).
14. Isbell, J. R. "An Optimal Search Pattern" *Nav. Res. Log. Quart.* **4**, 357–9 (1957).
15. Heyman, M. "Optimal Simultaneous Search for the Maximum by the Principle of Statistical Information". *Operations Res.* **16**: 1194–1205 (1968).
16. Koopman, B. O., "Search and Screening, O.E.G. Office of the C.N.O.," OEG Report 56 (ATI 64 627) (1946).
17. ——, "The Theory of Search: I. Kinematic Bases," *Operations Res.* **4**: 324–346 (1956a).
18. ——, "The Theory of Search: II. Target Detection," *Operations Res.* **4**: 503–531 (1956b).
19. ——, "The Theory of Search: III. The Optimum Distribution of Searching Effort," *Operations Res.* **5**: 613–626 (1957).
20. Larson, R. C., Urban Police Patrol Analysis, MIT Press, East Lansing, Michigan (1972).
21. MacQueen, J. and R. G. Miller, Jr., "Optimal Persistance Policies," *Operations Res.* **8**: 362–380 (1960).
22. Mela, Donald F., "Information Theory and Search Theory as Special Cases of Decision Theory," *Operations Res.* **9**: 907–909 (1961).
23. Morse, P. M. and G. E. Kimball, "Methods of Operations Research," OEG Report 54 (1946); 2nd Edn. MIT Press (1951).
24. ——, "Search Theory and Browsing," *The Library Quart.* **40**: 391–408 (1970).
25. Neuts, Marcel F., "A Multistage Search Game," *J. SIAM* **11**: 502–507 (1963).
26. Norris, R. C., "Studies in Search for a Conscious Evader," Lincoln Lab. MIT Tech. Report 279, (AD 294 832) (1962).
27. Pollock, Stephen M., "Optimal Sequential Strategies for Two Region Search when Effort is Quantized," Operations Res. Center, MIT, Interim Tech. Report 14, (AD 238 662) (1960).
28. ——, "Sequential Search and Detection," Operations Res. Center, MIT, Technical Report 5 (1964).
29. ——, "Search Detection and Subsequent Action: Some Problems on the Interfaces," *Operations Res.* **19**: 559–586 (1971).
30. Stone, L. D., "Total Optimality of Incrementally Optimal Allocations," to appear in *Nav. Res. Log. Quart.* **20** (September 1973).
31. —— and J. A. Stanshine, "Optimal Search Using Uninterrupted Contact Investigation," *J. SIAM* **20**: 241–263 (1971).
32. —— and C. A. Persinger, "Optimal Search in the Presence of Poisson-distributed False Targets," *J. SIAM* **23**: 6–27 (1972).

III-7

SIMULATION THEORY

Donald P. Gaver
Naval Postgraduate School

1. INTRODUCTION

This chapter is intended to furnish an account of various procedures for improving the quality of simulation studies. Special emphasis is placed upon the handling of random elements in operations research (OR) modeling: we try to show how the desired effects of randomness may be expeditiously represented and dealt with computationally, and we also present procedures for measuring the random error in the simulation experiments.

The treatment given will be in terms of specific simple problem types. It is believed that, with exercise of his imagination, a practitioner will be able to adapt some of the procedures described to his own uses.

2. STEPS IN A SIMULATION STUDY

It is useful to outline the succession of steps involved in a typical simulation study. In the process, we are led to discuss the alternatives to simulation, and, in fact, to assay an operational definition of the term "simulation." The reader is furnished with references for additional depth of details.

A broad outline of the activities involved in simulation might run as follows:

(1) Problem definition: identification of the important issues.
(2) Empirical information collection and data analysis; establishment of client contact.

(3) Model formulation: agreement upon abstractions, acceptable simplifications, and relevant responses and measures of performance.
(4) Model construction or selection: documentation of sub-models, and parameter determination.
(5) Model manipulation: computations to determine responses when model conditions vary; experimental design and "variance reduction."
(6) Validation studies: is computational outcome in conformity with input (e.g., are programming errors present) and is computational outcome consistent with "real world" experience?
(7) Communication of results to client: replay of parts of the above, depending upon what is learned.

The above activities are normally performed in order. Others, e.g., Naylor *et al.* [1966] express the steps in nearly the same way.

It is important to point out those features of the above steps for approaching a problem that *may* really involve what is currently meant by "simulation." These are essentially (3) through (7); the term and activity of *simulation* now commonly refers to the use of numerical computation and, in particular, statistical sampling on a mathematical model to arrive at results such as estimates of probabilities of certain responses. Certainly, steps (1) and (2) must be taken whenever an applied problem in OR or systems analysis is attacked. Model formulation, step (3), with consequent simplifications, must be undertaken with a view to manipulating the model, i.e., to calculating responses. Often, analytical calculations are infeasible unless oversimplifications are made. For example, a quick examination of the published theory of waiting lines and service systems reveals little of immediate utility when time-dependent or transient situations require study. Alternatives are numerical manipulation of probability equations, e.g., Koopman [1972]; numerical sampling procedures, or *simulation*; or the use of analytic approximations to probability equations, e.g., the employment of diffusion approximations cf. Iglehart [1965], Newell [1971], and Gaver and Shedler [1973]. Perhaps the reason for the popularity of the second (simulation) approach is that is seems to require less training and experience in mathematical probability theory and statistics than is required if a more mathematical approach to a complex problem is attempted. However, simulations of realistic systems, e.g., portions of a job shop or of a complex computer or traffic network, may involve extensive conceptual formulation effort, as well as computer programming and debugging time. Unless care is taken from the beginning, project resources may well be expended before many computer runs are made. Very often, excessive attention to detail in modeling (leading to programming difficulties) substitutes for a well-thought-out sequence of final, informative, computer runs and an adequate assessment of errors of estimation of system figures of merit. As is pointed out in the next chapter, programming languages adapted to commonly encountered problem types are an aid when dealing with complexity. In what follows, attention will be paid to methods by which randomness may be efficiently introduced (some new methods are superior to current package programs), and to methods for reducing variability and for data analysis and error assessment.

3. MODEL FORMULATION

3.1 Model Elements

Simulation models are often developed in terms of entities, e.g., servicing facilities, or customers, or jobs in a job-shop or queueing problems. Interactions between entities influence *state variables*, and at any time the *system state* is the value of the state variable; the latter may be a vector, so the state may be an ordered set of numbers. A model is a formal, mathematical, way of describing the way in which states change throughout time. For more detail see Fishman [1973].

3.2 Example: Model for a Population Growth

Suppose a population of animals or insects grows in proportion to size, but tends to be inhibited, by environmental conditions, from indefinite growth. A simple model is as follows: let Y_n = population size at end of year n, and

$$Y_{n+1} = Y_n + Y_n(a - bY_n) + \epsilon_{n+1} Y_n, \tag{1}$$

where a and b are positive constants and $\{\epsilon_n\}$ is a sequence of "random disturbances" representing environmental conditions. Each ϵ_n may be selected independently from an appropriate probability distribution (perhaps, but not necessarily, the Gaussian). Here Y_n represents system state; note that if Y_0 is given, successive state values may be generated easily. Such models may be made considerably more general and realistic.

3.3 Example: Models for a Simplified Job Shop

Suppose one machine (an entity) manufactures orders (also entities) that appear during the day. We are interested in delays that jobs may experience. One possible formulation is in terms of a *point stochastic process*: Let S_n denote the manufacturing time of job n, let A_n denote the time between arrival of job n and job $n + 1$, and let W_n denote the state variable giving the waiting time of job n. Then, for $n = 0, 1, 2, \ldots$

$$W_{n+1} = \max\,[W_n + S_n - A_n, 0], \tag{2}$$

and once values are given to W_1, S_n and A_n, the sequence of state values may be generated.

A simulation so developed makes state changes only at the occurrence of certain events, i.e., at arrivals and job completions. Such a simulation model, called *event-paced* or one utilizing the *next event* approach, is often quite efficient; see Gaver and Thompson [1973], or Fishman [1973]. On the other hand, if large numbers of events occur per unit time, it may be convenient to use *fixed increment timing*, in which states change at equal, perhaps arbitrary, times. For instance, in our job-shop problem we might split the day into 15 minute intervals, and characterize the number of new demands in t to $t + 15$ by $A(t)$, where $t = 0, 15, 30, \ldots$. Likewise, the number of jobs completed is $C(t)$. Thus, the net increase in jobs present from t to $t + 15$ is $Z(t) = A(t) - C(t)$. Then the number of jobs present at t is $Q(t)$, where

$$Q(t + 15) = \max\,[Q(t) + Z(t), 0]. \tag{3}$$

One can use data to estimate the distribution of $Z(t)$, and generate $Q(t)$ recursively. Very likely $A(t)$, and hence $Z(t)$, will have a mean that varies through the day, and whose random part is a sequence of correlated variables. Time series analysis may be required to develop models for $A(t)$ and $C(t)$; see the Box-Jenkins method exposited by Nelson [1973], and Section 1 of Chapter I-1 of the companion volume, *Handbook of OR: Models and Applications.* Note that if the backlog Q is generally high, daily time intervals may be quite sufficient.

4. RANDOM NUMBER GENERATION

The usual simulation model involves the use of random variables and processes to describe real events. In Eq. (1), $\epsilon_1, \epsilon_2, \ldots, \epsilon_n$ is represented as a sequence of random variables (r.v.'s) with a distribution or density function estimated from data; in Eqs. (2) and (3), S_n, A_n, and $Z(t)$ may be modeled as random variables or processes. When a digital computer is used to manipulate the program for the simulation model, realizations of these random processes must be obtained as conveniently as possible. Listed below are procedures for obtaining such realizations.

4.1 Uniform Random Numbers

Essential to the generation of r.v. realizations is access to a sequence of *uniform random numbers*, i.e., numbers that behave like independent realizations or samples from a r.v., R, uniformly distributed over the unit interval [0, 1]. Actually, what are available at computer centers are arithmetic codes for generating sequences of *pseudo random digits*, e.g., 3, 7, 5, 1, 9, 2, . . . , where each digit 0 through 9 occurs with approximately equal likelihood, and with, hopefully, no obvious or detrimental relationships. Consequently, the sequence can model successive flips of a fair ten-sided die. Such codes are called *random number generators.* Grouping together the digits generated gives psuedo random numbers having any required number of elements. The modifier "pseudo" signifies that the number sequence is initialized by use of a *seed* random number, and proceeds therefrom to generate successive numbers. The usual algorithm is a modification of the *multiplicative congruential method*, see Knuth [1969] for details. Critiques of random number generators have been given by Marsaglia [1968], including improved methods for generating random numbers and realizations of certain commonly required distributions (exponential, normal). Simulation languages for specific purposes, such as GPSS and APL, contain built-in random number generation capabilities, however, options are available if one programs in FORTRAN.

With the aid of a sequence of uniform random numbers (or simply random numbers, r.n.'s) one can generate sequences of realizations of r.v.'s having other distributions. Several methods are outlined below; one should note that alternative methods are always possible, certain alternatives being preferred for reasons of computational efficiency.

4.2 Transformation Method

Suppose we wish to generate a r.n. from distribution function $F(x)$, i.e., a *realization* of the r.v. X, where

$$P\{X \leqslant x\} = F(x)$$

Then it may be shown that if R is a uniform r.v. on the interval [0, 1], we have $F(X) = R$, and so $X = F^{-1}(R)$, where F^{-1} represents the *inverse* of F. Thus, if u_n is the nth in a sequence of uniform r.n.'s, generated as described above, $x_n = F^{-1}(u_n)$ is the nth in a sequence of X realizations. The utility of this method depends upon computational convenience: if the inverse is difficult to compute accurately, other available methods may require less computer time.

(a) *Exponential Numbers.* Let $F(x) = 1 - e^{-\lambda x}$ if $x \geqslant 0$, being zero otherwise. The times to device failure, and the time between successive calls for service, etc., are often modeled initially as exponentially distributed. An exponential r.n. is then

$$x_n = -\frac{1}{\lambda} \log_e (1 - u_n);$$

an identically distributed realization, but one that is slightly more computationallly efficient, is

$$x_n = -\frac{1}{\lambda} \log_e u_n.$$

The inverse transformation method is commonly used to generate exponential random numbers; however, more computationally efficient methods are available (see, for example, Ahrens and Dieter [1972]). Its practical success depends upon the existence of an easily computed inverse for F. If F is given only as an empirical distribution, then the same procedure, or an equivalent one, must be used.

(b) *Weibull Numbers.* Let $F(x) = 1 - e^{-\lambda x^{\alpha}}$ if $x \geqslant 0$, being zero otherwise; the parameter $\alpha > 0$. This is the *Weibull distribution*, often used in reliability studies. The inverse in this case is given by:

$$x_n = \left[-\frac{1}{\lambda}\log_e u_n\right]^{1/\alpha} \tag{5}$$

(c) *Normal (Gaussian) Numbers.* Let

$$F(x) = \frac{1}{\sqrt{2\pi}}\int_{-\infty}^{\frac{x-\mu}{\sigma}} e^{-z^2/2}\,dz,$$

the normal distribution with mean μ, and variance σ^2. The Box-Muller method for generating random normal numbers transforms pairs of uniforms: if u_n, u_{n+1} are the nth and $n+1$th of a sequence of uniform r.n.'s, then

$$\begin{aligned} y_n &= (-2\log u_n)^{1/2}\cos 2\pi\, u_{n+1} \\ y_{n+1} &= (-2\log u_n)^{1/2}\sin 2\pi\, u_{n+1} \end{aligned} \tag{6}$$

form a pair of uncorrelated normal r.n.'s each having mean zero and variance unity. It follows that

$$\begin{aligned} x_n &= \mu + \sigma y_n \\ x_{n+1} &= \mu + \sigma y_{n+1} \end{aligned} \tag{7}$$

form a pair of r.n.'s from a normal distribution having mean μ and variance σ^2. Alternative methods, more efficient than Box-Muller, in various senses, are presented in Ahrens and Dieter [1972].

(d) *Log-Normal Numbers.* A r.v. L, is log-normally distributed if its logarithm, $\log L = X$, is normal (the base of the logarithm should be specified—ours will be natural logs, i.e., to base $e = 2.718\ldots$ and will be denoted by ln). Thus, $L = e^X$, and so to generate a log normal r.n., l_n, first generate a normal r.n., x_n, and then $l_n = e^{x_n}$. If X has mean μ and variance σ^2, then L has mean and variance

$$E[L] = e^{\mu+\sigma^2/2};\ \mathrm{Var}\,[L] \equiv \sigma_L^2 = e^{2\mu+\sigma^2}(e^{\sigma^2} - 1) \tag{8}$$

Log-normal distributions resemble the gamma and the Weibull (with $\alpha > 1$) in that they are skewed to the right and unimodal. They often fit *time* measurements, e.g., service times and project completion times, rather well. Other transformations are also useful and easy: for instance, if N is Poisson, then $\sqrt{N}$

is more nearly normal (for large $\mu = E[N]$) than is N. Consequently $N \approx X^2$ where X is normal yields approximate Poisson numbers.

4.3 Composition

Realizations of many r.v.'s–examples from many distributions–are conveniently obtained by combining certain more easily generated variables. Such a method is called composition. Several examples are given below.

(a) *Gamma or Erlang Numbers.* If the distribution to be sampled has the gamma density, i.e., for $x > 0$

$$f_k(x) = e^{-\lambda x} \frac{(\lambda x)^{k-1}}{(k-1)!} \lambda, \tag{9}$$

where k is a positive integer, then a realization, y, may be obtained by adding together k exponential numbers

$$y = -\frac{1}{\lambda} \ln (u_1 u_2 u_3 \ldots u_k) = -\frac{1}{\lambda} \ln \prod_{i=1}^{k} u_i \tag{10}$$

The product form requires that the logarithm be computed only once. From (10) comes a string of numbers with mean k/λ and variance k/λ^2.

It is more difficult to obtain a gamma with $0 < k < 1$. Methods are described by Phillips and Beightler [1971] and Ahrens and Dieter [1974]. In practice, one might sometimes wish to substitute Weibull numbers, or log-normal numbers, which are easily obtained by transformation sampling. Sampling from a log normal or Weibull whose first two moments (mean and variance) equal those of the gamma may be practically adequate.

(b) *Poisson Numbers.* In order that $N = k$ Poisson events occur in $[0, t]$, a sum of k exponentials must be less than t, while $k + 1$ exceeds t. Hence, if we wish to generate a number having a Poisson distribution with mean λt, we may multiply together uniform r.n.'s until their product becomes less than $e^{-\lambda t}$: there are k Poisson events when the following hold.

$$\prod_{i=1}^{k} u_i > e^{-\lambda t}; \quad \text{and} \quad \prod_{i=1}^{k+1} u_i \leqslant e^{-\lambda t}. \tag{11}$$

If λt is "large," i.e., at least 25, then a normal (Gaussian) number, rounded to an integer value, may be a quite adequate approximation for many purposes.

(c) *Stuttering or Compound Poisson Numbers.* The Poisson stochastic process may be used to generate the total number of orders for inventory during a period, while another, independent, sampling generates the *size* of each order. It is convenient and sometimes realistic to let an exponentially distributed r.n. represent the size of an individual order, where λ^{-1} represents the expected (mean) size of orders. The total amount of material ordered during a time interval of length t is then the sum of a Poisson number of independent exponential numbers. One can similarly generate order sizes that are of any other distribution, e.g., gamma, or log-normal, and add up a Poissonian number of these.

(d) *Binomial Numbers.* If a random experiment with binary outcome (0 or 1, Success or Failure, Male or Female, etc.) is conducted N times, then the number of successes, X, has the binomial distribution. If we wish to realize X we may sum the outcomes of N repetitions: $i_1 + i_2 + \ldots + i_N$, where

$$\begin{aligned} i_j &= 1 \quad \text{if} \quad 0 \leqslant u_j < p \\ i_j &= 0 \quad \text{if} \quad p \leqslant u_j \leqslant 1 \end{aligned} \tag{12}$$

u_j being a r.n. and p the probability of success. This method requires N random numbers for each realization of x, and may be inefficient for N sizable and many realizations. An alternative is to store a table of the binomial and essentially use inverse transformation: if $p_X(x) = P\{X = x\}$ we realize $X = x$ if the r.n. u satisfies

$$\sum_{j=0}^{x-1} p_X(j) < u \leqslant \sum_{j=0}^{x} p_X(j) \tag{13}$$

4.4 Rejection

In principle, random variables (realization of r.v.'s) from any distribution may be obtained by the inverse transformation method. In practice, it may be easier to use an apparently more wasteful (of uniform r.n.'s) procedure, but one which requires less computation. Roughly speaking, the important *rejection method* draws samples from one easily-sampled distribution, and then randomly rejects certain of these to produce r.n.'s from a desired distribution.

Suppose X is a r.v. having distribution $F(x)$ and probability density $f(x) = dF/dx$. In order to generate samples by rejection, find a function $m(x)$ such that $m(x) \geqslant f(x)$, and convert $m(x)$ to a density by defining $m'(x) = \dfrac{m(x)}{\mu}$, and determining μ by $\int_{-\infty}^{\infty} m'(x)\,dx = 1$, or $\mu = \int_{-\infty}^{\infty} m(x)\,dx$. Now create two r.n.'s: u_1 and u_2. Use u_1 to draw a sample, x_1, from $m'(x)$; obviously, transformation is a possibility if $M'(x) = \int_{-\infty}^{x} m'(z)dz$ inverts readily. Now compare u_2 to $f(x_1)/m(x_1)$: if $u_2 \leqslant f(x_1)/m(x_1)$, retain x_1 as a sample from F; if $u_2 > f(x_1)/m(x_1)$, reject x_1, and start over with a new pair of uniforms, u_3 and u_4. On the average it will take μ pairs to create one sample from F.

The above procedure often provides very fast generation of realizations of distributions like the Gamma with shape parameter k non-integral; see Eq. (9). One can use the function

$$m(x) = \begin{cases} \dfrac{x^{k-1}}{\Gamma(k)} & \text{if } 0 < x \leqslant 1 \\ \dfrac{e^{-1}}{\Gamma(k)} & \text{if } x \geqslant 1 \end{cases} \qquad \text{for } 0 < k \leqslant 1 \tag{14}$$

to generate realizations from Eq. (9) with $\lambda = 1$, later multiplying by λ^{-1}. It turns out that

$$m'(x) = \begin{cases} \dfrac{ek}{e+k} x^{k-1}, & 0 < x \leqslant 1 \\ \dfrac{ek}{e+k} e^{-x}, & 1 \leqslant x \end{cases} \tag{15}$$

will do, and the expected number of steps required to accept a number is never greater than 1.37, according to Ahrens and Dieter [1974].

The same approach can be used to generate r.n.'s from the Beta density. Such numbers are often used to describe project completion times; see Moder and Phillips [1970].

5. SIMULATION DESIGN AND VARIANCE REDUCTION

The next technical subject to be considered is step (5) of section 2: model manipulations. In abstract terms, a simulation creates realizations of a *response*, W, that depends in some (complicated) way upon a number of other r.v.'s, $(X_1, X_2, \ldots, X_n, \ldots)$:

$$W = f(X_1, X_2, \ldots, X_n, \ldots). \tag{16}$$

Our examples (3.2) and (3.3) illustrate the situation. Usually, one will wish to investigage the distribution of W as the latter depends, for instance, upon (a) parameters of the distribution of the X_i's, (b) the initial conditions imposed upon the problem, and (c) the run lengths, e.g., the largest n-value (time, or customer number in Eqs. (1) and (2)) are at the simulator's disposal. For example, in a queueing problem, we may wish to stipulate that the servers are initially idle, or, alternatively, that a prescribed number of customers are present initially. Similar initial conditions with respect to stock on hand are of interest in inventory simulations, and an initial population is a requirement in Eq. (1).

Having settled upon the response variable of interest–one may wish to study several, and several functions of each, during one simulation run–it is time to mention some basic principles that are worth observing when simulations are carried out.

(1) Never simulate (sample) unnecessarily; that is, calculate what you can mathematically, making use of the special structure of the problem.
(2) Perform comparative simulations when possible.

To elaborate upon (1) by an example, it is clearly unnecessary to *simulate* in order to calculate the *expected* time, S, to pass through a two-stage process with processing times S_1 and S_2: the result is $S = S_1 + S_2$, and $E[S]$, the desired answer, equals $E[S_1] + E[S_2]$. The latter numbers can be directly computed from the input distributions of S_1 and S_2. More complex network problems can sometimes be broken down, and simulations performed only when necessary, e.g., when several paths are in parallel or in Wheatstone Bridge form; papers by Burt, Gaver and Perlas [1970], and Burt and Garman [1970] describe PERT network simulations in more detail. Carter and Ignall [1972] make use of the special structure of an inventory problem in order to improve sampling efficiency; see Fishman [1973] for discussion.

In order to illustrate the second principle above, suppose one wishes to compare two service systems that have different mean inter-arrival times, but otherwise are the same. If one can use the *same* sequence of uniform r.n.'s to generate the arrivals into each server for each realization, e.g.,

$$\begin{aligned} A_{n1} &= -\frac{1}{\lambda_1} \ln u_n \qquad n = 1, 2, \ldots \\ A_{n2} &= -\frac{1}{\lambda_2} \ln u_n \end{aligned} \tag{17}$$

in model Eq. (2), then the responses $W(1)$ and $W(2)$ will have a tendency to be positively correlated and the estimate of the difference $E[W(1)] - E[W(2)]$ given by sample means $\overline{W}(1) - \overline{W}(2)$ will tend to have a smaller variance than will that given by using independent r.n.'s (u_n and u_n') in (17). By this means, the estimation of the difference $E[W(1)] - E[W(2)]$, can be made more precise with a given number of realizations.

The point of both examples is that simulation results are statistical estimates, and that every reasonable attempt should be made to reduce the variability of the estimate. Of course, both analyst and client also deserve a realistic statement of the estimate's accuracy and precision.

We shall now describe several worthwhile general purpose sampling methods. For further details the references will be helpful. It is well to begin with the simplest.

5.1 Straightforward Sampling

Refer to Eq. (16) to see that to achieve one realization or sample from W we must obtain sample values from $X_1, X_2, \ldots$, and evaluate the function f or, equivalently, run out a simulated history. The procedure for obtaining X_i-realizations is given in the previous section, and the determination of f may be illustrated by the waiting-time problem; see Eq. (2). If $W_1 = 0$, then $w_2 = \max\,[s_2 - a_2, 0]$, w_2 being a realization of W_2 and s_2 and a_2 realizations of S_2 and A_2, respectively. Then $w_3 = \max\,[w_2 + s_3 - a_3, 0]$, etc. The responses of interest may be, for instance, $E[W_{10}]$ = the expected waiting time of the *10*th customer, or $E[W_{+10}]$ = the expected waiting time of the first ten customers, or $E[\max W_{10}]$ = the expected maximum waiting time among the final ten arrivals, etc.

It should be noted that several iterative steps are required to obtain one realized response value. If the X realizations, e.g., $s_2, a_2, s_3, a_3, \ldots, s_n, a_n, \ldots$ to obtain any one W realization, w, are all *independent* samples from w-realization to w-realization, we speak of *straightforward sampling*, and note than an unbiased estimate of $E[W]$ is obtained by simple averaging. If k independent realizations are run, starting from given initial conditions and proceeding to an end, then

$$\hat{E}[W] = \frac{1}{k}\sum_{j=1}^{k} w^{(j)} = \overline{w}. \tag{18a}$$

$w^{(j)}$ being the response value calculated on the jth realization. Since the samples are independent, the sample variance is an unbiased estimate of Var $[W]$:

$$s_w^2 = \frac{1}{k-1}\sum_{j=1}^{k} (w^{(j)} - \overline{w})^2. \tag{18b}$$

Perhaps more important, the variance of our estimate (17) is s_w^2/k. Note that since the sampling is independent across realizations, the variance of the estimated response only diminishes as k^{-1}, so tricky sampling procedures ("Monte Carlo swindles") are used in order to improve precision with fewer samples. We describe some of these, and point out that it may be worthwhile to use several of these ideas in combinations. Usually, the effectiveness of such a maneuver can only be estimated empirically, from a pilot run.

5.2 Antithetic Variables

In order to introduce this idea, examine model Eq. (2); notice that W_{n+1} increases if S_n increases, and decreases if A_n increases. It is intuitively clear that in many waiting time problems the waiting times are positively associated with service times, and negatively associated with inter-arrival times. Such direction of dependence (monotonicity) is noticeable in other situations, and may be exploited to obtain somewhat greater precision than that obtainable by straightforward sampling. To carry this out, let u be a uniform r.n. used (e.g., by transformation, as in (3)) to obtain a realization of X; for concreteness, think of $X = S_n$ in Eq. (2). Then, if u happens to be small, x may (*is* in Eq. 4) be small, while $1 - u$ is large, and $X(a)$—the negatively associated realization coming from $(1 - u)$—is large. The procedure is to create companion or *antithetic* realizations, leading to $W(1)$ and $W(2)$ as follows (illustrated in terms of Eq. (2)): let G be the distribution function (d.f.) of service times, and F the d.f. of inter-arrival times. Then for the

$$W(1) \text{ realization}, \quad s_n(1) = G^{-1}(u_n), \quad a_n(1) = F^{-1}(u_n'),$$

while for the (19)

$$W(2) \text{ realization}, \quad s_n(2) = G^{-1}(1 - u_n), \quad a_n(2) = F^{-1}(1 - u_n')$$

Here $\{u_n\}$ and $\{u_n'\}$ are mutually independent sequences of independent uniform r.v.'s. We mention that another antithetic idea, suggested by Page (1965), *exchanges* the random numbers across antithetic realizations:

$$\begin{aligned} W(1)&: \quad s_n(1) = G^{-1}(u_n), \quad a_n(1) = F^{-1}(u_n') \\ W(2)&: \quad s_n(2) = G^{-1}(u_n'), \quad a_n(2) = F^{-1}(u_n). \end{aligned} \tag{20}$$

(Why does this work?) In order to obtain the response estimate, simply average the responses from antithetic pairs:

$$w_A^{(j)} = \frac{w^{(j)}(1) + w^{(j)}(2)}{2} \tag{21}$$

and then

$$\hat{E}[W]_A = \frac{1}{k} \sum_{j=1}^{k} w_A^{(j)} = \overline{w}_A \tag{22}$$

The variance of the *estimator* (21) is estimated by

$$s^2_{\hat{E}[w]_A} = \frac{1}{k-1} \sum_{j=1}^{k} (w_A^{(j)} - \overline{w}_A)^2; \tag{23}$$

taking care to note that this does not estimate Var $[W]$; for the latter, an unbiased estimate is

$$\hat{\text{Var}}\,[W] = \frac{1}{2(k-1)} \left[\sum_{j=1}^{k} (w^{(j)}(1) - \overline{w}(1))^2 + \sum_{j=1}^{k} (w^{(j)}(2) - \overline{w}(2))^2 \right] \tag{24}$$

limited empirical evidence indicates that (20) is superior to (19) on heavily loaded systems.

5.3 Stratification

Instead of limiting consideration to two negatively associated responses, it may be worthwhile to deal with three or more, using a stratification idea. Consider running three parallel realizations, and address the problem of drawing three "separated" versions of an input variable X, called $X(1)$, $X(2)$, and $X(3)$. We first arrange to select a uniform subrange with equal probability (one-third) from among $(0, \frac{1}{3})$, $(\frac{1}{3}, \frac{2}{3})$, $(\frac{2}{3}, 1)$. Suppose $(\frac{1}{3}, \frac{2}{3})$ is selected. Then u_1 is a uniform r.n. over $(\frac{1}{3}, \frac{2}{3})$ and $x(1) = F^{-1}(\frac{1}{3} + u_1)$, while $x(2) = F^{-1}(\frac{2}{3} + u_1)$, and $x(3) = F^{-1}(u_1)$, F being the distribution of X; for the next realization, the subrange pick may well be $(0, \frac{1}{3})$, but the "spreading" effect is useful. Notice that two r.n.'s—one to select the subinterval, and the second to place the final number—provide input for three parallel realizations. Actually, one can anti-theticize within subintervals and obtain six realizations. Averaging across realizations yields the final estimate, and variances are calculated as in (18b).

5.4 Importance Sampling

The basic idea of *importance sampling* is that of sampling from a distribution or process other than that of immediate interest, and then correcting the result to achieve an unbiased estimator. Take as an illustration the problem of estimating the probability that a r.v. (e.g., an inventory demand) Z, having distribution $F(z)$ and density $f(z)$, exceeds a value h:

$$P\{Z > h\} = \int_h^\infty f(z)\, dz \tag{25}$$

This can be thought of as an expectation problem: let $I(z)$ be the function

$$I(z) = \begin{cases} 1 & \text{if } z \geqslant h \\ 0 & \text{if } z < h \end{cases} \tag{26}$$

and we seek $E[I(Z)]$. If we sample k times from F directly, then the simple estimate is

$$\widehat{E[I(Z)]} = \frac{\text{number of times } Z \text{ exceeds } h}{k}, \tag{27}$$

Clearly

$$\text{Var}\,\{\widehat{E[I(Z)]}\} = \frac{[1 - F(h)]\, F(h)}{k} \tag{28}$$

and the fractional error of the estimate is measured by

$$\frac{\sqrt{\operatorname{Var}\{\widehat{E[I(Z)]}\}}}{E[I(Z)]} = \sqrt{\frac{F(h)}{[1 - F(h)]\,k}} \tag{29}$$

Thus, as h becomes large, the probability that we seek to estimate becomes small, and the fractional error becomes large. In homely terms, this is the result of the fact that if $Z > h$ is quite improbable, $I(Z)$ will often be zero.

The importance sampling approach is to find another probability distribution that samples more frequently in the interesting region. Let $g(v)$ represent such a density. Now

$$P\{Z > h\} = \int_h^\infty f(z)\,dz = \int_h^\infty \frac{f(v)}{g(v)} \cdot g(v)\,dv$$

Let V be a r.v. with density g; then, clearly, the new response

$$I_V(v) = \begin{cases} \dfrac{f(v)}{g(v)} & \text{if } v \geqslant h \\ 0 & \text{if } v < h \end{cases}$$

has the proper expectation, and a clever choice for g can sometimes greatly improve the precision of the estimate.

5.5 Control Variables and Regression

If it is desired to estimate $E[W]$ by stimulating Eq. (16), improved precision can sometimes be achieved by identifying a similar problem that can be solved mathematically and using it as a crutch. That is,

$$W^* = f^*(X_1^*, X_2^*, \ldots, X_n^*, \ldots)$$

where perhaps f^* is a different function, or even $X_1^*, X_2^*, \ldots$ are r.v.'s with a different, more tractable, distribution from that of $X_1, X_2, \ldots$. Now, if we can arrange that realizations of X_1 and X_1^*, X_2 and X_2^*, etc., are dependent (perhaps positively correlated), then W and W^* will be dependent, and this can be exploited to create a new estimate that is (nearly) unbiased but with smaller variance than the straightforward sampling approach. Let the estimate be

$$\widehat{E[W]}_R = \overline{W} + \beta_0(\overline{W}^* - E[W^*]);$$

minimization of the variance of the estimate leads to

$$\beta_0 = -\frac{\operatorname{cov}[W, W^*]}{\operatorname{Var}[W^*]}.$$

The parameter β_0 must be estimated from available data. We can proceed as follows:

(a) simulate both W and W^* to obtain pairs of correlated realizations:

$$W_1, W_1^*; W_2, W_2^*, \ldots; W_k, W_k^*.$$

To do this one can use the same uniform r.n. to generate x_1 and x_1^*, etc.

(b) calculate $E[W^*]$ analytically; the auxiliary problem was chosen with this in mind.

(c) compute $\overline{w}$ and $\overline{w^*}$; compute s_{w^*}. If Var $[W^*]$ can be calculated analytically, so much the better.

(d) compute $\quad \hat{\beta}_0 = \dfrac{1}{k-1} \sum_{i=1}^{k} (w_i - \overline{w})(w_i^* - \overline{w^*}) \dfrac{1}{s_{w^*}^2}$

(e) estimate: $\quad E[\hat{W}]_R = \overline{w} + \hat{\beta}_0(\overline{w}_* - E[W^*])$.

Such an estimate is not unbiased since β_0 must be estimated from the data; approximate unbiasedness can be achieved by splitting the data or by use of the jackknife. More details on the jackknife are given in the following section. Use of that technique also makes it possible to put confidence limits on the unknown parameter.

5.6 Control and Recurrent Events Methods in Queueing Networks

One of the difficulties encountered in simulating and analyzing simulation data from many stochastic process models, is the considerable lack of independence that is present. However, it has been noticed by Crane and Iglehart [1974], Fishman [1973], and also by Lavenberg [1974] that in certain queueing networks, regeneration points occur; these have the effect of dividing the time history of the system into independent and identically distributed segments. For example, Lavenberg simulates a closed cyclic network of queueing stations in order to estimate the steady-state work rate at each stage (work rate is essentially the total time all servers at a stage are busy, divided by the time of examination). He shows that a properly weighted linear combination of the observed work rates at *all* stages provides a more precise (smaller variance) estimator of work rate at stage i ($i = 1, 2, \ldots, s$) than does the straightforward estimator of work rate at stage i alone. He is able to analytically derive the appropriate weights when service times are exponential, and to derive asymptotically valid confidence limits using his estimates. He then applies the exponential-appropriate weights to non-exponential distributions, and in both cases observes a satisfactory reduction in confidence interval widths.

6. STATISTICAL ANALYSIS OF DATA

Simulation studies often consume and produce prodigious amounts of data. Data related issues appear at initial study stages, at which time available information must be assembled, judged for relevance, checked for errors, and summarized and combined in the modelling process. Statistical data-analytical procedures, particularly those of an informal exploratory nature, cf. Tukey [1977], are profitable at this stage in order to suggest hitherto unsuspected facts about model inputs. (Are service times really independent of queue length? Do daily demands for inventory come from the same distribution?) Of less importance are formal methods, such as hypothesis testing: the effect of departing from a convenient if crude model (e.g., the exponential distribution) can probably best be assessed by a sensitivity test using the final simulation.

Data analytical complexities arise because many simulation *outputs* are realizations of a stochastic process, i.e. are *time series*. Consequently, successive observations are not independent, a fact that is not accounted for by most conventional statistical procedures. In addition, dependencies are often deliberately introduced for purposes of variance reduction, e.g. when the antithetic variables technique is applied. Finally, the interdependent observations are typically far from the comfortable normal or Gaussian form that supports the textbook derivations of standard statistical procedures such as Student's t statistic for comparing means, analysis of variance, and the like. An appropriate reexpression or transformation of the data is a useful and common way to deal with such problems; see Hald [1952]. Much of the data encountered in the practice of OR, e.g., pertaining to service times, order sizes, times between demands or arrivals, queue lengths and waiting times, etc., seems to come from asymmetric distributions with long right tails—exaggerated versions of the exponential or the log-normal. Thus, a logarithmic transformation may be indicated prior to further analysis.

It should be noted that the behavior of statistical procedures or estimates when confronted by non-standard data is now commonly studied by simulation. For an extensive reference see Andrews, *et al.* [1972].

We now discuss statistical analysis for certain prototypic simulation situations. Limitation of space prevents all but the most cursory commentary.

6.1 Independent Realizations

Suppose that one is interested in studying some random response variable, W, and does so by creating n independent realizations $w_1, w_2, \ldots, w_n$. First of all, graphical display of the outputs, in the form of histograms, sample cumulative distributions, perhaps on arithmetic (normal) probability paper or on semilog paper, are highly useful. For instance, extreme outliers or unsuspected clusterings are quickly detected; a computer programming error may be the culprit. Then standard statistical methods may be applied in order to (a) point estimate $E[W]$, possibly by $\overline{w}$, point estimate Var $[W]$, possibly by s^2, etc., (b) provide confidence interval estimates for $E[W]$, possibly by use of Student's t, or confidence intervals on Var $[W]$ but probably *not* by the usual χ^2 (chi-square) procedure, as the results are apt to be sensitive or non-robust to departures from normality by W. One useful solution here is the *jackknife procedure* of Quenouille-Tukey-Miller; see Miller [1964] for details. Confidence limits on other, more complex, estimates are also attainable via the jackknife, which, as the name implies, is a useful all-round tool.

The Jackknife. The jackknife procedure will be illustrated by using it to put approximate confidence limits around a parameter, utilizing a complicated estimator derived from a simulated sample. Here, the parameter is the variance of, say, the average waiting time of the first k customers in a single-server queue; see Gaver [1972]. If n independent realizations are available we can compute

$$s^2 = \frac{1}{n-1} \sum_{i=1}^{n} (w_i - \overline{w})^2,$$

where w_i = average waiting time for first k on ith realization, $\overline{w} = \frac{1}{n} \sum_{i=1}^{n} w_i$. The estimate, s^2, is an unbiased estimate of σ^2, the parameter of interest. Use of χ^2, to set approximate confidence limits, does poorly because of non-normality of w_i's. Proceed as follows:

(a) Compute $\theta(s^2)$, θ being a transformation that tends to symmetrize the sampling distribution of s^2: $\theta(\cdot) = \log(\cdot)$ or $\theta(\cdot) = \sqrt[3]{\cdot}$ tend to behave well, with $\theta = \log(\cdot)$ being the popular choice.

(b) Compute $\theta_{-j}(s^2)$, the estimate *omitting* the jth observation, w_j.

$$\text{E.g.}\quad \theta_{-1}(s^2) = \log\left[\frac{1}{n-2} \sum_{i=2}^{n} (w_i - \overline{w}_{-1})^2\right], \quad \overline{w}_{-1} = \frac{1}{n-1} \sum_{i=2}^{n} w_i.$$

There will be n such values.

(c) Compute the *pseudo-values*

$$y_j = n\theta(s^2) - (n-1)\theta_{-j}(s^2), \qquad j = 1, 2, \ldots, n.$$

(d) Compute the mean and variances of the y_j's:

$$\overline{y} = \frac{1}{n} \sum_{j=1}^{n} y_j$$

and

$$s_y^2 = \frac{1}{n-1} \sum_{j=1}^{n} (y_j - \overline{y})^2.$$

(e) Quote $\overline{y} = \widehat{\theta(s^2)}$ as an unbiased estimate of $\theta(\sigma^2)$, and $\theta^{-1}(\overline{y})$ as an approximately unbiased estimate of σ^2.

(f) Treat the pseudo-values as independent, and

$$t = \frac{\bar{y} - \theta(\sigma^2)}{s_y/\sqrt{n}}$$

as Student's t on $n - 1$ degrees of freedom. Hence

$$\left(\bar{y} - t_{1-\alpha/2}^{(n-1)} \frac{s_y}{\sqrt{n}},\ \bar{y} + t_{1-\alpha/2}^{(n-1)} \frac{s_y}{\sqrt{n}}\right)$$

is an approximate $(1 - \alpha) \cdot 100\%$ confidence interval for $\theta(\sigma^2)$, if $t_{1-\alpha/2}^{(n-1)}$ is the $(1 - \alpha/2) \cdot 100$ percentile of Student's t on $n - 1$ degrees of freedom.

6.2 Comparisons

Frequently, one wishes to compare responses: w_1 and w_2, for example. Again, preliminary graphical displays are to be recommended. In addition to those described in Section 6.1, one can cross plot x_{1i} vs x_{2i} or examine the conditional histogram of x_{1i}, given that x_2 lies in interesting ranges, etc. Specifically, we may wish to assess $E[W_1] - E[W_2]$. Then, if independent realizations are available, $w_{11}, \ldots, w_{1,n_1}$, and $w_{21}, \ldots, w_{2,n_2}$, a Student's t will supply confidence limits (or test hypotheses) for this difference. Complications arise if variances Var $[W_1]$ and Var $[W_2]$ differ; approaches to this so-called Behrens-Fisher problem are given by Scheffé [1970]. Also, a suitable transformation may be appropriate. It has been observed that if W_1 and W_2 are to be compared, and the same r.n.'s are used to generate comparison realizations, then $w_{1i} - w_{2i}$ seem often to yield confidence limits of greater validity than in the case of independent realizations; see Gaver [1972]. One should beware of using two-sample non-parametric tests (e.g., sign, or Wilcoxon) under the above (non-independent) circumstances; see Gastwirth and Rubin [1971] for an account of the effect of dependence.

6.3 Establishing Relationships and Dependencies

Simulations may be undertaken in order to establish the dependence of one or more responses upon certain underlying parameters. For instance, the effect of changing the expected service or processing time at a stage in a network upon expected total network transit time may be of interest. It may well be appropriate to attempt to explain $E[W]$ in terms of some parametric form involving $E[X_i]$. A common suggestion might be to "fit" a convenient function, such as

$$E[W] = \sum_{i=1}^{n} a_i E[X_i],$$

perhaps using the method of least squares. Such a fit can *always* be carried out by the all-too-convenient package programs available at most computer centers. Moreover, the procedure may be useful even if the strict mathematical conditions (Gauss-Markoff theorem) cannot be verified. The analyst should carefully check the adequacy of the fit by examining residuals, and should be cautious about extrapolations. Also, an approximate mathematical theory will help to express the fitting function appropriately. It is worth noting that new nonlinear fitting methods now, often usefully, replace least squares: the *robust* procedures of Andrews, *et al*, are adaptable to regression; see Huber [1973] for details.

6.4 Dynamic Processes

Simulation is often used to study dynamic many-stage service (transportation, computer system) processes, manpower and inventory systems, and production and inventory problems. For such problems, there may be a tendency towards a statistical equilibrium or steady-state condition. One sometimes wishes to estimate such steady-state process characteristics as the expected waiting and transit time (through the system) of customers, personnel, or goods. This can be done by averaging individual responses in one realization of the process, provided the steady state is essentially reached. Complications arise because of (a) uncertainty concerning the *practical* onset of equilibrium conditions, i.e., when to begin averaging, and, (b) because successive response variables are not independent. Concerning (b), dependency makes difficult the assessment of the variance of the sample mean, and hence the establishment of valid confidence limits.

Various approaches to this class of problem have been proposed. Crane and Iglehart [1974], and also Fishman [1973] have utilized special features of certain many-server problems, i.e. existence of recurrent events, to side-step the dependence question and arrive at confidence limits. Fishman [1973], p. 279, has suggested the use of statistical spectrum analysis for obtaining variance estimates in the face of dependence. Package programs at many computer centers now render such an approach feasible. The paper of Chipmen *et al.* [1968] comments on the efficiency of the sample mean as an estimator in just such situations, and proposes an alternative that may be worthwhile in many simulations.

Concerning (a), one should consider application of a smoothing technique (running average) and a graphical plot to indicate essential presence at equilibrium. If the process starts at zero, one might fit a growth curve, e.g., the logistic, to describe the approach to equilibrium in a simple fashion. In clossing, it should be remarked that considerable opportunity remains for useful work in this area.

REFERENCES

1. Ahrens, J. H. and U. Dieter, "Computer Methods for Sampling from the Exponential and Normal Distributions," *Communications ACM* **15, No. 10,** (October 1972).
2. —— and ——, "Computer Methods for Sampling from the Gamma, Beta, Poisson, and Binomial Distributions," *Computing* **13** (1974).
3. Andrews, D. F., P. Bickel, F. Hampel, P. Huber, W. Rogers, and J. Tukey, *Robust Estimates of Location*, Princeton University Press, Princeton, New Jersey (1972).
4. Burt, J. and M. Garman, "Monte Carlo Techniques for Stochastic Network Analysis," *Proc. Fourth Annu. Conf. on Applic. of Simulation* (1970).
5. Burt, J. M., D. P. Gaver, and M. Perlas, "Simple Stochastic Networks: Some Problems and Procedures," *Nav. Res. Log. Quart.* **17, No. 4** (December 1970).
6. Carter, G. and E. Ignall, "Virtual Measures for Computer Simulation Experiments," RAND Corp., P-4817, Santa Monica (April 1972).
7. Chipman, J., K. Kadiyala, A. Madansky, and J. Pratt, "Efficiency of the Sample Mean When Residuals Follow a First-Order Stationary Markoff Process," *J. Amer. Stat. Assoc.* **63** (1968).
8. Crane, M. and D. L. Iglehart, "Statistical Analysis of Discrete Event Simulations," *Proc. 1974 Winter Simulation Conf.* (1974).
9. Fishman, G. S., *Concepts and Methods in Discrete Event Simulation*; Wiley-Interscience, John Wiley and Sons, New York (1973).
10. Gastwirth, J. and H. Rubin, "Effect of Dependence on the Level of Some One-Sample Tests," *J. Amer. Stat. Assoc.* **66** (December 1971).
11. Gaver, D. P., "Methods For Assessing Variability, With Emphasis on Simulation Data Interpretation," *Proc. Int. Symp. on Uncertainties in Hydrologic and Water Resource Systems*, Univ. of Arizona, Tucson, Arizona (1972).
12. —— and G. S. Shedler, "Approximate Models for Processor Utilization in Multiprogrammed Computer Systems," *SIAM J. Comput.* **2, No. 3** (September 1973).
13. —— and G. L. Thompson, *Programming and Probability Models in Operations Research*, Brooks/Cole, Monterey, California (1973).
14. Hald, A., *Statistical Theory with Engineering Applications*, John Wiley & Sons, New York (1952).
15. Huber, P., "Robust regression: Asymptotics, Conjectures, and Monte Carlo," *Ann. Stat.* **1, No. 5,** (September 1973).
16. Iglehart, D. L., "Limiting Diffusion Approximations for the Many Server Queue and the Repairman Problem," *J. Appl. Prob.* **2, No. 2** (December 1965).
17. Knuth, D., *The Art of Computer Programming, Vol. II*, Addison-Wesley, Reading, Massachusetts (1969).
18. Koopman, B. O., "Air-Terminal Queues Under Time Dependent Conditions," *Operations Res.* **20, No. 6** (November–December 1972).
19. Lavenberg, S., "Efficient Estimation Via Simulation of Work Rates in Closed Queueing Networks," IBM Res. Lab., San Jose, California (1974).
20. Marsaglia, G., "Random Numbers Fall Mainly in the Planes," *Proc. Nat. Acad. of Sciences* **60** (1968).
21. Miller, R. G., "Jackknifing Variances," *Ann. Math. Stat.* **35, No. 4** (1964).
22. Moder, J. J. and C. R. Phillips, *Project Management with CPM and PERT*, Van-Nostrand Reinhold, New York (1970).
23. Naylor, T. H., J. L. Balintfy, D. S. Burdick, and K. Chu, *Computer Simulation Techniques*, John Wiley and Sons, New York (1966).

24. Nelson, C. R., *Applied Time Series Analysis for Managerial Forecasting*, Holden Day, San Francisco (1973).
25. Newell, G. F., *Applications of Queueing Theory*, Chapman-Hall, London (1971).
26. Page, E. S., "On Monte Carlo Methods in Congestion Problems, II," *Operations Res.* **13** (1965).
27. Phillips, D. T. and C. Beightler, "A Procedure for Generating Gamma Variates With Non-Integer Parameter Sets," *Proc. Fifth Annu. Conf. on Applic. of Simulation* (1971).
28. Scheffé, H., "Practical Solutions of the Behrens-Fisher Probelm," *J. Amer. Stat. Assoc.* **65** (December 1970).
29. Tukey, J. W., *Exploratory Data Analysis*, Addison-Wesley, Reading, Massachusetts (1977).

III-8

SIMULATION-COMPUTATION*

Geoffrey Gordon
IBM Corporation

Simulation in its broadest sense covers many possibilities. Such diverse topics as wind tunnels, airline pilot trainers, and war games could be included. The specific topic to be discussed here is the use of digital computers for discrete system simulation; in particular, the simulation of systems involving stochastic processes. Typically, such systems involve queuing for service from units that have random service times; they include decision processes for selecting the sequence of events and they are measured by such factors as the distribution of queue lengths and response times. Many applications of discrete system simulation are listed in the reference section at the end of this chapter.

Representing a system with stochastic processes implies that there are random events that change the state of the system by discrete steps at specific points in time. While other operations research (OR) techniques find methods of analyzing the stochastic processes, simulation simply follows the succession of events, tracking the changes of state chronologically. Discussed here are the programming techniques for representing and following complex sequences of events which occur randomly and asynchronously. The fact that the events result from stochastic processes requires generating and measuring random numbers, but these topics have been discussed in the previous chapter.

*This chapter is based, in part, on Chapter 2 of, Geoffrey Gordon, "The Application of GPSS V to Discrete System Simulation," Prentice-Hall Inc., Englewood Cliffs, New Jersey (1975).

1. SYSTEM SIMULATION

Essentially, simulation is a numerical computation technique. It is usually invoked when it proves impossible to formulate a problem in terms of a mathematical model that can be solved by other methods developed within the field of OR. Unlike those methods, simulation does not require that a model be presented in a particular format. It permits a considerable degree of freedom so that the model can bear a close correspondence to the system being studied. The simulation user is, in effect, put in the position of an experimenter operating the model in much the same way as he would have liked to operate the system itself. Correspondingly, the results obtained are much the same as observations or measurements that might have been made on the system itself. Whatever questions are to be asked about the system must be formulated in such quantitive terms. Questions such as: "What conditions optimize some factor of the system?" must be answered by testing many sets of conditions and observing which gives the optimum performance.

Many programming systems have been developed, incorporating simulation languages for describing models. Some of them are general-purpose in nature, while others are designed for specific types of systems. A number are listed in the references for this chapter. They incorporate algorithms for controlling the succession of events, and they carry out such 'housekeeping' routines as gathering statistics and preparing output reports. A substantial part of all simulation work is carried out using these simulation languages, since they allow the user to concentrate on the task of model building rather than the technical details of executing the simulation. Nevertheless, general-purpose scientific programming languages such as FORTRAN, ALGOL, and PL/1 are also used. In particular, there are some forms of simulation in which the processing of events is substantially simpler than that needed for representing stochastic processes and, consequently, there is no great burden involved in programming in a non-simulation language. This gives the advantages of using a familiar language and possibly having access to other programming packages which are specifically designed for the analysis of the type of system being simulated. Of course, the general-purpose simulation languages are equally applicable to the simpler forms of simulation.

One type of simplification occurs when the model does not involve time. A decision process, for example, may consist of a number of sequential steps where the only interest is in the final outcome. The inherent step-by-step computation method involved in simulation can be used to execute the sequential steps.

Monte Carlo methods constitute another particular type of simulation. These methods are concerned with studying mathematical equations by means of statistical trials. For example, if an analysis of a system leads to a complex, multi-dimensional integral, Monte Carlo methods can be used to evaluate the integral. From the point of view of simulation, such problems only involve the repeated execution of some random event. There are, of course, very significant problems in generating and measuring the random variates involved, as was discussed in the previous chapter.

Econometric models are examples of still another class of problem which, from the point of view of simulation, can be relatively simple. They do involve time, but usually in a synchronous manner. The values of variables are calculated at regular intervals, such as every year, and the control of the computations does not present any great difficulty. There are problems in deciding upon the order in which the equations should be evaluated when lagged variables are present, (i.e., the same variable evaluated at more than one time period appears in the model). However, these problems are more properly the concern of model definition, rather than of simulation techniques. Similar types of models, in which it is only necessary to update a set of equations at uniform intervals of time, occur in such fields as business studies, the life sciences, and the social sciences.

2. SYSTEM MODELS

Since the model used in a simulation does not have to conform to any rigid format, no definitive terminology for describing simulation models has evolved. However, three terms have come to be widely used, and they will be used here to clarify the discussion. An *entity* is taken to mean some object in the system of sufficient interest to be included in the model. Each entity is considered to have *attributes* that describe the properties or the state of the entity. There are *activities* which cause changes in the system, either by changing the value of attributes or by creating or destroying an entity.

Each simulation language has its own set of terms for defining simulation models, but the three basic concepts will be recognized, even though the specific terms, entity, attribute, and activity, may not be used.

The first task of a simulation user is to form a model of the system. The lack of formality leaves a great deal of freedom; an ever-present danger in applying simulation is that the realism possible can lead to a model with much more detail than is essential. Since simulation involves a step-by-step computation, and since a simulation study can involve many experiments with different conditions, the amount of computation increases very rapidly as the model size increases. It is important, therefore, to carefully consider what level of detail is essential to the questions being asked about the system and to keep the model to that minimal level. The most significant factor controlling the amount of computation is the total number of events to be simulated. The important simplifications to be sought are those that aggregate a number of detailed actions into some simplified form. For example, in representing the input of messages to a computer from a network of terminals, it is preferable to use a single message source with an inter-arrival pattern representing the combined load, and assign the message origin as an attribute, rather than to use individual sources for each terminal. The events concerned with scanning the terminals and detecting the presence or absence of messages can then be omitted.

The range of time scales on which various types of events occur is a significant indicator of the level of detail. In the example just quoted, using a single source might result in events occurring on a time scale of tenths of seconds, whereas representing the full scanning procedure would probably involve events on a time scale of milliseconds, co-existing with message arrivals on a time scale of tens of seconds or even minutes. Reducing the range of event time scales will produce simplifications that make a simulation faster and easier to control.

Studying the terminal scanning technique by itself would, of course, be a proper subject for simulation study, possibly leading to the inter-arrival statistics needed as input for a separate study of the computer system. This illustrates another way to search for simplifications; namely, to separate potentially large models into parts that are independent or only interact loosely.

In most systems, there is no particular difficulty in identifying the entities involved. When simulating a machine shop, for example, the machines and the parts to be machined are obvious entities. Even so, some important considerations can influence the complexity of a model. If, for example, there is a group of identical machines, each of which can be assigned interchangeably to machine parts, it will be preferable to define a single entity to represent the machines as a group, and assign as attributes the total number of machines and the number currently in use. Dealing with the single entity will involve less record keeping. The simplification, however, implies that a common waiting line feeds the group of machines whereas, in the actual system, there probably are individual waiting lines for the separate machines. The simulation user must decide whether the distortion this causes is significant. Similarly, if there are different part types, it must be decided whether to represent each type by a separate entity type or to use a common entity with the part type assigned as an attribute. In general, the latter choice will give a simpler model.

With other systems, it takes thought and ingenuity to define the proper entities, and it may be difficult to reduce the attributes to quantitative form. Social studies, for example, might have to break a population into rather arbitrary classes; a business system model might need to divide a market into a number of parts on the basis of type of customer or geographic region. Such qualitative factors as customer satisfaction, quality of life, or response to a political issue may have to be reduced to a set of numbers. There obviously can be a great deal of discussion on the validity of these representations but, since simulation is a numerical computation method, the reduction has to be made. In spite of having to use rather artificial numbers as input, such studies are usually justified on the ground that the results give relative results, such as the ranking of alternatives.

From a practical point of view, an important distinction to be made is whether an entity is permanent or temporary. The machine tools discussed previously are typical of permanent entities that remain throughout the simulation, while the parts being machined are typical of temporary entities which are created and destroyed during the simulation. Generally, different data representations will be used for the two types of entities. Permanent entities can be compactly and efficiently represented in tables, while temporary entities will be volatile records and are usually handled by the list processing technique described later.

3. A MACHINE SHOP EXAMPLE

To demonstrate the principles involved in executing a discrete simulation, a specific worked example will be given. Consider a simple machine shop, (or a single stage in the manufacturing process of a more complex machine shop). The shop is to machine five types of parts. The parts arrive at random intervals and are distributed randomly among the different types. There are three machines, all equally able to machine any part. If a machine is available at the time a part arrives, machining begins immediately. If all machines are busy upon arrival, the part will wait for service. On completion of machining, the parts will be dispatched to a destination depending upon their type. The progress of the parts will not be followed after they are dispatched from the shop. However, a count of the number of parts dispatched to each destination will be kept.

Clearly, there are two types of entity in the system: parts and machines. There will be a stream of temporary entities, representing the parts that enter and leave the system. There is no point in representing the different types as different entities; rather, the type is an attribute of the parts. As indicated before, it is simpler to consider the group of machines as a single permanent entity having as attributes the number of machines and a count of the number currently busy. The activities causing changes in the system are the generation of parts, waiting, machining, and departing.

4. SYSTEM IMAGE

A set of numbers is needed to record the state of the system at any time. This set of numbers is called the *system image*, since it reflects the state of the system. The simulation will proceed by deciding, from the system image, when the next event is due to occur and what type of event it is; testing whether it can be executed; and executing the changes to the image implied by the event.

The image must have a number representing clock time, and this number will be advanced, in uneven steps, with the succession of events in the system. For each part record, there will be four numbers to represent the part type, the arrival time, the machining time, and the time the part will next be involved in an event. The first three of these items are random variates derived by the methods described in the previous chapter. The next event time, in general, depends upon the state of the system, and must be derived as the simulation proceeds.

The organization that will be used for the system image is illustrated in Fig. 1. There are four frames in the figure, representing successive states of the system. The frames are to be read from left to right and top line first. The frame in the top left corner is the initial state. The description of the system image will be made in terms of that particular frame.

Frame 1 (top left)

	Part type	Machine time	Arrival time	Next event time
Next arrival	2	75	1002	1002
Waiting parts	4	52	992	—
	3	84	976	—
Parts being machined	3	43	972	1040
	1	21	936	1017
	2	62	896	1003
Clock Time				1000

	1	2	3	4	5
Counters	12	22	20	31	15

Frame 2 (top right)

	Part type	Machine time	Arrival time	Next event time
Next arrival	1	68	1018	1018
Waiting parts	2	75	1002	—
	4	52	992	—
	3	84	976	—
Parts being machined	3	43	972	1040
	1	21	936	1017
	2	62	896	1003
Clock Time				1002

	1	2	3	4	5
Counters	12	22	20	31	15

Frame 3 (bottom left)

	Part type	Machine time	Arrival time	Next event time
Next arrival	1	68	1018	1018
Waiting parts	2	75	1002	—
	4	52	992	—
Parts being machined	3	84	976	1087
	3	43	972	1040
	1	21	936	1017
Clock time				1003

	1	2	3	4	5
Counters	12	23	20	31	15

Frame 4 (bottom right)

	Part type	Machine time	Arrival time	Next event time
Next arrival	1	68	1018	1018
Waiting parts	2	75	1002	—
Parts being machined	3	84	976	1087
	4	52	992	1069
	3	43	972	1040
Clock time				1017

	1	2	3	4	5
Counters	13	23	20	31	15

Fig. 1. Machine shop example.

The top line of the system image represents the part due to enter the system next. As shown here, it is a type 2 part, will require 75 minutes of machining, and is due to arrive at time 1002. This, of course, is also its next event time.

Below the next arrival listing is an open-ended list of the parts that have arrived and are now waiting for service. Currently, there are two waiting parts. As indicated, they are listed in order of arrival. Because the waiting parts are delayed, it is not possible to predict a next event time for them. It will be necessary to see whether there is a waiting part when a machine finishes, and offer service to the first part in the waiting line.

The next level of numbers represents the parts being machined, in this case limited to three. Once machining begins, the time to finish can be derived and entered as the next event time. Three parts are occupying the machines at this time and they have been listed in the order in which they will finish. As will be seen, this is not necessarily the order in which machining started. Finally, a number represents the clock time, here set to an initial value of 1000, and there are five counters showing how many parts of each type have been completed. Note that it is not customary to pre-calculate all the random variates. Instead, each would be calculated at the time it is needed, so a simulation program will be continually switching between the examination and manipulation of the system image and the subroutines that calculate the random variates.

5. THE SIMULATION PROCESS

Looking now at the system image in Fig. 1, assume all events that can be executed up to time 1000 have been processed. It is now time to begin one more cycle. The first step is to find the next potential event by scanning all the event times. Because of the ordering of the parts being machined, it is, in fact, necessary only to compare the time of the next arrival with the first listed time in the machining section. With the numbers shown in frame 1, the next event is the arrival of a part at time 1002, so the clock is updated to this time in the second frame.

The arriving part finds all machines busy and must join the waiting line. The successor to the part just arrived is generated and inserted as the next future arrival, due to arrive at time 1018. Another cycle can now begin. The next event is the completion of machining a part at time 1003. The third frame of Fig. 1 shows the state of the system at the end of this event. The clock is updated to 1003 and the finished part is removed from the system, after incrementing by 1 the counter for that part type. There is a waiting part, so machining is started on the first part in the waiting line, and its next event time, derived from the machining time of 84, is calculated as 1087. In this case, the new part for machining has the largest finish time and it joins the end of the waiting line. The records in the waiting line and the machine segment are all moved down one line. There is then another completion at 1017 which, as before, leads to a counter being incremented and service being offered to the first part in the waiting line. In this case, however, the machining time is short enough for the new part to finish ahead of one whose machining started earlier, so, instead of being the last listed part, the new part becomes the second in the list. This is shown in the last frame of Fig. 1.

6. STATISTICS GATHERING

The purpose of the simulation, of course, is to learn something about the system. In this case only the counts of the number of completed parts by type has been kept. Depending upon the purpose of the simulation study, other statistics would be gathered. Simulation language programs include routines for collecting certain typical statistics. Among the commonly used types of statistics are the following:

(a) *counts* giving the number of entities of a given type, or the number of times some event occurred.
(b) *utilization* of equipment, in terms of the fraction of time it is in use, or in terms of the average number of units in use.
(c) *distributions* of random variates such as processing times and response times, together with their means and standard deviations.

7. LIST PROCESSING

In the machine shop example, it was convenient to describe the records as though they were located in one of three places corresponding to whether they represented parts that were arriving, waiting, or being processed. The simulation was described in terms of moving the records from one place to the next, possibly with some re-sorting. A computer program that used this approach would be very inefficient because of the large amount of data movement involved. Much better control and efficiency are obtained by using *list processing*. With this technique, each record consists of a number of contiguous words (or bytes), some of which are reserved for constructing a list of the records. Each record contains, in a standard position, the address of the next record in the list. This is called a pointer. A special word, called a header, located in a known location, contains a pointer to the first record in the list. The last record in the list has an end-of-list symbol in place of its pointer. If the list happens to be empty, the end-of-list symbol appears in the header.

The pointers, beginning from the header, place the records in a specific order, and allow a program to search the records by following the chain of pointers. These lists, in fact, are usually called chains. There may be another set of pointers tracing through the chain from end to beginning so that a program can move along the chain in either direction. It is also possible for a record to be on more than one chain, simply by reserving pointer space for each possible chain.

Removing or adding a record, or reorganizing the order of a chain, now becomes a matter of manipulating pointers. To remove C from a chain of the records A, B, C, D, . . . , the pointer of B is redirected to D. If the record is being discarded, its storage space would probably be returned to another chain from which it can be reassigned later. To put the record Z between B and C, the pointer of B is directed to Z and the pointer of Z set to indicate C. Reordering a chain consists of a series of removals and insertions.

As can be seen, list processing does not require that records be physically moved. It therefore provides an efficient way of transferring records from one category to another by moving them on and off chains, and it can easily manage lists that are constantly changing size; these are two properties that are very desirable in simulation programming. Therefore, list-processing is used in the implementation of all major discrete system simulation languages, including the GPSS and SIMSCRIPT simulation programs, which are described later.

8. SIMULATION LANGUAGES

Since simulation models do not follow any formal structure, it is not surprising that there is a wide variety of approaches used in simulation programming languages, making it impractical to review them here in any detail. For reviews, see Kiviat [1969a], Kleine [1970], Palme [1968], and Teichroew *et al.* [1966, 1967]. Nevertheless, two general approaches have emerged in the design of languages. They are exemplified by the General Purpose Simulation System GPSS: (Efron and Gordon [1964]), (Gordon [1961, 1962, 1975]), (IBM [1970]), (Gould [1969]), (Greenberg [1972]), (Herscovitch and Schneider [1965]), (Schriber [1974]); and SIMSCRIPT: (Dimsdale and Markowitz [1964]), (Karr *et al.* [1966]), (Kiviat *et al.* [1969]), and (Markowitz et al. [1963]).

These are probably the two most widely used simulation languages. Both are general-purpose in that they can be applied to a wide variety of problems. The following sections will describe the principles on which these two programming systems operate and will demonstrate their use with the machine shop example that has been discussed previously.

9. SIMULATION CONTROL ALGORITHMS

In addition to language differences, different methods have been used for controlling the sequence of events. The main differences are concerned with the handling of conditional events. In the case of the machine shop, for example, the end of machining is an isolated event if there is no waiting line, but when there is a waiting line, implied is removing a part from the waiting line and beginning machining on that part; all these changes occur at the same time. It is a matter of interpretation as to whether such interrelated changes should be regarded as a single complex event or as a set of simultaneous elemental events. In GPSS, the approach is the latter one. The example would be executed as three separate events. However, they are executed immediately, without intervention by events affecting other entities that happen to occur at the same time.

This has been referred to as a 'process interaction' form of control, Kiviat [1969]. A process is considered to be a set of time-oriented events through which an entity must pass. A process interaction control method will move each entity through as many events as it can at the current time. To be effective, it must be able to detect when an entity that has become blocked is able to move again, and immediately restart its advance through the process. Other simulation languages using the process interaction control method are SIMPL/1 (IBM [1972]), SIMULA (Dahl and Nygaard [1966]), and SOL (Knuth and McNeley [1963]).

In contrast, SIMSCRIPT uses another control method which is referred to as 'event scheduling'. Using this form of control, the machining would be considered one event, and a single routine would be responsible for executing all the changes that might occur as a result of that event. The routine must decide whether the event is just the simple event of ending a machining or whether it is a complex event, requiring also that another part be taken from the waiting line and committed to machining. Another simulation language using the event scheduling approach is GASP II (Pritsker and Kiviat [1969]).

A third general method of organizing a simulation control is called 'activity scanning'. In effect, it defines a separate clock for each entity in the system to record the time when that entity will next cause an event. The descriptions of activities include the conditions under which the activities will occur. As each event is considered, all activities are scanned to see if they should occur. The CSL language (Buxton and Laski [1962]) and its extension (Clementson [1966, 1972]) are characteristic of this organization.

10. ORGANIZATION OF GPSS

GPSS is based on a block diagram language. It uses a set of specific block types, each of which is, in effect, a macro-instruction, representative of a system activity. Transactions moving through the block diagram represent temporary entities, and an event corresponds to a transaction entering a block. The transactions carry parameters to record attributes of the temporary entities. Permanent entities are represented by program elements such as storages and queues; and their attributes, such as utilization or current length, are made available.

Returning to the worked example, the records, which in GPSS would be transactions, were logically located in three categories: arriving, waiting, and being machined. List processing could implement this organization by using three lists, but it is apparent that this is an organization specific to the particular model being used. A more useful organization is to divide the transactions into those that have future events times and those that are ready to move but are currently blocked. The position in the block diagram is then carried in the transaction. GPSS uses these two basic chains, calling them the future events chain and the current events chain. There are also other chains, as will be explained later.

In the machine shop example, the transactions for the parts being processed and the next arrival would be on the future events chain, arranged in chronological order. The transactions for waiting parts would be on the current events chain, arranged in order of arrival. Priorities may be assigned, in which case transactions on the current events chain will be organized in priority order, and order of arrival within priority class, while simultaneous future events transactions will be arranged in priority order. Each current event is dependent on some other event changing the state of the system. This may be a future event, such as the completion of machining a part, but in general it could be some other delayed event. Once an event occurs, therefore, it is possible for a series of current events, all due to occur simultaneously, to become unblocked. In particular, one entity may be involved in a series of events all due to occur at the same time. This would correspond in GPSS to a string of blocks, none of which involves time. The process interaction form of control used in GPSS will move each transaction through as many blocks as it can, before turning attention to other transactions.

Events that should occur simultaneously in the system must be processed sequentially in the simulation. Maintaining a logical sequence, particularly in the presence of priorities, presents difficulty. Clearly, the current events chain must be scanned periodically for transactions that can move. The scan, naturally, is conducted in priority order. At some point in the scan, a transaction could move, and, in doing so, cause a change that unblocks a higher priority transaction. Because the unblocked transaction is of higher priority, it will have been passed by the scan. If the scan simply continues down the chain, some lower priority transaction could take advantage of the change, either directly or indirectly, through intermediate events. Even if this does not happen, the higher priority transaction will not become aware of the change until the next scan, when the clock will have been advanced. The difficulty is further complicated by the new transactions that become current when the clock is updated. The priorities of these transactions need to be examined against the priorities of the blocked transactions.

To prevent violations of the priority rules, two actions are taken. First, all new transactions arriving from the future events chain are merged, in priority order, with the transactions on the current events chain, before an attempt to move them is made. Second, the scan is restarted whenever a change of state occurs that may have unblocked a higher priority transaction. To re-scan on every change of state would be very time consuming. In GPSS, almost all changes of state that unblock or reactivate a transaction, and therefore call for a rescan, can be detected. The program efficiency is greatly improved by rescanning only when these changes occur. This is achieved in two ways. Sets of transactions which are all waiting for some specific event, represented by a transaction entering a particular block, can be removed from the current events chain and returned only when that event occurs. Second, transactions waiting for a permanent entity to be in a particular state are left on the current events chain but rendered inactive. Meanwhile, they are placed on a subsidiary chain, which can be used to locate and reactivate them when the desired state occurs. Either of these two types of change will initiate a restart of the scan.

11. MACHINE SHOP EXAMPLE IN GPSS

Figure 2 shows a GPSS block diagram for the machine shop example. At the beginning is a GENERATE block which creates transactions, each representing a part to be machined. A function controls the inter-arrival time distribution. Transactions can have parameters to hold attributes of the entities they represent. The ASSIGN block places a part type number in one of the parameters, deriving the value from a distribution specified by a second function. The

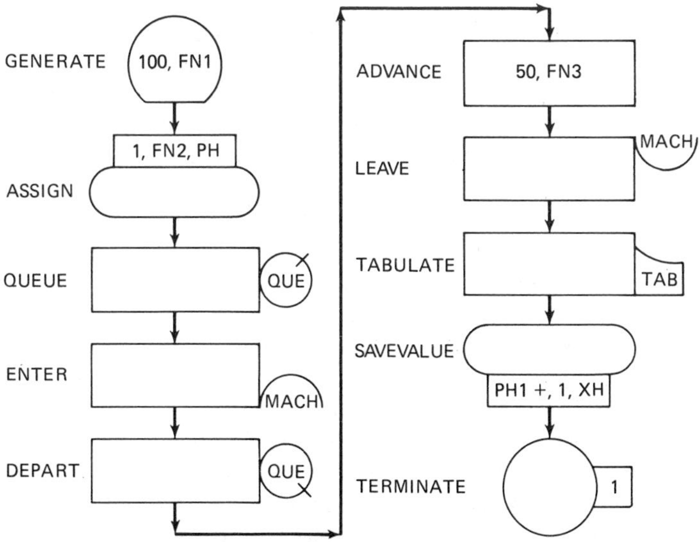

Fig. 2. Machine shop example in GPSS.

transaction enters a QUEUE block to join a waiting line until space becomes available in a permanent entity, called a storage, which is here named MACH, and set to a capacity of three. When space is available, the transaction takes the space by going into the ENTER block. It then immediately goes to the DEPART block to be removed from the waiting line, and then goes into the ADVANCE block to expend the machining time. In keeping with the process interaction organization of GPSS, if a machine is available when the part arrives, the transaction will immediately move through the blocks from the GENERATE to the ADVANCE block.

When the machining is finished, the transaction goes to a LEAVE block to give up a machine, enters a TABULATE block to record the processing time, goes to a SAVEVALUE block, which will increment a counter according to the part type, and finally goes to a TERMINATE block to be destroyed.

A single input statement is created for each block. Along with about eight control statements, this constitutes the program input. At the end of the simulation, the program will print a report which is generated automatically. In this case, the significant outputs will be statistics on the waiting line and the processing time distribution, together with statistics on the occupancy of the machines. Although the data is collected automatically, it is possible to edit the output by extracting only the information of interest and, if desired, to plot some of it in graphical form.

12. ORGANIZATION OF SIMSCRIPT

In contrast to GPSS, a SIMSCRIPT program has very little pre-arranged structure. Activities are represented by event routines, which are separately compiled subroutines describing the events that occur, or could occur, as a result of the activity. Data structures for representing the system entities are defined in a preamble section of the coding. Permanent entities are represented by individual words, arrays, or multi-indexed tables, to record attributes or gather statistics. Temporary entities are represented by records that can be organized in sets. Instructions create and destroy the temporary entities at different points of the model. Other instructions will file, locate, and extract them from the sets under a variety of queueing or logical conditions.

One particular type of temporary entity is called an event notice. Its purpose is to control the progress of the simulation; thus, it plays a role similar to a transaction in GPSS. However, an event notice does not necessarily pass through the complete process for an entity, as does a GPSS transaction. Event notices are usually destroyed upon execution of an event, and a new event notice is created for the following event. Each event notice carries the name of the event it is to schedule. When an event notice has been created, a special instruction schedules the notice to implement an event routine, either at the current time or at some time in the future. The simulation control algorithm files the event notices in chronological order, and proceeds by advancing the clock to the time of the next most imminent event notice.

The event routines are responsible for making all the changes of state implied by the event. As pointed out in Section 9, this can mean making tests to see what conditions prevail and deciding upon the type of change to be made. The event routines must also incorporate the processing needed to gather statistics, such as incrementing counters or marking times from which to calculate transit times. An event notice, having initiated an event routine, is usually destroyed. It may, however, be rescheduled, as might be done, for example, to generate a stream of arriving entities from the inter-arrival time statistics. If the execution of the event implies some other event, the routine must create the appropriate event notices and schedule them for execution, either immediately or at some future time.

The SIMSCRIPT program includes an extensive report generator which allows the user to describe how the report will appear, naming the items of data to be inserted, and giving instructions on the manner of printing repetitive information.

13. MACHINE SHOP EXAMPLE IN SIMSCRIPT

The SIMSCRIPT view of the machine shop example would see two main activities; the arrival and departure of parts. Fig. 3 shows event routines for handling the arrival and departure of parts. The example is taken (with slight modifications) from Fishman [1973], to which the reader is referred for the full example. It uses the SIMSCRIPT II version of the language, (Kiviat *et al.* [1969]). The example is for the case of a single server, but the changes for the multi-server case are simple. Also, it does not distinguish between different types of parts. The full example arranges to sample the queue length periodically and save the data for analysis after the simulation, using a separate FORTRAN program, called by the simulation program.

A preamble section (not shown) defines all the elements of the system, and a MAIN section (also not shown) initializes the program and starts and stops the simulation run. Shown in Fig. 3 are the two main event routines. The first, called ARRIVAL, uses an event notice which is not destroyed but is continually re-scheduled to represent arriving parts. (The MAIN routine schedules the first ARRIVAL event.) Statement 2 is responsible for the re-scheduling, and it uses an exponential function to generate a random inter-arrival time. Statement 3, and a similar statement in the DEPARTURE routine, is used to produce a time in minutes from a time that happened to be originally defined in units of days. Statements 4 through 6 are concerned with generating statistics. The notation *S* (*N*. QUEUE + SERVER + 1) selects a slot in an array called *S*, which was defined in the preamble. The variable *N*. QUEUE is the number of tasks waiting

Arrival Event

```
Line
 1 EVENT ARRIVAL SAVING THE EVENT NOTICE
 2 RESCHEDULE THIS ARRIVAL IN
   EXPONENTIAL.F(MEAN.INTERARRIVAL, 1) MINUTES
 3    LET T = TIME.V*1440
 4    ADD T-T.1 TO S(N.QUEUE+SERVER+1)
 5    LET T.1 = T
 6    LET MAX.Q = MAX.F(MAX.Q,N.QUEUE+SERVER+1)
 7 IF SERVER = BUSY,
 8    CREATE A TASK
 9    FILE THIS TASK IN QUEUE
10    RETURN
11 ELSE
12 LET SERVER = BUSY
13 SCHEDULE A DEPARTURE IN
   EXPONENTIAL.F(MEAN.SERVICE, 2) MINUTES
14 RETURN
15 END
```

Departure Event

```
 1 EVENT DEPARTURE
 2 LET T = TIME.V*1440
 3 ADD T-T.1 TO S(N.QUEUE+SERVER+1)
 4 LET T.1 = T
 5 IF QUEUE IS EMPTY,
 6    LET SERVER = IDLE
 7    RETURN
 8 ELSE
 9 REMOVE THE FIRST TASK FROM THE QUEUE
10 DESTROY THIS TASK
11 SCHEDULE A DEPARTURE IN
   EXPONENTIAL.F(MEAN.SERVICE, 2) MINUTES
12 RETURN
13 END
```

Fig. 3. Machine shop example in SIMSCRIPT. (Reprinted from George S. Fishman, *Concepts and Methods in Discrete Event Digital Simulation*, New York, 1973, by permission of John Wiley & Sons.)

in a set called QUEUE. Statement 7 tests whether the server is busy or not, and the routine proceeds differently according to the outcome. When the server is busy, a temporary entity called TASK is created, and filed in the set called QUEUE. If the server is not busy, an event notice called DEPARTURE is created and scheduled. The RETURN statement gives control to the simulation algorithm to find the next event.

When a departure becomes due, the second event routine, called DEPARTURE, is initiated. The event notice in this case is automatically destroyed. After extracting a statistic for a queue length histogram, the routine takes one of two courses, according to whether there are waiting tasks. If there are none, the server is simply made idle, but if there are, the first is removed from the set QUEUE and destroyed. A new DEPARTURE event notice is then created and scheduled. A final section of the program describes an output report.

With regard to simultaneous events, the following statement, appearing in the preamble, establishes the order in which events will be executed if they happen to occur simultaneously: PRIORITY ORDER IS ARRIVAL, DEPARTURE, COLLECTION AND END.OF.SIMULATION.

14. COMPARISON OF THE LANGUAGES

As was pointed out before, GPSS and SIMSCRIPT are to some extent representative of the different types of simulation languages that are available. It happens that they also provide a contrast between the process interaction and event scheduling approaches to simulation control. A comparison of these two languages, therefore, illustrates many of the choices made in constructing simulation programs.

The most striking contrast is that GPSS has a highly structured format, whereas SIMSCRIPT is extremely flexible. The relative inflexibility of GPSS often results in models that are more costly in storage space than a SIMSCRIPT model, particularly with large models. On the other hand, some programming is saved in GPSS, as the structure of the system image does not have to be declared, and the gathering of statistics and report writing are automatic.

The formal structure of GPSS makes the program easy to learn. The modeling of a system can usually be done by a systems analyst familiar with the system but not necessarily particularly skilled in programming. As might be expected, the special purpose simulation programs exploit this principle by defining languages that are closely related to the type of system for which they are designed.

The GPSS language essentially consists of a set of macro-instructions that are executed in an interpretive fashion, whereas SIMSCRIPT statements are compiled into efficient machine language code. This makes the execution of GPSS much slower than SIMSCRIPT. However, a slow running time is not always a significant factor. In the life of a simulation project, the cost of the time spent creating and testing a model will usually far exceed the cost of running the model.

The process interaction control method, at least as implemented in GPSS, has the advantage of providing a specific set of rules by which the execution of events can be interpreted. However, as indicated in Section 10, it can result in an extra expenditure of time through rescanning. The fact that the system action must be broken down into elemental events also tends to increase the programming overhead, and further slow the execution of the program. The event scheduling control used in SIMSCRIPT permits more efficient programming but it places much more responsibility on the user, since it is necessary to carefully consider all the possible interactions that might arise in the execution of an event.

REFERENCES

General Bibliographies

1. IBM Corp., "Bibliography on Simulation," Form No. 320-0924, 112 East Post Road, White Plains, New York (1966).
2. Malcolm, D. G., "Bibliography on the Use of Simulation in Management Analysis," *Operations Res.* **8:** 169–177 (1960).
3. Naylor, Thomas H., "Simulation and Gaming: Bibliography," *Computing Rev.* **10, No. 1:** 61–69 (January 1969). A listing of approximately 440 references on all aspects of simulation. (Also available as a reprint from ACM, Avenue of the Americas, New York, N.Y., 10601.)
4. Shubik, Martin, "Bibliography on Simulation, Gaming, Artificial Intelligence and Allied Topics," *J. Amer. Stat. Assoc.* **55:** 736–751 (1960).

General Textbooks

1. Beekman, M. and H. P. Kunzi, (eds.), *Digital Simulation*, (In German), Springer-Verlag, New York (1971).
2. Chorafas, Dimitris N., *Systems and Simulation*, Academic Press, New York (1965).
3. Emshoff, James R. and Roger L. Sisson, *Design and Use of Computer Simulation Models*, Macmillan, New York (1970).
4. Evans, George W., Graham F. Wallace, and George L. Sutherland, *Simulation Using Digital Computers*, Prentice-Hall, Englewood Cliffs, New Jersey (1967).
5. Fishman, George S., *Concepts and Methods in Discrete Event Digital Simulation*, John Wiley & Sons, New York (1973).
6. Gordon, Geoffrey, *System Simulation*, Prentice-Hall, Englewood Cliffs, New Jersey (1969).
7. Hollingdale, S. H. (ed.), *Digital Simulation in Operations Research*, American Elsevier, New York (1967).
8. Maisel, Herbert and Guiliano Gnugnoli, *Simulation of Discrete Stochastic Systems*, Science Research Associates, Palo Alto, California (1972).
9. Martin, Francis F., *Computer Modeling and Simulation*, John Wiley & Sons, New York (1968).
10. McLeod, John (ed.), *Simulation*, McGraw-Hill, New York (1968).
11. McMillan Jr., Claude and Richard Gonzales, *Systems Analysis: A Computer Approach to Decision Models*, (Revised Edition), Richard D. Irwin, Homewood, Illinois (1965).
12. Mize, Joe H. and J. Grady Cox, *Essentials of Simulation*, Prentice-Hall, Englewood Cliffs, New Jersey (1968).
13. Naylor, Thomas J., Joseph L. Balintfy, Donald S. Burdick, and Kong Chu, *Computer Simulation Techniques*, John Wiley & Sons, New York (1966).
14. Reitman, Julian, *Computer Simulation Applications: Discrete-Event Simulation for the Synthesis and Analysis of Complex Systems*, John Wiley & Sons, New York (1971).
15. Smith, John, *Computer Simulation Models*, Hafner, New York (1968).

16. Stephenson, Robert E., *Computer Simulation for Engineers*, Harcourt Brace Johanovitch, New York (1971).
17. Tocher, K. D., *The Art of Simulation*, D. Van Nostrand Co., Princeton, New Jersey (1963).

Simulation Languages

1. Buxton, J. N. and J. G. Laski, "Control and Simulation Language," *Computer J.* **5, No. 3:** 194-199 (1962).
2. ——, (ed.), "Simulation Programming Languages," *Proc. IFIPS Working Conf.*, Oslo (1967), North-Holland, Amsterdam (1968).
3. Clementson, A. T., "Extended Control and Simulation Language," *Computer J.* 9, **No. 3:** 215-220 (1966).
4. ——, "Extended Control and Simulation Language II," *User's Manual*, University of Birmingham, England (1972).
5. Connors, Michael M., Claude Coray, Carol J. Cuccaro, William K. Green, David W. Low, and Harry M. Markowitz, "The Distribution System Simulator," *Management Sci.* **18, No. 8:** 425-453 (1972).
6. Dahl, O. J. and K. Nygaard, "SIMULA–An ALGOL-Based Simulation Language," *Communications ACM* **9, No. 9:** 671-678 (1966).
7. Dewan, Prem Bhushan, C. E. Donaghey, and Joe B. Wyatt, "OSSL–A Specialized Language for Simulating Computer Systems," *Proc. AFIPS 1972 Spring Joint Computer Conf.*, 799-814, AFIPS Press, Montvale, New Jersey (1972).
8. Dimsdale, B. and H. M. Markowitz, "A Description of the SIMSCRIPT Language," *IBM Systems J.* **3, No. 1:** 57-67 (1964).
9. Efron, R. and G. Gordon, "A General Purpose Digital Simulator and Examples of its Application: Part 1–Description of the Simulator," *IBM Systems J.* **3, No. 1:** 21-34 (1964).
10. Gordon, Geoffrey, "A General Purpose Systems Simulation Program," *Proc. of EJCC*, 87-104, Washington, D.C., Macmillan (1961).
11. ——, "A General Purpose Systems Simulator," *IBM Systems J.* **1, No. 1:** 18-32 (1962).
12. ——, *The Application of GPSS V to Discrete System Simulation*, Prentice-Hall, Englewood Cliffs, New Jersey (1975).
13. IBM Corp., "GPSS V User's Manual," Form No. SH20-0851, 112 E. Post Road, White Plains, New York (1970).
14. ——, "SIMPL/1 User's Manual," 112 E. Post Road, White Plains, New York (1972).
15. Gould, R. L., "GPSS/360–An Improved General Purpose Simulator," *IBM Systems J.* **8, No. 1:** 16-27 (1969).
16. Granger, R. L. and G. S. Robinson, "COMSL–A Communication System Simulation Language," *Proc. AFIPS 1970 Fall Joint Computer Conf.*, 407-414 (1970).
17. Greenberg, Stanley, *GPSS Primer*, John Wiley & Sons, New York (1972).
18. Greenlaw, Paul S. and Michael P. Hottenstein, *PROSIM: A Production Management Simulation*, International Textbook, Scranton, Pennsylvania (1969).
19. Herscovitch, H. and T. Schneider, "GPSS III–An Expanded General Purpose Simulator," *IBM Systems J.* **4, No. 3:** 174-183 (1965).
20. Hills, P. R., "SIMON–A Computer Simulation Language in ALGOL," *Digital Simulation in Operations Research*, 105-115, American Elsevier, New York (1967).
21. Jacoby, Kathe, Diana Fackenthal, and Arno Cassel, "SMPS–A Toolbox for Military Communications Staffs," *AFIPS 1966 Spring Joint Computer Conf.*, 149-157, Spartan Books, Washington, D.C. (1966).

22. Karr, Herbert W., Henry Kleine, and Harry M. Markowitz, "SIMSCRIPT 1.5," California Analysis Center, Santa Monica, California (1966).
23. Kellev. D. H. and J. N. Buxton, "Montecode–An Interpretive Program for Monte-Carlo Simulations," *Computer J.* **5:** 88–93 (1962).
24. Kiviat, P. J., "Digital Computer Simulation: Computer Programming Languages," The Rand Corp., RM-5883-PR, Santa Monica, California (1969).
25. ——, R. Villanueva, and H. M. Markowitz, *The SIMSCRIPT II Programming Language*, Prentice-Hall, Englewood Cliffs, New Jersey (1969).
26. Kleine, Henry, "A Survey of Users' Views of Discrete Simulation Languages," *Simulation* **14, No. 5:** 225–229 (1970).
27 Knuth, D. E. and J. L. McNeley, "SOL: A Symbolic Language for General Purpose System Simulation," *IEEE on Electronic Computers* **EC-13, No. 4:** 401–414 (1963).
28. Levin, Herman, *Introduction to Computer Analysis: ECAP for Electronics Technicians and Engineers*, Prentice-Hall, Englewood Cliffs, New Jersey (1970).
29. Markowitz, Harry M., B. Hausner, and H. W. Karr, *SIMSCRIPT–A Simulation Language*, Prentice-Hall, Englewood Cliffs, New Jersey (1963).
30. Palme, Jacob, "A Comparison Between SIMULA and FORTRAN," *BIT* **8, No. 3:** 203–209 (1968).
31. Parslow, R. D., "AS: An ALGOL Simulation Language," in *Simulation Programming Languages*, 86–100, North-Holland, Amsterdam (1968).
32. Petrone, Luigi, "On a Simulation Language Completely Defined on to the Programming Language PL/1," in *Simulation Programming Languages*, 61–85, North-Holland, Amsterdam (1968).
33. Pritsker, Alan B. and Philip J. Kiviat, *Simulation with GASP II: A FORTRAN Based Simulation Language*, Prentice-Hall, Englewood Cliffs, New Jersey (1969).
34. Pugh III, Alexander, *DYNAMO II User's Manual*, MIT Press, Cambridge, Massachusetts (1973).
35. Schriber, Thomas J., *Simulation Using GPSS*, John Wiley and Sons, New York (1974).
36. Teichroew, Daniel and John Francis Lubin, "Computer Simulation–Discussion of the Technique and Comparison of Languages," *Communications ACM* **9, No. 10:** 723–741 (1966).
37. ——, ——, and T. D. Truitt, "Discussion of Computer Simulation Techniques and Comparison of Languages," *Simulation* **9:** 181–190 (1967).

Applications

1. Amstutz, Arnold E., *Computer Simulation of Competitive Market Response*, MIT Press, Cambridge, Massachusetts (1967).
2. Apter, Michael J., *The Computer Simulation of Behaviour*, Hutchinson and Co., London (1970).
3. Borko, Harold (ed.), *Computer Applications in the Behavioral Sciences*, Prentice-Hall, Englewood Cliffs, New Jersey (1962).
4. Boulden, James B. and Elwood S. Buffa, "Corporate Models: On-Line Real-Time Systems," *Harvard Bus. Rev.* **48, No. 4:** 65–83 (1970).
5. Conway, R. W., W. L. Maxwell, and L. W. Miller, *Theory of Scheduling*, Addison-Wesley, Reading, Massachusetts (1967). (Describes the simulation of job shops, using SIMSCRIPT.)
6. Coplin, William D., *Simulation in the Study of Politics*, Markham, Chicago, Illinois (1968).
7. Crecine, John P., "A Computer Simulation Model of Municipal Budgeting," *Management Sci.* **13:** 786–815 (1967).

8. Forrester, Jay W., *Industrial Dynamics*, MIT Press, Cambridge, Massachusetts (1961).
9. ——, *Urban Dynamics*, The MIT Press, Cambridge, Massachusetts (1969).
10. Fraser, Alex and Donald Burnell, *Computer Models in Genetics*, McGraw-Hill, New York (1970).
11. Fromm, Gary, and Lawrence R. Klein, "The Brookings-SSRC Quarterly Econometric Model of the United States: Model Properties," *Am. Econ. Rev.* **55**: 348–361 (1965).
12. Guetzkow, Harold (ed.), *Simulation in the Social Sciences*, Prentice-Hall, Englewood Cliffs, New Jersey (1962).
13. ——, Alger F. Chadwick, Richard A. Brody, Robert C. Noel, and Richard C. Snyder, *Simulation in International Relations: Developments for Research and Teaching*, Prentice-Hall, New York (1963).
14. Hamilton, H. R., S. E. Goldstone, J. W. Milliman, A. L. Pugh III, E. R. Roberts, and A. Zellner, *Systems Simulation for Regional Analysis*, MIT Press, Cambridge, Massachusetts (1969).
15. Harbaugh, John W. and Graeme Bonham-Carter, *Computer Simulation in Geology*, John Wiley & Sons, New York (1970).
16. Knight, Douglas E., Huntington W. Curtis, and Lawrence J. Fogel, (eds.), "Cybernetics, Simulation, and Conflict Resolution," Third Annual Symposium of the American Society for Cybernetics, Spartan Books, New York (1971).
17. Lowry, Ira S., "Seven Models of Urban Development: A Structural Comparison," *J. Amer. Inst. Planners* **31, No. 2** (1965).
18. MacDougall, M. H., "Computer System Simulation: An Introduction," *Computing Surveys* **2, No. 3**: 191–209 (1970).
19. Naylor, Thomas H., *Computer Simulation Experiments with Models of Economic Systems*, John Wiley & Sons, New York (1971).
20. Orcutt, G. H., M. Greenberger, J. Korbel, and A. M. Rivlin, *Microanalysis of Socioeconomic Systems–A Simulation Study*, Harper and Row, New York (1961).
21. Patten, Bernard C. (ed.), *Systems Analysis and Simulation in Ecology*, Academic Press, New York (1971).
22. Pool, Ithiel de Sola, R. Abelson, and S. Popkin, *Candidates, Issues, and Strategies: A Computer Simulation of the 1960 Presidential Campaign*, The MIT Press, Cambridge, Massachusetts (1965).
23. Schmidt, J. W. and R. E. Taylor, *Simulation and Analysis of Industrial Systems*, Richard D. Irwin, Homewood, Illinois (1970).
24. Seaman, P. H. and R. C. Soucy, "Simulating Operating Systems," *IBM Systems J.* **8, No. 4**: 264–279 (1969).
25. Taylor, Jean G. and Joseph A. Navarro, "Simulation of a Court System for the Processing of Criminal Cases," *Simulation* **10, No. 5**: 235–240 (1968).
26. Tomkins, S. S. (ed.), *Computer Simulation of Personality*, John Wiley & Sons, New York (1963).
27. Weber, J. H., "A Simulation Study of Routing and Control in Communication Networks," *Bell System Tech. J.* **43, No. 6**: 2639–2676 (1964).

III-9

DYNAMIC PROGRAMMING

Eric V. Denardo*
Yale University

1. INTRODUCTION

Dynamic programming (DP) has to do with sequential decision processes. A *sequential decision process* is loosely defined as an activity entailing a sequence of decisions taken toward some common goal. Sequential decision processes come in a myriad of forms as diverse as managing an inventory, preparing dinner, and guiding a spaceship. *Dynamic programming* is loosely defined as the set of mathematical tools used to analyze sequential decision processes. This identifies DP as a branch of applied mathematics, rather than anything more specific.

What gives DP its coherence? Curiously, when sequential decision processes as disparate as those just mentioned are submitted to mathematical analysis, certain themes recur. These themes are the guts of DP, and we shall attempt to lay them bare.

The origins of DP are nebulous; good ideas have deep roots. We cite six early works: a study of water resources by Massé [1946]; studies of sequential decision processes in statistics by Wald [1947] and by Arrow, Blackwell, and Girshick [1949]; studies of inventory theory by Arrow, Harris, and Marschak [1951] and by Dvoretzky, Kiefer, and Wolfowitz [1952]; and Bellman's [1952] study of functional equations. Surely, it was Bellman who seized upon the

*The research leading to this paper was supported by NSF Grant GK-38121.

principle of optimality and, with remarkable ingenuity, applied it to literally hundreds of optimization problems in mathematics, engineering, economics, operations research, and other fields. Many of these developments are compiled in Bellman [1957] or in Bellman and Dreyfus [1962]. Iscaas [1951], whose *tenet of transition* is another version of the principle of optimality, seems to merit partial credit for recognizing the key role that this idea plays.

This chapter is strangely annotated. Except for the preceding sketch of the subject's early history, no attempt is made at giving credit where it is due. Instead, references point to the most accessible sources of the indicated information. One of these is the author's book [1978] on DP and in cases where a reference reads "cf. [x]," you could also refer to it.

2. THE PROTOTYPE SEQUENTIAL DECISION PROCESS

Every sequential decision process is an elaboration of this prototype: a shortest route problem through a directed, acyclic network. We shall analyze this shortest route problem in a way that reveals the themes that give DP its coherence.

A short preliminary discussion of directed networks is in order. A *directed network* consists of a non-empty, finite set S of *nodes* and a subset T of $S \times S$. The elements of T are called *arcs*. Arc (i, j) is intended to connote the possibility of movement from node i to node j. A *path* $(i_1, i_2, \ldots, i_n)$ is a finite sequence of nodes with the property that (i_k, i_{k+1}) is a directed arc for $k = 1, 2, \ldots, n - 1$. A path with $i_1 = i_n$ and $n \geqslant 2$ is called a *cycle*. A network is called *cyclic* if it contains one or more cycles. Otherwise, it is called *acyclic*.

The nodes of a directed, acyclic network can always be labeled with integers 1 through N in such a way that every arc (i, j) has $i < j$. We assume this has been done. The network in Fig. 1 is acyclic and has 9 nodes. The *length* t_{ij} of arc (i, j) is written next to the arc; e.g., $t_{47} = 15$. We shall take the *path length* as the sum of the lengths of the arcs.

Suppose one wishes to find the shortest path from node *1* to node *9*. Pause to note that the shortest path from node *1* to node *9* is (*1, 3, 4, 5, 7, 9*) and that it length is 19 units. Having solved this problem by inspection, we shall now solve

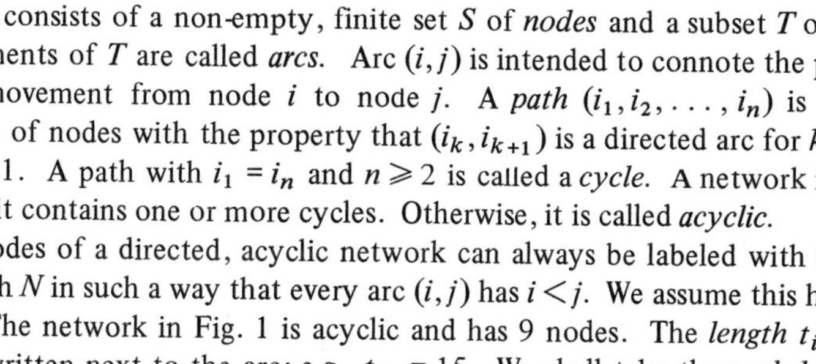

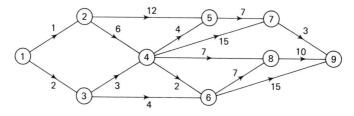

Fig. 1. A shortest route problem.

it by DP, the purpose of which is to provide insight into DP. Let

$$f_i = \text{the length of the shortest path from node } 1 \text{ to node } i.$$

By definition, $f_1 = 0$. Also, we have observed that $f_9 = 19$. Notice from the definition of f_i that

$$f_i + t_{ij} = \text{the length of the shortest path from node } 1 \text{ to node } j \text{ whose last arc is } (i, j).$$

The shortest path from node *1* to node j must have some arc as its final arc, and so

$$f_j = \underset{i|(i,j) \text{ an arc}}{\text{minimum}} \{f_i + t_{ij}\}. \tag{1}$$

Arc (i, j) is said to *emanate* from node i and *terminate* at node j. Notice that each arc (i, j) terminating at node j has $i < j$. This means that (1) can be used to evaluate f_j successively for $j = 2, 3, \ldots,$ and then 9. For instance, arcs *(4, 7)* and *(5, 7)* terminate at node 7, and f_7 can be computed from (1) as soon as f_4 and f_5 are known. This observation is recapitulated as an algorithm.*

Backwards Optimization:

1. Set $v_1 = 0$ and $v_k = \infty$ for $k = 2, \ldots, 9$. Set $j = 2$.
2. For each arc (i, j) terminating at node j,

$$v_j \leftarrow \min \{v_j, v_i + t_{ij}\}. \tag{2}$$

3. Stop if $j = 9$. Else, $j \leftarrow (j + 1)$ and go to step 2.

Step 2 of the above algorithm amounts to replacing v_j by $v_i + t_{ij}$ whenever the latter is smaller. This step is executed for every arc terminating at node j, in increasing j. Step 2 ends with $v_j = f_j$. If you have any difficulty understanding this, it will help to apply the algorithm to the network in Fig. 1. As just specified, backwards optimization computes the length of the shortest path, but not the path itself. To determine the shortest path, one need only keep the arc (i, j) attaining the current value of v_j.

Backwards optimization is an unfortunate name for this algorithm. In the current case, computation proceeds in the direction of the arrows. One could reverse the arrows, in which case computation opposes the direction of the arrows. "Backwards optimization" works when the network is acyclic. Moreover, one can start at *either* end of the network and work "backwards" toward the other.

Backwards optimization associates one operation, namely (2), with arc (i, j). A different algorithm prescribes the same operations, but executes them in a different sequence.

*The expression $x \leftarrow (y)$ means that variable x takes the value assumed by the variable y. For instance, $j \leftarrow (j + 1)$ increases j by 1.

Reaching:

1. Set $v_1 = 0$ and $v_k = \infty$ for $k = 2, \ldots, 9$. Set $i = 1$.
2. For each arc (i, j) emanating from node i,

$$v_j \longleftarrow \min\ \{v_j, v_i + t_{ij}\}. \tag{3}$$

3. Stop if $i = 8$. Else, $i \longleftarrow (i + 1)$ and go to step 2.

To see that reaching and backwards optimization are basically different, you might pause to apply them to the network in Fig. 1. Suppose step 2 of backwards optimization has been applied for $j = 2, 3$, and 4. Then the shortest paths to nodes *2*, *3* and *4* are known. Now suppose that step 2 of reaching has been applied for $i = 1$, 2 and 3. At this point, v_j is the length of the shortest path from node *1* to node j whose final arc (i, j) has $i \leqslant 3$. At this point in the calculation, $v_3 = 2$, $v_4 = 5$, $v_5 = 13$ and $v_6 = 6$. The shorter path (*1*, *3*, *4*, *5*) to node *5* will be found at the next iteration of step 2, when arcs emanating from node *4* are evaluated.

Though different, backwards optimization and reaching entail one addition and one comparison per arc. Each algorithm is exactly as fast as the other. There is, however, an important, though subtle, difference. Reaching associates arcs with nodes whose shortest paths are known; that is, arcs emanating from node i are considered at a point in the computation when $v_i = f_i$. Backwards optimization associates arcs with nodes whose shortest paths are as yet unknown; that is, arcs terminating at node j are considered at a point in the computation when f_j is as yet unknown.

This usually accords reaching the advantage. It can be adopted to exploit whatever structure exists on the set of shortest paths. An example is studied subsequently in which this is the case, and equation (6) will be used to accelerate reaching.

Notice that the longest-route through a directed acyclic network is easily found; simply replace "min" by "max" in (1), (2), and (3), and replace $+\infty$ by $-\infty$ in step 1 of the algorithms.

From a mathematical viewpoint, the model we have just analyzed is trivial. Even so, it encompasses a great many of the DP problems that arise in OR. The non-trivial part is to recognize a DP problem upon encounter, and the themes we now list should make them easier to spot.

3. SOME THEMES OF DYNAMIC PROGRAMMING

The shortest-route problem illustrates several features that are shared by much more elaborate sequential decision processes. These are enumerated here. Interest in the shortest-route problem lay initially in the computation of f_9 and of a path whose length is f_9. Yet this problem was not attacked directly. Instead, it was first embedded in a class of shortest-route problems; namely, computation of f_j for each j. This feature is characteristic of virtually every model of a sequential decision process; thus, it is displayed below.

> The problem of interest is *embedded* in a set of optimization problems, one problem per node.

In cases when only one problem in the family is of interest, embedding seems a step backwards. Still, it often leads to efficient computation, as we shall soon see.

> The set of solutions to the optimization problems is characterized by a *functional equation*, as in (1).

For current purposes, think of a "functional equation" as a system of equations, one per node, that interrelate the solutions to the several optimization problems. Moreover, these equations have, typically, optimization operators like *min* or *max* or *minimax* to the right of the equality sign, with variables like f_i and f_j on both sides.

> The solution to the set of optimization problems can be computed by a process called *backwards optimization*, which amounts to evaluating the constituent functional equations in an orderly sequence.

Notice that backwards optimization entails *exactly one* evaluation per arc. For instance, (2) is evaluated once per arc. So, one can hardly hope for a more efficient method than backwards optimization, *providing* the arcs are unrelated. This points out the strength and weakness of DP; it works for problems that have no particular structure, but it must be suspected of being inefficient when structure exists.

As noted earlier, backwards optimization works for acyclic networks. One can start at either end of the network and work toward the other. The same is true of reaching. Backwards optimization generalizes to problems whose evolution is affected by chance, but reaching does not.

The next theme we shall focus upon is the elusive principle of optimality. For this, we need to introduce the notion of a subpath. Path $(i_1, \ldots, i_n)$ has path $(i_p, \ldots, i_q)$ as a *subpath*, providing $1 \leqslant p \leqslant q \leqslant n$. For instance, path *(2, 4, 6, 8)* in Fig. 1 has several subpaths, including *(2, 4, 6)* and *(4, 6)*.

> *Principle of optimality* (1st version): A subpath of a shortest path is a shortest path.

We illustrate. Path *(1, 3, 4, 5, 7, 9)* is the shortest path from node *1* to node *9*. The principle of optimality asserts that *(3, 4, 5, 7)* is the shortest path from node *3* to node *7*. If you wish, you might check this by referring back to Fig. 1. But there is no need to do so, for if another path p from node *3* to node *7* were

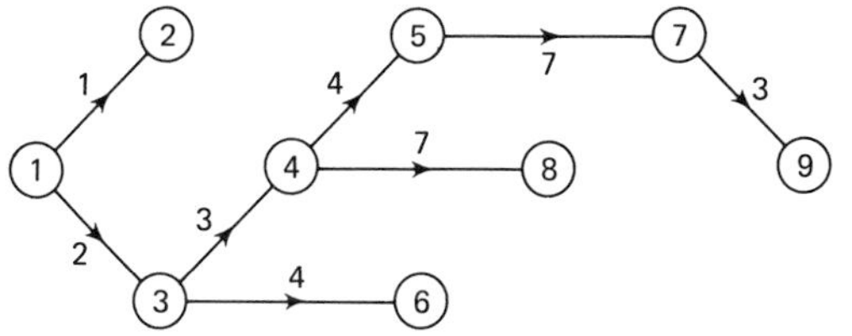

Fig. 2. An optimal policy.

shorter, then the composite path $(1,p,9)$ would be shorter than the shortest path from node *1* to node *9*. And that is impossible.

The principle of optimality and the functional equation are intimately interrelated. In many cases, each implies the other. However, if the path length were defined as the longest of its arcs (not their sum) then a subpath of a shortest path need not be a shortest path.

The preceding version of the principle of optimality applies, regrettably, only to network optimization models. A more ubiquitous version entails the notion of a policy. In the context of Fig. 1, a *policy* specifies for each node j, with $j \neq 1$, an arc (i,j) terminating at node j. (Node *1* is special in that no arcs terminate at it.) One policy is depicted in Fig. 2; there are 63 others. Notice that the policy in Fig. 2 specifies the shortest path from node *1* to every other node. A policy is called *optimal for node j* if the arcs it specifies contain the shortest route from node *1* to node j.

> *Principle of optimality* (2nd version): There exists a policy that is optimal for every node.

The second version of the principle of optimality asserts the existence of a policy that is optimal, simultaneously, for every node. One might have thought that trade-offs are involved–that in order to be optimal for some node, a policy need be sub-optimal for another node. Fig. 2 contradicts this intuition, and analogues of it occur in much more elaborate sequential decision processes.

One of the merits of the second version of the "principle" of optimality is that it is simple enough to state as the conclusion of a theorem. Indeed, a continuing line of research in DP consists of delineating the classes of optimization problems for which this version of the principle of optimality is true.

Discussion of the 3rd, and most traditional, version of the principle of optimality is deferred, temporarily, until another functional equation is in evidence.

4. AN EXAMPLE

The following example illuminates the themes just identified and enables us to introduce the central concept in DP. Consider this mathematical program:

Maximize $\{p_1(x_1) + p_2(x_2) + \cdots + p_N(x_N)\}$

subject to the constraints

$$c_1(x_1) + c_2(x_2) + \cdots + c_N(x_N) \leqslant K$$

$$0 \leqslant x_n \leqslant B \qquad n = 1, \ldots, N$$

$$x_n \text{ integer} \qquad n = 1, \ldots, N.$$

In the above, K and B are constants. Assume throughout this section that the function $c_n(x)$ is non-negative and integer-valued, with $c_n(0) = 0$. Assume also that function $p_n(x)$ has $p_n(0) = 0$, but is otherwise arbitrary. The functions c_n and p_n are data, and the variables are $x_1, \ldots, x_N$.

This program has several useful interpretations. We shall think of x_n as the number of units of commodity n produced, with attendant profit $p_n(x_n)$ and attendant consumption $c_n(x_n)$ of the resource. With this interpretation, the optimization problem is to obtain the maximum profit while consuming K or fewer units of the resource.

Time plays no central role here, and yet, we shall convert this problem to a sequential decision process by imagining the various commodities to be produced one after the other. Imagine that commodity 1 is produced first, then commodity 2, etc., ending with commodity N. Look at the situation after commodities 1 through $n - 1$ have been produced. There remains some number y of units of the resource. Since the resource is consumed in integer quantities, y must be some integer between 0 and K. These y units are to be allocated to the production of commodities n through N. Let

$f(n, y)$ = the maximum profit obtainable by allocating y units of the resource to produce commodities n through N.

The number $f(1, K)$ is the solution to the original optimization problem, which has just been *embedded* in a family of $N(K + 1)$ problems, namely the determination of $f(n, y)$ for $n = 1, \ldots, N$ and for $y = 0, \ldots, K$.

Given the situation depicted by the pair (n, y), we call production quantity x_n *feasible* if

$$c_n(x_n) \leqslant y, \qquad 0 \leqslant x_n \leqslant B, \qquad x_n \text{ integer}.$$

In other words, x_n is feasible if it does not utilize more of the resource than is available. Notice that

$p_n(x_n) + f[n + 1, y - c_n(x_n)]$ = the maximum profit obtainable by allocating y units of the commodity to production of commodities n through N, *providing* x_n units of commodity n are produced.

The above holds because the units that remain after production of commodity

n are, by definition, allocated optimally. Maximizing over x_n removes the proviso, and so

$$f(n,y) = \underset{x_n | x_n \text{ feasible}}{\text{maximum}} \; \{p_n(x_n) + f[n+1, y - c_n(x_n)]\}. \tag{4}$$

The above also holds for $n = N$, providing we define*

$$f(N+1, y) = 0 \qquad y = 0, 1, \ldots, K. \tag{5}$$

Recognize (4)-(5) as a *functional equation.* Notice that the equation with $f(n,y)$ on the left has on its right-hand side the values $f(n+1, z)$ for sundry z. So *backwards optimization* consists of evaluating (4) in decreasing n. That is, $f(N,y)$ is first computed for each y, then $f(N-1, y)$ is computed for each y, etc., ending with $f(1, K)$.

One can easily see that this is a longest-route problem through a directed acyclic network. Establish one node corresponding to each pair (n, y). An arc emanates from node (n, y) for each feasible production quantity x_n, and this arc terminates at node $[n+1, y - c_n(x_n)]$. Its length is $p_n(x_n)$, and the problem is to find the longest path from node $(1, K)$ to *any* node $(N+1, z)$, where the number z of unused resources is a free variable. The functional equation can also be solved by *reaching.* Indeed, the fact that producing nothing consumes nothing leads directly to the inequality

$$f(n, y) \leqslant f(n, y+1). \tag{6}$$

Moreover, (6) is enough to accord reaching the edge in speed of computation, as it allows one to eliminate arcs associated with nodes for which (6) fails to hold as a strict inequality. See Denardo [1978] for a discussion of this and of other instances in which reading can be accelerated.

5. STATES

States play a central role in DP, and the term 'state' is used throughout this chapter in a manner that preserves these properties.

> *Properties of states:* Transition occurs from state to state, and a state is a summary of the prior history of the process, that is sufficiently detailed to enable evaluation of current alternatives.

We illustrate. For the network model in Fig. 1, the nodes are states. The arcs emanating from a node depict the various decisions available for that node (state). With this interpretation, transition occurs from state to state, and the states are the points at which decisions are made. The displayed statement

*The assumption that what remains is valueless is often unrealistic. One could replace (5) by whatever disposal cost or profit function is appropriate.

means that the arcs emanating from a node have nothing to do with how that node was reached.

For the resource-allocation example, take the pair (n, y) as a state. Recall that state (n, y) depicts the situation of allocating y units of the resource to production of commodities n through N. Enough information is contained in the pair (n, y) to evaluate the current options, which are the various possible production quantities of commodity n. It is *not* necessary, for instance, to know how transition to state (n, y) occurred.

The elements of a state are often called *state variables.* For instance, the allocation model has two state variables, n and y. The states in a DP model often group themselves into "stages," with transition occurring from each stage to the next. In the allocation model, transition occurs from state (n, y) to state $(n + 1, z)$ for some z, so that n indexes the stage. With

$$S_n = \{(n, y) | y = 0, 1, \ldots, K\},$$

the set S_n of states is known as *stage* n, and transition occurs from stage n to stage $n + 1$. Stages are less ubiquitous than states. For instance, the shortest-route problem in Fig. 1 has states, but not stages, as it is impossible to group the states into sets in such a way that transition occurs from each set to the next.

The themes cited earlier have to do with states. Embedding amounts to establishing a *state space*, which is a set of states. The functional equation concerns the optimal return as a function of the starting state, and the principle of optimality interlocks the optimal returns for the various starting states.

One of the reasons why states and stages are important is that it is not easy to formulate optimization problems for solution by DP. This takes ingenuity. Virtually everyone encounters difficulty doing this, especially at the beginning. The key is to recognize the states, and the properties of states and stages serve as guideposts.

We are now equipped to state the 3rd and traditional version of the principle of optimality. A *policy* is now interpreted as a decision procedure specifying one decision per state. An *optimal policy* is a policy that is optimal, simultaneously for every state. The 2nd version of the principle of optimality asserts the existence of an optimal policy. The 3rd version of the principle of optimality concerns deviations from the optimal policy in which the first decision is changed, but not the others.

> *Principle of optimality* (3rd version): An optimal policy has the property that whatever the initial state and decision are, the remaining decisions constitute an optimal policy for the state resulting from the first transition.

This version is very nearly a transliteration of the functional equation into

English. To convince yourself of this, compare the 3rd version with the expression displayed just above equation (4). They are essentially the same.

6. UNCERTAINTY

Many sequential decision processes have the property that future states cannot be predicted with certainty. A retailer knows his current inventory, but does not know how many customers will require his product this month. Investments are made without knowing their outcomes with certainty. Insurance is bought and sold because the future is uncertain. Indeed, many of the most fascinating problems faced by mankind are sequential decision processes in which uncertainty plays a central role.

A simple, flexible model of sequential decision-making under uncertainty is presented here. This model has stages, and state (n, i) is an element of stage n. The data of this model are these:

$R_i^k(n)$ = the reward earned if state (n, i) is observed and if decision k is selected.

$P_{ij}^k(n)$ = the probability that transition occurs to state $(n + 1, j)$ given these conditions: state (n, i) is observed and decision k is selected.

The planning horizon consists of N periods, numbered 1 through N. Transition occurs from period n to period $n + 1$, and decision-making ends with period N. This model has a great many uses and interpretations, which, for lack of room, we shall not enumerate. (Cf. Howard [1960], Veinott [1975], Wagner [1970].) A model of this sort is called a *Markov* decision model; it blends the basic descriptive idea of Markov chains with DP.

The objective we select for this model is to maximize the expectation of the total income earned over the planning horizon. Let

$f(n, i)$ = the maximum expected income obtainable during periods n through N if state (n, i) is observed.

Notice that the quantity

$$R_i^k(n) + \sum_{\text{all } j} P_{ij}^k(n) f(n + 1, j) \tag{7}$$

is the expected income for starting at state (n, i), selecting decision k, and using an optimal policy for periods $n + 1$ through N. So this cannot be larger than $f(n, i)$. Moreover, the 2nd version of the principle of optimality asserts that if we maximize expression (7) over k, we obtain $f(n, i)$.

$$f(n, i) = \max_k \{R_i^k(n) + \sum_j P_{ij}^k(n) f(n + 1), j)\}. \tag{8}$$

The above holds for $n < N$ and also for $n = N$, providing we set*

$$f(N+1, j) \equiv 0. \tag{9}$$

You should recognize (8)-(9) as a functional equation. Backwards optimization amounts to solving it in decreasing n. Incidentally, reaching does not work for this model, whose evolution is uncertain.

Typical formulations of planning problems over time include interest rates. Let α be the per-period interest rate. Suppose each unit of income earned at period n can be invested to return $1 + \alpha$ units of income at period $n + 1$. So, with $(1 + \alpha)c = 1$, the decision-maker is indifferent between receiving one unit of income at period $n + 1$ and its *present value*, c, at period n. To compute the policy whose expected present value is largest, simply insert c after the "+" sign in (8).

7. A LANGUAGE FOR SEQUENTIAL DECISION PROCESSES

Notation is the language of mathematics. A good scheme of notation reveals the structure of the subject under study, and a poor scheme masks it. Some mathematicians have argued that devising the proper language for a particular subject is the most creative act in mathematics. In any event, sequential decision processes come in myriad forms, and it would be extremely desirable to design a language or scheme of notation that encompasses them all. Such a language would necessarily reveal the common structure of diverse sequential decision processes.

The notational scheme introduced here encompasses a great many of the sequential decision processes that are studied by operations researchers. (Exceptions consist mainly of control problems in continuous time, which could be handled by introducing derivatives.)

The set S of observable states is called the *state space*, and an element s of S is cabled a *state*. Each state s has a set $D(s)$ associated with it. An element d of $D(s)$ is called a *decision*. We assume that $D(s)$ is non-empty or, equivalently, that the states are the points at which decisions are made. A policy δ is a recipe specifying a feasible decision for each state. Specifically, *policy* δ assigns each state s an element $\delta(s)$ of $D(s)$. The *policy space* Δ is the set of all such δ. This means that selecting a decision for a particular state in no way restricts one's choice for the other states. (In essence, Δ is the Cartesian product of the sets $D(s)$ over s.)

One of the ideas of DP is that each policy δ should have associated with it a return function v^{δ}, where $v^{\delta}(s)$ is the aggregate return for starting in state s and using policy δ. "Using policy δ" means selecting decision $\delta(s)$ for state s, then

*As in (5), one could replace (9) by whatever terminal reward function is appropriate to the application.

function v^π is the best possible in the sense that

$$v^\pi(s) \geqslant v^\delta(s) \qquad \text{all } s \text{ in } S, \quad \text{all } \delta \text{ in } \Delta. \tag{15}$$

Mathematically, (15) amounts to asserting the existence of a policy whose return function is the upper envelope of the return functions of all the policies.

The 3rd version of the principle of optimality has to do with perturbations of policy π in which the "first" decision $\pi(s)$ is changed and all other decisions remain as they were. The 3rd version asserts that changing only $\pi(s)$ does not affect the income earned after transition, and so

$$v^\pi(s) \geqslant h(s, d, v^\pi), \qquad \text{all } s, \quad \text{all } d. \tag{16}$$

Combine (16) with (14) to obtain

$$v^\pi(s) = \max_d \{h(s, d, v^\pi)\}, \qquad \text{all } s. \tag{17}$$

So, it seems that the principle of optimality amounts to the assertion that the optimal return function v^π exists and is a solution to (17). Equation (17) is the *functional equation* of DP, written in rather general notation. From a mathematical viewpoint, the questions are these: (1) whether any solution to (17) exists, (2) whether exactly one solution exists and (3) whether that solution is the optimal return function. That is, the question is whether v^π, as defined by (15), is the unique fixed-point of the operator $\max_j \{h(s, d, \cdot)\}$.

Some central ideas of DP have just been expressed in terms of the local income function. The return function for any particular policy is supposed to be the unique solution to (14). A policy is supposed to exist whose return function satisfies (15). And that policy's return function is supposed to be the unique solution to (17). One might hope to prove these statements as theorems whose hypothesis consists of assumptions on the structure of the local income function. Such theorems would replace the principle of optimality, which concerns solutions to optimization problems, with a hypothesis concerning the structure of the underlying sequential process itself.

Conditions that support (14), (15) and (17) have indeed been discovered, and they continue to be discovered. The state of the research on this topic is too sophisticated to warrant inclusion here. For current purposes, it suffices to indicate that this is one of the main thrusts of research in DP. (Cf. Blackwell [1965], Blackwell, Freedman and Orkin [1974], and Denardo [1967].)

8. A MARKOV DECISION MODEL

This section concerns a much-studied, popular and useful model of decision-making under uncertainty. The model has finitely many states that, for convenience, are numbered 1 through m. Each state has finitely many decisions associated with it. The model's local income function is

$$h(i, k, v) = R_i^k + c \sum_{j=1}^{m} P_{ij}^k v_j. \tag{18}$$

(In the above, $v(j)$ has been abbreviated to v_j, which will turn out to be the jth element of the $m \times 1$ vector v.)

We interpret (18). Decision-making occurs at periods $0, 1, 2, \ldots$, without limit. The periods are equally spaced, and c is the per-period discount factor. It is natural to assume that

$$0 \leqslant c \leqslant 1, \tag{19}$$

which connotes a non-negative interest rate. Suppose state i is observed at period n and decision k is selected. The local income function indicates that reward R_i^k is earned immediately, and also that the probability of transition to state j at period $n + 1$ is P_{ij}^k. So (18) defines an infinite-horizon version of the Markov decision model whose functional equation was (8). It is now natural to assume that

$$\sum_{j=1}^{m} P_{ij}^k \leqslant 1. \tag{20}$$

This allows for the possibility of termination, rather than transition to some state at the next epoch.

Notice that decision-making begins at period 0 and has the potential for continuing indefinitely. The process lacks an "end" from which to initiate backwards optimization.

Policy δ specifies decision $\delta(i)$ for state i. The rewards for policy δ can be arrayed into the $m \times 1$ vector $\mathbf{R}^\delta$, and the transition probabilities can be arrayed into the $m \times m$ matrix $\mathbf{P}^\delta$ as follows:

$$(\mathbf{R}^\delta)_i = R_i^{\delta(i)} \tag{21}$$

$$(\mathbf{P}^\delta)_{ij} = P_{ij}^{\delta(i)}. \tag{22}$$

Discounted/Transient Case: This model is now analyzed under either of two hypotheses.

(I) $$c \sum_{j=1}^{N} P_{ij}^k < 1 \qquad \text{all } i, k.$$

Hypothesis (I) identifies the *discounted* case. It holds if (20) holds as a strict inequality or if $c < 1$. It is easy to test for. Hypothesis (II) is actually a generalization of hypothesis (I).

(II) For every policy δ, all eigenvalues of $c\mathbf{P}^\delta$ are below 1 in absolute value.

Hypothesis (II) identifies the *transient* case, and the literature does contain a simple test for it. (Cf. Veinott [1975].)

Either hypothesis (I) or (II) suffices for $(cP^\delta)^n \longrightarrow 0$ as $n \longrightarrow \infty$. So, with I as the $m \times m$ identity matrix, the Neumann series $I + (cP^\delta) + (cP^\delta)^2 + \cdots$ converges to the inverse of the matrix $(\mathbf{I} - c\mathbf{P}^\delta)$.

As there are m states, the return function for policy δ can be written as an $m \times 1$ vector $\mathbf{v}^\delta$, and the policy evaluation equation, (14), can be written in matrix notation. Specifically, with $\mathbf{R}^\delta$ and $\mathbf{P}^\delta$ as defined by (21) and (22), the policy evaluation equation becomes

$$\mathbf{v}^\delta = \mathbf{R}^\delta + c\mathbf{P}^\delta \mathbf{v}^\delta, \tag{23}$$

or, equivalently,

$$(\mathbf{I} - c\mathbf{P}^\delta)\mathbf{v}^\delta = \mathbf{R}^\delta. \tag{24}$$

We have observed that $(\mathbf{I} - c\mathbf{P}^\delta)$ is invertible, and so

$$\mathbf{v}^\delta = (\mathbf{I} - c\mathbf{P}^\delta)^{-1} R^\delta. \tag{25}$$

Equation (25) demonstrates that the policy evaluation equation has a unique solution when (I) or (II) holds.

Still assuming hypothesis (I) or (II), we consider the following linear program.* With $\alpha_1, \ldots, \alpha_m$ as any fixed, positive constants:

$$\text{Maximize} \quad \left\{\sum_i \sum_k\right\} R_i^k x_i^k$$

subject to the constraints

$$\sum_k x_i^k - c \sum_j \sum_k x_j^k P_{ji}^k = \alpha_i \qquad i = 1, \ldots, m$$

$$x_i^k \geqslant 0 \qquad\qquad \text{all} \quad i, k.$$

This program is known to be feasible and bounded, and any optimal basis for it has the following properties. For each i, the variable x_i^k is positive for exactly one k. Moreover, with

$$\pi(i) = k \quad \text{whenever} \quad x_i^k > 0$$

policy π is an optimal policy. That is, π satisfies (15) and the second version of the principle of optimality. Also, $\mathbf{v}^\pi$ is the vector of dual variables that satisfies complementary slackness with respect to any optimal primal basis. Incidentally, the linear program displayed above is a Leontief system, and a property of Leontief systems is that the same basis is optimal for all positive right-hand sides. This is the reason why the values α_i are immaterial, providing they are positive.

*When a range of summation is omitted, the entire range is indicated.

The literature contains three other approaches to the solution of this Markov decision problem. Two of these are *policy iteration* and *Newton-Raphson iteration*. (Cf. Howard [1960], Blackwell [1962].) Under hypothesis (I) or (II), these two methods prove to be precisely equivalent to each other, and both are identical to block pivoting in the dual simplex method, as applied to the above program. Since large-scale simplex codes are widely available, these special methods do not warrant presentation here. The third method is known as *successive approximations*, or sometimes as *value iteration*. It consists of starting with an $m \times 1$ vector $\mathbf{v}^0$ and, using the equation

$$\mathbf{v}_i^n = \max_k \left\{ R_i^k + c \sum_j P_{ij}^k \mathbf{v}_j^{n-1} \right\} \tag{26}$$

to compute vector $\mathbf{v}^n$ from vector $\mathbf{v}^{n-1}$, successively, for $n = 1, 2, \ldots$. It can be shown that $\mathbf{v}^n$ converges to $\mathbf{v}^\pi$, the optimal return function, as $n \longrightarrow \infty$. The literature also discusses two sorts of variants of (26). One amounts to using Seidel iteration. The other exploits the idea of computing a sequence of inner products quicker, by increasing the number of additions and decreasing the number of multiplications.

When compared with LP, successive approximations has the advantage of simplicity. Successive approximations does not readily yield the sensitivity information that LP codes produce, but for problems having an extremely large number of states and not too many decisions per state, successive approximations is faster. For details in support of these assertions, see Denardo [1978].

Undiscounted Case: Another useful version of the Markov decision model has no discounting and no probability of termination. In this version, hypothesis (III) is satisfied.

(III) $$c = 1, \quad \sum_j P_{ij}^k = 1 \qquad \text{for all } i \text{ and all } k.$$

Hypothesis (III) identifies the *undiscounted* case. Here, decision-making continues indefinitely, rewards are earned each epoch, and future income is not discounted. The aggregate return during the first n periods is likely to approach infinity as $n \longrightarrow \infty$, no matter what policy is employed. Therefore, total reward is an unselective performance criterion.

The most common performance criterion for the undiscounted case is to maximize the average rate at which income is earned per unit time. This is known as the *gain rate*. Maximizing the gain rate is not an entirely satisfactory criterion, as, for instance, income streams $(0, 0, 0, \ldots)$ and $(10^6, 0, 0, \ldots)$ both have gain rate of 0. We content ourselves here with the problem of maximizing the gain rate, although more sensitive criteria have been proposed and analyzed. (Cf. Veinott [1966].) Consider the following LP:

$$\text{Maximize} \left\{ \sum_i \sum_k R_i^k x_i^k \right\}$$

subject to the constraints

$$\sum_k x_i^k - \sum_j \sum_k x_j^k P_{ji}^k = 0 \qquad i = 1, \ldots, m$$

$$\sum_i \sum_k x_i^k = 1 \tag{27}$$

$$x_i^k \geqslant 0 \qquad \text{all } i, k.$$

The above program is feasible and bounded. Any optimal basis is known to have the following properties. For each i, the variable x_i^k is positive for, at most, one k, and the transition probabilities identified below form exactly one ergodic chain.

$$\{P_{ij}^k \mid x_i^k > 0\}$$

Moreover, the gain rate for this ergodic chain is the largest gain rate over all ergodic chains.

In short, the above program finds the ergodic chain with the best gain. This chain always yields the best gain rate for the states that comprise it. In most practical cases, these states are accessible from the others, and the aforementioned ergodic chain yields the best gain rate for all the states. However, in complex, multi-chain cases, it is necessary to use the above program repeatedly in a decomposition-like procedure, the details of which are too complex to warrant inclusion here. (Cf. Denardo [1970] and Denardo and Fox [1968].)

The best gain rate for the undiscounted model can also be found by policy iteration. In the very simplest cases, policy iteration amounts to block pivoting in the dual simplex method, just as in the discounted case. However, in more complicated cases, policy iteration and the simplex method behave quite differently, with the simplex method generally having the edge. (Cf. Blackwell [1962] Denardo [1978].)

Successive approximations can also be applied to the undiscounted model. Just use (26) with $c = 1$. Under favorable conditions, $v_i^{n+1} - v_i^n$ approaches the gain rate of the best chain. Even under favorable conditions, $\mathbf{v}^n$ drifts off to infinity. This causes serious computational difficulties that can be overcome by subtracting a constant, like v_1^n, from each element of $\mathbf{v}^n$ once in a while or after each iteration of (26).

Turnpike Theorems. Logic does not support the assumption of an infinite planning horizon; eventually, everything will be reduced to ashes. For many applications of DP, the planning horizon is long, but unknown. A *turnpike theorem* is a statement of the following sort: if the planning horizon is more than N periods, it suffices for the purpose of current decisions to assume that the planning horizon is infinite. Turnpike theorems allow us to make rational decisions without knowing the planning horizon, providing it is long enough. Turnpike theorems have been developed for this Markov decision model, as well as for a number of other sequential decision processes. These turnpike theorems are important, but rather involved, and we shall not delve into them here. (Cf. Veinott [1975].)

Markov Renewal Programs. The Markov decision model can be generalized in quite a variety of ways. Perhaps the most useful generalization is the one allowing unequal and/or variable transition times. In that model, we replace cP_{ij}^k by

$$Q_{ij}^k = P_{ij}^k \int_0^\infty e^{-\alpha t}\, dF_{ij}^k(t), \tag{28}$$

where

- $F_{ij}^k(\cdot)$ is the cumulative distribution of the time to transition given these conditions: state i is observed now, decision k is selected, and state j will be observed next.
- P_{ij}^k is the probability that state j will be observed next given these conditions: state i is observed now and decision k is selected.
- α is the interest rate, which is compounded instantaneously.

In this model, states are observed for instants, and transitions between states can take variable or random lengths of time. Whenever a state is observed, a decision must be selected, and the decision cannot be changed until the next state is observed. This model is a blend of Markov chains and renewal theory known as a *Markov renewal program.* Some readers will recognize it as a decision model over a semi-Markov process. In the case of exponential transition times, F_{ij}^k is the cumulative distribution function of the exponential distribution, whose parameter can depend on i, j, and k.

Everything said earlier about the discounted and transient cases of the Markov decision model applies directly to the Markov renewal program, providing only that cP_{ij}^k is replaced throughout by Q_{ij}^k. For instance, the LP has precisely the same interpretation as before, but with Q_{ij}^k replacing cP_{ij}^k in the constraints. (Cf. Jewell [1963].)

The undiscounted case of the Markov renewal program occurs when the interest rate α is 0. As a consequence, P_{ij}^k and Q_{ij}^k are identical. Let

$$t_i^k = \sum_{j=1}^m P_{ij}^k \int_0^\infty t\, dF_{ij}^k(t).$$

Notice from the above that t_i^k is the expected time to transition, given state i and decision k. The LP for the undiscounted case has the same meaning in the Markov renewal program as in the original model, providing constraint (27) is replaced with (29). (Cf. Denardo and Fox [1968].)

$$\sum_i \sum_k t_i^k x_i^k = 1. \tag{29}$$

9. RECAPITULATION

This precis of DP had three focuses. One was the computational tools used to solve DP problems; they consist primarily of backwards optimization, successive approximations and LP. The second was to lay bare the themes that unify the field and give it its coherence; they include the notion of a state, the properties of states, embedding, functional equations, the principle of optimality, and the local income function. The last was to reveal the sorts of issues that arise when one tries to discern the underlying structure of decision processes that give rise to functional equations; that involved the local income function and fixed-point equations.

Any precis of a field as broad as DP is, of necessity, selective. Virtually no mention was made of structured sequential decision problems whose solutions have interesting qualitative forms. (CF. Veinott [1975].) Two important topics were not discussed at all: the relationship between DP and the calculus of variations, and the relationship between the principle of optimality and Pontryagin's maximum principle. (See Bellman [1957], Dreyfus [1965].)

REFERENCES

1. Arrow, K. J., D. Blackwell, and M. A. Girshick, "Bayes and Minimax Solutions of Sequential Decision Problems," *Econometrica* **17:** 214–244 (1949).
2. ——, T. E. Harris, and J. Marschak, "Optimal Inventory Policy," *Econometrica* **19:** 250–272 (1951).
3. Bellman, R. E., "On the Theory of Dynamic Programming," *Proc. Nat. Acad. of Sci.* **38:** 716–719 (1952).
4. ——, *Dynamic Programming*, Princeton University Press, Princeton, New Jersey (1957).
5. —— and S. Dreyfus, *Applied Dynamic Programming*, Princeton University Press, Princeton, New Jersey (1962).
6. Blackwell, D., "Discrete Dynamic Programming," *Ann. Math. Stat.* **33:** 719–726 (1962).
7. ——, "Discounted Dynamic Programming," *Ann. Math. Stat.* **36:** 226–235 (1965).
8. ——, D. Freedman, and M. Orkin, "The Optimal Reward Operator in Dynamic Programming," *Ann. Prob.* **2:** 926–941 (1974).
9. Denardo, E. V., "Contraction Mappings in the Theory Underlying Dynamic Programming," *SIAM Rev.* **9:** (1967).
10. ——, "On Linear Programming in a Markov Decision Chain," *Management Sci.* **16:** 281–288 (1970).
11. ——, *Dynamic Programming: Theory and Applications*, Prentice-Hall, Englewood Cliffs, New Jersey (1978).
12. —— and B. L. Fox, "Multi-Chain Markov Renewal Programs," *SIAM J. Appl. Math.* **16:** 468–487 (1968).
13. Dreyfus, S. E., *Dynamic Programming and the Calculus of Variations*, Academic Press, New York (1965).
14. Dvoretzky, A., J. Kiefer, and J. Wolfowitz, "The Inventory Problem–I (and II): Case of Known (Unknown) Distributions of Demand," *Econometrica* **20:** 187–222, 450–466 (1952).

15. Howard, R. A., *Dynamic Programming and Markov Processes*, Technology Press of M.I.T., Cambridge, Massachusetts (1960).
16. Iscaas, R., *Games of Pursuit*, 257, The Rand Corporation, Santa Monica, California (1951).
17. Jewell, W. S., "Markov-Renewal Programming. I: Formulation, Finite Return Models; II: Infinite Return Models, Example," *Operations Res.* **11:** 938-971 (1963).
18. Massé, P., *Les Réserves et la Régulation de L'Avenir Dans la Vie Économique*, 2 vols., Herman, Paris (1946).
19. Veinott, A. F., Jr., "On Finding Optimal Policies in Discrete Dynamic Programming with No Discounting," *Ann. Math. Stat.* **37:** 1284-1294 (1966).
20. ——, "Markov Decision Chains," in *M.A.A. Studies in Mathematics* **10,** edited by J. B. Dantzig and B. C. Eaves, published and distributed by Mathematical Association of America, Washington, D.C., 1975.
21. Wagner, H. M., *Principles of Operations Research with Applications to Managerial Decisions*, Prentice-Hall, Englewood Cliffs, New Jersey (1970).
22. Wald, A., *Sequential Analysis*, Wiley, New York (1947).

AUTHOR INDEX

AUTHOR INDEX

SUBJECT INDEX

SUBJECT INDEX